world development report 2009

Reshaping Economic Geography

world development report 2009

Reshaping Economic Geography

THE WORLD BANK
Washington, DC

Softcover
ISSN: 0163-5085
ISBN: 978-0-8213-7607-2
eISBN: 978-0-8213-7608-9
DOI: 10.1596/978-0-8213-7607-2

Hardcover
ISSN: 0163-5085
ISBN: 978-0-8213-7640-9
eISBN: 978-0-8213-7608-9
DOI: 10.1596/978-0-8213-7640-9

Cover design and interior navigational graphics by Zefyr Design, info@zefyr.co.uk.

Typesetting, graphs, and page layout by Precision Graphics.

Printed in the United States by Quebecor World.

Contents

Contents   **vii**

A policy framework for integrating lagging and leading areas   238

The framework in action   245

Avoiding Balkanization: the political benefits of economic integration   258

**9 Winners without Borders:
Integrating poor countries with world markets   260**

Regional integration to scale up supply, global integration to scale up demand   262

Building integrated neighborhoods: a framework   265

The framework in action   273

*Geography in motion: Density, Distance, and Division
in Sub-Saharan Africa   284*

Bibliographical Note   287

Endnotes   291

References   305

Selected Indicators   331

Table A1   Geography and access   332

Table A2   Urbanization   335

Table A3   Territorial development   338

Table A4   International integration   340

Table A5   Other indicators   343

Sources and definitions   346

Selected World Development Indicators   349

Data sources and methodology   349

Classification of economies and summary measures   350

Terminology and country coverage   350

Classification of economies by region and income, FY2009   351

Table 1   Key indicators of development   352

Table 2   Millennium Development Goals: eradicating poverty and improving lives   354

Table 3   Economic activity   356

Table 4   Trade, aid, and finance   358

Table 5   Key indicators for other economies   360

Technical notes   361

Index   369

Boxes

Figures

Maps

Tables

Foreword

Production concentrates in big cities, leading provinces, and wealthy nations. Half the world's production fits onto 1.5 percent of its land. Cairo produces more than half of Egypt's GDP, using just 0.5 percent of its area. Brazil's three south-central states comprise 15 percent of its land, but more than half its production. And North America, the European Union, and Japan—with fewer than a billion people—account for three-quarters of the world's wealth.

But economic concentration leaves out some populations. In Brazil, China, and India, for example, lagging states have poverty rates more than twice those in dynamic states. More than two-thirds of the developing world's poor live in villages. A billion people, living in the poorest and most isolated nations, mostly in Sub-Saharan Africa and South and Central Asia, survive on less than 2 percent of the world's wealth.

These geographically disadvantaged people cope every day with the reality that development does not bring economic prosperity everywhere at once; markets favor some places over others. But dispersing production more broadly does not necessarily foster prosperity. Economically successful nations both facilitate the concentration of production and institute policies that make people's living standards—in terms of nutrition, education, health, and sanitation—more uniform across space. Getting the benefits of both economic concentration and social convergence requires policy actions aimed at economic integration.

Integration should begin with institutions that ensure access to basic services such as primary education, primary health care, adequate sanitation, and clean drinking water for everyone. As integration becomes more difficult, adaptive policies should include roads, railways, airports, harbors, and communication systems that facilitate the movement of goods, services, people, and ideas locally, nationally, and internationally. For places where integration is hardest, for social or political reasons, the response should be commensurately comprehensive, with institutions that unite, infrastructure that connects, and interventions that target, such as slum upgrading programs or incentives for producers to locate in certain areas.

Using these principles, *World Development Report 2009*, the 31st in the series, reframes the policy debates on urbanization, territorial development, and regional integration. The report analyzes the early experience of developed countries and draws practical implications for urbanization policies in today's developing countries. For the poorest countries in Africa and Asia that are landlocked or otherwise isolated from world markets, the Report discusses promising approaches to regional integration that combine institutional cooperation, shared infrastructure, and special incentives. In growing middle-income economies, general prosperity can camouflage areas of persistent poverty. For such countries, the Report outlines strategies to foster domestic integration and help the poor in the least fortunate places.

I expect that *Reshaping Economic Geography* will stimulate a much-needed discussion on the desirability of "balanced growth," which has proved elusive. And by informing some important policy debates, it will point the way toward more inclusive and sustainable development.

Robert B. Zoellick
President

Acknowledgments

This Report has been prepared by a team led by Indermit S. Gill, comprising Souleymane Coulibaly, Uwe Deichmann, Maria Emilia Freire, Chorching Goh, Andreas Kopp, Somik V. Lall, Claudio E. Montenegro, Truman Packard, and Hirotsugu Uchida. Important contributions were made by Homi Kharas, Marisela Montoliu Munoz, Andrew Nelson, Mark Roberts, Sebastian Vollmer, and Fang Xu. The team was assisted by Eduardo S.F. Alves, Brian Blankespoor, Maximilian Hirn, Siobhan Murray, and Catalina Tejada.

Bruce Ross-Larson was the principal editor.

The maps were created by the World Bank's Map Design Unit under the direction of Jeff Lecksell. Book production and printing were coordinated by the World Bank's Office of the Publisher, under the supervision of Stephen McGroarty, Susan Graham, Rick Ludwick, and Andres Méneses.

World Development Report 2009 is co-sponsored by the Development Economics Vice Presidency (DEC) and the Sustainable Development Network (SDN). The work was conducted under the joint guidance of François Bourguignon, Alan H. Gelb, and Justin Yifu Lin, DEC Senior Vice Presidents at various stages of the production and dissemination of this Report, and Katherine Sierra, SDN Vice President. Jean-Jacques Dethier, Jeffrey Lewis, Claudia Paz Sepulveda, Laszlo Lovei, and Antonio Estache also provided valuable comments.

World Bank Presidents Robert B. Zoellick and Paul D. Wolfowitz provided guidance and advice, and Managing Directors Ngozi Okonjo-Iweala and Graeme Wheeler have been invaluable sources of encouragement to the team.

Two panels of advisers provided excellent advice at all stages of the Report. The Academic Panel was chaired by the Chief Economist and DEC Senior Vice President and consisted of François Bourguignon, Paul Collier, Masahisa Fujita, Vernon Henderson, Philippe Martin, Ravi Kanbur, Lord Nicholas Stern, and Anthony Venables. The Policymaker Panel was chaired by the SDN Vice President and consisted of Lobna Abdellatif Ahmed, Newai Gebreab, Jerzy Kwiecinski, Shantong Li, Katharina Mathernova, Charbel Nahas, Enrique Peñalosa, Carolina Renteria, Kamal Siddiqui, Jorge Wilheim, and Natalia Zubarevich.

Many others outside and inside the World Bank contributed with comments and suggestions. The team benefited greatly from many consultations, meetings, and regional workshops held locally and in Côte d'Ivoire, Finland, France, Germany, India, Japan, Norway, Russia, South Africa, Sweden, Tanzania, Turkey, and the United Kingdom. The team wishes to thank participants in these and other workshops, videoconferences, and on-line discussions, which included academics, policy researchers, government officials, and staff of nongovernmental, civil society, and private sector organizations.

The team would like to acknowledge the generous support of the United Kingdom's Department for International Development, the multi-donor Knowledge for Change Program, the Government of Norway, the Japan Policy and Human Resources Development Trust Fund, the Institute for Environment and Sustainability in the Joint Research Centre of the European Commission, Germany's Federal Ministry for Economic Cooperation and Development, and the William and Flora Hewlett Foundation.

Rebecca Sugui served as senior executive assistant to the team, Ofelia Valladolid as program assistant, and Jason Victor and Maria Hazel Macadangdang as team assistants. Evangeline Santo Domingo served as resource management assistant.

Abbreviations and Data Notes

ACP	Africa, Caribbean, and Pacific
AMU	Arab Maghreb Union
ASEAN	Association Southeast Asian Nations
BELDES	Municipal Infrastructure Support Project (Turkey)
CACM	Central American Common Market
CARICOM	Caribbean Community
CEFTA	Central European Free Trade Agreement
CESIN	Center for International Earth Science Information Network
CKLN	Caribbean Knowledge and Learning Network
DR-CAFTA	Dominican Republic–Central America Free Trade Agreement
EAC	East African Community
EAP	East Asia and the Pacific
ECA	Europe and Central Asia
ECOWAS	Economic Community of West African States
ECSC	European Coal and Steel Community
ECTEL	Eastern Caribbean Telecommunications Authority
EEC	European Economic Community
EMU	European Monetary Union
ENEA	École Nationale d'Économie Appliquée (Dakar)
ENSEA	École Nationale de Statistique et d'Economie Appliquée (Abidjan)
EPA	economic partnership agreements
EU	European Union
FDI	foreign direct investment
FEU	forty-foot equivalent units
GATS	General Agreement on Trade in Services
GDP	gross domestic product
GIS	geographic information system
GNI	gross national income
GRP	gross regional product
GRUMP	Global Rural-Urban Mapping Project
IBRD	International Bank for Reconstruction and Development
ICT	information and communication technology
IDA	International Development Association
IIED	International Institute for Environment and Development (UK)
INEGI	Instituto Nacional de Estadística y Geografía
IOM	International Organization of Immigration
ISSEA	Institut Sous-Régional de Statistique et d'Économie Appliquée (Yaoundé)
IT	information technology
KÖYDES	Village Infrastructure Support Project (Turkey)

MERCOSUR	Southern Common Market (Latin America)
NAFTA	North American Free Trade Agreement
NEPAD	New Partnership for Africa's Development
NSDP	National Slum Development Program (India)
NUTS	Nomenclature of Territorial Units for Statistics
OECD	Organisation for Economic Co-operation and Development
OEEC	Organization for European Cooperation
PAFTA	Pan-Arab Free Trade Area
PPS	purchasing power standard
R&D	research and development
RASCOM	Regional African Satellite Communication Organization
SADC	Southern African Development Community
SAR	South Asia region
SASEC	South Asia Sub-regional Economic Cooperation
SEZ	special economic zone
SIC	Standard Industrial Classification.
SPARTECA	South Pacific Regional Trade and Economic Cooperation Agreement
TEU	twenty-foot equivalent units
TFP	total factor productivity
UPE	universal primary education
VAMBAY	Valmiki Ambedkar Awas Yojana
WAEMU	West African Economic and Monetary Union
WTO	World Trade Organization

Data notes

The countries included in regional and income groupings in this Report are listed in the Classification of Economies table at the beginning of the Selected World Development Indicators. Income classifications are based on gross national income (GNP) per capita; thresholds for income classifications in this edition may be found in the Introduction to Selected World Development Indicators. Group averages reported in the figures and tables are unweighted averages of the countries in the group, unless noted to the contrary.

The use of the word *countries* to refer to economies implies no judgment by the World Bank about the legal or other status of a territory. The term *developing countries* includes low- and middle-income economies and thus may include economies in transition from central planning, as a matter of convenience. The terms *industrialized countries* or *developed countries* may be used as a matter of convenience to denote high-income economies.

Dollar figures are current U.S. dollars, unless otherwise specified. *Billion* means 1,000 million; *trillion* means 1,000 billion.

The Report at a Glance—Density, Distance, and Division

Growing cities, ever more mobile people, and increasingly specialized products are integral to development. These changes have been most noticeable in North America, Western Europe, and Northeast Asia. But countries in East and South Asia and Eastern Europe are now experiencing changes that are similar in their scope and speed. **World Development Report 2009: Reshaping Economic Geography** *concludes that such transformations will remain essential for economic success in other parts of the developing world and should be encouraged.*

Seeing development in 3-D

These transformations bring prosperity, but they do not happen without risk and sacrifice. Look at three of the world's most prosperous places:

- The first is Tokyo, the largest city in the world with 35 million people, a quarter of Japan's population, packed into less than 4 percent of its land.
- The second is the United States, the largest economy in the world and perhaps also the most mobile, where about 35 million people change residences each year.
- The third is Western Europe, the most connected continent in the world today, where countries trade about 35 percent of their gross domestic product (GDP), more than half among neighbors.

Visitors to Tokyo can see people being crushed into trains by professional train-packers. Millions of people willingly subject themselves to the unpleasantness of such a crush. A map of Japan's economic density shows why. Tokyo generates a big part of Japan's wealth—to get a share of it, people have to live close by (see map G0.1). The most striking feature of this map is density—the concentration of wealth in Tokyo and Osaka.

In the United States, each year in the days before the Thanksgiving holiday, about 35 million people try to get back to their families and friends. It is

the start of winter in some parts of the country, so flights often are canceled. But Americans put up with the pain of leaving friends and family, because economic activity is concentrated in a few parts of the country (see map G0.2). To get a part of this wealth, you have to get closer to it. That is why 8 million Americans change states every year, migrating to reduce their distance to economic opportunity. The most striking feature of this map is distance.

Across the Atlantic, in Western Europe, another massive movement takes place every day—not of people but of products. One example is Airbus,

Map G0.1   Density—why it pays to be close to Tokyo
Economic production per square kilometer in Japan

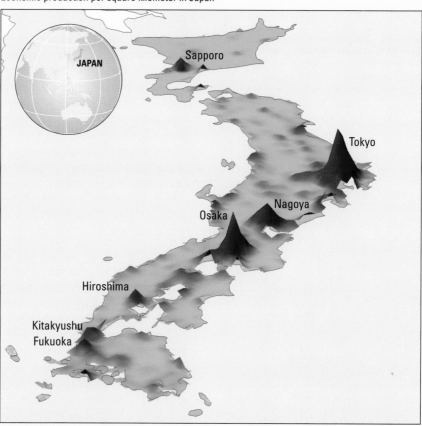

Source: WDR 2009 team and World Bank Development Research Group based on subnational GDP estimates for 2005. See also Nordhaus (2006).

Map G0.2   Distance—why Americans must be mobile
Economic production per square kilometer in the United States

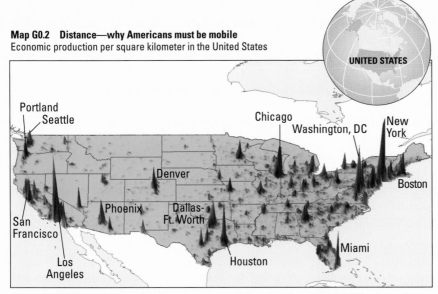

Source: WDR 2009 team and World Bank Development Research Group based on subnational GDP estimates for 2005. See also Nordhaus (2006).

which makes parts of planes and assembles them in France, Germany, Spain, and the United Kingdom as well as in other countries. Huge sections of aircraft are loaded onto ships and planes, as places specialize in making different parts and producing them in scale. Countries in

Map G0.3   Division—what prevents progress in Africa does not in Western Europe
Border restrictions to flows of goods, capital, people, and ideas

Source: WDR 2009 team (see chapter 3 for details).
Note: The width of borders is proportional to a summary measure of each country's restrictions to the flow of goods, capital, people, and ideas with all other countries.

a region that was divided not so long ago now trade with former enemies to become an ever-more-integrated European Union (EU). As this integration has increased, economic divisions have decreased, making specialization and scale possible (see map G0.3).

What is the payoff for this pain? A map of economic geography, which resizes the area of a country to reflect its GDP, shows the benefits of big cities, mobile people, and connected countries. The United States, Western Europe, and Japan dominate the world's economy (see map G0.4).

Cities, migration, and trade have been the main catalysts of progress in the developed world over the past two centuries. These stories are now being repeated in the developing world's most dynamic economies.

- Mumbai is not the largest city in the world, but it is the most densely populated. And it keeps growing.
- China is not the largest economy in the world, but it is the fastest growing and may be among the most mobile.
- Southeast Asia may not have formed a political union like Europe, but it trades parts of goods back and forth as the EU does.

People risk loss of life or limb on Mumbai's packed trains to take advan-

tage of economic density. Despite the crush among commuters and in such slums as Dharavi, Mumbai's population has doubled since the 1970s. Since the 1990s, millions of Chinese workers have migrated to get closer to economic opportunity concentrated along the coast. Just as Americans travel during Thanksgiving, more than 200 million people in China travel during the Chinese New Year. Regional production networks in East Asia are spread far wider than Airbus sites in Western Europe. East Asian countries may not trade airplane parts, but nations that once were enemies now trade parts of cars and computers with the same frequency and speed.

And what is the payoff? We can again recognize the shapes of China, India, and Southeast Asian countries on the map of the world's economic geography (see map G0.4). Contrast these shapes with that of the mighty continent of Africa, which shows up as a slender peninsula.

The *World Development Report* argues that some places are doing well because they have promoted transformations along the three dimensions of economic geography:

- Higher densities, as seen in the growth of cities.
- Shorter distances, as workers and businesses migrate closer to density.
- Fewer divisions, as countries thin their economic borders and enter world markets to take advantage of scale and specialization.

The United States and Japan reshaped their economic geography along these lines in the past. China is reshaping its economic geography now. This Report proposes that these will be the changes that will help developing nations in other parts of the world, most notably Africa.

Unbalanced growth, inclusive development

That is what this *World Development Report* proposes, and the Report is

Map G0.4   How markets view the world
A country's size shows the proportion of global gross domestic product found there

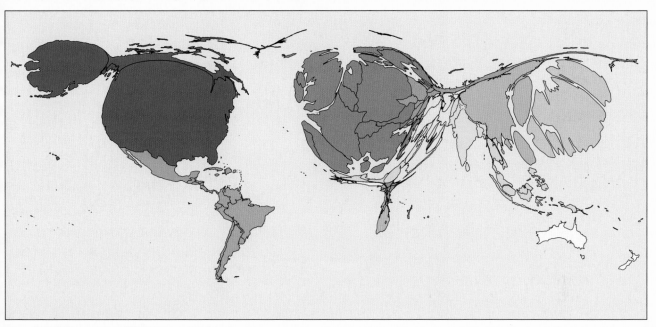

Source: WDR 2009 team using 2005 GDP (constant U.S. dollars).
Note: The cartogram was created using the method developed by Gastner and Newman (2004). This map shows the countries that have the most wealth when GDP is compared using currency exchange rates. This indicates international purchasing power—what someone's money is worth if spent in another country.

structured to bring out the message (see figure G0.1).

- Part one describes the changes along the dimensions of density, distance, and division—taking up each in turn. It summarizes the experience of the past century or so.
- Part two analyzes the drivers of these transformations—the market forces of agglomeration, migration, and specialization and trade. It distills the findings of policy research during the past generation or so.
- Part three discusses the policy implications of the experience and analysis in the first two parts. It provides a common framework for reframing three policy debates—on urbanization, on lagging areas within countries, and on regional integration and globalization.

The Report is structured and written in such a way that people interested in only one of these debates can read just some of it. That is, it can be read vertically. The chapters on density, agglomeration, and urbanization should

interest all countries—small and large, low income and middle income. The chapters on distance, factor mobility, and regional development may be of most interest to larger middle-income countries. And the chapters on division, transport costs, and regional integration may be of most interest to low-income and smaller economies.

Four spotlights on *Geography in Motion* examine the interplay between market forces and government policies in North America, Western Europe, East Asia, and Sub-Saharan Africa. By highlighting the interactions among the three dimensions, they also connect the Report's different parts.

Seen another way, the Report examines the most important policy issues of economic geography, from local, to national, to international. Locally, the policy issue in areas such as Lagos state in southern Nigeria is how to manage urbanization. Nationally, the policy issue in Nigeria is how to manage the disparities in resources and living standards in the north and the south. And internationally, the policy issue in West

Africa is how to make a better economic union that benefits both the landlocked and the coastal countries, the poorest and the more prosperous.

As the geographic scale increases from local to national to international, the specific policy issue changes. But the underlying problem is the same—some places do well, others do not. And it is difficult for anyone to accept this as inevitable.

The Report's main message is that economic growth *will* be unbalanced. To try to spread out economic activity is to discourage it. But development can still be inclusive, in that even people who start their lives far away from economic opportunity can benefit from the growing concentration of wealth in a few places. The way to get both the benefits of uneven growth and inclusive development is through economic integration.

Economic integration—local, national, and international

The Report makes it clear what economic integration means. It means one

Figure G0.1   The Report can be read by part or by policy

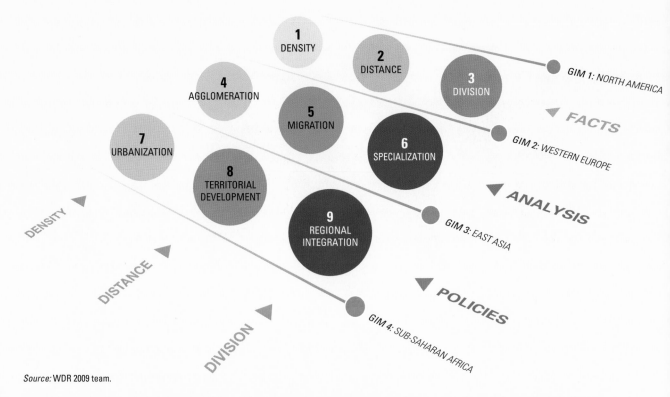

Source: WDR 2009 team.

thing to integrate rural and urban areas, and slums with other parts of cities. It means another to integrate lagging and leading provinces within a nation. And it means yet another to integrate isolated and well-connected countries. These notions of economic integration are central to three debates in development—urbanization, territorial development, and international integration.

Urbanization

The arguments and evidence in *World Development Report 2009* can set priorities for policies at different stages of urbanization, essentially providing the elements of an urbanization strategy. Each territory or area within a nation has a specific geography. But the principles are quite universal.

- In places mostly rural, governments should be as neutral as possible and should establish the institutional foundation for possible urbanization in some places. Good land policies are central, and so are policies to provide basic services to everyone. A good example is Costa Rica.

- In places urbanizing rapidly, governments must put in place, in addition to institutions, connective infrastructure so that the benefits of rising economic density are more widely shared. A good example is Chongqing, China.
- In places where urbanization has advanced, in addition to institutions and infrastructure, targeted interventions may be necessary to deal with slums. But these interventions will not work unless institutions for land and basic services are reasonably effective and transport infrastructure is in place. A good example is Bogotá, Colombia.

Territorial development

The principles also can reshape the debate on territorial or regional development. The tools of geography can identify which places are poor—the lagging areas—and where most of the poor live. Often, the two are not the same, because the poor have the most reason to move from poor places. The Report discusses how governments can tailor policies to

integrate areas within nations, while reducing poverty everywhere.

Lagging areas have one thing in common—they are economically distant from places doing well. But besides this, the economic geography of different areas is not the same:

- In some countries, such as China, lagging areas are sparsely populated. It does not make a lot of sense to spread expensive infrastructure into these places—or to give firms incentives to move to them. What makes much more sense is to provide basic services everywhere, even if it costs more to reach these distant areas. Encouraging mobility of people is the priority, and institutions that make land markets work better and provide security, schools, streets, and sanitation should be the mainstay of integration policy.
- In other countries, such as Brazil, lagging areas are densely populated. As in China, poor people have moved in the millions from the northeast to the southeast. Everyone speaks

the same language, and domestic mobility is not difficult. But many poor people still live in the northeast. Encouraging mobility of people from the northeast is important, but so is enabling access to markets in the dynamic southeast. In such cases, both institutions and infrastructure to connect the two coastal areas are necessary for economic integration.

- In a third group of countries, such as India, lagging areas are densely populated—almost 60 percent of India's poor live in these poor places—and people can find it difficult to migrate to places doing well, such as the capital area and the south. Language and cultural differences within some areas can be considerable. In such cases, institutions and infrastructure could be complemented by incentives to producers to locate in these lagging states. But these incentives should be carefully designed to avoid offsetting the unifying effects of common institutions and connective infrastructure. A promising

possibility is providing incentives to agriculture and allied activities that are appropriate for states that are still mostly rural.

Regional integration

Finally, the principles developed in this Report inform the debates on how to make globalization work for all countries. The same logic applied at the local and national levels can be used at the international level to classify world regions by the difficulty of economic integration in these regions. The common problem is division—thick economic borders. Aside from this, the task of integration varies in different parts of the developing world:

- Countries in regions close to world markets, such as Central America, North Africa, and Eastern Europe, face a relatively straightforward task of integration. Common institutions can help them become extensions of these large markets.
- Countries in regions distant from world markets, but with large home

markets attractive to investors, face a more difficult challenge. Good institutions and regional infrastructure can help them access these markets. Examples include East Asia and, increasingly, South Asia. Southern Africa and South America can also integrate globally by making their home markets bigger and more specialized through regional institutions and infrastructure.

- Integration is hardest for countries in regions that are divided, are distant from world markets, and lack the economic density provided by a large local economy. These countries include those nicknamed the "bottom billion"—East, Central, and West Africa; Central Asia; and the Pacific Islands. For these countries, all three instruments are needed—regional institutions that thin borders, regional infrastructure that connects countries, and such incentives as preferential access to world markets, perhaps conditioned on ensuring that all countries strengthen regional cooperation.

One thing is common to the policy debates on urbanization, area development, and globalization. In their current form, they overemphasize geographic targeting—what to do in rural areas or in slums, what to do in lagging states or remote areas, and what to do in the most poor or landlocked countries. The Report reframes these debates in a way that better conforms to the reality of growth and development. The reality is that the interaction between leading and lagging places is the key to economic development. The reality is that spatially targeted interventions are just a small part of what governments can do to help places that are not doing well. The reality is that, besides place-based incentives, governments have far more potent instruments for integration. They can build institutions that unify all places and put in place infrastructure that connects some places to others.

The Report calls for rebalancing these policy discussions to include all the instruments of integration—institutions that unify, infrastructure that connects, and interventions that target. And it shows how to use the three dimensions of density, distance, and division to tailor the use of these policy instruments to address integration challenges that range from the relatively straightforward to the most complicated.

Overview

Economic growth will be unbalanced, but development still can be inclusive—that is the message of this year's **World Development Report***. As economies grow from low to high income, production becomes more concentrated spatially. Some places—cities, coastal areas, and connected countries—are favored by producers. As countries develop, the most successful ones also institute policies that make living standards of people more uniform across space. The way to get both the immediate benefits of the concentration of production and the long-term benefits of a convergence in living standards is economic integration.*

Although the problems of economic integration defy simple solutions, the guiding principle does not have to be complex. The policy mix should be calibrated to match the difficulty of the development challenge, determined by the economic geography of places. Today, policy discussions about geographic disparities in development often start and end with a consideration of spatially targeted interventions. The Report reframes these debates to include all instruments for economic integration—institutions, infrastructure, and incentives. The bedrock of integration efforts should be spatially blind institutions. As the challenges posed by geography become more difficult, the response should include connective infrastructure. In places where integration is hardest, the policy response should be commensurately comprehensive: institutions that unite, infrastructure that connects, and interventions that target.

Place and prosperity

Place is the most important correlate of a person's welfare. In the next few decades, a person born in the United States will earn a hundred times more than a Zambian, and live three decades longer. Behind these national averages are numbers even more unsettling. Unless things change radically, a child born in a village far from Zambia's capital, Lusaka, will live less than half as long as a child born in New York City—and during that short life, will earn just $0.01 for every $2 the New Yorker earns. The New Yorker will enjoy a lifetime income of about $4.5 million, the rural Zambian less than $10,000.

A Bolivian man with nine years of schooling earns an average of about $460 per month, in dollars that reflect purchasing power at U.S. prices. But the same person would earn about three times as much in the United States. A Nigerian with nine years of education would earn eight times as much in the United States than in Nigeria. This "place premium" is large throughout the developing world.[1] The best predictor of income in the world today is not *what* or *whom* you know, but *where* you work.

Bumps, curves, and spills

These disparities in incomes and living standards are the outcome of a striking attribute of economic development—its unevenness across space. Somewhat unfairly, prosperity does not come to every place at the same time. This is true at all geographic scales, from local to national to global. Cities quickly pull ahead of the countryside. Living standards improve in some provinces

1

while others lag. And some countries grow to riches while others remain poor. If economic density were charted on a map of the world, the topography at any resolution would be bumpy, not smooth.

Location remains important at all stages of development, but it matters less for living standards in a rich country than in a poor one. Estimates from more than 100 living standard surveys indicate that households in the most prosperous areas of developing countries—such as Brazil, Bulgaria, Ghana, Indonesia, Morocco, and Sri Lanka—have an average consumption almost 75 percent higher than that of similar households in the lagging areas of these countries. Compare this with less than 25 percent for such developed countries as Canada, Japan, and the United States. In contrast, as a country grows richer, location becomes more important for economic production. Ghana, Poland, and New Zealand—three medium-size countries with land areas of about 250,000 square kilometers—have vastly different per capita gross national incomes of about $600, $9,000, and $27,000, respectively. The most economically dense 5 percent of the country's area produces about 27 percent of gross domestic product (GDP) in Ghana, 31 percent in Poland, and 39 percent in New Zealand.

Put another way, as countries develop, location matters less for families and more for firms. Development seems to give a place the ability to reap the economic advantages of rising concentrations of production, and to obtain the social benefits that come from a convergence in consumption. Economic development thus brings with it the conditions of even greater prosperity, in a virtuous circle.

Another stylized fact: neighborhoods matter. A prosperous city seldom leaves its periphery mired in poverty. A province's prosperity is sooner or later shared with those nearby. And neighboring countries share not just political borders but economic destinies. North America, Western Europe, and East Asia are now prosperous neighborhoods. Within these regions, all countries did not grow in lockstep. Within countries, some provinces did better, and within each province, prosperity came at different times to cities, towns, and villages.

Less widely appreciated is the fact that places near prosperous provinces, countries, and regions have invariably benefited. Prosperity produces congestion and causes economic activity to spill over, but only to places that are well connected to these prosperous parts. The detrimental effects of poverty, instability, and conflict spill over as well. To prosperous places, proximity is a blessing, to poor places, a curse.

These three attributes of development—geographic unevenness, circular causation, and neighborhood effects—have not always received much attention. They should, because they have radical implications for public policy.

- *Geographic unevenness*—the first attribute of development—implies that governments generally cannot simultaneously foster economic production and spread it out smoothly.
- *Circular causation*—the second attribute—provides hope for policy makers wishing to pursue progressive objectives. Rising concentrations of economic production are compatible with geographic convergence in living standards. And the market forces of agglomeration, migration, and specialization can, if combined with progressive policies, yield both a concentration of economic production and a convergence of living standards.
- *Neighborhood effects*—the third attribute—come with a principle for policy making: promote economic integration. Unevenness and circularity imply that it is more difficult for places left behind to catch up. But spillovers point to the promise for surmounting this handicap. Economic integration is an effective and the most realistic way to harness the immediate benefits from concentration to achieve the long-term benefits of convergence.

Putting this principle of economic integration into practice requires identifying the market forces and government policies that best support the concentration of economic mass and the convergence of living standards across different locations. It also requires recognizing that these market forces can be strong or weak depending on economic geography. Earlier *World*

Development Reports have studied these phenomena. This Report advances the influence of geography on economic opportunity by elevating space and place from mere undercurrents in policy to a major focus.

The problem—at three geographic scales

Depending on the "geographic scale," the market forces to be harnessed or supported differ. At a smaller scale—say, an area within a country (a province or state)—geography poses different challenges than at a larger geographic scale—say, a country. At an even larger geographic scale—say, a group of countries that form a geographic region—the market forces that work toward integration can be blocked by even greater geographic and political obstacles (see box 1).

Locally, the concentration of economic production as countries develop is manifest in urbanization. In East Asia, for example, if current trends continue, the urban population is expected to increase by about 450 million people over the next two decades, as countries in the regions grow, adding the equivalent of a Paris every month. In South and Central Asia, the increase is expected to be almost 350 million. And in Sub-Saharan Africa—if economies continue to grow—the urban population could increase by 250 million between 2005 and 2025. In other parts of the developing world, within-urban transformations will be as important.

The question is whether growing concentrations of humanity will increase prosperity, or produce congestion and squalor. Another concern is the divergence in living standards between those who benefit most from this geographic

---

BOX 1   *Three geographic scales: local, national, and international*

Consider the "neighborhoods" of Lagos State, Nigeria, and West Africa (see the maps below).

- *The first geographic scale is the area.* The state of Lagos in southwestern Nigeria has the five districts of Badagry, Epe, Ikeja, Ikorodu, and Lagos, covering about 3,500 square kilometers. Its estimated population density—with the smallest land area but among the two most populous in the nation—is about 2,600 persons per square kilometer. Metropolitan Lagos has a density more than three times that, fueled by

agglomeration economies and rural-urban migration.

- *The second geographic scale is the country.* With its 36 states and capital area and covering 924,000 square kilometers, Nigeria is the world's 32nd largest country. The distance from Lagos to the northeastern tip of Nigeria is almost 1,500 kilometers. The southern states have seaports and oilfields. The northern part, once a seat of ancient empires, now has higher poverty. Migration between the north and the south is not an easy matter because

of religious and linguistic differences. The sharing of oil wealth is a source of tension.

- *The third geographic scale is the region.* Nigeria's West African neighbors include Cameroon, the Central African Republic, Côte d'Ivoire, Equatorial Guinea, Ghana, Niger, and Togo. The region covers more than 6 million square kilometers, divided by some of the world's thickest borders.

Source: WDR 2009 team.

Three geographic units: area, country, and region
Lagos State, Nigeria, and West Africa represent the local, national, and international scales

The first geographic scale	The second geographic scale	The third geographic scale
The *area* around Lagos State	The *country* of Nigeria	The West African *region*

LAGOS STATE

LAGOS STATE

Source: WDR 2009 team.

Map 1   The biggest development challenges—at the local, national, and international geographic scales

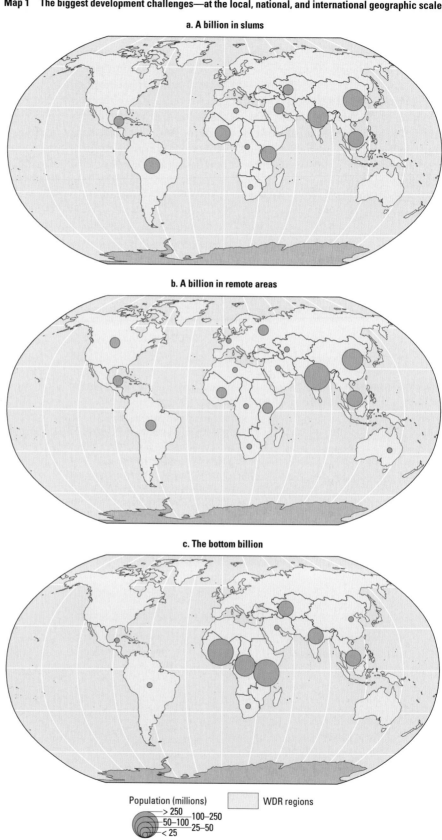

a. A billion in slums

b. A billion in remote areas

c. The bottom billion

Population (millions)
> 250
100–250
50–100
25–50
< 25

WDR regions

Sources: Panel a: United Nations 2006a; panel b: WDR 2009 team, based on household survey data; panel c: Collier 2007.

concentration—essentially urbanites in prosperous neighborhoods—and those left behind in villages and those living in slums, estimated to number about 1 billion in the developing world (see map 1, panel a). The (ineffective) policy responses so far have been to try to slow down urbanization.

At the national scale, economic growth displays a similar unevenness, as places close to large markets prosper sooner than places more distant. In China the coastal provinces—mainly in the three areas known as the Bohai Basin, the Pearl River Delta, and the Yangtze River Delta—accounted for more than half of the country's GDP in 2005, with less than a fifth of its area. In Brazil the south-central states of Minas Gerais, Rio de Janeiro, and São Paulo account for more than 52 percent of the country's GDP, with less than 15 percent of its land area. Greater Cairo produces 50 percent of the Arab Republic of Egypt's GDP, using just 0.5 percent of its land area.

Politicians generally view this economic imbalance disapprovingly. In communist Russia the government labored to reduce the economic share of the old industrial area of St. Petersburg, the Center, and the mid-Urals from 65 percent to 32 percent, forcibly shifting production to the eastern areas. It boosted the share of the east in economic production from 4 percent in 1925 to 28 percent at the end of communism, whose demise probably was hastened by the spatial inefficiency that these efforts engendered. Because governments care so much about domestic disparities, they jeopardize competitiveness and risk collapse. Policies to reduce interstate or provincial disparities in production and living standards are commonplace—but largely ineffective. About 1 billion people continue to live in these inhospitable lagging areas (see map 1, panel b).

At the international scale, economic growth has concentrated global production in a few regions, with commensurate differences in incomes. In 2000 about three-quarters of world GDP was concentrated in North America, Western Europe, and Northeast Asia. This concentration is not new. Three centuries ago, China and India accounted for about two-thirds of the world's wealth. What was different then

is that they also had more than half of the world's population; the European Union (EU), Japan, and the United States have less than one-sixth.

Today, the worry at the international level is the high poverty, illiteracy, and mortality in some parts of the world, set against the prosperity, literacy, and longevity in others. The policy responses include foreign aid and multilateral efforts to ease international trade and investment flows. But barriers to the agricultural exports of developing countries remain considerable, and apathy for people distant or distinct renders aid flows miniscule. Aid will be a small part of the solution. Even in the European Union, with a combined GDP of about €8 trillion, annual aid through the structural and cohesion funds will average less than €50 billion between 2007 and 2013. Foreign aid is less than 0.5 percent of the gross national income of giving countries, and not even a large fraction of the GDP of countries home to the "bottom billion" who have 12 percent of the world's population, but less than 1 percent of its GDP (see map 1, panel c).[2]

A billion slum dwellers in the developing world's cities, a billion people in fragile lagging areas within countries, a billion at the bottom of the global hierarchy of nations—these overlapping populations pose today's biggest development challenges. Seemingly disparate, they share a fundamental feature: at different spatial scales, they are the most visible manifestation of economic geography's importance for development.

Concern for these intersecting 3 billion sometimes comes with the prescription that economic growth must be made more spatially balanced. The growth of cities must be controlled. Rural-urban gaps in wealth must be reduced quickly. Lagging areas and provinces distant from domestic and world markets must be sustained through territorial development programs that bring jobs to the people living there. And growing gaps between the developed and developing world must be addressed through interventions to protect enterprises in developing countries until they are ready to compete.

World Development Report 2009 has a different message: economic growth is seldom balanced. Efforts to spread it

BOX 2   *The three dimensions of development: density, distance, and division*

This Report uses three geographic dimensions to describe the transformation of economies as they develop (part one) and the conditions to keep in mind when formulating policies (part three). The words are easy metaphors, since density, distance, and division summon images of human, physical, and political geography. But they can be measured. Consider this illustration.

In 2003 Nigeria had 45 million goats and kids, 28 million sheep and lambs, and 15 million cattle. In a typical year 8 million sheep, 7 million goats, and 0.5 million cattle are slaughtered, mostly in five northern states including Kano. More than half the hides are consumed as *pomo*. The rest are sold to tanneries. The demand from tanneries exceeds local supply, so animals are imported from nearby Chad, Niger, and Cameroon. Goat and sheep skins are good business—in 2001 Nigeria produced 30 million to 35 million of them, exporting almost all to Europe.

Density. Consider the market conditions for a tannery that produces leather in the city of Kano in Northern Nigeria. Officially, the population of Kano State is about 9 million, large enough to provide the skilled labor and infrastructure for its tanneries. Due to the concentration of people in and around Kano city, the area's economic density (GDP per square kilometer) was 35 times that of Nigeria in 1990. The capacity of the tanneries in and around the city even makes it worthwhile to illegally import live animals—the most important intermediate input—from neighboring countries. But Kano is neither large enough, nor rich enough, to consume more than a little of what is produced. The goods must be exported to people willing to pay enough to make production worthwhile.

Distance. Wealthy Europeans want goods made with "Morocco leather," a lot of which comes from Kano. To get to Europe, Kano's bulky exports must travel through Lagos, which along highways and railways is about 1,000 kilometers away. It might as well be 4,000 kilometers. A railway goes to Lagos through the cities of Kaduna and Ibadan, but it is narrow gauge and poorly maintained. Most commerce is by road, obstructed by roadblocks and piracy. Shipping companies charge more than $1,200 for a 30-ton trailer from Kano to Lagos. Once the goods get to Lagos, there are port fees, pilferage, and delays. It takes 26 days to get the goods onto a ship. The economic distance from Kano to Lagos, measured as money, is several times the Euclidean (straight-line) 829 kilometers.

Division. But the journey is not yet complete. The goods must surmount the division caused by differences in currencies and conventions between Nigeria and Europe. Between December 2007 and March 2008, Nigeria's currency depreciated from 170 naira to €1 to 180 naira, but appreciated from 246 naira to the British pound in November 2007 to 235 naira in March 2008. Buyers and sellers of leather goods have to contend with these fluctuations. They must also deal with two sets of laws and customs. The United Kingdom has 30 procedures for enforcing a contract, Nigeria 39. These divisions multiply the costs of doing business. Few cargo ships make landfall in Lagos, so it costs much more to transport goods from Lagos than from busier places such as Shanghai. It costs less than $400 to ship a container to the United Kingdom from China, more than $1,000 from Nigeria.

Low local density, costly internal distances, and international divisions conspire against Kano. Making matters more difficult are religious and other divisions within Nigeria.

Sources: World Bank 2007; Phillips, Taylor, Sanni, and Akoroda, (FAO 2004); Government of Nigeria 2003.

---

prematurely will jeopardize progress. Two centuries of economic development show that spatial disparities in income and production are inevitable. A generation of economic research confirms this: there is no good reason to expect economic growth to spread smoothly across space. The experience of successful developers shows that production becomes more concentrated spatially. The most successful nations also institute policies that make basic living standards more uniform across space. Economic production concentrates, while living standards converge.

Part one of the Report describes the geographic transformations that are necessary for development. Part two analyzes the drivers of these changes and identifies the markets that deliver both concentration and convergence. Part three proposes the principle of economic integration—between places that producers prefer and places where people live—to guide policy making. Using this principle, it reframes the debates on urbanization, territorial development, and international integration, calling for a change in orientation of policies away from geographic targeting toward integration.

By using a well-calibrated blend of institutions, infrastructure, and interventions, today's developers can reshape their economic geography. When they do this well, they will experience unbalanced growth and inclusive development.

The three dimensions of development

The geographic transformations for economic development can be characterized in three dimensions—density, distance, and division. These three words are not just metaphors for the policy challenges just outlined. They conform closely to the more technical notion of "market access" (see box 2). And they represent the dimensions of economic geography that have to be reshaped if the development challenges are to be met.

Understanding the transformations along the dimensions of density, distance, and division helps to identify the main market forces and the appropriate policy responses at each of the three geographic scales—local, national, and international (see table 1).

- **Density** is the most important dimension locally. Distances are short, and cultural and political divisions are few and shallow. The policy challenge is getting density right—harnessing market forces to encourage concentration and promote convergence in living standards between villages and towns and cities. But distance can be important as rapid urbanization leads to congestion, and divisions within cities can be manifest in slums and ghettos.
- **Distance** to density is the most important dimension at the national geographic scale. Distance between areas where economic activity is concentrated and areas that lag is the main dimension. The policy challenge is helping firms

and workers reduce their distance from density. The main mechanisms are the mobility of labor and the reduction of transport costs through infrastructure investments. Divisions within countries—differences in language, currency, and culture—tend to be small, though large countries such as India and Nigeria may be geographically divided because of religion, ethnicity, or language.

- **Division** is the most important dimension internationally. But distance and density are also relevant. Economic production is concentrated in a few world regions—North America, Northeast Asia, and Western Europe—that are also the most integrated. Other regions, by contrast, are divided. While distance matters at the international level, for access to world markets, divisions associated with the impermeability of borders and differences in currencies and regulations are a more serious barrier than distance. Having a large and dynamic economy within the neighborhood can help smaller countries, especially in regions distant from world markets. For economies in other regions such as Central Africa and Central Asia, international integration is hardest.

But the potential problem at each of these geographic scales is the same—people in one place, production in another. Places

Table 1   Density is most important locally, distance nationally, and division internationally

	Geographic scales		
	Local	**National**	**International**
Unit	**Area**	**Country**	**Region**
Examples	Guangdong (178,000 km^2) Rio de Janeiro State (44,000 km^2) Lagos State (3,600 km^2) Greater Cairo (86,000 km^2)	China (9.6 million km^2) Brazil (8.5 million km^2) Nigeria (933,000 km^2) Egypt, Arab Rep. of (995,000 km^2)	East Asia (15.9 million km^2) South America (17.8 million km^2) West Africa (6.1 million km^2) North Africa (6.0 million km^2)
Most important dimension	Density Of rural and urban settlements	Distance Between lagging and leading areas	Division Between countries
Second-most important dimension	Distance Because of congestion	Density Of population and poverty in lagging areas	Division To major world markets
Third-most important dimension	Division Between formal settlements and slums	Division Between areas within countries	Density Absence of large country in the neighborhood

Source: WDR 2009 team.
Note: Throughout the Report, "areas" are within-country economic neighborhoods or administrative units such as states or provinces, and "regions" are groupings of countries based on geographic proximity.

attract production and people at different speeds, and these differences determine geographic disparities in income. Across provinces, nations, and the world, development comes in waves and leaves behind a bumpy economic landscape—prosperity in some places, poverty in others.

The world is not flat

Development is neither smooth nor linear—at any geographic scale. Growth comes earlier to some places than to others. Geographic differences in living standards diverge before converging, faster at the local scale and slower as geography exercises its influence. These are the stylized facts, based on the experiences of successful developers over the last two centuries.

Economic production becomes more concentrated

As countries develop, people and economic activities become more concentrated. But the speed varies, depending on the spatial scale—economic forces do not operate in a geographic vacuum. The concentration of people and production is fastest locally, slowest internationally.

- *Concentration is fastest locally.* Economic concentration at the local scale is most conveniently measured by the rate of urbanization—the growth of economic and population density in towns and cities. A large part of this geographic transformation has been completed when countries reach per capita incomes of about $3,500, roughly the threshold for crossing into upper-middle incomes. The speed of this transformation is no different from what was seen in today's developed countries when they transformed. The implication is that all nations must manage a rapid growth of cities when they still have low incomes and nascent institutions.

- *Concentration is steadier nationally.* Here, it can best be measured by area development indicators—the accumulation of production and people in leading areas. A large part of this transformation generally is completed when countries reach per capita incomes of about

$10,000–$11,000, about the threshold for crossing into high incomes. This is the experience of successful developers. The implication is that developing countries should expect rising subnational disparities in income and production when they still have underdeveloped infrastructure and institutions.

- *Concentration is slowest internationally, and it continues longer.* Production and wealth continue to concentrate in countries beyond per capita incomes of $25,000, the upper reaches of the international income distribution. Neighborhoods of nations seem to grow or stagnate together—nearness to prosperity helps, while nearness to poor nations hurts. The implication is that growth strategies for later developers are not the same as the strategies that worked for those who have already grown to high-income levels; for today's developing countries, economic integration with the rest of the world—neighbors and distant countries—is even more essential.

Local concentration (in towns and cities) happens quickly. Consider first the rising concentration of people in towns and cities. As countries develop, the economic density in some places increases as more people move to live in or near towns and cities (see figure 1, panel a). The urban share of the population rises sharply—from about 10 percent to 50 percent—as countries grow from low income to lower-middle incomes of about $3,500. (It is difficult to make international comparisons because countries define "urban" differently.[3]) Between 2000 and 2005, the average urban population growth for low-income countries was 3 percent a year, more than twice the rate for middle-income countries and more than three times the rate for high-income countries. Sometimes, this can mean rapid growth of a single city, such as Bangkok, Thailand, producing even greater concentration.

The share of urban residents in total household consumption rises too. Urbanites in Malawi, Jordan, and Panama—countries with per capita GDPs of about $160, $1,600, and $5,600 respectively—account for 36, 63, and 80 percent of aggregate consumption.

These spatial transformations are closely related to the sectoral transformation of countries from agrarian to industrial and then, in a postindustrial economy, to services. Today's high-income countries experienced a similar rush to urbanize as they industrialized (see chapter 1). All the evidence indicates that the shift from farming to industry is helped, not hurt, by healthy agriculture, which helps towns and cities prosper.[4] People move to make their own lives better. But when agriculture is doing well, migration makes not just them better off, but also the villages they leave and the cities in which they settle.

National concentration (in leading areas) continues for longer. What is true of cities is also true of areas within countries, but at a slower speed. With development, people and production become concentrated in some parts of countries, called "leading" areas. Economic density grows in these parts—Marmara in Turkey, for example—while incomes in places economically distant—such as southeastern Anatolia in the east—can lag far behind. This concentration is hard to quantify, but it appears to slow or stop at per capita incomes between $10,000 and $15,000 (see figure 1, panel b).

Initially, the concentration increases rapidly. The share of total consumption of the leading areas in countries with incomes ranging between $500 and $7,500—Tajikistan, Mongolia, El Salvador, and Argentina—increases from 30 percent to 65 percent. Comparing GDP concentrations in countries with the same land area— Lao PDR, Ghana, Poland, and Norway—but with incomes from $600 to $27,000 shows concentration rising as incomes increase.

This is nothing new. Production in today's developed economies grew more concentrated until they reached high incomes. Concentration in France's leading area quadrupled between 1800 and 1960, and French incomes grew from $1,000 to $6,000. But at some point, nations continue to grow wealthier but not more concentrated—about when they enter the ranks of high-income countries. There are no reasons to expect greatly different patterns today (see chapter 2).

Figure 1   At all three geographic scales, the patterns of concentration of economic activity are similar

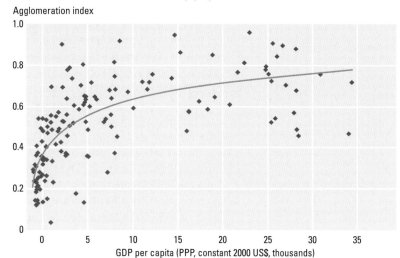

a. As nations start to develop, people concentrate in towns and cities

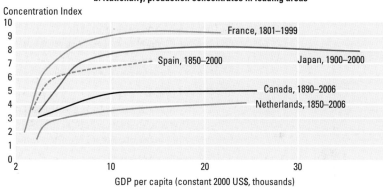

b. Nationally, production concentrates in leading areas

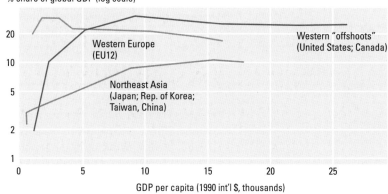

c. Internationally, wealth concentrates in some regions

Sources: Panel a: WDR 2009 team (see chapter 1 for details); panel b: WDR 2009 team (see chapter 2 for details); panel c: WDR 2009 team (see chapter 3 for details).

International concentration (in some world regions and leading countries) continues for a while. A similar concentration of economic mass has occurred internationally. Today, a quarter of the world's GDP can fit into an area the size of Cameroon, and a half into one the size of Algeria. In 1980 the shares of the EU15, North America, and East Asia added up to 70 percent; in 2000 the sum was 83 percent.[5] Within these regions, economic activity became more concentrated in a few countries over time before it became more dispersed. The shares of France, Germany, and the United Kingdom in the EU15 regional GDP rose to about two-thirds by 1940, before falling to about half today. In East Asia, the share of Japan in the region's GDP rose to 83 percent in 1975 and then fell to 62 percent by 2000.

There is no reason to expect that, when they prosper, other parts of the world will not experience the same patterns—a rising concentration in some countries, before overflowing to their neighbors (see chapter 3).

Living standards diverge before converging

As incomes increase, living standards converge between places where economic mass has concentrated and where it has not, but not before diverging.

- *Essential household consumption converges soonest.* Rural-urban gaps in essential household consumption diminish quite rapidly. Even for countries that have urban shares of about 50 to 60 percent, these differences can be small. Area differences in poverty rates are more persistent, international differences even more so. But as the world has developed, these gaps have diminished at all geographic scales.

- *Access to basic public services converges next.* Rural-urban gaps in basic education, health, drinking water, and sanitation persist until countries reach upper-middle incomes. But within-city disparities in these services—most visible as slums—persist well past high levels of urbanization and upper-middle incomes.

- *Wages and incomes converge last.* Indeed, wages and incomes diverge between lag-

ging and leading areas of a country as it grows through low and lower-middle incomes, the same range of per capita incomes needed for territorial concentration to increase. And global divergence in wages and wealth appears to go on for much longer. East Asia saw per capita incomes diverge between 1950 and 1970 as Japan pulled ahead. Then, Japan's prosperity spilled over into the neighborhood, and incomes converged as countries in the region that integrated internationally prospered. Among the countries of West Asia, by contrast, there was no divergence in incomes—nor was there rapid growth.

Convergence in living standards, like concentration of economic activity, takes place faster at the local geographic scale and slowest at the international. But this happens only in prosperous neighborhoods. Even in such places, some measures of living standards (such as per capita consumption, income, or earnings) take a long time to converge, sometimes even with an initial divergence (see figure 2). For others, such as education and health indicators, it can be quicker.

Locally, convergence in basic living standards sets in early. Urban-to-rural gaps in consumption levels rise until countries reach upper-middle-income levels (see figure 2). But they fall soon after, and become small even before they get to high-income levels of around $10,000 per capita. Access to water and sanitation in urban areas is more than 25 percent higher in urban areas for the less urbanized countries. For countries with urbanization rates of about 50 percent, such as Algeria, Colombia, and South Africa, the disparity in access is about 15 percent. For such countries as Brazil, Chile, Gabon, and Jordan, the disparity is less than 10 percent.

This pattern is also seen within countries. Provinces that are more prosperous and urbanized have smaller rural-urban gaps in living standards. This is true even in countries at low levels of income, such as China, India, and the Philippines. But within highly urbanized areas, gaps in basic living standards such as sanitation and schools tend to persist. Despite the best efforts of governments, for example, slums mark the urban landscape in countries well after they reach high-income levels. It is common for one-third of a developing city's population to live in slums.

Nationally, divergence in living standards happens quickly, but convergence is slower. At early levels of income, provincial or interarea disparities in basic living standards can be small. But they increase quickly as countries grow. In low-income Cambodia, for example, the gap between leading and lagging areas in consumption of otherwise-similar households is almost 90 percent. In middle-income Argentina, the gap is 50 percent; but in contemporary Canada, it is just 20 percent. In the rapidly growing East Asian and Eastern European countries, for example, these gaps have increased rapidly.

A few countries such as Chile have been exceptions. Between 1960 and 2000, it experienced geographic convergence while its GDP per capita more than doubled to about $10,500. In Colombia, the ratio of GDP of leading Bogotá to lagging Choco fell from 10 to 3 between 1950 and 1990. Less exceptional is convergence in poverty, basic health, nutrition, and education levels between areas within countries. Fast-growing countries everywhere have been able to quickly translate economic progress into spatial equity in these more basic living standards.

Internationally, divergence in incomes continues a while, and convergence is slowest. Global GDP per capita has increased almost tenfold since 1820. Life expectancy has doubled. Literacy rates have increased from less than 20 to more than 80 percent. But these gains have not been shared equally. Europe and its offshoots—Australia, Canada, New Zealand, and the United States—and more lately Japan and its neighbors have seen enormous increases in income and living standards.

For incomes, the convergence has happened only in the fastest-growing regions of the world. The pattern has been uneven within these countries—a few countries lead, resulting in divergence within the neighborhood, and then growth appears to spill over into their neighbors. In other regions such as Western Asia, there is no divergence—cold comfort because

Figure 2   At all three geographic scales, the patterns of convergence in living standards are similar

a. Locally, first divergence, then convergence, in rural-urban gaps

Ratio of urban to rural per capita consumption

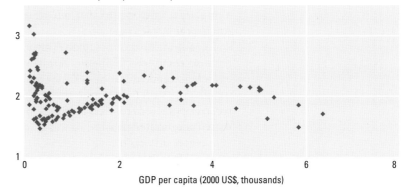

b. Nationally, divergence, then convergence, in incomes between leading and lagging areas

Coefficient of variation of regional wages or income

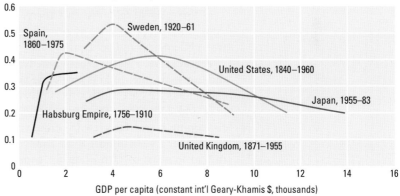

c. Internationally, divergence, then convergence—but only in growing regions

Coefficient of variation of GDP per capita

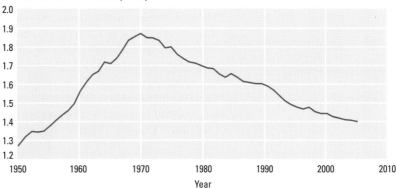

Source: Panel a: WDR 2009 team estimates from more than 120 household surveys for more than 75 countries; Panel b: WDR 2009 team (see chapter 2); Panel c: WDR 2009 team (see chapter 3).

these regions have been falling behind Europe, the European offshoots, and Japan. The importance of neighborhoods is shown most graphically by a comparison of the southern cone nations of Latin

America—Argentina, Brazil, Chile, and Uruguay—with Italy, Portugal, and Spain in southern Europe. Between 1950 and 2006, convergence within southern Europe took place at 1 percent per year, but in South America at just 0.3 percent.

In contrast to incomes, global inequality in access to basic living standards—life expectancy and education—has been falling since 1930. These improvements have picked up pace since 1960 and have been shared across all regions.

The world is different today, but the past provides useful lessons

The general patterns of concentration and convergence are likely to remain the same for today's developing countries as they were for early developers. But there are some differences because of reasons that are technological and political.

Bigger cities. Thanks to better medicine and transport, the world is now more populated and cities are much larger. Between 1985 and 2005, the urban population in developing countries grew by more than 8.3 million a year, almost three times the annual increase of 3 million for today's high-income countries between 1880 and 1900, when their incomes were comparable. If China and India are excluded, though, the annual increase is less than 4.5 million, about 50 percent more than a century ago. The big difference is that the world's largest cities are today much larger. London had fewer than 7 million people in 1900; the largest city among low-income countries today (Mumbai) is three times that size. So is Mexico City, the largest city in middle-income countries. The average size of the world's largest 100 cities has grown to almost 10 times their size in 1900 (see figure 3, panel a), and almost two-thirds of these cities are in developing countries.

Wider markets. Because of advances in communications and transport technology, the notion of markets is more global. Global trade as a share of production is now more than 25 percent, almost five times more than in 1900 (see figure 3, panel b). The openness to trade and capital flows that makes markets more global also makes subnational disparities in income larger

and persist for longer in today's developing countries. Not all parts of a country are suited for accessing world markets, and coastal and economically dense places do better. China's GDP per capita in 2007 was the same as that of Britain in 1911. Shanghai, China's leading area, today has a GDP per capita the same as Britain in 1988, while lagging Guizhou is closer to Britain in 1930. China's size, the openness of coastal China to world trade, and Shanghai's location are the reasons.

More borders. While markets are becoming more international because of better transport and communications, the world has become more politically fragmented. In 1900 there were about 100 international borders (see figure 3, panel c). Today, there are more than 600, as nations in Asia and Africa gained independence from European colonizers, and the Soviet Union and other communist countries broke up into smaller nations. The fragmentation of the world into more nations means smaller domestic markets. But at the same time, the potential for accessing foreign markets has been growing. In any case, thinner borders between countries now bring greater payoffs for producers and workers.

Do such differences in technology mean that the past provides no lessons? Are cities in developing countries too large, and would these countries be better off if urbanization were slowed? Should today's developing countries be more concerned about regional disparities in production and income than developed countries were at a comparable stage of development? Is it easier today for all developing countries to access global markets and offset the disadvantages associated with greater fragmentation? This Report shows why the answer to all these questions is no.

Markets shape the economic landscape

Rising densities of human settlements, migrations of workers and entrepreneurs to shorten the distance to markets, and lower divisions caused by differences in currencies and conventions between countries are central to successful economic development. The spatial transformations along

Figure 3   Later developers face a different world

a. Cities are more populous

Millions of people, world's largest cities

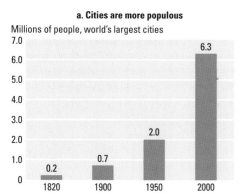

b. Markets are more international

Global trade as share of global GDP (%)

c. But the world is more fragmented

Number of borders

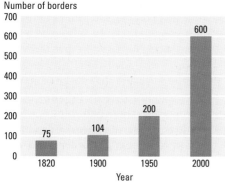

Source: WDR 2009 team.

these three dimensions—density, distance, and division—have been most noticeable in Japan, North America, and Western Europe. Fast and frequent movements of people and products have helped North America, Western Europe, and Northeast Asia account for about three-fourths of global production with less than a sixth of the world's people.

The same market forces of ***agglomeration, migration,*** and ***specialization*** are changing the economic landscape of today's most successful developing countries, in ways similar in scope and speed. Growing cities, mobile people, and vigorous trade have been the catalysts for progress in the developed world over the last two centuries. Now these forces are powering the developing world's most dynamic places.

The realm of "agglomeration economies"

A trip on National Highway 321 east from Chengdu in Sichuan province to Shenzhen in Guangdong is a journey through economic development. Migrating workers who travel these highways often leave their families behind. But they also help their families escape poverty and propel China through the ranks of middle-income countries. As they travel eastward, they leave an agrarian realm in which they receive few benefits from working in proximity to others. Instead, they enter the realm of "agglomeration economies," in which being near other people produces huge benefits.

Shenzhen attracts young workers—90 percent of its 8 million residents are of working age. It specializes in electronic goods. But it makes them in enormous quantities. In 2006 its exports exceeded India's, making its seaport the fourth busiest in the world. Propelled by the forces of agglomeration, migration, and specialization, and helped by its nearness to Hong Kong, China, Shenzhen has grown the fastest of all cities in China since 1979, when it was designated a special economic zone.

This story is being replayed in India. In 1990 Sriperumbudur was known mostly as the place where Prime Minister Rajiv Gandhi was assassinated. In 2006 his widow, Sonia Gandhi, watched as Nokia's telephone plant churned out its 20-millionth handset.[6] The plant had begun production just earlier that year. With neither Shenzhen's favored administrative status nor its infrastructure, Sriperumbudur may be on its way to becoming a national, perhaps even regional, hub for electronic goods. The key is the town's proximity to Chennai, just as Shenzhen's proximity to Hong Kong, China, was instrumental in its growth.

In 1965, when independence was thrust on Singapore, it was not near any prosperous or peaceful place. Instead, it lay between Malaysia and Indonesia, two poor countries that had been ravaged by war between colonizers. Three-quarters of Singapore's population lived in tenements. By 1980 it had industrialized, specializing in electronics, much as Shenzhen is doing now. By 1986 it was the world's busiest container port and Southeast Asia's financial hub. Along the way, by instituting land markets, building efficient transport infrastructure, and intervening to improve housing, it cleaned up its slums. Prosperity spilled over into neighboring Malaysia. Malaysia's manufacturing-led prosperity in turn helped more than 2 million Indonesians who streamed in to fill jobs in construction and services. Singapore's businessmen jet around Asia, fueling growth in places farther than Shenzhen and Sriperumbudur. The "little red dot" on a map—as reportedly derided by a neighboring president[7]—has transformed itself, integrated its neighborhood, and overtaken Britain, its former colonizer (see map 2).

Singapore, Shenzhen, and Sriperumbudur show how scale economies in production, movements of labor and capital, and falling transport costs interact to produce rapid economic growth in cities and countries both large and small. These are the engine of any economy, with a role so fundamental in prosperity and poverty reduction that they are the subject of the first three chapters of the most influential economics text ever written, Adam Smith's *The Wealth of Nations.*

The economies of scale emphasized by Smith can be categorized into three types—those exclusive to firms, those shared by firms in the same industry and location, and those more generally available to producers in a larger urban area.

- With fewer than 17,000 people, Sriperumbudur was large enough for Hyundai to set up a big plant there in 1999. By 2006 the town had helped Hyundai produce its millionth automobile. Basic education and health services, proximity to a port, and basic infrastructure were all it needed to facilitate plant-level scale economies. The evidence is that internal scale economies are high in such heavy industries as shipbuilding, and low in such light industries as garments. The town has enough workers to enable matching workers and jobs in big plants. So towns like Sriperumbudur are large enough to facilitate *internal economies.*

- Shenzhen Special Economic Region—with an area of just 300 square kilometers but a population of almost 3 million—is home to a bustling electronics industry. With a ready supply of skilled and semi-skilled young workers, the area is investing in better education and research facilities to ensure that the city supplies what the industry needs. Its port ships in intermediate inputs and ships out final products. It shares expensive facilities, such as top-notch container ports and convention centers, and matches workers to the growing number of jobs as firms rapidly expand their operations. Proximity to Hong Kong, China, provides access to finance, though Shenzhen is home to a rapidly expanding financial sector. And competition for customers among the multiple suppliers of inputs produces cost savings. The area excels in providing, in economic jargon, *localization economies.*

- Singapore has passed through these stages and is now one of the world's top centers of commerce. By providing a stable economic environment, excel-

Map 2   Settlements of varying size facilitate different scale economies

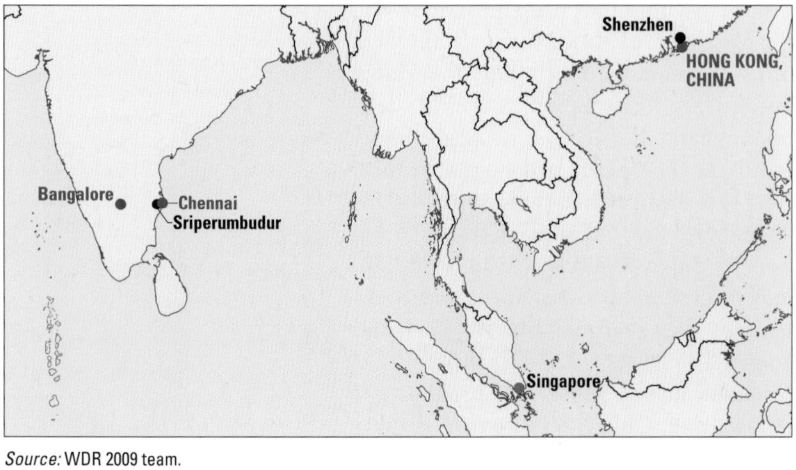

Source: WDR 2009 team.

lent transport links, livability, and efficient finance, it provides services to the entire Asia-Pacific region. These services are used by a wide range of industries, from shipping to manufacturing, to education, and to finance, insurance, and real estate. They thrive on economic density. With fewer than 5 million people packed into less than 700 square kilometers of space, Singapore is the world's most densely populated country. In 2006 its exports of $300 billion approached those of the Russian Federation, which has more than 16 million square kilometers. Singapore's diversity facilitates sharing, matching, and learning, providing what economists call *urbanization economies.*

In most countries, such towns and cities coexist. Brazil's Rio de Janeiro state has about 14.5 million people. Volta Redonda, not too far from Rio city, originally supplied goods and services just to meet the needs of CSN, the largest steel plant in Latin America. Duque de Caixas, about 15 kilometers from Rio, meets the needs of an industry producing petrochemicals. And the diversified Rio de Janeiro metropolis, with about 6 million people, supplies financial services to settlements that surround it. And with other metropolises like São Paulo, Rio connects Brazil to the rest of Latin America and the world. The pattern is so familiar that it is almost a law of urban economics.

The functions and fortunes of settlements are linked. Industrialized places are different from their agrarian predecessors not just because they are more concentrated but also because they are more specialized. The largest cities may be well suited for startup enterprises; the smaller ones may be better suited for those more established. In agriculture, sowing and reaping must happen in the same place. Not so for industry and business services. Falling transport and communications costs allow firms to spatially separate sowing and reaping. Products may be designed and financed in large cities—and produced in small towns.

As firms adjust to changing market conditions, places have to perform different functions or risk decay. The most immobile of all inputs to production—land—must become mobile between uses. Access to oceans and rivers might be the reason a place is settled, but the nimbleness of its land markets will largely determine how much it will grow. Governments may not be good at picking places that will prosper. But how well they institute regulations, build infrastructure, and intervene to make *land use* efficient will decide the pace of prosperity for the entire neighborhood.

Depending on what type of agglomeration economies they deliver, places can be large or small. Function is far more important than size. But locating farther away from economic density generally reduces productivity. Doubling this distance in Brazil apparently reduces productivity by 15 percent and profits by 6 percent. Better infrastructure reduces economic distance. But in a developing country, the most natural way for workers and entrepreneurs to close this distance is to move closer.

Migrating to profit from proximity

Agglomeration economies attract people and finance. Today, capital tends to move quickly over long distances to exploit opportunities for profit. People also move, but they move more quickly to nearby agglomerations than to those far away. Once plants and people come to a place, others follow.

- Locally, the move toward density is quick in fast-growing economies, manifest in a rapid rural-urban migration that accompanies the shift from agriculture to industry. As the Republic of Korea grew between 1970 and 1995, the urban share of population quadrupled to 82 percent, with migration accounting for more than half the increase in the 1960s and 1970s.

- Nationally, workers move to reduce distance to markets in parts that are prospering. About 3 million people moved in the second half of the 1990s from the lagging Indian states of Bihar and Uttar Pradesh to leading Maharashtra and prosperous Punjab (see map 5). In Vietnam, a much smaller country, more than 4 million people migrated internally during the same period.

- Internationally, regional migration is a big part of labor mobility. Migration among neighbors is considerable. Côte d'Ivoire, India, and the Islamic Republic of Iran have been among the top destinations for their neighbors. Germany, Italy, and the United Kingdom still rank among the top 10 sending countries. But interregional migration is sluggish. Fewer than 200 million of the world's 6.7 billion people live outside their region of birth. And just 2 million people move from poorer countries to the developed every year, half of them to the United States.

Map 3   Migrating to reduce distance to density: Despite the obstacles, Chinese workers have migrated in the millions

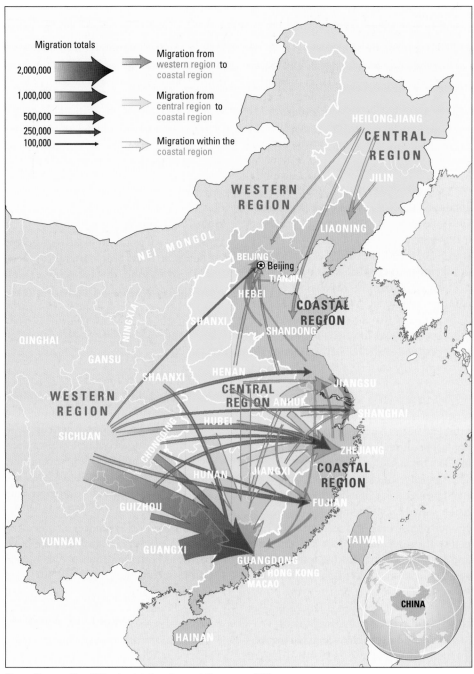

Source: Huang and Luo 2008, using data from the population census of China.

This sum is not likely to increase, even though the gains from greater migration from developing to developed countries are considerable.[8] International migration has been high in the past: fully 20 percent of Europeans emigrated to new lands in the Americas, Australia, and South Africa. Today, these movements have slowed. Just 500,000 Chinese emigrated abroad in 2005. But internal migration has picked up in the developing world. More than 150 million people moved internally in China despite restrictions (see map 3). In Brazil's high-growth years during the 1960s and 1970s, almost 40 million people left the countryside for cities; even today, young workers migrate in large numbers (see map 4). Vigorous internal migration is not new. Between 1820 and 2000 per capita incomes in the United States multiplied 25-fold, and Americans earned the reputation of being among the most footloose of people. In Japan internal migration peaked in the 1960s, as it grew to become the world's second-largest economy.

Despite aggressive area development policies, 1.7 million people—more women than men—have left East Germany for the West, helping to make incomes more equal. Since the transition to market economies, firms and people have picked places better suited for production. More than a million people—about 12 percent of

Map 4   Migrating to reduce distance to density: Brazil's young workers move in thousands to get closer to economic density

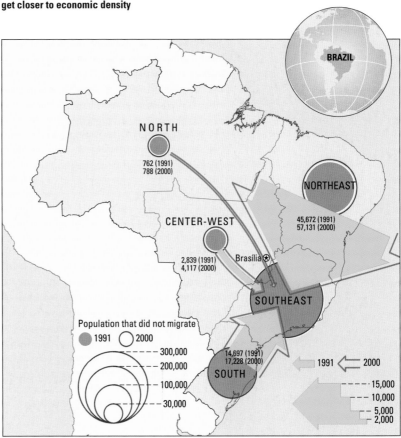

Source: WDR 2009 team, based on census data from the Instituto Brasileiro de Geografia e Estatística.

Map 5   Migrating to reduce distance to density: Migration in India has been less frenetic

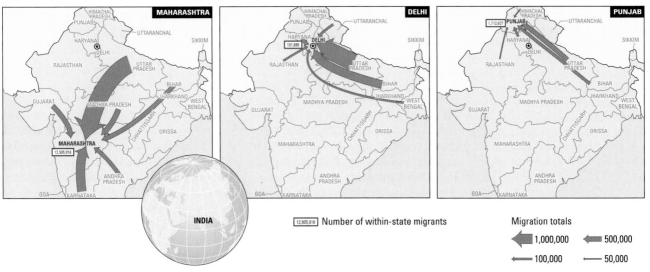

Source: WDR 2009 team, based on census data from the Census of India.

residents—have left Siberia and the Russian North and Far East for the western parts of Russia.

West Africa has sustained regional labor mobility through institutional cooperation. But independent Africa is generally less integrated. Africans—especially the most skilled—have been leaving the continent, seeking and getting higher rewards in the North. Other parts of the world show how to deal with this brain drain. Educated workers will be pulled toward places where other skilled people agglomerate. This is beneficial for both places. But when people are pushed out by the lack of security or basic services, migration is beneficial for the migrant but not always for the nation. Pull migration is better than push, but both are hard to stop or slow. Policy makers are realizing that the challenge is not how to keep people from moving, but how to keep them from moving for the wrong reasons.

China illustrates the benefits. Except for a brief period during the Cultural Revolution, China has treated its diaspora well, according them both rights and respect.[9] Internally, its policies have gone back and forth, but now they are shifting from trying to discourage people from moving to delivering basic services to people wherever they live. The policies are paying dividends. As Chinese migrants are moving to the coast by the million, many of the 57 million overseas Chinese are bringing finance and expertise back to some of the same places. Internal and international migrants are coming together in a way that is not accidental. The willingness of the Chinese to move—leaving the country for other parts of the world to escape war and squalor in the first part of the twentieth century and then bringing finance and know-how to coastal China during the last quarter—promises to bring to southeast China a "reversal of fortune" rivaling the U.S. Northeast (see "Geography in Motion: Overcoming Distance in North America").

Countries do not prosper without mobile people. Indeed, the ability of people to move seems to be a good gauge of their economic potential, and the willingness to migrate appears to be a measure of their desire for advancement. Governments should facilitate **labor mobility.** For decades since independence, India treated its 40 million emigrants as "not required Indians." Encouraged by a change in attitude since the 1990s, expatriate Indians are pulling distant places like Bangalore and Hyderabad closer to world markets, just as the overseas Chinese did for Shanghai and Guangzhou more than a decade earlier. Falling costs of transport and communications have helped greatly.

Specializing and trading as transport costs fall

Transport and communication costs have indeed fallen rapidly over the last century, especially in the last 50 years. Since the 1970s, railroad freight costs are down by half. Road transport costs, despite higher energy and wage costs, are down by about 40 percent. For worldwide air freight, the price has fallen to about 6 percent of its 1955 level. The price for tramp shipping services is half that in 1960. A three-minute phone call from New York to London was almost $300 in 1931. Today, the same call can be made for just a few cents.

With falling domestic transport costs, economic production should have become more evenly spread within countries. With lower costs of transporting and communicating internationally, countries should have traded more with distant partners. What happened was the opposite. Falling transport costs have coincided with greater economic concentration within countries. And while countries now trade more with everyone—exports as a share of world production quadrupled to 25 percent over the last three decades—trade with *neighbors* became even more important.

Why did this happen? The answer lies in the growing importance of scale economies in production and transport (see chapter 6). As transport costs have fallen, they have allowed greater specialization and radically altered the location of firms and the nature of trade. With high transport costs, firms had to be near consumers. But as transport costs fall, they can avail of internal, local, and urban economies of scale, and transport the product to consumers. Internationally, the same thing. With high transport costs, England imported only what it could not grow or produce at reasonable cost—spices from India and beef from Argentina in exchange for British textiles and china. As transport costs fell, it imported more spices and beef. But it also traded more with France and Germany—Scotch whisky for French wine, English ale for German beer. Trade to fulfill basic needs was joined and soon overtaken by trade to satisfy a variety of wants.

Falling costs of transportation and communication have made the world smaller. But they have also made economic activity more geographically concentrated.

- Locally, with falling costs of commuting and a greater potential for exploiting scale economies, towns and cities can grow bigger and denser.
- Nationally, as leading and lagging areas within countries are connected through better modes of transport, production is more concentrated in the more economically dense areas to take advantage of agglomeration economies.
- Internationally, countries that have lowered the costs of transport more have benefited most from greater trade. Greater specialization has made these countries more competitive still, concentrating trade and wealth in a few parts of the world.

Scale economies are evident in the transport sector, too. More trade means lower costs of transportation, which in turn means more trade. This is especially true for intraindustry trade, which has been the most rapidly growing part of international trade during the last half-century. Since 1960 the share of intraindustry trade in the world's total has doubled from 27 percent to 54 percent. Within-region intraindustry trade is low in most regions, and high in a few. It is close to zero for Central Africa, Central Asia, East Africa, Northern Africa, South Asia, and Southern Africa. It is highest for Australia, East Asia, New Zealand, North America, and Western Europe (see figure 4).

Regional cooperation has advanced much faster and further in these parts of the

Figure 4   Intraindustry trade is high in North America, Western Europe, Oceania, and East Asia

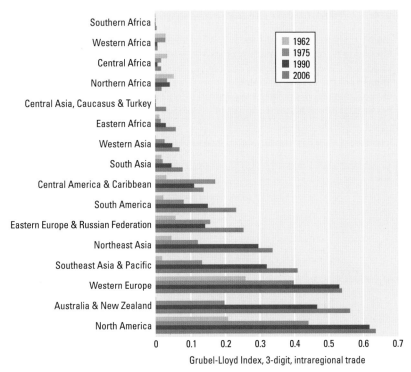

Source: Brülhart 2008 for this Report.
Note: The Grubel-Lloyd Index is the fraction of total trade that is accounted for by intraindustry trade.

world, explaining why the friction of borders on trade has fallen. Aided by a deepening integration, the intraregional share of trade in the EU has risen above 60 percent (see "Geography in Motion: Overcoming Division in Western Europe"). In East Asia, the fastest-growing region, the share of regional trade is now more than 55 percent (see "Geography in Motion: Distance and Division in East Asia").

Development in a world of greater specialization and concentration is even more challenging. Developing countries have higher transport costs and small markets, which do not support specialization. But several countries—mainly in East Asia—have shown that these markets are accessible for low-income countries. The answer lies in the fastest-growing component of intraindustry trade: trade in "intermediate inputs" of production (see box 3).

In agriculture, industry, and services, the potential for fragmenting production is almost without limit. Thailand may not be able to make a television set better than Japan, but it could make parts of televisions

BOX 3 *Intraindustry trade and intermediate inputs*

More than half of world trade today is intraindustry trade, with industries classified in 177 (3-digit) categories, up from about a quarter in 1962. So countries are becoming more similar in their economic structures. This trade consists of final and intermediate goods, with both having increased considerably over the last 50 years. This rise in intraindustry trade is not just for manufacturing. Intraindustry trade in machines and transport equipment is the highest, but the largest increase is in food and live animals. Consumers like variety for farm produce, and that means profit in trade between two countries that raise similar food and animals (see figure at left).

But the largest rise is for intermediate inputs—the produced means of production. Marginal intraindustry trade—a reliable measure of change—is highest in intermediate inputs. This is not just for manufacturing. Agriculture needs inputs, too. And falling communications costs have resulted in greater fragmentation of services into "components," supplied to final consumers from different parts of the world.

Trade in intermediate goods is more sensitive to transport costs than is trade in final goods. Consider the following illustration: if intermediate inputs are two-thirds of the value added for a good, a 5-percent increase in transport costs can mean the equivalent of a 50-percent tax. Little wonder that intermediate goods trade has increased fastest in parts of the world that have reduced trade and transport costs the most.

Intraindustry trade has risen for primary, intermediate, and final goods

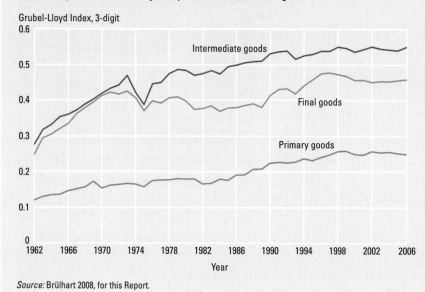

Source: Brülhart 2008, for this Report.

Source: WDR 2009 team.

equally well and much cheaper. Anchored by China and Japan, countries in East Asia have developed production networks that trade intermediate goods back and forth. By specializing in a small part of the production chain, they have broken into this most lucrative and fastest-growing component of trade in manufactures.

Countries in other regions can also benefit from the growing *trade in intermediate goods*. The key for most is making a concerted effort to lower the costs of transport. This means more concentration within developing countries, but—by allowing them to specialize at earlier stages of development and exploit economies of scale—it will help them converge to the incomes and living standards in the developed world. Over the last two decades, such interactions between scale economies, mobility of capital and labor, and transport costs have occupied the interest of researchers (see box 4).

Their insights should change what to expect from the markets. They should also inform what governments can do to promote the geographic transformations necessary for development.

Putting development in place

Prosperity will not come to every place at once, but no place should remain mired in poverty. With good policies, the concentration of economic activity and the convergence of living standards can happen together. The challenge for governments is to allow—even encourage—"unbalanced" economic growth, and yet ensure inclusive development. They can do this through economic integration—by bringing lagging and leading places closer in economic terms.

BOX 4 *New insights from a generation of analysis*

Researchers have been taking a fresh look at industrial organization, economic growth, international trade, and economic geography, having incorporated the effects of scale economies in production. The results can be surprising for those schooled in conventional economic analysis. Here are some of the new insights:

Plants have to be big to exploit economies of scale, but places do not have to be big to generate them. Increasing returns to scale arise because of fixed costs of production (internal to a firm) and proximity to workers, customers, and people with new ideas (external to a firm, even an industry). The size of settlements matters less than their function.

The reason: with reasonable transport costs, towns can be large enough to facilitate internal scale economies. Medium-size cities are often large enough for "localization" economies that come from

thick input markets, but not for "urbanization" economies—especially those involving knowledge spillovers—generated mainly by large cities (see chapter 4).

The implication: policy makers should focus on the functions of cities.

Human capital moves to where it is abundant, not scant. Conventional economic analysis implies that people should move to where their skills are scant. But the opposite seems to happen: educated migrants seek places where many others have similar skills. Among the 100 largest metropolitan areas in the United States, the 25 cities with the highest share of college graduates in 1990 had, by 2000, attracted graduates at twice the rate of the other 75.

The reason: educated workers gain from proximity to others (see chapter 5).

The implication: policies should not fight the market force that pulls skilled people together.

Falling transport costs increase trade more with neighboring, not distant, countries. With a decline in transport costs, countries should trade more with countries that are farther away. But trade has become more localized than globalized. Countries trade more with countries that are similar, because increasingly the basis of trade is the exploitation of economies of scale, not the differences in natural endowments.

The reason: falling transport costs make specialization possible (see chapter 6).

The implication: falling transport costs change the composition of international trade and make it even more sensitive to such costs. Policies to reduce trade and transport costs should be a big part of growth strategies for late developers.

Recognizing scale economies and their interaction with the mobility of people and products implies changing long-held views about what is needed for economic growth. *Source:* WDR 2009 team.

This integration can best be done by unleashing the market forces of agglomeration, migration, and specialization, not by fighting or opposing them. How well markets and governments work together determines the speed and sustainability of geographic transformations. Look at what is happening in Bogotá, Turkey, and West Africa:

- Bogotá has almost 7 million citizens, but migration from rural Colombia continues. A third of its population growth is due to rural migrants, who mostly settle in poor, crowded neighborhoods as the city grows denser. Since 2000 a new public transportation system, the *TransMilenio*, has eased congestion, now carrying a million passengers a month. For the poor neighborhoods especially, it has reduced the distance to economic opportunities. But many people still live in slums, and crime and violence are getting worse. A municipal initiative has addressed these social divisions since 2003, helping almost a million people integrate into the city and change their neighborhoods.

- Turkey is trying to change neighborhoods too, in a different way. The country of 70 million has been looking toward integration with the EU. Because of higher agglomeration economies and lower transport costs, areas near Istanbul and Izmir may be better suited for integrating with Europe. The more distant areas of eastern and southeastern Anatolia and the Black Sea have 40 percent of the land but less than 20 percent of the national product, with a GDP per capita about half that of the western areas. The disparities persist despite government efforts to spread economic mass toward the east. Meanwhile, public investments in social services help lagging areas, while fiscal incentives for firms to locate in those areas seem ineffective.[10]

- The Economic Community of West African States (ECOWAS) has a protocol that allows free movement of its 250 million people between member states. This has helped the neighborhood maintain regional labor mobility at preindependence levels, even as it fell in East and Southern Africa. But trade is another story. In the most dynamic parts of the world, the exchange of similar goods and services—intraindustry trade—has been rising rapidly. But in West Africa, international borders are thickened by red tape and illicit checkpoints, which divide the region and thwart the efforts of ECOWAS members to specialize and trade.

As the lens of economic geography is widened, different movements, stresses, and strains come into view.

- Locally, in places like Bogotá, land must accommodate more and more people. If **land markets** work well, land will be mobile between uses and allocated productively. The cities that do this best will grow, and even more people will be attracted to their economic density.
- People and products move much faster in and around Bogotá than they do in Turkey. But even in Turkey, the western areas will become more prosperous and dense, if at a slower pace. Spatial disparities in incomes and poverty rates between the west and the east will likely rise and then diminish as people move to take advantage of economic density. If **labor markets** in Turkey are fluid, people will reduce their economic distance to these agglomerations.
- Internationally, these movements are likely to be fewer and even slower. If regional and global markets were integrated, countries in West Africa would specialize in a few tasks and become competitive in world markets. As divisions diminish, neighboring countries

trade similar goods and services, motivated more by the benefits of specialization and scale than by differences in natural endowments. Trade can only partially offset the immobility of land and labor, but it will help convergence when developing countries can tap into the most rapidly growing component: **trade in intermediate goods.**

Private motives are the main shapers of the economic landscape, but it can be reshaped by collective action, most potently by governments. Seen through the lens of economic geography, land use, labor mobility, and intermediate goods trade come into focus (see table 2). Governments should pay special attention to land, labor, and product markets. When they do not work well, the forces of agglomeration, migration, and specialization weaken, and the economy stagnates. When they do, land, labor, and input markets bring the economic efficiency that comes with geographic concentration, and the equity associated with converging living standards.

A rule of thumb for economic integration

The concern of policy makers is that production will concentrate in some places, people in others. Cities will have economic density, and the countryside most of the poor. Leading areas will have the economic mass, while the poor are massed in lagging areas. Some countries will have much of the world's wealth, others most of the world's poor. Even if this were temporary, it seems unfair. But the disparities may be long lasting, destabilizing parts of a country, entire nations, and even some world regions.

Governments have many reasons to worry about disparities in welfare in and among countries. They also have many policy instruments for promoting economic integration to reduce those disparities.

- *Institutions*—shorthand in the Report for policies that are *spatially blind* in their design and should be universal in their coverage. Some of the main examples are regulations affecting land, labor, and international trade and such social

Table 2   Agglomeration, migration, and specialization are the most important forces—and land, labor, and intermediate inputs the most sensitive factor markets

	Geographic scales		
	Local	**National**	**International**
Economic force	**Agglomeration** Speeded by migration, capital mobility, and trade	**Migration** Influenced by agglomeration and specialization	**Specialization** Aided by agglomeration and factor mobility
Key factor of production	**Land** Immobile	**Labor** Mobile within countries	**Intermediate inputs** Mobile within and between countries

Source: WDR 2009 team.
Note: Throughout the Report, "areas" are within-country economic neighborhoods or administrative units such as states or provinces, and regions are groups of countries based on geographic proximity.

services as education, health, and water and sanitation financed through tax and transfer mechanisms.

- *Infrastructure*—shorthand for policies and investments that are *spatially connective*. Examples include roads, railways, airports, harbors, and communication systems that facilitate the movement of goods, services, people, and ideas locally, nationally, and internationally.

- *Interventions*—shorthand for the *spatially targeted* programs that often dominate the policy discussion. Examples include slum clearance programs, fiscal incentives for manufacturing firms offered by state governments, and preferential trade access for poor countries in developed country markets.

Today, policy debates often begin and end with discussions of spatially targeted incentives. The debate on how to promote healthy urbanization is polarized between those who emphasize villages, where a majority of the world's poor still live, and those who believe the way out of poverty lies in cities, where much of the world's wealth is generated. As urban poverty increases, the focus is shifting from villages to slums. Motivated by within-country geographic disparities in living standards, the debate on territorial development is similarly fixated on economic growth in lagging areas. At the international level, preferential market access for

the least developed countries can end up dominating policy discussions.

This Report calls for a rebalancing of these debates to include all the elements of a successful approach to spatial integration—institutions, infrastructure, and incentives. Using the findings in part one and the analysis of market forces in part two, part three reframes these debates, calling for a shift from spatial targeting to spatial integration.

The world is complicated, and the problems of economic integration defy simple solutions. But the principles need not be complex. The bedrock of integration policies should be spatially blind institutions. Where the integration challenge spans more than one geographic dimension, institutions must be augmented by public investments in spatially connective infrastructure. Spatially targeted interventions are not always necessary. But where the problem is low economic density, long distances, and high divisions, the response must be comprehensive, involving spatially blind, connective, and targeted policies.

For each spatial dimension, an instrument of integration (see table 3). The rule of thumb: "an I for a D."

- For a one-dimensional problem, the mainstay of the policy response should be (spatially blind) institutions.
- For a two-dimensional challenge, both institutions and (spatially connective) infrastructure are needed.

Table 3 "An I for a D?" A rule of thumb for calibrating the policy response

Complexity of challenge	Place type—local (L), national (N), and international (I) geographic scales	Policy priorities for economic integration		
		Institutions Spatially blind	Infrastructure Spatially connective	Interventions Spatially targeted
One-dimensional problem	L. Areas of incipient urbanization N. Nations with sparse lagging areas I. Regions close to world markets	●		
Two-dimensional challenge	L. Areas of intermediate urbanization N. Nations with dense lagging areas I. Regions distant from world markets	●	●	
Three-dimensional predicament	L. Areas of advanced urbanization that have within-city divisions N. Nations with dense lagging areas and domestic divisions I. Regions distant from markets with small economies	●	●	●

Source: WDR 2009 team.
Note: Throughout the Report, areas are within-country economic neighborhoods or administrative units such as states or provinces, and regions are groupings of countries based on geographic proximity.

- For a three-dimensional predicament, all three instruments are needed—institutions, infrastructure, and (spatially targeted) interventions.

The primary dimension at the local geographic scale is density; nationally, it is distance; internationally, division. At each of these geographic scales, policies designed without explicit consideration to space should be seen as the primary instrument. In some places, these can be a large part of integration policies. The task of integration is relatively straightforward in areas of incipient urbanization (as in lagging states in many low-income countries), in countries with mobile labor and capital (such as Chile), or in regions that are close to world markets (such as North Africa). In such places, the integration challenge can be seen as one dimensional. Explicitly spatial policies are not generally necessary. Universal or spatially blind institutions—made available to everyone regardless of location—form both the bedrock and the mainstay of an effective integration policy.

As the task becomes more complicated, these institutions must be assisted by infrastructure. Locally, rapid urbanization can congest the area, increasing economic distance and choking off agglomeration economies. In places such as Mumbai, whose population has doubled since the 1970s, rising congestion has to be met by investments in transport infrastructure, so that the benefits of density are shared more widely. Nationally, changing economic and political fortunes can leave behind a misplaced density of populations in lagging areas, so that in some countries (such as Brazil) lagging areas have higher poverty rates *and* high population densities. Internationally, developing regions are all deeply divided, but some also may be distant from world markets. Even if regional institutions take hold and make South Asia a more integrated region, some countries (such as Nepal) may need concerted policy action to improve the infrastructure to reach growing regional and international markets. For places that face two-dimensioned integration challenges, investments in infrastructure that connects lagging to leading places and aid market access should supplement the institutions that bring people together.

The integration challenge is greatest where adverse density, distance, and division combine to pose a "three-dimensional challenge." In highly urbanized areas (such as Bogotá), the fear is that economic density and population density may not coincide. Within-city divisions may prevent the integration of slums and spawn problems of crime and grime. In some countries (such as India), ethnic, religious, or linguistic divisions discourage the poor in densely populated lagging areas from seeking their fortunes elsewhere. And in the most fragmented and remote regions (such as Central Africa or Central Asia), a clustering of small and poor nations can lead to spillovers of the wrong kind—disease, conflict, or corruption.

Slums in large cities, densely populated poor areas in divided nations, and the "bottom billion" countries—approximating the three billions discussed at the beginning—are the most difficult challenges for integration. The policy responses should not be timid. But they should also be deliberate.

Efficient and inclusive urbanization

No country has grown to middle income without industrializing and urbanizing. None has grown to high income without vibrant cities. The rush to cities in developing countries seems chaotic, but it is necessary. It seems unprecedented, but it has happened before (see figure 5). It had to have, because the move to density that is manifest in urbanization is closely related

Figure 5 In charted waters: the pace of urbanization today has precedents
Change in urban shares since 1800

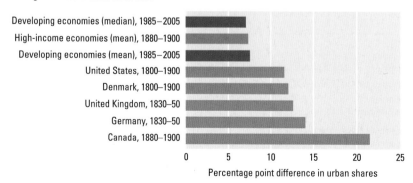

Source: WDR 2009 team calculations based on data from various sources (see figure 1.13).

to the transformation of an economy from agrarian to industrial to postindustrial.

Governments can facilitate the spatial transformations that lie behind these sectoral changes. Depending on the stage of urbanization, sequencing and priority-setting require paying attention to different aspects of the geographic transformation. What does not change is that a foundation of institutions must be universal and come first, investments in connective infrastructure should be both timed and located well and come second, and spatially targeted interventions should be used least and last.

The approach requires the discipline of following the integration principle set out earlier. The payoff is a spatial transformation that is both efficient and inclusive (see chapter 7).

The principles outlined in the Report help to prioritize policies for different stages of urbanization, providing the elements of an urbanization strategy. Map 6 shows three areas in Colombia, each with a specific geography. But the principles are quite universal.

- *Incipient urbanization.* In places that are mostly rural, governments should be as neutral as possible and should

establish the institutional foundation of possible urbanization in some places. Good land policies are central, and so are policies to provide basic services to everyone. For example, the universalization of land rights in Denmark at the turn of the eighteenth century contributed greatly to the nation's take-off into industrialization a few decades later. Indeed, policies to strengthen rural property rights are seen as instrumental for higher agricultural productivity in sixteenth-century England, which freed workers to migrate to towns to work in manufacturing and services. A close complement to the institutions for better land markets is the universal provision of basic social services—security, education, health services, and sanitation. In 1960, the Republic of Korea had a per capita income level that Benin has today. Seventy-five percent of its people lived in rural areas, more than a third of Korean adults had no schooling, and fewer than 5 percent of children had been immunized against preventable diseases such as measles. By 2000, more than 80 percent had urbanized, almost everyone was literate and immunized, and the Republic of Korea's income had

Map 6   As urbanization advances, policies must evolve

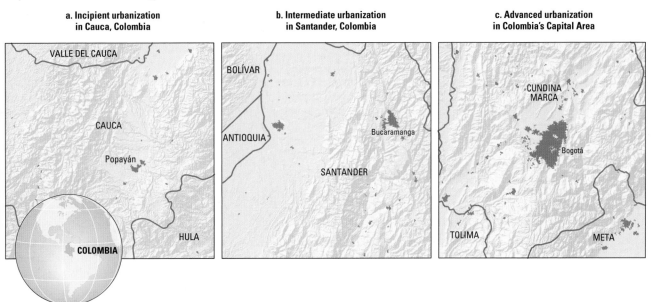

|a. Incipient urbanization in Cauca, Colombia|b. Intermediate urbanization in Santander, Colombia|c. Advanced urbanization in Colombia's Capital Area|

Source: WDR 2009 team, using data from Schneider, Friedl, and Potere 2008.

Concentration without congestion in western China: Chongqing and Chengdu

An experiment in China might change the future of urbanization policy in the developing world. Policy makers should take notice.

China is taking inland the urbanization strategy that was successful in the leading coastal areas in the 1980s and 1990s. The "area approach" is being implemented in two places—Chongqing and Chengdu, both located in the near west. At about 40 percent, they have the same urbanization ratio as the average for China. The aim is to increase that to 70 percent by 2020, promoting both concentration and rural-urban convergence.

Chongqing has a population of about 40 million, with a portfolio of a capital city, six large cities, 25 small and mid-size cities, 95 central townships, and 400 townships. Chongqing has been accorded the status of a special municipality, as Beijing, Shanghai, and Tianjin have had for some years. Like them, it will enjoy greater financial autonomy. Chengdu is smaller, a sprawling metropolitan area with 11 million people. Along with the 2,000-year-old capital city of Sichuan province, it has eight medium-size cities, 30 central townships, 60 townships, and 600 villages.

The urbanization strategy involves "three concentrations" of land, industry, and farmers. The idea is to reap the benefits of scale economies, promote the mobility of goods and workers, and improve the well-being of new migrants to cities. Consistent with the policy priorities outlined for areas with intermediate urban shares of about 40–50 percent, the emphasis in both places is on universal institutions and connective infrastructure, not spatially targeted interventions.

Better institutions. The emphasis is on coordination across government levels to manage land use and conversion. In the countryside, the plan concentrates rural land by transferring use rights to firms and farmers. In towns and cities, the creation of industrial zones is a key part of the wider framework. Large and medium cities are developing high value-added manufacturing, while smaller cities and towns are specializing in labor-intensive industries, pulling in labor from nearby villages, and facilitating localization economies.

More infrastructure. Massive trunk infrastructure is planned. Chongqing will spend billions on infrastructure, from the central government and through increased private investment from Hong Kong, China, and from Singapore. In Chengdu, about 117 billion yuan will be invested in 71 infrastructure projects, including rural-urban transport networks, and water and sanitation projects in both rural and urban areas. Another 16.5 billion yuan will be invested in 34 social projects to improve the living standards of lagging rural residents.

If markets favor the two places as much as the government has, they will improve the lives of millions in the Chinese hinterland. The integration already has had a local impact. In Chongqing, rural incomes in 2007 increased faster than those of urban residents. In Chengdu, farmer concentrations are believed to have led to a productivity increase of 80 percent, as industry has been absorbing about 100,000 farmers a year.

Source: WDR 2009 team.

reached that of modern-day Portugal. Another good example is Costa Rica.

- **Intermediate urbanization.** In places where urbanization has picked up speed, in addition to these institutions, governments must put in place connective infrastructure so that the benefits

of rising economic density are more widely shared. Industrialization involves changing land use patterns as activities concentrate, and requires moving goods and services around quickly. Land use regulations can affect location decisions, and they continue to be the institutional priority. Spatially blind social services should continue as part of rural-urban integration, so that people are pulled to cities by agglomeration economies, not pushed out by the lack of schools, health services, and public security in rural areas. But even if these services are provided, transport costs can rise quickly because of growing congestion, affecting the location choices of entrepreneurs. Connective infrastructure is needed to keep such areas integrated. State and central governments that work well together can provide the trunk infrastructure necessary to ensure that prosperity is widely shared. Making the administrative jurisdiction wider can help in coordinating infrastructure investments. A good example is Chongqing in western China (see box 5).

- **Advanced urbanization.** In highly urbanized areas, besides institutions and infrastructure, targeted interventions may be necessary to deal with the problem of slums. Services and learning require people to be in proximity to livable surroundings. This is the stage in which slums can compromise a city's ability to deliver the economies that come from proximity. Slum-improvement programs may not be a priority at earlier stages of urbanization, but at this stage they become necessary. The lesson from assessments of slum-improvement initiatives is that targeted interventions will not be enough by themselves. These interventions will not work unless institutions related to land and basic services are reasonably effective, and transport infrastructure is in place. A three-dimensional challenge must be met by a three-pronged policy response, requiring coordinated policies at the central, state, and city levels of government. Singapore's success shows the advantages of such coordination in a city-state. More recent examples are Shanghai and Guangzhou in China. An even more recent (and perhaps more generally applicable) example is Bogotá in Colombia.

The experience of successful urbanizers indicates that the basis of successful rural-urban transformations is a set of spatially blind policies—"institutions" in the shorthand of this Report. Investments in infrastructure that connects places form the second tier. Geographically targeted interventions should be used only when the challenge is especially difficult, but should always be used together with an effort to improve institutions and infrastructure.

Area (territorial) development policies that integrate nations

Some parts of a country are better suited for agriculture, others for industry, and still others for services. And as industry and services flourish, the spatial distribution of economic activities must change.[11] No country has grown to riches without changing the geographic distribution of its people and production.

A rising concentration of people and production in some parts of a country has marked economic growth over the last two centuries. To fight this concentration is to fight growth itself, and policy makers must show patience in dealing with these imbalances. But aided by government policies, successful development also has been marked by falling disparities in living standards between places favored by markets and those less fortunate. Policies can speed up the convergence in basic living standards, so that people in the least-fortunate places do not have to wait for basic public amenities until their nations reach high income levels. The experience of successful developers also justifies impatience in equalizing basic living standards.

Consider Malaysia. Economic growth and government policies have reduced poverty and improved living standards, speeding progress toward meeting the Millennium Development Goals. But in the early years of growth (between 1970 and 1976), poverty rates between different states diverged briefly, to later converge as they declined for all states (see figure 6). Health indicators (infant mortality) declined more

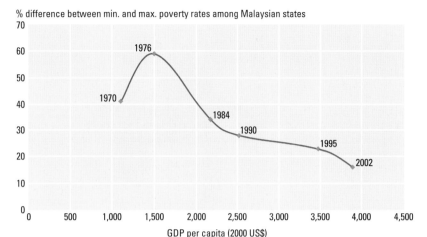

Figure 6   Quicker geographic convergence in basic living standards in Malaysia

% difference between min. and max. poverty rates among Malaysian states

Source: Malaysia Economic Planning Unit 2008.

in the slower-growing states, implying that tax and transfer mechanisms worked well. Such impatience with spatial inequality in living standards is paying off in other countries such as China, Egypt, Indonesia, Mexico, Thailand, and Vietnam.

But not all countries have experienced geographic convergence in the Millennium Development Indicators, such as child mortality, maternal health, basic education, safe water, and sanitation. What should they do?

The answer lies in integrating lagging and leading areas, using policies that are tailored to the level of difficulty of integration. While economic motives are important, social and political conditions influence the speed of these spatial changes. The location choices that people make reflect the strengths and inclinations of societies and political structures. Poverty maps provide a snapshot of where the poor are concentrated (high poverty mass—that is, the "poor people"), and which places are the poorest (high poverty rate—that is, the "poor places"). These maps can tell us a lot about the social and political conditions in a country: the movement of poor people may best reflect the constraints to mobility, because they have the most reason to move and the fewest resources to do so.

Using information on where poor people are located and which places are poor, the policy response can be calibrated to country conditions.

- *Countries with sparsely populated lagging areas.* In China the highest poverty rates

Map 7   Three types of countries, differing challenges for area development

a. China: Poverty rates are high in the west, but most poor people are in the east

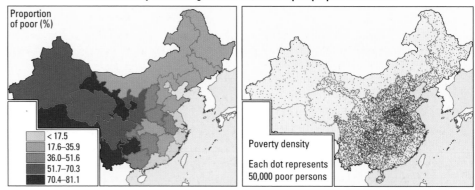

Proportion of poor (%)

< 17.5
17.6–35.9
36.0–51.6
51.7–70.3
70.4–81.1

Poverty density

Each dot represents 50,000 poor persons

b. Brazil: Poverty rates are high in the north and northeast, but most poor people live along the coast

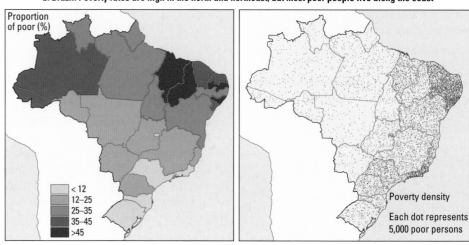

Proportion of poor (%)

< 12
12–25
25–35
35–45
>45

Poverty density

Each dot represents 5,000 poor persons

c. India: Poverty rates are high in the central states, and many poor people live there

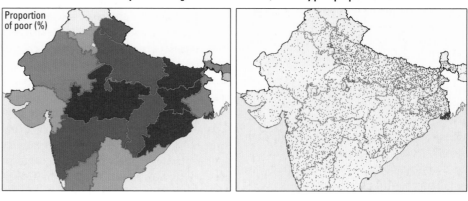

Proportion of poor (%)

6.4–9.7
9.8–16.7
16.8–24.8
24.9–35.4
35.5–46.6
no data

Poverty density

Each dot represents 50,000 poor persons

Source: WDR 2009 team (see chapter 8 for details).

are in the western provinces, but the poor are concentrated in the southeast and central areas (see map 7, panel a). Economic density and population density overlap. The country has few divisions—linguistic and other barriers are not high—and people, including the poor, can move to reduce their distance to density. Spatially blind institutions that ensure well-functioning land markets, enforce property rights, and deliver basic social services such as schooling and health care can be the mainstay of an economic integration strategy to reduce the economic distance between lagging and leading areas. Chile, Egypt, Honduras, Indonesia, Russia, Uganda, and Vietnam are other examples of countries where the area development challenge is unidimensional—the main problem is distance.

- *Undivided countries with densely populated lagging areas.* In Brazil the poverty rates are highest in the north and northeast: eight of the ten poorest states are in the northeast, the other two are in the north (see map 7, panel b). But the economic mass and the concentration of poverty are highest in the urban agglomerations near the coast, from the poor northeast to the thriving southeast. Economic and population densities coincide only partially. The poverty-related symptoms are those of a country where within-country divisions such as ethnolinguistic differences and political fragmentation are low, but where population densities are—for historical and policy-related reasons—in the "wrong places." Bangladesh, Colombia, Ghana, and Turkey have similar conditions. In such places the pull of agglomeration economies in leading areas and the mobility of labor may not be strong enough to induce concentration and convergence. The problems of "long distance and wrong density" must be met by a two-pronged policy of economic integration: spatially blind institutions should be augmented by spatially connective infrastructure, such as interregional highways and railroads and improved telecommunications.

- *Divided countries with densely populated lagging areas.* In India more than 400 million people live in the central lagging states, home to more than 60 percent of the nation's poor (see map 7, panel c). People live there for a reason: it is a fertile plain and was the cradle of Indian civilization. But their location is less fortunate now, as the world has changed. Labor mobility is limited because of linguistic and class divisions. Mobility has not been helped by policies that sought to revive growth in these lagging provinces through subsidized finance and preferential industrial licensing. The debate is now shifting toward economic integration—policies more consistent with mobility of labor such as interregional infrastructure and better health and education services. These policies and the interstate migration they encourage will, if given time, reduce the divisions that have made the distances long between leading areas and densely populated lagging areas. In the meantime, these areas may need a helping hand—from geographically targeted incentives that encourage local production. Another country with a three-dimensional integration agenda of distance, densely populated poor areas, and domestic divisions may be Nigeria. In such places, the policy response has to be a blend of spatially blind, connective, and targeted policies.

Governments should not be faulted for being impatient with markets, and for trying to help lagging areas. But targeted interventions should be designed to work with the institutional reforms and the investments in infrastructure. Experience suggests that incentives should not be provided for activities that depend on agglomeration economies or international market access. Incentives for agriculture are prime candidates in these largely rural and agrarian areas. Relying mainly on targeted incentives for industry—as India did for decades—will not help the lagging states improve living standards to levels in the leading states.

Regional integration to increase access to global markets

The merits of global versus regional trade agreements have been debated for years. The debate is now largely concluded. Where

Figure 7   Northeast, Southeast, and South Asia have been catching up to developed nations
Average annual growth rates of GDP per capita, 1960–2006

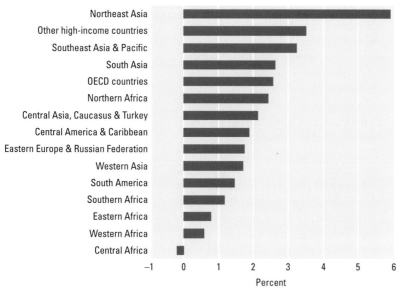

Source: WDR 2009 team.

if the scale of production is big, and that requires reaching the big markets of the Northern Hemisphere.

What do late developers have to do to accelerate development? The common condition is division—that is, thick borders. What differs is their distance from large world markets and whether or not there is a large country in their neighborhood (see map 8, panel b).

- *Countries in regions near large world markets.* For countries near large markets, regional and global integration does not require geographic differentiation. Spatially blind measures such as improving economic policies and the investment climate will attract capital and technology from the more sophisticated markets nearby. Their underused talent and cheaper labor are powerful draws. Whether they lag or lead within the region is hardly relevant; the presence of a sun nearby makes them all small planets. Mexican exports to the United States are about 1.7 percent of the U.S. economy. Mexico should build even stronger links with the United States. But for other countries in Central America, the payoffs to infrastructure connections to Mexico are small—the market in North America dwarfs all of Central America's. And market access likely depends most on economic stability. Spatially blind institutions should be able to integrate Central America with world markets. The same is true for Eastern Europe and North Africa. Countries in these regions have better-than-average market access, though depending on their economic policies and regulations, this access is not uniform even within these regions (see map 8, panel c).

- *Countries in regions distant from large world markets that have a large economy.* To integrate regions more distant from large world markets but with a sizable economy—East Asia, Latin America, Southern Africa, and South Asia—such spatially blind measures are just as necessary, but they may not be sufficient. For lagging countries in these regions, such as Mongolia,

regional or bilateral pacts do not discourage trade with countries in other regions, and where they are accompanied by measures to facilitate the flows of goods, people, and finance—such as infrastructure and compensatory mechanisms—they can help. Otherwise, they are not worth the trouble.

This Report does not reopen that debate. Instead, it takes up the question of how developing countries can best gain access to markets within their neighborhoods and across the world. Geography matters greatly in deciding what is needed, what is unnecessary, and what will fail. But with the right mix of policy actions, even countries in parts of the world that have been left far behind can overcome their geographic disadvantage. The way to tell if the actions are paying dividends is whether market access improves noticeably.

Some regions of the world have done better than others (see figure 7). Countries in these regions now have thinner economic borders (see map 8, panel a). They can afford to have thin borders, because their neighbors are prospering too. For them, regional markets are world markets. Others, like the East Asians, have allowed production relationships to grow strong and cut paths even through thick borders. But specializing can increase efficiency only

Map 8   Market access distinguishes world regions

a. Borders are thicker in developing regions

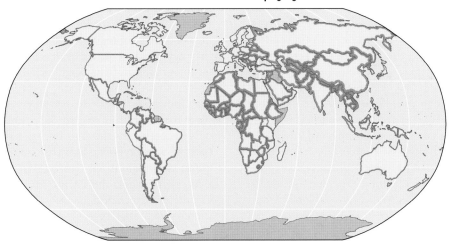

b. The size and access to markets differs greatly by region

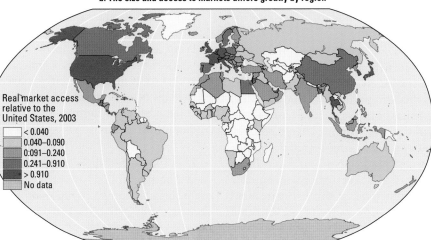

Real market access
relative to the
United States, 2003

- < 0.040
- 0.040–0.090
- 0.091–0.240
- 0.241–0.910
- > 0.910
- No data

c. The three D's suggest a simple taxonomy of the world's neighborhoods

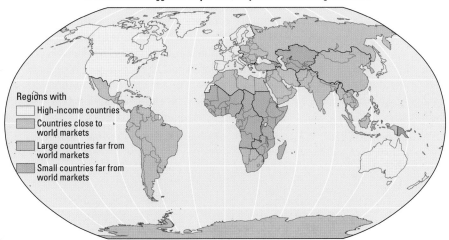

Regions with

- High-income countries
- Countries close to
  world markets
- Large countries far from
  world markets
- Small countries far from
  world markets

Sources: Panel a: WDR 2009 team (see chapter 3 for details); panel b: Mayer 2008 (see chapter 9 for details); panel c: WDR 2009 team (see chapter 9 for details).

Nepal, Paraguay, and Zimbabwe, some of the paths to world markets may go through their larger neighbors. Brazil, China, and India are attractive to investors because of their potential market size, and these "home market effects" can generate the impetus for specialization and help their enterprises compete in world markets. A qualification: for market access, the relevant measure of distance is economic, not Euclidean. With a combination of bilateral accords, inspired transport policies, and aggressive specialization in primary products, Chile reduced distance to North America and built global rather than regional links. But such cases are exceptions. For the smaller countries in these regions, both institutional reforms and regional connectivity will be necessary for economic integration.

- *Countries in regions distant from world markets without large economies.* The most difficult challenges are for the countries in parts of the world divided by thick borders, distant from world markets, and without a large country that can serve as a regional conduit to world markets, as Brazil and India might. For these regions, economic geography poses a three-dimensional challenge. Côte d'Ivoire or Tanzania can hardly be blamed for worrying most about their own poor, and not their less fortunate neighbors such as Burkina Faso or Burundi. Indeed, seeing the benefits of regional cooperation, they have made repeated efforts to foster integration in their neighborhoods. The ECOWAS even includes a clause that allows workers to cross borders, a stage of integration rivaled only (and only recently) by the EU. It also has tried to share regional infrastructure. Other such regions are Central Africa, Central Asia, and the Pacific Islands. Countries in such regions face a three-dimensional challenge (see "Geography in Motion: Density, Distance, and Division in Sub-Saharan Africa"). A combination of efforts to improve institutional cooperation and regional infrastructure investments is needed—but it is not enough. Targeted incentives also will be necessary, through preferential access to developed country markets, perhaps made conditional on regional collaboration to improve institutions and infrastructure.

Everyone should support the efforts of these "bottom billion" countries to integrate their economies, within and across borders. A billion lives depend on it.

We are familiar with the sectoral transformations needed for economic growth—the changes in work and organization as agrarian economies become industrialized and service oriented. This Report discusses the spatial transformations that also must happen for countries to develop. Higher densities, shorter distances, and lower divisions will remain essential for economic success in the foreseeable future. They should be encouraged. With them will come unbalanced growth. When accompanied by policies for integration calibrated to the economic geography of nations, these changes also will bring inclusive development—sooner, not much later.

Navigating This Report

In 1971 Simon Kuznets, a Russian émigré who had built his career in the United States, was awarded the Nobel Prize in Economics "for his empirically founded interpretation of economic growth, which has led to new and deepened insight into the economic and social structure and process of development."[1] In his prize lecture, Kuznets summarized the structural changes that accompany economic growth, emphasizing "the shift away from agriculture to nonagricultural pursuits and, recently, away from industry to services."[2] These are the sectoral changes in production needed for nations to prosper. Nations do not develop by merely doing more of the same thing. They must do different things, and do them better.

Over the years, this has been confirmed so often that it now seems almost obvious. Less obvious but no less important are the *spatial* transformations needed for these structural shifts. Some places are suited for farming, others for industry, yet others for services. As economies become industrialized and more people are employed in services, their shapes must change, too. These changes, involving social adjustment as much as the economic, can take time. The economic world is not frictionless. The "what" and "how" of economic production cannot be decided without deciding the "where."

For policy makers, especially, it is important to understand these changes and to appreciate the market forces that shape them. This understanding can be the difference between prosperity and stagnation. It may even be one of the main lessons of the twentieth century. After Kuznets left Russia in 1922, Soviet planners implemented one approach to economic geography, and the United States implemented another. The Soviet strategy forced people to move to the north and east and to spread out economic production. Meanwhile, Americans moved voluntarily toward the south and the west, but production became more concentrated. Within five years of Kuznets' death in 1985, the Soviet Union would collapse. At the time, Russia's per capita income was a quarter that of the United States. Spatial inefficiency was not the only reason why the Soviet Union fell. But it could not have helped.

As Russia has moved from plan to market, spatial efficiency increased. Between 1989 and 2004, almost all new firms chose locations with the best access to Moscow, St. Petersburg, and international markets.[3] Over the past three decades, researchers have been documenting the changes in economic geography needed to stay spatially efficient as technology advances and production structures change. They have studied the effects of larger populations, globalizing markets, and international borders on the location of people and production. They are starting to assess how governments can help or hurt these transformations. This Report draws on this work and its implications for public policy.

Government policies are important. With development, people and production become more concentrated—in towns and cities, and in areas of countries closer to domestic and international markets. While economic activity concentrates in some parts of a nation or the globe, many people may be spread out over the countryside or in places distant from prosperity, perhaps opening sizable geographic disparities in living standards. This Report discusses why this happens, and assesses what has been most effective in altering the economic geography of developing countries. Economic activity will concentrate in any case. But managed one way, as the United States did, it can foster growth and integration. Managed another way, it can result in disintegration and despair, and even conflict.

The Report covers a broad and seemingly disparate set of phenomena that span the spectrum from local to national to international scales, from human to physical to political geography, and from national and global institutions to targeted interventions. To keep the inquiry disciplined requires emphasizing some aspects of spatial transformations and leaving others out. The rest of this chapter summarizes the Report's scope, clarifies its terms, and outlines its structure.

Scope

Governments intervene (usually incorrectly) to spread the benefits of economic growth more evenly across space. Even when the imperatives are political, they have economic consequences. And even if the objectives are economic, they have social and environmental effects. Policy makers thus face sharp tradeoffs and must compromise. The economic costs of mistakes can be large and lasting: recognizing the importance of economic geography means realizing that once producers and people make decisions on where to locate, they can be difficult to reverse.

Governments can do better by promoting the market forces that deliver both the concentration of economic production and the convergence of living standards, and augment them with policies to ensure affordable basic services everywhere. They can do this by helping people and entrepreneurs take advantage of economic opportunities, wherever they arise. The market forces that help most are agglomeration, migration, and specialization. Their economic benefits are the subject of this Report. Their social and environmental implications are not considered in detail (see box 0.1). The unintended social and environmental effects of market forces are important policy matters. But they deserve more space than can be covered in a report that shows how *economic* geography is reshaped during development.

The Report describes the geographic transformations needed for development. It analyzes these changes using the insights from economic history and recent research. It then revisits the policy debates on urbanization, regional development, and international integration. This is the 31st *World Development Report,* and the issues it covers have been visited by earlier Reports. But here the facts, analysis, and policies related to spatial transformations are the major focus, and the Report is structured accordingly.

Terms

To formulate simple messages that are useful to policy makers requires an uncomplicated

---

BOX 0.1 *What this Report is not about*

To keep the Report focused, several important aspects of the spatial transformations do not get the attention they would in a fuller study. The main aspects not considered—except when emphasizing or qualifying the most important messages—are the *social and environmental effects* of a changing economic geography.

Agglomeration—the growth of cities—can have social and environmental effects that are beneficial and some that are detrimental. Cities help to break down societal stereotypes and increase cohesion. Most progressive movements throughout history have had urban origins. But so have the most violent. The propensity of people to commit crimes is believed to be greater in cities. And while cities allow individualism and creativity and break down social barriers, they also break societal ties:

The cities have always been the cradles of liberty, just as they are today the centres of radicalism. Every man of the world knows that isolation and solitude are found in a much greater degree in a crowded city than in a country village, where one's individual concerns are the concern of everyone.[a]

Migration also can have vastly different effects across societies, both in the places people leave and to those places they go. It almost always brings economic rewards, but as the anti-immigrant sentiments in many countries show, it also means more risk.

Specialization of production made possible by falling transport costs can come at an environmental price. Cod is caught off Norway, transported by plane to China to be cleaned, and then flown back to Norway to be sold. Such specialization based on natural endowments (fish in Northern Europe, people in China) helps both Norwegian consumers and Chinese workers, but the cod now has a longer carbon trail. The environmental effects of urbanization and transport are considered in this Report, but only when they qualify the Report's messages.

a. Weber 1899, p. 432.

terminology. The Report uses some terms that may not be familiar to readers, introduces others, and uses yet others as shorthand. This section clarifies the terms that the rest of the Report uses consistently.

Spatial scales—area, country, and region

Throughout the Report, the analysis is provided at three geographic scales—local, national, and international. The policy concerns that correspond to these spatial scales are, respectively, the speed and sustainability of the rural-urban transformation, the territorial disparities in production and welfare within countries, and the same disparities across countries and world regions. The units that correspond to these spatial scales are area, country, and region. These terms are used consistently throughout the Report. An "area" is the same as a "territory," the target of territorial development policies. In Anglophone countries, it is the same as a "region" within a country, as in the debates on "regional development." Area is used here to avoid confusion with another spatial scale, the international, because "region" also describes a group of countries, such as South Asia, which includes India and its neighbors.

To fix the terms, consider the three geographic scales of the Shanghai metropolitan area, the country of China, and the East Asia region (see map 0.1):

- **Area.** The local scale is the municipality of Shanghai—which includes the city of Shanghai and neighboring cities, towns, and villages in an area of about 7,000 square kilometers, with a population

density of about 3,000 persons per square kilometer. The population density in the city is about 13,000 persons per square kilometer.

- **Country.** The national scale encompasses the 23 provinces, five autonomous regions, and four municipalities (Shanghai is one of them) that make up China, covering about 9.6 million square kilometers. The distance between the western province of Xinjiang and the dynamic coastal areas in the east is more than 4,000 kilometers. Restrictions on internal migration can make the *economic* distance seem much longer.

- **Region.** The international scale consists of China and its East Asian neighbors including Japan, Mongolia, and the Republic of Korea. The region is divided by borders, some thick, some thin.

This Report uses the notion of "natural" neighborhoods, defined by elements of human, physical, and political geography. The World Bank commonly classifies all low- and middle-income countries into six regions, and groups all high-income countries together, regardless of their location. This Report classifies the world into 16 regions that include both developed and developing countries, using geographic proximity as the most important criterion (see box 0.2). It is also more detailed. Sub-Saharan Africa, for example, has four regions—West, Central, East, and Southern. East Asia and the Pacific has three—Northeast, Southeast, and the Pacific Islands. The

Map 0.1   Three geographic scales—area, country, and region
Shanghai, China, and East Asia exemplify the local, national, and international scales

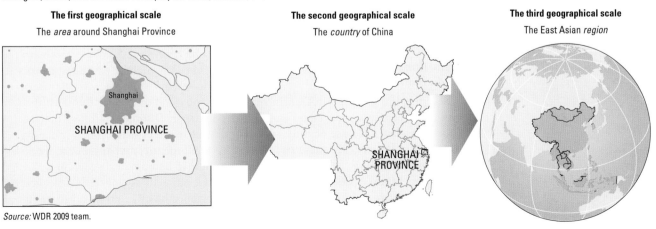

| The first geographical scale | The second geographical scale | The third geographical scale |
| The *area* around Shanghai Province | The *country* of China | The East Asian *region* |

Source: WDR 2009 team.

BOX 0.2 *This Report's regions are more detailed than the World Bank's*

This Report is about geography and economic development, focusing more on spatial variability of conditions and outcomes than economic analysis usually does. Where appropriate, it uses countries or areas within countries as the units of analysis. But where the emphasis is on regional integration and interactions between neighboring sovereign states, the Report uses an aggregation of countries that is more detailed than the six standard World Bank regions, which can hide significant variation.

Adapting the United Nations geographic regions but remaining consistent with World Bank regions yields the 16 regions displayed here. Depending on the context, the analysis in this Report ignores the income of countries within a region—say, where regional growth spillovers from industrial to developing countries are of interest—or treats the Organisation of Economic Co-operation and Development (OECD) and other high-income economies separately.

Regions used in this Report

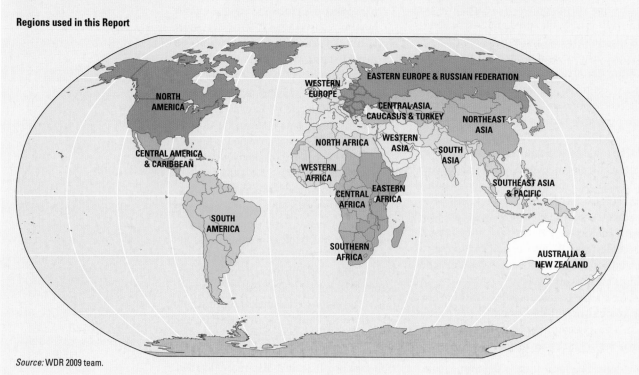

Source: WDR 2009 team.

term "region" is used throughout the Report to refer to these 16 groups of countries.

While the choice of area or region can be arbitrary, these spatial scales conform well to the levels of policy making. This Report aims to inform policy making at these three levels—subnational, national, and international.

Spatial dimensions—density, distance, and division

To describe the geographic transformations that accompany development, the Report introduces the use of three spatial dimensions—density, distance, and division. These dimensions help the reader see development in real space—in three dimensions, in other words. The terms are easy metaphors, but they also have a technical interpretation. *Density* generally signifies the intensity of economic activity on a unit of land, say, a square kilometer. Data limitations can force compromise: since production and population densities are closely related, and production data are less easily available, population density is sometimes used as a proxy for economic density. It can get a bit confusing. London is probably the city with the highest economic density in the world, but Mumbai, with 30,000 people per square kilometer, is the most densely populated. *Distance* signifies the costs of getting to places with economic density.

While density and distance relate closely to human and physical geography, *division* refers more to sociopolitical geography. Religion, ethnicity, and language are among the main attributes that lead to divisions between places. While divisions are greatest across nations, they can be considerable within countries as well.

These dimensions are measurable. But unlike height, length, and breadth, for example, the geographic dimensions are not orthogonal. Better analogs for the three dimensions are a person's height, weight, and age, which are related. Likewise, as distances increase, it is likely that divisions also get stronger. Density, distance, and division are best illustrated by market access, an indicator of economic opportunity for a location that tells the size of the potential markets in its vicinity, and the ease of reaching them. Market access across geographic scales determines where economic activity can thrive and thus where firms will locate and populations will grow.

Using this concept of market access, the three dimensions are defined as follows:

- **Density** indicates the size of economic output or total purchasing power per unit of surface area—say, a square kilometer. It is highest in large cities where economic activity is concentrated and much lower in rural neighborhoods.
- **Distance** measures the ease of reaching markets. It determines access to opportunity. Areas far from economically dense centers in a country are more likely to lag.
- **Division** arises from barriers to economic interactions created by differences in currencies, customs, and languages, which restrict market access. It is most relevant in an international context.

The concept of distance is also relevant internationally. The difference between distance and division is that distance modulates access to economic opportunity in a more continuous way—a distance decay. Division, by contrast, presents discrete barriers to access and economic integration. It can be seen as increasing economic distance or travel time for a unit of physical (or Euclidian) distance.

These definitions are not scientifically exact. But the terms are used consistently in the Report. When "density" is used, it means economic density: production per area of land. When any other measure of density—such as the population per square kilometer (as in chapters 1 and 7) or the places where more of a nation's poor people live (as in chapters 2 and 8), it is qualified accordingly.

Distance can be measured with some precision, but where infrastructure is sparse, straight-line distance is different from road or rail distance. Many other factors, such as the availability and affordability of transport services, determine actual accessibility. Where such information is available, it is used. Chapter 1, for example, reports a uniform measure of urbanization based on places that both have minimum levels of population density and are within an hour's travel time to sizable settlements. In computing this "agglomeration index," the quality of transport infrastructure is taken into account. Division is associated with international borders, because they usually impede the ease of exchange or travel. But not all borders imply divisions. Those in the European Union (EU), for instance, have increasingly ceased to reflect divisions between countries. And not all divisions imply international borders. Where religious, ethnic, and linguistic differences are manifest spatially, there can be divisions within countries.

There is a correspondence between the geographic scales and dimensions. Locally, within an area, the most important dimension is density, because generally distances are short and divisions few. Nationally, the most important dimension is distance to density; divisions within countries tend to be fewer, though they can be serious in some countries. Internationally, across a regional or global spatial scale, distances and divisions are usually more serious.

Using these three dimensions, the Report summarizes the geographic transformations needed for development (part one). It shows how market forces drive these transformations (part two). And it assesses how governments can augment these forces to sustain growth and reduce poverty (part three).

Instruments for integration— institutions, infrastructure, and interventions

Through good policies, governments can promote economic integration between places where economic production is concentrated and places that are lagging. Some of these policy instruments are spatially explicit, like a slum-upgrading program in a city, a Brazilian state's fiscal incentives to a U.S. automobile company, or the EU's structural and cohesion funds. Others are intended to be universal in their coverage, including compulsory and free basic education for all children, such labor market regulations as minimum wage laws, and the enforcement of property rights. Between these spatially targeted programs and "spatially blind" policies are investments and regulations that connect places, such as roads, airports, and communications systems.

In their current form, the debates on how governments can foster rural-urban transformation, help lagging areas reduce poverty, and—in the poorest nations in the world—improve access to world markets all emphasize geographic targeting. The debate on how to promote healthy urbanization is polarized between an emphasis on villages, where a majority of the world's poor still live, and a belief that the way out of poverty lies in cities; if urban poverty increases, the focus shifts from villages to slums. Motivated by within-country spatial disparities in living standards, the debate on territorial development tends to be similarly fixated on promoting economic growth in lagging areas. At the international level, preferential market access for the least developed countries can end up dominating policy discussions. Part three of the Report reframes these debates, calling for a shift from spatial targeting to integration.

The policy instruments for economic integration can be classified in three categories, based on how explicitly place is considered in their scope and design:

- **Institutions** is shorthand for all the policy instruments that are *spatially blind*. These are the amenities that governments should provide to everyone, regardless of place. The word "institutions" connotes universality, and includes mechanisms for financing and delivering such basic amenities as the administration of justice, public security, the regulation of land, labor, and capital markets, primary

education and health, and electricity, water, and sanitation. Systems for collecting taxes and financing the spending associated with these services are also best designed without specific places in mind.

- **Infrastructure** is the summary term for all *spatially connective* investments and the associated rules and regulations. It includes roads and railways, airports and air transport systems, telecommunications, and the Internet.

- **Interventions** is shorthand for all *spatially focused* incentives. These include regulations and investments that favor some places, such as export processing zones. They also include place-based programs—such as slum-upgrading schemes like Rio de Janeiro's *Favela Bairro,* or Superintendency for the Development of the Northeast (SUDENE), Brazil's development agency for the lagging Northeast, or the *Everything But Arms* initiative of the EU, which gives the least developed countries preferential trade access to European markets.

Because these definitions do not conform strictly to common usage, additional clarification is necessary:

- First, spatial blindness does not mean spatial *neutrality*. A progressive tax system, for example, may not be neutral in its effects or outcomes. Cities may end up contributing more in taxes than the countryside, and richer states may contribute more than those that are poorer. But the guiding principle is that tax rates differ not by place alone, but by the attributes of firms and families that happen to be located there.

- Second, in the common use of the term, infrastructure includes nonconnective investments such as water supply and energy. In this Report, infrastructure is reserved for the spatially *connective* components. Nonconnective public utilities are included in institutions, as for such basic services as sanitation.

- Third, each of these categories includes all three tools of government policy—taxes, transfers and public expenditures, and regulations.

- Finally, government initiatives can include more than one instrument. Slum development can include steps to make urban land markets work better by formalizing property rights, improving streets, and offering monetary incentives for some of the slum-dwellers to relocate.

Structure

The main finding of this Report—at all three spatial scales—is that economic development is not smooth, linear, or neat. The processes of economic growth leave behind a bumpy landscape, with economic mass concentrated in some places. Living standards in such places—especially rising prosperity, good access to education and health facilities, and safe shelter, water, and sanitation, some of the most urgent among the Millennium Development Goals—improve faster than where there is less economic activity, widening the spatial disparities in welfare. But where there is sustained economic growth, the convergence in living standards begins to supplant divergence. Nations become both spatially efficient and equitable (see box 0.3). The challenge of development is to institute policies that allow—even encourage—"unbalanced" economic growth and yet ensure geographically balanced development outcomes.

The facts

Part one of the Report presents the facts about the spatial transformations—the changes in economic density, distance, and division. Chapter 1 shows that development is accompanied by the rising density of human settlements: no country has reached high income without this rise in density. Chapter 2 expands the scale and shows that development is also accompanied by the greater concentration of economic activity in areas of countries closer to economic density. Chapter 3 incorporates international divisions that slow, but do not prevent, the concentration of economic activities in some countries. At the local, national, and international scales the pattern is similar: rapidly rising concentrations at the early stage and then a slowing down.

BOX 0.3 *This Report's message is not anti-equity*

Policies for spatially balanced growth are often justified by equity. The EU describes its territorial policy as governed by the principle of solidarity because it "aims to benefit citizens and regions that are economically and socially deprived relative to EU averages."[a] The policy seems to equate social and spatial equity—equality across individuals, and the equality of living standards across states and countries. This Report, by contrast, argues in favor of the benefits from geographic concentration of economic production. But it shows that in the earlier stages of development, increased concentration is associated with spatial divergence in living standards such as income. So is this Report's message anti-equity?

No. It is important to distinguish between three types of disparities: spatial disparities in economic production, spatial disparities in living standards, and social inequality.

Spatial disparities in economic activity. In both the United States and the EU-15 countries, gross domestic product (GDP) and population have lumpy spatial distributions. In the United States, three states (California, New York, and Texas) generated 21 percent of national GDP in 2005. The same three states have 19.8 percent of the U.S. population, but only 12.8 percent of the country's land. Meanwhile, 10 EU subnational areas were responsible for 20.5 percent of the EU's GDP in 2005. These areas have 16.9 percent of the EU-15's population, but only 8 percent of its land. So, in both cases, economic activity and population are concentrated. But spatial inequality of production and population is higher in the United States than in the EU.

The Gini coefficient for the spatial inequality of GDP is 0.53 for the United States and 0.41 for the EU. For population, the coefficients are 0.54 and 0.32, respectively. For subnational areas in the EU and states in the United States, the numbers change, but the conclusion is the same.[b]

Spatial disparities in living standards. EU-15 countries have greater spatial inequality in per capita income and unemployment rates, two common indicators of individual living standards in high-income countries. GDP per capita, for example, exhibited greater variation across EU areas than it did across U.S. states in 2005. Although production is more concentrated geographically in the United States, people are also more likely to live where production is, so GDP per capita varies less. The same is true of unemployment rates. In the United States, the state with the highest unemployment in 2007 (Michigan) had an unemployment rate of 7.2 percent, 2.8 times the lowest unemployment state (Hawaii). But in the EU in 2006, the ratio was 8.1. There is less spatial inequality in living standards in the United States.

Social inequality. While spatial inequality in living standards is greater in the EU than in the United States, the opposite is true for social inequality between individuals. During the past few decades, the Gini coefficient for the United States has been about 0.40, compared with 0.33, 0.28, and 0.23 for the United Kingdom, Germany, and Austria, respectively.[c]

Contributed by Mark Roberts.
a. http://europa.eu/pol/reg/overview_en.htm.
b. Puga 2002.
c. Burkey 2006.

The long experience of countries shows that income differences between leading places and following places first diverge and then converge, but only in the more dynamic areas, countries, and regions. At each of the three spatial scales, it pays to be in dynamic neighborhoods. Economic growth leads to congestion in cities—and to the growth of towns and cities that are well connected to fast-growing agglomerations. This pattern is repeated at the national and international levels. Expanding economic activity spills over to areas and countries that are—in economic terms—near places doing well.

The insights

The second part of the Report is the "engine room." It exploits the main insights from a quarter century of work spanning several subdisciplines in economics, such as industrial organization, urban economics, international trade, and economic geography. Distilled to its essence, the engine works through a three-way interaction between scale economies, the mobility of workers and entrepreneurs, and the costs of transporting and communicating between places (see figure 0.1).

Firms are generally more productive when they locate in large places and when they operate at a relatively large size. If it is relatively easy to transport produce, the scale can be even higher, since the potential market is bigger. Workers move to these places, bringing with them both a supply of labor and a demand for goods and services. As people become more mobile and as transport and communications costs fall, these economies of scale create a circular and cumulative causation, where economic activities become even more concentrated spatially. Rising concentration inevitably leads to congestion, which slows the process and eventually reverses it. Declines in transport costs first make concentration possible, and then, when they fall low enough, they make it unnecessary.

Part two discusses these interactions in some detail, summarizing more than a century of experience and the novel insights that come from a generation of research recognizing how factor mobility and falling transport costs feed economies of scale (see box 0.2). They should change what we can expect from the markets, and what governments can and should do to facilitate the concentration of production and promote the convergence in living standards.

Chapter 4 provides evidence of agglomeration economies—increasing returns to scale associated with places, not plants—in producing goods, services, and ideas. Places of different sizes provide varying agglomeration benefits, and congestion associated with spatial concentration leads to a portfolio of places that facilitate economic growth, with different parts in the lead depending on the stage of development.

Chapter 5 explains the interaction between scale economies and factor mobility, focusing on the migration of workers. Chapter 6 explains the nonlinear relationship between transport costs and the geographic concentrations of production, focusing on intraindustry trade, which is especially sensitive to transport costs. These chapters summarize the new insights provided by the three-way interaction between scale economies, factor mobility, and transport costs—and their implications for development policy (see box 0.4).

The policy framework

Circular causation, unevenness, and spillovers make for a world in which policies can promote economic growth and improve social welfare beyond what markets yield, because well-executed policies can set these transformations in motion or speed them up.

These features of economic development also make policy making a difficult enterprise. Part three of the Report reframes three important policy debates, using a principle derived from its first two parts: for developing countries to realize the benefits of both spatial concentration of production and convergence in consumption, development is best facilitated by economic integration. Using the three dimensions—density, distance, and division—described in part one, and the (mal) functioning of pivotal markets at each spatial scale—land, labor, and intermediate inputs—analyzed in part two, the chapters in part three provide a simple framework and illustrate its workings through real-world policy experience. At each of the geographic scales, the response rule is the same—*an instrument per dimension*. Here is a somewhat oversimplified summary, using examples from only the local scale (chapter 7):

BOX 0.4 *Fresh insights from economic geography: concentration, convergence, and integration*

Over the past two decades, new analysis has changed the way we think about the location of production, trade, and development. The analysis builds on two elements. First, large markets are disproportionately attractive for firms producing with scale economies. Firms with a larger home market have more sales that, with scale economies, imply lower unit costs and more profits, which encourage existing firms to expand and attract new firms. Second, large markets are big partly because many firms and consumers locate there. Market access and mobility creates a circular and cumulative causation. A large market attracts firms and workers—and the demand for intermediate inputs by firms and the demand for final goods by workers make the market even larger, attracting more firms and workers, and so on.

This is both good and bad news for places with poor initial conditions. It is good because it means that firm location is not as constrained by nature as theories based on comparative advantage would have us believe. Places with poor endowments can sustain concentration of activity. It is bad news because the circle of market access and mobility produces persistence. Once a place gets far ahead, it is difficult for lagging areas to catch up. While agglomeration raises the cost of labor, firms do not move to low-wage areas, because this would mean forgoing the benefits of proximity to suppliers and customers.

Concentration is the rule. The strength of the agglomeration forces created by market access and mobility depends on transport costs, but the relationship is not linear. When these costs are high, firms avoid shipping their output long distances by spreading out their production. Firm location is then mostly determined by local access to immobile demand, such as from farmers and miners. For intermediate values of trade costs, it becomes feasible to supply markets from a distance, and places that get an advantage in market size build on it and take off relative to other places. When trade costs fall to low levels, it matters little whether one sells and buys locally. Firm location is then determined mostly by the local cost of immobile features, including the cost of land and housing, but also by the ability to have face-to-face interactions or to find a good match in a specialized labor market. So once trade costs decline sufficiently, some activities will spread out in response to cost differences, and others will remain concentrated.

Convergence is the objective. The forces of market access and mobility have implications for the way we think about convergence. The view of development as smooth and linear gives way to a lumpier nonlinear process. As a country grows, new producers locate close to existing production, widening the production differences between lagging and leading places. When wage gaps become wide, industry starts to spread to places that have low wages. But this does not lead to steady development of all places. Instead, development takes place in waves, where some areas or countries are drawn in sequence out of poverty and are pulled rapidly through the development process. In the neoclassical world, being behind can be an advantage—places lagging farther can catch up faster. But with agglomeration economies, the farther behind an area, country, or region, the tougher it is to catch up. What should lagging places do?

Integration is the answer. Because both high and low trade costs can encourage production to spread out, lagging areas, countries, or regions could in principle turn to either import substitution or export-oriented industrialization. But import substitution becomes less feasible as a development strategy over time. Why? Because it limits foreign access to local immobile demand, whereas export-oriented industrialization reduces the cost of purchasing foreign intermediates for processing and export. The falling share of agriculture and the tendency of manufacturing and services to agglomerate have reduced the share of demand in lagging places. And the fragmentation of production has made access to intermediate inputs more important. Both make development strategies based on fencing off local immobile demand hopeless. The observation that some developed countries or provinces industrialized while being closed to trade is of little help to lagging areas, countries, or regions today. The ones left behind are so small relative to the world economy that isolation is no longer a feasible option.

Contributed by Diego Puga.

- For one-dimensional problems, a calibrated response would be spatially blind policies. In areas experiencing incipient urbanization, for example, the policy objective should be to facilitate rising *density*, and policy makers should pay special attention to *institutions* to improve the functioning of (rural and urban) land markets.

- For two-dimensional problems, the response should include both spatially blind and connective policies. For example, in areas of a country undergoing rapid urbanization, the policy problems are not only to facilitate the increase in *density*, but also to alleviate the problem of *distance* caused by growing congestion. The response includes improvements in *institutions* to facilitate rising density as just outlined—and investments in *infrastructure* to address the growing problem of economic distance.

- For three-dimensional problems, the response should include spatially blind, connective, and targeted policies. In highly urbanized areas of a country, for example, the problems of *density* and *distance* are compounded by *divi-*

sions within urban areas, most noticeably between formally settled parts of a metropolis and slums, where land markets use informal conventions. An effective policy response includes *institutions, infrastructure,* and *interventions.*

At the national level, a similarly graduated policy response can help to integrate lagging and leading areas (chapter 8), and at the international level, it can help to integrate poor countries with world markets (chapter 9).

At all three geographic scales, policy debates have one thing in common: currently, they begin and end with discussions of spatially targeted interventions. This Report calls for a rebalancing of these debates to include all the elements of a successful approach to spatial integration—institutions, infrastructure, and incentives.

This Report takes a long-term perspective, chronicling spatial disparities in today's developed economies when they were at incomes comparable to those of today's low- and middle-income countries. It also systematically documents the relationship between spatial disparities and development for a large set of countries. In its conclusions, it makes a sharper distinction between spatial disparities in economic production and those in welfare. And it recommends using agglomeration rents in leading areas to push up social welfare in lagging areas—and not, except in special circumstances, to push economic production out to those places.

- At the local spatial scale, the policy objective should be to improve the quality of urbanization to maximize its growth effects. Chapter 7 discusses how the priorities of policy makers should change as urbanization advances. It pays special attention to *land use,* where the potential for market malfunctioning is greatest.
- At the national spatial scale, the policy objective should be to improve the market access of workers and entrepreneurs, especially in a world in which diminished distance has changed the notion of markets from local to global. Discussing how policy makers can reconcile the political objective of national unity with

economic concentration, chapter 8 pays special attention to *labor mobility,* for which the potential for market malfunctioning is greatest.

- At the international spatial scale, the policy objective should be to promote convergence in living standards in a world in which divisions hamper the movements of labor and capital. Discussing how developing countries can gain access to world markets, chapter 9 emphasizes specialization and intra-industry trade, in addition to exploiting comparative advantage based on natural endowments. It pays attention to trade in *intermediate goods,* which is especially sensitive to transport costs.

The Report draws on both experience and analysis to discipline the inquiry in a policy area as broad and difficult as development itself, and it should be useful for a wide readership. But the Report is structured to be friendly to readers interested only in specific aspects of this inquiry:

- The Report has descriptive, analytical, and prescriptive parts and progresses gradually from the positive to normative. Each part is a section of an integrated inquiry, but each can be read separately. Policy makers pressed for time can read just the overview and the three policy chapters in part three. Students interested in the world's spatial transformation can read just the three chapters of part one, which provides a three-dimensional tour of economic development.
- The Report progressively widens the spatial scale for addressing the policy questions posed by economic geography, from local to national to international, with the specialized reader in mind. Readers interested in just the policy debate on urbanization in developing countries can read just the three density cluster chapters—1, 4, and 7. Those who are mostly interested in the policy discussion on territorial development and geographic disparities within countries can read chapters 2, 5, and 8—the distance cluster. Readers interested in regional integration can read just chapters 3, 6, and 9 in the division cluster.

Figure 0.1   A navigational aid for the reader

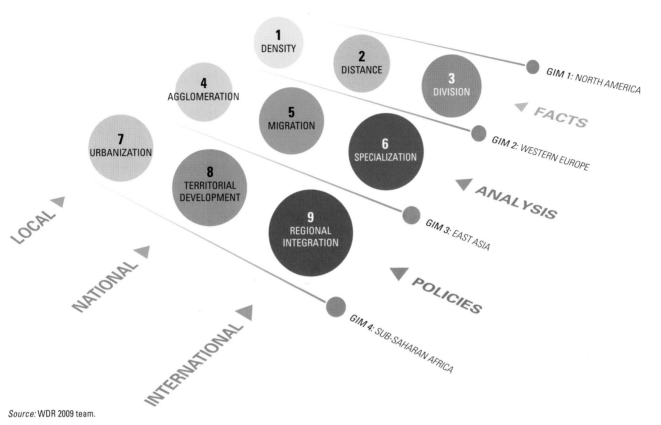

Source: WDR 2009 team.

- Chapters 1 through 9 slice the problem of economic development into digestible bites, each serving a pedagogical function. The arguments in the Report are punctuated with four notes on "Geography in Motion," which connect the different components by spotlighting the experiences of North America, Western Europe, East Asia, and Sub-Saharan Africa. Readers interested in the chal- lenges posed by geography for develop- ment—and some clues to how geography was reshaped—can read these notes on different parts of the world.

Figure 0.1 shows how the Report can be read horizontally (facts, analysis, and poli- cies, respectively) or vertically, according to the policy interest of the reader.

Overcoming Distance in North America

When Europeans began to colonize beyond their shores, the prospects for economic growth in North America seemed remote. During the Seven Years' War (1756–63), as the French and British battled over Canada, Voltaire wondered why they should fight over "a few acres of snow." They should have been more interested in the economic potential of the Caribbean, where climate and soil were good for growing sugarcane, and they were. Manhattan was famously traded away by the Dutch in exchange for land around Suriname. But over time, it has been the few acres of snow and the rocky landscape of Plymouth (Massachusetts) that gave birth to the "reversal of fortune" between frigid northeastern America and the warmer south.[1]

To understand how this reversal happened, one has to understand how North Americans managed the growing density, the vast distances in the continent, and the sharp divisions between slaves and their owners, between natives and colonialists, between French and English—in short, how North America's economic geography has been reshaped.

Size and American economic ascendancy

Size is the most obvious feature of the United States' economic geography.[2] In 1800 5.3 million individuals lived on the 865,000 squares miles of land given to the fledgling nation under the Treaty of Versailles (1783). By 1900 a little more than 2 million square miles had been added through outright purchase, spoils of war, or treaty. Today the United States has more than 300 million people and a territory of 3.5 million square miles. Since 1790 the population *density* of the country has multiplied nearly 18 times.

The challenges of distributing population and production over such a vast space are enormous. Both people and productive land have moved west and south. In 1800 the population was centered in Maryland, on the eastern seaboard (see map G1.1). By 1900 the center had moved to Indiana. Over the twentieth century, the center veered

southwest, ending up in Missouri in 2000. By this time, America's population had settled mostly on its two coasts. Americans are as physically distant as they have ever been.

How did America overcome these vast physical distances? Initially, institutional mechanisms to allocate land and secure property rights were paramount. The Constitution and the Northwest Ordinance (1787) provided the procedural mechanisms for transforming unsettled areas into states. Public land was disposed of through sales to private individuals and outright grants. Eminent domain was used to put land to its best use, especially when required for railroads.

Map G1.1   The U.S. geographic center of population gravity moved 1,371 kilometers between 1790 and 2000

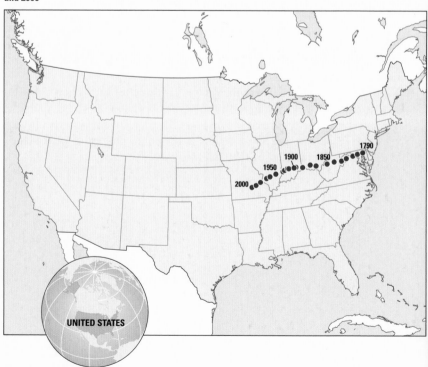

Source: Geography Division, U.S. Census Bureau.

The first transcontinental railroad was completed in 1864. Indigenous populations were removed forcibly, where necessary, by the U.S. Army. States and local governments encouraged Americans to move by offering land, building canals, and supplying schools, roads, and other public goods. These local governments competed with each other to attract people and firms, offering tax and other incentives.

People and firms were also encouraged to move by the commerce clause of the U.S. Constitution, which explicitly prohibits state governments from engaging in restraint of trade across state boundaries. The institutional structure thus permitted the free movement of people (except slaves), capital, and goods, with attendant property rights so that movement could occur without economic loss.

In this policy environment, the "transport revolution" of the nineteenth century and growing density permitted a fundamental change in American economic structures. The combination of rail, canals, and steamboats vastly reduced the costs of medium- and long-haul transport compared with wagon transport alone.[3] The country became more urban and dense, while regional economic structures diverged. New England, which had been 80 percent agricultural in 1800 despite its poor soils and climate, started to develop manufactures, while the Midwest specialized in food. By the beginning of the twentieth century, the United States had become the largest manufacturer in the world.

The growing density and the migration of people and firms were driven largely by market forces. Most settlement was cautious. Railroads were built when (and where) investors thought they could make a profit and moved incrementally across the country. Occasionally settlement did "leapfrog," jumping over large expanses of land to get someplace else, as in California after the discovery of gold in 1849. But that simply accelerated the pace of reallocation of labor in America.

Convergence in living standards

The American Civil War had long-lasting economic effects that *divided* the country. Per capita incomes fell sharply in the South after the Civil War, both absolutely and relative to the rest of the country. In 1900 per capita income in Alabama was still half of the national average. In 1938 Franklin Roosevelt famously remarked that the South was the nation's "number one economic problem." America had its lagging areas. But the twentieth century experience was one of steady convergence of living standards.

In the United States, a clear negative relationship exists between the level of per capita income in a state in 1900 and the income growth in that state over the next century. That is, poorer states grew faster than richer states between 1900 and 2000, a phenomenon known as "beta-convergence." The main explanation for this phenomenon is migration of people. In the twentieth century, the dominant pattern of movement was from poorer to richer states. Probably the most important example is the migration of African Americans from the rural South to the urban North (and West), beginning in earnest during World War I and becoming a tidal wave during and just after World War II. States such as Mississippi and Louisiana now rank lowest in disposable income, but it is easy to imagine that they would have been much worse off without this migration.

Convergence has been aided by reductions in transport costs. Many of the most important inventions in transport and communications happened in the United States. In the twentieth century, the network expanded with the diffusion of the airplane, the automobile, and electronic communications. Today, 16 of the 30 busiest airports in the world are in the United States, and there are more than 75 automobiles for every 100 Americans.

Map G1.2   America's large cities are in the Northeast and on the two coasts

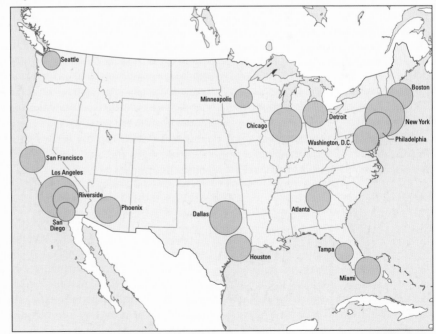

Population, 2007 (millions)

Source: Population of Metropolitan Statistical Areas; U.S. Census Bureau.

The invention and diffusion of the automobile led to the enlargement of cities through a pronounced "flattening" of urban density as one moves from the center city to the suburbs. This helped magnify agglomeration economies, but it also produced social *divisions*. The U.S. system of local public finance, relying on local property taxes to fund services, is poorly designed to effect income redistribution. Rich and middle-class households can avoid subsidizing others by moving to new suburbs. Race also plays a role—the central city is predominantly "black" whereas the suburbs are "white."

For better or for worse, growth in automobiles benefited from the Federal Highway Act of 1956, which authorized building of the Eisenhower Interstate System of highways. In a famous speech, President Eisenhower recounted how as a young officer he participated in the first transcontinental motor convoy from Washington, D.C., to San Francisco in 1919. The trip took 62 days, encountering every type of delay imaginable along the way. Today, courtesy of the system, a driver can cover the 2,819-mile journey in two days. Recent research shows that the 47,000-mile network of highways has integrated formerly isolated rural areas into the national economy and fostered metropolitan growth.

What have these connections done to the distribution of population and economic activity? Paradoxically, as the center of gravity moved toward the interior of North America, the interior—except for its metropolises—has hollowed out. Missouri has just 5.5 million people, more than half of them in the greater St. Louis area. Spreading out the transport infrastructure has not spread people out, but it has allowed growth from agglomeration economies to occur in more cities across the country. The distribution of population in 2000 is clustered in cit-ies, in the Northeast and on the coasts, producing what is known as "sigma-convergence," a reduction in the income inequality across states (see map G1.2). By one measure, the dispersion across states in per capita income had fallen to one-third its 1880 level by 2000.

Rising density, falling disparities, persisting divisions

The long-run economic performance of the United States is exemplary. Per capita income growth has averaged 1.8 percent per year for the last 180 years, leading to a cumulative 26-fold improvement in living standards. Alongside this growth, income inequality across states has fallen. America has realized economies of scale—first at the plant level, then at the local level as towns specialized in manufacturing, and later at the metropolis level in the major urban agglomerations in places like Los Angeles and New York.

The United States today is composed of a highly effective set of national markets in goods and factors of production. Place still matters in determining income, but it matters in the short run, not the long, and the short run is much shorter than it was a century ago. Major local shocks like Hurricane Katrina have far less impact on local growth prospects than before. After the Mariel boatlift brought 125,000 Cuban refugees to Miami in the early 1980s, regional wages did not experience a perceptible impact.

The result is a seeming paradox: wages in America (corrected for human capital) are similar in different locations, while economic activity is highly unequal across space. Europe is lauded for having lower *social* inequality, but North America is more *spatially* equal. And it has a more spatially efficient distribution of economic production. The reason: a mobile labor force. Every year about 8 million Americans move across states; over a decade, more than a quarter of the population changes its state of residence. By overcoming distance and division, and by permitting population and production to be uneven across space through free mobility, per capita incomes in the United States today are both high and remarkably similar across the different states.

A remaining challenge for the United States is the removal of divisions. The North American Free Trade Agreement (NAFTA) is a step in this direction. But it is a modest step. Consider Canadian-U.S. market integration. One study found that trade among Canadian provinces was much larger than between Canada and the United States, controlling for distance and the economic size (gross domestic products) of the trading partners, in this case, states and provinces.[4] Given California's size, for example, its trade with Ontario should have been 10 times Ontario's trade with British Columbia, California's closest Canadian neighbor. In fact, Ontario's trade with British Columbia was three times its trade with California. Even one of the thinnest borders in the world has a large negative influence on trade.

Along its northern boundary, the United States and Canada share 3,987 miles, the longest unguarded international border in the world. The situation is markedly different along the southern border with Mexico. The border is guarded—not closely enough for many U.S. citizens—to keep potential illegal immigrants from entering. There are even proposals to build a fence stretching across the 1,933 mile border. Such barriers are an obstacle to convergence between countries in the North American continent.

Contributed by Robert A. Margo.

PART ONE
SEEING DEVELOPMENT IN 3-D

As the world's economy grows, people and production are concentrating, pulled as if by gravity to prosperous places—growing cities, leading areas, and connected countries. As it did decades ago in today's high-income countries, the drive to density in low- and middle-income countries can increase the sense of deprivation as the economic distance between prosperous areas and those left behind widens. And although rapid advances in transport and communication increasingly bind together geographically distant communities around the world and open new opportunities for exchange, political divisions that obstruct the flow of people, capital, and goods remain. Part one of this Report defines the spatial dimensions—density, distance, and division—and describes their evolution with economic development. Chapters 1, 2, and 3 show how the economic geography at the local, national, and international scales is changing, and how the scope and pace of these changes compare with transformations in the economic geography of North America, Europe, and Japan when they were at similar stages of development. This broad sweep of stylized facts informs the analysis in part two and the policy discussions in part three of the Report.

CHAPTER 1

Density

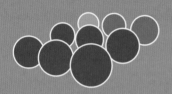

Mostly off the world's radar, on a dusty plain in West Africa, is a city of 1.6 million people. Bisected by the River Niger, its two halves—with about 800,000 people each—are linked by only two bridges. The pressure of movement is so strong that every morning one of these bridges is dedicated to incoming traffic: minibuses, bicycles, motorbikes, pedestrians, and occasionally private cars. In the evenings, to leave the center means joining an exodus of people toward the minibus depots. Green vans loaded with passengers file out to residential neighborhoods as far as 20 kilometers away. This is Bamako, Mali. It contracts into its center every morning and breathes out again in the evening.

With each breath Bamako grows bigger. It happens to be one of the fastest-growing cities in the world. Natural demographic growth is supplemented by migration from the countryside and other Malian cities. Its population in 2008 is 50 percent larger than 10 years ago, making it the same size as Budapest, Dubai, or Warsaw. It has 10 times more inhabitants than the next biggest Malian city and accommodates 70 percent of the country's industrial establishments.[1] New neighborhoods—*quartiers*—formerly villages, become consolidated with the rest of the city, toward the south, east, and west. Some of Bamako's people are now moving out into surrounding neighborhoods in search of cheaper land and some tranquility, but they remain within reach of the city because it provides their livelihoods.

Despite its industriousness, Bamako is one of the sleepier cities in West Africa. Many of the manufactured staples come 1,184 kilometers by road from one of the region's metropolises, Abidjan, which has more than twice Bamako's population. Abidjan seems small beside Lagos, where activity is so concentrated that its residents speak of living in a pressure-cooker. Some families rent rooms to sleep for six hours and then turn them over to another family that takes their place. Shopping does not necessarily require travel: goods are brought on foot and cart to drivers stuck in Lagos's interminable traffic jams. To some, like the authors of Lagos's 1980 master plan written when the city had just 2.5 million residents, the continuing growth of the city is "undisciplined."[2] What can possibly be so attractive about living in Lagos that, despite its congestion and crime, it continues to draw migrants?

The short answer: economic density. Lagos is not the most economically dense city in the world, nor even the most densely populated. Those distinctions belong to Central London and Mumbai, respectively. Even so, Nigeria's economic future and Lagos's growth are as inextricably tied as Britain's economy is with London's growth. No country has developed without the growth of its cities. As countries become richer, economic activity becomes more densely packed into towns, cities, and metropolises. This geographic transformation of economies seems so natural that—at an impersonal aggregate level—it is taken for granted. But moving to economic density is a pathway out of poverty both for those who travel on it and, ultimately, for those left behind. Jane Jacobs, the noted urbanist, did not have Bamako and Lagos in mind when she wrote, "A metropolitan economy, if it's working well, is constantly transforming many poor people into middle-class people, many illiterates into skilled people, many greenhorns into competent citizens. Cities don't lure the middle class. They create it."[3] She might as well have written: as Lagos and Bamako grow, they will fill in West Africa's missing middle.

This chapter introduces density, the first of the geographic dimensions of development, defined as the economic mass or output generated on a unit of land. Surveying the evolution of density with development, the chapter presents stylized facts about how density in a country rises with urbanization, rapidly at first, and then more slowly. These changes are associated initially with a divergence of living standards between places with economic density and those without, later with a convergence. Living standards thus eventually converge between areas of different density, such as urban and rural. Even within cities, densely populated slums amid formal settlements, the differences slowly disappear with development. But this convergence does not happen by itself. It requires the institutions to manage land markets, investments in infrastructure, and well-timed and executed interventions.

The main findings:

- ***The concentration of economic activity rises with development.*** The world's densest areas or settlements are in developed countries. But the path to these levels, "urbanization" in this Report, is not linear. The share of a country's population settled in towns and cities rises rapidly during its transformation from an agrarian to an industrial economy, which generally coincides with its development from low to middle income. The pace of urbanization slows after that, but economic density continues to increase in a postindustrial economy because services are even more densely packed than industry.

- ***Rural-urban and within-urban disparities in welfare narrow with development.*** In the early stages of development, geographic disparities in welfare are large. With development, these gaps may increase initially. Rural-urban gaps in income, poverty, and living standards begin to converge as economies grow, faster for access to social services, and faster in areas of more vibrant growth. Within-city gaps in welfare and housing—most obvious in informal settlements or slums—persist for much longer, and narrow only at later stages of development.

- ***Neither the pace of urbanization nor its association with economic growth is unprecedented.*** Today's developing countries are sailing in waters charted by developed nations, which experienced a similar rush to towns and cities. The speed is similar, and the routes are the same. What is different today is the size of the ship: the absolute numbers of people being added every year to the urban populations of today's developing countries are much larger than for even the most recent industrializers such as the Republic of Korea and Taiwan, China. Later chapters of this report investigate the policy implications of these similarities and differences.

Defining density

Density refers to the economic mass per unit of land area, or the geographic compactness of economic activity. It is shorthand for the level of output produced—and thus the income generated—per unit of land area. It can, for example, be measured as the value added or gross domestic product (GDP) generated per square kilometer of land. Given that high density requires the geographic concentration of labor and capital, it is highly correlated with both employment and population density. Density is the defining characteristic of urban settlements.

The economic world is not flat

The geographic distribution of economic activity, at any resolution, is uneven. No matter the geographic scale examined, be it the country or a subnational area such as a province or district, there is a hierarchy of density. At the top is the primary city, and at the bottom are agricultural lands or rural areas. Between them is a continuum of settlements of varying density.

The geographic unevenness of economic mass, or bumpiness, tends to increase with a country's land area. But even the economic geography of small countries is bumpy. The Belgian city of Brussels has a land area of 161 square kilometers, of which 159 square kilometers are used for nonagricultural purposes. On this small area, a GDP of €55 billion is generated by about 350,000 workers—that is, the average square kilometer of land has more than 2,000 workers annually producing almost €350 million of services and goods. Brussels not only has high densities of GDP and employment; it also has the highest population density of any European (EU27) area classified as NUTS1 (Nomenclature of Territorial Units for Statistics)—more than 6,000 people per square kilometer, 18 times the average for Belgium.[4] For the sake of comparison, the population density of London and Madrid is about 5,000 people per square kilometer.

This density contrasts markedly with the agricultural areas of Belgium. In the Flemish Flanders (Vlaams Gewest) area, 6,323 square kilometers of land are used for agriculture. Its area is almost 40 times that of Brussels, but its employment is just 13 percent of Brussels and its GDP a mere 4.5 percent, translating into employment and GDP densities of only seven workers and €330,000 per square kilometer. The ratio of output density between Brussels and Flanders is 1,000 to 1. In between metropolitan Brussels and rural Flanders is a range of settlements, each with a different density (see map 1.1). The cities of Antwerp, Brugge, Gent, and Leuven have an average output of €22 million and employment density of 342 workers per square kilometer.[5]

In both developed and developing countries, then, the economic landscape is bumpy. But the topography does not correspond to a simple urban-rural dichotomy. A continuum of density gives rise to a portfolio of places. At the head is a country's leading, primary, or largest city. Below the primary city is a spectrum of settlements—secondary cities, small urban centers, towns, and villages (see figure 1.1). In some countries, such as France and Mexico, the size difference between the top two cities is phenomenal. With a population of 10 million, Paris dwarfs second-ranked Marseille with just 1.5 million. And with a population

Map 1.1   The landscape of economic mass is bumpy, even in a small country like Belgium

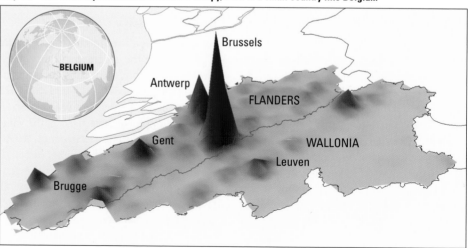

Source: WDR 2009 team and World Bank Development Research Group, based on subnational GDP estimates for 2005. See also Nordhaus 2006.

of 22 million, Mexico City is more than four times as populous as Guadalajara, Mexico's second city. Conversely, in India and the United States, the size difference between the two biggest cities is relatively small. With populations of more than 22 million people, Mumbai and New Delhi stand shoulder to shoulder. New York has a population of 22 million, Los Angeles 18 million.[6, 7]

An evolving portfolio of places

Although the growth of cities appears chaotic, the underlying patterns have a remarkable order (see figure 1.2). A country's urban hierarchy is characterized by two robust regularities:

- The "rank-size rule"—the rank of a city in the hierarchy and its population are linearly related.
- Gibrat's law—a city's rate of population growth tends to be independent of its size.

According to a special case of the rank-size rule, known as Zipf's law, the population of any city is equal to the population of the largest city, divided by the rank of the city in question within the country's urban hierarchy (see box 1.1).[8] As early as 1682, Alexandre Le Maître observed a systematic pattern in the size of cities in France.[9] For all classes of country, the relative size distribution has remained stable over time, even as incomes and populations grew (see figure 1.2). Concerns about "urban

Figure 1.1 From dichotomy to continuum: a portfolio of places

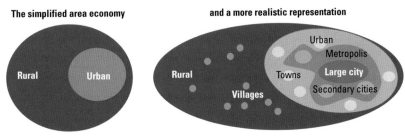

Source: WDR 2009 team.

primacy" notwithstanding, the "portfolio of places" is an enduring feature of economic development.

Settlements of different sizes complement one another. Metropolises, secondary cities, market towns, and villages are all linked through their complementary functions (see box 1.2). The primary city is often but not always the national administrative center and the seat of political power: Cambodia's Phnom Penh, Cameroon's Yaounde, and Colombia's Bogotá. A country's leading city also tends to be its most diversified, both in the provision of goods and services and in cultural and other amenities. For the cultural amenities, think of Broadway in New York City, the Opera House in Sydney, and the Louvre in Paris. But think also of Trinidad and Tobago's Port of Spain, famous for the annual carnival that attracts large numbers of visitors.

Just as a primary city forms the core of a country's metropolitan area with other adjacent cities, other large urban centers or

Figure 1.2 Almost a law: relative size distributions of settlements remain stable over time

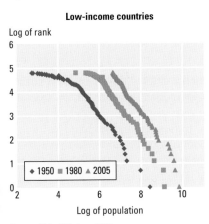
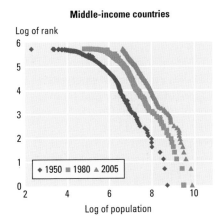
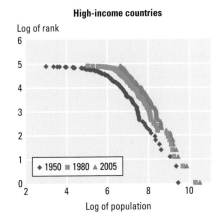

Source: United Nations 2006c.
Note: Each data point represents an agglomeration area of population size of 750,000 or more.

BOX 1.1 *Two laws and a rule: the empirical regularities of a country's city-size distribution*

The rank-size rule, discovered in 1913, can be expressed as the rank *r* associated with a city of size *S* is proportional to *S* to some negative power. The special case in which the estimated power equals –1 is known as Zipf's law, named after a linguist, George Zipf. Evidence on the pervasiveness of the rank-size rule comes not only from large cities belonging to countries of different income classes, but also from the experience of individual countries. The remarkable westward and southward expansion of the U.S. urban hierarchy notwithstanding, the rule provides a good description of the size distribution of U.S. cities for every decade between 1790 and 1950.[a] Indeed, even today, the rank-size rule continues to describe well the size distribution of U.S. cities (see figure below). This is so despite evidence that the shape of the rule has changed over time, becoming slightly flatter so that the overall distribution of

U.S. city sizes is more even—and that the rule fails to hold at the extremes of the U.S. city-size distribution, a common finding for many countries.[b] Moreover, the rank-size rule also holds for countries as diverse as Kazakhstan and Morocco, providing further evidence of its universality (see the figure below).

Whether the rank-size rule is really a rule with underlying theoretical structure is still under debate. It can be shown to follow from Gibrat's law, which implies that cities grow in parallel.[c] This is consistent with the absence of any systematic growth differences between cities. But this does not imply that policy is incapable of influencing a city's size and economic performance. Cities can and do move up and down their national urban hierarchies as a result of good and bad policy choices. And even transitory departures from a parallel growth

path can have important long-term repercussions for the welfare of a city's inhabitants. On whether the power in the rank-size rule equals –1, so that Zipf's law holds, many researchers seem to agree that, in general, it does not.

The robust message from the rank-size rule is that, for a given country or area, a wide range of city sizes coexists. Even the most developed countries have a portfolio of settlements of different sizes, ranging from the small to the large, as opposed to a single megacity or a collection of cities, all of similar size. Agglomeration is a balancing act between centripetal and centrifugal forces. The balancing point differs depending on the sector, the economic activities, and the type of industries.

Contributed by Mark Roberts.
a. Madden 1956, cited in Kim and Margo 2004.
b. Gabaix and Ioannides 2004, p. 14.
c. Gabaix and Ioannides 2004, pp. 16–17.

The rank-size rule, for nations as diverse as the United States, Morocco, and Kazakhstan

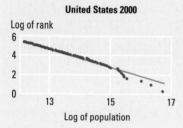

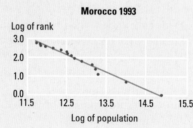

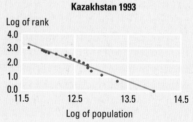

Sources: The graph for the United States is from Rose (2005); the graphs for Kazakhstan and Morocco are based on data for cities and urban agglomerations from Brakman, Garretson, and Marrewijk (2001).

secondary cities act as regional foci for both the economy and society. For example, they are the local centers for the financial sector, which serve the areas around them. Düsseldorf, Hamburg, Hanover, and Munich are all home to regional stock exchanges, as well as local concentrations of venture capital firms.[10] Dallas and Atlanta emerged as regional centers of commerce and finance in the lower South of the United States, and both host regional offices of the Federal Reserve Bank.[11] Large urban centers and secondary cities also act as local political centers, and provide advanced public health, education, and cultural facilities. Hyderabad, the state capital of Andhra Pradesh, with numerous universities, leading institutes for technical education, and

private medical colleges, is a seat of learning in southern India.

These large regional cities are connected to smaller cities or major towns. The Ruhr area of Germany, the Randstadt area of the Netherlands, and the Padang-Medan hub in Indonesia's Sumatra represent alliances of cities. Smaller cities within these areas constitute more specialized urban centers, typically focusing on manufacturing and the production of traditional and standardized items. Symbiosis is the ruling order: just as the larger cities help to serve the smaller cities, so the reverse is true. For instance, the larger cities depend on the smaller ones for the daily provision of workers through commuting.[12]

Just as there are mutually beneficial links between larger and smaller cities, the same is

BOX 1.2 *The Republic of Korea's portfolio of places*

Illustrating a well-developed portfolio of places are seven settlements in the Republic of Korea's urban hierarchy: Seoul, Pusan, Daegu, Ansan, Gumi, Jeongeup, and Sunchang.

Seoul is at the pinnacle of the hierarchy. Located 50 kilometers from the Republic of Korea's border with the Democratic Republic of Korea in the Han River basin, it is the country's capital and home to a quarter of its population (that is, 9.76 million people). It serves as the nation's political center and cultural heart. Also typical is its specialization in business services, finance, insurance, real estate, and wholesaling and retailing. Overall, services account for 60 percent of the local economy. Seoul is also highly specialized in publishing and printing and in fashion design and high-end apparel, with the two industries employing more than half the city's 465,000 manufacturing workforce.

Next in the urban hierarchy are Pusan and Daegu. With a population of 3.7 million, Pusan is the Republic of Korea's second largest city. In the southeastern corner of the Korean Peninsula, its seaport, one of the world's largest, handles more than 6.5 million container ships a year. Daegu is a metropolitan area of 2.5 million, dominated by textile and clothing manufacturing and automotive parts manufacturing and assembly. Since 1970, the Gyeongbu Expressway has connected Pusan to Seoul through Daegu. About 20 flights operate daily between Seoul and Daegu, and since 2001, the two cities have been linked by a high-speed train.

Much farther down the hierarchy, Ansan and Gumi are secondary cities, with populations of around 679,000 and 375,000, respectively. In Gyunngi province, Ansan belongs to the Seoul National Capital Area, as part of Seoul's suburban area. Gumi is in Gyungbok province, in the southeast. As tends to be the case with secondary cities, Ansan and Gumi are more specialized in

manufacturing, especially standardized manufacturing, than cities farther up the hierarchy. Although both cities serve as manufacturing centers, they differ in their specializations. Gumi is heavily specialized in the radio, television, and communication equipment industry, which by itself accounts for more than 50 percent of local manufacturing employment. Ansan is specialized in such high-tech industries as electrical machinery and computers and office machinery. It also has agglomerations in several heavy industries: almost 14,000 workers, or 14.7 percent of the local manufacturing workforce, are employed in the fabricated metal products industry.

At the bottom of the hierarchy, Jeongeup and Sunchang, both in the Jeonbuk province, are close to the interface between rural and urban. So while Jeongeup has a relatively large population (129,050), one in four of its inhabitants is a farmer. Likewise, Sunchang is a rural town: half of the 32,012 residents are farmers. To the extent that they exhibit any specialization in manufacturing, it is either in traditional resource-related industries, as in Jeongeup, or in the manufacture of food and beverage products, as in Sunchang.

Contributed by Park Sam Ock.

Seoul heads the hierarchary of settlements in the Republic of Korea

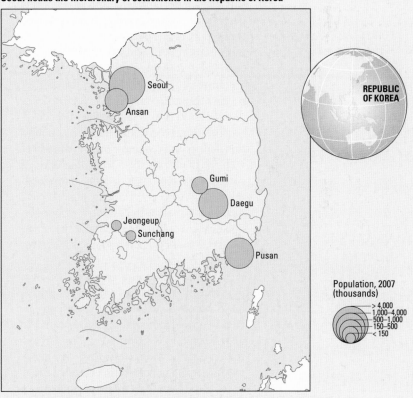

Sources: WDR 2009 team, using data from the National Statistical Office of the Republic of Korea.

true for smaller cities and towns, and towns and rural areas. Towns are the connective tissue between rural and urban areas. They act as market centers for agricultural and rural output, as stimulators of rural nonfarm activity, as places for seasonal job opportunities for farmers, and as facilitators of economies of

scale in postsecondary education and health care services. Symbiosis is again the rule. Towns draw sustenance from the agricultural activity of rural areas, but their prosperity also spills over to villages by providing nonfarm employment opportunities. Farmers in Vietnam migrate seasonally to work in urban construction, returning to invest the money earned in their farms.[13] Farmers in Makueni, Kenya, use nonfarm income to invest in terracing, planting trees, clearing bush, building houses, and educating their children. Farmers in the semiarid Diourbel region of Senegal have responded to growing urban demand for meat by diversifying away from groundnut production into animal husbandry.[14]

Measuring density

Measures of gross product at a refined spatial scale, such as a district or a city, are difficult to come by. Even for developed countries, output estimates tend to be available only for rather broadly defined subnational areas (first level and administrative units, such as provinces or states). At this level, important variations in economic density are likely to average out. Fortunately though, as illustrated earlier for Belgium, output and population density are closely correlated. Reliable population estimates are more easily available, even for villages or townships, because in most countries, a population census is taken every decade.

The strong correlation between population density and economic mass is consistent with urban areas being a conglomeration of consumers and producers, of buyers and sellers, and of firms and workers. For a typical metropolitan area, the gradient of population density for distance from the city center is similar to the corresponding gradient for employment density.[15] As implied above, the extent to which a country's population lives in urban areas bears a strong relationship to how "bumpy" its economic geography is. Density goes from smoothly spread out to quite uneven as a country develops. Urbanization is thus synonymous with a tendency toward greater agglomeration within a country. A country's urban share is a good proxy for the proportion of its population living in areas of high density and, therefore, for the "bumpiness" in its economic geography.

This Report proposes the use of an agglomeration index computed using geographic information systems as a measure of density. Measures of urbanization are nonuniform across countries, which makes comparability and aggregation a challenge. The index allows for a more consistent comparison of the level of urbanization—or,

interchangeably, agglomeration, density, or geographic concentration of economic activity—across countries.

The index identifies an area of 1 square kilometer as urban, agglomerated, or dense if it satisfies the following three conditions:

- Its population density exceeds a threshold (150 persons per square kilometer).
- It has access to a sizable settlement within some reasonable travel time (60 minutes by road).
- The settlement it has access to is large in that it meets a population threshold (more than 50,000 inhabitants).

Box 1.3 summarizes the rationale and methodology underpinning the index.

One advantage of the agglomeration index is that it incorporates both density and the local distance to density. Based on the criteria of population density and accessibility to a sizable market, the index also comes closer to providing an economic definition of an area that can both benefit from and contribute to agglomeration economies. Although economic density is both a cause and a consequence of agglomeration economies, accessibility to this economic mass from the outer parts of the city facilitates the exploitation of such benefits to proximity. This is especially true in the service sector in which face-to-face interactions are often necessary. By reducing the need to allocate valuable land area to residential uses in and near urban centers, transport infrastructure facilitates economic density.

Going to work by car or by high-speed public transportation is a luxury that developed country commuters do not always share with their counterparts in developing countries. For any given geographic distance, therefore, accessibility to a city tends to be lower in developing countries because of the need to rely on alternative, more time-intensive modes of transportation, such as walking, cycling, or inefficient public transportation operating on poor-quality roads. In Mumbai, India, 44 percent of people walk to work,[16] and in Hefei City, China, more than 70 percent either walk or cycle.[17]

Such variations in accessibility determine both the shape and form of a city. When most people walk to work, a city is more likely to be monocentric and densely

BOX 1.3   *Computing the agglomeration index*

The United Nations maintains the *World Urbanization Prospects* database, a treasure trove of information. It provides urban shares and population data for 229 countries stretching back to 1950. But these data are based on country definitions, which can be quite different. This Report proposes a new measure of agglomeration, based on a uniform definition of what constitutes an "urban" or agglomerated area, using the technique outlined in Chomitz and others (2007) and elaborated in Uchida and Nelson (2008).

This should not be read as implying that *World Urbanization Prospects* data are flawed. A better interpretation is to see the challenge of measuring urbanization as analogous to the measurement of poverty. Each country has its own poverty line and criteria to track changes in national poverty rates. But these measures do not allow reliable comparisons of poverty between countries, and they cannot be used to aggregate poverty for groups of countries. The merit of a uniform poverty measure—such as those living below US$1 or US$2 a day,

adjusted for purchasing power differences between countries—is that it allows international comparisons and calculations that aggregate poverty for regions and the world. The agglomeration index allows the same comparisons and aggregation.

The methodology underlying the calculation of the agglomeration index can be summarized as follows:

- *Specify thresholds*. To be classified as "urban" using the agglomeration index, an area must satisfy three criteria based on (1) minimum population size used to define a sizable settlement, (2) minimum population density, and (3) maximum travel time, by road, to the sizable settlement.
- *Locate the centers of sizable settlements*. This mapping is done for cities that meet the minimum population size criterion using data from the Global Rural-Urban Mapping Project (GRUMP) human settlements database.[a]
- *Determine the sizable settlement's border*. The border surrounding a sizable

settlement center is calculated based on the maximum travel time to the center.

- *Create population density grids*. These are created at a 1-kilometer spatial resolution using two global grid-based population data sources, GRUMP and LandScan.[b]
- *Identify the areas*. Identify the grid cells that satisfy thresholds for all three criteria.
- *Aggregate grid cell populations*. The result is analogous to urban population. The proportion of this number to that country's total population is the agglomeration index, a summary measure of the proportion of the population living in areas of high density.

In calculating the index, this Report uses a base case set of thresholds of 50,000 for minimum population size of a settlement, 150 people per square kilometer for population density, and 60 minutes for travel time to the nearest large city.

The density and travel time thresholds are those employed in Chomitz, Buys, and Thomas (2005). The density threshold is the same as the one used by the Organisation for Economic Co-operation and Development (OECD). The threshold of 50,000 for a sizable settlement is reasonable for developing and developed countries. Many developing nations have more than 10 percent of their total population in urban centers of between 50,000 and 200,000. Some examples include Chile in 2002, Brazil in 2000, and Malaysia in 2000, all with around 17 percent of their national population living in urban centers of 50,000–200,000 inhabitants. Of India's urban population in 2001, 20 percent lived in settlements of this size.

According to the *World Urbanization Prospects* database, the worldwide urban share in 2000 was 47 percent. Using the base case criteria, this ratio is 52 percent, but using 100,000 as the minimal settlement size, it is 44 percent, according to the agglomeration index. But country level estimates can be further apart (see figure at left).

The internationally comparable agglomeration index can yield different urban shares than those from country-specific definitions

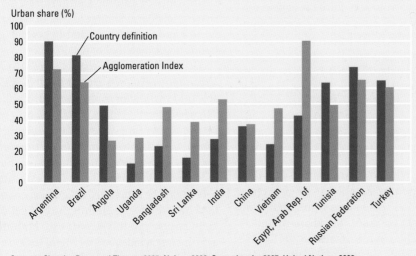

Urban share (%)

Sources: Chomitz, Buys, and Thomas 2005; Nelson 2008; Satterthwaite 2007; United Nations 2006c.
a. The GRUMP human settlements database was developed by the Center for International Earth Science Information Network (CIESIN) at Columbia University (http://sedac.ciesin. columbia.edu/gpw/index.jsp).
b. LandScan was developed by Oak Ridge National Laboratory (http://www.ornl.gov/sci/landscan/).

populated at its core. In Mumbai, half of all workers commute less than 2 kilometers, implying that they live close to their places of work. Similarly, to obtain the advantages of

agglomeration in industrial districts, workers in nineteenth-century Britain had to live nearby. The centers of industrial towns were densely populated, and overcrowded housing was common. Not until the electric tram was introduced did this change.

In determining accessibility, and thus the shape and form of cities, features of physical geography can also be important. Manhattan Island in New York City is difficult to get to, simply because of geography, so it has skyscrapers and a classic monocentric structure, with half its employment within a three-mile radius of Wall Street. By contrast, in Los Angeles, one has to widen the area to a radius of 11 miles from the center to find as large a share of employment.[18] The implication: economic density in New York City is $1.44 billion of gross product per square kilometer, in Los Angeles it is $0.49 billion.[19]

In the United Kingdom, Stevenage, Basildon, and Crawley are commuter towns that serve London. About 11 percent of London's GDP is generated by commuters from suburban areas.[20] Similarly, in the United States, a daily tide of workers commute into Washington, D.C., from the neighboring states of Maryland and Virginia. In 2005 the net contribution of commuters from these two states to Washington, D.C.'s output was $36.4 billion. Maryland's Montgomery County—within easy commutable distance of the district—alone contributed $6.4 billion to Washington's gross product.[21]

The biggest advantage of the agglomeration index is its comparability across countries. Here the index has an advantage over the United Nations' *World Urbanization Prospects* database, which contains the "de facto population living in areas classified as urban according to the criteria used by each area or country."[22] The heterogeneity across countries can makes cross-country comparisons misleading. A few examples:

- *India.* With the criterion for an urban area used by Zambia or Saudi Arabia, defined as settlements with populations of 5,000 or more, the share of India's population in urban areas in 1991 would be 39 percent instead of the official figure of 26 percent. This is because 113 million inhabitants of 13,376 villages would be reclassified as urban.
- *Mexico.* Based on Mexico's official criterion of settlements of 2,500 or more as urban, the country's urban share in 2000 was 74.4 percent. But if the settlement population threshold were to be

redefined as 15,000 (Nigeria and Syria, for example, have cutoffs of 20,000), that share would drop to 67 percent.
- *Mauritius.* In 2000 about a quarter of Mauritius's population lived in settlements with between 5,000 and 20,000 inhabitants. Some of these settlements are district capitals, but none of them are classified as urban. If they were, the urban share would have been more than two-thirds rather than less than half.

At a regional level, according to *World Urbanization Prospects* data, South Asia poses the paradox of being the least urbanized region (27 percent urban) in the world while also the most densely populated. Using the agglomeration index, South Asia's urban share in 2000 was 42 percent, making it more urbanized than both Sub-Saharan Africa and East Asia and the Pacific (figure 1.3). The *World Urbanization Prospects* also pose a puzzle for Latin America and the Caribbean. The urban share in this region in 2000 was greater than that in Eastern Europe and Central Asia and almost on par with the OECD's. The OECD has an average GDP per capita more than six times that of the average Latin American country. More reasonably, the agglomeration index indicates that Latin America and the Caribbean's urban share in 2000 was similar to that of Eastern Europe and Central Asia, and 15 percentage points lower than that of the OECD.

Despite these drawbacks, the *World Urbanization Prospects* data are the only available information for comparisons over time. The agglomeration index is available only for 2000, because time-series data on road networks, necessary to estimate travel time, are not readily available. So, the agglomeration index and *World Urbanization Prospects* database should be considered as complementary data sources for examining urbanization and density, and this Report uses both the agglomeration index and the *World Urbanization Prospects* data.[23] Calculating comparable urban share measures for at least some countries in the past is possible; going forward, it should be a priority for all countries.

Economic concentration— the richer, the denser

In the early stages of development, when an economy is primarily agrarian, people live spread out on farmland. Even the largest towns and cities are small. Urban settlements are likely to be small port cities and market towns, serving the rural needs and trading surpluses of agriculture. Industrialization brings with it a rapid process of urbanization—new cities are born, and existing cities expand. As people crowd into these cities at a faster rate than their boundaries expand, population and economic density increase. Quite early in a country's development, this leads to a hierarchy of places.

So, two transitions characterize economic development. The first involves the movement from a primarily agrarian economy to a much more manufacturing-oriented economy. The second transition, taking place at a much higher level of development, involves the transformation to a service-oriented economy. The first phase of urbanization, which occurs at a faster rate, coincides with the transition from a rural to an urban economy. The second phase of urbanization, at a slower rate and a much higher level of development, is linked to a within-urban evolution. In most countries, these transformations happen at the same time but in different areas.

To measure concentration, we have to define an area. The policy debate often involves a discussion of urban primacy, such as whether developing country cities are too big or too small. More academic discussions use a purer geographic notion of space. This chapter uses both spatial units—primary cities and the densest grid cell of 1° longitude by 1° latitude of a country—to measure concentration.

Historically, rapidly rising concentration, then a leveling off

By one definition, a city is a geographic area characterized by a concentration of economic actors.[24] Globally, the top 30 cities, ranked by GDP, generated around 16 percent of the world's output in 2005, while the top 100 generated almost 25 percent. The urban agglomerations of Tokyo and New York have estimated GDPs (in purchasing power parity) broadly similar to those of Canada and Spain, respectively, whereas London has a higher estimated GDP than either Sweden or Switzerland. Similarly, primary cities in developing countries account

Figure 1.3   The agglomeration index helps to compare urbanization across regions

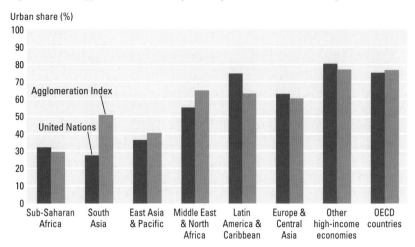

Sources: Chomitz, Buys, and Thomas 2005; Nelson 2008; Satterthwaite 2007; United Nations 2006c.

for disproportionate shares of their national GDP. In 2005, Mexico City contributed 30 percent of Mexico's GDP despite occupying only 0.1 percent of its land. Luanda contributed a similar share of Angola's GDP, while occupying 0.2 percent of its land. Likewise, the largest cities in Hungary, Kenya, Morocco, Nigeria, and Saudi Arabia—Budapest, Nairobi, Casablanca, Lagos, and Riyadh—contributed about 20 percent of their country's total GDP while taking up less than 1 percent of land.[25]

Density, defined as GDP in purchasing power parities per square kilometer, rises with the level of development, and the densest places in the world are in the richest countries. Dublin, London, Paris, Singapore, and Vienna ranked at the top, in 2005, with more than $200 million in gross product per square kilometer. Likewise, Tokyo-Kanagawa, New York–New Jersey, Oslo–Akershus-Vestfold, and Vienna-Mödling were the densest grid cells of 1° longitude by 1° latitude, generating more than $30 million of gross product per square kilometer (figure 1.4).

A century of data on aggregate urban shares, and two centuries of population estimates for primary cities, suggest that urbanization is initially rapid before slowing. Developing countries—especially those in Africa and Asia—are at phases during which urban shares increase sharply. People in Western Europe and North America, which went through the same phase a century ago, have understandably forgotten. Emerging economies such as the Republic of Korea that

Figure 1.4   The richer a country, the more concentrated its economic mass

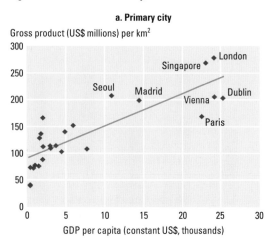

a. Primary city

Gross product (US$ millions) per km²

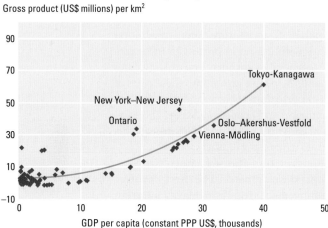

b. Area of 1° longitude by 1° latitude

Gross product (US$ millions) per km²

Sources: WDR team estimates based on World Bank (2007j), and databases from www.citymayor.com and www.gecon.yale.edu.

Figure 1.5   Developing countries have a pace of urbanization similar to that of early developers

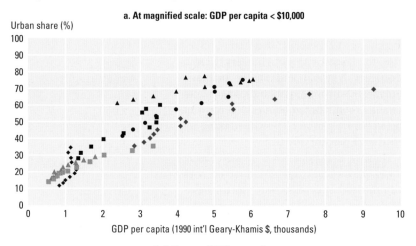

a. At magnified scale: GDP per capita < $10,000

Urban share (%)

GDP per capita (1990 int'l Geary-Khamis $, thousands)

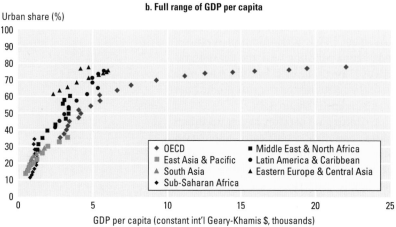

b. Full range of GDP per capita

Urban share (%)

- ◆ OECD
- ■ East Asia & Pacific
- ▲ South Asia
- ◆ Sub-Saharan Africa
- ■ Middle East & North Africa
- ● Latin America & Caribbean
- ▲ Eastern Europe & Central Asia

GDP per capita (constant int'l Geary-Khamis $, thousands)

Sources: Maddison 2006; United Nations 1969; United Nations 1949; United Nations 1952; Historical Database of the Global Environment; United Nations 2006c.

developed rapidly provide the best case studies for understanding the pace and pattern of geographic concentration. Their experience traces the initially rapid and the more gradual growth of today's wealthiest nations.

At the aggregate level, using the population shares in urban areas, the urbanization pattern of developing countries in Asia, Africa, Middle East, and Latin America over the last 50 years closely tracks the first part of the historic path earlier traversed by OECD countries between 1900 and 2000 (figure 1.5). The urbanization in Asia mirrors the rapid phase of urbanization that OECD countries experienced in the nineteenth century. Likewise, the geographic transformations in Latin America and the Caribbean, in Eastern Europe and Central Asia, and in the Middle East and North Africa are qualitatively similar to those experienced by the OECD in the first phase of urbanization. Quantitatively, the urban shares for Latin America and the Caribbean and for Eastern Europe and Central Asia regions are higher than those for the OECD at comparable incomes.

This may, however, be an artifact of the data. Data from the *World Urbanization Prospects* database systematically overstate—purely as a definitional matter—the urban shares of Latin America and the Caribbean, Eastern Europe and Central Asia, and Sub-Saharan Africa. The safest conclusion may be that the pattern of urbanization—the

BOX 1.4 *Africa's urbanization reflects industrialization*

Between 1970 and 1995, the urban populations in Sub-Saharan Africa were growing at 5.2 percent a year while their GDP per capita was shrinking at 0.66 percent a year. Since the work by Fay and Opal (2000), many have argued that urbanization does not necessarily accompany development, with Sub-Saharan Africa in mind (Commission for Africa 2005). But Satterthwaite (2007) questions the validity of the urban population numbers in most studies. Since many were based on projections, some may have been grossly overestimated.

The problem is the lack of regular population censuses. For Chad and Eritrea the population projections spanning 1950 through 2030 were based on one population census. Those for the Democratic Republic of Congo were derived from two observations, the most recent for 1984. It is thus reasonable to consider only countries with at least two censuses during the period examined (1970–95), a census post-2000 for more accu-

rate population estimates, a population of at least 1 million in 1995, and data on sectoral value added for 1970 and 1995.

This whittles the sample down to just 10 countries: Benin, Botswana, Central African Republic, Ghana, Mauritania, Niger, Rwanda, Senegal, Zambia, and Zimbabwe. Of these 10 countries, five experienced conflict at least once, and the other five were peaceful throughout the period. The results do not appear to differ systematically between these two sets of countries. The main findings follow:

- Except for Botswana, the countries experienced on average a doubling of population, but only 60 percent cumulative growth in GDP. Population growth outpaced increases in gross value added, and GDP per capita fell.
- Urban population growth and total GDP growth are positively correlated. Countries with the fastest growth

in total GDP—a doubling of their economies—also witnessed the fastest growth in urban population—a four-fold increase. The leaders in the sample were Benin and Zimbabwe.

- The pace of urbanization was positively correlated with growth in industries and services, activities predominant in urban areas.

These patterns do not support the claim of African urbanization without growth. In contrast, countries with higher GDP growth experienced faster urbanization, and rapid urbanization came hand-in-hand with higher growth in industries and services. A counterfactual of an Africa without urbanization is one with even slower economic growth, greater GDP per capita losses, and increases in poverty.

Sources: Fay and Opal 2000; Satterthwaite 2007; United Nations 2006c.

relationship between economic growth and urbanization—is not unprecedented. Even in Sub-Saharan Africa, faster urbanization between 1970 and 1995, albeit with negative GDP per capita growth, was associated with higher total GDP growth. Urbanization also came hand-in-hand with rapid growth in industries and services (see box 1.4).

At a disaggregated level, the primary city's population share of a country displays a similar, nonlinear pattern of initially rapidly rising concentration, followed by a subsequent leveling (figure 1.6). This intensification of economic mass within a country's largest cities is seen for a wide range of incomes, from Budapest, Cairo, Kuala

Figure 1.6 Density intensifies rapidly in the early phase of urbanization before leveling off

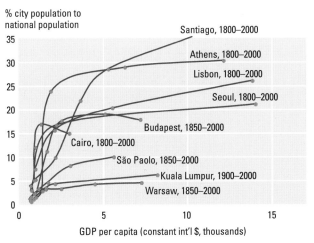
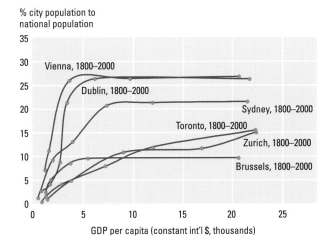

Sources: WDR 2009 team estimates, based on the Staff City Population Database, Human Settlements Group, International Institute for Environment and Development (IIED). Data from 1950 to the present, primarily from United Nations (2006c); data before 1950, primarily from Chandler and Fox (1974), Chandler (1987), and Showers (1979). Latin America drew on a review of 194 published censuses.

Lumpur, and Warsaw to Athens, Lisbon, Santiago, and Seoul. These evolutions have also been observed in Brussels, Dublin, Sydney, Toronto, Vienna, and Zurich over the two centuries since 1800.

Again today, rapidly rising concentration, then a leveling off

A similarly shaped pattern reappears in contemporary comparisons between a country's level of development and the concentration of density. During 2000–05, the average urban population growth for low-income countries was 3 percent a year—faster than upper-middle-income countries at 1.3 percent and high-income countries at 0.9 percent. The relationship is robust. It holds for a variety of concentration measures, ranging from the agglomeration index, to population, gross product, and household consumption density. It is robust to geographic scale: an area of 1 square kilometer, a city, a grid cell of 1° longitude by 1° latitude, and an aggregated urban sector.

Local 1-square kilometer areas. Estimated agglomeration indexes produce a pattern similar to the historical time series: rapidly rising density for countries during the early phase of urbanization (figure 1.7). This strong positive relationship between

urban share and development holds until a GDP per capita of around $10,000. This incipient urbanization is associated with a rapid shift in the number of people moving from rural to urban areas. Subsequently, the pace of urbanization slows and density levels off as the urban share surpasses 60 percent, and the level of GDP per capita surpasses $10,000. With only a handful of exceptions, countries with GDPs per capita above $25,000 have an agglomeration index above 70 percent.

Administratively defined areas. Taking individual cities as the geographic unit, a positive concave relationship exists between a country's level of development and its primacy—the share of urban population living in the country's primary city, a widely used concentration measure. Similar to the relationship between agglomerations and the level of development, primacy also rises rapidly before stabilizing during the latter stages of urbanization (see figure 1.8, panel a). Population and output density are highly correlated, but population density understates the geographic concentration of economic mass. Agglomeration economies, the benefits that firms and workers enjoy as a result of proximity, make it likely that output density will increase more than proportionally with employment or population density.

1° longitude by 1° latitude. Using the terrestrial grid cells to estimate concentration as the share of the densest cell's gross product in the country's GDP, concentration of economic mass rises rapidly among countries with a GDP per capita of less than $15,000, and then stabilizes and tapers off among higher-income countries (see figure 1.8, panel b).

Urban areas of countries. Concentration measured by consumption, rather than by population or GDP, suggests the same concave relationship with the level of development. For instance, the urban shares of household consumption in Malawi and Cameroon at GDPs per capita of $150 and $700, respectively, are 36 percent and 48 percent. At about 63 percent, the shares are higher for Jordan and the Arab Republic of Egypt with GDP per capita of around $1,600, and rise to 80 percent in Panama and Poland

Figure 1.7 Shares of population living in urban agglomerations rise with the level of development

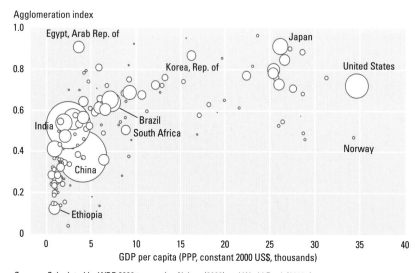

Sources: Calculated by WDR 2009 team using Nelson (2008) and World Bank (2006g).
Note: The size of each circle indicates the population size of that country. PPP = purchasing power parity. The agglomeration index uses the following criteria: density of 150 persons per kilometer or more, access time of 60 minutes or less to a sizable settlement, defined as one that has a population of more than 50,000.

Figure 1.8   Geographic concentration of population, gross product, and household consumption rises sharply with development, then levels off
Cross-country evidence, late 1990s and 2000s

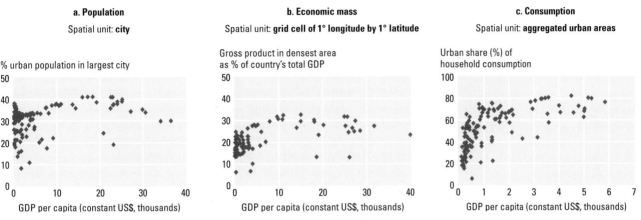

a. Population	b. Economic mass	c. Consumption
Spatial unit: **city**	Spatial unit: **grid cell of 1° longitude by 1° latitude**	Spatial unit: **aggregated urban areas**

Sources: WDR 2009 team estimates, based on World Bank (2007j), Nordhaus (2006), and more than 120 household surveys for more than 75 countries.

with GDPs per capita of $3,500 and $5,000, respectively (see figure 1.8, panel c).[26]

A portfolio of bigger and denser places

It follows from these stylized facts of geographic transformation that high-income countries have a portfolio of places with a higher proportion of large settlements and a lower proportion of small settlements than do middle-income countries. And the middle-income countries have a significantly higher proportion of medium-size settlements than do low-income countries. In low-income countries, about three-quarters of the population live in small settlements of less than 20,000 people, and only 10 percent live in urban agglomerations of more than 1 million people. In high-income countries, the opposite is true. Less than a quarter of the population live in small settlements of less than 20,000 people, and about half of the population live in settlements of more than 1 million people (see table 1.1).

At an incipient stage of urbanization, the portfolio of places in a small country or part of a larger country, such as a province or even a large district, can be approximated as 75 percent rural and 25 percent urban, all settlements of relatively low density. As urbanization accelerates—still predominantly a rural-urban transformation driven by industrialization—and the area or province grows toward a GDP per capita of $10,000, its distribution of settlements

will approximate a 50/50 urban-rural split. During more advanced urbanization—now a within-urban transformation in a postindustrial area—the distribution of population can be approximated as 75 percent urban and 25 percent rural.

This generalization corresponds well to the experience of the United States. In 1690, when the average GDP per capita was a mere $500 (1990 international dollars),[27] the primary city in colonial British America was Boston. With a population of 7,000, however, Boston was by modern-day standards little bigger than a small town. In the urban hierarchy, only three other cities had populations greater than 2,500, two of them New York and Philadelphia. The early phase of American industrialization brought with it an increase in the urban share from 7 percent in 1820 to 20 percent in 1860, as GDPs per capita rose from $1,257 to $2,170 (1990 international dollars). During this time, the population of the primary city, now New York, expanded from 123,706 to 805,651. Its rapid growth allowed the urban hierarchy to expand and stretch out.

Table 1.1   The size of urban settlements grows with development

Population size	Low-income countries (%)	Middle-income countries (%)	High-income countries (%)
Small settlements: less than 20,000	73	55	22
Medium settlements: 20,000 to 1 million	16	25	26
Large settlements: more than 1 million	11	20	52

Source: World Bank 2007j.

The number of cities with a population greater than 1 million increased from just one, New York, in 1820 to nine in 1860. All these cities were in the Northeast, where industrialization began. As the geographic transformation wore on, and the United States completed its transition to a mature industrial economy, population density in a consistent sample of U.S. cities with populations greater than 25,000 increased from 7,230 persons per square mile to 8,876 per square mile. The average land area of a city increased from about 19 square miles to 40 square miles.[28] Cities became more packed and more sprawling at the same time.

Convergence—rural-urban and within cities

A "bumpy" economic geography distributing production and people unevenly across the space in a country is a natural feature of the working of a market economy. This bumpiness tends to become more pronounced as a country develops. The question often asked is: what does this do to the geographic distribution of poverty, consumption, and other living standards? The answer can determine the political and social sustainability of the process of concentration.

Rural-urban disparities in well-being— first wide, then narrow

Rural-urban disparities in productivity, wages, and well-being can be expected to be large and increasing in the earlier stages of development. With the rapidly increasing concentration of economic mass in a country's towns and cities in the earlier stages of development, significant disparities in productivity, wages, and basic welfare occur between urban and rural areas. The agglomeration of capital, consumers, and workers quickly brings production advantages, and transport costs restrict the benefits to the locality. These larger local markets enable firms to spread the fixed costs of production across a wider number of consumers, producing cost and productivity advantages.[29] This means higher wages in towns and cities, and greater availability of a more diversified range of goods and services.

The concentration of mass also helps to ensure a better supply of basic infrastructure and public health facilities in urban areas. Along with diverging wages, this promotes divergence in more basic measures of welfare between urban and rural areas.[30] But rural-urban disparities begin to narrow as the urbanization process slows, and governments become more capable. The exodus of people and workers from rural areas to towns and cities reduces surplus labor from the land in agriculture—and reduces competition between workers in rural labor markets. And labor-saving technological progress releases labor for migration to urban areas and improves productivity. In time, investments and fiscal redistributions give rural residents better local access to basic amenities, such as a clean daily source of running water, sanitation, and electricity, as well as schooling and health care. Indeed, with development and the passage of time, a country's economic geography approximates a "natural" balance that equalizes welfare between urban and rural residents. In this situation, people choose to live where they expect to be best off in material and nonmaterial well-being. The Islamic Republic of Iran illustrates this rural-urban convergence (see box 1.5).

Evidence from today's industrial countries suggests that development has largely eliminated rural-urban disparities. High urban shares and concentrated economic density go hand in hand with small differences in rural-urban well-being on a range of indicators. The 15 countries that joined the European Union (EU) before 2004, all with GDPs per capita in excess of $13,000 (1990 international dollars), consider the unemployment rate an important policy target.[31] But rural-urban unemployment differences should not be a concern. The unemployment rates are 10.1 percent for urban areas, and 9.9 percent for rural areas. This is also evident for youth: 19.4 percent in urban areas compared with 18.7 percent in rural areas. The rates of labor force participation in urban and rural areas are 68.3 and 69.4 percent, respectively.[32] For England, the high degree of rural-urban equality in well-being is reflected in similar disposable incomes: indeed, at £522, weekly disposable income in villages is 10 percent higher than the £476 in cities.[33]

BOX 1.5 *Urbanization and narrowing rural-urban disparities in the Islamic Republic of Iran*

Rural-urban disparities have narrowed in the Islamic Republic of Iran. In 1976, on the eve of the Iranian revolution, the mean per capita household income in rural areas was 44 percent of that in urban areas. By 2005, it had increased to 63 percent.

The Shah's government favored cities over the countryside. Price controls for essential foods depressed agricultural incomes. High tariffs, import bans, and licensing for industrial goods propped up prices of manufactured goods and depressed farmers' purchasing power. An inward-looking development strategy oriented toward final domestic demand amplified internal migration to Tehran and a few other large cities. For every indicator of development, the center performed far better than the periphery. In 1973, the poverty rate was 23 percent in the central region and 42 percent for the country. This spatial inequality matched the nation's ethnic map, fueling tensions.

What has happened since the commitment in 1979 to address spatial disparities?

• First, the share of the urban population has increased from 49 to 67 percent between 1979 and 2005. This is a continuation of a longer-term trend: the urban population had grown by 5.4 percent per year (and in Tehran by 6 percent) between 1966 and 1976.

• Second, the rural-urban gap in household incomes has narrowed. Between 1976 and 1984, agricultural value added grew by 31 percent, twice the rate of the nonoil economy. One reason for this growth was that farmgate prices rose 55 percent. Another reason was that more was spent on projects to increase the productivity of small and medium-size farms. Growth could also be attributed to the fact that agricultural production in the Islamic Republic of Iran is dominated by the private sector, whereas large industrial enterprises and service providers were nationalized after the revolution, which hindered their efficiency.

• Third, rural and urban human development indicators improved, even in the lagging provinces. Between 1976 and 1996, the female literacy rate rose from 17 to 62 percent, while for urban women it rose from 56 to 82 percent. During 1994–2000, infant mortality and under-5 mortality fell fastest in the poorest provinces.

• Finally, overall poverty has fallen. The national poverty rate was at 8.1 percent in 2005, with relatively modest differences in rural and urban poverty of 10 and 7.1 percent, respectively. But poverty rates still vary a lot between provinces, ranging from 1.4 to 23.3 percent.

The political commitment to spatial equity has produced mixed outcomes during the last 30 years: overall poverty declines and a convergence in rural-urban standards of living, but persistent differences in interprovincial living standards.

Based on a contribution by Anton Dobronogov, Alexander Kremer, and others.

For 21 of the 30 OECD countries, the higher the GDP per capita in 2003,[34] the lower the ratio of GDP per capita in predominantly urban areas to that in rural areas (see figure 1.9).[35] For the Czech Republic, Hungary, Poland, the Slovak Republic, and Turkey, with an average GDP per capita below $10,000 (1990 international dollars), GDP per capita in urban areas is two to three times higher. But for OECD countries with average GDPs per capita above $10,000, the ratio is between one and two (except for Norway). Given the well-developed fiscal redistribution mechanisms in OECD countries, and differences in age-demographic profiles between urban and rural areas, these disparities in GDP per capita will overstate rural-urban differences in, say,

Figure 1.9 Rural-urban disparities in GDP per capita tend to be smaller in richer OECD countries

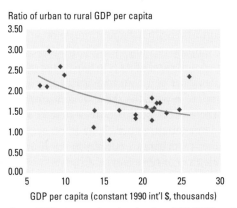

Source: WDR 2009 team, based on data from OECD (2007), pp. 1–256.

Table 1.2   Rural-urban disparities in earnings, wealth, and consumption characterize development over the last two centuries

Country (year)	Rural-urban disparity (%)	Description and country sample
Sweden (1805)	221.0	Wealth per male adult in urban and rural areas.
Finland (1805)	146.0	Wealth per male adult in urban and rural areas.
England (1830s)	73.2	Urban wages are wages per laborer in the building trades, and rural wages are for agricultural laborers.
France (1882) France (1911)	29.0 51.0	Urban wages are for unskilled wages in the regional capital city (department *chef lieu*), and rural wages are based on average farm wages .
United States (1925) United States (1935)	28.0 75.0	Urban earnings are manufacturing earnings, and rural earnings are agricultural earnings.
Developing countries (nineteenth century)	51.2	Urban wages are for unskilled general laborers, and rural wages are agricultural wages, including payments in kind. The countries included are Argentina 1872; Australia 1887; Denmark 1872; France 1892, 1801; Hungary 1865; Japan 1887; and the United States 1820–29, 1890.
Developing countries (twentieth century)	41.4	Urban wages are based on wages for unskilled construction workers, and rural wages are agricultural cash wages. There are 19 countries (1960–70) underlying this average: Argentina, Cameroon, Chile, Costa Rica, Côte d'Ivoire, Guatemala, Kenya, Pakistan, Malawi, Malaysia, Mexico, Morocco, Panama, Sri Lanka, Tanzania, Trinidad and Tobago, Tunisia, Uruguay, and R. B. de Venezuela.
Developing countries (twenty-first century)	42.0	Based on per capita household consumption, after controlling for household characteristics. There are 72 countries (2000–05) underlying this average disparity: Armenia, Angola, Bangladesh, Belize, Benin, Bhutan, Bolivia, Brazil, Burkina Faso, Burundi, Bulgaria, Cambodia, Cameroon, Chad, Chile, Colombia, Dem. Rep. of Congo, Costa Rica, Côte d'Ivoire, Croatia, Djibouti, Ecuador, Arab Rep. of Egypt, El Salvador, Ethiopia, The Gambia, Georgia, Ghana, Guatemala, Guinea, Guyana, Honduras, Hungary, India, Indonesia, Jamaica, Jordan, Kyrgyz Republic, Madagascar, Malawi, Maldives, Mali, Mauritania, Mexico, Moldova, Mongolia, Morocco, Mozambique, Nepal, Nicaragua, Nigeria, Pakistan, Panama, Paraguay, Peru, Philippines, Poland, Romania, Russian Federation, Rwanda, Senegal, South Africa, Sri Lanka, Swaziland, Tajikistan, Tanzania, Thailand, Timor-Leste, Uganda, Ukraine, Vietnam, and Zambia.

Sources: Sweden and Finland 1805: Soltow 1989, table 1, p. 48; England 1830s: Williamson 1987, table 3, p. 652; France 1882, 1911: Sicsic 1992, table 2, p. 685; United States 1925, 1935: Alston and Hatton 1991, table 3, p. 93; Developing countries (nineteenth century): Clark 1957, table II pp. 526–31; Developing countries (twentieth century): Squire 1981, table 30, p. 102; Developing countries (twenty-first century): WDR 2009 team estimates based on individual country's household survey for 72 countries; the data set is described in detail in Montenegro and Hirn (2008).
Note: Rural-urban disparity (in nominal terms) is computed as the difference in wages, earnings, wealth, or consumption between urban and rural areas relative to the rural averages.

average levels of personal disposable income and consumption. The agglomeration index produces the same qualitative pattern.

Rural-urban disparities in these countries were wide throughout the nineteenth and early twentieth centuries. Wealth per male adult in nineteenth century Sweden was more than 200 percent higher in urban areas than in rural areas, and 150 percent higher in Finland (see table 1.2). Meanwhile, for rapidly urbanizing England, urban wages were more than 70 percent higher than rural wages in the 1830s. France and the United States saw big increases in the urban wage premium from 1882 to 1911 and from 1925 to 1935. Indeed, in the United States, the premium increased almost threefold in a decade.[36] For developing countries in the nineteenth century, including Australia, Denmark, France, Japan, and the United States, urban nominal wages were 50 percent higher.

Today's developing countries are still in the first phase of urbanization and, not surprisingly, have large rural-urban disparities in productivity and income. For a sample of developing countries in the 1960s—among them Malaysia, Mexico, and Trinidad and Tobago, which have since reached upper-middle-income or high-income status—urban wages exceeded rural wages by more than 40 percent. Similar gaps can be observed in per capita consumption between urban and rural areas for a recent sample of 72 developing countries.

The rural-urban discrepancy between economic mass and population distributions diminishes with urbanization. Another way to examine consumption disparities between urban and rural areas is to look at the population share of a country's urban areas and compare it with the share of consumption in these areas. If this ratio is greater than one, consumption per capita is, on average, higher in urban areas than in rural areas, while the converse is true if the ratio is less than one.

Rural-urban disparities in consumption fall with density in today's developing

Figure 1.10   Rural-urban gaps in per capita consumption become smaller with urbanization

Ratio of urban consumption share
to urban population share

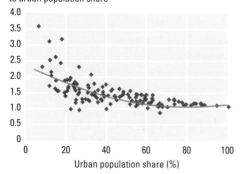

Source: WDR 2009 team estimates from more than 120 household surveys for more than 75 countries.

countries (see figure 1.10).[37] In Malawi and Sri Lanka the ratio is around two: urban areas account for about 10 percent of the population but 20 percent of consumption. For countries with higher levels of urbanization, the spatial distribution of population more closely resembles that of production. Madagascar and Tanzania have urban population shares of around 20 to 25 percent and urban consumption shares of about 30 to 35 percent. By the time a country enters an advanced stage of urbanization, population is more or less proportionately distributed with economic mass, so that the ratio is close to one. In Chile 85 percent of the population reside in urban areas, and these urban residents account for 92 percent of national consumption. In Brazil 80 percent of people live in urban settlements, and these 80 percent are responsible for 85 percent of consumption. As development progresses and the concentration of economic activity in areas of high density increases, rural-urban disparities narrow. A downward sloping line at all levels of urbanization is a good omen: most developing countries may have passed the peak in their rural-urban disparities.[38]

What is true for private consumption is true for basic amenities. Among low-income countries with urban population shares of less than 25 percent, access to water and sanitation in towns and cities is around 25 percentage points higher than in rural areas.[39] But for more urbanized countries, such as Algeria, Colombia, and South Africa, the disparity in access is 15 to 20 percentage

points. For countries where urbanization is advanced and the urban share is approaching its natural maximum, almost no difference exists between urban and rural areas in access to basic services. Equalization of access to basic services can be expected to promote a corresponding convergence in nonmaterial indicators of welfare and living standards (see table 1.3).

Narrowing rural-urban disparities is important, but the progress in absolute measures of basic welfare in the rural areas of the world's poorest countries is even more important. Rising rural-urban disparities are consistent with an absolute improvement in basic welfare in both rural and urban areas. The overall evidence is encouraging. Over the past decade, most low- and middle-income countries have experienced absolute improvements on a range of basic welfare indicators, including infant and under-5 mortality rates, malnutrition, immunization, and school participation in rural and urban areas. Of 32 low-income countries, three-quarters reduced infant and under-5 mortality rates and the incidence of severe stunting and severe underweight, especially in rural areas.[40] And since 1990, school attendance rose in four-fifths of these countries, especially in rural areas.[41] Both

Table 1.3   Rural-urban disparity in basic services narrows with development

Urban population share (mean GDP per capita)	Disparity in access to clean water (percentage points)	Disparity in access to sanitation (percentage points)	Examples of countries in the sample
75% or higher (mean GDP per capita: $21,602)	8	8	United States, Norway, Switzerland, Spain, Germany, Canada, Mexico, Chile, Brazil, Argentina, Gabon, R. B. de Venezuela, Djibouti, Lebanon, Jordan, United Kingdom
50%–70% (mean GDP per capita: $9,672)	15	20	Estonia, Panama, Turkey, Hungary, Ecuador, Colombia, Malaysia, Syria, Azerbaijan, South Africa, Rep. of Congo, Algeria, Tunisia, Bolivia
25% or lower (mean GDP per capita: $2,585)	24	26	India, Rep. of Yemen, Madagascar, Chad, Tajikistan, Bangladesh, Tanzania, Kenya, Nepal, Cambodia, Malawi, Uganda, Sri Lanka, Bhutan

Source: World Bank 2007j.
Note: Disparity refers to the percentage point difference between urban and rural areas.

Figure 1.11   Even at the subnational level, rural-urban disparities fall as density increases

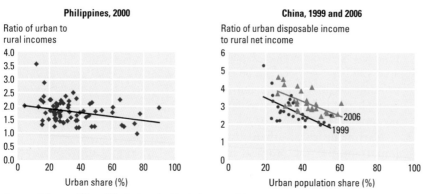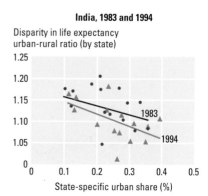

Sources: Balisacan, Hill, and Piza forthcoming; Yao forthcoming; Cali 2008.

urban and rural areas in these nations have achieved progress toward the Millennium Development Goals.

Rural-urban convergence takes place sooner in more urbanized subnational areas. In both China and the Philippines, urbanized provinces exhibit lower internal urban-rural disparities in incomes (see figure 1.11). In China the entire relationship has shifted upward over the past decade so that, in general, rural-urban disparities have increased over time, consistent with China's early stage of development, which is marked by rapid urbanization. In India rural-urban gaps in life expectancy were smaller in the more urbanized states in both 1983 and 1994. But the entire relationship has shifted downward over time.

Slums—divergence and convergence within cities

In poor countries, higher average living standards in cities do not rule out poverty

and deprivation. Disparities within cities can be large. In Nairobi poverty is high in the inner city but much lower in the rest of the city and the suburbs (see figure 1.12). In Mombasa, Kenya's second-most-populous city, marked geographic divisions in the poverty rate are evident (see map 1.2). South African cities also show internal disparities in the poverty rate. Cape Town has a low poverty rate in the coastal areas, but a higher poverty rate in the interior of the city. Similarly, both Johannesburg-Pretoria-Tshwane and Durban have visible divisions. But the geography of poverty in Durban is different from that in Cape Town and Johannesburg: the poverty rate is, in general, higher outside the city boundaries than inside.

The most obvious sign of divisions within cities is slums. Slums have chronically overcrowded dwellings of poor quality in underserved areas. The reason for the lack of basic public services and infrastructure is the inability or unwillingness of many urban

Figure 1.12   Slums grow with the pace of urbanization, and fall with its level

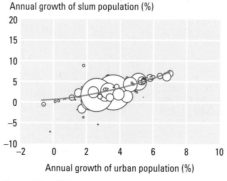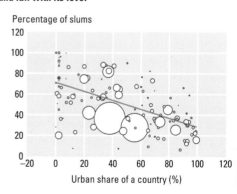

Source: Kilroy 2008.

Map 1.2   Local divisions—spatial disparities within urban settlements can be large
Poverty rates in African cities

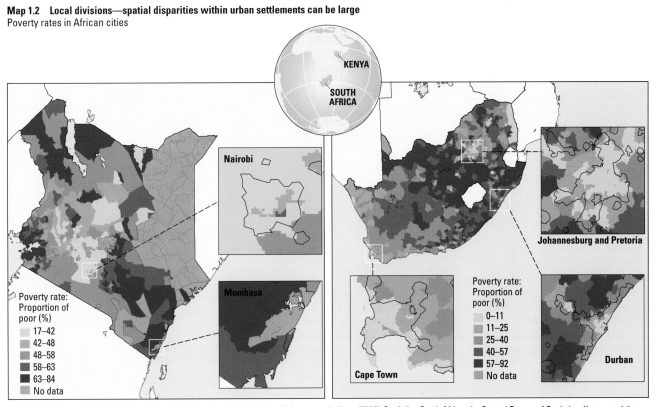

Source: The Poverty Mapping Project, Columbia University, using data from Alderman and others (2002); Statistics South Africa; the Central Bureau of Statistics, Kenya; and the Ministry of Planning and National Development, Kenya.

governments, utilities, and service providers to operate in slums, generally because of the informality and illegality of such settlements.[42] So living standards, especially health, security, and sanitation, are lower in slums than in formal settlements close by. Mumbai's Dharavi, believed to be Asia's biggest slum, has "maybe a million residents . . . crammed into a square mile of low rise wood, concrete and rusted iron . . . a family of 12 living in a 90-square-foot room." In Shiva Shakti Nagar, again in Mumbai, each community tap is shared by roughly 100 people.[43]

The growth of slums in major cities is characteristic of rapid urbanization. Because rapid population growth cannot be satisfactorily accommodated, slums and shantytowns grow bigger and more visible. This contributes to wide and increasing geographic divisions in well-being within urban areas. Development—both economic and institutional—and better infrastructure, combined with focused interventions, eventually bring about a convergence in living standards in urban areas.

Slums are part of rapid urbanization, and it is not uncommon for a fifth to a third of a city's population in a contemporary developing country to reside in slums (see figure 1.12).[44] Goiâna, the capital of the Brazilian state of Goiàs, a medium-size city of 40,000 in 1950, is today a city of more than 1 million, with much of the population increase accommodated in slums.[45] Since 1950, Delhi's population has risen more than tenfold, from 1.4 million to 15.6 million,[46] accompanied by an increase in the number of slum clusters from 200 to 1,160.

"A dirtier or more wretched place he had never seen. The street was narrow and muddy, and the air was impregnated with filthy odors. . . . Covered ways and yards, which here and there diverged from the main street, disclosed little knots of houses, where drunken men and women were positively wallowing in filth." A contemporary description of a developing country slum such as Nairobi's Kibera or Huruma, Abidjan's Washington, Delhi's Majboor Nagar or Kanchan Puri, Buenos Aires's San Fernando,

The term "slum," probably originating from an old English or German word meaning a poorly drained or muddy place, was applied to housing in the early Industrial Revolution in the United Kingdom before the railways were in place, when canals transported heavy goods along the length and breadth of the country. During Britain's rapid industrialization, most factories were built beside canals, the main channel for transporting coal for their steam engines and other inputs of production.

Poor workers, migrating to cities for factory jobs, could ill afford to walk long distances to and from their places of work. Before electric trams, other forms of transport were expensive. So workers settled close to factories. Cheap housing grew around these factories in low-lying, poorly drained areas. Housing was overcrowded. Sanitation was inadequate and in most cases nonexistent. And air quality was poor, with soot and other pollutants. Sickness was commonplace. Diarrhea, typhus, respiratory diseases, measles, and scarlet fever cut the life expectancy of those born in cities by 12 years compared with those born in rural areas.

The growing public health hazards in Britain's urban slums exacted a terrible health toll that eventually reached out beyond the working class, finally motivating strong political action. But rather than attempting to stop more workers from coming, or clearing out these areas of disease and poverty, the government in the 1870s passed legislation for strict building regulations, prescribing the dimensions of streets and houses, and making it mandatory that all dwellings be connected to newly built sewerage systems. Major municipal investments in water works, sewage facilities, and public health dramatically reduced mortality in Britain's cities between 1874 and 1907.

Despite atrocious and filthy conditions, millions of migrants keep leaving rural areas for the teeming economic opportunity offered in the cities of poor and middle-income countries. Even though health hazards and mortality rates are far worse in the shanties around many cities in Africa, people there are trading, working, and sending large sums of money home. The challenge facing policy makers today is similar to that faced by the Victorians in London: how to nurture these agglomerations with functional land markets, better transport, and public health infrastructure to capture the benefits of economic growth.

Sources: Satterthwaite and others 2007; Crafts 2008; *The Economist* 2007a.

in multistory tenements arranged along narrow, unlit foot passages. This "housing was hopelessly inadequate in all respects—in quantity, in quality and environmental amenities, if needs as basic as clean water and safe sewage disposal can be described as amenities."[47] Apart from the obvious misery, slums were prone to deadly outbreaks of measles and scarlet fever and high rates of mortality attributable to diarrheal diseases, typhus, and respiratory diseases.[48]

Yesterday's slums are today's world-class cities. Britain is not the only industrial country to suffer from slums and wide intracity divisions in welfare during the earlier phases of development and rapid urbanization (see box 1.7). The stylized pattern of divergence followed by convergence is a hallmark of other modern-day developed countries as well. Slums for these cities are now much a thing of the past. Aided by improving land markets, investments in infrastructure, and targeted incentives, within-city welfare disparities tend to narrow, but only in the more advanced stages of urbanization. Indeed, for "world" cities such as London, New York, Paris, Singapore, and Tokyo, slums can, with the benefit of hindsight, be viewed as part of their "growing pains." Britain cleaned up its Dark Satanic Mills over a century, and if it had started the cleanup sooner, the working class would have suffered from slower wage growth and lower consumption.[49]

The emergence and growth of slums in the early and intermediate stages of a country's development can be explained by the interaction of functioning labor markets with dysfunctional land markets. In the rapid phase of urbanization, the labor market signals higher labor demand in urban areas, the higher demand that arises from growth in industries and services. Labor responds by moving to towns and cities.

As a reflection of this, slum dwellers in developing countries are often productively engaged, taking advantage of the economic opportunities the city offers. Mumbai's Dharavi has 15,000 "hutment" factories, and "the clothes, pots, toys and recycled materials its residents produce earn the factories millions of dollars a year." Many slum residents started businesses after the state government provided them with limited

or Rio de Janeiro's Rocinha? No, this is an excerpt from Charles Dickens's *Parish Boy's Progress,* published in 1838, describing the rapidly expanding city of London in the nineteenth century (see box 1.6).

London was by no means the only city or urban area in nineteenth century Britain with large slum settlements. Chronically overcrowded and inadequately serviced housing was a common feature of British cities and industrial towns of the time. In Edinburgh rapid population growth and a first wave of suburbanization by the then-rising middle classes meant that by the 1860s, the core of the city had a large slum area with population densities as high as 600 persons per acre. Residents in this area lived

BOX 1.7 *Many of today's world-class cities were littered with slums*

"In **Antwerp** and in most Belgian towns the basic problem in matters of working class housing was . . . no individual sanitation or individual water supply. . . . The three heavy cholera epidemics of the 19th century had terrific effects in these slums . . . "

"The first encampments of **Baltimore**'s poor were at the water's edge. Time and again, outbreaks of yellow fever, malaria, cholera, typhoid fever swept the town. These epidemics seemed peculiarly associated with the low-lying encampments of the poor. The yellow fever epidemic of 1797, for example, was said to have begun in the stagnant waters of the Fells Point cove and to have spread . . . to the huts and hovels on the banks of the Jones Falls and thence on to the shacks and shanties at the foot of Federal Hill."

"By the 1890s, Polish immigrants had supplanted the Irish and Germans, creating a ghetto of a new dimension. Single dwellings housed from six to eight families, one [family] to a room. . . . Fells Point was described by a health official as an Augean stable . . . a mass of nuisance . . . Open drains, great lots filled with high weeds, ashes and garbage accumulated in the alleyways, cellars filled with black water, houses that are total strangers to the touch of whitewash or scrubbing brush, human bodies that have been strangers for months to soap and water . . . that's Pigtown."

"The slums of **Dublin** were among the worst in Europe, rivaled only by **Glasgow**. Tall town houses, originally built as elegant homes for the rich in the eighteenth century, fell into the Tomae hands of avaricious and pitiless landlords who filled them to bursting point with the desperate and impoverished urban poor. Conditions were often unspeakably vile, with massive over-crowding and utterly inadequate sanitation."

"Katajanokka's transformation in its entirety from a low-income housing area to an enclave for the city's civil service elite and bourgeoisie represented an urban growth pattern that emerged for the first time in the history of **Helsinki**. A former slum had become a prestigious residential area for the privileged classes."

"Here the background embraces the pauper burial-ground, the station of the **Liverpool** and **Leeds** railway, and, in the rear of this, the Workhouse, the "Poor-Law Bastille" of **Manchester**, which, . . . looks threateningly upon the working-people's quarter below. . . . Passing along a rough bank, among stakes and washing-lines, one penetrates into this chaos of small one-storied, one-roomed huts, in most of which there is no artificial floor; kitchen, living and sleeping-room all in one. In such a hole, scarcely five feet long by six broad, I found two beds—and such bedsteads and beds!—which, with a staircase and chimney-place, exactly filled the room."

"**Melbourne**'s most infamous slum, Little Bourke Street, . . . by the 1880s . . . was crowded, bustling and growing. . . . The lane is completely filled up with all kinds of filth comprising garbage tips, putrid liquid, straw rags, and other rubbish. A most disagreeable odor arose from this offensive mass . . . the loathsome mass . . . exposed and allowed to rot and spread its contaminating influences."

"About 200 years ago, Lower **Manhattan** was adorned by a pretty five-acre lake known as the Collect. . . . By the mid-1700s, however, the Collect was already rimmed with slaughterhouses and tanneries. The effusions from these bloody businesses were poured directly into the lake and more industries, more trash, quickly followed. By 1800 the Collect was a reeking cesspool. By 1813 it had been entirely filled in and by 1825 something entirely new stood on the site—America's first real slum, the Five Points."

"Although this is a hugely expensive area in **Paris** to live today, in Victor Hugo's day it was a slum area, close to the Bastille Prison."

"[T]he lawyer Derville ventures into the slums of Saint Marceau, the poorest section at the outskirts of **Paris**. Taking his coach through the filthy rutted lanes, he arrives at a broken-down building, made entirely of second-hand materials and poorly built, where Colonel Chabert is lodged with the cows, goats, rabbits and impoverished family of a former regimental soldier turned milkman, Vergniaud. There the Colonel lives in a single room with a dirt floor and a straw bed."

"Between 1815 and 1851 France's population grew from 29 to 36 million . . . it was the cities that absorbed the thousands of migrants unable to find work in the countryside. . . . But there were simply not enough jobs. Unemployment and overcrowding created appalling living conditions. Only one in five houses had running water. In 1832 cholera wiped out some 20,000 Parisians."

"Like so many other European cities, **Paris** suffered from chronic post-war housing shortages. Of the 17 slum areas designed for clearance, most were still intact in the 1950s."

"One of the worst outrages of industrialism in China against humanity is the herding of these workers in noisome slums in the factory districts, . . . so foul and revolting . . . in **Shanghai**. . . . There are no sanitary provisions of any kind, and the passages between the rows of houses are practically open latrines. Overcrowding exists to a distressing extent. The many children who are reared in these filthy quarters are covered with running sores from dirt and bodily neglect."

"In the 15 years between 1930 and the end of the war, the population of **Singapore** doubled to a million people. The population explosion had generated a housing shortage of epidemic proportions. Small shophouses gave shelter to as many as 100 people. The average living space was 9 feet by 9 feet, about the size of a prison cell."

"All of the ghettos of the 1920s within the city of **Tokyo** were products of Tokyo's urban development and Japan's modern economic growth. . . . The sheer size of these ghettos was astonishing. . . . Poverty pockets re-emerged in all parts of the metropolis of Tokyo after the Second World War, even in the midst of the old city of Tokyo."

Sources: Belgium: Lis; Baltimore: Garrett 2002; Dublin: Kearns 2006; Helsinki: Mäkinen; Manchester: Engels 1987; Melbourne: Mountford; Manhattan: Baker 2001; Paris: Sanderson, Villon 2000, *The Economist*; Shanghai: Schwenning 1927; Singapore: Baker 1999; Tokyo: Koji 1969.

rights over their dwellings in 1976 and began to supply water and power to parts of the settlement. Because Dharavi is sandwiched between the city's two main railway lines and is surrounded by six stations, it also acts as Mumbai's transportation hub.[50] In short, slums arise in many developing countries as low-income households take advantage of spatially concentrated employment opportunities and as businesses take advantage of their location in a land-constrained environment. Consistent with today's industrial countries, the correct response is not to slow, stop, or reverse urbanization. It is to tackle dysfunctional land markets.

The interplay of such market forces and responses from rational market actors can also be seen in many Sub-Saharan African countries. But inefficient land markets, often thanks to misguided urban planning and zoning, produce only a limited and unresponsive supply of affordable, legal land sites for building housing to keep pace with the demand.[51]

What's different for today's developers?

At the beginning of the nineteenth century, one person in every 10 in today's developed European countries lived in urban settlements of 5,000 inhabitants or more.[52] In this respect, at least, little had changed from the previous five centuries. So the takeoff into urbanization over the next century broke dramatically from the past.

The pace and pattern of urbanization is similar

It started in Great Britain. In 1800 Britain's urban share stood at 19.2 percent, about twice the European average. But in the first two decades of the century, the number of people living in urban areas doubled. By 1820 the urban share was 40 percent. By the close of the century, seven of every 10 Britons were living in urban settlements. Britain was joined in its headlong rush into urbanization by other early European industrializers. By the second half of the nineteenth century, urbanization spread beyond the Old World to the United States and Canada. By World War I, four of every 10 Americans were living in urban settlements with populations of 5,000 or greater; just 60 years earlier, the ratio was one in 20.

So if anything is different for today's developers, it is certainly not the pace of urbanization. Indeed, the average pace of

Figure 1.13   Urbanization's speed has precedents

Percentage point difference in urban population, 1985–2005 (except where specified)

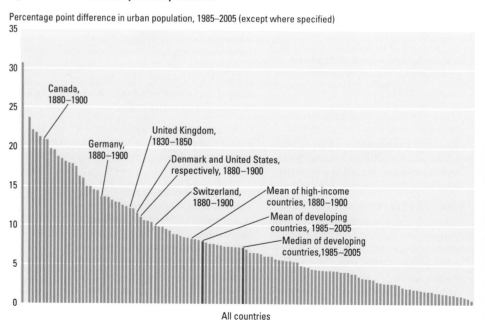

All countries

Sources: WDR 2009 team calculations based on data from the United Nations (2006c); historical data for Canada, the United Kingdom, and industrial countries' averages are from Bairoch and Goertz (1986) and Dumke (1994).

urbanization for developing countries over 1985–2005 is remarkably similar to the average for European and North American countries[53] between 1880 and 1900 (see figure 1.13).[54] For the early developers the average absolute increase in the urban share over the 20 years was 7.7 percentage points, and for current developers the respective median and mean absolute increases were 7.1 and 8.0 percentage points. The pace of urbanization among most of the early developers in the last two decades of the nineteenth century ranked in the top quartile of the contemporary distribution of urbanization speeds.

The volume of urbanization is greater for today's developers

What then is different? One difference is the unprecedented absolute increases in urban populations in many developing countries in recent decades. Today's developing countries simply have larger populations than the industrializing countries of the nineteenth and early twentieth centuries. The urban population today, estimated at 3.3 billion, is far greater than the world's total population as recently as 1960. It took more than 10,000 years for the urban population to reach 1 billion in 1960, 25 years to add the second billion, and only 18 to add the third.[55] According to the UN projection, it will take just 15 years to add the fourth.[56] In East Asia alone, 500 million people will join today's 750 million urbanites over the next 25 years, essentially adding another Paris or Kuala Lumpur every month.

Between 1985 and 2005, China added 225 million people to its towns and cities, almost the entire population of the United States. Yet China for the same time period, ranked only fifteenth in its absolute increase in urban share. In India the number of people in towns and cities rose by 137.8 million, adding a Germany and an Italy to its urban areas in just two decades.

Today's developing countries had an average increase in their urban population of 8.3 million over 1985–2005, almost three times the increase for many of today's high-income European and North American countries between 1880 and 1900. But when China and India are excluded from the group, the average urban population increase in recent decades has only been 4.4 million, about 50 percent more than the average for the early developers during 1880–1900 (see figure 1.14).[57]

Correspondingly, megacities in developing countries are unprecedented in their size. Through the nineteenth century the world's largest city was London. But its 1900 population of 6.6 million was only a third that of modern-day Mumbai or New Delhi, the largest cities in low-income countries. The London of 1900 and, indeed, even the London of today are also smaller than modern-day Shanghai (10 million), the largest city in lower-middle-income countries, and several others (Cairo, Jakarta, and Manila) among the more successful developers. With more than 22 million people, Mexico City, the largest city in upper-middle-income countries, is three

Figure 1.14   The population increment in urban areas of today's developing countries is much larger

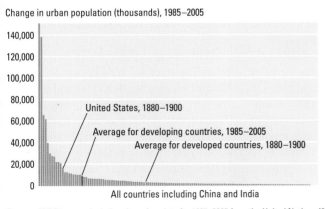

Change in urban population (thousands), 1985–2005

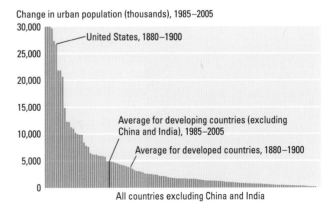

Change in urban population (thousands), 1985–2005

Sources: WDR team calculations based on data for 1985–2005 from the United Nations (2006c) plus historical data from Bairoch and Goertz (1986).

times the size of London at the start of the twentieth century.

Urbanites today enjoy both higher private earnings and better public services

Cities now do better than rural areas in both income and nonincome indicators of well-being. In 2000 the infant mortality rate in rural Malawi was 117 per 1,000 live births, in urban Malawi it was 83. Urban Benin did much better than rural Benin in lowering under-5 mortality rates and reducing diarrhea and acute respiratory infections.[58] Urban Ugandan women were less likely to suffer from anemia or malnutrition. Superior health indicators are repeated in urban areas throughout the developing world—from Chad and Cameroon in Sub-Saharan Africa, to Nepal in South Asia, Kazakhstan in Central Asia, and Nicaragua in Latin America, and to Morocco and Egypt in North Africa and Middle East.[59]

But the opposite was true for the developers of the nineteenth and early twentieth centuries. Migrants to cities could expect better material standards of living, offset by poorer health and shorter lives for them and their children. In 1881–91 life expectancy at birth was 51 years in English and Welsh villages, but only 44 years in London and 39 years in large towns.[60] In 1850s Britain the infant mortality rate in cities with populations greater than 100,000 was, at 196 per 1,000 live births, far higher than the 138 per 1,000 live births in rural communities.[61]

Even as late as 1937, George Orwell saw it fit to characterize industrial towns and cities as places where "one always feels that the smoke and filth must go on for ever and that no part of the earth's surface can ever escape them."[62] It is perhaps no surprise, then, that the absence of respiratory diseases attributable to poor air quality in the cities would have resulted in life expectancies 4.7 years longer in the England and Wales of 1861–70. In the absence of cholera, diarrhea, dysentery, and typhus, life expectancy might have been 1.7 years longer, and the absence of measles and scarlet fever, common in the cities, would have added 2.3 years to life expectancy.[63] Thus in the 1830s, while

workers in London earned an urban real wage premium of 67 percent, a large part of this premium was compensation for the evident health hazards of city living.[64]

In Germany during the second half of the nineteenth century, infant mortality rates in rural areas were about 150 per 1,000 live births. But expanding Berlin had the highest infant mortality in the Kaiserreich era, hovering around 300 per 1,000 live births in the 1860s, and peaking at 410 per 1,000 live births in the 1870s. The rural-urban gap in physical well-being remained for decades during the nineteenth century.[65]

As the U.S. economy industrialized and urbanized, people living in high-density areas at the turn of the twentieth century were exposed to infectious and parasitic diseases. In 1880 urban mortality for adults was 50 percent higher than rural mortality, and two decades later, the urban mortality rate was still 18 percent higher. The rural-urban mortality difference was even greater for infants and young children. For infants, excess urban mortality was 63 percent in 1890 and 49 percent in 1900, and for young children ages one to four, the respective figures were 107 percent and 97 percent. In 1900 male life expectancy was 10 years shorter in urban areas than in rural areas.[66]

That the cities and towns of modern-day developing countries do better than villages on indicators of health, while the opposite was true for the developed countries at similar incomes in the nineteenth century, reflects advances in public health and medicine, and improvements in sewers and water systems. It also reflects the public benefits that today's cities in developing countries confer. So the advantages of high density are not limited to income generation and wealth creation—they also include social services.

With these differences in private and public sources of well-being, it should hardly be a surprise that cities and towns in the developing world are growing rapidly. The surprise is that this move to density is not faster. And the policy implication? Any strategy for a less desperate and more deliberate urbanization must include efforts to improve public services in rural areas.

Distance

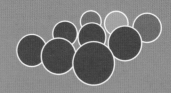

Deng Xiaoping, generally seen as the architect of China's resurgence as an economic superpower, insisted on openness to world markets. He also insisted on concerted development of the country's coastal areas, like Shanghai and Guangzhou, as launching grounds for connecting to these markets. When asked about the growing wealth disparities between the coast and the interior, he reportedly countered, "If all of China is to become prosperous, some [areas] must get rich before others."

This chapter shows that all successful developers support Deng's insight. But his wisdom may have eluded leaders in the developing world, even the few lauded as visionaries, as later chapters in the Report will show. For decades, "spatially balanced growth" has been a mantra of policy makers in many developing countries. It was an obsession of planners in the former Soviet Union (see box 2.5). And it has been the objective of governments of various political hues in the Arab Republic of Egypt, Brazil, India, Indonesia, Mexico, Nigeria, the Russian Federation, South Africa, and other great developing nations. There has even been a strong commitment to spatially balanced development in the economic history of many developed countries. The United Kingdom pursued it between the late 1920s and 1980s,[1] and Canada did so between the late 1950s and late 1980s.[2] But in these cases, even with the popularity of these policies, Deng's insight remained valid.

Indeed, the concentration of economic activity and the convergence of living standards can happen in parallel. Development in the United States was accompanied by a rapidly rising concentration of manufacturing activity in a relatively small area of the northeast and eastern part of the Midwest at the turn of the twentieth century.[3] Throughout this process, U.S. states witnessed a slow, if sometimes halting, convergence of per capita incomes.[4] Today, roughly half of the U.S. population is in only five states,[5] but long-term unemployment disparities among states have been fairly small since World War II.

The convergence of living standards in the United States has been assisted by the willingness of workers to "pull up their roots" and relocate.[6] But basic welfare indicators have converged even in countries where such a willingness has been less evident, because development has been accompanied by the spread of public services. Take France and Germany. Even though Paris generates 28 percent of France's gross domestic product (GDP)[7] using only 2 percent of its land, infant mortality rates in the country show little spatial variation. The lagging area of Lorraine had the highest rate, 4.5 deaths per 1,000 live births in 2005, but this is not much higher than the national average of 3.8.[8] In Germany the leading area of Hamburg—with an economic density of €114 million of GDP per square kilometer—enjoyed a GDP per capita more than twice that of the northeastern lagging area of Mecklenburg-Vorpommern and an economic density more than one hundred times higher. Despite the phenomenal differences in economic density between these areas, there is no difference in basic welfare. The numbers of physicians and hospital beds per 1,000 habitants in both Hamburg and Mecklenburg-Vorpommern closely track the national averages.[9]

This chapter presents stylized facts about economic concentration in parts of a country, usually called "leading areas," and the convergence in living standards between households in these areas and those in distant or disconnected parts, called "lagging areas," in the same country. It introduces the concept of economic distance, which is related to but not the same as physical distance. When supplemented with the economic density discussed in chapter 1, distance helps characterize the spatial transformations that accompany development and that may be necessary for rapid economic growth.

The main findings:

- *As countries develop and integrate internally, location matters more for economic activity but less for social welfare.* Greater economic mass (which accumulates where firms carry out production) and higher living standards (reflected in household consumption, poverty, and access to basic services) are not spatially synonymous. During the early phases of development, infrastructure and social services tend to be confined to areas of economic mass. But as countries develop and integrate internally, the distinction between leading and lagging areas becomes sharper for economic mass and more blurred for living standards.

- *The spatial concentration of economic activity first rises and then levels off.* As an economy changes from agrarian to industrial, the spatial distribution of people and economic production becomes more compact. Within a country, agglomeration and city-periphery integration give rise to metropolitan areas and leading areas of dense economic mass. This process eventually levels off, and the spatial distribution of economic activity stabilizes.

- *Spatial disparities in living standards follow an inverted-U path, widening in the early stages of economic development, and remaining high for a long period before slowly converging.* As a country industrializes, it concentrates its limited initial human and physical capital in leading areas, those with high growth potential. Areas distant from the new density lag. Spatial disparities in productivity and income can persist for generations, even with mobile labor and capital. History points to persistent spatial divergence in living standards in today's developed countries in their earlier stages of development, followed by slow convergence many years after they attained high income.[10]

- *Technological progress and globalization have increased market potential in the leading areas of developing countries, intensifying concentration and amplifying spatial disparities.* Although the basic forces shaping the internal economic geography of developing countries are the same as those that earlier shaped the economic landscapes of today's developed countries, the magnitudes have changed. Larger international markets, better transportation, and improved communication technologies mean that leading areas in open developing countries have greater market potential than industrial countries did in their early development. So the forces for spatial divergence between leading and lagging areas are now stronger.

Defining distance

Density, discussed in chapter 1, is also relevant at the country level. Denser concentrations of economic activity increase choice and opportunity. They ensure greater market potential for the exchange of goods, services, information, and factors of production. This chapter examines the disparities in economic mass and welfare between areas within countries, linking these disparities to the distance from economic density. So while chapter 1 discussed changes at the local scale—where the most relevant spatial dimension is density—this chapter addresses the spatial transformations at the country scale, where both density and distance are relevant. Chapter 3 will propose that although density and distance also matter for world regions, the most important dimension at the international scale is division—political barriers to the flows of goods, entrepreneurship, people, and information between nations.

As the crow flies? Distance as an economic, not Euclidean, concept

Distance refers to the ease or difficulty for goods, services, labor, capital, information, and ideas to traverse space. It measures how easily capital flows, labor moves, goods are transported, and services are delivered between two locations. Distance, in this sense, is an economic concept, not just a physical one. Although economic distance is generally related to Euclidean (straight-line) distances between two locations and the physical features of the geography separating them, the relationship is not always straightforward. One reason is that distance for the exchange of goods is different from that for the migration of people.

For trade in goods and services, distance captures time and monetary costs. The placement and quality of transport infrastructure and the availability of transport can dramatically affect the economic distance between any two areas, even though the Euclidean distance between them could be identical. Two villages may have the same straight-line distance to a city, but one could be near a national highway, the other on an unpaved rural road. Based on straight-line distance, most of India is well connected to markets in dense settlements. But people in many parts of India have difficulty getting to markets because of the travel time, determined by the type and quality of roads and other transport infrastructure (see map 2.1).

For labor mobility, distance also captures the "psychic costs" of separation from familiar territory. Between 1985 and 1995, the share of migrants in a Chinese province originating from another province fell as distance between the provinces increased. And additional costs exist for migration between non-neighboring provinces.[11] So, as with trade, economic distance for migration is related to, but not synonymous with, physical distance. In this Report, the destination of interest is a location with the greatest economic density or highest market potential. Distance is thus a metaphor for access to markets.

Manmade barriers, including policies, can also increase distance. Roadblocks and local barricades—improvised "toll stations" for local police and others to extract payments—are common for journeys by road in many Sub-Saharan countries.[12] And where local political autonomy is high, there may be territorial fragmentation as policies of protection are pursued at the local level. Map 2.2 shows the time to human settlements, assuming few or no manmade barriers. Distances can be long, even in high-income countries.

Map 2.1 Access to markets is not a straight line

a. Based on Euclidean distance	b. Based on economic distance	c. Roads and settlements

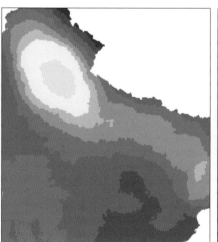 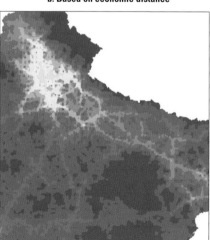 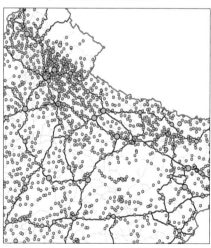

Source: WDR 2009 team.
Note: The lighter color represents greater access to places with economic mass.

Map 2.2   **Distances can be long even in the developed world**

Travel time to sizable settlements, by subnational administrative area

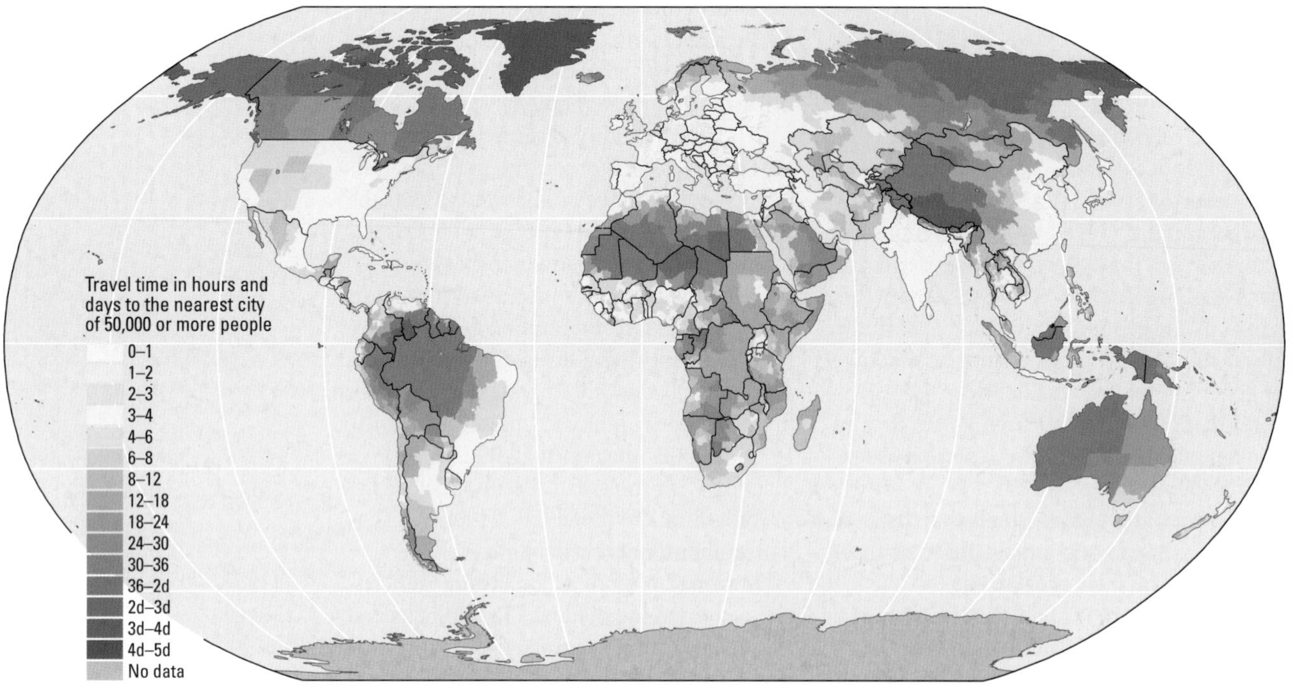

Travel time in hours and
days to the nearest city
of 50,000 or more people

0–1
1–2
2–3
3–4
4–6
6–8
8–12
12–18
18–24
24–30
30–36
36–2d
2d–3d
3d–4d
4d–5d
No data

Contributed by Andrew Nelson; see Uchida and Nelson (2008) for this Report.

Locations close to markets have a natural advantage

Provincial governments in 1980 in China heightened their administrative powers under decentralization reforms. They used these powers to protect local firms—raising tariffs and imposing bans on shipments from other provinces. Imports between provinces fell from 50 percent of GDP to 38 percent between 1992 and 1997, while local absorption of goods within provinces rose from 68 percent to 72 percent. The magnitudes are similar to those for goods crossing the U.S.–Canada border and international borders in the European Union (EU).[13] China's *hukou* system of permanent household registration—linking place of residence with access to consumer goods, employment opportunities, and social protection—similarly reduced internal migration.[14]

Distance to density affects spatial movements in goods, services, information, knowledge, and people. Commuting, migration, telecommunication, information flows, and shipments of goods connect originating and receiving areas. Most spatial interactions, such as learning and trade, are beneficial. But some are harmful, such

as the spread of disease. The main determinant of the strength of these interactions is distance. Waldo Tobler's *First Law of Geography* states that "everything is related to everything else, but near things are more related than distant things."[15] Areas closer to economic density have easier access to beneficial interactions and exchanges.

In Indonesia better road connections shorten travel time and the distance to economic centers, creating larger agglomerated areas. Because of good roads and easier access to markets, villages 60 kilometers from the district center generate as much manufacturing activity as the district center itself, and the well-connected periphery becomes part of the agglomerated area. But in poorly connected peripheries, the density of economic activity falls off rapidly beyond 25 kilometers from the center (figure 2.1).

Spillovers from proximity to density show up in both developed and developing countries. In European manufacturing, an area's total factor productivity growth is positively and significantly related to the density of manufacturing production in neighboring areas. And faster demand growth in neighboring areas stimulates, through spillovers,

Figure 2.1   Manufacturing activity in Indonesia flourishes in areas with shorter economic distance to density

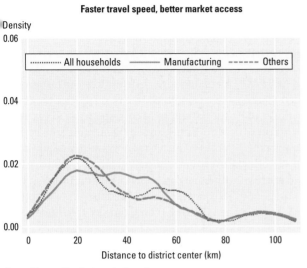
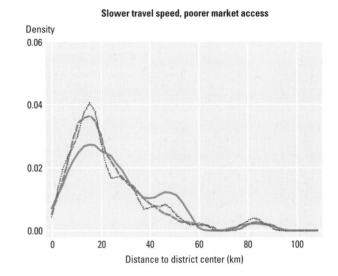

Source: Yamauchi and others, forthcoming.

faster total factor productivity growth.[16] In Canada, North York and Waterloo are, thanks to proximity and local research universities, becoming an extended part of the Toronto information and communication technology (ICT) hub. Firms closer to Toronto do better than those farther away.[17]

The phenomenon is repeated in emerging economies. When a network of highways surrounding Jakarta was built in the 1980s, many firms moved out of the center to save on land and congestion costs. But they stayed near the metropolitan region to have access to the large market.[18] Similar but less pronounced is the pattern in other Indonesian agglomerations, where growth has been strongest in peripheral areas surrounding megacities.[19] In Brazil industries moved out of greater São Paulo to the lower-wage populated periphery. Following the transport corridors, these industries moved through São Paulo state and into the neighboring state of Minas Gerais. In the Republic of Korea the early decentralization of manufacturing from Seoul was to peripheral locations within an hour's drive. Only in the 1990s did industries decentralize to towns and rural areas.[20]

The natural way to reduce distance is for people to migrate

A leading area of dense economic activity, through its market opportunities, creates incentives for firms and workers to move

there. Responding to these incentives, firms and workers enlarge the market opportunities available in the dense area. The result is a circular and cumulative process of dense areas continually gaining workers and firms from less dense areas. In this process, migration balances the distribution of population against the spatial disparity in economic density. Reducing distance-related costs or spatial frictions increases movements of people, firms, and ideas—as well as those of goods and services—and thus brings less developed areas into the national system of production. With trade, the mobility of people is probably the most potent mechanism for integrating areas of low economic density with markets of high density. But for internal migration to bring about a convergence in living standards, large population movements may be necessary over generations.

Every year, approximately 40 million people in the United States change residences, and 8 million people change states.[21] The reason for this mobility is that economic production is concentrated in a few parts of the country, and accessing this economic density generally means moving closer to it.

People moving to economically dense areas contribute to production and boost their incomes. But they also increase competition among workers in dense areas, reducing it in less dense areas, and contributing to the convergence of living standards between low- and high-productivity areas.

Among today's industrial countries, the quickest convergence occurred between 1870 and 1913, largely driven by the largest flows of people from Europe to emerging markets in Asia and the Americas. For Ireland between 1851 and 1908, mass outmigration contributed at least a third to the catch-up in Irish real wages with those in the United States and Britain—by reducing competition in the domestic labor market. The virtual cessation of catch-up or convergence among the industrial countries between the two world wars was attributed largely to more restrictive immigration policies.[22,23]

Density in leading areas, distance for lagging areas

Subnational areas, when compared, should ideally be defined according to economic criteria that correspond to fairly self-contained labor markets and zones of economic activity. But data on such functionally defined economic areas are hard to come by.[24] So subnational areas are more commonly defined by administrative or political boundaries. Such definitions can bias econometric analysis (see box 2.1), but they have the advantage of corresponding to the areas for defining and implementing subnational policy. This chapter examines administratively or politically defined areas based on different data sources, ranging from national accounts and household surveys to terrestrial grid cells of 1° longitude by 1° latitude.

In this Report, leading areas have a high economic density, and lagging areas have a long distance-to-density. An area is more likely to be lagging the farther it is from

---

BOX 2.1 *Defining an area: impossible or NUTS?*

Subnational policy analysis relies on data for areas that range from small primary sampling units to districts, and to states or provinces. Typically, these areas are defined administratively or politically, reflecting historical characteristics more than current patterns. For instance, the existing administrative structure of the EU's member states generally consists of two levels, such as *länder* and *kreise* in Germany, *regions* and *départements* in France, *comunidades autónomas* and *provincias* in Spain, and *regioni* and *provincie* in Italy. The *Nomenclature of Territorial Units for Statistics* (NUTS) provides a single uniform classification of territorial units for producing regional statistics for the EU. The first two administrative levels in most member states correspond to NUTS 2 and NUTS 3. NUTS 1, a larger unit representing the major socioeconomic regions, often does not correspond to existing administrative units within member states.

Which spatial scale to use, or how best to define a subnational area, depends on the issue and the information available. But the choice can dramatically affect the conclusions drawn from studying social and economic conditions across different parts of a country—for two reasons.

• First, areas are not defined keeping in mind the policy issues. For instance, within-area differences in employment or poverty can be as large as between-area differences. Any change in the boundaries between areas could change the results. The potential implications are succinctly summarized by the title of a classic paper on this topic, "A Million or So Correlation Coefficients."[a]

• Second, analytical findings depend on the aggregation or spatial scale, the ecological fallacy of inferring characteristics of individuals from aggregate data. The classic study by Robinson (1950) illustrates this problem.[b] A broader aggregation will yield smaller differences between units of analysis—and lower variances. So, results can differ significantly depending on the size of the units.

The figure below shows the density of economic activity for Germany's 16 provinces (*länder*) and 439 districts (*kreise*). The highly aggregated data indicate that 30 percent of GDP is produced on 10 percent of the country's area, and the more disaggregated data show that almost 60 percent of GDP is produced on the same 10 percent. Aggregate information can be useful, but be mindful of these biases.

Source: WDR 2009 team.
a. Openshaw and Taylor 1979.
b. Using state level data for the United States, the study showed that the proportion of foreign-born people is positively correlated with the proportion literate in English, suggesting that native-born Americans were more likely to be illiterate. Analyzing the same relationship using individual data showed a negative correlation.

Different spatial scales yield different results because of an aggregation bias

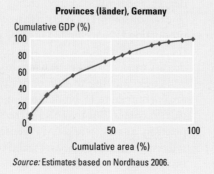

Provinces (länder), Germany

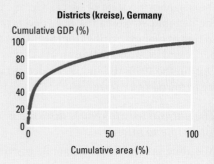

Districts (kreise), Germany

Source: Estimates based on Nordhaus 2006.

leading areas because greater distance-to-density implies a lack of integration into the economy of leading areas. It also implies poorer access to the "thick" markets of capital, labor, goods, services, and ideas, and the spillovers of knowledge and information they provide. A lagging area is usually a remote part of the country with one or more of the following features: high poverty, low productivity and income, high unemployment, and stagnant growth, which are typically the criteria governments use to define lagging areas.

In developing countries, lagging areas tend to be remote places where basic needs, such as access to sanitation and electricity, are not met. In developed countries, lagging areas are locations with poorer job prospects than leading areas, but no differences in basic welfare. So distance and market access, in this Report, capture a wide range of criteria that different countries use to define a lagging area (see box 2.2).

It follows that distance-to-density is the cause of low income per capita, labor productivity, and real wages—and of the high rates of poverty and unemployment. In the United Kingdom, economic density in the leading London and southeast areas produces a wage premium of 18 percent, which

---

BOX 2.2 *How developed and developing countries define lagging areas: a quick survey*

In this Report, a lagging area is defined as a place distant from density. How does this definition compare with how policy makers in developing and developed countries have, today and historically, defined lagging areas?

Usually, the criteria national governments use to classify an area as "lagging," "disadvantaged," or "backward" are linked to explicit strategies or policies for spatial or regional development. The criteria might be vague or precise. They might relate to a single indicator of economic performance or to a weighted average of several. And they might reflect the definition of lagging areas at different spatial scales.

- *Vague.* UK regional policy in the 1980s classified a lagging area as being either a "development area" or an "intermediate area." But the law was vague in the criteria it set to designate such areas. "In exercising his powers under the preceding provisions of this section [in the designation of development and intermediate areas] the Secretary of State shall have regard to all the circumstances actual and expected, including the state of employment and unemployment, population changes, migration and objectives of regional policies."[a]

- *Precise and simple.* EU regional or "cohesion" policy for the period 2007–13 defines lagging areas as those qualifying for assistance under the "convergence objective," equated with NUTS2 areas with a GDP per capita of less than 75 percent of the EU average.[b] These areas are budgeted to receive

around 71 percent of funds under the convergence objective. But, even in EU regional policy, funding is available on more favorable (and complicated) terms for those areas whose GDP per capita is not only less than 75 percent of the EU average, but which are in a country whose GDP per capita is less than 90 percent of the EU average. These areas are considered to be "more lagging."[c]

- *Precise and complicated.* Between 1982 and 1987 Canada's Department of Regional Industrial Expansion used a development index to classify areas for allocations under its Industrial and Regional Development Program. The index assigned a 50 percent weight to an area's unemployment, a 40 percent weight to its personal income, and a 10 percent weight to the fiscal capacity of the province to identify 15 percent of the "least developed."[d]

- *Sophisticatedly defined and measured.* To identify areas considered as lagging, Mexico's microregional strategy uses a "marginalization index" based on indicators of access to such basic services as electricity and drinking water, and indicators of the quality of dwelling conditions and the proportion of the local working population that is poorly paid.[e] It is mainly targeted at remote rural communities in the south, because the "remoteness of rural communities often translates into conditions of poverty and a substantial lack of access to a wide range of basic public services."[f]

Mexico is noteworthy not only because of the sophistication of the measure used to identify lagging areas, but also because of the sophisticated manner of defining areas. Rather than using crude administrative boundaries to define areas, geographical information system (GIS) techniques are used to consider an area's geographical proximity, ethnic and cultural identity, and geoeconomic characteristics.

So the criteria that different countries use to identify lagging areas depend on the level of development and on domestic political considerations. High levels of poverty and marginalization define lagging areas in developing countries, and a high rate of unemployment often defines them in developed countries.

India's 10th Five-Year Plan (2002–07) identifies the northeastern region as "backward" and "disadvantaged" and thus deserving special policy attention. EU regional policy, under its convergence objective, makes special provisions for "the outermost regions," deemed to require additional assistance.

This Report's definition of lagging areas—as distant from density—captures this wide range of criteria.

Contributed by Mark Roberts.
a. Industrial Development Act 1982, chapter 52, part I, para. (3); bold emphasis added.
b, c. http://europa.eu/pol/reg/index_en.htm, "Activities of the European Union—Regional Policy," 2008.
d. Atkinson and Powers 1987.
e. Villarreal 2005; OECD 2003, p. 6.
f. OECD 2003.

distant areas in the north and southwest of England and in Scotland and Wales do not enjoy.[25] In Indonesia the potential profitability of firms in textiles and other sectors is negatively related to distance-to-density: more distance, less profit. This is true for distance-to-density within the country and for distance to an international port and thus to the density in international markets.[26] Again, lagging areas unable to attract investment and employment are those with a high distance-to-density.

As in today's rich countries, distance-to-density affects incomes in emerging market countries. In China good market access produces higher individual wages, even after controlling for individual, sector-, and province-specific attributes, living cost differences, and human capital externalities.[27] In Brazil lagging areas economically distant from São Paulo and other large markets

have lower wages, and improving an area's growth prospects largely depends on reducing distance.[28] In Brazil's leading area, economic density implies a wage premium of 13 percent, comparable to that in European countries.[29,30] In Mexico the southern rural areas—distant from the economic density in Mexico City and the United States—have the lowest wages and highest poverty.

Lagging areas in many countries are home to ethnic minorities. Tribal, racial, and religious differences in access to resources show up as spatial disparities. In a vicious cycle, disparities between areas that coincide with different ethnic groups can deepen political divisions and fuel tensions, contributing to greater divergence in living standards. They can even fuel civil conflict that is difficult to extinguish, causing "development in reverse" (see box 2.3).[31]

BOX 2.3 *Dangerous disparities: when divisions aggravate distance*

The academic literature argues that internal labor migration is the strongest force for convergence in economic and other measures of household welfare across areas of a country. But differences in language, religion, ethnicity, and race are probably one of the strongest barriers to internal migration, a troubling dilemma for policy makers. The ethnic, linguistic, and religious barriers that may keep households from taking advantage of many opportunities to arbitrage geographic differences for employment and earnings can be the same barriers that cage poor people in lagging areas, perpetuate their poverty, and sharpen spatial disparities.

Disparities in East Asia. In Thailand 17 percent of people in the northeast are poor, compared with 0.5 percent in Bangkok. About half of Thailand's ethnic minority groups live in the Northeast. In Indonesia poverty and welfare indicators are persistently worse in West Kalimantan—home to such ethnic minorities as the Dayak, Bugis, and Sambas—than in Java, home to Indonesia's ethnic majority.

Disparities in South Asia. In India the states of Arunachal Pradesh, Assam, Manipur, Meghalaya, Mizoram, Nagaland,

Sikkim, and Tripura make up the lagging northeast. Except for the Assamese, the population is predominantly tribal, speaks Tibeto-Burman and Austro-Asiatic languages, and has a strong genetic similarity with the people of East Asia. Hinduism is the dominant religion, but the proliferation of Christianity has set the area apart from the rest of India. By conventional measures of economic welfare and development, northeastern states rank among the lowest in India.

Disparities in Africa. A study of 11 Sub-Saharan countries found that ethnicity was on its own a strong predictor of differences in child mortality, but when combined with geography, it continued to predict the probability of survival among children. For instance, in Côte d'Ivoire, mortality among two year olds fell much faster from 1970 to 1994 for the Baoule than for other ethnic groups. Children of Ashanti women in Ghana were about 20 percent less likely to die than other children. In Uganda, Baganda children under five were a third less likely to die than children of other ethnic groups.

A 2005 study on spatial inequalities by the World Institute for Development

Economics Research at the United Nations University in Helsinki (UNU-WIDER) conjectured that "Spatial inequality is a dimension of inequality overall, but it has added significance when spatial and regional divisions align with political and ethnic tensions to undermine social and political stability."[a] These somewhat abstract words chillingly foreshadowed the violence in Kenya in early 2008, which left 1,500 people dead and another 250,000 displaced. Violence began over the disputed outcome of a presidential election in late December 2007, quickly exposing deep ethnic cleavages that demarcate Kenya's economic and political geography. Communal fighting was most pronounced around the town of El Doret in the Rift Valley, and on the outskirts of Kisumu in the Western district of the country. The Rift Valley and Western districts are among Kenya's economically lagging areas and are the traditional home places of the minority Kalenjin, Luo, Kisi, and Luhya tribes, who along with other ethnic minorities in these areas harbor resentments related to economic deprivation and neglect.

Source: Brockerhoff and Hewett 2000.
a. Kanbur and Venables 2005.

Lagging areas have higher poverty rates, leading areas have more poor people

The rate of poverty (the poverty headcount) is related to distance, and the mass of poverty is related to density. Lagging areas tend to have a higher proportion of poor residents, and the leading areas tend to contain a higher share of the country's poor people, because of the dense population in leading areas. Vietnam's lagging inland areas have the highest poverty rate, but its prosperous leading areas contain the mass of poor people (see map 2.3). And in Honduras the country's poverty mass is concentrated in its two leading areas of Tegucigalpa and San Pedro Sula, while distant eastern areas generally have a high poverty rate (map 2.4).

Economic concentration in leading areas

As economies develop, economic activity generally becomes more concentrated, not less. In about a quarter of the world's nations—such as Botswana, Brazil, Norway, Russia, and Thailand—more than half of national income is generated on less than 5 percent of the land area. In half of all nations—such as Argentina, Saudi Arabia, Slovenia, and Zambia—a third or more of national income is generated on less than 5 percent of land. Only one country in 10 has a dispersed economic mass, with less than a tenth of national income generated on 5 percent of its land. Among the few countries with this high spatial dispersion: Bangladesh, the Democratic Republic of Korea, the Netherlands, and Poland.[32]

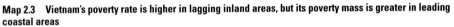

Map 2.3   Vietnam's poverty rate is higher in lagging inland areas, but its poverty mass is greater in leading coastal areas

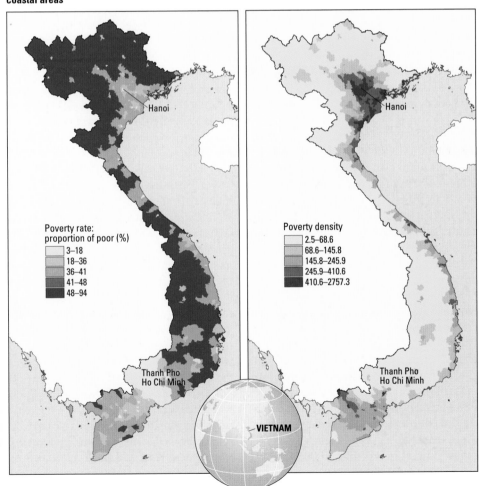

Source: The Poverty Mapping Project. Columbia University, using data from Minot, Baulch, and Epprecht 2003.

Map 2.4   The poverty rate is high in distant eastern Honduras, but the poor are concentrated in the two largest metropolitan areas

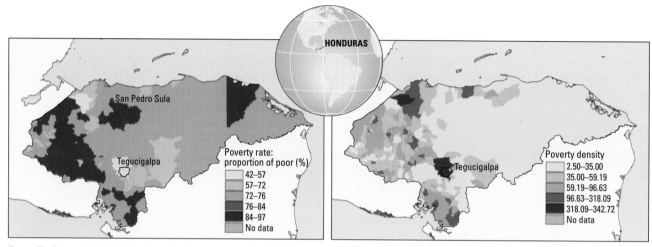

Source: The Poverty Mapping Project. Columbia University, using data from Robles 2003.

This section presents the historical experience of selected industrialized countries. Spanning more than a century, this section shows how these countries experienced rapidly rising spatial concentrations, followed by a leveling off. It then turns to a large sample of developed and developing countries to document how the concentration of economic mass rises with a country's development.

Rapidly rising concentration in the early stages of development, then a leveling

It is difficult to come by data that track the evolution of spatial concentrations of economic activity.[33] The information available reveals that economic development, in its early stages, is accompanied by a rapidly rising spatial concentration in a country. Not only does the volume of economic activity grow, but its generation becomes more compressed into a smaller land area. Leading areas benefit most from this compression and growth.

Economic concentration in the Ile de France—the leading area of France, with about 2 percent of the country's land—increased rapidly from a value of around two times the hypothetical share in 1801 to three times in 1851 and to six times by 1910.[34] It continued to rise, but less rapidly, to nine times that share in 1960. French GDP per capita grew from less than $1,000 in 1801 to $7,000 in 1960. From 1960 on, however, its economic concentration stabilized, even though its GDP per capita tripled. In Canada and the Netherlands the increases were

not as dramatic, but both countries experienced the same pattern of rapidly rising concentrations at low levels of development, followed by a leveling off as GDP per capita rose past $10,000 (see figure 2.2).[35]

Patterns are similar in today's developing countries. As Thailand industrialized and grew rapidly, the concentration in the leading Bangkok metropolitan area increased from 1.8 in 1975 to 3.1 in 2004, while GDP per capita increased fourfold. In Brazil too, the concentration in the leading São Paulo area edged upward from 7.3 in 1960 to 8.4 in 2004, as the country's GDP per capita almost tripled.

For Japan during its post–World War II industrialization, the concentration in its leading area of greater Tokyo increased from a high of 7.1 in 1955 to about 8 in 1970 as its GDP per capita more than doubled. This increasing spatial concentration eventually levels off, as the spatial distribution of economic activity in a country stabilizes. After 1970, the concentration in greater Tokyo stabilized.

In the United States as GDP per capita rapidly increased from $1,806 in 1850 to $4,091 in 1900,[36] concentration came in the manufacturing belt of Green Bay–St. Louis–Baltimore–Portland ME, which accounted for three-quarters of U.S. manufacturing employment. Over the next 60 years, the belt's share of manufacturing employment remained stable at two-thirds to three-quarters.[37] Despite structural changes in the U.S. economy and shifting patterns of economic concentration, that concentration remained stable after 1960.

Figure 2.2   Rising density of economic mass accompanies development over decades, even centuries

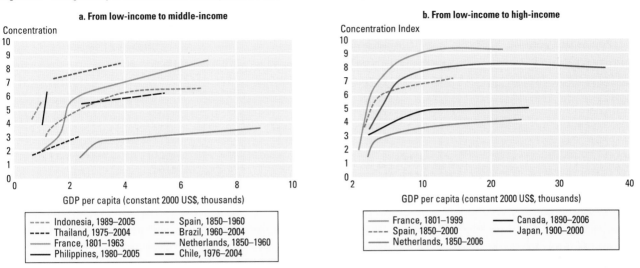

a. From low-income to middle-income

Concentration

GDP per capita (constant 2000 US$, thousands)

b. From low-income to high-income

Concentration Index

GDP per capita (constant 2000 US$, thousands)

- - - - Indonesia, 1989–2005   - - - - Spain, 1850–1960
- - - - Thailand, 1975–2004   - - - - Brazil, 1960–2004
——— France, 1801–1963   ——— Netherlands, 1850–1960
——— Philippines, 1980–2005   —— — Chile, 1976–2004

——— France, 1801–1999   ——— Canada, 1890–2006
- - - - Spain, 1850–2000   ——— Japan, 1900–2000
——— Netherlands, 1850–2006

Sources: WDR team estimates based on national accounts—statistical yearbooks of various years in respective countries. 1890 data for Canada come from Green (1969). Data on France are based on population numbers from Catin and Van Huffel (2003); Barro and Sala-I-Martin (2004). Data on Japan, the Netherlands, and Spain came from the Staff City Population Database, Human Settlements Group, International Institute for Environment and Development (IIED).

Another corroborative piece of evidence of rising concentration comes from the falling share of land area occupied by 80 percent of the U.S. population in the densest counties from 25 percent of the U.S. land areas in 1900 to 17 percent in 2000.[38]

As countries grow beyond $10,000 GDP per capita, concentration tends to stabilize, with the details differing. The concentration in the leading area is greater in Canada, France, and Japan than it is in the Netherlands and the United States. For developing countries too, Brazil, Indonesia, and the Philippines seem to be on paths toward greater spatial concentration than either Chile or Thailand.

International comparisons of concentration today support historical trends

The relationship between a country's development and its spatial concentration holds for countries at different levels of development. It holds for countries based on administrative areas (Canadian provinces, Japanese prefectures, Russian oblasts, and U.S. states), statistical areas (the nine census regions of the United States, the three regions in Ecuador), and land areas (terrestrial grid cells of 1° longitude by 1° latitude). And it holds for different measures of concentration.

Administrative areas. Different countries have different numbers of administrative areas, which may be of different geographic sizes. But controlling for these factors, a comparison of 24 developing countries—ranging from Mozambique with a GDP per capita of $211 to Greece with more than $12,000—reveals the same pattern as the historical experiences of Canada and France. The share of national GDP produced in the leading administrative area tends to increase with the level of development (see figure 2.3, panel a).

Statistical areas. Statistical areas, broad census regions, can differ from administrative areas. The United States has nine statistical areas but 50 states; Canada has five statistical areas but 10 provinces and three territories. A country's statistical office generally uses these areas to stratify its sampling frame for household surveys, with the areas corresponding to the geographic partitions of a country such as east and west.[39] Despite the difference in aggregation, the data for statistical areas suggest the same relationship between concentration, measured by consumption rather than GDP, and development (see figure 2.3, panel b).

Land areas. Terrestrial grid cells of 1° longitude by 1° latitude, each corresponding to a land area of 100 square kilometers can provide purer geographic resolution.[40] Spatial concentration within a country can then be measured as the share of national GDP generated on the densest 5 percent of

Figure 2.3 Measures based on national accounts, household surveys, and geoscaled economic data confirm the historical pattern of a rising concentration of economic mass with the level of development

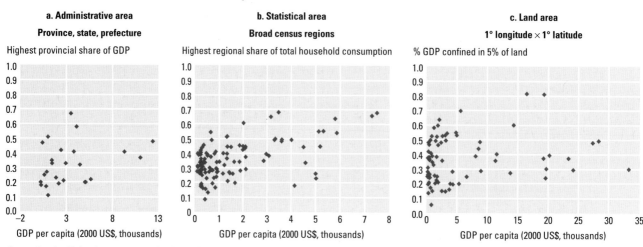

Source: Panel a: National accounts at national statistical office Web sites or Yearbooks; panel b: World Bank staff estimates of more than 120 household surveys in 75 countries (data set is described in detail in Montenegro and Hirn 2008); panel c: World Bank staff estimates from http://gecon.edu.yale.

its land.[41] The stylized pattern of rising concentration of GDP with development using historical data is the same as that using contemporary data. The relationship between development and economic concentration is positive and roughly linear when comparing developing countries with a GDP per capita of less than $10,000. But this relationship starts to level off when higher-income countries are included in the sample (figure 2.3, panel c).

The rising concentration of production with economic development is not an artifact of the number of subnational areas across countries or of the different sizes of land area in the countries (see table 2.1). Consider Tanzania, Italy, France, and Sweden, with similar numbers of administrative areas (21 or 22). Tanzania's leading area of Dar-es-Salaam generates 15 percent of national GDP, Italy's leading area of Lombardia, 21 percent. France and Sweden, each with a higher GDP per capita than Italy, also have higher concentrations in their leading areas.

For a set of countries partitioned into five statistical areas—ranging from Argentina to Tajikistan—the concentration of consumption in the leading area increases with development. Among medium-size countries with about 300,000 square kilometers of land area, Ghana and Lao People's Democratic Republic (both low-income countries) have markedly lower spatial GDP concentrations measured by spatial Gini coefficients[42] than Poland (a lower-

middle-income country) and New Zealand (a high-income country). Poland and New Zealand have lower spatial Gini coefficients than richer Norway and the United States. The pattern also holds for small and large countries.

Divergence, then convergence—between leading and lagging areas

When production is primarily agrarian, economic activity tends to be evenly distributed across space. Productivity differences are also moderate, varying naturally with soil quality and climate. But as an economy develops and production expands in manufacturing and services, some areas become more attractive to firms and workers. Some are endowed with natural or "first nature" geographic advantages.[43] For example, a strategic coastal location makes an area a natural choice for a port (as with New York and Philadelphia in the United States). For others areas not so blessed by nature, their economic pull might be linked to a "second nature" historical accident. An example is Boston, saved from economic decline by an influx of immigrant labor fleeing the Irish potato famine. For Irish immigrants it was cheaper to travel from Liverpool to Boston than to New York.

Economic development brings with it greater market integration, which facilitates the mobility of people and capital and allows for greater trade, forces benefiting the leading

Table 2.1 Administrative, statistical, and geographic area measures all point to rising spatial concentrations of economic activity with development

Administrative areas	Country	GDP per capita	Number of administrative areas	Share of GDP in the leading area (%)
	Tanzania	324	21	15
	Italy	19,480	21	21
	France	22,548	22	29
	Sweden	31,197	22	29

Statistical areas	Country	GDP per capita	Number of statistical areas	Share of household consumption in the leading area (%)
	Tajikistan	204	5	30.2
	Mongolia	406	5	34.6
	El Salvador	1,993	5	43.9
	Brazil	3,597	5	51.6
	Argentina	7,488	5	64.7

Land areas	Country	GDP per capita	Land area (km^2)	Spatial Gini coefficient
	Ghana	211	227,540	0.48
	Lao PDR	231	230,800	0.48
	Poland	3,099	311,888	0.52
	New Zealand	11,552	267,990	0.55
	Norway	27,301	304,280	0.64

Sources: Administrative area information for Tanzania is from http://www.nbs.go.tz/nationalaccount/index.htm; information for France, Italy, and Sweden are from the Annex in *Growing Regions, Growing Europe.* Statistical area information is from more than 120 household surveys fielded during the 2000s for more than 80 countries (data set described in detail in Montenegro and Hirn 2008). Land area information is from http://gecon.edu.yale, which is based on 1990 information.
Note: GDP per capita estimates are in 2000 U.S. dollars for the particular year of the household survey.

areas. And by attracting people and firms, leading areas fuel agglomeration economies, becoming centers for innovation and growth and driving the national economy. But the process does not go on forever. Agglomeration economies start to be offset by congestion and pollution, the diseconomies of agglomeration. So the spatial concentration in leading areas starts to level off.

What, then, of the income and welfare disparities that accompany this pattern of first rising and then stable economic concentration? Is there a tendency for lagging areas to catch up with leading ones as economic development progresses? What is the role of government policies in facilitating this convergence?

For today's developed countries, spatial inequalities in income and welfare rose early, followed by slow convergence

In today's developed countries, per capita incomes initially diverged between subnational areas, and convergence began to set in as GDPs per capita approached $10,000, following an inverted-U relationship (see figures 2.4 and 2.5 and table 2.2).[44]

Across areas of the United Kingdom, the coefficient of variation of GDP per capita increased by almost 40 percent between 1871 and 1911.[45] During this period, Britain went from a modern-day Namibia to a Jordan or the former Yugoslavia.[46] After World War II, GDP per capita across areas of the United Kingdom displayed a slow convergence, continuing until the late 1970s, when spatial inequalities stabilized.[47]

In the United States, the dispersion of per capita income across states increased between 1840 and 1880, coinciding with the rise of the manufacturing belt in the North, and the Civil War and its aftermath. The end of the Civil War marked the beginning of integration between states in the North and the South, and spatial dispersion in per capita income began to narrow. Because the southern states remained more dependent on agriculture, lagging areas of the United States suffered a setback in the 1920s because of a sharp drop in the relative prices of agricultural goods. Once this shock dissipated, the slow convergence between lagging and leading areas resumed with few interruptions until the 1990s, when disparities among states stabilized.[48]

Figure 2.4   Spatial inequality rose and remained high before slowly declining as economies approached $10,000 in GDP per capita

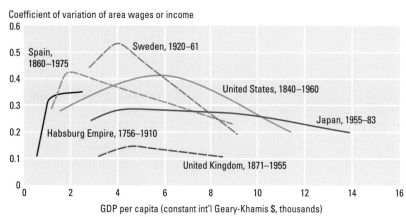

Sources: United States: Williamson 1965; Habsburg Empire: Good 1986; Sweden: Williamson 1965; Spain: Martinez-Galarraga 2007; Japan: Mutlu 1991.

Figure 2.5   Subnational disparities in income and wages persisted for more than 70 years in Canada and France

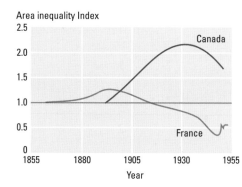

Sources: Canada: Green 1969; France: Williamson 1965.
Note: Canada data are based on provincial per capita gross value added; France data are based on department agricultural wages.

Table 2.2   Spatial inequality varied through different phases of development

Country	Spatial disparity measure	Phase of economic development			
		Early	Middle		Advanced
United States		1774	1790	1840	1860
	Relative deviation regional GDP per capita from U.S. average	30	31	56	66
Italy		1861	1911	1936	1951
	Index of regional percent agriculture labor force	6.55	9.41	12.7	14.2
Canada		1901	1911	1941	1951
	Index of regional percent agriculture labor force	7.14	9.88	12.6	10.2
England		1767	1795	1867–70	1898–1914
	Maximum-minimum in county agriculture wages	3s 11d	8s 2d	11s 0d	7s 4d
Austria		1869	1890		1910
	Maximum-minimum regional percent agriculture labor force	0.32	0.35		0.40
Spain		1860	1914	1955	1975
	Maximum-minimum ratio regional GDP per capita	1.76	2.33	2.22	1.74
Australasia		1860	1880		1900
	Coefficient of variation regional GDP per capita	0.30	0.35		0.10

Sources: United States: Good 1986; Italy: Williamson 1965; Canada: Williamson 1965; England: Hunt 1986; Austria: Good 1986; Spain: Martinez-Galarraga 2007; Australasia (Australia, New Zealand, and Tasmania): Cashin (1995).
Note: For Spain, the maximum is the top five and the minimum is the bottom five. For England, the currency is in shillings (s) and pence (d).

Canada and France also exhibit the same inverted-U-shaped pattern of rising spatial disparities in the early stages of development—spanning two generations—followed by slow convergence (see figure 2.5). In France the spatial dispersion of wages across *départements* increased between 1855 and 1900, when convergence set in. In Canada the spatial dispersion of average gross value added between areas increased between 1890 and 1910, carrying over to 1929 and starting to fall by 1956.[49] In Italy, Germany, and Spain, the convergence in per capita income gradually set in many years after these economies reached high income—after World War II—followed by stable income disparities (see figure 2.6).

Government policies can facilitate this convergence. In Japan, for example, investments in social services in lagging areas were increased as concentration of economic production accelerated. By making

BOX 2.4 *Correcting geographic disparities in postwar Japan*

In 1970, Prime Minister Eisaku Sato and the Cabinet initiated the New Economic and Social Development Plan and the New Integrated Spatial Development Plan (Shin-Zenso). The objective was to address disparities in living standards, as a result of accelerated growth in industrial areas around Tokyo, Nagoya, and Osaka along the Pacific Coast during the early postwar years. An excerpt in the Shin-Zenso summarized the government's vision:

Among many problems concerning spatial disparities, disparities in living standards are more serious than those in per capita income. From this standpoint, the construction of the basic services and social institutions must be accelerated in rural towns, and new policies must be adopted to improve the living conditions of their surrounding areas above a certain minimum level.

These plans continued to provide public investment in basic services and social institutions (for example, public utilities, medical facilities, and school buildings) to industrialized areas. But additional investments were made in the less developed areas, to achieve at least a minimal level of living standards for all places. The result was a rapid catch-up in investment in basic services and social institutions in less developed areas relative to the more industrialized areas (see the figure immediately to the right).

Both the general account budget of the central government and the Fiscal Investment and Loan Program were instrumental in mobilizing financial resources. The general account budget of the central government provided earmarked budget transfers to local governments in addition to nonearmarked transfers. Among the earmarked budget transfers, a substantial amount was allocated for investments in basic services (for example, rural roads) and social institutions under cost-sharing arrangements with the local government.

The Fiscal Investment and Loan Program pooled public funds from such sources as postal savings and public pension insurance premiums and then channeled them for investments in housing and social institutions to improve welfare in less developed areas. These policies were effective in corralling large investments toward achieving universal attainment of basic living standards. Per capita income converged between leading and other areas during the 1970s (see the figure on the right, below). Labor migration from rural to large urban areas was pronounced throughout the 1950s and 1960s, but it tapered off after the mid-1970s.

Sources: Cabinet Council 1972; Hayashi 2003; Kamada, Okuno, and Futagami 1998; Ministry of Finance 2008; Nakajima 1982; Okuma 1980; Overseas Economic Cooperation Fund 1995; Policy Research Institute for Land 2001; Sakamaki 2006.

Rising investments in social services facilitate convergence in incomes

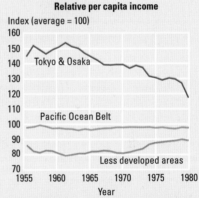

Contributed by Keijiro Otsuka and Megumi Muto.

the labor force more mobile, this led to falling geographic disparities in incomes (box 2.4).

For developing countries, spatial disparities in living standards between subnational areas first rise and then fall with development

Comparing a large number of countries at different levels of development reveals that spatial disparities in per capita product and welfare diminish with level of development (see figure 2.7). This is consistent with most developing countries being clustered on the upward-sloping section of the inverted-U-shaped relationship between development and spatial inequality—and with the developed countries on the

Figure 2.6   Spatial disparities have narrowed slowly in Europe since World War II

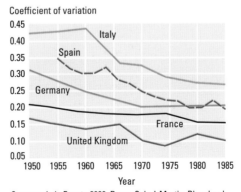

Sources: de la Fuente 2000; Barro, Sala-I-Martin, Blanchard, and Hall 1991.

Figure 2.7 Contemporary comparisons of countries indicate that disparity in welfare among subnational areas fall with economic development

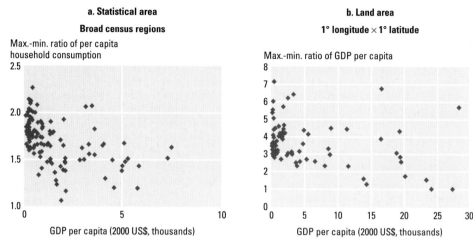

Source: Panel a: World Bank staff estimates of more than 120 household surveys fielded during 2000s in more than 80 countries; panel b: World Bank staff estimates from http://gecon.edu.yale, which is information in 1990.

downward-sloping part of the relationship. The conclusion is based on two sources of information. The first source comes from more than 120 household surveys covering more than 80 developing countries, from the Democratic Republic of Congo with a GDP per capita of less than $100,

to Argentina with more than $7,500. The second source is based on the geophysically scaled economic data of terrestrial grid-cells of 1° longitude by 1° latitude for 90 countries that span the full spectrum of development, from Ethiopia with a GDP per capita of less than $200, to Japan with a GDP of more than $30,000.[50]

The household survey data offer an added advantage because individual household consumption is a better measure of welfare than income. Similar households in different areas of a developing country can have an average gap in household consumption of 70 percent simply as a result of location.[51] In Nicaragua, a six-person household headed by a primary-educated 40-year-old male in the lagging area of Matagalpa-Jinotega consumes half of what an equivalent household consumes in the leading area of Managua. In Canada and the United States a household in the lowest GDP per capita area consumes 20 percent less than an equivalent household in the highest. In Japan the area of residence means even less for the gap in consumption.

As countries become more developed, the disparities in welfare purely attributable to location diminish.[52] This pattern holds after controlling for the land area of a country and its number of administrative areas. Among countries partitioned into five areas,

Table 2.3 Household survey and subnational gross product data corroborate the pattern of declining spatial disparities in welfare with development

Statistical area	Country	GDP per capita	Number of statistical areas	Leading-lagging area disparity in household consumption (minimum-maximum ratio)
	Cambodia	234	5	1.89
	Bangladesh	286	5	1.73
	Colombia	1,989	5	1.54
	Thailand	2,109	5	1.52
	Argentina	7,489	5	1.48
	Canada	23,392	5	1.22

Land area	Country	GDP per capita	Land area (km²)	Leading-lagging area disparity in per capita gross product (minimum-maximum ratio)
	Philippines	920	300,000	5.43
	Poland	3,099	311,888	4.63
	New Zealand	11,552	267,990	3.35
	Norway	27,301	304,280	1.78
	Japan	33,280	364,600	0.35

Sources: Estimates of consumption disparity are from more than 120 household surveys fielded during the 2000s for more than 80 countries. Estimates of disparity in gross product are from, which comes from information gathered in 1990.
Note: GDP per capita estimates are based on constant 2000 U.S. dollars for the particular years of the surveys.

Bangladesh and Cambodia, both with GDP per capita less than $300,[53] had spatial gaps in consumption between their leading and lagging areas of 89 percent and 73 percent, respectively. For Colombia and Thailand (with GDPs per capita of approximately $2,000) the equivalent gaps are about 50 percent. For Canada (with a GDP per capita of $20,000) the gap is less than 25 percent. Among the medium-size countries, spatial disparities in welfare follow the same pattern, falling across the spectrum from developing to industrialized countries. The same is true for larger and smaller countries (see table 2.3).

Fast-growing countries see spatial disparities in income widen

East Asian growth has outstripped both the world economy and the growth of other developing regions. As they moved from plan to market, Eastern European and Central Asian countries have also grown faster than the world (see figure 2.8). As in the early stages of development in today's industrialized countries, development in East Asia, Central Asia, and Eastern Europe has brought widening gaps. In Southeast Asia the disparities in incomes per capita between leading and lagging areas has grown wider (see figure 2.9). In China too, the spatial dispersion in GDP per capita increased over the last decade (see figure 2.10). All this is consistent with the findings of the UNU-WIDER research program.

In Eastern Europe and Central Asia, too, disparities among subnational areas in labor productivity and income widened. In Russia income per capita in the lagging subnational area in 1985 was half the national average, and that in the leading area, twice the national average. Since then, income per capita in the lagging area has fallen to a quarter of the national average, while that in the leading area increased to five times the national average.[54] This divergence occurred during a reshaping of Russia's economic geography as state industries in remote areas collapsed, and economic activity started to respond to spatial variations in market potential (see box 2.5). Similarly, the Czech Republic, Hungary, Poland, and the Slovak Republic have

Figure 2.8   Economic growth in East Asia and Eastern Europe is faster than the world's growth

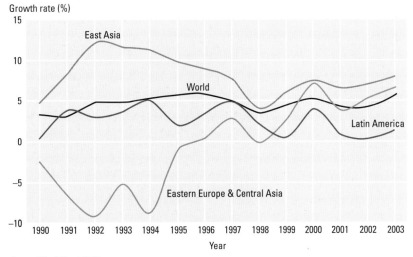

Source: World Bank 2005e.

Figure 2.9   Disparities in per capita gross product have been rising between leading and lagging areas in Southeast Asia

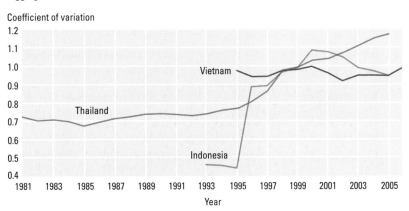

Source: Hamaguchi forthcoming.

Figure 2.10   Steady rise in inequality of per capita provincial gross product in China since 1990

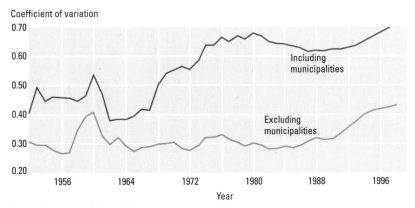

Source: Demurger and others 2002.

BOX 2.5 *Spatial inefficiency and the downfall of the Soviet Union*

The Earth hosts many vast and harsh spaces, but few governments have put as much energy into the development of such places as Russia did under the Soviet government.

The effort to develop Russia's eastern areas was substantially increased under Stalin's rule. A forced industrialization attempted to shift production to the east and create new economic bases in the country's geographic heart. Equalization of economic (especially industrial) mass across Russia was seen as the way to make development uniform across space. "Balanced industrial growth" remained a slogan for a long time. In the 1930s the new areas received more than 50 percent of the central investment, financed mainly by expropriating wealth from agriculture. The new areas absorbed only capital at first. Visible effects appeared during World War II, although the most productive zones were close to the front, like the Ural-Volga, where 58 percent of factories evacuated from the west of the USSR were placed.

An accounting of this centralized, directive effort to spread out economic mass is depressing. Alexei Mints, the Soviet geographer, dismissed as propaganda the claims that directed investment boosted backward areas and created cities "from zero" under the five-year plans. The reality was more prosaic: the "opening up" of eastern raw material fields coincided with the growth of manufacturing in the west. The shift eastward, Mints wrote, occurred mostly in the European part.[a] In reality, Russia's demographic and economic geocenter had moved only as far east as the river Belaya in Bashkiria by 1990; eight of Russia's 11 time zones lay to the

east of the Belaya. Industrial Siberia grew in absolute terms, but its share did not exceed one-fifth under the Soviet price system that favored final goods at the expense of raw materials, transportation, and energy (see the table below).

The Soviet social infrastructure over-lapped with industrial development. Health centers, schools, recreational, cultural, sports, and communal-housing facilities—called *sotscultbyt*—generally belonged to enterprises. This overlap was especially evident in large companies in remote areas, such as the transpolar city of Noril'sk. This tradition was combined, somewhat paradoxically, with a vigorous redistribution of funds between sectoral and regional departments. Profits were seized and then given back—not necessarily to the same place—in capital goods and assets. The share of enterprises under the all-Union jurisdiction reached 70 percent in the reigns of Stalin and Brezhnev. The central government (Sovmin) controlled less than 20 percent of industrial profits obtained on Russian soil.

Industrial deconcentration, together with price system distortions and an expensive arms race, would bring the Soviet system down. In the late 1980s both the elite and the masses in almost every area or republic claimed that it bore the burdensome duty of a land that "fed the others." The slogan of regional *khozraschet* (self-repayment and economic accounting) soon grew into political separatism and contributed to the demise of the Soviet Union.

After the Soviet Union collapsed, the Russian Federation became more integrated with the world market. Russia

found itself more resource abundant, but also less populated. The market revaluation of resources and assets shrank the economic mass of distant zones and poles, but deteriorating infrastructure did not reduce, and in some cases, increased economic distance. Industry-tied public services also collapsed in the 1990s, as firms were privatized or transferred to their *sotscultbyt* to municipal authorities. For some time under Yeltsin, the revenues of federal and regional/local budgets were officially equal (50:50). In the 2000s, though, the rules were changed in favor of the Federation (60:40 when the external debt payments were made, reduced later to 55:45). But expenditures stayed at 50:50 because of growing transfers.

Today, center-region financial relations are again based on the principle of redistribution, though less so than in the Soviet Union. But industry is now more fuel and material based. After decades of equalization plans, the economy sees widening disparities in regional per capita product.

The figures on the next page show this for 1990 and 2005, using old Soviet net material and new gross regional product (GRP) methods and prices. The two leaders, Tyumen oblast in Western Siberia and Moscow in the center, remained the same. But the gap between leading and lagging areas skyrocketed from 5 to 43. With redistribution, the leading-lagging gap in each area's average personal income in 2005 was 11. Only 20 of 88 regions exceed the Russian average in per capita GRP, and only 22 in income. Most poor areas reduced the gap in living standards with the help of transfers.

Spatial shifts in the Russian Federation, 1900–2000

Indicator/region	1900	1925	1950	1975	2000	1900	1925	1950	1975	2000
	Number of workers, millions					Production, billion rubles, in 2000 prices				
Absolute figures	1.9	2.2	10.8	21.4	13.3	22	37	579	4,705	4,759
By type of region[a]	Percent					Percent (in current prices)				
Old industrial[b]	64	61	42	40	33	50	65	68	42	32
New European	30	33	39	41	47	33	31	27	38	40
Eastern (Asiatic)	6	6	19	19	20	17	4	5	20	28

a. Author's calculations based on various statistical and literary sources. b. Includes St. Petersburg and suburbs, the center (including Nizhniy Novgorod) and the mid-Urals.

BOX 2.5 *Spatial inefficiency and the downfall of the Soviet Union—continued*

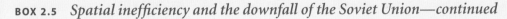

Differences in regional product widened
Current prices, percent of Russian average

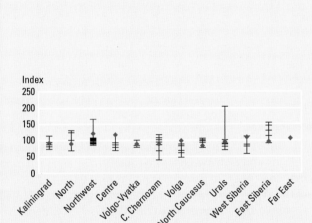

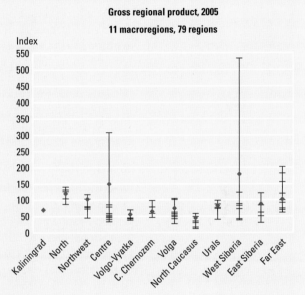

Note: Vertical lines show range of values within an area, and diamonds represent the area mean.

Welfare in remote areas has become less dependent on economic mass in contemporary Russia. The trend is not seen as satisfactory by some Russian observers and policy makers, but what should be done about it is not clear. The policy debate ranges between two polar visions: reinforcing the redistributive system

across space based on a wider sharing of oil and gas profits, or a forced diversification of regional economies based on military-industrial activities and research and development initiatives. While the debate continues, Russia's experience under the Soviet government offers policy lessons. Particularly for a country with the world's

largest land area, spatial policy choices and their efficiency could mean the difference between economic progress and stagnation.

Contributed by Andrei Treyvish.
a. Mints 1974, pp. 20–54.

all witnessed increased spatial disparities across subnational areas since the beginning of transition (see figure 2.11).

The East Asian and Eastern European countries appear to be on the rising part of the inverted-U curve. Economic activity is still concentrating in a small number of favored leading areas, with agglomeration economies increasing their productivity, wages, and income per capita. The lagging areas, insufficiently integrated into the national economy, have not yet captured spillovers from the leading areas.

The dynamics of geographic divergence in East Asia, Eastern Europe, and Central Asia have generally been a "race to the top." All subnational areas experienced gains in average wages and household incomes, though the biggest gains have gone to the

Figure 2.11 Income disparities between areas widened as Eastern European nations moved from plan to market

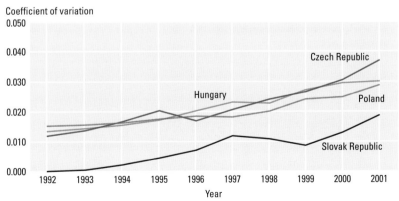

Source: Ezcurra and Pascual 2007.

leading areas.[55] Among the poorest provinces in China, the southwest region had GDP per capita growth of 7.7 percent over 1979–98, the central region 7.8 percent, and the northwest region 8.4 percent.[56] East Asian countries saw phenomenal declines in poverty from more than 450 million poor living on less than $1 a day in 1990 to about 120 million in 2007.[57] For Eastern Europe and Central Asia, the divergence between 1998 and 2003 was associated with a fall of 40 million in the region's poor living on less than $2 a day, mainly because the mass of poverty is in leading areas.[58]

Some relatively closed or middle-income countries had incomes converge

In upper-middle-income Brazil, the dispersion of state per capita income around the national mean fell from a coefficient of variation of 0.65 in 1970 to 0.49 in 1995.[59] Chile witnessed spatial convergence in GDP per capita across subnational areas between 1960 and 2001, when its GDP per capita more than doubled from $4,270 to $10,538.[60] Upper-middle-income South Africa also had per capita incomes converge between its towns and cities from 1990 to 2000.[61] For Colombia, a relatively closed economy, the ratio of GDP per capita in the leading *departamento* of Santafé de Bogotá to the lagging *departamento* of Choco fell from 10 to 6 during 1950–60 and to 3.1 in 1990.[62]

As incomes diverge, health and education converge

Many developing countries have had subnational Millennium Development Indicators across areas converge, so even though disparities in income and material well-being widened, basic welfare has become more equal. In Indonesia the coefficient of variation across provinces for average years of schooling fell from 0.43 in 1971 to 0.15 in 2000, and that for the poverty rate fell from 0.42 to 0.35.[63] In Thailand infant mortality rates narrowed from a minimum-maximum gap of 6 percentage points between the leading and lagging areas in 1980 to 0.7 percentage points in 2000,[64] around a national mean of six deaths per 1,000 live births. In Vietnam the gap in malnutrition rates between leading and lagging areas fell from 20 percentage points in 1998 to 15 percentage points in 2004, accompanying an overall improvement for all areas.[65] In China territorial disparities in the human development index declined between 1995 and 2003. The disparity between the best-performing province (Beijing) and the worst-performing province (Tibet) declined from 0.26 in 1995 to 0.19 in 2003 for life expectancy, and from 0.50 to 0.32 for the human development index. The gap for literacy rates also declined between 1990 and 2003, from 58 to 51 percentage points.[66] The convergence of basic welfare in rapidly growing East Asian countries is epitomized by Malaysia (see figure 2.12).

Figure 2.12   In Malaysia, geographic convergence in basic welfare accompanied economic growth

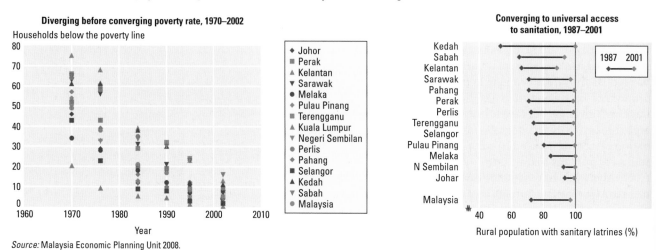

Source: Malaysia Economic Planning Unit 2008.

For Mexican states, rates of adult literacy and infant mortality converged from 1940 to 2002, as did life expectancy and enrollment rates from 1990 to 2002.[67] In Egypt the gap in female primary school enrollment rates between the best- and worst-performing governorates narrowed from 41 percentage points in 1995 to 25 in 2004, as did the literacy rate and the gender gap in literacy between 1986 and 2001.[68]

Not all countries have experienced spatial convergence in the Millennium Development Indicators. Countries in South Asia and Africa still have wide internal disparities. In India and Sri Lanka the disparities across states remained large between 1981 and 1991,[69,70] though there have been absolute improvements both nationwide and in the country's lagging areas. In Sri Lanka poverty was reduced in all provinces between 1991 and 2007, with the fastest reduction in its leading western province.[71] In Kenya provincial gaps in primary and secondary school enrollment rates remained large between 1999 and 2004, but more important, all areas made progress, including the lagging Northeast.[72]

What's different for today's developers?

In *The Wealth of Nations,* published in 1776, Adam Smith wrote, "It is upon the sea coast, and along the banks of navigable rivers, that industry of every kind naturally begins to sub-divide and improve itself, and it is frequently not till a long time after that those improvements extend themselves to the inland parts of the country."[73] What Smith wrote in 1776 could apply equally to the spatial processes in China's modern economic development. What, if anything, is different for today's developing countries?

In some fundamental respects, very little. Smith's key point was that a country's economic development, in its early stages, tends to be led by subnational areas that provide the greatest potential access to markets and thus to density. But subnational areas distant from density, inland areas in Smith's example, tend to be left behind. Only later in the development process do these lagging areas share more of

the benefits of development as a slow subnational convergence in living standards sets in. This basic thesis holds true today.

But there are some important differences for modern-day developing countries:

- Given the phenomenal size of today's global market, development relies more on pursuing an outward-oriented strategy in which leading areas compete and trade globally.
- The rapid transformation of internal economic geography—and the spatial disparities in today's developing countries—will likely be greater than in industrial countries during their early stages of development.
- Because redistributive mechanisms take time to build and mature, labor mobility and market connectivity are more potent mechanisms to integrate lagging areas into national economies. Globalization and technological progress in transportation and communication potentially provide a wider range of means to bridge the economic distance between leading and lagging areas.

Global markets are more important. Because of greater integration today, global markets are more important than domestic markets than at any time in history. The market potential of leading areas is higher in today's developing countries than it was in today's developed countries during the nineteenth and early twentieth centuries, thanks to the rapid growth of trade since the end of

Figure 2.13   Today's developing countries face a more integrated world

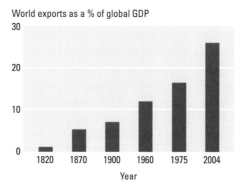

Source: Chase-Dunn, Kawano, and Brewer 2000.

World War II. Indeed, the growth of trade has been about twice that of world income in recent decades.[74] Trade as a proportion of world GDP is now more than 25 times its level in 1820 (see figure 2.13). So development under protectionist policies might have been a viable (if not optimal) strategy in the nineteenth and early twentieth centuries.[75] But a protectionist strategy is much less likely to be viable today, especially in the light of recent failures of such policies in Latin America and Sub-Saharan Africa.

When a country is relatively closed, an area's market potential is determined mainly by its distance to density within the country. But once it is open, distance or access to international markets also becomes important, and border and coastal areas tend to gain in their shares of economic activity. Structural shifts in patterns of trade can alter the topography of market potential in a country: previously leading areas, perhaps favored by policy, lose out and decline as their distance to new leading areas increases. This is illustrated by Britain, China, and Mexico.

Openness matters for distance. Before Mexico liberalized trade in 1985, the distance to Mexico City was the primary determinant of an area's market potential. But with liberalization, distance to density in

the United States also became important, and border areas such as Ciudad Juarez, Mexicali-Calexico, Nogales, and Tijuana had large increases in market potential and growth, whereas Mexico City had some depopulation and dispersion of its manufacturing activity.[76]

In China, during Mao's era of self-sufficiency, heavy industries were promoted in interior provinces, which received 71 percent of state investment between 1966 and 1970. Many companies in Shanghai and other coastal cities were relocated to the interior and mountainous provinces of Guizhou, Hubei, and Sichuan.[77] But since China has become more open to foreign trade and investment, coastal areas flourished as gateways to overseas markets, but many interior areas floundered. Export-oriented industries (garments, electronics, leather) are concentrated in coastal provinces, while domestic market-oriented industries (metals, nonferrous smelting) are dispersed (see map 2.5).[78]

The costs of transport and telecommunications matter more. Sea coasts and navigable rivers are natural locations for leading areas because, in Smith's day, shipping was the most cost-effective way of transporting goods to domestic and international

Map 2.5   Exporting industries concentrate in coastal areas to minimize distance to the global market

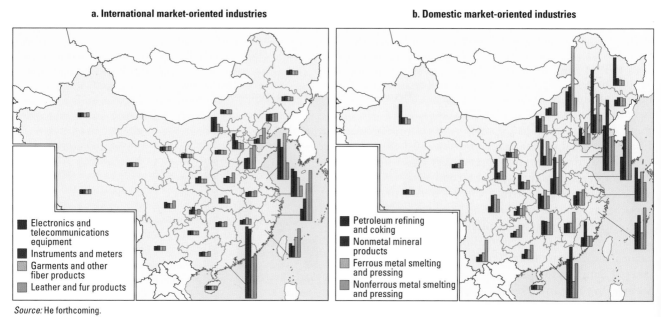

a. International market-oriented industries

b. Domestic market-oriented industries

- Electronics and telecommunications equipment
- Instruments and meters
- Garments and other fiber products
- Leather and fur products

- Petroleum refining and coking
- Nonmetal mineral products
- Ferrous metal smelting and pressing
- Nonferrous metal smelting and pressing

Source: He forthcoming.

markets. But technological progress has led to large reductions in the cost of transporting goods and in telecommunications (see chapter 6). New (non-water-based) modes of transport and the information technology revolution have reshaped the landscape of economic density.

Access to knowledge is easier. So today's developing countries can take advantage of world markets of unprecedented size and can access these markets with greater ease. At the same time, greater flows of foreign direct investment, expanding twice as fast as world trade, increase access to knowledge at the world's technological frontier.[79] For the most successful developing countries (mainly in East Asia) of recent decades, the result has been national growth—driven by leading areas—far faster than that of today's developed countries in the early stages of their development.

With such rapid growth in leading areas, the geographic disparities in today's developing countries are far larger. Take China, for example, whose GDP per capita is roughly equivalent to that of Britain in 1911. London then had a GDP per capita around 1.7 times the national average, whereas East Anglia had a GDP per capita two-thirds that average.[80] In China today, the comparable figures are 3.3 for the leading area of Shanghai and one-third for the lagging area of Guizhou.[81] Shanghai has a GDP per capita ($16,044), roughly equivalent to the British average in 1988, while Guizhou has a level ($1,653) close to the British average in 1830.[82]

Although comparisons between China and Britain need to be made with caution because of the different geographic scales of the two countries, the basic point remains. When today's rich countries were developing during the nineteenth and early twentieth centuries, the growth of their leading areas was constrained to the rate of growth of their domestic markets and the world technological frontier. These constraints limited the extent to which spatial disparities could increase in their early stages of development. In sharp contrast, for today's developing countries, these constraints no longer exist. Although the absence of these constraints helps developing countries, the potential disparities that can arise between leading and lagging areas in the early stages of development are much larger.

Although the spatial inequality between leading and lagging areas in today's developing countries will follow the same inverted-U shaped path, the features of this path will differ. The ascent is likely to be steeper in the initial stages of development. Set against this faster rise in disparities, however, is the opportunity for faster convergence between lagging and leading areas as development progresses—because modern information and communications technologies offer a wider range of methods to bridge the economic distance between leading and lagging areas.

CHAPTER 3

Division

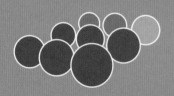

Density and distance, the dimensions of economic geography examined in the two previous chapters, matter for the development of countries and regions. Over the past two centuries, global gross domestic product (GDP) has grown about 2.3 percent a year, an almost 50-fold increase in constant dollars.[1] But growth has not been uniform. Half of global GDP today is produced on just 1.5 percent of the world's land, which would fit comfortably into Algeria. This dense economic mass is home to about a sixth of the world's people.[2]

High density reflects the self-reinforcing benefits of proximity between economic agents across spatial scales—local, regional, and international. Distance also matters for countries and world regions. For the past 50 years, by far the largest share of global economic activity has been concentrated in North America, Western Europe, and Northeast Asia (see map 3.1). Being near these largest markets for products and supplies opens great opportunities. Indeed, the correlation between access to markets and economic growth is strong.

But it is the persistence of divisions between nation-states that sets the processes of economic geography apart for countries and regions. The latest wave of globalization, which began after World War II, has been associated with a borderless world. In 1990 Kenichi Ohmae famously pronounced that "borders have effectively disappeared."[3] For some world regions and some transactions across borders, this reflects reality. But borders, rather than disappear, have tripled in the past 50 years. There are now about 600 land borders between nations (see figure 3.1).[4] And their number may continue to increase if federated states split apart, if minorities within nations achieve self-determination, and if some of the remaining 70 dependencies seek independence.[5]

This chapter shows how divisions affect economic development, how geography and cultural history contribute to persistent divisions, and how countries impose barriers to productive interaction with their neighbors and the rest of the world. Economies benefit from gradually lowering barriers, and rich countries tend to have the lowest barriers to trade and factor mobility. Countries that have integrated *regionally* benefit from growth spillovers, larger home markets, and scale economies in production and some types of public services. Some countries within a region may initially prosper more than others, but living standards eventually converge in regions that have integrated. And in a world with economic activity and purchasing power concentrated in a few regions, countries that have integrated *globally* benefit from access to those markets and sources of investment. This chapter makes the case for countries to promote such integration.

The main findings:

- ***Divisions between countries make for thicker borders in the developing world.*** Borders restrict the flow of goods, capital, people, and ideas everywhere. But larger countries with big markets may get by with more restrictive borders. Small countries have to worry more.

Some types of divisions, like being land-locked, are beyond the control of individual countries. Others are self-imposed. And as countries develop, they gradually lower almost all types of barriers.

- *Economic mass is concentrated in North America, Western Europe, and Northeast Asia.* And only East Asia has significantly increased its share of global GDP in recent decades. This global concentration matters greatly for the development prospects of today's lagging world regions, and increasing their access to these large world markets must be a priority for global development policy.

- *Within world regions, economic development tends to be accompanied by an initial divergence in living standards between countries, followed by convergence.* Basic health and education indicators show improvements in almost all world regions, but there is some divergence in incomes between the richest and poorest countries. The increasing inequality between countries within a region reverses as lagging countries benefit from growth spillovers from leading countries.

- *Overcoming divisions between countries regionally and globally is essential for sustained progress.* This points to the importance of facilitating access to global markets and promoting regional integration in all its many forms (see chapters 6 and 9).

Defining division

Borders and divisions are not synonyms. National borders enclose people with shared characteristics, providing a sense of place and belonging that contributes to social welfare. They also generate manageable units for governing society. And well defined and settled, they provide security and stability, yielding considerable economic benefits. Divisions, by contrast, arise when borders are poorly managed. They range from moderate restrictions on the flow of goods, capital, people, and ideas to more severe divisions triggered by territorial disputes, civil wars, and conflicts between countries. Borders are not a problem in themselves. But the consequences for economic development are quite different when the countries separated by

Map 3.1 Global GDP is concentrated in a few world regions, 2006

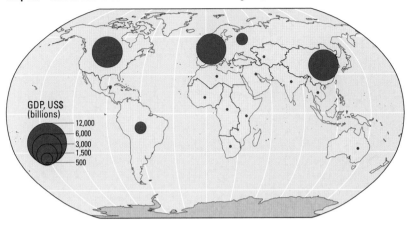

Source: World Bank 2007j.

Figure 3.1 The number of borders between nations tripled in the past 50 years

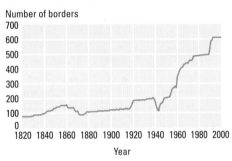

Source: Stinnett and others 2002.

those borders are integrated in a functional economic community (the Czech Republic and the Slovak Republic) or divided by conflict, reducing the scope for further integration (Eritrea and Ethiopia).

Viewed through an economic lens, some borders are much wider than others (see map 3.2). The width or thickness of each country's borders is proportional to restrictions that each country imposes on the flow of goods, capital, people, and ideas with all other countries.[6] The wider the border, the more the country limits trade, travel, and the flow of factors of production.

- Economic borders are narrow in North America, Western Europe, Japan, Australia, and New Zealand; are wide in Asia, Africa, and Eastern Europe; and are in between in Latin America. Countries with wide borders include emerging economies in East Asia and countries in Sub-Saharan Africa, which for decades have had low growth.

Map 3.2   Some borders are much wider than others

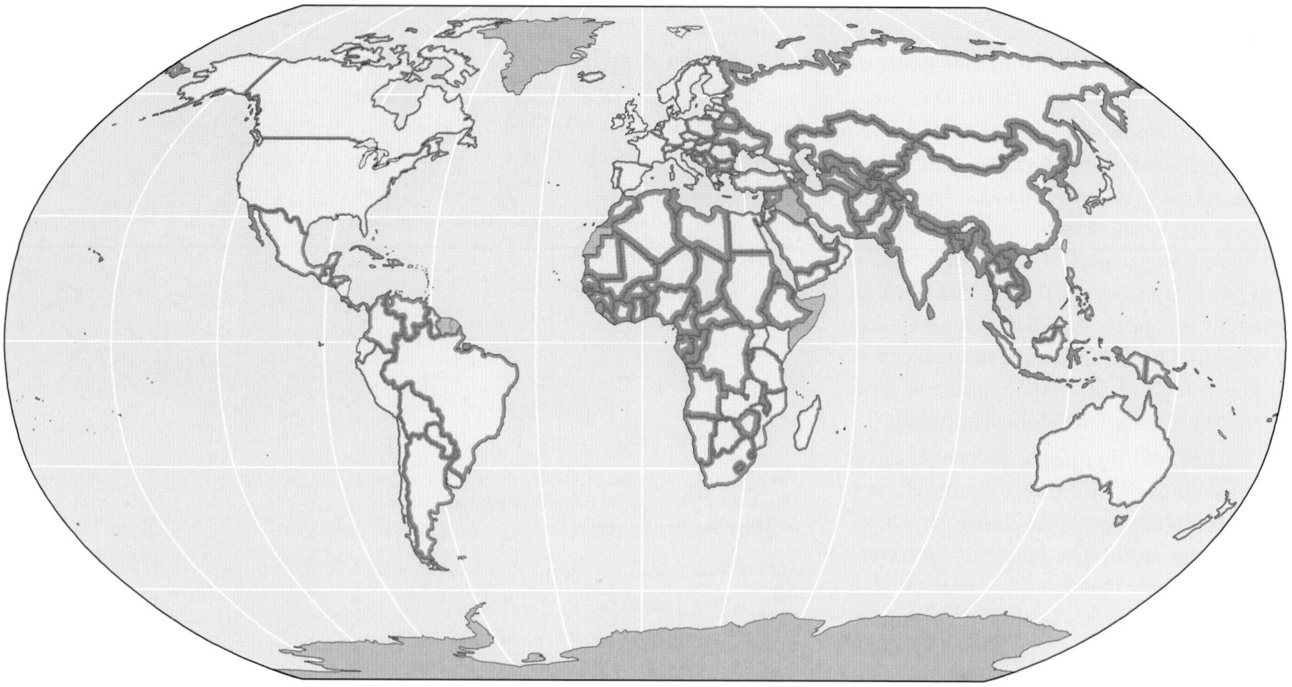

Source: WDR 2009 team.
Note: The width of borders is proportional to a summary measure of each country's restrictions to the flow of goods, capital, people, and ideas with all other countries. Gray areas = insufficient data.

- Borders of the same width appear narrower around larger countries. This reflects the reality that large countries can often get away with more restrictive policies. Small countries depend more on openness to overcome small markets and production scales.

- Some countries with narrow borders are surrounded by countries with restrictive policies, making it more difficult for them to benefit from openness than for countries in more open neighborhoods.

- This is true more for countries that are open but landlocked, such as Armenia, Uganda, and Zambia, than for those that are open and coastal, such as Chile or Georgia. Some coastal countries, by contrast, have such high restrictions that they might as well be landlocked.

Comparing border widths with economic status confirms that wealthier countries typically have lower border restrictions (see figure 3.2).[7] As a country develops, it strengthens the institutions that manage its borders and regulate the flow of goods and factors of production. It also becomes more integrated into the global economy and opens its borders to benefit from interactions with other countries, promoting further development. But there are exceptions. Some upper-middle-income countries maintain high restrictions—all of them oil exporters: Equatorial Guinea, Gabon, Libya, and Saudi Arabia (upper right of figure 3.2). And some poorer countries have greatly reduced border restrictions, among them the landlocked countries of Armenia, Uganda, and Zambia, as well as the coastal countries of The Gambia, Georgia, Haiti, Kenya, Madagascar, and Nicaragua (lower left).

How countries maintain divisions

Countries choose how permeable their borders are, affecting the flows of goods, capital, people, and ideas. And the effects of division change as countries become more open to some flows and restrict others.

Goods and services. Borders reduce trade. A study in the mid-1990s found that trade between Canadian provinces is, on average, more than 20 times greater than trade between those provinces and equally distant places in the United States. That implies a "border-width" equivalent to increasing the trade distance by 10,500 miles.[8] More recent

Figure 3.2 Rich countries tend to have lower border restrictions

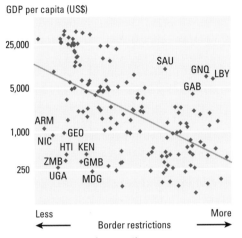

GDP per capita (US$)

Source: WDR 2009 team (see note 6).
Note: GDP per capita is for 2005 in 2000 U.S. dollars from a series used in later sections of this chapter and based on World Bank (2007j) and Maddison (2006). ARM = Armenia; GNQ = Equatorial Guinea; GAB = Gabon; GMB = The Gambia; GEO = Georgia; HTI = Haiti; KEN = Kenya; LBY = Libya; MDG = Madagascar; NIC = Nicaragua; SAU = Saudia Arabia; UGA = Uganda; ZMB = Zambia.

estimates suggest that international borders reduce trade between industrial countries by a still significant 20–50 percent.[9] The reductions are even larger for developing countries, which tend to have higher trade barriers.

Countries that encourage exports and are open to imports of goods and services grow faster and reduce poverty more than countries that do not encourage exports. When exports are concentrated in labor-intensive manufacturing, trade increases the wages for unskilled workers, benefiting poor people. It also encourages macroeconomic stability, again benefiting the poor, who are more likely to be hurt by inflation. And through innovation and factor accumulation, it enhances productivity and thus growth.[10] There may be some empirical uncertainty about the strength of trade's relationship with growth.[11] But essentially all rich and emerging economies have a strong trade orientation.

A country's openness to trade is often measured by a country's sum of exports and imports as a share of GDP. But a more direct measure is the average tariff rate, which fell globally from close to 30 percent in the early 1980s to about 10 percent in 2005.[12] Tariffs are highest in Africa, South Asia, and Western Asia and lowest in member countries of the Organisation for Economic Co-operation and Development

(OECD) (see figure 3.3). Quotas, subsidies, antidumping duties, licensing, and idiosyncratic or confusing regulations affect trade as well.[13] Using tariff and nontariff barriers, poor countries restrict trade more than rich countries. They also face higher barriers to their exports. Nontariff barriers, on average, represent more than two-thirds of total trade barriers, with higher proportions in rich countries than in poor.

Capital. Restrictions on capital flows in 2005[14] are lower in industrial than in developing countries (see figure 3.4) and are greatest in Africa, Central Asia, and South Asia. Recent empirical work—much prompted by the financial crises of the 1990s—provides qualified evidence that financial globalization benefits developing countries and that greater financial openness does not by itself contribute to more severe economic crises.[15] By reducing the cost of capital in receiving countries, freeing capital account transactions increases the availability of resources for productive investment. It can also promote portfolio diversification, thus mitigating risk, and encourage sound monetary management. From 1955 to 2004, freeing capital accounts had a positive association with growth in both developed and emerging economies.[16] Liberalizing equity markets

Figure 3.3 Tariffs are highest in Africa, South Asia, and Western Asia
Average tariff, 2005

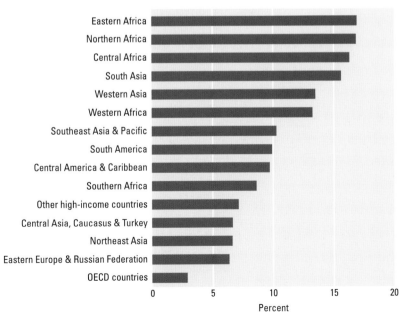

Source: World Bank 2006f.
Note: The figure reflects the unweighted mean of country average tariffs.

Figure 3.4   **Capital restrictions are highest in Africa, South Asia, and Central Asia**

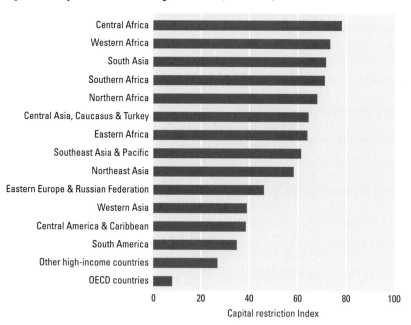

Source: Chinn and Ito 2006.

added 1 percentage point to annual GDP growth.[17] But short-term debt flows, which include portfolio bond flows and commercial bank loans, can be highly volatile. In countries where the financial sector is underdeveloped, governments and financial institutions may increase their exposure to short-term debt and thus their vulnerability to sudden outflows.

The indirect benefits of global integration and free capital flows may be greater than the direct effect of capital accumulation and portfolio diversification. Open markets can enforce monetary discipline, macro-economic stability, and financial development. They can also strengthen institutions and governance structures. And they can increase integration with the global economy.[18] Where markets and governance are well developed, financial globalization contributes to GDP and productivity growth and reduces financial vulnerability. Where they are not, the impacts on growth are ambiguous, and the risk of a financial crisis is high.

People. Migration flows have increased with globalization, but much less than trade or capital flows. Global estimates suggest that 11 million people move annually for longer-term employment or to settle in another country. About 3.5 million of them are low-skilled workers, many migrating to the Gulf

States or other middle-income countries.[19] Migrants move for higher wages, greater education opportunities, or a better quality life (see chapter 5). Sending countries receive remittances, shed surplus agricultural labor, and benefit from return migration by those who have acquired skills or capital abroad. Receiving countries, many with aging populations or chronic labor shortages, increase their labor pool by admitting unskilled workers and their productivity by attracting highly qualified migrants.

The economic benefits from more migration could be great.[20] The pool of potential migrants is likely to remain large given prevailing wage differentials between poor and rich countries, three to four times those triggering the mass migration of Europeans to North America in the late-nineteenth century.[21] Yet, despite the potential benefits and the ready supply of migrants, most countries restrict in-migration, largely because of perceived negative effects on domestic labor markets.

Comparable information on migration restrictions is not available. But countries also regulate admission of short-term visitors. Each country faces a tradeoff in allowing people from some nations to visit for business or pleasure, while deterring residents of other nations for economic, political, or security reasons. This produces a complex system of "unequal access to foreign spaces"[22] that reflects similar restrictions for people seeking to migrate. Residents of richer countries face fewer visa requirements than those from poorer countries (see figure 3.5). But poorer countries also restrict entry by visitors from other nations. Exit can be regulated as well. Many countries make it difficult for their citizens to leave.[23] Passport costs across countries are as high as 125 percent of per capita gross national income (GNI), and higher costs are associated with lower migration rates.

Ideas. Basic labor-intensive manufacturing is a stepping stone for countries to improve their economic fortunes. But to maintain growth that outpaces population and reduces poverty, an economy needs to move from low-margin activities to the development and production of new or improved products, a process associated with moving from low-income to middle-income status.

Endogenous growth theory stresses that new ideas support this transition, generating economic rents that enable the accumulation of private and public capital. China—for the past two decades a producer of low-margin, standardized manufactured goods—now exports more than $300 billion worth of information and communication technology (ICT) goods a year. So far, most of these exports have been assembled from imported components, with the largest rents captured by foreign firms that develop innovative technologies and control marketing and sales. Of the retail proceeds from an iPod® music player assembled in China, more than half goes to Apple's profits and the retail and distribution costs.[24] Assembly and testing account for only about 2 percent of the final sale value.

Freedom of access to all types of information is necessary for an atmosphere that induces innovation and productivity. Ideas and knowledge spread through the research and development (R&D) investments by firms and governments and through the global stock of existing knowledge accessible through publications, patents, and so on.[25] Governments do not restrict the flow of purely technical information, although poorer countries have limited access to such information because of cost or language barriers.

The link between the free flow of ideas and economic development is somewhat ambiguous and not well researched. A free press generally reduces corruption and increases public accountability.[26] An indicator of press freedom reported annually since 2002 by Reporters without Borders covers freedom and security in reporting, government control of media, restrictions on Internet providers, and censorship of content.[27] Western industrial countries generally have a high degree of freedom. Many low-income countries have high restrictions on the media and Internet traffic. Significant restrictions persist in parts of Africa, East Asia, the Middle East, and the former Soviet Union.

Some divisions are beyond the control of individual countries

Countries for the most part are free to determine their openness to the outside world. But geography and history produce divisions over which countries have little or

Figure 3.5   Residents of richer countries face fewer visa requirements

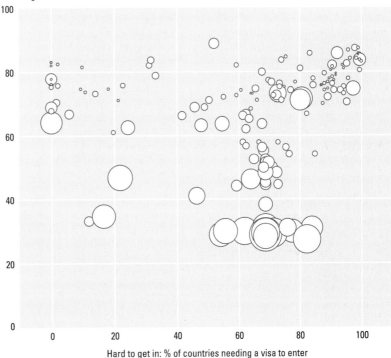

Hard to get around: % of countries for which a visa is needed

Hard to get in: % of countries needing a visa to enter

Source: Neumayer 2006.
Note: Circles are proportional to GDP per capita; visas available at the border are not included.

no control. These include being landlocked, being in a remote location (especially if combined with small size), and having a high degree of ethnic or cultural heterogeneity within and across borders.

Landlocked. There are 43 landlocked countries in the world. Being landlocked reduces growth by at least half a percentage point.[28] Boxes 3.1 and 3.2 illustrate further the costs of being landlocked. Small surprise then, that many landlocked countries are among the world's poorest. But being landlocked in itself is not a cause of poverty—look at Botswana, Luxembourg, and Switzerland. The problem is being landlocked with poor neighbors or being landlocked far from markets.[29] Often the two go together. Africa has the most landlocked countries (15), and Eastern Europe and Central Asia the highest proportion—about half (see map 3.3). Bhutan, Lao People's Democratic Republic, and Nepal in Asia, and Bolivia and Paraguay in South America are other poor landlocked countries.

Country size. A large land area is often associated with abundant natural resources (see box 3.3). A large population

BOX 3.1 *A country's neighborhood matters: regional integration and growth spillovers*

Spillovers of growth from across borders are among the main benefits of regional integration.[a] In a more integrated economic space, the long-run growth prospects of countries become interlinked as markets of neighboring countries become more accessible. Growth in neighboring countries enhances domestic growth, which benefits neighbors. This spatial multiplier enhances the rewards to good policy and contributes to convergence in living standards.

Quantifying the benefits of growth spillovers

From 1970 to 2000, membership in a common regional trade agreement (RTA) among neighbors was associated with a growth spillover of 13.6 to 15.3 percent, so every percentage point increase in the average growth rate of RTA partners brought a "growth bonus" of 0.14 percent to supplement domestic growth. Associated with this is a spatial multiplier of 1.14 to 1.18, with regional integration increasing the effectiveness of growth-promoting domestic policies by 14 to 18 percent.

In Europe and East Asia, where regional integration has been strongest, the benefits over the past few decades have been even larger. For these countries the

average growth spillover between 1970 and 2000 was 15.3 to 17.0 percent. This contributed to a slow, but steady, convergence in living standards, with the gap in prosperity between the poorest and richest OECD countries closing at an average rate of 1.59 to 1.85 percent a year. Along with this, the effectiveness of growth-promoting domestic policies has been supplemented by 18.1 to 20 percent.

In Sub-Saharan Africa the average growth spillover has been far weaker, signaling the relative lack of regional integration despite a plethora of RTAs. The growth spillover is estimated at only 2.9 to 3.9 percent, implying a spatial multiplier of only 1.01 to 1.04. This finding of virtually no growth spillovers holds when neighbors are defined by contiguity rather than RTA membership. A typical Sub-Saharan country's growth rate was basically independent of the growth rates of its neighbors.

Implications for landlocked and resource-poor countries in Sub-Saharan Africa

Under current conditions, if the Sub-Saharan countries whose natural endowments are most favorable sustained a growth takeoff, the landlocked and

resource-poor countries of Central Africa would be left further behind.

If Switzerland had been subject to the same low spillovers experienced by the Central African Republic between 1970 and 2000, its GDP per capita in 2000 would have been 9.3 percent lower, with a cumulative GDP loss of $334 billion (2000 constant U.S. dollars), or 162 percent of Swiss GDP (see the figure below).

Putting Switzerland in Africa would have cost it $334 billion

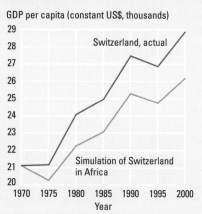

GDP per capita (constant US$, thousands)

Source: Roberts and Deichmann 2008.
a. Collier and O'Connel forthcoming.

BOX 3.2 *Bolivia and Chile's border—from wide to narrow?*

Bolivia illustrates the economic dependence of a landlocked country on its neighbors and how economic integration could help overcome these divisions. After a war with Chile in the late-nineteenth century, Bolivia lost its access to the Pacific, and Peru, Bolivia's ally, also lost territory to Chile.

Chile and Bolivia have not had diplomatic relations since 1978, but they are now talking. A motive for Chile is natural gas. Since 1995 it has relied almost exclusively on gas from Argentina, but supplies have been limited by high demand in Argentina.

Bolivia has South America's second-largest natural gas reserves. So economic integration could be an incentive for resolving regional disputes. Chile would gain from energy imports from Bolivia; Bolivia would benefit from better access to ports, which would make it easier to export. Peru would likely be involved in any agreement because it provides an alternative, though less economic, route to the coast for Bolivia and because any corridor through Chile would likely pass through former Peruvian territory in Chile.

Sources: The Economist 2007b, Malinowski 2007.

provides a ready market and large labor force. Conversely, small countries lack the scale, capacity, and stock of production factors to achieve high economic growth by themselves. But as with being landlocked, size by itself is not a determining factor. What determines economic prosperity is a country's economic integration with the rest of the world.[30] Luxembourg ranks 167th in population but has the world's highest GDP per capita. Fully integrated in the European Union (EU), its highly specialized financial sector operates globally. Small countries should thus favor economic integration, because they will gain most from freer trade and openness.

In world regions that are more highly integrated, parts of a country therefore have less incentive to remain within a nation dominated by another cultural or ethnic group. Devolution in the United Kingdom and separatist movements in Spain confirm this. Similarly, the "re-balkanization" of Southeastern

Map 3.3   Forty-three countries do not have direct access to the coast

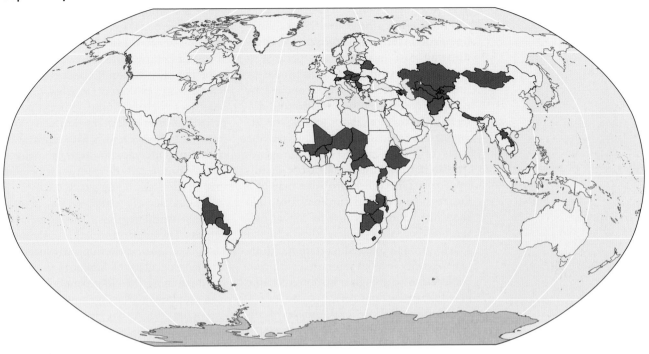

Source: WDR 2009 team.

Europe with the disintegration of the former Yugoslavia was in part facilitated by the prospect of EU accession for the newly independent countries. Noneconomic considerations can dominate, however. Eritrea and Timor-Leste have seceded from their larger neighbors (Ethiopia and Indonesia) without the benefit of integration with a larger economic association.

Sea-locked countries. Being landlocked can generate an island effect, preventing a country from benefiting from neighboring suppliers and markets. Small islands in remote locations suffer similar isolation; they are essentially "sea-locked." They face high transport costs for exports and imports, higher costs for energy and intermediate inputs, and typically higher wage costs and rents. The problems are acute for the small island nations of the Pacific.[31] Trade preferences to support them until they become competitive in world markets have generated large and unsustainable inefficiencies in production. And large per capita aid flows have had only limited impact on their competitiveness. Closely linking up with wealthier "patron" countries and increasing labor mobility may be the only strategies.[32] Small island states in the Caribbean, by

contrast, have more diversified economies and, being closer to rich markets, benefit more from tourism and trade.

Mauritius shows that good policy can overcome small size and remote location. It now has the second highest GDP per capita in Africa despite being more than 900 kilometers from the nearest mainland. Its location among the Middle East, South Africa, and India allows it to capture offshoring activi-

---

BOX 3.3   *The benefits of size*

Five benefits of being a large country:

- Smaller per capita cost of providing many public goods, such as a judicial system or embassies.
- Larger home market, which can increase productivity and thus benefit economic growth.
- Stronger buffer to regional economic shocks—if a region that specializes in, say, agriculture suffers a recession, the impacts can be reduced through transfers from other regions, and workers can seek employment elsewhere in the country.

- More effective redistributive schemes to reduce gaps in after-tax incomes between rich and poor regions.
- Better ability to provide security, as the per capita cost of defense declines.

A possible disadvantage is the greater heterogeneity of preferences and thus the larger coordination costs in large democracies. Diversity also makes it harder to overcome collective action problems.

Source: Alesina and Spolaore 2003.

ties in manufacturing and banking, as well as a thriving stopover tourism industry.

Ethnic and cultural divisions. Ethnolinguistic heterogeneity imposes a coordination cost on countries, because it often reflects differences in attitudes or interests that need to be reconciled by national governments. Consider the differences in opinion about joining the EU among the French- and German-speaking parts of Switzerland. This heterogeneity also has implications for labor mobility. For instance, the Euro zone may be a less resilient common currency area than the United States, because its higher cultural heterogeneity hinders adjustments to shocks through internal migration. Ethnic heterogeneity is often associated with civil conflict and with high costs for economic growth.

Empirical evidence for the impact of cultural diversity is mixed (see also box 3.4). Ethnic fragmentation is negatively associated with the quality of government and with economic growth.[33] The relationship between ethnic heterogeneity and conflict

is statistically significant only in countries where one group is in the majority but the minority groups are still powerful—for example, Burundi and Iraq.[34] In most cases ethnic or cultural differences are unlikely to be the cause of conflict. But ethnic differences are exploited to achieve other objectives, such as gaining political power or control over resources. Ethnicity also interacts in complex ways with other facets of society. Autocracy, for example, reduces growth in ethnically diverse countries more than in ethnically homogenous ones.

Linguistic diversity varies greatly between world regions. The *Ethnologue* database includes information on almost 7,000 languages, including their location. The heterogeneity of language groups is very high in Africa and generally increases with proximity to the Equator (see map 3.4 and figure 3.6). Although empirical cross-country studies suggest that linguistic fractionalization hurts economic performance, a regional trading language has traditionally helped overcome the divisions: Hindi and Urdu in a large part of South Asia,

Map 3.4   Language diversity is very high in Africa

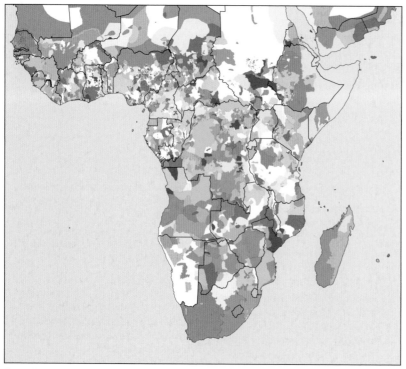

Source: World Language Mapping System, *Ethnologue* 2004.

Figure 3.6   Globally, language diversity is highest near the equator

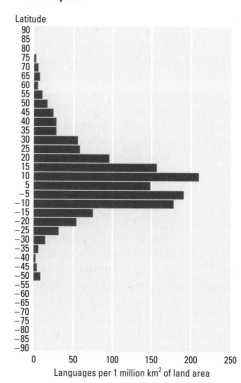

Source: World Language Mapping System, *Ethnologue* 2004.

Indonesian and Filipino in Southeast Asia, Arabic and Persian in the Middle East, Swahili in Eastern Africa, and Hausa in Western Africa. English, French, and Spanish have done the same, but in many countries they are used predominantly by an educated minority.

Economic costs of conflict and territorial disputes

Impermeable borders tend to reduce economic growth. But full political unification between countries would not necessarily improve economic performance.[35] A full merger of two countries has a positive country size effect but an overall slightly negative impact on growth due to reduced trade with the rest of the world. Only in a few instances would both partners benefit from full political and economic integration. But integration of neighboring markets without political integration, on average, would increase growth across countries significantly.

Borders further reduce economic benefits where divisions are aggravated by conflict within or between countries. Even when conflict does not involve military action, the cost can be significant. Territorial disputes impose high international economic transaction costs because of insecure property rights and jurisdictional and policy uncertainty. Economic models suggest that the territorial dispute between Argentina and Chile reduced trade between the two countries by $33 billion between 1950 and 1995.[36] The competing claims between Japan and Russia over the Kurile Islands lowered trade by $535 billion between 1952 and 1995. And those between Indonesia and Malaysia cost $11.5 billion between 1980 and 1995. Similar disputes exist over maritime boundaries, only about one-third of which are settled by treaty.[37]

When disputes turn to military confrontation, the costs are considerably higher—not only in loss of life, but also in economic terms. The cost of a "typical" civil war is about $64 billion, and an average annual worldwide cost of about $100 billion far exceeds global aid flows.[38] A civil war in a neighboring country is estimated to reduce a country's annual growth by about half a

BOX 3.4 *Artificial states?*

Gathered in Berlin in 1884–85, the colonial powers determined Africa's borders with little concern for social or economic divisions. Many borders in the Middle East were similarly drawn at the end of World War I.[a] Alesina, Easterly, and Matuszeski identify "artificial states" with a measure of how straight a country's border is and whether these borders partition ethnic groups into two or more countries.[b] Northern Africa, Northeast Asia, and South Africa have the most artificial (straight) borders, while South Asia and Western Africa are the most partitioned. Eastern and Central Africa are among the top four regions in both categories.

Empirical analysis suggests that artificial borders hurt economic and social outcomes. But this link is less significant after controlling for colo-nial origin or location in Africa. Artificial borders are not associated with a higher probability of war, reflecting similar results on ethnic diversity and conflict found by Paul Collier.[c]

So, avoiding economic and political problems associated with ethnic diversity would require cultural homogeneity within countries. In Africa this would imply a far larger number of countries. Yet the already small size of many African countries is perhaps a more severe problem—it prevents countries from reaching sustainable economic scale. As argued in this Report, the appropriate response to small size and ethnic diversity is closer integration and more permeable boundaries.

Source: WDR 2009 team.
a. MacMillan 2003.
b. Alesina, Easterly, and Matuszeski 2006.
c. Collier 2004.

percentage point. It causes neighbors to increase their military spending by 2 percent. Other costs include refugee flows and disruption of preferred trade routes. The civil war in the Democratic Republic of Congo closed river access to the sea for timber exports from the Central African Republic.

Economic concentration

Economic output is spatially concentrated—by any measure and across geographic scales. Looking at grid cells, a quarter of the world's GDP is produced on just 0.3 percent of the land area (about the size of Cameroon), half on 1.5 percent, and nine-tenths on 16 percent.[39] China, Japan, and the United States produced about half of global GDP in 2006, and the 15 largest economies produced about 80 percent.

Early in the Industrial Revolution, at the beginning of the nineteenth century, GDP per capita in today's industrialized countries was about twice that of today's developing and emerging countries (see table 3.1). But total GDP in China and India, which had far larger populations, was more than twice that in today's G7 countries. By

Table 3.1   The concentration of GDP and population growth shifted between 1820 and 1998

	Share of world GDP (%)			Share of world population (%)			Average annual GDP growth rate (%)	Avergage annual population growth rate (%)	Excess growth rate (GDP per capita growth)
	1820	1950	1998	1820	1950	1998	1820–1998		
G7	22.7	50.9	45.5	13.4	18.1	11.6	2.6	0.9	1.7
China and India	49.0	8.7	16.5	56.7	35.9	37.5	1.6	0.7	0.8
Rest of Asia	7.3	6.8	13.0	8.6	15.5	19.8	2.5	1.4	1.1
Latin America	2.0	7.9	8.7	2.0	6.6	8.6	3.0	1.8	1.2
Africa	4.5	3.6	3.1	7.1	9.0	12.9	2.0	1.3	0.7
Eastern Europe and the former Soviet Union	8.8	13.0	5.3	8.8	10.6	7.0	1.9	0.8	1.1

Source: Maddison 2006.
Note: The rest of Western Europe, Australia, and New Zealand are not included.

Figure 3.7   Concentration increases at the global level, then a leveling off
Shares of world GDP at different levels of GDP per capita, 1820–1998

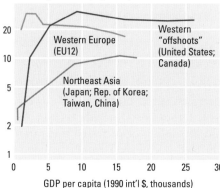

Source: Maddison 2006.

the middle of the twentieth century, the G7 countries accounted for more than half of global output (about 60 percent if the other western industrial countries are included). North America and Japan grew the fastest at 3.5 and 2.8 percent a year between 1820 and 1998.[40] The four largest European economies grew at an annual average of about 2 percent, not very different from growth rates in Africa, Eastern Europe, and the smaller Asian developing countries. But while GDP growth exceeded population growth by 1.7 points in the G7, it did so by only 0.8 points in China and India and by 0.7 points in Africa. Over the 180 years to the end of the twentieth century, these different growth rates moved the concentration of economic production more toward the northern industrialized countries.

How did this concentration come about?

The concentration of economic mass in today's western industrialized countries and Japan has its roots in eighteenth-century economic and technological innovation. Europe's economic growth accelerated greatly during the Industrial Revolution, with modern manufacturing starting in Great Britain in the mid-eighteenth century and gradually spreading across the continent. At the beginning of this process, Western Europe had less than 20 percent of global GDP.[41] By the end of the nineteenth century, it had more than 30 percent, three-quarters of it in the four largest economies—France, Germany, Italy, and the United Kingdom (see also figure 3.7).

This growth occurred against a backdrop of frequent conflict between neighboring countries, constant changes of alliances, and mergers and disintegrations of countries. At the beginning of the nineteenth century, Germany included about 300 individual states. It had 1,800 customs borders, with Prussia alone having 67 local tariff zones.[42] Only in the 1870s did Germany fully integrate domestically. Even with a patchwork of economic regions in Europe, trade flows had always been large, thanks to local or regional agreements. These expanding trade links inspired the work of David Ricardo, who in 1817 famously described the exchange of textiles and port wine between Great Britain and Portugal in his theory of comparative advantage. Ricardo's work motivated further trade liberalization by governments, most of all Britain's.

Formal economic integration did not begin until the middle of the twentieth century. Motivated by political as much as economic objectives, six European countries, accounting for about a quarter of world GDP, joined in a treaty liberalizing trade in coal and steel. Annual GDP growth accelerated in subsequent years to around 4.5 percent, up from only around 1 percent in the 35 years after World War I. Although the relative shares of European countries in world GDP dropped somewhat, the combined EU economy maintains a share of 25 percent, largely through enlargement to its current 27 member countries.

Europe's economic progress was exported to English-speaking "offshoots" in Australia, New Zealand, and North America. Between 1820 and the late-twentieth century, their economies grew by about 3.6 percent, almost twice the population growth of 1.9 percent, driven by massive migration mostly from Europe and Asia. Their share of global GDP increased from 2 percent to 25 percent during that time, the lion's share by the United States (22 percent). Cultural proximity and close trade ties meant that innovations crossed the Atlantic quickly in both directions.

Japan started to industrialize fairly late. In 1820 its GDP per capita was half that in North America and Western Europe, a ratio that did not change until the twentieth century. GDP growth between 1820 and 1870 was 0.4 percent a year. Industrialization began to accelerate after the Meiji Restoration in the 1860s. The fastest growth rates were in the second half of the twentieth century. Between 1950 and 1973, as the country opened to the world economy, Japan's economy grew at a rate of almost 9 percent a year. By the late 1980s, its GDP per capita was higher than Western Europe's.

How did the rest of the world do?

The share of the largest industrial economies in world GDP has fallen slightly, from 51 percent in 1950 to 46 percent in 1998.[43] Among emerging economies, Eastern Europe and Russia reduced their share from almost 5 percent to 2.4 percent in the late 1980s and early 1990s. The smaller shares of industrial countries and Eastern Europe are largely due to increases in Asia (see figure 3.8). Southeast Asia and the Pacific doubled its share

Figure 3.8   Only Asia's share in world GDP has risen noticeably since 1980
Shares of world GDP of developing and emerging economies, 2000 constant dollars

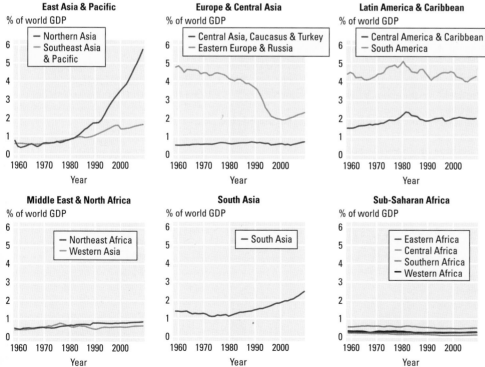

Sources: World Bank 2007j; Maddison 2006.

to about 1.8 percent, and South Asia's share of global GDP rose from 1.4 to 2.4 percent. The largest increase has occurred in Northeast Asia since the mid-1980s, essentially in China, where the share of global GDP rose from less than 1 percent to about 5.5 percent. Shares in the remaining *World Development Report 2009* regions remained essentially unchanged despite considerably higher population growth.[44]

Why does this matter? The importance of market access

The distribution of economic production globally matters greatly for the development prospects of countries because of the interaction of *density* and *distance* at a global scale. This is demonstrated by the close empirical relationship between trade as a driver of growth and two variables that define the well-known gravity model of trade: (1) the distance between trading partners, and (2) their economic size as measured by GDP

(see box 3.5). Trade decreases with distance and increases with GDP, so any country will trade more with nearby countries and with countries that have a larger GDP. Despite reductions in transport and communication costs, the trade-reducing impact of distance increased until about a half century ago, remaining "puzzlingly" high since then (see, for example, for Brazil in figure 3.9).[45]

This empirical evidence may be at odds with the rapidly increasing long-distance trade between, say, China and the United States or between Japan and Europe. But this increase in trade may not be so much due to trade cost reductions. It is largely driven by the other factor in the gravity trade relationship: economic output.[46] China's GDP has increased, providing the economic mass to export goods to international markets and to import consumer goods, capital equipment, and intermediate inputs. Increasing trade, in a self-reinforcing process, generates scale economies in

---

BOX 3.5 *Market access and per capita incomes*

Quantifying market access (sometimes called "market potential") is not just of theoretical interest. Empirical studies have shown that market and supplier access have a significant impact on growth and income. For instance, halving a country's distance from its trading partners is associated with a 25 percent increase in per capita income—more than the combined effect of a coastal location and open trade policies.[a] Trade benefits a country by raising factor incomes (wages) through expenditures by trading partners for goods produced in that country. The level of expenditures is in large part determined by the size of the trading partner's economy (*density*) and by physical market access, largely determined by proximity to trading partners (*distance*) and the effect of borders (*division*).[b]

Between 1970 and 2003, the distribution of per capita income spread out, reflecting greater global inequality among countries—the poorest countries now have smaller incomes relative to the United States (see the figures at the right). The distribution also moves to the right, implying that market potential is increasing almost everywhere as a result of global GDP growth. And its slope is getting steeper, so

the returns to market potential are increasing—the same amount of market potential buys more per capita income—at least for some countries.

There continues to be a large variance of GDP per capita at any given market potential. Haiti's market potential is higher than New Zealand's. Its proximity to the United States raises its market potential, reflecting the interaction between economic size

and distance from markets. For any given level, the size of the economy determines how well a country can take advantage of market access. Rich countries like Australia and New Zealand can compensate for a remote location by offering a fairly large market and supply capacity.

a. Redding and Venables 2004.
b. See Mayer 2008.

Market potential for countries has become more unequal

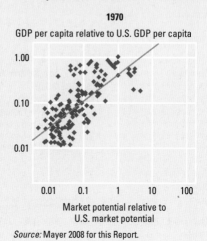

1970

GDP per capita relative to U.S. GDP per capita

Market potential relative to U.S. market potential

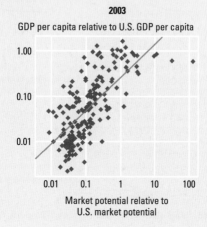

2003

GDP per capita relative to U.S. GDP per capita

Market potential relative to U.S. market potential

Source: Mayer 2008 for this Report.

Figure 3.9 The effect of distance between Brazil and its trading partners has remained considerable

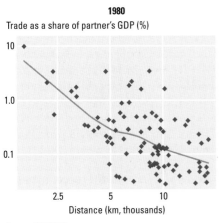

1980
Trade as a share of partner's GDP (%)

2005
Trade as a share of partner's GDP (%)

Source: IMF 2007.

the trade infrastructure and services, such as efficient ports and frequent container shipping links (see chapter 6). Larger economies and richer countries can thus overcome the friction of long trade distances with higher economic density.

Divergence, then convergence

The changing geographic distribution of world economic output reflects the concentration of economic mass initially in Western Europe and later in North America. More recently, some deconcentration has occurred as first Japan and then other economies in the East Asia region have grown. China and India are reclaiming their position among the countries and regions with the highest shares of global GDP. Country access to input and output markets influence the geographic distribution of absolute levels

of economic output. As these distributions change, so too do the prospects of national economies. These, in turn, influence development outcomes at the regional and country levels, reflected in levels and changes in income, health, and human capital. This human capital, most often considered an input contributing to human development, is also a development outcome that raises the quality of life for individuals.

Three broad trends:

- A general increase in income and basic living standards globally, but with some big exceptions.

- Considerable divergence of incomes between the richest and the poorest countries, but some global convergence in health and education.

- Some convergence within the faster growing regions.

Table 3.2 GDP per capita increased tenfold, 1500–1998
1990 international dollars

	1500	1820	1870	1913	1950	1973	1998	1998:1500
Western Europe	774	1,232	1,974	3,473	4,594	11,534	17,921	23.2
Western offshoots	400	1,201	2,431	5,257	9,288	16,172	26,146	65.4
Japan	500	669	737	1,387	1,926	11,439	20,413	40.8
Asia (excluding Japan)	572	575	543	640	635	1,231	2,936	5.1
Latin America	416	665	698	1,511	2,554	4,531	5,795	13.9
Eastern Europe and the former Soviet Union	483	667	917	1,501	2,601	5,729	4,354	9.0
Africa	400	418	444	585	852	1,365	1,368	3.4
World	565	667	867	1,510	2,114	4,104	5,709	10.1
Interregional spreads	2:1	3:1	5:1	9:1	15:1	13:1	19:1	

Source: Maddison 2006.

General improvements

Today's generation, by almost any global summary measure of income and welfare, is better off than any previous generation in human history. GDP per capita in 1990 international dollars increased tenfold from $565 to $5,700 over the last 500 years, while population grew from 400 million to more than 6 billion (table 3.2). Since 1820 output growth has been about 2.2 percent a year, bringing with it a considerable rise in living standards. Life expectancy at birth rose from 26.5 years in 1820 to 32.8 years in 1910 to about 68 years in 2005.[47] In the last 35 years alone, average global life expectancy grew by about 10 years. And a much larger share of the world's population now has access to basic education. In 1870 the mean years of schooling was 1.1 years, and the adult literacy rate 25.5 percent.[48] By 1929, schooling had increased to 2.5 years, and by 2000, to 6.7 years, and literacy to 43.8 percent and then to 78.3 percent (see figure 3.10).

Considerable income divergence between the richest and poorest countries, but improvements in health and education

Over the past 500 years, per capita output increased 40-fold in Japan and 65-fold in Australia, Canada, New Zealand, and the United States (see table 3.2).[49] In Africa it increased only threefold, and in Asia (not including Japan), fivefold. Spreads between the poorest and the richest regions increased from a factor of 2 in 1500 and 5 in 1870 to almost 20 by the end of the twentieth century. During the past two centuries, the Gini coefficient of inequality increased by 30 percent. Per capita income inequality among world citizens increased by 60 percent, as measured by the Theil index, largely because of income divergence between countries rather than within countries.[50]

The main story is one of an enormous increase in per capita incomes in Europe and its offshoots. More recently this has happened in East Asia, with Japan, whose GDP per capita has increased tenfold since 1950, and was followed by the Republic of Korea; Taiwan, China; China; and countries in South Asia. GDP per capita in China, though still low in absolute terms, grew at 8.4 percent a year between 1990 and 2005. At the low end of the income distribution, total GDP in the Central Africa region increased threefold between 1960 and 2006, compared with Northeast Asia's 30-fold increase (see figure 3.11). With population growth outpacing economic growth, per capita incomes in Central Africa fell by 8 percent in constant prices. Incomes in the poorest countries in the world—mostly landlocked and many in Africa, home to the "bottom billion" of the world's population—declined by 5 percent during the 1990s.[51]

Figure 3.10   Education outcomes have improved
Global average, 1870–2000

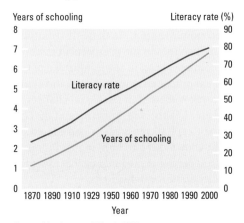

Source: Morrisson and Murtin 2005.

Figure 3.11   East and South Asia have been the only regions catching up
Average annual growth rate of GDP per capita, 1960–2006

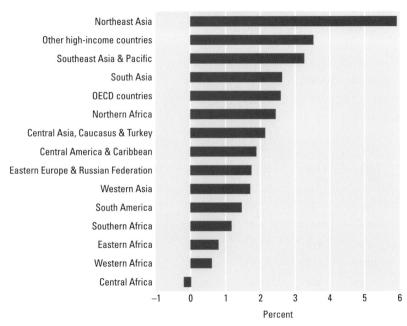

Source: World Bank 2007j.

Between 1960 and the late 1980s, almost every country in the world showed continual increases in life expectancy at birth.[52] In South Asia it increased from 42 years to 60, and in Northern Africa from 47 years to 65. The exception was in Sub-Saharan Africa. Until the late 1980s, life expectancy increased slowly in Western, Central, and Eastern Africa and slightly faster in Southern Africa, where it rose from 46 years to about 60. Since then, however, the HIV/AIDS epidemic has caused a large increase in mortality, bringing life expectancy in Southern Africa below its level in 1960. In Central and Eastern Africa, life expectancy is down less dramatically, and Western Africa contained the epidemic and saw only a slight decline in the rate of improvement. Nine of the 10 countries showing the worst trends are in Sub-Saharan Africa, and most of these are in Southern or Southeastern Africa (see figure 3.12).

Figure 3.12 Life expectancy decreased significantly in many African countries

Countries with largest increase/decrease in life expectancy, 1970–2005

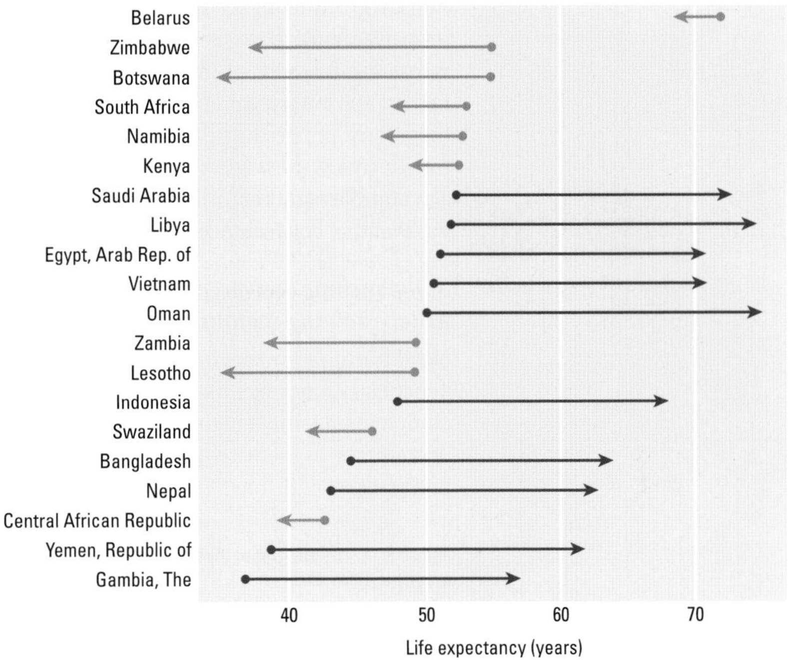

Source: World Bank 2007j.

Similar to life expectancy, global inequality in access to education fell sharply from a Gini coefficient for years of schooling of 0.79 in 1870 to 0.39 in 2000.[53] The high Gini coefficient in the nineteenth century was largely due to near-universal primary education in Western Europe and its offshoots. Other world regions started expanding education much later, and inequality dropped considerably after 1930, when primary education was expanded in many developing countries.[54] Between 1960 and 2000, the years of schooling among the working-age population increased across all world regions and income

Figure 3.13 Education has become more equal since the 1980s

Years of schooling for 15–46-year-olds (population-weighted averages)

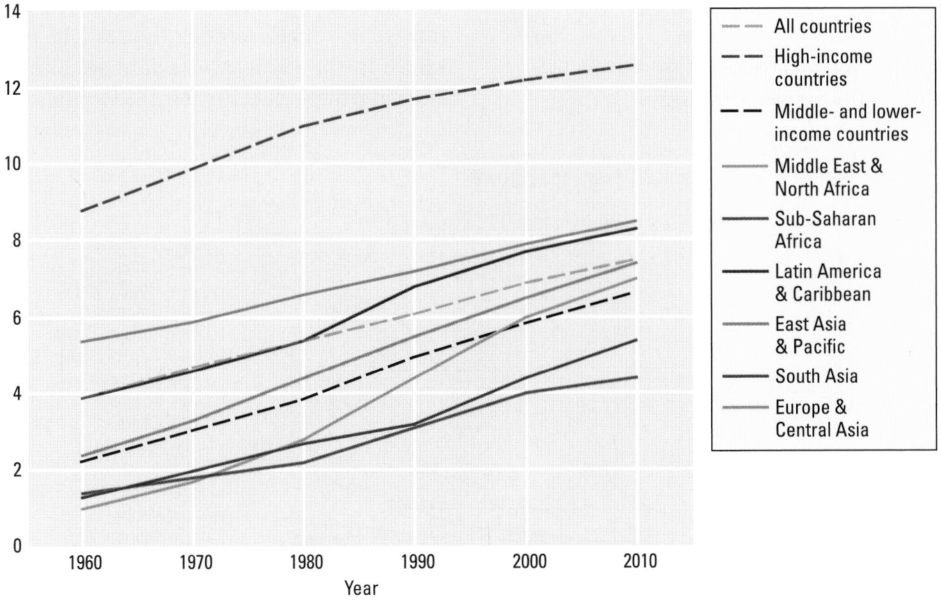

Source: Cohen and Soto 2007.

groups (see figure 3.13).[55] The ratio of highest to lowest population-weighted average education dropped from 9.7 years to 3.1.[56] These improvements have been fairly uniform across regions, so the difference between the highest and lowest region has remained essentially constant. Because poorer countries start from a far lower level, however, their percentage improvements are much higher, suggesting eventual convergence.

Some income convergence within faster-growing regions

Neighboring countries can provide mutually beneficial economic linkages, spillovers, and complementarities that allow whole groups of countries to increase their incomes. If this increases growth rates in poorer countries,

economies should converge over time. Will poor countries eventually catch up with the rich? The question received considerable attention among growth economists in the late 1980s and 1990s.[57] They produced tools and techniques to analyze convergence, relating growth to initial income, with the expectation that lower initial status is associated with higher growth rates. But there has been little, if any, convergence between countries globally over the past five decades (see figure 3.14). There is even some indication of divergence, though the trend is weak. Within world regions, the evidence is much more differentiated.

Regional integration and temporal dynamics make the study of convergence important. First, economic fortunes are shaped by what neighboring countries do, and successful economic integration—overcoming divisions— can pull weaker countries toward incomes that they cannot achieve in isolation. Higher convergence would be expected in regions that have integrated. Second, in fast-growing regions, there initially is divergence as the leading regional economies pull away, but later there is convergence as poor countries benefit from growth spillovers and begin to catch up over time.

In East Asia, the fastest-growing world region in recent years, convergence followed initial divergence. From 1950 to 1970, incomes diverged sharply as first Japan; and later Hong Kong, China; and then Singapore grew at very high rates (see figures 3.15 and 3.16a). In the 1970s other countries joined the fast-growth club, notably the Republic of

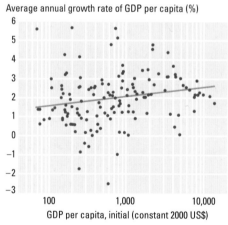

Figure 3.14   Slight global divergence in per capita incomes, 1950–2006
Countries with populations greater than 1 million

Average annual growth rate of GDP per capita (%)

GDP per capita, initial (constant 2000 US$)

Source: World Bank 2007j, Maddison 2006.

Figure 3.15   Divergence, then convergence in East Asia, 1950–2006
Countries with populations greater than 1 million, coefficient of variation and GDP per capita growth

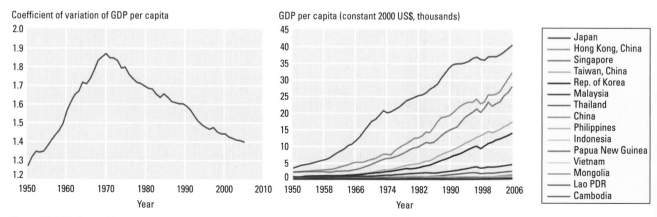

Source: World Bank 2007j, Maddison 2006.

Figure 3.16 The East Asian growth experience had two distinct phases
Countries with populations greater than 1 million, in 1950–70 versus 1976–92

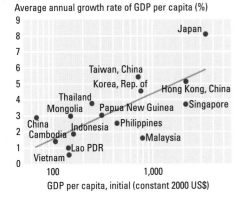

a. 1950–70

Average annual growth rate of GDP per capita (%)

b. 1976–92

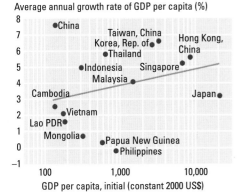

Average annual growth rate of GDP per capita (%)

c. 1976–92

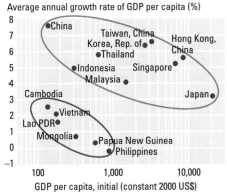

Average annual growth rate of GDP per capita (%)

Source: World Bank 2007j; Maddison 2006.

Korea and Taiwan, China. Between 1976 and 1992, what looked like moderate divergence (see figure 3.16b) actually represented two groups of countries on separate but closely linked convergence paths (see figure 3.16c). Overall, this led to a strong regional convergence as the variation among country GDPs per capita—while still large—dropped to

levels last seen in 1960. This convergence has much to do with market policies in China and Vietnam as well as with a special blend of regional economic integration against a backdrop of globalization.

There are few signs of convergence where growth has been sluggish and regional integration limited, as in Western Asia and Eastern Europe (see figure 3.17). Western Asia includes resource-rich countries, with low and high populations, as well as resource-poor countries, such as Jordan. Low levels of intraregional trade indicate low levels of integration. Eastern Europe shows low variation in per capita income until about 1990.[58] After the disintegration of the Soviet Union and the fall of the Berlin Wall, per capita incomes dropped drastically in some countries and moderately in others. This divergence was reinforced as the western-most countries reoriented their economic linkages toward Western Europe, eventually joining the EU. Belarus and initially Ukraine, by contrast, maintained close links to the Russian Federation, which only recently began benefiting from natural resource–driven economic growth.

The southernmost economies in the Latin America and Caribbean region experienced relatively low growth and limited convergence (see box 3.6). At the northern end of the region, in 1994, Mexico entered the first major regional free trade pact that includes both industrial and developing countries. The North American Free Trade Agreement (NAFTA) eliminated tariffs on most products traded between the United States, Canada, and Mexico. The evidence since then illustrates three points about formal regional integration processes:[59]

- Formal integration followed many years of preparation, gradual informal integration, and domestic policy changes. Mexico unilaterally reduced trade barriers and implemented regulatory changes long before the agreement took effect.

- The agreement led to large increases in trade and foreign direct investment (FDI) flows. Economic analysis suggests that without NAFTA, Mexico's global exports would have been about 50 percent lower and its FDI 40 percent lower. This likely contributed to significant poverty reduc-

Figure 3.17 Western Asia and Eastern Europe have had little integration—and little convergence

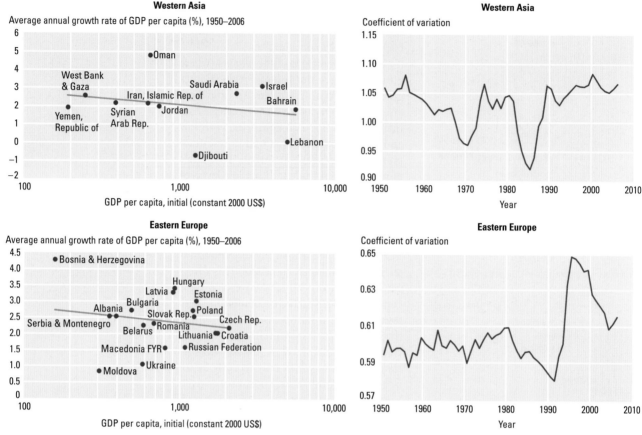

Western Asia

Average annual growth rate of GDP per capita (%), 1950–2006

GDP per capita, initial (constant 2000 US$)

Western Asia

Coefficient of variation

Year

Eastern Europe

Average annual growth rate of GDP per capita (%), 1950–2006

GDP per capita, initial (constant 2000 US$)

Eastern Europe

Coefficient of variation

Year

Source: World Bank 2007j; Maddison 2006.

Figure 3.18 Mexico and other LAC countries have not been catching up with the United States
GDP per capita in the largest LAC economies relative to U.S. levels

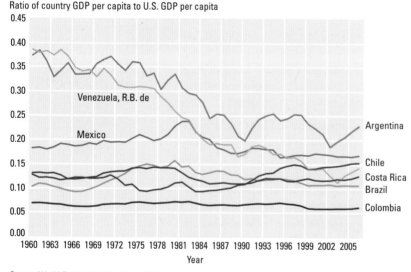

Ratio of country GDP per capita to U.S. GDP per capita

Year

Source: World Bank 2007j; Maddison 2006.
Note: LAC = Latin America and the Caribbean.

tion and income growth. GDP per capita in 2002 may have been as much as 4 percent lower without NAFTA.

- Despite these positive impacts on the Mexican economy, the agreement has not produced rapid convergence in incomes (see figure 3.18). Mexico has avoided major economic crises, suggesting greater stability that can have significant welfare effects.[60] But its performance relative to the U.S. economy has not differed much from that of several other Latin American economies.

The large differences in economic output will likely remain significant for some time. In fact, steady-state convergence estimates suggest that Mexican incomes will reach only about half of U.S. incomes. Among the main reasons are significant differences in the quality of domestic institutions, in the innovation dynamics of firms, and in the skills of the labor force. These will all

BOX 3.6 *Neighborhoods matter: Southern Cone versus Southern Europe*

Half a century ago the countries in the southern cone of South America—Argentina, Brazil, Chile, and Uruguay—had per capita incomes similar to or higher than the three Southern European countries with which they had strong cultural bonds—Italy, Portugal, and Spain. The two groups have since followed different growth trajectories. For most of this period, the Southern Cone countries, except Chile, followed similar protectionist policies. Between 1950 and 2006 the

four countries' GDP per capita grew by an average 1.7 percent a year.

Economic dynamics in Southern Europe unfolded differently. Italy was one of the founding members of the European Community, and Portugal and Spain joined in 1986 after emerging from a long period under authoritarian regimes. From lower levels, they grew at more than 3 percent a year, far outpacing Latin America. While incomes converged in both regions, they did so faster in Western

Europe at around 1 percent a year than in South America at 0.3 percent. Italy, Portugal, and Spain benefited from regional growth spillovers, proximity to large markets, and cohesion policies within a single integrated Western European market. In the Southern Cone, regional integration was slow, and integration with wealthy markets in the Western Hemisphere was neglected for long periods.

Source: WDR 2009 team.
a. Lucas Jr. 2007;

The economic fortunes of Latin America and "Latin Europe" have diverged

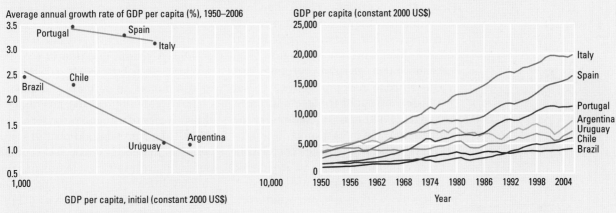

Source: World Bank 2007j; Maddison 2006.

Convergence in South America has been moderate; in Europe strong

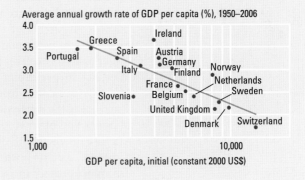

Source: World Bank 2007j; Maddison 2006.

benefit from closer integration with Mexico's northern neighbors, but the process will take considerable time.

Geography, globalization, and development

Four main aspects explain the persistent regional concentration of economic wealth over the past few centuries, with

new countries or regions only occasionally breaking into the ranks of the rich. First, physical geography has helped some countries become rich initially but continues to hold back others. Second, the forces of economic geography—starting from an initial advantage, such as technical innovation during the Industrial Revolution—facilitated agglomeration economies and reinforced the concentration of economic activity. Third, regional spillovers increased economic activity in other countries within a region, further increasing the scale and scope of economic production. Fourth, entirely new regions of economic concentration emerged—as a response to congestion and a shift in established regions from manufacturing to services, "freeing up" manufacturing opportunities elsewhere. What does this imply for the prospects in today's lagging world regions?

How much does geography matter today?

First-nature geography. Physical endowments influence the development prospects of countries. For instance, agricultural intensification in areas of good agroecological endowments generates surpluses that can be shifted to more productive uses. But these assets are not distributed uniformly. As Landes (1998) puts it: "Nature like life is unfair, unequal in its favors." Researchers have found a strong correlation between economic output and geographic characteristics. A simple regression of output density (GDP per square kilometer) on geographic variables—mean annual temperature, mean annual precipitation, mean elevation, terrain "roughness," soil categories, and distance from coastline—captures 91 percent of the variability in the density of economic production.[61] A similar analysis explains 20 percent of the difference in per capita output between tropical Africa and industrial regions, and 12 percent of the difference between tropical Africa and other tropical regions. Climate also interacts with other factors, such as disease. Vector-borne diseases strike disproportionately in tropical countries, reducing productivity. Malaria is estimated to cause approximately 1 million deaths and more than 200 million clinical events among Africans each year.[62] Other purely geographic factors—such as being landlocked, which shaves half a percentage point off annual GDP growth, or a remote location—were discussed earlier.

Does this mean that geography dictates the destiny of countries? No. Physical geography helps explain initial growth differences and some of the variation in economic outcomes. But most of these constraints can be overcome with enough resources. They are thus a proximate rather than an ultimate cause of underdevelopment. High levels of malaria, for instance, may be as much a symptom of persistent poverty as a cause (see box 3.7). They are a grave concern for development interventions but insufficient to explain global patterns of economic wealth or to predict future growth potential by themselves.

Second-nature geography. An alternative but complementary explanation for global development patterns shows how small initial differences between countries and regions (for instance, natural endowments) can, over time, generate large disparities. A central question in economic development is how much growth is due to differences in human and physical capital accumulation, and how much to the efficiency of using these factors.[63] Evidence from a growing number of studies confirms that levels of capital accumulation alone are insufficient to explain cross-country differences in growth and income. Instead, total factor productivity (TFP)—how efficiently factors of production are combined—tends to better explain differences in growth and income between countries.[64]

TFP is, however, a vague concept that subsumes several aspects of economic production. Most generally, it relates to better technology for combining inputs to generate products or services. This leads to cost reductions and thus increased competitiveness. Complementarities, spillovers, and economies of scale also explain differences in TFP. Geographically, these externalities imply benefits for producers to locate close to each other. Combined with scale economies that favor larger production units, the concentration of economic activities increases across geographic scales. European economic growth during the modern era was initiated by the industrial revolution, which generated major technological advances. Improved technology and population growth reinforced scale economies leading to concentrated centers of industrialization. These centers attracted workers

BOX 3.7   *The influence of first-nature geography: is it possible to eradicate malaria?*

The species of Plasmodia that cause human malaria most likely reached their maximum global extent in 1900. Since that time the affected area has been progressively reduced by a regionally variable mixture of improving human conditions and deliberate control. The map below shows the difference between the widest hypothesized extent of the distribution of all types of human malaria around 1900[a] and the contemporary limits of *Plasmodium falciparum*,[b] the most clinically severe and epidemiologically important form of human malaria, in 2007. The formerly malarious areas are concentrated in the temperature latitude extremes of the parasite's ancestral distribution, in both the Northern and Southern Hemispheres.

Researchers have documented the strong inverse correlation between the economic prosperity of nations and their contemporary malaria burden.[c] Richer countries have less malaria, poorer countries more. This work also documents the many mechanisms, from individual to macroeconomic, for malaria to contribute to poverty. What if the constraint of malaria were lifted? Is it possible to eradi-

cate malaria? The question has never been satisfactorily answered at the global scale.[d]

But it is possible to start addressing the problem. In the map below, risk is classified as stable if more than 0.1 case is recorded per 1,000 population each year, unstable if below this figure, and zero if no cases have been recorded within the three most recent years of records. When overlaid on a population map for 2007,[e] 2.37 billion people were found to live in areas with any risk of *P. falciparum* transmission. Globally, almost 1 billion people lived under unstable, or extremely low, malaria risk. Conditions of low risk are typical in the Americas and in South and East Asia but are also common in Africa.

For 1 billion people at risk of unstable malaria transmission, malaria elimination is epidemiologically feasible. Epidemiological feasibility was determined by reference to historical experience during the global malaria eradication program and by inferring, through modeling, that transmission could be interrupted by taking insecticide-treated bednets to scale.[f] There are many reasons in many regions why elimination may not be a simple mat-

ter of epidemiological feasibility. Political instability and geographic accessibility are obvious examples, but these are operational and not technical obstacles.

What can be achieved with the 1.37 billion people suffering stable risk? Initial evidence suggests that a substantial fraction of those affected will be living in areas of very low prevalence.[g] A detailed investigation with mathematical models could estimate the impact from the existing toolkit of interventions. When this estimate combined with a detailed analysis of the data on the efficiency of historical interventions, considerable insight could follow. These approaches will help determine whether malaria is eradicable and, if so, under what time frame and with what resources.

Contributed by Simon Hay, David L. Smith, and Robert W. Snow.
a. Hay and others 2004; Lysenko and Semashko 1968.
b. Guerra and others 2008.
c. Sachs and Malaney 2002.
d. Roberts and Enserink 2007.
e. Balk, Deichmannand others 2006.
f. Hay, Smith, and Snow, forthcoming.
g. Guerra 2008.

Currently prosperous parts of the world were formerly malarious

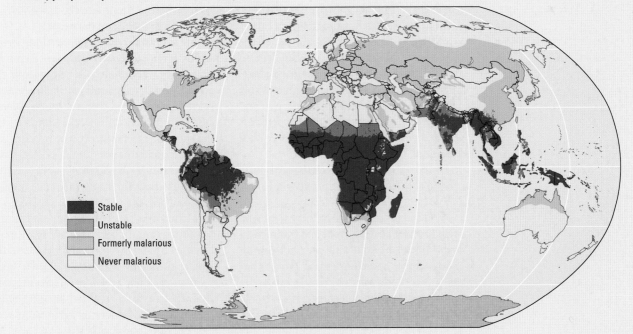

- ■ Stable
- ■ Unstable
- ■ Formerly malarious
- □ Never malarious

Source: Malaria Atlas Project (MAP), Kenyan Medical Research Institute, and University of Oxford.

and new firms, instigating a virtuous, self-reinforcing process that led to even greater concentration.

Development is contagious, tending to spread across regions. Although growth centers may start within specific areas in a country—the industrial belt in the northwest of England or the mill towns in New England—dynamic centers tend to spread out. At the international level, growth spreads to neighboring states, giving rise to regional growth centers. With enough openness and interaction between countries, the mechanisms for spreading growth are technological spillovers and increasing specialization, breaking up production processes. This makes it more likely that some of the demand for intermediate products will be satisfied from neighboring countries. This can greatly expand trade, which produces scale economies and steep increases in economic productivity. The larger labor and capital pools and the greater market size that emerge due to gradual improvement of transport links can lead to the rapid takeoff of a regional economy.[65]

New regions of growth and wealth can emerge. This happens when growth in a core region has reached a point at which congestion and rising wages encourage entrepreneurs to seek new locations for production in nearby regions. This happened in Western Europe, when firms relocated manufacturing capacity to Central and Eastern European countries, and in North America, when Mexico attracted investment in manufacturing capacity for the U.S. and Canadian markets. This contagion model of region building would suggest that all economic activity remains within an expanding contiguous zone—but it does not.

Under some conditions, economic growth may leap to an entirely new region.[66] The location of this new center of global manufacturing depends on many factors, including market size, trade and transaction costs, initial human and physical capital endowments, and competition from other potential growth regions. This leapfrogging model matches the emergence of East Asia as a global hub initially for labor-intensive production and later for technologically more advanced production. Half a century

ago, Japan would have seemed an unlikely source of inexpensive electronics and consumer goods for the U.S. market given the distance between the two countries. But the emergence of containerized shipping allowed Japanese producers to be competitive in North American markets and later in the European markets.[67] The Republic of Korea and Taiwan, China, followed in Japan's footsteps. Manufacturing investments spread from there to South Asia, particularly Malaysia and Thailand, and then, after economic liberalization, to China.

What do we learn from this?

Size matters a lot. To generate scale economies, a certain population and an economic mass need to be in place. In Europe during the Industrial Revolution, a relatively large and concentrated population provided both the labor that produced manufactures and the market that consumed them. North America, when it shifted from natural resources to industry, had a large population along its eastern seaboard, which grew quickly with immigration from Europe and elsewhere. East Asia has a vast population, with first Japan and later China serving as engines of manufacturing growth in the region. Each region benefited from a large home market, but much of the production was soon destined for export both within the region and to the rest of the world.

Few countries have lifted their economic fortunes based only on exports of primary commodities. Botswana, a sparsely populated country with large mineral wealth and good policies, is one exception. Well-managed mineral resources can help generate capital that can be invested in other sectors, but few countries have done this successfully. Agriculture—important for subsistence, for rural income generation, and for specific regions in a country—cannot by itself lift poor countries to middle- or high-income status. Rural activities are either too small in scale to provide sufficient surplus for export—or, in cases in which agricultural production has sufficient scale, it often benefits only a few large landowners or agribusinesses. The verdict on services is still out. But it is unlikely that poor countries have enough skilled white-collar workers to generate broad-based growth spillovers. India has a large export-oriented service sector, but it employs only about 560,000 of its more than 1 billion inhabitants, most in jobs in constant-return customer support and back-office tasks.[68]

Manufacturing remains important. Each successful world region has, at some point, made significant and broad-based gains with basic labor-intensive manufacturing. This process initially led to a diversification of production as countries grew richer and consumers demanded more varieties. As economies in these regions expanded, production and employment in individual countries started to specialize in what they were best at, giving rise to interlinked networks of production trading intermediate goods among countries within the region. This is the point at which China and some of the other "second-wave" economies in East Asia have arrived. In Europe and other regions that industrialized earlier, the share of manufacturing in the economy has fallen quite rapidly, with only highly specialized manufacturing remaining, such as machine tools or information technology (IT) equipment. In these countries, the service sector, including the research and design of products that will be manufactured elsewhere, now accounts for the largest share, by far, of employment and economic output.

Openness helps a lot—but it has to be introduced with care. Each of today's successful regions initially developed its manufacturing sector behind a fairly substantive wall of tariffs and other protections. Only as their economies matured and became more dependent on foreign inputs and markets for their products did they gradually open their borders and integrate regionally and globally. The rise of interlinked production networks that cross international borders within each region required more coordination and cooperation among countries, not just for trade in goods and services, but also to settle on common standards and regulations.

The process proceeded somewhat differently in each region, most formally within Europe, where the EU's political and economic integration superseded a patchwork

> **BOX 3.8** *Integration takes a long time, and its benefits do not come overnight*
>
> In Europe, after the diffusion of modern industrial technology and the expansion of trade links in the early nineteenth century, it took more than 100 years before formal integration processes began in the 1950s. Even then, the efforts were limited to agreements on narrowly focused economic issues between six countries. Gradually they expanded into additional areas of cooperation such as customs and nuclear energy. It took 16 years before these agreements were consolidated in the European Community in 1967. Membership expanded slowly, with three countries joining each decade between 1970 and 2000, and finally the addition of 12 Eastern and Central European countries by 2007. Just as the initial Coal and Steel Community formalized long-established economic and cultural ties between the member countries, each subsequent expansion followed a long period of ever-closer interaction between members and accession countries.
>
> Formal, *de jure*, integration thus followed *de facto* integration, providing a framework and structure for deepening already close relations. This gradual process allowed institutions to develop and gave labor, financial, and product markets time to prepare for possibly harsh adjustments, particularly for recently joining countries with much smaller economies. Bulgaria and Romania, which joined in 2007, added 8.6 percent to the EU's land area and 6.3 percent to its population but only 1 percent to its GDP.[a] So the convergence of social and economic outcomes across member countries will also take longer. Assessing the benefits from integration thus requires a long time horizon, as increased labor mobility, investment in private and public capital, and other structural changes accelerate growth in lagging member countries.
>
> *Source:* WDR 2009 team.
> a. European Union 2007.

of bilateral agreements among a fairly large number of countries (see box 3.8). East Asia, by contrast, has created tightly linked entrepreneurial production networks with relatively little formal protocol. Initial integration in North America was facilitated by a shared language and cultural background between Canada and the United States. The relatively recent addition of Mexico has removed some divisions between economies of greatly different per capita incomes.

Openness and integration are most beneficial for smaller or landlocked countries whose access to world markets depends on neighboring countries. Luxembourg's small size does not matter, because it is tightly integrated in the European economy and thus operates more like a specialized city in a large country. Switzerland's being landlocked has not constrained the development of highly specialized manufacturing and service sectors. It can connect to world markets by air or through neighboring countries, and its neighbors are significant destinations for its outputs. Integration has enabled the two countries to benefit from specialization and scale economies that would otherwise be achievable only in far larger countries.

To facilitate integration, industrial regions invested heavily in physical infrastructure that promotes intraregional trade. Initially, sea and river transport was most important for exporting manufactured products, requiring good coastal and river ports. More recently, interrelated production processes require more timely availability of intermediate products, which has moved a larger proportion of trade to road, rail, and air links.

What's different for today's developers?

Are the conditions today different, or is this just a continuing or recurring phase of globalization similar to that of a hundred years ago? In fact, goods and factor markets may be no more closely linked today than they were a century ago. They may be somewhat more integrated for trade, no more integrated for capital, and less integrated for labor.[69] So how can lagging regions and countries join the group of leading world regions? Do they need to wait their turn, or are there ways for them to break out of a geographic determinism?

Some clear differences in the current phase of globalization and economic development relate to the dynamics of economic geography and the persisting divisions between countries. First, the scale and speed of economic integration in recent decades have been unprecedented. The economic liberalization in China and India, as well as in Russia and South America, adds huge numbers of unskilled workers to global production capacity.[70] In many ways this is a reemergence of those regions (Asia accounted for almost 60 percent of world GDP as recently as the early nineteenth century).

China and India, because of the enormous size of their home markets, are essentially world regions of their own. With no formal internal divisions, they benefit from scale economies and provide the incentive for investors and trading partners to overcome their significant external barriers—the thick borders in the map that opened this chapter (see map 3.2). Smaller countries do not have this luxury. They must learn to manage their borders more rapidly to achieve economic integration with their neighbors to attain competitive production scale and to access world markets. Countries and regions that do this faster will have an advantage, but it will not be easy. By providing a vast unskilled labor pool—and relatively little human or physical capital—countries like China and India can absorb new manufacturing capacity for a long time. These are precisely the types of activities that might provide a path to middle income for the poorest countries. China also demonstrates the benefits of its economic rise for its neighbors. Almost all East Asian countries have sometimes significant trade surpluses with China in most manufacturing sectors.[71]

Second, there has been an unprecedented fragmentation of production processes. This includes not only the intrafirm division of manufacturing steps across several places, but more important the intraindustry trade of increasingly specialized components and services, sometimes over long distances. Advances in communications technology facilitate these complex buyer-supplier networks. Although integrated in global markets, production tends to be regionally concentrated. For smaller countries, this may be both a threat and an opportunity. The threat is that smaller countries with poor infrastructure and low skills will remain outside global trading networks. The opportunity is that, while spatial concentration remains beneficial for production, increasing specialization allows concentration and scale economies within subsectors in which even small players can carve out a niche.

In 1999 India's then-prime minister, Atal Behari Vajpayee, remarked on some of the same issues that have been discussed in this chapter: "We can change history but not geography. We can change our friends but not our neighbors."[72] Is he correct? On one level, certainly. Countries cannot just pack up and move to a better neighborhood the way individuals can. But in an economic and political sense, countries can change their neighborhoods. Japan and the United States overcame deep divisions of history and geography to become close neighbors by developing extensive transport links and increasing economic interdependence. Mexico and Turkey may be changing neighborhoods by reorienting economic ties from their traditional cultural backyards to more prosperous countries in another part of their neighborhood. European integration ended centuries of division and war. Since December 2007, travel from the Portuguese Algarve to Estonia is possible without once showing identification.

Many world regions continue to face the impacts of significant division. But this Report shows that countries can improve their economic fortunes by changing their neighborhoods virtually and practically. For this, they must do two things. First, they must overcome the limitations and barriers of geography by developing close trade and transport links with markets and sources of investment in rich and emerging regions of the world (see chapter 6). And second, they need to seek strength in numbers by "thinning" their borders and integrating their economies with their physical neighborhood (see chapter 9).

Overcoming Division in Western Europe

The day will come when you France, you Russia, you Germany, all you nations of the continent, without losing your distinct qualities and your glorious individuality, you will merge into a superior unit, and you will constitute European fraternity.

—Victor Hugo, from a speech at the 1849 International Peace Congress

Victor Hugo was laughed at when he said this, as were several of his predecessors who proposed European integration. It took the catastrophe of two world wars to get people to take the idea seriously and make policy makers ready for radical change. The scale of devastation and misery is the key to understanding the drive for integration: on top of the horrifying death toll, the war caused enormous economic damage. The war cost Germany and Italy four or more decades of growth and put Austrian and French gross domestic products (GDPs) back to levels of the nineteenth century.[1]

Overcoming division and its dramatic consequences was the objective of European leaders after World War II. Destructive nationalism—and its economic dimension, protectionism—were indeed partly blamed for the disaster. Economic integration was thus viewed as the best way to avoid another war. That it should come through peaceful means and with the main objective of maintaining peace was—and remains—a unique endeavor. In this respect, European integration is a clear success. But it was not clear in the 1940s and 1950s that this vision of "Peace through Integration" would succeed, particularly because it came at the same time as the Cold War's division between the East and the West.

Under American pressure, 13 European countries created the Organization for European Economic Cooperation (OEEC) in 1948 to implement the Marshall Plan. Its mandate was to reduce trade barriers, particularly quota restrictions. Europe in the early postwar years was a tariff- and quota-ridden economy. Removing trade barriers fostered the rapid growth of trade. Between 1950 and 1958, manufacturing exports grew by almost 20 percent a year in West Germany, 9.2 percent in Italy, and 3.8 percent in France. Additionally, average annual GDP growth was 7.8 percent in West Germany, 5 percent in Italy, and 4.4 percent in France. Correlation is not causality, and reconstruction was a strong engine of growth. But the rapid growth as European trade was

Map G2.1   The division in Western Europe has gradually dissipated
Stages of economic integration

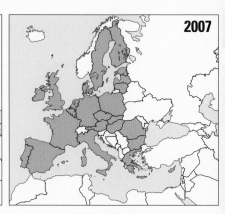

Source: WDR 2009 team.

Figure G2.1 The stairway to success
The institutional index of integration for the European Economic Community Six

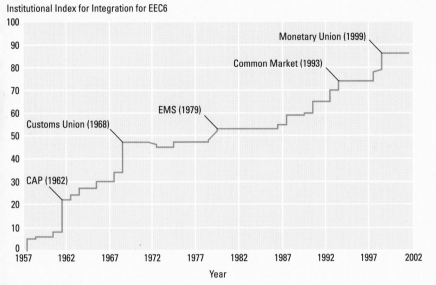

Institutional Index for Integration for EEC6

Source: WDR 2009 team.

a custom union remove all tariffs for intra-EEC trade and establish a common external tariff, but also a unified economic area would promote free labor mobility, integrated capital markets, free trade in services, and several common policies. This degree of economic integration was not feasible without deep *political* integration. So, in retrospect, "using economics as a Trojan horse for political integration worked like a charm."[2] As "guardians of the Treaty," the Court and the European Commission would control those countries (especially France when de Gaulle returned to power) that came to reject the level of supranationality implied by the Treaty. From 1966 to 1986, however, the deep integration promised by the Rome Treaty stalled (see figure G2.1). Europeans began to erect barriers that took the form of technical regulations and standards, fragmenting markets—a classic reaction by lobbying industries to defend their rents.

The Single European Act (1986) relaunched the process of deepening economic integration—all the more stunning given the slow disintegration during the 1970s. Emphasizing the mobility of capital, the Single Act was also partly responsible for the birth of the European Monetary Union (EMU). Indeed, the fixed exchange rate of the European Monetary System implied, with free capital mobility, the loss of monetary sovereignty. This made the EMU more politically palatable for countries committed to fixed exchange rates.

Overcoming division means reducing the impact of borders on trade flows. Has this been so in the European Union (EU)? One way to answer the question is to compare the volume of trade within borders with the volume of bilateral trade between countries. The ratio of the two is the "border effect." Fontagné, Mayer, and Zignago (2005) do this for the EU-9, the six founders plus Denmark, Ireland, and the United Kingdom. The border effect for reported intra-EU trade fell from around 24 in the late 1970s to 13 in the late 1990s—a

liberalized was changing the minds of European policy makers. European integration was not just a political project—it also made economic sense.

The European Coal and Steel Community (ECSC) was launched by France and Germany, who invited other nations to place these two sectors under its supranational authority. The project was both political and economic because it applied a supranationality onto two sectors that were considered strategic for economic and military

reasons. Belgium, Italy, Luxembourg, and the Netherlands joined the project in 1951, and these six would become the driving force behind European integration (see map G2.1). The ECSC showed that economic cooperation was more feasible than political or military integration.

The Treaty of Rome in 1957 created the six nations of the European Economic Community (EEC). The move committed the six to unprecedented economic integration. Not only would

Figure G2.2 Border effects between the European Union and the United States remain more than twice that within the European Union

Ratio of trade within borders to trade across borders

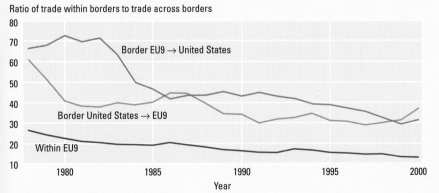

Source: Fontagné, Mayer, and Zignago 2005.
Note: The border effect is the reverse of the volume of trade within natural borders to the volume across borders.

substantial increase in integration (see figure G2.2) unmatched in the world. The border effect between the EU-9 and the United States, while decreasing fast during the period, remains more than twice that within the EU. Borders in the EU have become thinner, but they have not disappeared.

The European regional integration process has spread. As the EU deepened and enlarged, the cost of discriminatory treatment (the natural implication of any regional integration process) for outsiders increased, creating a "domino dynamic of regionalism."[3] Even European countries that most valued their sovereignty applied for membership. That the EU with its unmatched supra-nationality remains so attractive for outsiders is evidence of an enduring success.

Contributed by Philippe Martin.

PART TWO
SHAPING ECONOMIC GEOGRAPHY

In the past generation, there has been a slow revolution in economic thought, brought about by the recognition of imperfectly competitive markets, due mainly to increasing returns to scale, spillovers, and circular causation. A new way of thinking has transformed the classical analysis of industrial organization, economic growth, and international trade, and has delivered what were at first controversial, but now widely accepted, implications for the progress of developing countries. Part two of the Report illustrates the interplay between scale economies, factor mobility, and transport costs to explain the formidable forces that shape the spatial transformation described in part one. Chapters 4, 5, and 6 are the stops in a tour of the "engine room," each spotlighting a different facet of the interactions among agglomeration, migration, and specialization.

CHAPTER 4

Scale Economies and Agglomeration

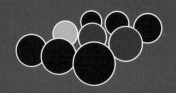

The most celebrated example in economics is perhaps the simplest. On the first page of *The Wealth of Nations*, published in 1776, Adam Smith wrote of the benefits of dividing labor to make pins. A single unskilled worker without the benefit of machines might make fewer than 20 pins in a day. But in a pin factory that Smith visited, 10 workers, who divided among themselves the 18 operations involved in making a pin, were producing 48,000 pins a day. Rather than struggling to produce just a few pins a day, each worker was turning out almost 5,000. Later in Smith's classic work are two important qualifiers: the gains from dividing labor are limited by market size, and not all activities exhibit increasing returns to scale.

The ability to transport products widens the market, so cities are located near the most natural and efficient of transport systems—waterways. Places blessed with this natural infrastructure often do well, while other places must bide their time. As Smith wrote,

> There are in Africa none of those great inlets, such as the Baltic and Adriatic seas in Europe, the Mediterranean and Euxine seas in both Europe and Asia, and the gulphs of Arabia, Persia, India, Bengal, and Siam in Asia, to carry maritime commerce into the interior parts of that great continent: and the great rivers of Africa are at too great a distance from one another to give occasion to any considerable inland navigation.[1]

Besides, not all activities exhibit scale economies, and some do not need large markets to thrive. Subsistence farming is one such occupation, fruitfully carried out in villages. But such trades as manufacturing and commerce can be carried out only in bigger settlements, because they require access to both workers and customers.

Caveats notwithstanding, the benefits of producing large quantities in a single plant or place have increased as transport costs have fallen in the two centuries since Smith visited the pin factory. Those who doubt the awesome potential of scale economies and how access to world markets helps exploit them should visit Dongguan, a city halfway between Guangzhou and Shenzhen in Southeast China. Until the 1980s it was a collection of sleepy villages in China's Pearl River delta. Since then it has rushed headlong into the world of increasing returns (see box 4.1). Every year, millions of people in the developing world enter this new realm and the implications, for them and for policy makers, are nothing short of revolutionary.

This chapter summarizes the experience of entrepreneurs over the last two centuries in exploiting economies of scale in production. It focuses on "agglomeration economies," whose exploitation requires locating in areas densely populated by other producers. It next provides a brief synopsis of about two decades of work by economists seeking to understand these scale economies—work that has diminished the disconnect between research and the real world, and that yields valuable policy insights. It then assesses whether policy makers in the developing world have been learning from this experience and analysis.

BOX 4.1   *Scale economies in an almost unreal world: the story of Dongguan, China*

In 1978 what today is the city of Dong-guan in China's Guangdong province was but a collection of villages and small towns spread over 2,500 square kilometers on the Pearl River, midway between Guangzhou to the north and Shenzhen and Hong Kong, China, to the south. The area's population of 400,000 relied on fishing and farming and—though not the poorest in China—was not especially prosperous.

Today Dongguan is home to about 7 million people. More than 5 million of its residents are migrants who work in the thousands of factories that dot the city, churning out a wide range of products in such huge volumes that recent media accounts have assigned Dongguan the label of "factory of the world." Dongguan's economy has grown at more than 20 percent annually since 1980, and in 2004 its gross domestic product (GDP) was about $14 billion—greater than Iceland's. If one includes only registered urban residents (as in official statistics), Dongguan's GDP per capita of $9,000 in 2004 made it the wealthiest city in China. Even if the city's floating population of migrant workers is included, its GDP per capita in 2004 was still more than $2,000.

Dongguan's development since the 1970s, and particularly in the last decade, exemplifies (perhaps in exaggerated fashion) the economic forces shaping East Asia's middle-income economies (see the table below).

Location and favorable factor prices undoubtedly spurred Dongguan's early growth. For the first decade and a half after China's reforms began, small and medium enterprises from both Hong Kong, China, and Taiwan, China, were attracted to Dongguan by plentiful supply of land and low-cost labor, and by its proximity to both Guangzhou and Hong Kong, China. Despite these factors, Dongguan's rapid growth in the 1990s can best be understood through ***economies of scale,*** whether in the production of intermediate goods or differentiated products, and ***agglomeration effects,*** within and across industries. Combined with reductions in transport costs and improvements in logistics, technological progress demonstrates that such effects have emerged as important characteristics of global production.

The internal scale economies are obvious. In 2005 a single plant in Dongguan manufactured more than 30 percent of the magnetic recording heads used in hard disk drives worldwide. Another produced 60 percent of the electronic learning devices sold in the U.S. market. A third produced nearly 30 million mobile phones, more than enough to provide a mobile phone for every man, woman, and child in Peru or República Bolivariana de Venezuela.

Agglomeration or external scale economies are equally visible. The knowledge spillovers and lower logistics costs from locating close to input providers and export traders have produced globally important industry clusters for knitted woolens, footwear, furniture, and toys. But the cluster that has dominated the industrial landscape of Dongguan since the mid-1990s is telecommunications, electronics, and computer components. Of the parts and components used in manufacturing and processing personal computers, 95 percent can be sourced in Dongguan, and for several products, Dongguan's factories account for more than 40 percent of global production.

Contributed by Shubham Chaudhuri.
Source: Gill and Kharas 2007.

Dongguan in numbers

Average annual GDP growth, 1980–2005 (%)	22.0	GDP (US$, billions)	14.2
Population: registered residents (millions)	1.6	Population: total, estimated (millions)	7.0
GDP per registered resident (US$)	8,999	GDP per capita (US$)	2,070
Exports (US$, billions)	35.2	Imports (billion US$)	29.3
Government revenues (US$, billions)	1.0	Government expenditures (US$, billions)	1.2
Electricity consumption (kWh, billions)	35.2	Water consumption (ft^3, billions)	1.5

Environmental impact indicators

Sulfur dioxide emissions (tons, thousands)	199.4	Industrial waste water (tons, millions)	225
Sulfur dioxide emissions meeting standards (%)	92.9	Industrial water discharge meeting standards (%)	90.1
Industrial solid wastes (tons, thousands)	28.6	Industrial solid wastes meeting standards (%)	86.5

Global market share in 2002 of computer and electronics components manufactured in Dongguan (%)

Magnetic heads and computer cases	40	Scanners and mini-motors	20
Copper-clad boards and disk drives	30	Keyboards	16
AC capacitators and fly-back transformers	25	Motherboards	15

Source: Dongguan Government 2005.

The main findings:

- *Developing economies are entering a new realm of agglomeration.* A century of experience indicates that as countries develop from agricultural to industrial to service-oriented production, entrepreneurs and workers leave behind not just their villages and their agrarian occupations, but also a world in which scale does not matter much. More and more of them enter not just larger and denser settlements, but also a world in which scale matters—where production and distribution enjoy scale economies, especially those associated with places. Proximity matters more, not just for access to markets for goods and services, but also for access to ideas.

- *A portfolio of places is needed for economic growth.* Research over the last generation indicates that different forms of human settlement facilitate agglomeration economies for different forms of production. A somewhat-oversimplified (but not altogether incorrect) generalization would be that market towns facili-

tate scale economies in marketing and distributing agricultural produce, medium-size cities provide localization economies for manufacturing industries, and the largest cities provide diverse facilities and foster innovation in business, government, and education services.

- *Policy makers have often misjudged the potency of market forces.* Many policy makers perceive cities as constructs of the state—to be managed and manipulated to serve some social objective. In reality, cities and towns, just like firms and farms, are creatures of the market. Just as firms and farms deliver final and intermediate goods and services, towns and cities deliver agglomeration economies to producers and workers. So city administrators are better advised to learn what their city does, and to help it do this well, rather than try to abruptly change the course of their city's destiny. Planners and policy makers should see their role as prudent managers of a portfolio of places, to get the most from agglomeration economies.

Table 4.1   A dozen economies of scale

Type of economy of scale			Example
Internal		1. Pecuniary	Being able to purchase intermediate inputs at volume discounts
	Technological	2. Static technological	Falling average costs because of fixed costs of operating a plant
		3. Dynamic technological	Learning to operate a plant more efficiently over time
External or agglomeration	*Localization*	Static	4. "Shopping"	Shoppers are attracted to places where there are many sellers
			5. "Adam Smith" specialization	Outsourcing allows both the upstream input suppliers and downstream firms to profit from productivity gains because of specialization
			6. "Marshall" labor pooling	Workers with industry-specific skills are attracted to a location where there is a greater concentration.[a]
		Dynamic	7. "Marshall-Arrow-Romer" learning by doing	Reductions in costs that arise from repeated and continuous production activity over time and which spill over between firms in the same place
	Urbanization	Static	8. "Jane Jacobs" innovation	The more that different things are done locally, the more opportunity there is for observing and adapting ideas from others
			9. "Marshall" labor pooling	Workers in an industry bring innovations to firms in other industries; similar to no. 6 above, but the benefit arises from the diversity of industries in one location.
			10. "Adam Smith" division of labor	Similar to no. 5 above, the main difference being that the division of labor is made possible by the existence of many different buying industries in the same place
		Dynamic	11. "Romer" endogenous growth	The larger the market, the higher the profit; the more attractive the location to firms, the more jobs there are; the more labor pools there, the larger the market—and so on
		12. "Pure" agglomeration		Spreading fixed costs of infrastructure over more taxpayers; diseconomies arise from congestion and pollution

Source: Adapted from Kilkenny 2006.
a. For a formalization, see Krugman 1991a.

This chapter discusses, in general terms, the implications of experience and analysis for reshaping urbanization strategies in the developing world. Chapter 7 continues this task of reframing the debate over urban strategies.

A guide to scale economies

The benefits of increasing scale can be either internal or external to an individual firm or farm. External economies are synonymous with "agglomeration economies," which include the benefits of localization (being near other producers of the same commodity or service) and urbanization (being close to producers of a wide range of commodities and services). Consumption externalities also are associated with agglomeration, but these are not yet well studied in the literature.[2] So, this chapter deals with production-related scale economies (see table 4.1).[3]

- *Internal economies* arise from the larger size of a plant to better exploit fixed costs (numbers 1 through 3 in table 4.1). A larger steel mill can get volume discounts from suppliers—implying fixed costs of transport and trade—and reap the benefits of dividing labor within the firm.

- *Localization economies* arise from a larger number of firms in the same industry and the same place (numbers 4 through 7 in table 4.1). Spatial proximity helps because immediate access to competitors in the same sector allow firms to stay abreast of market information in negotiating with customers and suppliers.[4] Clustered firms can also share a larger and more dependable pool of specialized labor.

- *Urbanization economies* arise from a larger number of different industries in the same place (numbers 8 through 11 in table 4.1). A management consulting company can benefit from locating near business schools, financial service providers, and manufacturers.

Agglomeration economies depend not just on size (a big city or industry) but also on urban interactions. They are traditionally classified as localization economies arising from *within-industry* economic

interactions, and as urbanization economies, arising from *between-industry* interactions.[5] The reasons for producers to gain from proximity to others depend on the sharing of capital inputs, information, and labor. They also depend on improving the matches between production requirements and types of land, labor, and intermediate inputs—and learning about new techniques and products (see box 4.2).

Internal scale economies are higher in heavier industries

Internal increasing returns to scale are found in manufacturing and services, based on various sources of data. The internal scale economies range from negligible or low among light industries, to high among heavy and high-technology industries (see table 4.2). Based on engineering estimates, a summary of sector-specific studies that examines the minimum efficiency scale of production and cost-saving finds significant increasing returns in motor vehicles, other

BOX 4.2 *Sharing, matching, and learning*

Three reasons explain why firms in a particular industry often locate close to each other. Geographic concentration helps in—

- *Sharing.* Broadening the market for input suppliers, allowing them to exploit internal economies of scale in production (average costs decline as the scale of production rises). This sharing of inputs also permits suppliers to provide highly specialized goods and services tailored to the needs of their buyers. The result is higher profits for all, accompanied by easier access to a broader range of inputs.
- *Matching.* Expanding the availability of the range of skills required by employers to facilitate better matching to their distinctive needs. At the same time, workers find it less risky to be in locations with many possible employers.
- *Learning.* Accelerating spillovers of knowledge and allowing workers and entrepreneurs to learn from each other.

The ability to go beyond industry-specific sharing, matching, and learning (localization economies) to citywide processes (urbanization economies) requires additional mechanisms. These include the effects of cumulative causation and the interpenetration of production and trade across industries. They also include gains from the cross-fertilization of ideas. The concentration of workers and suppliers leads to a concentration of consumer demands.

If economies of scale are large and unexhausted, and if firms can compete not only on price but also through product differentiation, strong centripetal forces come into play. In addition, by formally introducing distance (the cost of shipping inputs and outputs), the framework used in this Report provides useful insights into the centrifugal forces that explain spatial dispersion in a country.

Sources: Gill and Kharas 2007, based on Duranton and Puga 2004.

Table 4.2   Internal scale economies are low in light industries and high in heavy industries

Findings	Data source
Constant returns to scale: apparel, leather, footwear, textiles, wood products	Based on trade data (Antweiler and Trefler 2002)
High increasing returns to scale: machinery, pharmaceuticals, instruments, iron and steel, petroleum and coal products	
Constant returns or low increasing returns to scale: leather goods, footwear and clothing, timber and wood, textiles	Based on engineering estimates to examine cost gradients and changes in minimum efficiency scale (Junius 1997, cited from Prateen 1988 and Emerson and others 1988)
High increasing returns to scale: Motor vehicles, other means of transportation, chemicals, engineering, printing and publishing	
Low increasing returns to scale: footwear, apparel, food products, leather	Based on markups in manufacturing industries for 14 OECD countries (Junius 1997, cited from Oliveira and others 1996)
High increasing returns to scale: tobacco, pharmaceuticals, office and computing machinery, railroad equipment	
Low increasing returns to scale: apparel, leather products, textiles	Based on markups of prices over marginal costs for two-digit sectors in the United States covering 1953–84 (24 sectors) (Roeger 1995)
High increasing returns to scale: electric, gas, and sanitary services, motor vehicles and equipment, chemicals, tobacco	
Low increasing returns to scale: textiles, milk products, lumber mills, fish oil and meal products	Based on production function estimates for 1963 Census of Manufacturing Establishments in Norway (27 industries) (Griliches and Ringstad 1971)
High increasing returns to scale: basic metal, transport equipment, cement products, fixtures, beverages	
Low increasing returns to scale: clothing, knitting, leather, textiles	Based on cost and profit data in (167 industries) four-digit SIC manufacturing industries for 1970 in Canada (Baldwin and Gorecki 1986) and labor productivity and output estimates for 90 four-digit industries in Canada between 1965 and 1970 (Gupta 1983)
High increasing returns to scale: petroleum, basic and fabricated metal, transport equipment	
Low increasing returns to scale: apparel, wood products	Based on estimates of firm-level production function estimates for 6,665 plants in Chile during 1979–86 (Levinsohn and Petrin 1999)
High increasing returns to scale: other chemicals, food products, printing and publishing	

Source: WDR 2009 team.
Note: OECD = Organisation for Economic Co-operation and Development; SIC = Standard Industrial Classification.

transport equipment, chemicals, machinery, engineering, and paper and printing. In the three-digit product category, the highest returns to scale are in books, bricks, dyes, and aircraft.[6] By contrast, internal scale economies are negligible in rubber and plastics, leather and leather goods, footwear and clothing, and textiles.[7]

Based on cost and value added estimates, different sources point to similar findings. A sample of 5,000 manufacturing firms in Norway shows evidence of scale economies at the individual industry level.[8] For Canadian industries at the four-digit level, returns to scale average 10 percent for 107

manufacturing sectors, with clothing, knitting, leather, and textiles at the lower end of the spectrum.[9] Increasing output cuts costs in U.S. manufacturing, in the industries of middle-income countries (Chile), and in the European car, truck, and consumer durables industries.[10,11]

Based on trade data, a third of all goods-producing industries have increasing returns to scale.[12,13] Manufacturing industries with the highest plant-level economies and industry-level externalities are petroleum and coal products, petroleum refining, pharmaceuticals, machinery, and iron and steel. Industries with constant returns include footwear, leather, textiles, apparel, and furniture.

Markups are another source of information. Because increasing returns to scale confer market power on firms, markups of price over marginal cost can be a proxy for plant-level scale economies. Studies find a range of markups for U.S. manufacturing, from 15 percent in apparel to more than 200 percent in the electric, gas, and sanitary services. For 36 manufacturing sectors across 19 member countries of the Organisation for Economic Co-operation and Development (OECD), the highest markups are in tobacco, drugs and medicines, and office and computing machinery—and the lowest in footwear, apparel, and wood products.[14]

While manufacturing data dominate the literature, increasing returns in services also are evident. The best-studied sector is electric power generation, where the internal increasing returns to scale are considerable.[15] The highest markups are in utilities and sanitary services.[16] Scale economies also are found in banking and finance.[17] A study of commercial banks in 75 countries shows that banks with larger loans and deposits have lower average costs—and that banks operating in larger financial systems require less proportionate increases in financial capital and have lower risk management costs.[18]

Localization economies arise from input-sharing and competition within the industry

Localization economies come from geographically concentrated groups of firms, linked by the technology they use, the markets they serve, the products and services they provide, and the skills they require. Competitive pressures that force firms in the same sector to innovate or fail also lead to productivity growth. Conditions tend to be competitive when upstream and downstream firms and associated institutions in a particular industry (say, electronic machinery or petrochemicals)—including universities and trade associations—"cluster" together. Other channels for localization economies are the less easily measured "Marshall-Arrow-Romer externalities,"[19] which come mainly from knowledge spillovers.

Proximity to similar firms influences the location decisions of firms. Consider the hosiery industry in the United States. Shortly after 1900 New York City became the U.S. center for garment production and distribution. But after World War II garment production moved south, to North Carolina.[20] Many knitting and weaving mills moved to be closer to the supply of yarn and to take advantage of cheaper power, labor, and land.

Today, the hosiery industry, localized in North Carolina, boasts many brands—among them, *Sheer Energy, Silken Mist, Just My Size,* and *No Nonsense*—all competing in a $2 billion market. According to the U.S. Census Bureau, about 150 establishments producing women's full-length and knee-length hosiery in the early 2000s, half the nation's total, were located in North Carolina. They shipped $973 million worth of hosiery, about 75 percent of the national total, and employed 13,497 people, including 11,567 production workers.[21] Adding men's socks and stockings, more than half of a $6 billion industry is in North Carolina.

One reason textile producers went to North Carolina was to exploit productivity gains from proximity to upstream yarn producers. The yarn and pantyhose industries are tightly knit—in relationships delicately stitched together at each step of production—but fiercely competitive. Macfield, a textile giant and a leading producer of yarns for pantyhose, socks, outerwear, upholstery, and industrial products operates five plants in North Carolina and employs about a quarter of the yarn industry's labor force. About six of every 10 pairs of sheer hosiery sold in the United States were knitted with Macfield yarn.[22] Together with other large North Carolina producers (Unifi, Regal, and Spanco), they make up more than three-quarters of the industry's $3.7 billion worth of textured yarn products.[23] The localization of the yarn and hosiery industries in North Carolina is a powerful manifestation of intra-industry external economies.

Urbanization economies come from industrial diversity that fosters innovation

As cities grow, urbanization economies become more important.[24] Urban diversity can foster the exchange of ideas and technology to produce greater innovation and growth.[25] Firms in different industries can share indivisible facilities or public goods, a wider variety of intermediate input suppliers, a larger pool of narrowly specialized workers, and risks. The evidence of greater importance of across-industry knowledge spillovers can be seen in established cities. In fairly mature cities, such as Los Angeles, and Philadelphia, competition and city diversity help employment growth, indicative of urbanization economies of between-sector innovation.[26] On New York's Wall Street and in the city of London, financial firms, insurance companies, and banking syndicates benefit from being close to one another. And co-location stimulates the growth of other specialist services, such as legal, software, data processing, advertising, and management consulting firms. These clustered firms, by providing a thicker market for highly educated individuals, benefit from drawing on the same large pool of human capital. They also gain from the generation and diffusion of knowledge amongst one another.

Evidence of urban agglomeration economies comes primarily from developed countries.[27] But there is also evidence of external economies in developing countries, wherever data are available. A survey of 12,400 manufacturing firms in 120 cities in China points to the higher productivity of firms in more populous cities.[28] Agglomeration economies in Indonesian

---

BOX 4.3 *Agglomeration economies in Indonesia*

Much of the rigorous evidence of agglomeration economies comes from developed countries. An exception is Indonesia, where recent research helps to identify the determinants of industrial concentration. The analysis focuses on four broad groups—chemicals (including petroleum, rubber, and plastics); textiles (including garments, leather, and footwear); nonmetallic minerals (including glass, ceramics, and cement); and machinery (including electrical and nonelectrical machines, transportation equipment, and instruments). It sheds light on how the size and type of scale economies influence the extent and pattern of agglomeration in a developing country.

Localization economies—the benefits of locating near other firms in the same industry—have been more important than urbanization economies for manufacturing, and static agglomeration economies are more important than dynamic (or learning related) externalities. The sector-specific findings of tests for static externalities show that

- Localization economies are strong for textiles and chemicals.
- Urbanization economies are strong for nonmetallic minerals and machinery, though weak during some periods.

Activities subject to urbanization and dynamic economies are poor candidates for policies that seek to spread out economic mass within a country (see chapter 8 for a more detailed discussion). Such firms prefer to stay put, since this helps learning, and they thrive in fairly large and diverse cities. The agglomeration economies for textiles and chemicals (largely static and local) indicate that policies to deconcentrate production in these industries might succeed if accompanied by improvements in infrastructure and governance in the areas chosen for relocation. The agglomeration economies make the nonmetallic minerals and machinery (essentially static and urban) likely to resist relocation to smaller urban centers.

Source: Kuncoro, forthcoming.

---

manufacturing between 1980 and 2003 vary over time; however, in the broadest terms, these benefits are mainly static rather than dynamic and somewhat more likely to arise from localization than from urbanization (see box 4.3).

A different realm

Countries develop by shifting their economies from traditional subsistence-based agricultural activities to higher-value manufacturing and services. Along the way, firms rather than farms become the dominant production unit. The production of differentiated manufactured goods and services increases as a share of the economy's output. Between 1900 and 2000 the share of the global population in industrial or service-dominant urban localities rose from 15 percent to 47 percent. The global employment share in agriculture among working-age

people fell from just over 55 percent in 1960 to about 33 percent in 2004. Production technology shifts away from constant returns to increasing returns to scale. And over time, scale-augmenting technical change boosts scale economies. Imperfect and monopolistic competition become the dominant forms of market structure.

The world is more urban, and the concentration of economic mass in the densest urban centers is greater as well. In 1900 the number of people in the largest 100 cities added up to just 4.3 percent of the world's population. The same 100 cities now have 7.5 percent of the total, and the largest 100 cities, almost 10.5 percent. Despite ample open space, almost all recent development in the United States has been less than 1 kilometer from earlier developments.[29] Even today, only about 2 percent of the land area of the United States is built up or paved. Only agglomeration economies can explain this extreme clustering of firms and workers in cities.

As producers seek scale economies, agriculture disperses but manufacturing clusters

As economies develop, farms spread out to exploit scale economies in production. In the United States about 1,500 kilograms of agricultural products are produced annually to feed each American, whereas the Chinese make do with about 600 kilograms per person. In 2005 the average cropland in the United States was 20.4 hectares per farmer, in Australia it was 45 hectares, and in Canada it was 47 hectares. Average farm size in Brazil is about 19 hectares.[30] But scale economies in agriculture are generally difficult to obtain in low-income countries. The cropland per farmer was a fraction of that in developed countries: 0.16 hectares in China, 0.30 in Bangladesh and Indonesia, and 1.20 in Nigeria.[31]

As economies develop, manufacturing and services become more important, firms cram in closer together to harness agglomeration economies. In France, the United Kingdom, and the United States, 75–95 percent of industry is localized (clustered or concentrated relative to overall economic activity), while less than 15 percent is dispersed.[32] In the United States more than a third of aerospace engines are produced in three cities: Hartford with about 18 percent of total employment, and Cincinnati and Phoenix with another 18 percent together.[33] Over time the spatial concentration of industries in U.S. states has increased.[34] Using continuous space without considering administrative boundaries and based on concentration of plants, more than half of the United Kingdom's 122 four-digit industries are localized, and only 24 percent are dispersed. The rest are randomly distributed.[35]

Spatial clustering is more pronounced with high-skill and high-technology industries (electronic computing machinery, process control instruments, semiconductors, and pharmaceuticals) than light industries. This is consistent with the documented findings of higher-scale effects in heavier industries. High-skill and high-tech industries have more capital-intensive production technology. They are also likely to benefit more from the various mechanisms that generate external economies (discussed earlier).

In the Republic of Korea the ranking of industries by their localization economies follows the ranking of industries by their spatial concentration across cities. Heavy and transport industries (metals, chemicals, and transport equipment) tend to be concentrated in a few highly specialized cities to take advantage of local scale externalities, while traditional or light industries with low scale externalities (food and textiles) are more dispersed.[36] High-tech industries (computers, aircraft, medical instruments, and electronic components) tend to be more concentrated than durable-good, machinery-related industries (metal works, industrial, refrigeration, and machinery and equipment).[37] Cities in the Republic of Korea have also become more specialized.[38]

Services become even more densely clustered than manufacturing

As countries move to a more mature phase of development, their economies become more knowledge based and service oriented. The spatial concentration of activity also rises (see chapter 2).[39,40] The important types of agglomeration economy change as development progresses. In particular, as an economy becomes more knowledge based, knowledge spillovers, which require proximity, become more important. Evidence suggests that knowledge industries are spatially concentrated.[41]

Services are even more spatially concentrated than manufacturing—for two reasons. First, they tend to use less land per employee. Banks, insurance companies, hospitals, and schools can operate comfortably in high-rise buildings that economize on land and allow for high density. Second, because of external economies, business services have even greater potential for agglomeration, as firms serve one another: every bank needs advertising, every advertising firm a bank account. The potential for codependence and agglomeration is thus intrinsic to services.[42]

Services are prominent among the most agglomerated industries in the United States.[43] Larger cities have been amassing service jobs from areas less than 20 kilometers away.[44] Between 1972 and 1992, jobs in the United States became more spatially concentrated, driven primarily by the rising localization of service activities in larger cities,[45] as small and medium-size counties lost jobs to the more urban areas.[46] For instance, in Suffolk County, Massachusetts, which includes Boston, 35 percent of the workforce is in business services, nearly twice the national average of 18 percent.[47] In the United Kingdom nearly 60 percent of all venture capital offices are in London.[48] London-based venture capital offices favor investment in London-based small and medium enterprises to get better information: they can easily visit and monitor these enterprises. As communication costs fall, services become more tradable, allowing providers to take advantage of narrower specialization and agglomeration economies. For instance, financial services can be disaggregated into more refined categories of retail banking, consumer credit and financing, commercial and corporate banking, investment banking, and so on. And within investment banking, there is further specialization in mergers and acquisitions, corporate finance, fixed income, debt management, and the like.

Cities facilitate scale economies of all types

A plant in an isolated location can benefit from internal scale economies, but unless it is situated in an area of density, it cannot enjoy the competitive benefits associated with localization or urbanization economies. Towns and cities bring together large pools of skilled labor and suppliers of specialized intermediate inputs and by doing so, enhance employer-employee and buyer-seller matches. Input-sharing is an important channel for agglomeration economies.[49] Density of activity allows more refined specialization and a wider variety of intermediate inputs. Averaging across industries, a firm's relocation from a less-dense location (of 499 or fewer neighboring employees in the same industry) to a denser location (of 10,000–24,999 neighboring employees) results in a 3 percent increase in purchased input intensity.[50] The composition of a city emerges from the scope for agglomeration economies and their interaction with other aspects of microeconomic behavior.

Large cities with more firms allow workers to hedge against sector-specific risks. Smaller specialized cities expose workers to greater industry-specific shocks but provide favorable match-specific advantages. In both cases the concentration of economic activity lowers the search costs between firms and workers, which results in fewer unfilled vacancies, lower risk of job loss, and shorter durations of unemployment. The large variety and quantity of inputs to share in cities also implies better quality-matching. For instance, because of the better matching possible, married couples with university education, are increasingly found in large cities, up from 32 percent in 1940 to 50 percent in 1990.[51] Cities make it easier for producers to find inputs and for customers to experiment and discover new possibilities. Examples of easy diffusion of information and social learning range from the congregation of diners in certain restaurants, to the propagation of

rumors, to the word-of-mouth learning in neighborhoods.[52]

Learning mechanisms also explain agglomeration in cities.[53] As Alfred Marshall implied, when knowledge spillovers exist, "The mysteries of the trade become no mysteries but are as it were in the air."[54] Knowledge spillovers are difficult to measure, because they can seldom be traced through transactions. With patent citations, however, it is possible to identify a paper trail for some knowledge spillovers. U.S. patent citations are spatially concentrated, with citations 5 to 10 times more likely to come from the same standard metropolitan statistical area as originator patents.[55] Another strand of research focuses on workers as the primary vehicles of knowledge, implying that economies with substantial labor mobility across industries will exhibit a greater spread of ideas and growth.[56]

Agglomeration economies are amplified by density and attenuated by distance

Cities obviously reflect the demand for density. People choose to live close to one another, paying high rents and tolerating crime and congestion. This density helps reduce distances of all types. Cities are thus a natural market creator and a conduit for internal and external scale economies. Firms are drawn to dense areas concentrated with people and infrastructure by the possibility of serving a large local market from a large plant at low transport costs.[57] Increasing return-to-scale production technology leads to large factories with many workers. The sizable workforce forms a large local market. By reducing transport costs, cities with a large local demand attract firms in different industries. So a self-reinforcing process of agglomeration that begins with the expanding local market further raises industry productivity.

Plants in dense economic environments tend to be larger.[58] As local market scale increases, firms are more likely to outsource their service functions to local suppliers.[59] This outsourcing further encourages competition and diversity in the local business service market, which reinforces outsourcing. Firms are attracted to locations with large concentrations of other firms in their industry and with large demand.[60] The large and growing academic literature suggests that doubling city size will increase productivity by 3–8 percent.[61] In the Republic of Korea, a plant in a city with 1,000 workers could, without altering its input mix, increase output by 20–25 percent simply by relocating to a city that has 15,000 workers in the same industry.[62] And the spatial concentration of people reduces the cost of producing knowledge because information transmission, competition, spying, imitation, learning, innovation, and the commercialization of new ideas are easier.[63] In the United States a staggering 96 percent of innovations occur in metropolitan areas.[64]

Agglomeration economies are influenced by geographic scope, and the density of economic activity and the distance between economic agents influence the productivity gains from scale economies (see table 4.3). For example, doubling the density of economic activity in European Nomenclature of Territorial Units for Statistics (NUTS1) regions can increase total factor productivity growth by 0.42 percentage points a year.[65] Evidence from Brazil and the United States indicates that doubling the distance to dense metropolitan centers reduces productivity by 15 percent; doubling the distance from 280 to 550 kilometers reduces profits by 6 percent. The concept of distance can be generalized, in this context, from distance in physical space to distance in industrial space. For example, spillovers between industries are more likely if industries share related scientific facilities.[66] Furthermore, the extent to which distance attenuates agglomeration economies differs for different types of agglomeration. For example, knowledge spillovers that rely on face-to-face communication decay more quickly with distance than the home market effect.[67]

A portfolio of places

Adam Smith introduced scale economies, factor mobility, and transport costs as central to understanding the nature and causes of the wealth of nations. But until the 1980s most economists were happier to anchor their inquiries on another concept

Table 4.3   Scale economies amplify with density and attenuate with distance

Finding	Data sources
Scale economies amplify with density . . .	
Doubling economic density increases productivity by 6 percent	1988 data on output per worker in U.S. states (Ciccone and Hall 1996)
Doubling employment density increases productivity by 4.5–5.0 percent	Data for the late 1980s on nonagricultural private value added per worker in European NUTS regions (Ciccone 2002)
A one-standard-deviation increase in the share of own-industry local employment in the first period will raise that industry's employment level by 16–31 percent in a later period	Data on five traditional manufacturing industries in 224 U.S. metropolitan areas between 1970 and 1987 (Henderson, Kuncoro, and Turner 1995)
A 10-percent increase in local own-industry employment results in 0.6–0.8 percent increase in plant output, for the same level of inputs	Republic of Korea city-industry data for 1983, 1989, 1991–93 (Henderson, Lee, and Lee 2001)
and attenuate with distance.	
Increasing distance from the city center by 1 percent leads to a 0.13 percent decline in productivity	1980 data for 356 new manufacturing firms in Brazil (Hansen 1990)
Doubling the distance to a regional market center lowers profits by 6 percent	Firm data in auto-component and agricultural machinery in Brazil and the United States (Henderson 1994)
Doubling travel time to a city center reduces productivity by 15 percent	Data for eight industries in Brazil (Sveikaukas and others 1985)
Own-county (lagged and contemporaneous) effect on plant productivity, but no effect from neighboring county	Plant-level data on productivity, 1972–92, in 742 U.S. counties (Henderson 2003b)
Effects of own-industry employment on new plant openings attenuate rapidly within the first five 1-mile concentric rings	12 million U.S. establishments from Dun & Bradstreet Marketplace database (Rosenthal and Strange 2003)

Source: WDR 2009 team.

introduced in *The Wealth of Nations,* that of the "invisible hand" of perfect competition.[68] But perfect competition is an artificial theoretical construct: it assumes a large number of infinitesimal firms with negligible influence over market prices, even in the immediate vicinity of the firm's location. Its assumption of constant returns to scale further implies the so-called problem of "backyard capitalism."[69] That is, in the world of constant returns to scale, small-scale production is as efficient as large-scale production, so every household should be producing a fully diversified range of goods and services in its own backyard. Economics professors, when pressed by students to give a real-world example of such an industry, would offer subsistence agriculture—small farms producing wheat or rice, whose produce could not be distinguished from those of others. Never mind that most people no longer worked on small farms in countries that had grown out of poverty. It led to convenient characterizations of the economy in which all firms and workers were identical, so one firm or worker could be considered representative of all. Scale economies were inconvenient—they required acknowledging that specialization differentiated people and products.

Occasionally, the contradiction between internal increasing returns and perfect competition would surface, but because of the technical difficulties it raised, it quickly would be buried again.[70] Then, during the 1970s, two economists at Princeton University proposed a technical solution to model increasing returns to scale, opening a door for researchers to the same realm that so many firms and workers had inhabited since the industrial revolution.[71]

By the late 1980s scale economies were standard features of the explanations for international trade. By the early 1990s, growth theorists had accepted the need to incorporate imperfect competition among firms into aggregate formulations of an economy. By the mid-1990s, theorists were beginning to show how these ideas could be used to understand the spatial distribution of economic activity, including the rise of towns and cities. With the new economic geography, researchers came to realize that the dichotomy between internal and external economies is often false. Why? Because, in modeling the microfoundations of agglomeration economies, the source of external economies have often been found in the interaction of internal scale economies with other influences, such as transport costs.

Table 4.4   Thirty years of theoretical advance recognize the importance of scale economies

Subject	Main insights	Key publications
Industrial organization, 1970s	Increasing returns to scale and imperfect competition can be incorporated into formal economic models	Spence 1976; Dixit and Stiglitz 1977
Urban economics, 1970s	External economies within cities and systems of cities; different levels of agglomerations are related to city functions	Mills 1972; Diamond and Mirrless 1973; and Henderson 1974
International trade, 1980s	Increasing returns and imperfect competition explain intraindustry trade between countries with similar endowments; initial endowments may, through trade and specialization, influence the long-run rate of growth; trade unleashes forces of both convergence and divergence	Krugman 1980, 1981; Ethier 1982; Helpman and Krugman 1985; Grossman and Helpman 1995
Economic geography, 1990s	Increasing returns-to-scale activities are characterized by agglomeration and imperfect competition, while constant returns-to-scale activities remain dispersed and competitive, helping to explain spatial distribution of economic activity and growth of cities	Krugman 1991; Fujita, Krugman, and Venables 1999; Henderson 1999
Endogenous growth, 1980s	Perfect competition and knowledge-related or human capital–related externalities imply aggregate increasing returns and explain why growth rates may not fall over time and why wealth levels across countries do not converge	Romer 1986; Lucas Jr. 1988
Endogenous growth, 1990s	Imperfect competition explains why the incentive to spend on R&D does not fall, and knowledge spillovers explain why R&D costs fall over time, resulting in more and better products that fuel growth	Romer 1990; Grossman and Helpman 1991; Aghion and Howitt 1992
Endogenous growth, 2000s	Imperfect competition and Schumpeterian entry and exit of firms, with entrants bringing new technologies, explain how a country's growth and optimal policies vary with distance to the technology frontier; knowledge accumulation in cities leads to growth	Aghion and Howitt 2005; Rossi-Hansberg and Wright 2007; Duranton 2007

Source: Adapted from Gill and Kharas 2007.

Recognizing scale economies: recent theoretical advances

The literature on the microeconomic foundations of agglomeration economies flourished in the last 20 years by combining models in the paradigms summarized in table 4.4 and insights about urban economics that emphasize the tension between benefits from the concentration of economic activity and costs arising from that spatial concentration.[72] In general, researchers have progressively recognized that economic growth has different impacts on firms and workers depending on their sector and location. The underlying reason is the love for variety in consumption and the economies of scale in production; the proximate reasons are product differentiation, monopolistic power, specialization, and location externalities.

The formal recognition of scale economies, externalities, and imperfect competition makes economic theory conform more closely to the world in which policy makers live. The policy implications of this work arise from the way economic production relates to trade, ideas, and cities.

- *Intraindustry trade.* The main insight coming from a formal recognition of increasing returns to scale and product differentiation is that trade may take place between economies that are similar in factor endowments: both interindustry *and* intraindustry trade may profitably take place. The main implication is that countries may, in theory, encourage some activities and ensure comparative advantage.

- *Idea-driven economies.* The insight is that the nonrival nature of ideas makes them different from other factors of production, such as capital, land, and labor, in that the market may underinvest in the creation of new ideas. The main implication is that governments should, theoretically, subsidize some strands of research and development (R&D), such as those that will ensure the continuance of the comparative advantage a country has acquired in certain areas.

- *City-based growth.* The main insight is that activities that display increasing returns generated by factors external to a firm tend to be concentrated in cities, while those displaying constant returns remain more dispersed. The main implication is that policies to keep cities business-friendly and livable become more important as economies develop.

Urban systems exhibit some stylized patterns. Larger cities tend to be more diversified and service oriented: they innovate, invent, breed new firms, and expel mature industries.[73] Smaller cities tend to be industrially specialized: they produce or manufacture and receive relocated industries from diversified cities.[74] The relative city-size distribution and industrial concentration in specific cities tend to be stable over time. An urban system tends to be made up of a few large diversified cities and many smaller, more specialized, cities.[75]

The stylized observation in most countries is an urban hierarchy of a few large cities and many smaller cities with varied economic functions.[76] At the global level, "world cities" at the top of the hierarchy, such as New York, London, Paris, and Tokyo, are characterized by a diverse industrial structure, predominantly service based, and a labor force with a wide range of skills.[77]

Smaller cities specialize, receiving industries as they mature and relocate

Even after controlling for natural comparative advantage, externalities are still important in explaining the patterns of specialization and diversity among cities (see table 4.5). The production of nontraditional items is more concentrated in diverse U.S. cities, while standardized traditional goods are concentrated in smaller specialized cities. Similarly, in Japan, smaller cities are specialized, while low-tech activity and standardized high-tech production processes are located offshore. Likewise, in the Republic of Korea, large cities are more service oriented and smaller cities, manufacturing oriented.[78]

Mid-size cities tend to specialize in mature industries, not new ones, and larger cities specialize in services not manufacturing.[79] Improved infrastructure and falling transport costs have encouraged standardized manufacturing production to move out of high-rent centers to smaller cities.

Table 4.5 Agglomeration economies vary by city size and profile, and by the industry life cycle

Main finding	Data
Localization economies are more important for heavy industries; urbanization economies are more important for light industries	Data for two-digit manufacturing industries in Japan (Nakamura 1985)
Localization economies become less important, giving way to urbanization economies, as cities expand in size	Cross-sectional data for the United States and Brazil (Henderson 1986)
Scale economies from labor pooling are stronger in newer and expanding markets, while those from knowledge spillovers and specialized asset-sharing are more important in mature markets	Annual firm employment data for four U.S. metropolitan areas and three two-digit industries (Hammond and Von Hagen 1994)
For mature capital goods industries, there is evidence of localization economies but none of urbanization economies; for new high-tech industries, there is evidence of both localization and urbanization economies	Panel data of 742 urban counties for 1970–87 (Henderson, Kuncoro, and Turner 1995).
For all industries both localization and urbanization effects are important. For traditional industries most effects die out after four or five years, but for high-tech industries, the effects can persist longer. The biggest effects are typically from conditions of three to four years ago, in the county and metropolitan area	Data for five traditional and three new high-tech manufacturing industries in 224 metropolitan areas between 1970 and 1987 (Henderson 1997)
The historical industrial environment of cities matters. In fairly mature cities urbanization economies encourage industrial growth	Growth data for the largest industries (1956–87) in 170 U.S. cities (Glaeser and others 1992)
For high-tech industries a 1-standard-deviation increase in diversity of the local manufacturing base increases productivity by 60 percent, but diversity has no effect on standard industries (such as textiles, or food).	City-industry data for the Republic of Korea, 1983, 1989, 1991–93 (Henderson, Lee, and Lee 2001)

Source: WDR 2009 team.

Production in large cities focuses on services, nonstandardized manufacturing, and R&D.[80] The relocation of manufacturing to the suburbs has been documented in Colombia, Indonesia, the Republic of Korea, and Thailand.[81] It is common to find that services do not deconcentrate from city centers to their surrounding suburbs.[82]

Large cities diversify, incubate new ideas and firms, and push out mature industries

New firms often start in diverse cities, but they move to specialized ones after they mature. Of all new plants in France, for example, 84 percent were created in cities with above-median diversity.[83] Some 72 percent of firm relocations are from an area with above-median diversity to an area with above-median specialization. In the United States almost all product innovations are in metropolitan areas. Industrial diversity and city size are both good for innovative output.[84] Trial plants are based in large cities in Japan, but mass production plants are in small cities or rural areas. Young firms appear to need a period of experimentation to determine their ideal production process.[85] In the early learning phase, diversified cities act as "nurseries" for firms to try out a variety of processes. Once a firm identifies its ideal process, it can begin mass production in specialized cities, where all firms share similar processes or specializations (see box 4.4).

The different economic functions that cities serve can be seen in the clustering of headquarters from different sectors and concentrations of business services in a few large cities while production plants from each sector congregate in smaller specialized cities. In 1950 there was little difference across U.S. cities in their proportions of managers and production workers. Although the largest cities already housed more managers, there was no clear ranking by city size. By 1980, however, the differences across cities had increased substantially, and a clear ranking by size had emerged. Larger cities had become specialized in management and information-intensive activity, which benefit from face-to-face contacts, and smaller cities had become specialized

in production. This pattern became even more marked during the 1990s.[86]

Many business and economic historians have argued that the extra costs of coordinating and monitoring multilocation firms relative to integrated firms have come down significantly following key developments in transport and communication technologies, as well as new management practices.[87] Technological progress in transport and telecommunication made it less costly for firms to separate their production facilities from their headquarters and management facilities. Firms can locate their production facilities in environments with same-sector specialization, and their headquarters in a metropolis with a concentration of business service employment. Furthermore, the reduced communication costs that make transportation of service industry outputs (through electronic transmittal) cheaper did *not* imply the "death of distance" and the fading of cities into obscurity, contrary to many predictions.[88] In this context, while distance has become less important for transmitting information, it has become more important for transmitting knowledge. Telecommunication can be a complement to, but it is certainly not a strong substitute for, face-to-face interactions, which involve several forms of communication simultaneously, notably body language and verbal conversation (see box 4.5).[89] The geographic distribution of commercial Internet domains suggests that the Internet is a complement to face-to-face interactions (primarily within-city) as well as a substitute for longer-distance communication, such as phone or postal mail.[90]

Activities that cities specialize in are stable, and so are city-size distributions

Externalities imply that history matters. That is, modern-day location patterns for an industry are strongly influenced by the historical industrial environment of cities and thus by the localization economies. Such intangibles include the local stock of knowledge relevant for an industry or a labor force with specific acquired skills. Two otherwise-identical enterprises in the same city could benefit differently from the local agglomeration depending on how long

BOX 4.4 *When sowing and reaping happen in different places: rising interdependence of cities*

Urban specialists and economists have long debated whether specialized or diverse cities are more conducive to growth. Cities that are narrowly specialized create greater economies of agglomeration, so a firm's productivity increases with proximity to similar firms. Meanwhile, a diverse mix of activities makes cities more likely to grow, particularly in new sectors. The main conclusion: both diversity and specialization are important, but at different points in a firm's life cycle. A "balanced" urban system is not one in which all cities are similarly specialized or diversified, but one in which both diversified and specialized cities coexist.

For young firms, urban diversity is more important. A new businessman may not know all the details of the product to be made, what components to use, where to source them, which workers to hire, and how to finance the venture. Firms using similar technologies in different sectors are more likely to share information about new practices and technologies than firms in the same sector. For firms in more standardized or mature industries, urban specialization is more important. These firms typically benefit less from the flexibility from urban diversity, and by locating in a specialized environment, they can better reap the benefits of urban agglomeration economies. For example, auto firms in Detroit lower their costs by sharing parts suppliers, and garment manufacturers in cities like San Pedro Sula in Honduras benefit from thick labor markets that help workers move between fac-

tories as the market adjusts to the whims and fancies of fashion.

Clusters of similar firms are sometimes promoted as the best environment for innovation. But studies find instead that diverse metropolises do better in breeding new products and processes. For example, the adoption of computer-controlled machinery for cutting metals has been faster in situations in which many firms (ranging from furnace manufacturers to aircraft producers) have similar technical needs but are not direct competitors. Firms for which innovating is important (such as electronics producers) prefer diversity during the early innovative phases, and then they relocate to specialized cities for mass production. For manufacturing and services, unlike agriculture, "sowing" and "reaping" can take place in different locations.

Just as product development and mass production increasingly take place at different locations, so too does management and production. Half a century ago the difficulties associated with managing businesses from a distance made firms keep their headquarters and management offices close to their factories. Falling transport and communications costs have made it much easier to manage production from far away (see chapter 6).

As a result, many firms have separated management and production spatially, searching for the best possible conditions for each. For headquarters, this means locations with other headquarters where these firms can, for example, share legal

services or advertising agencies; for production facilities, this means places with other such plants. Headquarters are usually in bigger cities, because professional services tend to exhibit greater economies of agglomeration, are less land-intensive, and employ highly educated employees willing to pay for big-city amenities. If land markets work well, the ensuing increase in land prices prompts production establishments to relocate to smaller, more specialized towns and cities.

Cities in the United States provide a good illustration. In 1950 the ratio of managers to production workers was similar across cities of different sizes. By 1990, however, cities with between 75,000 and 250,000 people had 20 percent fewer managers per production worker than the national average; cities with 1.5 to 5 million people had 20 percent more managers per production worker; and those larger than 5 million people were 50 percent above the national average. A similar trend can be seen in other countries such as France and Germany.

Policy makers should be aware of these developments. Since this growing interdependence manifests itself in plant relocations away from large cities, governments may be tempted to take away resources from them. This would kill the goose that lays the golden eggs, since such relocations to smaller specialized cities are just a later part of a life cycle of firms that large, diverse cities helped give birth to.

Contributed by Diego Puga.

each has been in the city. Similarly, two otherwise identical cities would offer different types of external economies depending on their histories.[91]

The influences of history and specialization are consistent with the observed stability in the relative city-size distribution and the industrial concentration in specific cities over time. Within countries the relative sizes of cities tend to remain unchanged. Among urban specialists, this phenomenon is often represented as a recurring relationship between a city's size relative to the largest city in the country,

known as Zipf's law: a city's population size relative to the primate city is inversely proportional to its rank in the national hierarchy of cities.[92] There is also persistence in the industrial concentration in specific cities.[93]

Among mature industries the persistence in employment patterns across cities is high over time, and the convergence in individual industry employment across cities is slow. This persistence occurs despite high plant and employment turnover rates for individual manufacturing industries, and despite strong evidence that plants

---

BOX 4.5 *Cities continue to thrive as telecommunication costs fall*

As telecommunications improve, cities become more important as a platform for interactions and knowledge transfers. Recent studies in the United States and Japan document the complementary roles of telecommunications and face-to-face interactions: people closer to one another physically call each other more often.

One interpretation is that face-to-face interactions generate more demand for telephone interactions. Since the mid-1980s, when faxes and e-mail became prevalent, business travel has risen more than 50 percent. Another evidence of increased face-to-face interactions with falling telecommunication costs is the phenomenal growth of co-authored articles in economics—from 12 percent in the 1960s to 56 percent in the 1990s. Local, out-of-state, and international co-authorships all rose. Better telecommunications increase long-range interactions, but not at the expense of local interactions.

As ideas become more complex and difficult to communicate, the value of intensive face-to-face interaction rises, and cities become even more important. And if cities are centers of telecommunication technology, improvements in information technology will increase their economic role. The rise of the New York multimedia industry may signal the comparative advantage of large cities in facilitating the difficult information flows in cutting-edge industries. In the developing world, the rise of Bangalore is a case in point.

Sources: Gaspar and Glaeser 1998; Huber 1995; Sassen 1991; and Gottman 1977.

---

relocate as local wages and demand conditions change.[94] Historically, some cities have undergone major sectoral overhauls, but they have tended to be the exceptions.[95]

The persistence of an industry's employment concentration in specific cities, which implies the "lock-in" of industrial structure, can be explained by localization economies. These cities can better compete for and, over time, retain plants and employment in that industry. A larger scale of own-industry activity historically means that firms in that locality today will operate more productively with greater accumulated knowledge about technology, sources of supply of different quality inputs, and local culture and its effect on the legal, business, and institutional climate. These localization advantages are relevant for more traditional manufacturing industries.[96] They explain the longevity of many industrial clusters in certain locations—such as the world-class cutlery cluster in Solingen, Germany, since 1348.[97]

There is also evidence of persisting concentration of particular services in specific cities. The American mutual fund industry began in Boston in 1924, when the Massachusetts Investment Trust was founded. Today, Boston is still home to almost a third of U.S. employment in mutual fund and asset management services. The Hartford insurance industry began even earlier, in the late-eighteenth century. Local merchants insured each other's overseas trading expeditions by sharing their profits and losses. These informal arrangements eventually grew into large insurance companies, starting with the Hartford Fire Insurance Company in 1810. Other major Hartford insurers, including Aetna, Connecticut General, and Travelers, were founded in the early and middle 1800s. Hartford is still known today as the "insurance city," with a wide range of related services such as life insurance, medical insurance, fire/marine/casualty insurance, and pension funds.[98]

Apprehension of market forces

Over the past century, producers and workers in the developing world have sought, and often found, their fortunes in towns and cities. In the past three decades, researchers have analyzed and increasingly understood the gains from urban agglomerations of all shapes and sizes. But it is not yet clear that policy makers appreciate the sheer strength of these market forces and the benefits that come from harnessing them.

More than half the developing world's governments surveyed in 2005 by the UN Population Division expressed a desire to make major changes to the spatial distribution of their populations. Almost three-quarters of developing country officials expressed a strong desire to implement policies to reduce migration into urban areas or to take actions to reverse rural-urban migration trends.[99] Many in developed countries are equally fearful of urbanization in developing countries. "The explosive growth of cities around the world—especially the rise of huge, nation-sized Third World metropolises—has U.S. scientists and officials worried. Chief among their concerns: "megacities increasingly will serve as incubators of diseases, economic disruptions, and endless political crises."[100] This worry was reflected in the goal of the 2006 World Urban Forum, held to discuss "mega-cities with mega problems."[101] The prevalent view was that "cities in the developed world have historically been engines of economic growth. But many cities in the Third World are so dysfunctional that they have become drags on economic progress."[102]

Some of the favored solutions: slow the massive migration to cities, decongest the largest cities in the developing world by establishing new cities, and make the biggest cities centers for cleaner high-technology activities. These solutions all represent a potentially costly misreading of the market forces that drive the spatial transformations for economic development.

A misplaced fear of urbanization

Economic activities in urban areas account for as much as 80 percent of GDP in more urban and industrialized countries. The urban share of economic activity in less developed countries is about 50 percent. Just the 10 largest metropolitan areas in Mexico, which account for a third of the country's population, generate 62 percent of its national value added.[103] In Vietnam, where the share of the urban population is 30 percent, the share of cities in national output is 70 percent. In China 120 cities account for three-quarters of the country's GDP.[104] Clearly cities make a dominant contribution to economic production, even in poor and middle-income countries.

There is also ample evidence that urban areas in developing countries, including those in the poorest countries in Africa, deliver external economies. Consumption in urban and rural households in a broad cross-section of developing countries shows that people with similar observable characteristics enjoy higher consumption attributable purely to their urban location. The gains range from 2 percent in Hungary, the Krygyz Republic, and Poland, to 30 percent in Costa Rica, Ethiopia, India, Romania, and Tanzania, and to more than 80 percent in Angola, Bolivia, and Rwanda (see figure 4.1).

These magnitudes make it futile for policy makers to try to restrict the flow of people to urban areas. Even when restrictions have stemmed migration flows, the

Figure 4.1 The urban premium for household consumption can be considerable

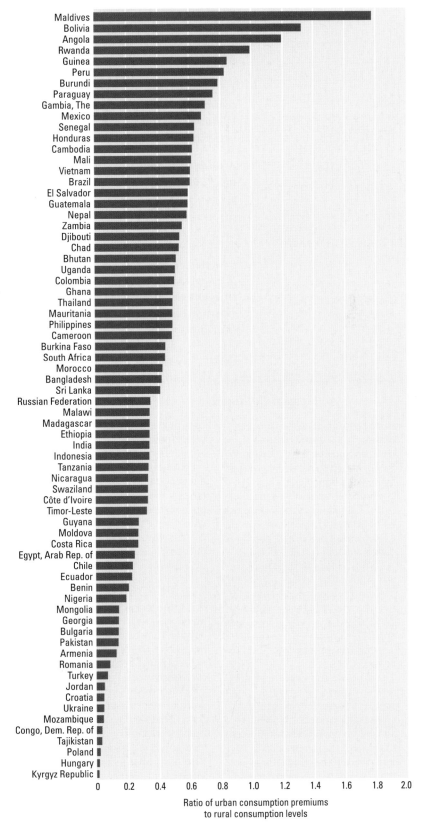

Source: WDR 2009 team calculations, using 120 household surveys in 75 countries.

economic costs have been high. China's policies to restrict rural-urban migration until the late 1990s stunted urbanization, with between half and two-thirds of Chinese cities remaining too small. For the typical city in China, being too small is estimated to result in a loss of about 17 percent in net output per worker; for at least a quarter of the cities, these losses may range between 25 and 70 percent.[105]

A misplaced preoccupation with size, not function, of cities

A city's prospects for prosperity and even survival are determined by how nimbly the same piece of land is adapted to changing market demands. Given that land is an immobile factor critical to the production of any activity, the real estate choices that cities provide influence the magnitude of external economies and the nature and specialization of city economies. To be attractive to investors, a city must satisfy the demands of its dominant or growing industries for both real estate and facilities. For example, professional services and financial services require large amounts of office space, which can be more efficiently provided vertically in high-rise office buildings. Manufacturing requires large amounts of land for factories to produce goods, and for warehouses to store products and materials. And the recreation, tourism, and entertainment sectors require highly visible, pedestrian-friendly areas of cities and retail space.

The ability and ease of a city to adapt its land to different uses according to changing market needs will enable its sustainable growth. The last 800 years in Hong Kong, China, and the last 300 in New York show the importance of markets in signaling and implementing this urban renewal (see boxes 4.6 and 4.7). In New York the mercantile trade grew out of the early shipping industry. In turn, the mercantile trade industry would help give birth to the city's modern finance industry. Traders in New York City in the late-nineteenth century thrived by sharing access not only to physical transportation infrastructure (the harbor, canals, and railroads), but also to intermediate inputs of specialized services not available elsewhere (such as scheduled sailings, wholesalers, and ship brokers). Later, these inputs to trade became the foundations for shared inputs in finance, with maritime insurance underwriting the subsequent basis for other forms of investment.[106]

Cities that provide fluid land and property markets and other supportive institutions—such as protecting property rights, enforcing contracts, and financing housing—will more likely flourish over time as the needs of markets change. Successful cities have relaxed zoning laws to allow higher-value users to bid for the valuable land—and have adopted flexible land use regulations to adapt to their changing roles overtime.

The benefits of agglomeration economies arise from the density of economic activity. These are the advantages for an information technology startup locating in Silicon Valley or a bookstall owner

---

BOX 4.6 *Hong Kong, China: market forces led the way, government followed*

Hong Kong, China, with a land area of about 1,000 square kilometers, less than a quarter the size of Rhode Island, started out as a fishing village. In the 1200s Hong Kong, a hilly and barren island, saw its first population boom as Chinese fled the mainland to escape war and famine. People made a living on salt production, pearl diving, and fishery trades. Between the 1650s and the 1800s, Hong Kong was also a military outpost and naval base, and its economy continued to rely on trade. By the end of World War II in 1945, the population in Hong Kong, China, had been reduced to less than half the prewar total of 1.6 million.

In the 1950s and 1960s, Hong Kong took up manufacturing buttons, artificial flowers, umbrellas, textiles, enamels, footwear, and plastics. Squatter camps provided homes for the masses. The camps led to disasters—like the Shek Kip Mei fire—until the governor responded by putting up multistory residential buildings. Conditions in public housing were basic, with communal cooking facilities. For many decades, the private sector showed more commitment to and interest in urban redevelopment.

Between 1960 and 1980 the government experimented with urban renewal and comprehensive redevelopment to improve environmental conditions, traffic circulation, and community facilities. Over subsequent decades, the flexibility in land use planning and the participation of the private sector would prove crucial to satisfying the demands on land for housing, commerce, industry, transport, recreation, and community use. This combination enabled Hong Kong, China, to flourish into the regional center of business and financial services that it is today.

Consistent with the tradition of minimal government intervention in Hong Kong, China, the private sector has been the driving force behind urban transformation. The government contracted out urban redevelopment to a specialist organization dominated by private development interests.

Source: Adams and Hastings 2001.

BOX 4.7   *Reinvention and renewal: how New York became a great city*

New Amsterdam was founded as a Dutch colony in 1614. It passed into British hands and became New York in 1664. Manhattan, the Bronx, Brooklyn, Queens, and Staten Island were brought together in 1898 in the form we know today. Throughout its history, New York has continually rebuilt, reinvented, and renewed itself. Once a fur-trapping and shipping hub because of its natural harbor, New York City is today a global financial center and a regional powerhouse in mass media, arts, information and communication technology (ICT) innovation, and medical research. The New York metropolitan area is home to more than 18.7 million people with a GDP of $1,133 billion, making it the second-largest urban agglomeration in the world, after Tokyo. New York had a gross metropolitan product of $950 billion in 2005, making it the largest regional economy in the United States. If it were a country, New York City would be the world's seventeenth largest, ahead of Switzerland. At more than $56,000, it has the second highest per capita production in the world.

A tour of four neighborhoods reveals the city's versatility and vibrancy.

SoHo. In the 1700s SoHo was farmland. By the early 1800s it was primarily residential, inhabited by the wealthy and, soon after, by the middle class. In due time rapid development attracted many businesses. Hotels, theaters, stores, mansions, minstrel halls, casinos, and brothels appeared along Broadway. Starting in the 1880s the textile industry settled in the area. By the 1950s artists flocked to the area because of low rents, a result of people, industry, and commerce shifting uptown. In October 1962 the City Club of

New York characterized SoHo as a commercial slum. But today the area, once called Hell's Hundred Acres, is a busy commercial and retail district and home to New York University.[a]

Wall Street. The financial district is one of the city's best-known and oldest neighborhoods. Today's Wall Street neighborhood is part of Manhattan Community District 1, which extends south from Canal Street to the tip of Manhattan at Battery Park and includes Governor's Island. It is home to the New York Stock Exchange and the NASDAQ, the world's two largest stock exchanges.

The street's name was originally De Wall Straat in reference to the Walloons, Belgian farmers who were the majority of the residents living in New Netherland around Fort Amsterdam in 1630. The beaver belt was the single most important commodity in New Netherland. Trade encouraged new activity in the production of food, timber, tobacco, and eventually slaves. In the late-eighteenth century there was a buttonwood tree at the foot of Wall Street under which traders and speculators gathered to trade informally. In 1792 this arrangement was formalized with the Buttonwood Agreement, which laid the groundwork for the New York Stock Exchange.

Meatpacking district. In 1969, when Vincent Inconiglios moved to a loft on Gansevoort Street in the meatpacking district, it was a no man's land. The neighborhood was defined by a stench that overpowered the senses. Down the street from Mr. Inconiglios was a pickle factory, and an importer of Spanish melons occupied the shop downstairs. The area was teeming with barrels of bones, meat, and men in bloody white coats. Within

a generation, the transformation in the meatpacking district was as stark as the contrast between night and day.[b] Today, more than 35 wholesale meat companies still operate there. But the area is now also home to world-class restaurants, art galleries, a fashionable retail corridor, and night clubs that take advantage of the enormous former factory spaces. Real estate prices have skyrocketed. Mr. Inconiglios paid $50 a month when he moved to the meatpacking district. In 2007 the Carlyle Group and Sitt Asset Management acquired a pair of buildings on West 14th Street for $70 million.[c]

Williamsburg. This neighborhood reinvented itself from a booming trade port to a rich industrial town after the Civil War. With the construction of the Williamsburg Bridge in 1903, many Jewish families who lived in Manhattan's Lower East Side crossed the East River to a better life in Williamsburg. When industries left the area in the 1960s and 1970s, Williamsburg became an immigrant ghetto. But the cheap rent also made the neighborhood an artistic hub. The neighborhood evolved into a mix of Italian, Polish, Hispanic, and Hasidic residents. In 2005 New York City approved zoning changes that would allow for open spaces, parks, affordable housing, and light industry. Today, prices average $700–$900 per square foot, and prominent waterfront developments range in the millions.[d]

Sources: Seeman and Siegfried 1978; Shaw 2007; Biedermann 2007; Lynch and Mulero 2007.
a. Seeman and Siegfried 1978.
b. Shaw 2007.
c. Biedermann 2007.
d. Lynch and Mulero 2007.

locating close to other bookstalls on Dadabhai Naoroji Road in Mumbai, India. While the financial sector of London is largely concentrated in a few square miles of the City and Canary Wharf, financial firms also benefit from being located anywhere in Greater London. Firms benefit from locating close to other firms in either the same or different industries and unless all of them move together, they will become less profitable, even if the location

they are moving to has lower wages and cheaper land.

But bigger city size and economic density bring their own problems. For people and firms, city living comes at a price in both developing and developed countries. Traffic in central London moves at only 11 miles per hour[107]—the same speed as horse drawn carriages a hundred years ago. Beijing is notorious for its pollution-induced smog. Land in Mumbai is among the most expensive in the world. High levels of crime are an accepted feature of city living around the world. Millions of city dwellers live in overpopulated slum housing, with little or no access to basic amenities and services. These are the costs of density, the diseconomies of agglomeration.

The main source of diseconomies is the paucity of land in places where agglomeration economies take hold. Land is limited and as economic growth occurs, it has to be used with increasing intensity. Take Manhattan in New York City, which has an area of less than 35 square miles. In 1800 it had a population density of just under 3,000 people per square mile. By 1850 this had risen to about 23,500, peaking in 1910 with a population density of more than 100,000. Today, the population density is about 70,000. With land in fixed supply, its use eventually can offset any further benefits from agglomeration economies. The way to offset the fixed supply of a factor of production is to substitute other factors for it, and the rise of skyscrapers in many large urban areas is an illustration of this substitution of capital for land. The building of subway systems in many of the developed countries' larger cities is another example. But such substitution has its limits, and the increasing shortage of land in cities leads to higher rents and congestion costs for workers and firms.

Better transport can, by reducing the economic distance to density, in essence make land a less-binding resource. Indeed, with the long-term decline in transportation costs, cities have expanded. In 1680 London was only 4 square miles and, because of the difficulties of traveling, more than 450,000 people were crammed into this small area. By 1901 the city had expanded to 24 square miles, and the average population density had fallen to 79,000. In 2001 London's 627 square miles had a population density of 13,203 people per square mile. An expanding city meant that millions of commuters have to be transported from the suburbs, large volumes of retail goods have to be delivered to shops, and manufactured products have to be shipped out. All of this leads to congestion or diseconomies of scale

that reduce the gains from agglomeration economies.

But restricting the growth of cities is not the answer. There is no evidence that the agglomeration economies of megacities have been exhausted. Indeed, evidence suggests that the growth of vehicles in the developing countries is increasing with per capita income along a path similar to that followed by the richer countries.[108] The problem has more to do with the spatial structure of the city and investments in infrastructure. Vehicle ownership is rising 15 to 20 percent annually in much of the developing world.[109] But most countries have not matched this growth with a parallel expansion of transportation infrastructure, so traffic congestion is severe. Cities in developing countries only devote half as much land space to roads as in the United States. But it is not just a matter of increasing this capacity. In cities such as Bangkok and Manila, it is the management and the use of road space that is important. Part of the problem is that in many cities the responsibility for road infrastructure has devolved from central to local governments, which do not always have the necessary resources.

Combined with the differing propensities of industries to benefit from agglomeration economies, the resulting constraints explain why the spatial distribution of economic activity within a country is not restricted to a single center, but rather consists of multiple centers of differing sizes. For policy makers the challenge is to best relax the constraints generated by the congestion and overcrowding of land and resources so that the benefits of agglomeration can be maximized. In many cases these constraints have been tightened by misguided land use policies and planning failures, only adding to congestion (see chapter 7).

A misplaced fascination with "new" cities

The land Chicago was built on is not all that different from the more sparsely developed places around Lake Michigan. Yet the difference in economic production and household earnings between Chicago and other settlements on the lakefront in Wisconsin and Indiana is stark. And along the 10-hour drive through Texas on Interstate Highway 75, wages and land rents spike in Fort Worth, Austin, and San Antonio and drop off sharply at points in between. It is hard to reconcile these huge differences in economic density with the minor differences in physical geography; it is as if the areas of Fort Worth and San Antonio cast a shadow over the points in between. A better understanding of economic geography, characterized by external economies, is required to harness economic forces. But it is not always obvious that developing country governments understand economic geography or appreciate these forces.

A survey of new city initiatives in the Arab Republic of Egypt, Brazil, Hungary, India, and República Bolivariana de Venezuela is sobering. Brazil transferred its capital city from the coast to the midwestern interior more than 900 kilometers away. República Bolivariana de Venezuela picked Ciudad Guayana in the 1950s, a city in the southern part of the country, to be the industrial "growth pole" of the central and southern region and to attract people and jobs from the already rapidly growing metropolitan region in the north. In many formerly planned economies, the more common practice was building industrial towns to accelerate industrialization. In Hungary, Dunaujvaro was designed as a "steel town," Tiszaújváros as a "chemistry town," and Kazincbarcika as a "mining and heavy industry town." The Soviet Union built Magnitogorsk into a steel town in an area with huge reserves of iron ore to challenge its capitalist rivals.

Some new towns were built around metropolitan areas to alleviate the pressures that the large cities faced. Navi Mumbai was established in 1972 with the hope of developing a twin city for Mumbai, and to decongest Mumbai. Egypt started a comprehensive new town construction program around Cairo and away from Cairo to create a "new population map of Egypt" starting in the 1970s, and the construction is still ongoing. Many of these cities were created

for economic reasons, but some were created for political reasons. Have these new towns and cities, met their goals? Generally not.

- New cities do better when they are located near larger successful cities. But they often suffer from the same government-related failures that led the government to establish them, especially the failure to manage large cities well. That is, governments that do badly in managing large old cities also do badly in managing small new cities.

- New cities attract residents, sometimes even more than anticipated, but often not the people intended. That is, governments can set up (noncapital) cities, and they sometimes become viable, but not for the reasons the government envisaged.

- These cities attract people because of the circular causation that the new economic geography emphasizes: workers and entrepreneurs come to seek markets, and then more people come because this is where the markets are. But there may be huge opportunity costs, because the counterfactual could be more organic growth of settlements. That is, it makes sense for private agents to come to these cities since others are already there, but large efficiency losses may result from the country's point of view. Once a "bad" location is picked, it may not fail entirely because of circular causation, but that means the economic costs of the mistake are greater, not smaller, since the country will pay these costs for a long time.

- New noncapital cities that seem to succeed are those where the purpose and location are chosen over time by markets and in cases in which the government hastens the pace of growth by coordinating investments in infrastructure, housing, and general governance.

For these reasons, cities and towns should be seen as market agents that, just like firms and farms, serve market needs.

CHAPTER 5

Factor Mobility and Migration

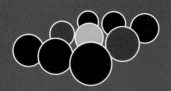

The largest movement of people in the world occurs every year around the beginning of February, as millions in China travel to be with their families for the Lunar New Year. In 2006, to mark the Year of the Dog, about 11 million people traveled out of Shanghai alone, and 10 million traveled into the city; 60 million people traveled on the last day of the festivities. In February 2008 ice and snow storms frustrated the plans of an estimated 200 million people trying to travel across China to be with their families for the New Year. Similarly, in the United States during the Thanksgiving period, millions take to the roads, airports, bus and train stations. The number of trips longer than 50 miles increases by half, with about 10 million people a day traveling over the holiday weekend, almost twice the daily average during the rest of the year.[1] The rising volume of holiday travelers in almost every country, rich or poor, is a telling reflection of just how many people live and work in a place other than where they were born.

This chapter is about the mobility of labor and capital, how their movements help to concentrate economic activity, and how these flows mitigate differences in welfare that can accompany economic concentration. It emphasizes movements of labor, especially, for two reasons. First, although many countries and regions are still thirsty for investment, national reforms and international agreements since the 1970s have eliminated most restrictions on the flow of capital. The scarcity of capital in some places now has less to do with actual barriers and more to do with unfavorable investment conditions.[2] In a globalizing economy capital is mobile and will move quickly. Labor, by contrast, tends to be less mobile for cultural and linguistic reasons. Second, a strong policy consensus supports the free flow of capital for foreign direct investment, even if this consensus is not always fully manifested in the policies of the many countries where external and internal obstacles remain. Relative to capital, labor is subject to more political restrictions and to explicit and implicit barriers. Some novel insights come from considering agglomeration economies and human capital together. Based on these insights, this chapter makes a case for facilitating the voluntary movement of people.

Textbooks teach us that the factors of production—capital and labor—move to places where they will earn the highest returns, and that these are the places where each factor is scarce. But by recognizing that increasing returns to scale are important, policies can be made better. Unlike unskilled labor and physical and financial capital, skilled labor—embodying human capital, a person's education, and endowment of skills and talent—earns higher economic returns where it is abundant, not scant. This explains the clustering of talented people in cities, the migration of entrepreneurs to leading areas within countries, and the rising number of skilled migrants moving to wealthy countries, all places where their skills seem plentiful but are nonetheless highly rewarded. Recognizing the growing benefits to human capital in areas where it has already accumulated changes the thinking about how governments should try to raise growth and achieve spatial convergence in living standards.

But policy makers in many developing countries—particularly in South Asia and in Sub-Saharan Africa—have been conditioned by an early literature on migration to worry about the specter of rising urban unemployment, overburdened city services, social tensions in economically vibrant areas, and a "brain drain." As a result, many countries still restrict the movement of people. Yet direct and indirect restrictions, although not effective at stemming the flow of people, create unnecessary friction and impose the cost of forgone opportunities for economic growth and convergence in living standards.

Although researchers are now less skeptical about the benefits of labor migration, policy makers in both developing and developed countries are not so sure. What can they learn from each other? This chapter documents the disconnect between the implications of recent research and the migration policies in developing and developed countries, showing how they are changing.

Keep in mind three points:

- *The facts about labor migration can be surprising. Although international migration still captures the greatest attention in the media, by far the largest flows of people are between places in the same country, and not from villages to cities, but from economically lagging to leading rural areas.*[3] Although the movement of people to cities is on the rise, particularly in South and East Asia, the most sustained pattern of internal mobility within developing countries has been from lagging rural areas, like Western Kenya and Bihar in India, to leading rural areas in those countries, like the Central Highlands and Punjab, and a large share of this migration is temporary.[4] And when people move across national borders, they do not go far.[5] Most international migration takes place within world regional "neighborhoods," particularly between developing countries.[6]
- *Movements of capital and labor are driven by the benefits of agglomeration.* Early migration theories were based on surplus labor, fixed "exogenous" rates of growth, and job creation—and these theories viewed the outmigration of skilled people as both socially traumatic and an economic loss. New theories recognize that migration, when driven by economic forces, is a positive and selective process. The interactions between agglomeration and labor migration power places forward.
- *The policy challenge is not how to keep households from moving, but how to keep them from moving for the wrong reasons.* Instead of trying to fight the pull of agglomeration economies on workers and their families, governments should work to eliminate the factors that push people out of their home areas. By doing so they can improve the quality of migration and encourage economic growth. Labor mobility driven by economic reasons leads to greater concentration of people and talent in places of choice and adds more to agglomeration benefits in these places than to congestion costs.

From mercantilism to globalization to autarky, and back again

Restrictions on the flow of capital, labor, and goods fragmented the world economy between the two world wars, but globalization picked up speed after the end of the Cold War in 1990, loosening the restrictions and integrating the world economy. Capital mobility within and across countries increased. International labor mobility—particularly unskilled labor—declined after the mass movements in the nineteenth century and only recently began to rise. But the mobility of people within countries has accelerated. So, for the movement of labor over the last century, distance has diminished, but divisions not only have increased (many more borders) but indeed may have become more obstructive (many more restrictions).

Capital flows—up sharply since the 1970s
The mobility of capital across borders, particularly investment capital, has increased since the 1970s. The world is returning to an age of capital mobility abandoned at the onset of World War I. From 1880 to 1914, a growing share of the world economy operated under the classic gold standard and a global financial market centered in London.

WORLD DEVELOPMENT REPORT 2009

148

The gold-standard fixed exchange rates and underpinned a stable and credible regime that enforced discipline on countries. Interest rates tended to converge and capital to flow with relative ease across borders, constrained only by the limits of technology. Many rapidly industrializing countries outside Europe—in the Americas and in Asia—took part in an increasingly global economy.[7]

The fluid economic environment was destroyed by two world wars and the global economic retraction in between. From 1914 to 1945, monetary policy was used to pursue national aims, domestic policy goals, and "beggar-thy-neighbor" trade strategies that encouraged strict capital controls. International capital flows petered out, and investment from abroad was viewed with suspicion. So prices and interest rates across countries fell out of sync. Even during the Bretton Woods era from the end of World War II to 1971, as countries attempted to rebuild the global economy, fears of mobile capital that had taken hold during the interwar years proved difficult to dispel. Indeed, capital controls were sanctioned to prevent currency crises.

Figure 5.1 International capital flows have surged since the 1970s
Gross private capital flows

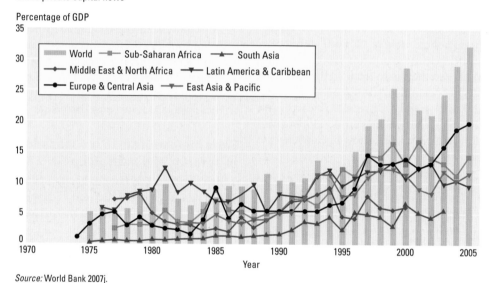

Source: World Bank 2007j.

Figure 5.2 A large share of capital now flows as direct investment
Foreign direct investment, net inflows

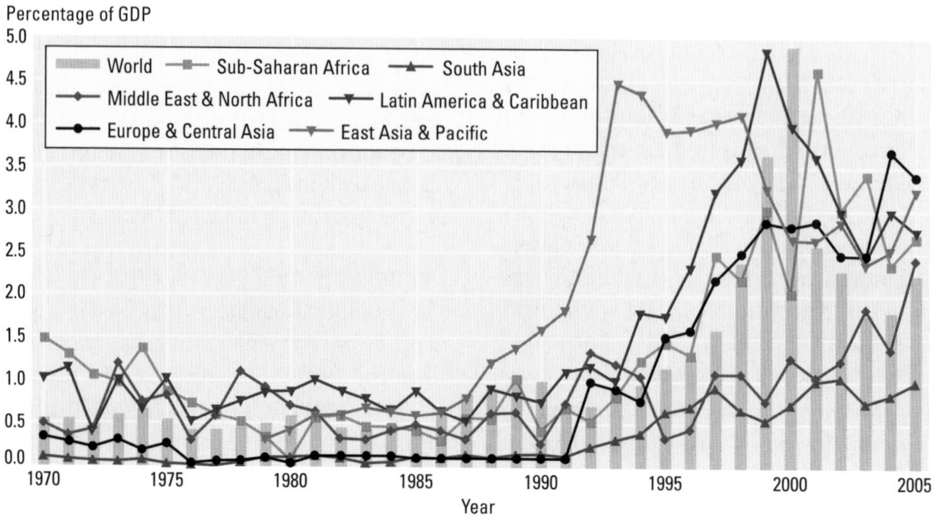

Source: World Bank 2007j.

But the growing volume of trade made it difficult to constrain the flow of capital, and in the early 1970s, the constraints began to loosen. Fixed exchange rates were abandoned, creating an international economic environment that could accommodate capital flows and market development. Political stability, structural reforms, and regulatory structures lowered the risks to foreign investment in developing countries, and capital markets responded with enthusiasm (see figures 5.1 and 5.2). By 2000, capital mobility returned to levels seen in 1914.[8]

Capital has become the most mobile factor of production. Converging real interest rates, declining spreads between deposit and lending rates, and shrinking risk premiums on the sovereign debt of developing countries are evidence of an international environment in which capital can go where it wants to, even if it does not always go where people wish it would. Indeed, recent comparisons of the marginal product of capital between high-income and lower-income countries show little evidence of friction preventing the flow of capital to poor countries. Instead, the lower capital ratios in poor countries are explained by lower efficiency and a lack of complementary factors.[9]

Labor flows across borders—blocked for much of the twentieth century

In a pattern similar to that of capital flows, from a peak in the late-nineteenth century, the mobility of labor across borders declined for most of the twentieth century, with the rise of economic barriers at the onset of the Great Depression and World War II. Geographers have long recorded the movement of humankind, from the earliest migrations out of Africa to Europe and Asia,[10] to the resurgence of movement across borders. They categorize the modern history of international migration into four distinct periods: mercantile, industrial, autarkic, and postindustrial.[11]

During the mercantile period, from 1500 to 1800, the movement of people around the world was dominated by Europeans. Agrarian settlers, administrators, artisans, entrepreneurs, and convicts emigrated out of Europe in large numbers. During the industrial period that followed—sometimes referred to as the first period of economic globalization,

an estimated 48 million emigrants, between 10 and 20 percent of the population, left Europe (see table 5.1).[12] Unlike international migration today, the movement of people across borders in the first and second periods of labor migration was not driven by a lack of economic growth or development in the sending countries. Indeed, the first country to industrialize and the most advanced at the turn of the twentieth century—Great Britain—was by far the largest sending country. Economic analysis shows a positive correlation between emigration and the extent of industrialization in the sending country.[13]

A long period of autarky and economic nationalism began in 1910. Unprecedented restrictions were placed on trade, investment, and immigration, stifling the international movement of capital and labor. The trickle of international migrants consisted mainly of refugees and displaced persons, unrelated to economic development.

The postindustrial period of migration began in the 1960s, characterized by new

Table 5.1   In the late-nineteenth century most international migrants came from better-off Europe
Top sending countries in 1900 and 2000

Top emigrant-sending countries in 1900	Percentage of sending country's population in 1900	Top emigrant-sending countries in 2000	Percentage of sending country's population in 2000
British Isles	40.9	Mexico	10.0
Norway	35.9	Afghanistan	9.9
Portugal	30.1	Morocco	9.0
Italy	29.2	United Kingdom	7.1
Spain	23.2	Algeria	6.7
Sweden	22.3	Italy	5.7
Denmark	14.2	Bangladesh	5.0
Switzerland	13.3	Germany	4.9
Finland	12.9	Turkey	4.5
Austria-Hungary	10.4	Philippines	4.3
Germany	8.0	Egypt, Arab Rep. of	3.5
Netherlands	3.9	Pakistan	2.4
Belgium	2.6	India	0.9
Russian Federation–Poland	2.0	United States	0.8
France	1.3	China	0.5
Europe	**12.3**		
Japan	0.9		
Total (Europe and Japan)	11.1	Total (of countries listed)	1.9

Sources: Massey 1988, Parsons and others 2007, in Ozden and Schiff 2007.

forms, no longer dominated by flows out of Europe. People began to move from lower-income countries to wealthy countries, with a surge in migrant labor from Latin America, Africa, and Asia. In the 1970s, countries that had been major sources of migrating labor to Northern Europe and the Americas—such as Italy, Portugal, and Spain—began to receive immigrants from Africa and the Middle East. The growing wealth of oil-rich countries in the late 1970s made economies in the Persian Gulf new destinations. And by the 1980s, migration to East Asian countries spread beyond Japan to Hong Kong, China; the Republic of Korea; Malaysia; Singapore; Taiwan, China; and Thailand.

Today, about 200 million people are foreign born, roughly 3 percent of the world population.[14] The flows of new international migrants have varied—from a 2-percent increase between 1970 and 1980, to 4.3 percent from 1980 to 1990, and to 1.3 percent from 1990 to 2000. Poor and middle-income countries now send the most emigrants, led by Bangladesh, China, the Arab Republic of Egypt, India, Mexico, Morocco, Pakistan, the Philippines, and Turkey (see table 5.1). But Italy, Germany, and the United Kingdom still rank near

the top, each accounting for between 3 million and 4 million emigrants.

The volume and flow of international migration is no longer mainly associated with population growth or demographic pressure. Unlike the 1960s and 1970s, international immigrants are not from the poorest, least developed countries. Voluntary international movements of people tend to originate from countries with rapidly growing economies and falling fertility rates. Emigration today is the outcome less of desperation and more of integration.[15]

The pattern of international migration is also shifting, from South-North to South-South.[16] Although the top three receiving countries are members of the Organisation for Economic Co-operation and Development (OECD)—the United States, Germany, and France, in that order—Côte d'Ivoire, India, the Islamic Republic of Iran, Jordan, and Pakistan are now among the top 15 destinations. But migration of labor from the low- and middle-income countries of the South to the wealthy countries of the North is still large, 37 percent of international migrants in 2000. Movement between Northern countries made up 16 percent of

Table 5.2   Close to home: the largest international flows of labor are between neighboring countries
Percentage of world migrants recorded as a bilateral movement between pairs of countries/regions, circa 2000

Countries/ regions of origin	Destination countries/regions												
	USA	Canada	UE15 & EFTA	AU & NZ	Japan	HI MENA	LAC	ECA	MENA	AFR	EAP	SAS	Total
USA	n.a.	0.16	0.34	0.04	0.02	0.03	0.43	0.04	0.05	0.03	0.15	0.02	1.29
Canada	0.54	n.a.	0.10	0.02	n.a.	0.01	0.02	0.01	n.a.	0.01	0.01	0.01	0.74
EU15 & EFTA	2.22	0.98	5.59	1.13	0.01	0.14	0.68	0.78	0.16	0.39	0.20	0.19	12.47
AU and NZ	0.06	0.02	0.16	0.23	n.a.	n.a.	n.a.	0.01	n.a.	0.01	0.03	0.01	0.55
Japan	0.28	0.02	0.06	0.02	n.a.	n.a.	0.04	0.01	n.a.	n.a.	0.05	0.01	0.50
HI MENA	0.10	0.03	0.06	0.01	n.a.	0.12	n.a.	0.02	0.72	0.01	0.04	0.03	1.14
LAC	10.22	0.36	1.45	0.05	0.13	0.10	2.07	0.17	0.08	0.14	0.14	0.25	15.15
ECA	1.27	0.39	4.75	0.26	n.a.	0.92	0.07	16.98	0.33	0.34	0.18	0.41	25.88
MENA	0.47	0.17	2.85	0.10	n.a.	1.49	0.04	0.16	1.79	0.28	0.05	0.12	7.52
AFR	0.41	0.12	1.58	0.10	n.a.	0.25	0.02	0.11	0.18	7.00	0.03	0.16	9.97
EAP	3.32	0.71	1.09	0.63	0.54	0.48	0.06	0.14	0.14	0.09	3.86	0.27	11.32
SAS	0.83	0.31	1.13	0.12	0.01	2.66	0.02	0.13	2.07	0.14	0.37	5.67	13.46
Total	19.71	3.25	19.14	2.72	0.74	6.22	3.45	18.56	5.53	8.44	5.10	7.15	100

Source: Parsons, Skeldon, Walmsley, and Winters 2007.
Notes: AFR = Africa; AU = Australia; EAP = East Asia and Pacific; ECA = Europe and Central Asia; EU15 = European Union 15; EFTA = European Free Trade Association; HI MENA = High-income countries in the Middle East and North Africa region; LAC = Latin America and the Caribbean; NZ = New Zealand; SAS = South Asia; n.a. = not applicable.

migration and that between Southern countries accounted for 24 percent, with Argentina, China, Côte d'Ivoire, India, the Islamic Republic of Iran, Jordan, Pakistan, and South Africa as important destinations.

There is a strong tendency for labor to move between countries in the same world neighborhoods, particularly for South-South migration (see table 5.2). Migration of labor is usually from countries with a shared land border.[17] While only 30 percent

of immigrants to the United States, 20 percent to France, and 10 percent to Germany come from countries with which they share a border, 81 percent of immigrants to Côte d'Ivoire, 99 percent to the Islamic Republic of Iran, and 93 percent to India are from neighboring countries.

International migrants tend to stay within regional neighborhoods, particularly in developing world regions, most notably in Sub-Saharan Africa (see figure 5.3). Almost

Figure 5.3 Migrants from East Asia, Latin America, and the Middle East and North Africa go mainly to OECD countries, but most in South Asia and Sub-Saharan Africa stay close to home

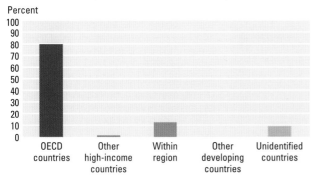

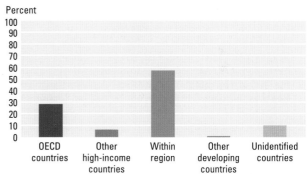

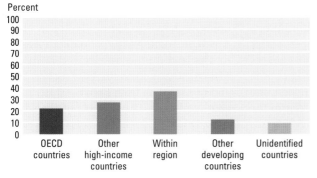

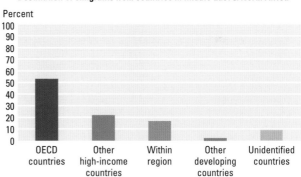

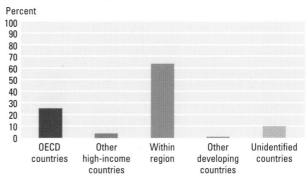

Source: Ratha and Xu 2008.

BOX 5.1 *Regional labor mobility has been falling in Sub-Saharan Africa*

The rate of labor migration within developing regions is highest in Sub-Saharan Africa, but it has fallen since the 1960s. More than 60 percent of emigrants from Sub-Saharan countries move to other countries in the region. The higher rate of labor movement within the region relative to other developing world regions is partly a consequence of the large number of land borders, but also of the relative permeability of these borders and the difficulty of monitoring the flow of people crossing them, despite numerous legal restrictions.

Migrants represented just over 3.5 percent of the population in Sub-Saharan Africa in 1960 but only 2.3 percent by 2000. In 1960 the stock of migrants relative to the population was much higher in Southern Africa than in other corners of the region, but it has since fallen to about the level of migrants in Western Africa (see the table below). In Eastern Africa and Central Africa the stock of migrants has fallen significantly.

Voluntary migration across borders in Sub-Saharan Africa is motivated by the same reasons that prompt people to move within a country: to pursue job opportunities and to diversify risks to income. Indeed, the economic rationale for movement from a lagging to a leading area of the same country is virtually indistinguishable from that for moving across a border in a region like Sub-Saharan Africa, where these movements are over relatively small distances and for the most part unmonitored. But many migrants also move across borders within a framework of formal agreements between countries. Since the 1960s, a web of bilateral and multilateral agreements has grown in an attempt to reap the benefits and control the costs of labor mobility within subregional neighborhoods.

In West Africa governments have attempted to manage population movements within the Economic Community of West African States (ECOWAS), which has had the most influence on the flow and composition of migration in Sub-Saharan Africa. Established in 1975, ECOWAS includes a protocol allowing the free movement of people and the right of residence and establishment for the citizens of its member countries.

The Southern African Development Community (SADC), a loose alliance of nine countries of Southern Africa formed in 1980, coordinated development projects to lessen economic dependence on South Africa during the Apartheid era. Part of this alliance was a provision for the flow of labor between member countries. The recent anti-immigrant violence in South Africa is a setback for regional integration and migration.

Kenya, Tanzania, and Uganda have formed the East African Community (EAC), a regional intergovernmental organization for interterritorial cooperation with roots extending to 1948 before independence. The EAC, gaining strength as a framework for economic integration since 1999, recently introduced East African passports and temporary passes to speed the movement of labor.

The movement of labor across borders in Sub-Saharan Africa's neighborhoods could be encouraged. During economic contractions, policy makers in these neighborhoods feel the same xenophobic political pressures as governments in rich countries do to favor native workers and ration public services to nonnatives. Less than one-third of governments in Sub-Saharan Africa have ratified the International Convention on the Protection of the Rights of All Migrant Workers and Members of Their Families. To really reap the benefits from labor mobility for faster economic growth with convergence across Sub-Saharan Africa's regional neighborhoods, much more can be done to welcome migrants and open channels for the flow of remittances to their home countries.

Source: Lucas 2006.

Sub-Saharan Africa's stock of migrants has fallen since 1960
Per 1,000 population, by regional neighborhood

Neighborhood	1960	1970	1980	1990	2000
Eastern Africa	37.3	31.6	35.3	31.2	17.9
Central Africa	40.7	44.2	35.9	20.6	16.0
Southern Africa	49.7	40.6	33.3	34.5	30.6
Western Africa	28.0	27.3	34.6	28.5	30.0
Sub-Saharan Africa	35.6	32.8	35.0	29.0	23.0

Source: UN Population Division, in Lucas 2006.

17 percent of recorded international migration around 2000 occurred within Europe and Central Asia, though a large part of this resulted from border changes and changes in the definition of who was "foreign born" in these countries. The second highest rate of labor mobility between countries in the same region was for Sub-Saharan Africa (see box 5.1).

Cross-border migration within subregional neighborhoods flows to countries that act as economic engines of growth in developing regions—to Côte d'Ivoire in West Africa, to South Africa in Southern Africa, to Thailand from countries in the Greater Mekong Region in South Asia (see box 5.2), and to Argentina from Bolivia, Chile, Paraguay, and Peru. Distance is not the whole story. Divisions, in the form of language and culture, also determine the pattern of international migration, with more than half of migrations occurring between countries with a common language. Of course, a common language and other cultural factors reinforce the neighborhood effects.

Immediately after World War II—when economies were growing rapidly, wage inequality was falling, and the volume of labor movement across borders was low—international migration was not really a thorny political issue. But after 1975—as growth in high-income countries slowed, wage inequality increased, and the volume of international migrants swelled—immigration became a heated topic of debate in electoral politics. Indeed, selective "managed immigration" policies first introduced in Australia and Canada in the 1980s are becoming popular in other high-income destination countries.[18]

With the return to globalization since the end of the Cold War, the movement of labor across borders resumed, but governments still restrict the number and influence the characteristics of immigrants. This contrasts sharply with the "first era of globalization" in the nineteenth century, when the flows of labor were free of obstruction. Restrictions on immigration arise and are sustained by wage inequality in receiving countries, rather than by unemployment or absolute wages. They are more likely to be tightened when international labor flows increase and to be loosened in periods of domestic support for trade.[19]

Internal labor mobility—growing rapidly, despite restrictions

With improvements in transport technology and infrastructure, the mobility of labor within countries rose steadily throughout the twentieth century, accelerating in its last two decades. The volume and velocity of internal voluntary migration, of concern to policy makers for decades, are growing despite predictions to the contrary.[20] Declining agriculture and rising manufacturing have changed the distribution of labor in low-income and emerging middle-income countries since the mid-twentieth century in South Asia and Sub-Saharan Africa, and long before in East Asia and Latin America. Migration of labor from lagging to leading rural areas remains the dominant internal movement

---

BOX 5.2   *Cross-border migration in the Greater Mekong Subregion*

The Greater Mekong Subregion (GMS), with 315 million people, comprises Cambodia, the Lao People's Democratic Republic, Myanmar, Thailand, Vietnam, and the Guangxi and Yunnan provinces of China. Despite marked disparities in economic development among its members, the subregion is extremely dynamic, with annual growth rates averaging above 6 percent in recent years.

Thailand's higher wages, faster growth, and more favorable social and political climate attract people trying to escape poverty in Cambodia, Lao PDR, and Myanmar. For Thailand the migrants are a reservoir of cheap and flexible labor and a boost to its competitiveness in some sectors. And Thailand alone is estimated to have 1.5 million to 2 million regular and irregular migrants from the GMS. Removing them could reduce Thailand's GDP by around 0.5 percentage points a year.

By some estimates, more than half of migrants enter Thailand holding legal documentation and then overstay, becoming illegal. Migrants are disproportionately young, of working age, and male. Those from Myanmar are, on average, less educated and less literate than the average for the populations of origin, indicating a push to migrate, or negative self-selection. But self-selection is positive among migrants from Cambodia, who have slightly higher education attainment than the population back home.

Remittances from Thailand to Cambodia, Lao PDR, and Myanmar are estimated at $177 million to $315 million a year. In Cambodia they are important for 91 percent of the households interviewed in one of the main sending provinces.

Much of this migration, however, will remain irregular and unregulated, increasing the vulnerability of migrants, the majority of whom do not use social services because they fear deportation. One of the biggest problems is ensuring access to schooling for children, who also suffer from a lack of health care. For the same reasons that migrant adults rarely receive health treatment, migrant children rarely receive vaccinations.

Despite the benefits of labor mobility, facilitating legal flows of people has been slow. Sending countries generally lack the capacity to manage the mass export of labor and to protect the rights of their nationals abroad. Receiving countries have fairly weak migration frameworks, often implemented hastily as an "after-the-fact" response to large numbers of migrants. The absence of an adequate legal and policy framework, typical of regional neighborhoods in developing country regions, increases the costs (and risks) of migration and reduces its benefits.

Source: World Bank 2006e.

---

in most of the developing world,[21] except in Latin America, where movements between cities dominate.[22] Rural-to-rural migration, difficult to document, has been largely ignored.[23]

Migration from rural areas to cities has been gaining importance since the mid-1970s, especially in the urbanizing economies of South and East Asia, with the rapid rise of manufacturing and services. In India, where movements from poor to rich

BOX 5.3 *From facilitating to restricting to (again) facilitating labor mobility in China*

In the second half of the twentieth century, China undertook some of the most active internal migration policies ever observed, initially to great economic benefit, but increasingly to the detriment of growth and development. Now, these policies are changing again.

In the 1950s the government sought to stimulate industrialization through policies that encouraged rapid urbanization. Households were given incentives to move to cities, and rural workers responded en masse, answering the demand to participate in reconstruction and industrial development. As a result of these efforts, the urban population of China had by 1953 grown by a third, to 78 million. The first Five-Year Plan (1953–58) promoted urban development, creating forces that pulled people to the cities, complemented by the collectivization of agriculture and the establishment of the commune system.

In apparent response to a larger-than-expected flow from villages, the government tried to stem the flow, centralizing hiring, restricting travel, and rationing grain in cities. But these measures failed to slow the outflow of Chinese rural workers, and the pressure on cities grew so much that the government mobilized to move

millions back to the countryside. Then, with the Great Leap Forward (1958–60), the government abandoned all attempts to control the flow of labor, again seeking to accelerate industrial development, motivating another surge of workers to China's cities. By 1960 China's urban population had doubled from that in 1949.

In the 1960s and first half of the 1970s, the urban population fell, a consequence of the relocation of intellectuals and urban elites to the countryside during the Cultural Revolution (1966–76). Then, with an abrupt shift in policy in 1976, the flow of people to the cities surged anew.

In the early 1980s the government became particularly preoccupied with the speed of urbanization. Although rural-to-urban migration was responsible for only 20 percent of the growth of China's cities from 1949 to 1980, evidence of burdened infrastructure and services in Shanghai and Beijing occupied the attention of policy makers.

The *hukou* household registration system became the main policy tool to regulate the flow of workers. It has four tenets:

- Migration, especially to urban areas, should be allowed only if compatible with economic development.

- Rural-to-urban migration must be controlled strictly.

- Movements between settlements of similar population size need not be controlled.

- Flows from larger to smaller settlements or between rural areas should be encouraged.

Under the *hukou,* each individual has an official place of residence, and the documents verifying residence are similar to a passport. People are allowed to work legally, to receive social security benefits including health coverage, and to access food rations only in their place of residence. A change in official place of residence can be granted only by permission, similar to a local authority granting a visa. But some forms of legal temporary migration would be allowed to meet shifts in labor demand.

As the government's preoccupation with the size of China's cities and the pace of urban growth changed, the *hukou* was tightened or loosened—for example, by relaxing the residency requirement to receive food rations or extending the rights of temporary migrants. Despite the controls, lax

China's industrial growth and concentration has been accompanied by massive movements of workers
Internal labor migration between 1995–2000

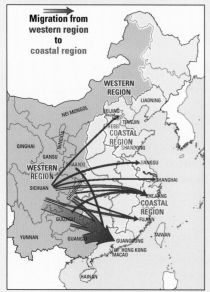

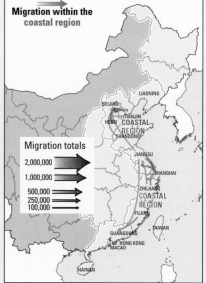

Source: Huang and Luo forthcoming, using data from the Population Census of China.

BOX 5.3 *From facilitating to restricting to (again) facilitating labor mobility in China—continued*

enforcement allowed large flows of migrant workers to settle in cities under "temporary" status. Indeed, in the past 30 years, the labor force requirements to fuel China's spectacular growth performance have relied on migrants who are temporary under law but in fact permanent residents.

Today the movement of people from rural areas to cities is again surging. One in five rural workers migrates, and migrants account for a third of urban employment. In 2005 average incomes in cities were three times the rural average. The mechanization of farming has added

to the pool of surplus labor. And China's industries are in constant need of low-cost labor.

Recognizing the growth dividend from allowing labor to flow freely, the government has been loosening the *hukou* in recent years, even facilitating migration. Migration restrictions have declined. The labor market has become more efficient. And mobility decisions are much more responsive to economic factors.[a] Beginning with pilot programs in selected municipalities, migrants from rural areas will be given access to health and social protection services, training, labor market

information, and job search assistance, and recourse to legal action in cases of employer abuse.

Recent research suggests that the restrictions have taken a toll: many Chinese cities are smaller than they should be.[b] In many areas, such as Chengdu and Chongqing, governments are again facilitating a rapid rural-urban migration (see chapter 7).

Source: WDR 2009 team.
a. Poncet 2006.
b. Au and Henderson 2006a.

rural agricultural areas have historically been the dominant form of internal migration, movements from villages to cities have increased sharply in recent years. Migration from the poor Indian state of Bihar has doubled since the 1970s, mainly to cities, and not to the agriculturally prosperous states in India's Northwest, as before. In Bangladesh two-thirds of all migration from rural areas is to cities. And in China, with the easing of residency restrictions, migration from rural areas to cities now predominates (see box 5.3).

Uniform measures of internal migration are rare. Because there are so few household surveys that regularly measure labor mobility, and the questions asked about migration vary, comparable indicators can be calculated for only a few countries. Questions about migration are more likely to be asked in countries that experience large movements of labor and with governments that are concerned about migration. Among the countries included in table 5.3, for example, are stable nations (such as Argentina and Costa Rica), where migration is more likely to reflect economic motives, as well as countries that have recently experienced conflict (such as Bosnia and Herzegovina, the Democratic Republic of Congo, Rwanda, and Sierra Leone), where internal mobility is also due to flight from the threat of violence.

Skills—the motor of internal and international migration

A rush of labor matching the migrations out of Europe at the turn of the twentieth century has not yet taken place, and perhaps it never will. But unlike the flow of unskilled labor, that of skilled labor—with human capital—has been on the rise. Globalization and selective migration policies are likely to ease travel for skilled labor within countries and across borders.

Within countries, education attainment continues to determine who moves and who does not—certainly from rural areas to cities. People with more education are more likely to migrate in their own country (see figures 5.4 and 5.5).[24] Many temporary, seasonal migrants with little or no education also migrate.[25] But education boosts the velocity of labor mobility, by opening employment opportunities farther afield and shortening the job search at migrants' destination.[26]

Education also increases the likelihood of people moving abroad. The international migration of skilled workers relative to that of unskilled workers has been rising since the 1970s for every developing world region (see figure 5.6). The highest proportions of skilled emigrants (as a percentage of the educated workforce) are from Africa, the Caribbean, and Central America. Many Central American

Table 5.3 Rates of labor mobility vary widely across countries in the developing world

Country and year of survey (ranked by stock of migrants)	Internal migrants (% of working-age population)	Recent migrants (less than five years, % of total working-age population)	Recent migrants (% of internal migrants)	Country and year of survey (ranked by stock of migrants)	Internal migrants (% of working-age population)	Recent migrants (less than five years, % of total working-age population)	Recent migrants (% of internal migrants)
Bosnia and Herzegovina 2001	52.5	12.8	24.5	Costa Rica 2001	19.9	2.5	12.4
Paraguay 2001	39.0	7.3	18.7	Brazil 2001	19.5	3.3	16.7
Bolivia 2005	37.7	5.0	13.3	Sierra Leone 2003	19.0	3.7	19.3
Morocco 1998	33.4	6.0	18.1	Nicaragua 2001	18.6	3.1	16.9
Azerbaijan 1995	33.2	19.4	58.4	Guatemala 2006	17.5	3.3	19.1
Honduras 2003	29.0	5.5	19.2	Haiti 2001	17.5	2.8	15.8
Venezuela, R. B. de 2004	28.3	3.0	10.7	Argentina 2006	17.2	1.4	8.1
Congo, Dem. Rep. of 2005	27.1	7.8	28.9	Kyrgyz Republic 1997	16.2	4.7	29.2
Dominican Republic 2004	26.9	4.0	14.9	Romania 1994	15.1	1.9	12.8
				Croatia 2004	14.7	1.2	8.0
Armenia 1999	24.5	22.4	91.7	Bulgaria 2001	14.3	1.4	10.0
Mauritania 2000	24.2	2.9	12.0	Cambodia 2004	14.2	2.8	19.4
Albania 2005	23.9	4.1	17.3	Tajikistan 2003	9.9	1.5	15.7
Ecuador 2004	22.7	5.3	23.4	Mongolia 2002	9.8	0.0	0.4
Vietnam 1992	21.9	3.1	14.3	Kazakhstan 1996	9.3	1.4	14.7
Rwanda 1997	21.5	5.9	27.6	Madagascar 2001	9.3	0.0	0.0
Colombia 1995	20.1	5.3	26.3	Mozambique 1996	8.1	0.0	0.2
				Malawi 2005	2.7	1.1	43.2
				Micronesia 2000	1.2	0.3	23.6

Source: WDR 2009 team, estimates using household surveys.
Note: Internal migrants are individuals who are not living in the same district in which they were born. This definition does not count returnees as migrants—that is, persons who moved away from their place of birth in the past, but returned by the time of the survey. *Recent migrants* migrated in the five years before the year of the survey.

Figure 5.4 In Latin America and the Caribbean internal migrants are more educated than those who stay behind
Education comparison between internal migrants and nonmigrants at place of origin and at time of migration

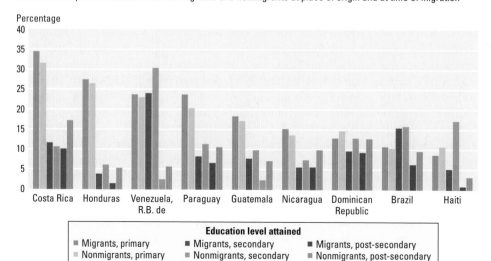

Source: WDR 2009 team drawing from selected household surveys.

and island nations in the Caribbean had more than half their university-educated citizens living abroad in 2000. And close to 20 percent of skilled workers have left Sub-Saharan Africa.[27] This could be taken as evidence that human capital is becoming more mobile internationally—or that "selective" immigration policies in wealthy countries are biasing the composition of international migration toward those with skills. But the increase in the migration of skilled labor is due to the rise in higher levels of education worldwide, most notably for countries sending the majority of international migrants. In relative terms, the cross-border movement of skilled labor has remained fairly constant as a share of the stock of skilled labor in sending countries. Rather than human capital becoming more mobile, more human capital is simply available, propelling larger volumes of migration.[28]

The rapid development of telecommunications and other forms of information and communication technology has separated the mobility of human capital from the mobility of labor. In a trend likely to accelerate, more services in the production processes of industries based in wealthy countries are being located "offshore" in low- and middle-income countries, where human capital is cheaper. What began with the export of software development and maintenance services from the Indian city of Bangalore to firms across the world has developed into a burgeoning trade in services requiring a wide array of skills, from simple customer communications—particularly from countries like India and the Philippines, where English is widely spoken—to financial accounting and computer maintenance. There is, as yet, no evidence that the export of "disembodied" human capital over telephone lines and the Internet will substitute for the flow of skilled workers. But by creating the possibility of separating human capital from labor, information and communication technology has further increased the mobility of skills relative to people.

Figure 5.5 Internal migrants are more schooled than workers in the places to which they move
Comparison between internal migrant and nonmigrant workers at migrant's place of destination

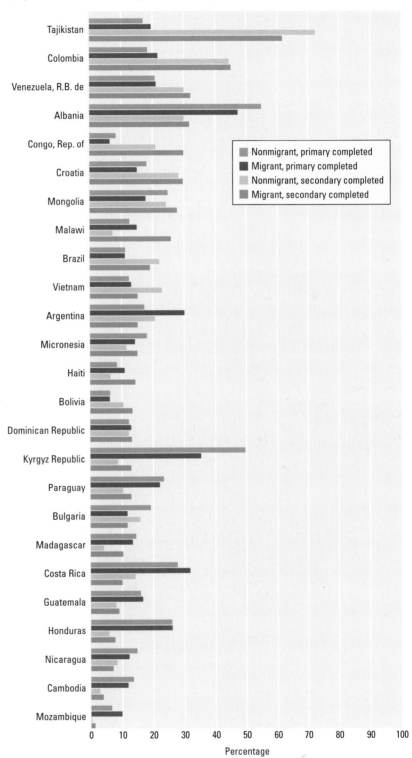

Source: WDR 2009 team drawing from selected household surveys.

Figure 5.6   Migration from developing countries is becoming more skilled

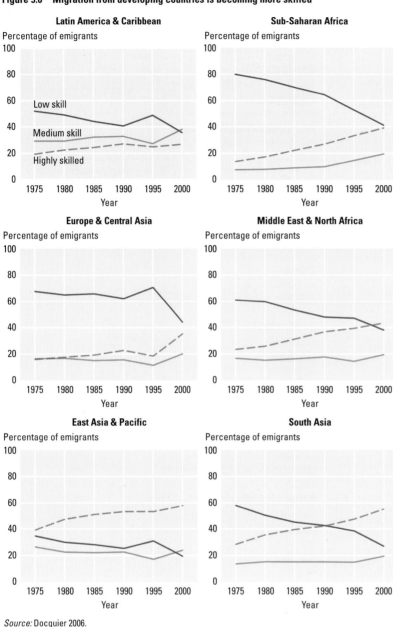

Source: Docquier 2006.

Labor mobility: learning from a generation of analysis

Until recently, two strands of economic literature—labor migration and economic growth, each with a powerful impact on developing-country policy makers— have evolved along separate tracks and diverged. But as shown in the arguments and evidence on agglomeration economies in chapter 4, the two phenomena are closely intertwined in the real world.

Labor mobility and voluntary migration for economic gain are the human side of the agglomeration story.

As for firms, localization and urbanization economies arise from knowledge spillovers between people in proximity. For this reason, people are often more economically productive when they are around others, especially for people with skills. Migration and agglomeration feed off each other. Whether this is agglomeration in leading places within a geographic area, in leading areas within countries, or in leading countries within regions, human capital flows to economically leading places. At every spatial scale, migration is the way that people who invest in education and skills realize the returns on their investment.

An important insight of the agglomeration literature—that human capital earns higher returns where it is plentiful—has been ignored by the literature on labor migration. Preoccupied with urban unemployment and squalor in the fast-growing cities of the South, early research on labor migration advocated restrictions.[29] Governments often acted on these prescriptions, instituting migration abatement policies, but to little effect: flows from the countryside to cities and from lagging to leading provinces continued unabated. The only effect of restrictions may have been forgone economic growth and slower spatial convergence in living standards.

Increasing returns to scale and spillovers from clustering—especially human capital-related spillovers—make clear the growth and welfare payoffs of policies that facilitate movements of labor from lagging to leading places. The implications for policy are powerful. Rather than an impending destructive tide of humanity, the swelling flows of people from villages to cities could be a boon for economic growth and the convergence of welfare. Moving from the local spatial scale, to the national, and then to the international, the benefits from clustering are the same—and the problems facing policy makers grow and become more complex. Put plainly, they do not want to lose people and human capital.

Economic theory now recognizes that governments should not try to hold on to people. The pull of agglomeration forces in prosperous places is simply too strong for any opposing measure to be sustained. Another aspect of the pull of agglomeration has been well studied by economists but is often overlooked by governments. Migrants who move to cities, to leading areas, or to leading countries are rarely disconnected from their home places. Most migrants maintain strong and active links with their home communities and send remittances. And they do much more than remit capital. They send back information and technical assistance, and when a place is ready, they often bring back ideas, knowledge, expectations of good governance, and links to leading markets. Sending governments that put the right policies in place can capture these benefits for faster growth and faster convergence in living standards.

Migration theory now recognizes the benefits of agglomeration

Economists' notions about what motivates people to move and what such movements mean come from theories of economic growth and convergence. Whether couched in a classical framework[30] or in the recent models of "endogenous growth,"[31] where people are free to move, they will move to compete away differences in wages between locations. Since higher wages at the destination reflect an initial shortage of workers relative to capital—or a large endowment of capital per worker—the arrival of new migrants will slow the accumulation of capital per worker and the growth of wages. In contrast, the accumulation of capital per worker in the places migrants leave will speed up as they go, accelerating wage growth for workers who stay behind. By this mechanism, incomes in different locations are predicted to eventually converge.

The first theories of labor migration originated in the analysis of economic growth in developing countries.[32] These early theories partitioned a developing economy into a traditional agrarian rural sector and a modern manufacturing sector centered in urban areas. The main idea was that with economic development, particularly with progressive mechanization of agriculture, labor in rural areas is always

in surplus. But in the growing modern manufacturing sector it is not. So, in rural areas, every additional worker, irrespective of innate talents or education attainment, has zero marginal productivity, but each potentially has a positive marginal productivity in manufacturing. This opens a gap in earnings and an incentive for labor to migrate from rural areas to cities in search of manufacturing jobs. Agriculture supplies an unlimited labor force to manufacturing, and the transfer of labor between the two sectors takes place through rural-urban migration. This migration continues until the "disguised unemployment" of workers in rural areas is absorbed into manufacturing in urban areas.

Movements from rural to urban areas were considered desirable when accompanied by economic growth. In what has become known as the Todaro class of migration models,[33] prospective migrants decide whether to move by comparing the expected future income streams they could earn in the city and in the rural home, after taking into account the costs of actually moving and searching for a job.[34] A key feature of the early Todaro models is that the economy's rate of growth—and by extension the rate of employment creation in the modern manufacturing sector—was assumed to be constant and set independent of the model. This classical framework—with an exogenously determined rate of economic growth and constant rate of employment creation in the manufacturing sector—explained rising urban unemployment in cities like Nairobi. But it also created what came to be known as the Todaro Paradox: any policy to improve urban economies could lead to more urban unemployment because the improvements would induce even more migration from rural areas.

Few economic models have had as much impact on policy makers in developing countries as these early labor migration theories. Across the developing world, but especially in South Asia and Sub-Saharan Africa, the Todaro Paradox provided a basis for strong disincentives and even outright restrictions on the movement of labor.[35] The Todaro model suggested that prohibiting internal migration over and above what

BOX 5.4 *Labor and social policies restrain migration in Eastern Europe—not good for growth*

Internal migration increased in several countries in Eastern Europe and Central Asia at the beginning of the transition away from planned economies. But this may have been a one-time phenomenon. Much of the sudden increase in migration in the Commonwealth of Independent States appears to have been driven by the return of people to their ethnic homelands and the departure of workers from areas they had been sent to by central planners. More than 1 million people relocated from Siberia and the Russian North and Far East to the more central parts of the Russian Federation, about 12 percent of the populations of these areas.

These movements may have run their course. Migration has slowed despite differences in income and the quality of life. Internal migrants in the Czech Republic, Poland, and the Slovak Republic represent less than 0.5 percent of the working population, much less than 1.5 percent in Germany, and nearly 2.5 percent in France, the Netherlands, and the United Kingdom.

People of working age in Europe's economically depressed areas mainly don't move because extensive unemployment benefits and social assistance reduce the pressure to migrate from declining areas. Under Poland's unemployment insurance, qualified workers receive fairly generous benefits for periods ranging from six months in areas with low unemployment to 18 months in areas with high unemployment. In addition,

unemployed workers close to the retirement age receive preretirement benefits linked to their pensions. Low-income households are also eligible for guaranteed temporary social assistance benefits. Housing policies may discourage migration. During the transition, homes typically were transferred to their occupants at little or no cost. So the cost of remaining in one's home is low. At the same time, rent control discourages new construction, driving up the cost of housing in regions that are expanding economically. The high cost of housing in economically prosperous places can whittle away at the income gains workers might expect from migration.

Also discouraging migration are uniform national minimum wages unadjusted for costs of living, collective bargaining arrangements, and job protection laws. In other regions where the informal economy is dominant, labor market regulation is less binding. But in the formerly planned economies of Central and Eastern Europe, minimum wage and job protection regulations matter. In Poland, where the minimum wage is relatively high, national wage-setting appears to inhibit the migration of workers from economically depressed areas. Elsewhere in the region, where legislated minimum wages are relatively low, they do not appear to have a similar effect on internal labor mobility.

Sources: Dillinger 2007, Paci and others 2007.

is required for full employment in manufacturing could increase national welfare because output in both agriculture and manufacturing can be maintained at optimal levels.

In the late 1970s and early 1980s, however, economists began to question the classical models, pointing out the weaknesses of the Todaro framework, which failed to capture the dynamic nature of

labor movements. It minimized differences in the appetite for risk among prospective migrants. It did not account for differences in education attainment and how these differences can influence job searches. It ignored pertinent motivations and household characteristics that could influence a family's choice of who will migrate. And it neglected the possibility of migration for jobs in the urban informal economy and the pull these could exert independently of the modern manufacturing sector.[36]

In parallel, some economists in the mid-1980s began to think differently about economic growth, mainly by reformulating the way classical growth models treated technical progress. Human capital and ideas were different from other factors of production—they exhibited increasing returns to scale.[37] And because the generation of ideas and human capital are in essence social activities—clustering people in a way that has no comparison in the process of accumulating physical capital—these models could explain why cities are important. They also could explain why human and financial capital do not move from where they are already abundant—rich countries, leading areas in countries, and cities—to where they seems to be scarce—poor countries, lagging areas, and rural communities.[38]

If there are external effects from clustering human capital, cities can jump-start and maintain economic growth. Although urban specialists had long held this view,[39] it was sufficiently novel for economists. Researchers in urban economics enthusiastically took up the hunt for the theorized positive external effects from human capital spillovers. Theoretical and empirical studies sought to quantify what happens to productivity, wages, and land prices when the aggregate stock of human capital in a city increases.[40] Evidence began to emerge of social returns to education accruing to specific geographic areas, supporting arguments in favor of a greater concentration of economic activity, if not the clustering of labor specifically.[41]

These arguments did not themselves spill over into the mainstream labor migration literature until the turn of the century. This should come as little surprise: the fundamental assumptions for the classical migration models are at odds with those embraced by the new growth theorists and by those emphasizing agglomeration economies (see box 5.5).

Migration, growth, and welfare: divergence or convergence?

In a world with increasing returns to scale, will selective, voluntary migration lead to economic divergence or convergence? A large volume of empirical work from developed and developing countries bolsters an emerging consensus that governments should not see voluntary internal population movements as a threat. Indeed, internal migration offers societies an opportunity for economic growth and the convergence of welfare.

In contrast to the emerging consensus on migration within countries, the benefits and costs of international migration are still the subject of debate. The preeminence of place in determining the return on an individual's investment in human capital is most dramatically observed in the difference the simple act of crossing a border can make to earned income. An adult male Bolivian with nine years of schooling in Bolivia will earn roughly US$460 per months in dollars that reflect purchasing power at U.S. prices. But a person with the same education, talent, and drive would earn about 2.7 times that much if he worked in the United States. A similar Nigerian educated in Nigeria would earn eight times as much by working in the United States rather than in his native country. This "place premium" is large throughout the developing world.[42] Although the benefits to an individual from migrating from a poor country to a wealthy country are clear, is the accelerated flow of skilled labor out of developing countries more likely to help or to hinder their growth and convergence prospects? The answer is disputed.

But what is not disputed is the growing volume of internationally remitted earnings, which now outpace all other capital flows to poor and middle-income countries. In 2007 the flows of remittances to many developing countries surpassed those of foreign direct investment and equity for the

first time.[43] And these are only the flows of remittances that governments and researchers can observe—just a fraction of what is actually sent through formal and informal channels. Allowing the freer flow of skilled and unskilled labor across national borders would probably do more to reduce poverty in developing countries than any other single policy or aid initiative.[44]

BOX 5.5 *From Lewis to Lucas: the economic perspective on migration has changed*

The insights from economists that have had the greatest impact on how policy makers view migration share similar origins, in theories of economic growth. The evolution of economic thought on migration—and particularly on the growth payoff from clustering labor and talent in cities—spans the work of two Nobel Laureate economists, W. Arthur Lewis and Robert E. Lucas, Jr.

Lewis laid the foundations for the study of labor migration with his two-sector model of economic growth in developing countries. But theorists studying economic growth since Lewis took a different path from those who used his insights to focus narrowly on labor migration.

The classical migration models inspired by Lewis assumed an exogenously determined and constant rate of economic growth. In sharp contrast, the new growth theorists—inspired by Lucas's contention that there are positive external spillovers from clustering human capital—internalized growth in models that allowed for increasing returns to scale. The classical theories modeled each additional migrant as lowering the probability of employment, contributing to urban unemployment, and raising congestion costs. The new growth theorists and later the proponents of urban agglomeration economies could imagine in that migrant an additional source of human capital to drive the agglomeration engine of growth.

In 2002 Lucas bridged the gaps between these diverging strands of the development literature, in a theo-

retical study of migration from rural to urban areas in low- and middle-income countries.[a] He posited a transfer of labor from a traditional sector, employing a land-intensive technology, to a modern human capital-intensive sector, with an unending potential for economic growth. In Lucas's model, cities are places where new immigrants can accumulate skills required by modern production technologies. In the conclusion to the paper, referring to the attraction to cities driven by gains from agglomeration, he writes:

"Even in the rapidly growing economies of the post-colonial world, the passage from a 90 percent agricultural economy to one that is 90 percent urban is a matter of decades. Since everyone has the option to migrate earlier rather than later, something must occur as time passes that makes the city a better and better destination."[b]

The new insight from theories that acknowledged spillovers from clustering human capital is that, while the returns to scale in agriculture are constant, the returns to scale in manufacturing and services are increasing. The policy implications of adopting one view or the other are profoundly different. A policy maker persuaded by the classical view would restrict the movement of labor, particularly flows of migrants from villages to towns and cities. In contrast, a policy maker who recognizes the external benefits of human capital would do exactly the opposite, facilitating migration and clustering, particularly of workers with skills.

Source: WDR 2009 team.
a. Lucas Jr. 2004.
b. Lucas Jr. 2004.

Labor migration promotes growth.
Within countries, the accumulated empirical evidence shows that labor migration increases the earnings prospects of people who move. It also shows that labor migration contributes to aggregate growth by improving the distribution of labor, driving concentration. And by clustering skills and talent, migration drives agglomeration spillovers. In the United Kingdom the estimated long-run wage premium for men who migrate is about 14 percent, and for women about 11 percent.[45] Wage premiums ranging from 7 percent to 11 percent have been found among internal migrants in the United States.[46] These gains for individual migrants translate into gains for the broader economy. In many countries high rates of internal labor mobility have been associated with periods of sustained economic growth, as in the United States from 1900 to 2000,[47] Brazil from 1950 to 1975,[48] Japan from 1950 to 1975,[49] the Republic of Korea from 1970 to 1995,[50] and China from 1980 to 2005. Among a selection of developing countries with comparable measures of internal migration drawn from household surveys, a positive association is found between internal labor mobility and economic growth (see figure 5.7).

Research in Bangladesh, China, the Philippines, and Vietnam suggests that internal migration has helped to drive growth.[51] In Brazil internal migration has raised productivity by allowing producers to reap the benefits of agglomeration.[52] Conversely, in China, restrictions on the movement of labor impede growth by constraining city size. Because Chinese cities are kept artificially smaller than they might otherwise be, the country has experienced welfare losses from forgone higher growth rates.[53] And in India past restrictions on the movement of labor may have kept the size of Indian cities inefficiently small, at a cost in forgone growth (see box 5.6).[54] Internal migrants are clearly economically active. In 24 of the 35 countries with comparable survey indicators, migrants are as or more likely than locally native people of working age to be employed (see figure 5.8).

In today's developed countries, leading and lagging areas converged. As for earnings and living standards between the leading and lagging areas, historical evidence of the impact of the internal labor movement during the nineteenth century in today's developed countries supports convergence.

At the start of the nineteenth century, the majority of nonindigenous people in the United States lived on the eastern seaboard. By century's end, more than 2 million square miles had been added to the country's original land area (see "Geography in Motion 1: Overcoming Distance in North America"). Robust institutions were critical in settling such a large land mass. The U.S. Constitution along with the Northwest Ordinance (1787) provided the framework for transforming unsettled areas into states. Factor mobility was enhanced by the commerce clause in the Constitution, explicitly prohibiting state governments from restraining trade across state boundaries. State and local governments provided public goods and infrastructure to attract settlers. In the 1820s real wages of "common" (unskilled) nonfarm labor were about 33 percent higher in the Midwest than in the Northeast. Between 1820 and 1860, the Midwest's share of the unskilled northern labor force rose from 23 to 45 percent. As the Midwest's share of

Figure 5.7   **Internal labor mobility and economic growth often go together**

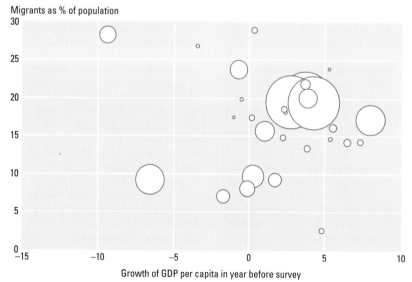

Migrants as % of population

Growth of GDP per capita in year before survey

Source: WDR 2009 team estimates using selected household surveys.
Note: Marker shows land area of country. Marker in the upper-left-hand corner is República Bolivariana de Venezuela in 2004.

BOX 5.6   *Implicit barriers to mobility: place-based entitlement and divisions in India*

Policy barriers to internal mobility in India are imposed by omission rather than by commission, exemplifying the implicit obstacles to migration in many developing countries. Current policies do not allow communities to fully capture the benefits of labor mobility. The costs and risks of migration would be significantly lowered by greater flexibility in the way households use public services and social entitlements, and in the deployment of targeted assistance for mobile populations. Negative attitudes held by government and ignorance of the benefits of population mobility have caused migration to be overlooked as a force in economic development.

Recent evidence shows that population mobility in India—having stabilized in the 1970s and 1980s—is rising. India's 1961 census classified 33 percent of the population as internal migrants—people living and working in a place other than where they were born. The share of migrants is larger in cities (about 40 percent of the population) than in rural areas (about 30 percent). But by far the largest flows of migrants—within districts, across districts, and across states—are from lagging rural to leading rural areas. Since the 1960s rural-to-rural migration flows typically have been more than twice the volume as the next largest flows, from rural areas to cities. Rural-rural migration accounted for roughly 62 percent of all movements in 1999–2000. Workers from lagging states like Bihar, Orissa, Rajasthan, and Uttar Pradesh routinely travel to the developed green revolution states of Gujarat, Maharashtra, and Punjab to work on farms.

In India both distance and division limit labor mobility. The highest levels of movement are recorded within the same district. The flow of migrants across state lines is a trickle. Since 2001 there has been a slowdown in permanent or long-term migration (see the map below). The share of lifetime (permanent) interstate migrants—at about 4 percent—is much lower than the total migrant population. Most of these permanent migrants live in cities. In addition to geographic distance, the strong differences in culture and language can discourage movement far from a person's home place.

Although official data sets indicate a slowdown in permanent rural-urban migration, microstudies find that circular migration is emerging as a dominant form of migration among the poor. Short-term migrants have been estimated to number 12.6 million but recent microstudies suggest that the figure is 30 million and rising.

The economic benefits of migration are not always recognized by policy makers. Two forms of policy have been attempted to counter migration in India. The first response has been to increase rural employment, in an attempt to stem movement out of rural areas. This policy implicitly assumes that deteriorating agriculture leads to out-migration and that improved employment opportunities in lagging rural areas can reduce or reverse migration. These measures include the recently introduced National Rural Employment Guarantee Program, which promises 100 days of wage labor to one adult member in every rural household who volunteers for unskilled work, numerous watershed development programs that aim to improve agricultural productivity, and programs to develop small and medium towns.

The second policy response is implicit. Because of the perceived negative effects, local governments remain hostile toward migrants, while employers routinely disregard laws to protect their rights and needs. In many cases welfare policies and social services are designed for a sedentary population. This is best exemplified by location-specific entitlements to social services, housing subsidies, food rations, and other public amenities especially important to working poor people.

Internal migrants in India flow to prospering Delhi and Maharashtra
Internal migrant flows reported in 2001 census

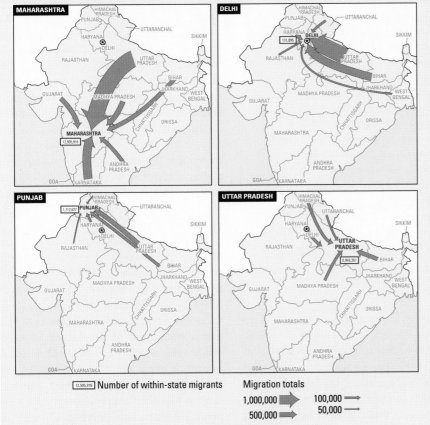

☐ *12,505,916* **Number of within-state migrants**

Migration totals

1,000,000 ➡
500,000 ➡
100,000 →
50,000 →

Source: WDR 2009 team, based on census data from the Census of India.

Figure 5.8   Internal migrants are more likely to work than natives
Comparison of internal migrants and native workers

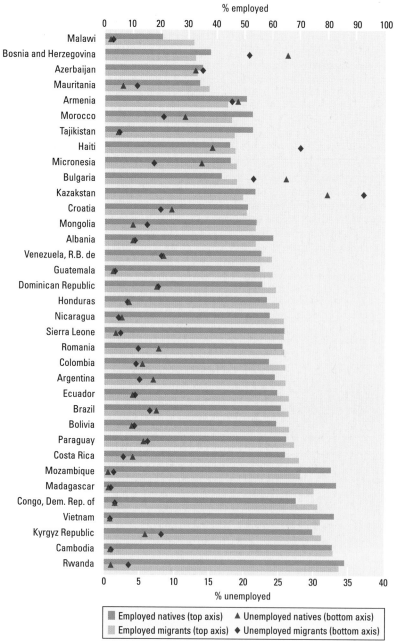

Employed natives (top axis)   ▲ Unemployed natives (bottom axis)
Employed migrants (top axis)   ◆ Unemployed migrants (bottom axis)

Source: WDR 2009 team using household surveys.

large in the mid-nineteenth century, eroded as labor poured into the city. More generally, wage differences across French *départements* narrowed significantly over the second half of the nineteenth century. Across Canadian cities, wage differences evolved precisely as would be expected if Canadian migrants treated the entire country as a single labor market.[56] And across England wage differences did not erode much during industrialization. This was not because the labor force was immobile, as history shows English labor moved freely from low- to high-wage areas. Rather, it was because the forces that sustained industrial development in various parts of England were so persistent that internal migration in any one period was not enough to cause wage gaps to decline.[57]

Throughout the twentieth century, labor mobility continued to be integral to concentration and convergence across the two geographically expansive and economically prosperous countries of North America. In the United States labor mobility was greater than in Europe, distributing labor from low- to high-wage states, converging state per capita incomes through most of the twentieth century.[58] With the notable exception of the U.S. South (see box 5.7), regional convergence in wage rates coincided with cross-regional labor market institutions and information flows.[59] Similarly, in Canada, labor mobility continued to narrow per capita income differences among Canadian provinces from 1910 to 1921. And when internal migration petered to a trickle between 1921 and 1960, convergence in income also slowed.[60]

Disparities in income and welfare between places were higher in the 15 countries of Western Europe where labor mobility has been much lower than in North America throughout the twentieth century. The variation in employment across subnational areas of the United States is much lower than that across subnational economic areas of the European Union (EU). In parts of the EU where employment is highest, the employment rate is 60 percent higher than where it is lowest. In the United States the difference is only 22 percent.[61] The greater equity in employment outcomes in the United States is a

the labor force increased, its wage advantage eroded to roughly 17 percent in the 1850s, and to 10 percent in the four decades after the Civil War. State data on farm wages point to a long-term narrowing of geographic wage differences in response to internal migration, a process that can be dated back even before the Civil War.[55]

In France wage differences between the Paris metropolitan area and the countryside,

Factor Mobility and Migration

165

direct consequence of higher labor mobility and a more tightly integrated national labor market.[62]

Convergence, after divergence, in developing countries. More recent empirical studies show the positive impact of net migration on income convergence in Japan.[63] So do estimates from India, the Russian Federation, and the United Kingdom.[64] These studies may underestimate the full impact of migration on the convergence in living standards by failing to take into account the differing skills of migrants flowing in and out of areas, and by ignoring the indirect negative impact of housing and labor market rigidities. Analysis that distinguishes between (1) the flow of skilled and unskilled migrants and (2) the levels of human capital in migrants' places of origin and destination shows a large impact of labor mobility on convergence.

Much of the empirical evidence of the impact of internal migration from low- and middle-income countries is consistent with expected convergence, after an initial divergence. As Japan grew, regional income inequality followed a bell-shaped curve, initially increasing in 1955–61, but then falling in 1961–75. Research attributes the convergence to labor migration.[65] In China after the economic reforms of 1978, income differences between subprovincial areas initially widened after economic reforms from 1978–96, but later declined with greater integration and internal labor migration.[66] In India and Indonesia higher internal labor mobility is associated with lower income inequality,[67] and migration increased equality in Mexico. But in Chile, lower-than-expected rates of internal migration may be to blame for high income inequality.[68] And in Brazil, where both social inequality and spatial mobility of labor are high, some research suggests that inequality would be even higher if not for internal migration.[69]

Most early research on internal migration and convergence across areas within countries focused only on a small part of migration as an economic force: labor market adjustments and changes in wage differences between areas. The impact of remittances was ignored. Yet in Sub-

---

BOX 5.7 *Why did the U.S. South take so long to catch up? Division.*

Researchers have long questioned why wages and incomes in the U.S. South were so different from the rest of the country for so long. Although wages and incomes in the South have caught up, particularly since the Great Depression, the process seems to have been remarkably slow before the 1940s (see "Geography in Motion 1: Overcoming Distance in North America").

Before the New Deal, the southern labor market was isolated from the rest of the country, with large wage gaps. Yet, there was little migration out of the southern states, even among African Americans who suffered the lowest wages and the most social discrimination and political disenfranchisement. Before the 1920s demand for low-skilled labor in the industrializing North was satisfied by migrating workers from Europe. Employers in northern factories showed a preference for low-skilled European immigrants over blacks, and the abundance of European migrants made it affordable to indulge this preference. This would change with the restrictions on movement across borders, tightened in the 1930s.

Until World War II, there were few established flows of either information or labor between the South and the North. Given the cumulative dependence of migration corridors, this impeded the movement of low-skilled workers of all races out of southern states. Southern work-

ers found opportunities by moving westward.

Even when the flows of migrants from the South to the North began to grow, wage and income differences persisted. Scholars explain that the Great Migration of rural southern blacks to northern cities involved a disproportionately educated segment of the population. After World War II, the selective migration of African Americans moderated, with return migration associated with economic growth in the South.

With the gradual buildup of information and migration corridors between North and South, the elimination of legal racial discrimination in the wake of the civil rights movement, and the improvement in the education of African Americans students with the racial integration of schools, the wages and incomes in southern states gradually converged with those in northern states. Indeed, since the 1970s, labor migration between the North and the South and other areas of the United States has been a safety valve easing economic pressure during recessions. The differing impact of economic downturns across areas of the country have spurred large movements of workers from states where the economy was contracting to other, more prosperous areas. In the early 1990s, a sizable number of workers migrated from the Northeast to states in the South.

Sources: Rosenbloom and Sundstrom 2003; Margo 2004; and Vigdor 2006.

Saharan Africa, remittances account for 15 percent of rural income. In Uganda labor mobility has a positive effect on household expenditure. Comparable households enjoy much higher per capita spending if they migrate within their own district or to another district than if they stay in their native area. The incomes of Ugandans who migrate from lagging to leading areas are 10 to 60 percent higher than nonmigrants in origin or destination areas.[70] In Tanzania, in the Kagera region between 1991 and 2004, internal migration added 36 percentage points to consumption growth.[71]

Remittances from internal migration have a positive impact in other developing regions as well. In Bangladesh temporary migrants to Dhaka send up to 60 percent of their income to family members in their home places, covering a large share of the household budgets of migrant-sending households. In several Latin American countries remitted earnings not only augment the consumption of receiving households, but also lower the incidence of poverty in their communities[72]

and increase the investment in education.[73] And in East Asia remittances from migrant family members increase investment in education and capital-intensive household enterprises in the Philippines.[74] In China the ministry of agriculture expects that the remittances of migrant workers will soon be more than earnings from agriculture for rural households.

For the communities left behind, internal migration is critical for overcoming poverty and smoothing household consumption in the wake of unexpected shocks. Indeed, World Development Report 2008 *Agriculture for Development* identifies internal migration as an important "pathway out of poverty" for rural households that can no longer rely solely on agriculture for their livelihood.[75] Even in situations in which supporting the permanent resettlement from villages to cities may be fairly costly, within the means of only better-off households, seasonal and temporary migration can more immediately mitigate downward shocks to consumption in rural areas than even the best-designed social assistance program.[76]

Members of rural households in Bangladesh migrate to cities to diversify household income when harvests are lower than expected. Internal migration in China raises the consumption of households in migrants' home communities, and the increase is greater for poorer households. And the out-migration of Chinese workers allows those who remain in rural areas to work more. The gains associated with internal migration increase housing wealth and consumer durables as well as agricultural production.[77] Indeed, the selective phenomenon that determines who moves seems to work both ways. Those with higher academic achievement choose to migrate to jobs in China's cities, and people who are better at farming choose to stay.[78]

Pulled or pushed? The development benefits of migration are seen when people move voluntarily. Large numbers of people—particularly in the poorest countries—are also forced to move by deteriorating living conditions and conflict. People are "pushed" off their land when agriculture is in decline, by the pressures of population growth, and when

Table 5.4 Most migrants move for economic reasons, but many are pushed out by poor services

	Percentage of internal migrants reporting reason for migration		
	To seek employment or join family	For education, health, or better living conditions	For sociopolitical or other reasons
Malawi	95	1	4
Morocco	91	2	7
Romania	87	10	3
Ecuador	86	12	2
Nicaragua	84	5	11
Albania	82	11	7
Mozambique	81	4	15
Vietnam	80	7	13
Armenia	78	1	21
Tajikistan	78	10	12
Kazakstan	77	14	9
Bolivia	77	17	6
Dominican Republic	76	21	3
Cambodia	75	2	24
Paraguay	74	24	2
Guatemala	72	24	4
Bulgaria	71	28	0
Congo, Dem. Rep. of	69	6	25
Kyrgyz Rep	69	28	3
Madagascar	62	28	11
Bosnia & Herzegovina	55	1	43
Rwanda	54	5	41
Azerbaijan	44	5	52
Mongolia	41	28	30
Sierra Leone	23	3	74
Mauritania	23	74	4

Source: WDR 2009 team estimates using household survey data.
Note: "Sociopolitical" refers to different circumstances and events, depending on the country and year specified, that lead to involuntary internal displacement.

environmental change makes continued cultivation of certain areas no longer viable. Historically, droughts have had sudden and prolonged impacts on the distribution of the population, particularly in Sub-Saharan Africa[79] and South Asia.[80]

Another important "push" that propels internal migration—mundane, but no less critical—is the lack of adequate public services (see table 5.4 and box 5.8).

In many developing countries, schools, health care centers, hospitals, and public and private amenities are located in areas of economic activity. With a concentration of economic mass, public services can be withdrawn from smaller towns and villages.[81] Several studies document the migration to large economic centers by people in search of better education and health services.[82] This movement, though voluntary,

BOX 5.8 *Migrating to economic density: rational decisions or bright lights?*

Twenty percent of poor men born in Brazil's Northeast—one of the country's lagging areas—now live in its prosperous Southeast. A large demographic shift occurred from villages to towns and cities in the 1970s, and from towns to cities in the 1990s.

Economists have long argued that migration decisions are motivated by

the possibility of earning higher wages. But since many migrants do not find jobs after moving, this attraction may be irrational. Some policy makers in developing countries believe that rather than adding to the economy in their new neighborhoods, migrants subtract from them by worsening the problems of livability. This

belief has resulted in deterrents ranging from disincentives to draconian regulations to limit the movement of people.

Recent empirical evidence from four decades of Brazilian census data shows something different. Working-age men migrated not only to look for better jobs but also to get better access to basic public services such as piped water, electricity, and health care. Results from models of migration behavior that focus only on the migrant's desire to move in search of better jobs can be biased, because places with better public services also have more job opportunities. Firms like to locate where workers would like to live. By ignoring the importance of public services, some econometric estimates may overstate a migrant's willingness to move in response to wage differences.

To determine how much public services matter, a rich data set of public services at the municipality level was combined with individual records from the Brazilian census to evaluate the relative importance of wage differences and public services in the migrant's decisions to move. Predictably, wage differences are the main factor influencing migration choices. For the better off, basic public services are not important in the decision to move. But for the poor, differences in access to basic public services mattered. In fact, poor migrants are willing to accept lower wages to get access to better services. A Brazilian minimum wage worker earning R$7 per hour (about US$2.30 in February 2008) was willing to pay R$420 a year to have access to better health services, R$87 for better water supply, and R$42 for electricity. Poor migrants are rational.

Contributed by Somik Lall and Christopher Timmins.

Brazilians move to the prosperous Southeast
Internal migration of adults, ages 25–35, based on reported region of birth in 1991 and 2001 censuses

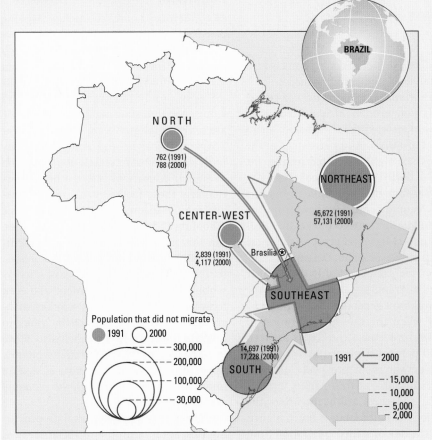

Source: WDR 2009 team, based on census data from the Instituto Brasileiro de Geografia e Estatística.

BOX 5.9 *Too early to tell? The impact of African emigrants on Africa*

The brain drain is debated most heatedly for Sub-Saharan Africa. Concern is justified, but emigrants and diaspora groups have contributed much to Africa's development.

Early accounts of voluntary migration from Africa tell of small numbers of Africans going abroad to study in religious schools and monasteries in Europe in the 1700s. Many of these students translated the Bible into African languages. In doing so, they produced some of the earliest attempts to introduce written text to what were predominantly oral-language traditions. One such student, Jacobus Capitein, who emigrated from what would become Ghana to study in the Netherlands, is credited for spreading the use of the written word in his native country.

Another Ghanaian, Kwegyir Aggrey, from a later generation of emigrants, traveled to the United States to study at Columbia University. With the support of American philanthropists, he returned to Ghana to found the country's first nondenominational school, which would later become the University of Ghana. Many of the region's seats of learning have similar origins.

Most of Africa's independence leaders were part of what might have been termed a brain drain in the 1930s and 1940s. Kamuzu Banda, Jomo Kenyatta, Julius Nyerere, and others were from a generation of students who emigrated to the United States and Europe and formed plans to fight for independence.

The economic and social contribution of these emigrants to their countries of origin are difficult to quantify but impossible to deny, and have made all the difference to the development prospects of Sub-Saharan Africa.

Source: Easterly and Nyarko 2008.

is more likely to add to congestion costs in cities than to agglomeration benefits.

International brain drains—or gains? There is concern about the volume of skilled workers leaving Sub-Saharan Africa and the Caribbean. As a percentage of the total stock of highly educated people, the number of skilled emigrants looks high. On the whole, though, most skilled migrants to high-income countries come from the larger middle-income countries like Brazil and India. Migration prospects in these countries induce more human capital accumulation, increasing not only the number of skilled migrants but also the skills of the global workforce generally.[83] A "brain gain" is likely when the rate of emigration of skilled workers from a country is between 5 and 10 percent. Concern arises for the stunted development prospects of some countries in Sub-Saharan Africa, Central America, and the Caribbean, where the emigration of skilled labor is much higher. In 2000 the rate of skilled emigration from Sub-Saharan Africa was 13.1 percent, from

Central America it was 16.9 percent, and from the Caribbean it was 42.8 percent.[84]

Critics of the "brain drain–brain gain" debate point out that it ignores real-world patterns of international migration. Skilled workers do not "drain away" as much as "circulate" among countries in the world economy. The benefits of attracting and retaining skilled people do not have to be distributed in a zero-sum game among countries. In addition to the large flows of international remittances, many skilled migrants work hard to return to their countries with improved prospects as entrepreneurs, armed with capital, new skills, and ideas. Several political, academic, and business leaders in developing countries began as emigrants (see box 5.9). Cross-country research on the determinants of economic growth has not found evidence of a negative impact associated with the emigration of people with skills.[85]

Practical policies for managing migration

Not everyone chooses to migrate. Moving can be a costly, difficult, and disruptive decision. Indeed, a generation of research shows that the movements of labor—from villages to towns, between towns and cities, across borders in the same region, and from poor to distant wealthy countries—are selective. Migrants are not the same as people who stay behind. And while many individuals move in search of a better job or higher education, many others—particularly those in the rural areas of low- and middle-income countries—seek basic schooling and health care for their families. But this migration is economically inefficient. By overlooking the provision of basic social services in outlying areas—such as schools, primary health centers, and even basic public infrastructure—policy makers can unwittingly influence the choice to migrate, motivating households to move for reasons other than to exploit economic opportunities. While the move is welfare improving for these families, the economy may end up worse off.

By focusing more attention on providing education, health, and social services in outlying, economically lagging areas,

Table 5.5 What does a practical policy toward migration do? Recognize agglomeration benefits.

	Migration of unskilled labor	Migration of skilled labor
Internal migration	**Neutral,** but discouraging if agglomeration economies are unlikely. Policies should encourage migration for economic reasons and discourage migration in search of public services. Remove explicit and implicit restrictions as well as place-based service entitlements.	**Strongly supportive,** particularly to capture agglomeration gains where these are likely. Invest in services in peripheral areas to build portable human capital. Increase the flow of labor market information, so migrants arrive better informed of employment possibilities.
Cross-border migration within regional neighborhoods	**Supportive,** particularly for welfare and diversification gains from remitted earnings.	**Supportive,** where markets in regional neighborhoods are integrated and gains from agglomeration can spill over to the sending country.
Cross-border migration outside regional neighborhoods	**Supportive,** particularly for welfare gains from remitted earnings.	**Neutral,** as there is a possible foregone agglomeration from an accelerated brain drain, but possible gains from knowledge transfer of return migrants, and strong incentives for human capital investment from the prospect of migrating.

Source: WDR 2009 team.

governments can go a long way toward eliminating some of the reasons households are pushed to migrate. These efforts can, in turn, improve the quality of migration. Labor mobility that leads to greater concentration of people and talent in locations of choice will contribute more to agglomeration benefits than it adds to congestion.

The impact of policies on the welfare of migrants and the broader economy should fuel skepticism of attempts to restrict labor mobility. Encouragingly, there is a growing shift away from restrictions on population mobility and toward facilitation and encouragement. But other than allowing people to move and settle where they will earn the highest return on their labor and human capital, can governments do more to help capture the benefits of agglomeration?

Migration results from forces that "pull" as well as those that "push" individuals to leave. One big pull is the agglomeration economies in cities. But people are also pushed out by the lack of social services. In Africa disparities in school enrollment and neonatal care between cities, towns, and villages are attributable to the near absence of schools and health facilities in outlying areas.[86] Evidence from Central Asia shows that in the isolated parts of Tajikistan, schools are inadequately heated, drinking water is scarce, and arrangements to clear garbage and sewage are lacking.[87] In China the government is emphasizing a more even distribution of basic services to address the gaps in living standards between the coast and the interior. By prioritizing education, health, and social services in outlying areas

over other investments, governments can eliminate some of the reasons households are pushed to migrate. These efforts can shape the composition of migration in a way that growing concentrations are more likely to add to agglomeration economies, rather than pile up congestion costs.

By recognizing the selective nature of voluntary labor migration, and the implications of increasing returns to scale, the economic arguments and empirical evidence in this chapter support a more positive view of labor mobility than that held by policy makers in poor and middle-income countries in the past. From this perspective, a practical policy stance will differ according to the human capital endowment of prospective migrants and whether the agglomeration spillovers from clustering talent can be captured and taxed by governments (see table 5.5).

All the evidence on the benefits of education suggests that policy makers should be concerned about the rapid loss of talent to countries far outside their regions. But the potential costs in forgone human capital from outright restrictions on skilled emigration are high. A far more practical and sustainable policy stance would operate along two tracks. First, raise the private, individual costs of acquiring human capital to match the private individual returns from migration of skilled workers abroad. Second, reap the benefits from diaspora communities in the world's prosperous places, by encouraging their economic and political participation at home, and by making it easy for them to retain citizenship, vote, and eventually resettle if they so choose.

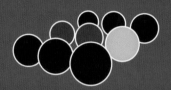

CHAPTER 6

Transport Costs and Specialization

The sharpest insights sometimes come from piecing together bits of information that separately can be innocuous and unsurprising. In the mid-1970s overseas transport costs had fallen to a fraction of what they were in 1900, thanks to such inventions as steam power and the telegraph. And the share of trade between neighboring countries in Europe had risen relative to their trade with countries more distant. In 1910 British exports were spread quite evenly between Europe (35 percent), Asia (24 percent), and other regions (31 percent). By 1996, 60 percent of Britain's exports went to Europe and only 11 percent to Asia.[1]

Singly, neither fact is surprising. Together, they are exactly the opposite of what standard economics would predict. After all, transport costs should be a larger part of the cost of goods shipped from half a world away than for goods traded with neighbors. So a fall in transport costs should have meant *more* trade with distant partners than with neighbors, not less. What had happened?

Research in the 1980s provides the answer.[2] Two waves of globalization—a euphemism for falling transport and trade costs—were responsible. During the first wave from about 1840 to World War I, transport costs fell enough to make large-scale trade possible between places based on their comparative advantage. So Britain traded machinery for Indian tea, Argentine beef, and Australian wool; trade increased between distant and dissimilar countries. During the second wave after 1950,

transport costs fell low enough that small differences in products and tastes fueled trade between similar countries, at least in Europe and North America. Neighbors traded different types of beer and different parts of cars, such as wheels and tires. Trade in parts and components grew to take advantage of specialization and economies of scale. The first wave of globalization was characterized by "conventional," inter-industry trade that exploited differences in natural endowments, the second by a "new international trade" driven by economies of scale and product differentiation.

Transport costs and scale economies interact to produce the trade flows observed in the past half-century.[3] The main insight from research is that the relationships between transport costs, production locations, and trade patterns are nonlinear. Falling transport costs first led to countries trading more with countries that were distant but dissimilar. When they fell further, they led to more trade with neighboring countries. Similarly, when transport costs fell from moderate levels, production concentrated in and around large markets.

In East Asia, as the costs of transporting goods by sea and air fell, the production of manufactured goods spread from Japan to neighboring economies such as Hong Kong, China; the Republic of Korea; and Taiwan, China. Production then moved to Southeast Asia, and now it has moved to China. With a fall in telecommunication costs, large cities in the United States and Europe reaped the rewards of growing markets. But as the costs of telecommunications fell further, services such as accounting and call centers moved to smaller cities in Europe and North America, and then, as they fell further, to cities in distant India and the Philippines.

Intraindustry trade—the exchange of broadly similar goods and services—is perhaps the most important economic development since World War II. Countries trade Samsung, Motorola, and Nokia phones; casings for television remotes; and buttons and stitching for textiles. Such trade is now more than half of global trade, up from a quarter in 1962. The share of intraindustry trade has gone up for all types of goods and services, from such primary goods as oil and natural gas, to such intermediate inputs as auto parts and computer help-lines, to such final goods as food and beverages (see figure 6.1, panel a).

This is important because of the border-related divisions identified in chapter 3. These divisions are barriers to movements of capital and labor. If all that countries could trade were final goods, such as televisions and cars, then convergence in living standards would be slow at best. With trade in intermediate inputs, the potential for specialization and trade increases significantly. The efficiencies generated through specialization and scale economies in production and transportation have indeed benefited the world. But these benefits have not been shared evenly (see figure 6.1, panel b). East Asia, North America, and Western Europe account for much of the world's intraindustry trade.

This chapter explains why these regions account for this trade and what this means for developing countries. In good measure the reasons have to do with the interactions between scale economies and transport costs. Transport and trade costs influence trade volumes. A 10-percent increase in trade costs is estimated to reduce trade volumes by 20 percent.[4] Trade in intermediate goods is especially sensitive to transport costs. If the share of imported intermediate inputs in final demand is large, small changes in transport costs can have large effects on the volume of trade flows—the "trade friction" increases. For instance, a 5-percent increase in transport costs can produce trade friction equivalent to an ad valorem tax of almost

50 percent, when the share of intermediate inputs in value added is 70 percent.[5] As transport costs fall, then, trade in intermediates would also increase rapidly.

"Circular causation" also affects transport. Trade volumes influence transport costs. On the trans-Pacific route, cost differences between a "Panamax" unit of 4,000

Figure 6.1   Intraindustry trade is becoming more important for all types of goods, but not in all world regions
Evolution of global intraindustry trade, by 3-digit product group, 1962–2006

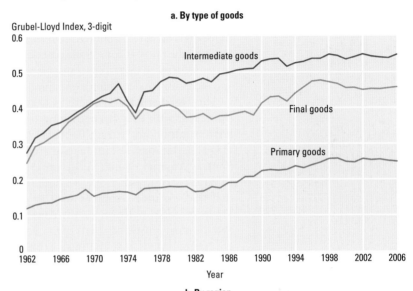

a. By type of goods

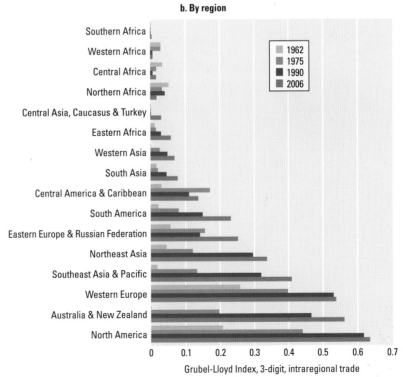

b. By region

Source: Brülhart 2008, for this Report.
Note: The Grubel-Lloyd Index is the fraction of total trade that is accounted for by intraindustry trade.

TEU (20-foot equivalent units, a measure of shipping tonnage) and a mega post-Panamax unit of 10,000 TEU are 50 percent. But exploiting these cost advantages requires large trade volumes and high capacity, because economies of scale are available not just in the production of goods and services but also in their transport. It costs about $400 to ship a container to the United States from China, about $800 to ship from India, and $1,300 to ship from Sierra Leone.[6] China's enormous trade is almost certainly a reason for low transport costs, just as falling transport costs have encouraged countries to move production to China. Scale economies in transport mean that falling transport costs and increasing trade reinforce one another.

The Northern Hemisphere is heavily trafficked, with ever-strengthening trade links as intraindustry trade flourishes (see map 6.1). But ships sail through or around Central America, South Asia, and Sub-Saharan Africa, going only to countries that have natural resources such as oil. Trade passages between South America and the most prosperous parts of the world are narrow roads, not the busy expressways between East Asia, North America,

and Western Europe. Global air and Internet traffic maps show a similar imbalance. These developments should be disconcerting for developing countries not integrated into these self-reinforcing production and trade networks. Scale economies in production and transport will make it more difficult, not easier, for developing countries to enter these highly competitive markets.

A world of nonlinear relationships and cumulative causation is a world with thresholds. Knowing how developing countries can get past these thresholds depends on where they are, what they produce, and the costs that traders must pay. In the developed world, the total trade and transport costs as a share of the value of goods can be split into 20 percent transport costs, 45 percent border-related trade costs, and 55 percent retail and wholesale distribution costs. These costs multiply, piling up to a 170 percent tax on the value of goods and services traded.[7] What they show is that lower international transport costs have reduced distance but that trade costs due to *international division* remain high. Meanwhile, transport costs due to *internal distance* have stayed high even in the developed world.

Map 6.1 Busy seafaring in the North, little landfall in the South
Intensity of shipping routes during one year beginning October 2004

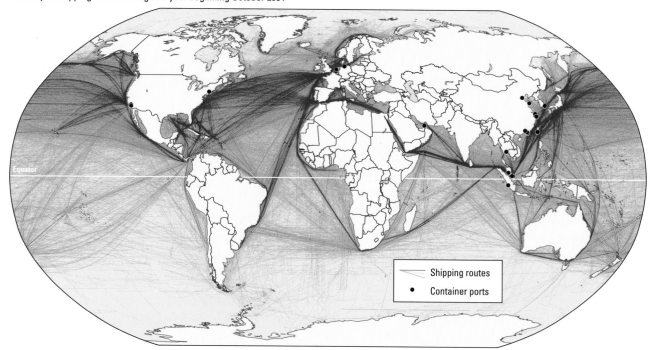

Sources: Data from the World Meteorological Organization (WMO) Voluntary Observing Ships' (VOS) scheme, processed by Halpern and others 2008.
Note: Container ports shown are the 20 largest by TEU of total containers handled in 2005 (Heideloff and Zachcial 2006).

Developing countries can learn how countries have reduced transportation costs, including how trade has been stimulated and new technologies developed. From the analysis of the past two decades, they can learn how spatial concentration of production may change as transport costs fall. What does this mean for latecomers to economic development? The main points:

- *Better transport technologies developed over the past two centuries have increased the volume of trade and radically altered its nature.* Before World War I transport costs declined enough to make large-scale trade possible, but only between countries that were dissimilar. They happened to be countries that were distant, because big differences in climate and natural endowments usually meant the countries were in different parts of the world (Indonesia and the Netherlands, for example). During the second wave following World War II, transport costs fell enough for small differences in products and tastes to fuel trade. This led to a rise in trade between countries that are similar (for instance, Argentina and Brazil), which often happen to be neighbors.[8] As transport costs fall, physical geography matters less. But with economies of scale in production, economic geography matters more.

- *A decline in transport costs—with increasing returns to scale—generally means more spatial concentration of production.* Recent thinking in economics has emphasized the importance of transport costs in development. With high transport costs, large economies of scale will remain unexploited, and production inefficient. Efficient production is more specialized. When transport costs fall, spatial differences in production and economic growth will increase, both within and between countries.

- *Developing countries should pay more attention to transport and communications regulations to reduce transport and trade costs.* The new economic geography has inadvertently contributed to an exclusive policy focus on "hard" infrastructure. The most critical policy-related aspects—the naturally monopolistic nature of transport—have been assumed away. Developing countries should do more to address the negative effects of market structure in the transport sector. And for some aspects of the agenda, they will need international support.

What has happened: two centuries of experience

Falling transport costs in the 100 years or so before World War II brought closer economic integration within and between countries. Then, as in the twentieth century, the fall was caused by large infrastructure investments and breakthroughs in transport technology.

From the early nineteenth century to the beginning of World War I, the global economy went through what economic historians call the "first era of globalization." Domestically, canals and then railways greatly reduced transport costs, leading to larger integrated home markets and to converging prices for manufactured and agricultural goods. The routing of these transport links greatly influenced the rise and decline of urban agglomerations. Internationally, steamships lowered maritime transport costs and increased the speed and reliability of service. The results were narrower intercountry price differences, expanding trade on routes that the new shipping technology could serve, and the emergence of large-scale interindustry trade.

Domestic transport. Inland waterways and railways reduced intercity and interarea transport costs dramatically in the first half of the nineteenth century. Before the railway era, which started around 1830 in Europe, most transportation was on roads or—50 to 75 percent cheaper—on water. In the United States massive investment in canal construction completely changed interregional trade and shaped a new urbanization pattern. The construction of the Erie Canal between 1817 and 1825 reduced the cost of transport between Buffalo and New York City by 85 percent, cutting the journey time from 21 days to 8. Productivity in the U.S. internal transportation sector grew at an annual average of 4.7 percent in the four decades before the Civil War. British navigable waterways quadrupled between 1780 and 1820. French canal construction boomed similarly, and continental European countries made a big step toward overcoming division when the Congress of Vienna recognized the freedom of navigation on the Rhine in 1815. Steamships appeared on important rivers and lakes in the early nineteenth century, drastically reducing travel times.

The major nineteenth-century development in transport was the expansion of railroads, which quickly surpassed inland waterways and "performed the Smithian function of widening the market."[9] Cities no longer just provided public services—they attracted industries with increasing returns to scale, reaping productivity effects from the more specialized inputs and larger labor markets. In the United States the expansion of the railways had strong effects on the geographic distribution of economic activity. Illinois, Michigan, and Ohio had marked increases in population, construction, and manufacturing with the new rail lines within and across their borders. One canal after another was abandoned. In 1850 boats carried six times the freight of railroads; by 1890 railroads carried five times the freight of boats. The drop in transport costs narrowed price differences for agricultural goods between local markets dramatically. The spread in the wheat price between New York City and Iowa fell from 69 percent to 19 percent from 1870 to 1910, and between New York City and Wisconsin from 52 percent to 10 percent.[10]

Railways expanded less in Europe than in the United States, reflecting the national scope of rail systems and the smaller size of European countries.[11] The higher freight transport intensity of U.S. rail propelled a further productivity increase. In 1910 the labor productivity in American railways was 3.3 times that in Britain, a gap that had doubled since 1870.[12] Russian railway construction took off after the mid-1860s, spreading wheat and rye production with the narrowing of regional price differences. The export share of Russian agriculture increased from 29 percent of the grain produced in European Russia to more than 42 percent between 1906 and 1910.[13]

India's rail expansion had even bigger impacts. In the 1860s the prices in some districts were 8 to 10 times higher than in others, and famines were common. The rail system reduced transport costs by about 80 percent, and the coefficient of variation of wheat and rice prices fell from more than 40 percent in 1870 to below 20 percent in the decade before World War I.[14] Lower transport costs had little effect on industrial development, however. At the turn of the eighteenth century, modern industry employed 2 to 3 percent of India's industrial workers (about 10 percent of the workforce). Modern factories were concentrated in two maritime trading hubs, Bombay and Bengal.[15]

International transport. The investments in domestic transport created large and integrated home markets. Tariff barriers remained low, and international trade benefited from technical and organizational progress, mostly in shipping. Ocean shipping rates differed substantially for routes and commodities, reflecting cost differences in harbor technologies, ship types, and stowage opportunities.[16] But overall the trade costs for grain, the main internationally traded good, fell by 40 percent between 1880 and 1914 within Europe and between the United States and Europe. This substantially reduced the price differences between exporting and importing countries.

Liverpool wheat prices exceeded Chicago prices by 58 percent in 1870, 18 percent in 1895, and 16 percent in 1913.[17] For nonagricultural products, the reduction in price differences was no less impressive. The Boston-Manchester cotton textile price gap fell from 14 percent in 1870 to −4 percent in 1913, while the pig iron price gap between Philadelphia and London fell from 85 percent to 19 percent.[18] International prices also converged in European trade. The steamboat initially shifted the relative importance of trade relations from European and Asian routes to the North Atlantic routes. Steamships could not serve Asia until the opening of the Suez Canal because coal was not available on the long route around Africa.[19]

During this first era of globalization, increasing competition from abroad due to declining transport costs gave rise to protectionist trade policies. In North America, during the Civil War, tariffs reduced the financial burden on the federal government, and they remained high after the war ended. Continental Europe shifted away from liberal trade policies in the late 1870s in response to cheap American and Russian grain. Tariffs were reintroduced on finished manufactured and agricultural goods.

Increasing "transport intensity" and intraindustry trade in the modern era

Freight costs have about halved since the mid-1970s,[20] driven by investments in transport infrastructure, better capacity use, and technological progress. Recent trends differed from those in the first era of globalization:[21]

- The major cost declines have been in road and air transport. Maritime transport went through the containerization revolution without reducing costs overall.
- The surge in international trade has been within industries, not between them, as in the first episode of falling trade costs.
- Reduced trade friction has been less a consequence of falling transport costs than of a drop in freight costs as a share of the value of goods traded. Most of the increase in trade has been in easily substitutable goods.[22]
- Transport reforms and falling trade barriers have contributed substantially to the fall in transport costs.
- Falling communication costs, interacting with falling transport costs, have been instrumental in fragmenting production processes and outsourcing intermediate goods production. Relative wage differences have become more important because of the lower costs of managing production processes over long distances.

Road transport costs. Road transport costs have fallen substantially, by almost 40 percent over the past three decades, despite higher energy and wage costs. (Comprehensive statistics on prices for transport services do not exist, and the implementation of price indexes as part of the system of national accounts is still in its infancy.

Empirical assessment therefore depends on the estimation of transport costs.) One study in France shows that truck transport costs fell by 33 percent between 1978 and 1998,[23] with substantial regional variation due to the differences in the quality of roads and the charges for road use. The main contributors were the deregulation of the trucking industry (a reduction of 21.8 percentage points) and the lower vehicle costs (–10.9 percentage points). Transport infrastructure (–3.2 percentage points) and declining fuel costs (–2.8 percentage points) were much less important.

Rail freight costs. Rail costs fell much less than road costs. Technical progress was uneven across rail submarkets, and the monopoly power of large, mostly state-owned enterprises slowed cost reductions (see box 6.1). Obligations to serve regions with small transport, for instance, have

---

BOX 6.1 *Biggest in the world: size and social obligations of Indian Railways*

The railway industry exhibits increasing returns to scale in two ways. First, network economies and economies of density lead to size advantages at the firm level. Second, rail transport operations are almost universally combined with the supply of infrastructure services, granting rail firms a natural monopoly, at least locally. Given the importance of the railways for economic development and the enormous market power of rail firms, it is not surprising that many rail companies are state owned.

The biggest of these mammoths is Indian Railways. The *Guinness Book of World Records* lists it as the world's largest commercial or utility employer, with more than 1.6 million employees. It moves more than 16 million passengers and more than 1 million tons of freight each day. In 2002 it ran 14,444 trains daily, 8,702 of them for passengers, and owned 216,717 wagons, 39,263 coaches, and 7,739 locomotives.

Founded in 1853 as a system of 42 rail systems, it was nationalized as one unit in 1951. Vertical integration of Indian Railways is not confined

to the bundling with infrastructure services. It owns and runs factories for locomotives, coaches, and even their parts. Long transport distances on the Indian subcontinent should give the railways a stronger competitive edge over roads. Indeed, Indian Railways makes 70 percent of its revenues and most of its profits from freight, cross-subsidizing the loss-making passenger sector. The overpricing of freight services is one reason it has lost business to roads in recent years.

Curtailing the potential to provide low-cost freight transport over long distances are extensive social obligations. Net social service obligations in 2005–06 were more than Rs 47 billion, plus welfare costs of Rs 9.6 billion. The service obligations include shipping essential commodities (sugar cane, livestock, paper) below cost, having freight subsidize passenger and other coaching services, and opening new unprofitable lines. A major part of the passenger transport deficits covered by freight are urban and suburban losses in Chennai, Kolkata, and Mumbai.

Source: WDR 2009 team.

motivated demands for public subsidies and cross-subsidies from profitable routes.

Rail costs are specific to the commodity shipped. For the United States, this has been shown to depend on price discrimination by the freight railroads among shippers of different commodities.[24] There was no uniform development of rail freight rates from 1981 to 2004. Markups for coal and grain have increased significantly. Markups in intermodal traffic have been lower because of competition from trucking and rail-to-rail competition between major cities. Decreasing or flat rates had been observed for shipping chemical products and automobiles. This mainly indicates the high value of these goods. Freight demand is a derived demand, and the prices shippers are willing to pay increase with the value of the shipments.

Air transport costs. With the arrival of the jet engine, air transport costs came down quickly from the mid-1950s to the early 1970s. Jet engines were faster, more reliable, and more fuel efficient than the piston engines they replaced (see box 6.2). Quality-adjusted real prices of aircraft fell by 13 to 17 percent annually from 1957 to 1972.[25] Technical progress slowed considerably after 1972, but prices were still falling by 2 to 4 percent a year from 1972 to 1983.

Between 1955 and 2004, air freight prices fell from $3.87 per ton-kilometer to less than $0.30, in 2000 U.S. dollars. Average revenue per ton-kilometer fell 8.1 percent a year in 1955–72 and 3.5 percent a year in 1972–2003. Despite this significant decline in nominal air freight rates, the trade friction in air transport did not fall as dramatically. The price of air shipping in real U.S. dollars per kilogram increased 2.9 percent annually from 1973 to 1980, in part due to oil price increases, and then declined by 2.5 percent annually from 1980 to 1993. The post-1980 decline varied substantially among routes, with longer routes and North America showing the largest drops.[26] After 2001 the real price of inbound air freight to the United States rose sharply, possibly reflecting higher security costs.

Maritime transport costs. Two submarkets have developed differently over the past decades. Tramp shipping is used for large quantities of bulk commodities on charter, with shipping prices set in spot markets. There are no fixed schedules or routes, so shipping is determined by current market demand. Liner shipping is used for general cargo on fixed trade routes and on a fixed timetable. The liner trade is organized into cartels, or conferences, which discuss and coordinate prices and market shares.

Technical progress and institutional changes have reduced prices in both submarkets. The most important are the growth of open registry shipping, the scale effects from the enormous increase in maritime transport demand, the introduction of containers, and the resulting changes in port logistics. Open registry shipping is the practice of registering ships under flags of convenience (Liberia and Panama) to circumvent higher regulatory and manning costs imposed by wealthier nations. Open registry fleets did 5 percent of world shipping tonnage in 1950, 31 percent in 1980, and 48 percent in 2000.[27] It is estimated that vessel expenses for open registry ships are 12 to 27 percent lower than those of traditional registry fleets, with most of the cost differences coming from labor costs.[28]

Cost reductions because of scale effects come from greater vessel capacity and institutional changes. The rapid expansion of maritime transport demand seems to have accommodated these changes and reduced the danger of preemptive competition.[29] The increase in vessel size seems to have allowed for hub-and-spoke economies—smaller vessels move cargo to a hub, where shipments are aggregated into much larger and faster ships for longer hauls. Prime examples are Hong Kong, China; Rotterdam; and Singapore.

Vessels for bulk commodities, refrigerated produce, and automobiles are profitable on individual routes. Since the mid-1980s, dedicated "juice tankers" have cemented Brazil's dominant position in the global export market for orange juice, almost all produced in São Paulo State. Standardized containers provide cost savings across transport modes—long-distance truck, inland waterways, rail, and short-distance truck—because goods do not need to be

BOX 6.2 *The jet engine*

An estimated 320 million people meet annually at professional and corporate events after traveling by air. Of the world's $12 trillion of merchandise trade, 35 percent by value was shipped by air in 2006.[a] The estimated economic rate of return from investments in aviation infrastructure and services is 56 percent in Kenya, 28 percent in Jordan, and 19 percent in Cambodia.[b] The reason for all this is the jet engine, perhaps the most significant innovation in long-distance transport ever. The jet is safer, easier to maintain, better suited for longer distances, and more fuel efficient than the propeller. Since it revolutionized air travel in the 1960s, it has become so closely identified with aircraft propulsion that one wonders how the aircraft industry managed to make so much progress with pistons.

But as with many path-breaking inventions in transport technology, the gestation period between invention and economic success was long. Frank Whittle in Great Britain, in 1929, and Hans von Ohain, a German physicist, in 1933, independently developed concepts for jet propulsion. Jet engine technology progressed quickly after World War II. The breakthrough in commercial passenger travel arrived with the Boeing 707 and Douglas DC-8. Earlier jet aircraft were noisy and had higher operating costs than advanced piston-engine aircraft. They could compete only on speed and greater seat capacity. But in the early 1960s, technology improvements (the so-called by-pass engine) rang in the end of propeller-powered long-distance travel. Within five years, prices per ton-kilometer fell by about 40 percent.

Jet aircraft have a much higher power-to-weight ratio, which enables longer range, faster travel, and bigger payloads. Higher quality and lower cost had a large impact in many sectors.

- *Supporting buyer-supplier networks over long distances.* Most global trade is by maritime shipping, but air transport fills an important niche in just-in-time production systems. While shipments by sea are routine, firms use air cargo to fine-tune intermediate input flows and to ship goods with high value-to-weight ratios. Even for Brazil, known for its primary goods exports, air cargo in 2000 accounted for 0.2 percent of total export volume by weight, but almost 19 percent by value.[c] Incidentally, Brazil is also home to the world's third-largest airplane maker, Embraer. Prime examples of sectors benefiting from air transport are semiconductors and fashion. Shipments of semiconductors are so highly correlated with air freight overall that they are considered a key leading indicator for the sector's health. Product cycles in the fashion industry have shortened so much that one Spanish clothing chain ships merchandise straight from factory to store, replacing designs twice a week. The need to respond quickly to changing customer tastes has led to the relocation of some of its production from East Asia to Spain and nearer countries like Morocco and Turkey. From there, clothes are sent to stores elsewhere in the world: "Planes from Zaragoza, Spain, land in Bahrain with goods for Inditex stores in the Middle East, fly on to Asia, and return to Spain with raw materials and half-finished clothes."[d]

- *Enabling exports of perishable goods over long distances.* Inexpensive and frequent air service has allowed countries like Chile, Colombia, and Kenya to sell agricultural and horticultural products to markets in Europe, the Middle East, and North America. A prime example is Kenya, which today has a third of the global market for cut flowers. Naivasha in central Kenya hosts a highly efficient cluster of growers, showing that localization economies also exist in agriculture. Flowers picked in the morning arrive on Amsterdam's markets by evening. Horticulture is now among the top three export earners (with tourism and tea). In 2007 the sector's free on-board (FOB) export value was 43 billion Kenyan shillings (about US$650 million), and the Kenya Flower Council estimates that the livelihood of 1.2 million people depends directly or indirectly on the industry. By contrast, Bangladesh's lack of cold storage facilities and refrigerated air cargo capacity has blunted its opportunities to export high-value fruits and vegetables to the Middle East.[e]

- *Mass tourism in developing countries.* In 2005 tourism receipts in low- and middle-income countries were about $200 billion,[f] thanks mostly to inexpensive air travel. Charter flights provide even larger cost reductions through packaging with other services and high-capacity use. Airport construction in tourist areas generates clusters of development with a high density of complementary services and thick and specialized labor markets. Between 1990 and 2005, tourist arrivals in Sub-Saharan Africa increased by 8 percent a year—from 6.8 million to 23.6 million—and tourism receipts, from $4.1 billion to $14.5 billion. Tourist arrivals in China grew almost 10 percent annually. Cambodia now receives more than 2 million tourists a year, Vietnam about 4 million—16 times as many as in 1990.

Source: WDR 2009 team.
a. International Air Transport Association 2007b.
b. International Air Transport Association 2007a.
c. Sanchez and others 2003.
d. Rohwedder and Johnson 2008.
e. Dixie 2002.
f. World Tourism Organization (UNWTO) 2006.

unloaded and reloaded (see box 6.3). Containerization reduces direct port costs for storage and stevedoring. It also reduces the indirect capital costs of idle capacity during long port stops, which previously made up half to two-thirds of a ship's lifetime.[30] And it allows for larger and faster ships, which reduce the costs per ton-mile while the ship is steaming. These cost reductions on the ocean leg have more than compensated for

BOX 6.3 *The big box*

About 90 percent of nonbulk cargo worldwide is transported in containers stacked on trucks, rail wagons, and freight ships. In 2007 more than 18 million containers made more than 200 million trips. Containerization has even changed how port and ship capacity or maritime transport services are measured. Cargo shipped is now measured in TEU or 40-foot equivalent units (FEU). A TEU is the measure of a box 20 feet long and 8 feet wide, with a maximum gross mass of 24 metric tons.

The revolution is popularly attributed to Malcom McLean.[a] He owned a trucking firm in New Jersey and had a simple insight: packages being shipped generally need to be opened only at origin and destination, but unloading and repacking costs a lot of money. In 1956 he inaugurated the Sea-Land Service, with his converted tanker ship, the *Ideal-X,* setting sail from Newark, New Jersey, for Houston, Texas, carrying 58 aluminum truck bodies in frames installed atop its deck.

The idea did not spread widely until more than a decade later, when the U.S. armed forces needed efficient military transport to Vietnam. Against considerable resistance, McLean won contracts to build a container-port at Cam Ranh Bay and to run containerships from California to Vietnam. Without the containers, the U.S. military would have had a tough time feeding, housing, and supplying the 540,000 soldiers, sailors, marines, and air force personnel in Vietnam in 1969. From almost nothing in 1965, Sea-Land's Defense Department revenues rose to $450 million between 1967 and 1973. Routes to Okinawa and Subic Bay in the Philippines were added later, but McLean's business remained restricted to military logistics.

The Japanese government was the first to support the expansion of containerization. In 1966 the Shipping and Shipbuilding Rationalization Council urged the Ministry of Transport to eliminate excessive competition to benefit from the new technology. It persuaded the government to build container terminals in the Tokyo-Yokohama and Osaka-Kobe areas. The first container cranes began operation in 1968. But highway regulations barred full-size containers, and the Japanese National Railway was not equipped to carry containers longer than 20 feet.

In the United States, Matson Navigation won government approval to operate an unsubsidized container service between the U.S. West Coast and Hawaii and East Asia. The company had visions of unloading cargo at Oakland directly onto special trains that would carry it east. On the return trip, the company planned to carry military cargo for the U.S. bases in Japan and the Republic of Korea. Business could not start before Matson entered a joint venture with a Japanese partner, and the containership that completed its maiden voyage in 1968 from Japan to the United States was owned by Nippon Yusen Kaisha Line. Six weeks later, McLean's Sea-Land Services started a regular service between Yokohama and the U.S. west coast.

Once the infrastructure facilities were in place, container traffic took off. By the end of 1968 the Japan–U.S. route was crowded with containerships, seven companies competing for fewer than 7,000 tons of eastbound freight each month. The speed of expansion was determined by port and rail infrastructure. In the United States, rail intermodal traffic tripled between 1980 and 2002, from 3.1 million trailers and containers to 9.3 million.

Container transport has continued to increase at enormous rates. The boxes keep getting larger, with the standard FEU size giving way to 48-foot and 53-foot boxes that allow trucks to haul more freight on each trip. The world's fleet is expanding steadily, with the capacity of pure containerships rising by 10 percent annually between 2001 and 2005. The size of the vessels has been increasing, too. Dozens of vessels able to carry 4,000 FEU joined the fleet in 2006, and even larger ones were on order. The *Emma Maersk* (396 meters long), launched in 2006, can carry more than 14,500 TEU. Of all traffic, 26 percent now originates in China.

Geography and topography limit the ever-increasing size of ships: Because the Panama Canal lost more traffic with the old locks unable to accommodate vessels larger than 5,000 TEU, it now is being expanded to allow ships up to 12,000 TEUs to pass. Most of the container ships are too large for the Suez Canal as well. Container ships have an absolute size, limited by the depth of the Straits of Malacca, linking the Indian Ocean to the Pacific Ocean. This "Malacca-max" size constrains a ship to dimensions of 470 meters long and 60 meters wide.

And what happened to Malcom McLean's company? Sea-Land grew and was the biggest shipping company in 1995. The Danish company Maersk was second, followed by Evergreen. Four years later, Sea-Land was acquired by Maersk. By 2000 Maersk-SeaLand had a slot capacity of about 850,000 TEU. McLean's big box is here to stay.

Source: WDR 2009 team.
a. Levinson 2006.

higher investment costs and higher costs for slack time in ports.[31]

But containerization has also concentrated shipping capacity in a few global ports. Most developing countries have been slow to containerize, because of their small trade volumes and different factor prices. Where capital is scarce and labor abundant, the capital cost of specialized cranes, storage areas, and rail heads is higher, and the

port cost savings of containers are much lower.

How did this technological change affect shipping costs? When adjusted for inflation, the real price for tramp services in 2004 was about half the real price in 1960.[32] But when deflated using the commodity price index, there are large fluctuations but no downward trend. This means that the trade friction resulting from transport costs for bulk commodities typically shipped by tramp trip charters has not gone down—the price of transporting a dollar's worth of iron ore or wheat has not fallen. Liner prices show a steady rise before peaking in 1985, based on long time-series from the German Ministry of Transport. The price index for liner shipping emphasizes general cargo, including containerized shipping and manufactured merchandise. It also covers loading and unloading expenses, which are particularly relevant because reductions in cargo handling costs are thought to be a major source of gains from containerization. Measured relative to the German GDP deflator, liner prices declined until the early 1970s, rose sharply from 1974 to reach their peak in the 1983–85 period, and declined afterward.

These trends in shipping costs run counter to public perceptions of continually falling trade costs. Two possible explanations: First, these price trends do not capture the true cost savings of containerization, since they do not factor in the total cost of door-to-door transportation. In 1956 the loading of loose cargo cost $5.83 a ton. When containers were introduced in that year, the loading cost was less than $0.16 a ton.[33] So the main savings came from lower intermodal transfer costs. Containerization allowed goods to be packed only once and shipped over long distances using maritime, rail, and road transport. Second, the quality of transport and logistics services increased markedly, particularly their speed and reliability. The absence of a more significant price decrease is thus explained, at least in part, by a greater willingness to pay for higher quality services.

Small declines in transport costs, but a big easing in trade friction

Cost information suggests that international transport costs have not dropped as much as is commonly believed. Real prices of air and maritime transport have not fallen or risen much since the 1970s and early 1980s. But the ad valorem transport charge—the cost of transport as a share of the value of the traded good—has gone down. Explaining the decline are changes in the composition of traded goods and the composition of trading partners.[34] One change is the

reduced weight-value ratio in all international transport. A second is the lower price of air transport relative to maritime transport. Goods that traditionally have been transported by sea are now shipped by air. After accounting for the changes of the weight-value ratios, the modal shift, and the changes of routes, the ad valorem tax equivalent of maritime transport fell more than that of air transport (see figure 6.2).[35] Changes in the composition of goods and trading partners reduced the market friction of transport, not its costs.

Logistics, time, and international trade. Transport services are not a homogeneous good, and transport costs are not product- or place-neutral. The revenue figures and price indexes do not indicate quality or speed. Shipping containers from Europe to U.S. destinations still requires two or three weeks—from Europe to Asia five weeks. But air shipping requires a day or less to almost anywhere in the world. With the decline in air transport costs, the price of speed has fallen dramatically.

This matters for trade. Every day in ocean travel that a country is distant from the importer reduces the probability of sourcing manufactured goods from that country by 1 percent.[36] And exporting firms are willing to pay 1 percent of the value of the good per day to avoid time losses associated with maritime transport. With the recent increase in the intensity of international trade, the demand for speed has increased. Goods with the highest time sensitivity have seen the fastest increase in trade. Examples are perishable agricultural goods and those with short product cycles such as fashion articles, where consumer preferences shift, or electronics, where the latest technology earns a premium. Such cycles are important not just for Europe, North America, and Northeast Asia but also for China, India, and Southeast Asia.

Faster transport can speed the changes in the geography of trade. Production locations for textiles and electronics were initially driven by wage costs. But with short product cycles, shorter transport times may outweigh higher wage costs, leading to relocations. Some apparel production outsourced from the United States to Asia has relocated to

Figure 6.2 Air freight costs are down less than ocean freight costs

Air freight

Ocean freight

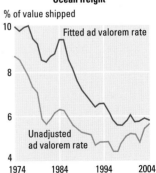

Source: Hummels 2007.
Note: The unadjusted ad valorem rate is the ratio of freight costs to import good value. The fitted ad valorem rate is derived from a regression and controls for changes in the mix of trade partners and products.

higher wage locations in the Caribbean and Mexico.[37] Short product cycles, and more generally uncertain demand, are forces for agglomeration as firms need to locate near suppliers.[38] But with more predictable demand, faster speed might contribute to outsourcing stages of production (component production, research and development [R&D], and assembly) to other countries according to comparative advantage.

Communication costs. The cost of a three-minute phone call from New York to London fell from $293 dollars in 1931 (in 1993 dollars) to around $1 in 2001 for a much better connection—and to just a few cents today (see figure 6.3). The Internet and other telecommunication advances have lowered communication costs, reducing even more the trade friction for physical goods, especially intraindustry trade. But they have had an equal if not greater impact on the trade in services. Yet many tasks that require intensive communication hardly have been affected. Direct personal interaction and face-to-face contact remain an important agglomerative force, especially and paradoxically in the most communication-intensive industries.

Lower communication costs facilitate the coordination of international production

networks.[39] But there are two more direct effects. The first is to reduce search costs. Because knowledge about potential customers or suppliers in foreign countries is imperfect, trade relations start with the search for trading partners. The search depends on the quality of the communication infrastructure, which is largely a fixed cost and therefore increases the intensity of international trade as it reduces the search cost for trading partners.[40] The second is to reduce variable trade costs. These costs arise from the need of consumers and producers to interact on product specifications, quality control, and timing.[41] They are low for homogenous goods traded on organized exchanges or with reference prices. But they are high for differentiated goods.[42] Since these kinds of goods are most prominent in trade within more disaggregated production processes, the line for communication costs played a big role in the recent surge in intraindustry trade (see figure 6.1).

Low communication costs make it possible to control production processes over long distances by computer-aided control systems and online communication, reducing the need to co-locate management and technical staff with unskilled workers. This allows vertically integrated companies to outsource production to low-wage countries. But it also facilitates the breakup of production processes into supply chains of different companies distributed across countries and continents.[43]

Low communication costs are particularly important for offshoring tasks that do not require the shipment of physical products, such as business, professional, and technical services, including accounting, bookkeeping, computer programming, and information and data processing. U.S. imports of these services increased by more than 66 percent in real terms between 1997 and 2004. The shift of jobs to foreign countries has stirred fears among white-collar workers of massive labor market adjustments and has reduced political support for open trade regimes.[44] Contrary to these fears, business service imports in rich countries have remained fairly low. In the United States, the import share of computing and business services reached only 0.4 percent

Figure 6.3   The costs of communicating have fallen to a fraction of what they were a decade ago
Average cost of a telephone call to the United States

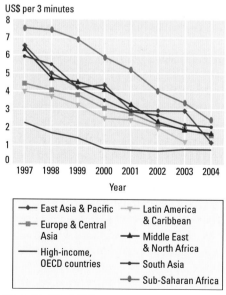

Source: World Bank 2007j.

in 2003, and exports of these services are even higher.

The biggest outsourcers, in relation to local value added of these services, are small countries like Angola, Mozambique, Papua New Guinea, and the Republic of Congo. Among the advanced economies, Germany, a country with high absolute imports in business services ($39 billion in 2002), ranks 59th with a share of 2.9 percent. The United States, with the highest absolute import value in business services ($41 billion in 2002), ranks 115th. But the United States was the biggest exporter of services ($58 billion in 2002) and so was a substantial net exporter. Ireland shows that trade in immaterial services tends to be within industries rather than between them. It is the largest exporter of computer and information services and the fourth-largest importer. Still its ratio of exports to the local value added of computer and information services was only 16 percent (9 percent of GDP).

So the relocation of back-office services to foreign countries is not a large threat to employment in advanced countries. Trade balances in business services in almost all developed countries have been positive and increasing from 1981 to 2001. India, seen to attract many business services from rich countries, had a smaller increase in output in this sector from 1995 to 2001 than did the United Kingdom.[45] In short, the impression that services drive economic dispersion across countries is not confirmed by the evidence. Trade in these services has increased a lot, but for both imports and exports. For most countries, the share in local services remains small. And when business has been outsourced, much of it has remained concentrated in a few places. Low communication costs have had little effect on creative activities and high-value services that require frequent personal interaction.

Transport costs and scale economies: two decades of analysis

The evolution of transport costs, a critical factor in economic geography, helps explain the experience in the previous section. A fall in transport costs increases the concentration of people and firms because it allows more efficient sharing of facilities and services. Recent research also explains two somewhat unexpected consequences of falling transport costs: (1) at the international level, trade increases with nearby countries, not with those farther away, and (2) within countries, improving transport infrastructure may lead to more concentration of economic activity, not less.

Research has been far less successful in showing why falling transport costs may make it more difficult for developing countries and lagging regions to break into world trade—indeed, increasing returns in the transport sector have often been ignored in formal models. But just as falling transport costs facilitate economies of scale in production, higher production and trade produce economies of scale in transport.

Falling transport costs create bumpy economic landscapes

Before the recent accelerated drop in transport costs, natural or "first-nature" geographic conditions (such as waterways) largely determined the location of settlements and the spatial arrangement of production and trade. Shared investments then created increasing returns to scale that shaped economic geography. Such investments could include local health and education facilities or markets and other services that reduce trade and transaction costs—such as enforcing property rights, resolving contract disputes, or identifying market opportunities. The more the people who use a facility or communal service, the lower the costs per user. The larger the settlement, the more the people who share the fixed costs. To use the service, people and goods have to travel. So as transport costs fall, access increases, scale increases and the unit cost of provision drops. This is how transport costs define the geographic size of markets and the reach and scale of communal services.

As more facilities and services are provided centrally in larger cities, smaller communities become less attractive and spatial disparities emerge—the size distribution of towns and cities changes. First-nature geography and the lumpiness of urban infrastructure investments result in irreversible dynamics that determine how the economic landscape first becomes rough, then bumpy.

Economic historians had long recognized that these processes, driven by changing transport costs, are critical for economic development.[46] And geographers and planners formalized the effect of indivisible communal facilities in differentiating city functions and sizes in the "central place theory."[47] Economists went beyond first-nature geography and public goods. They realized that increasing returns to scale in the production of manufactured goods and ideas further influence the distribution of economic activities in geographic space. With urbanization, manufacturing and allied services become the drivers of growth, as discussed in chapter 4. These forces interact with transport costs to determine the spatial evolution of economies, at all spatial scales—international, national, and local.

Falling transport costs increase trade between neighbors

The growing demand for varieties of similar goods helps explain the paradox that falling transport costs have led to more trade between countries that are close by and have similar characteristics. In fact, over the past 40 years, distance has become a larger deterrent to trade while divisions—border effects—have become less of a deterrent (see figure 6.4).

Traditional trade theory did not consider the increasing returns to scale and the differentiation of demand. It predicted more intensive trade in goods that are different, favoring trade between countries with different endowments. Countries traded because they could not produce the imported products themselves—bananas from Central America to Europe for cars in return. But with differentiated goods, trade is within classes of goods rather than between them. Countries trade because they want slightly different versions of similar goods—Japan and Sweden trade Toyotas for Volvos. In other words, in the old trade theory and with high transport costs, countries trade only what they *need to*. In the new trade theory and with scale economies, a love of variety, and low transport costs, countries trade because they *want to*.

International trade surged between (often nearby) countries of the Northern Hemisphere in the 1960s and 1970s, even though these countries have essentially similar resource endowments. Trade between rich and poor countries was initially dwarfed by these developments. In the beginning of the 1980s intraindustry trade between medium- and high-income countries expanded—and later between other categories of countries (see figure 6.5). The differentiation of demand—that is, the love of variety—and intraindustry trade did not remain confined to rich countries.

Accompanying the surge in intraindustry trade was a large increase in trade in intermediate goods relative to final goods. Intraindustry trade in intermediate goods requires an especially efficient transport sector. The ability to coordinate and control production processes in real time by computerized systems has been central to the vertical disintegration of production processes in the high-income countries and the outsourcing to medium-income countries.[48] So lower transport costs, changes in goods traded, and lower communication costs reinforce each other.

One might expect that goods with low value-to-weight ratios would be traded mainly over short distances. But product cycles for knowledge-intensive intraindustry goods and for consumer items such as electronic gadgets and fashion articles have become shorter. This greater time sensitivity helps explain why the distance-dependence of trade goes up rather than

Figure 6.4   Distance has become more of a deterrent, divisions less
Coefficients for distance and national borders in trade models, 1960–2005

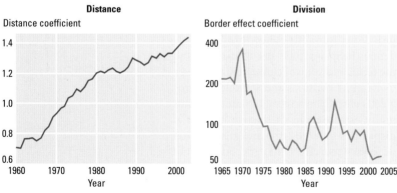

Source: Mayer 2008 for this Report.

down. If countries want to benefit from current trends of globalization, regional coordination of infrastructure investment and transport policies becomes even more important.[49]

How do increasing returns to scale in production, the love of variety for consumer and intermediate inputs, and lower transport costs drive concentrations of economic activities in geographic space? First, differentiated products and increasing returns to scale will increase productivity more in larger areas or countries than in smaller ones, even if they have identical per capita resources and access to the same technology. The important dimension of size is the volume of overall demand or economic mass, not the size of the land area. When such agglomeration forces are considered, both Hong Kong, China, and Singapore are viewed as "large."

Second, the larger a region, the more varieties or intermediates will be produced locally. Compared with smaller regions, fewer goods have to be imported, saving on transport costs. People with equal nominal incomes thus have a higher real income in the larger regions, and firms realize cost savings.

Third, the higher real incomes will lead to in-migration, putting pressure on local wages. Lower wages will attract more firms, making the larger market even larger and leading to a new round of circular causation of firm relocation, higher real incomes, and a larger market. Chapter 9 discusses in more detail how developing countries can address the challenging task of regional integration, learning from the experiences with institutional cooperation, regional infrastructure, and coordinated incentives around the world.

Falling transport costs lead to concentration within countries

The productivity and income benefits of agglomeration, driven largely by lower transport costs, are often difficult for planners and policy makers to accept. But they explain the second counterintuitive implication of falling transport costs. There is a strong belief that an equal distribution of transport infrastructure will induce an

Figure 6.5   Global intraindustry trade is no longer confined to rich countries

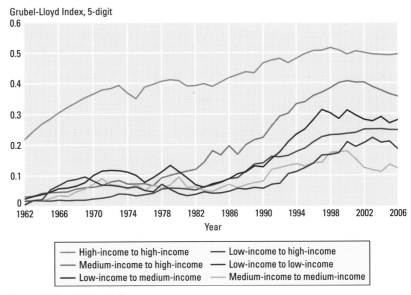

Grubel-Lloyd Index, 5-digit

Source: Brülhart 2008 for this Report.
Note: The Grubel-Lloyd index is the fraction of total trade that is accounted for by intraindustry trade.

equal geographic distribution of economic activities. High concentration is seen as a problem, and the spatial redistribution of economic mass is expected to promote overall development. Massive transport infrastructure investments have been the central policy instrument to induce firms to move to lagging regions. But the outcomes were usually the opposite—the target regions lost production and workers to the leading regions (see box 6.4).

Knowledge-sharing is another force shaping the economic geography of countries and areas. Technical know-how can be used by more users at no or small extra cost. It is embedded in an experienced workforce, and the accumulated stock of knowledge leads to innovation. Larger local labor markets increase knowledge spillovers between workers and thus increase productivity nonlinearly.[50] In big cities the benefits may not fully materialize because congestion and fragmentation hinder interaction. But well-functioning urban transport systems can increase the effectiveness of the labor market and spread the results of learning on the job (see box 6.5).

Falling transport costs enhance localization economies in the production of knowledge and information—say, for business,

BOX 6.4 *Italy's intervento straordinario: an unexpected response to falling transport costs*

Regional disparities are caused by the unequal distribution of infrastructure, and infrastructure investment in lagging areas will reduce these imbalances. That is the common assumption. But, frequently, the industries intended to prosper from these investments move elsewhere, accompanied by a mass out-migration of workers. A prime example is the Italian regional policy to reduce the development differences between the North and the South. The *Mezzogiorno* has become a generic term for a region that suffered from the good intentions of regional policy.[a]

A short-term *intervento straordinario* was managed by a special agency, the *Cassa per il Mezzogiorno,* set up in 1950. It was supported by the International Bank for Reconstruction and Development (IBRD), led by Paul Rosenstein-Rodan, who developed the Big Push Model of economic development in the 1940s. The development impact was to come from massive infrastructure investment, with much emphasis on road building and railways. It soon became obvious that short-term success would not be achievable, leading to repeated redefinitions of the strategic directions. By the mid-1950s, the *Cassa* shifted its focus to supporting industry investment, concentrating on "nuclei" and priority areas.

The result was that through the 1950s about 2 million workers left the target regions. By the end of the 1960s, the emigration was perceived to be the main development problem, and infrastructure investment and subsidies were concen-

trated on the areas where emigration was, in fact, highest.[b] From the beginning of the 1980s, when the original mandate of the *Cassa* ended, it was kept alive by 11 ministerial decrees. In 1986 the "extraordinary intervention" was refinanced up to 1993.

The total annual expenditures of the *Cassa* rose to a peak of 3,750 billion lire (US$4.5 billion) in 1976, declining to 2,650 billion lire (US$2.1 billion) in 1991, and collapsing afterward. The money had little effect on economic indicators in the *Mezzogiorno* (see box table).

The unemployment rate fell until the beginning of the 1970s because of the out-migration of millions of workers to Northern Italy and other countries. It then more than doubled up to the end of the 1980s, indicating a rapidly growing dependence of the South on fiscal transfers from the North.

Scandals surrounding the *Cassa per il Mezzogiorno* were disclosed as part of *tangentopoli* ("bribesville") by the efforts

of the *mani puliti* ("clean hands") of the country's judiciary. These scandals contributed to the dissolution of the Christian Democratic Party and the Socialist Party and to the emergence of the Northern League, which demanded the separation of the North from the South to end the waste in the *Mezzogiorno.* An intervention to make the country more uniform may have increased internal divisions.

Chapter 8, "Unity, Not Uniformity," discusses how countries have promoted national integration by using a calibrated blend of spatially blind institutions, connective infrastructure, and spatially targeted interventions.

Source: WDR 2009 team.
a. Boltho, Carlin, and Scaramozzino 1997; Sinn and Frank 2001.
b. By that time, some critics of the Mezzogiorno policy demanded that funds assist outmigration (Lutz 1962).

Economic development of the *Mezzogiorno*

	1951–60	1961–70	1971–80	1981–90	1990
The South's share of the national total (%)					
Population	37.2	36.0	35.1	36.1	36.6
GDP per capita	54.5	56.6	58.6	58.2	56.7
Fixed investment	26.0	29.0	31.2	29.0	26.9
Unemployment					
South	9.1	6.4	9.6	16.3	19.7
Center-North	6.8	4.5	5.2	7.6	6.5

Source: Faini, Giannini, and Galli 1993.

professional, and technical services. Lower communication costs might be expected to lead to a footloose tradable service sector. But most communication-intensive industries remain strongly agglomerated.[51] A main reason for the persistence of agglomeration economies in knowledge production is that verifying the quality of information requires understanding and relationships of trust. Informal networks work as screening devices to build up trust in a group of knowledge producers.[52] And lower urban transport costs increase the size of networks.

What to do: transport policies in the developing world

What do these events and insights mean for developing countries? Trade costs have fallen because of lower transport and communication costs, higher quality, and faster speed. But all countries have not benefited equally. Transport costs have fallen faster where the demand for transport services is greater. Increasing scale in traded production has raised competitiveness and allowed scale economies in the transport sector. The resulting lower trade and transport costs encourage trade and allow greater

BOX 6.5 *Mobility with density in Hong Kong, China*

Hong Kong, China, in the second half of the 1970s, had real growth of about 10 percent a year, an influx of immigrants, and roaring demand for private cars. Car registrations more than doubled in a decade. The results were huge time losses for passengers and freight transporters and health costs of air pollution. The Transport Department in Hong Kong, China, reacted with draconian measures. In 1979, it defined a transport policy to increase road capacity, expand and improve the mass transit system, and better manage the road capacity.

The government trebled the annual license fee for cars, doubled the first registration fee (to 70 to 90 percent of the import price of a vehicle), and doubled fuel taxes. Private and public vehicle ownership fell quickly. In 1985 the share of private cars in registered cars had fallen to 50 percent, 10 percent of them taxis.[a] The public transport system consists of a 74-kilometer underground mass-transit railway, a 34-kilometer heavy rail line (linking Kowloon with China), a 32-kilometer light-rail system in the northwest of the New Territories, and a

16-kilometer tram in the North Side of Hong Kong Island. Five private bus companies operate franchised services with more than 6,000 buses. They are complemented by minibuses (public light buses) with fixed fares and exclusive rights to provide service on certain routes. Entry to this submarket is strictly regulated, with a maximum number of minibuses set for the city's quarters.[b] Switching between different modes or submodes does not lead to big time losses.

Road pricing failed politically in 1985. One reason was the opening of the Island Route of the Mass Transit Railway, which carried about a quarter of all public transport boardings in 1988, and the Island Eastern Corridor a year earlier. Both eased congestion. Today, road charges in Hong Kong, China, are seen as a device not to reduce congestion but to curtail air pollution and maintain the city's attractiveness. It ranks fifth in the infrastructure index of the global competitiveness report, with a score of 6.2 out of 7, and first in product market efficiency and financial market sophistication.

The experience in Hong Kong, China, provides these lessons for the rapidly growing cities in the developing world:

- There is a limit to mobility and accessibility by private car in megacities. Even without congestion charging and the pricing of parking, strong fiscal disincentives can contain motorization in a phase of rapid income growth and limit the share of private cars in urban transport.
- Buses, and particularly minibuses, can be regulated to avoid congestion and high travel costs. Even with regulation, almost all public transport can be profitable.
- Along with policies to contain motorization, new traffic management instruments can make more effective use of existing infrastructure.

Chapter 7 discusses, for countries at various stages of urbanization, the institutions, infrastructure, and incentives that can facilitate concentration without congestion.

Source: WDR 2009 team.
a. Hau 1990.
b. Cullinane 2002.

specialization and exchange. Some countries such as China and Chile have broken into international markets and benefited from lower transport costs. But most of the others have not. In much of Africa, this cumulative causation has hurt, not helped, because agglomeration economies in Africa's divided neighborhoods remain small.

By increasing local market interactions and reducing intercity and interarea distances and international divisions, transport policies in developing countries can get these virtuous circles started. Improving physical infrastructure is an indispensable part of transport policy. Indeed, chapters 7, 8, and 9 discuss the need for spatially connective infrastructure in the local, national, and international contexts. But other important aspects of transport and communications policies are often neglected.

The new economic geography has highlighted what transport costs do for economic growth. Inadvertently, though, it

has contributed to an exaggerated focus of transport policy on *physical* improvements. And by using techniques that essentially assumed away the internal workings of transport—the goods to be transported are seen as an iceberg to be hauled from one place to another, and transport costs are the part of the iceberg that melts away—the most critical policy-related aspects also have been assumed away. The fundamental features that deserve the attention of policy makers are the scale economies in the transport sector that tend to create monopolistic behavior, and the circular causation between lower transport costs and greater trade and traffic. Another underemphasized aspect is the external cost of transport and communications, notably the congestion, pollution, and safety-related hazards.

The two neglected policy priorities are (1) reducing the negative effects of market structure in the transport sector and (2) improving trade facilitation and regional coordination. Both will promote agglomerative forces and will sometimes provide greater payoffs than more physical infrastructure investments. A third policy priority is to address the negative externalities in transport.

Regulating transport to get the benefits of scale economies

Markets for transport services rarely are perfectly competitive, with major differences between the different modes. Competition in the trucking industry increased because of deregulation,[53] but there is a tendency toward consolidated ownership in many countries. In railways and airlines, markets remain dominated by state-owned enterprises.[54] In the airline and maritime transport industries, market segmentation allows providers to discriminate between different goods.[55] These observations suggest firm-level size advantages in transport operations.

Transport providers consolidate power by owning infrastructure. In 1980 the top 20 percent of the world's carriers controlled just 26 percent of the global port slot capacity. By 1992 this had increased to 42 percent, and by 2003, to 58 percent. It may be even higher today.

Infrastructure services are not provided in competitive markets because the indivisibility of infrastructure facilities naturally precludes competition. At early stages of development, the demand for ports, roads, and telecommunication equipment does not exhaust minimum capacities. As traffic increases, so does productivity. This is ultimately balanced by increasing time losses caused by congestion—as diseconomies of scale set in. Recent developments have made the advantages of large ports and airports even more pronounced—and the technological progress in shipping has reinforced the cost advantages of large ports (see box 6.3). Assessing the size of these scale effects is a daunting task, but studies have confirmed economies of scale and spotlighted the indivisibility of transport infrastructure.[56]

A second reason for limited competition arises from "network economies." Adding a link to a road or rail network does not just provide the benefits of connecting two places—it increases the value of all other related connections by enhancing overall connectivity. These effects can be large. One estimate of the infrastructure-productivity link for India found a sizable externality of transport infrastructure. By providing a 5 percent rate of return on road infrastructure investment over and above the direct payoff, the network-related benefits accounted for almost a quarter of the overall increase in infrastructure productivity.[57]

The absence of effective regulation limits competition in the transport sector and can reduce the construction of new infrastructure. It may cause underinvestment in maintenance of existing infrastructure. A number of studies have confirmed the tendency to underprovide transport and telecommunication infrastructure in developing countries.[58] Underinvestment in infrastructure maintenance can be even more severe. Actual expenditures for road maintenance in Africa, for example, appear to have systematically fallen short of planned figures.[59] It was estimated that $45 billion was lost in road stock value during the 1970s and 1980s, which could have been avoided by spending $12 billion for preventive road maintenance. Badly maintained roads increase transport costs by increasing costs of maintaining vehicles and reducing their speed. The direct costs of badly maintained roads are thus higher than the losses in cost-based road asset values as recorded by the road administrations. On top of this, higher transport costs slow the spatial transformation and reduce gains from specialization.

The monopolistic sector also encourages corruption. In smaller markets, users often have no substitutes for the services of large ports and airports. The higher these substitution costs, the higher the potential for high markups or bribes, depending on whether the infrastructure is private or public. How much rent-seeking increases transport costs is difficult to estimate. But a recent World Bank study that reviewed the main road corridors in all the regions of Sub-Saharan Africa reveals big gaps between prices for transport services and their costs (see table 6.1). The surplus is shared among bribes, regulatory rents, and transport company profits.

Table 6.1   Prices, costs, and profit margins are all high on Africa's transport corridors

Corridor (countries)	Route (gateway–destination)	Price[a] (US$ per kilometer)	Variable cost (US$ per kilometer)	Fixed cost (US$ per kilometer)	Profit margin[b] (percent)
West Africa (Burkina Faso, Mali, and Ghana)	Tema/Accra–Ouagadougou	3.53 (2.01)	1.54 (0.59)	0.66 (0.64)	80
	Tema/Accra–Bamako	3.93 (1.53)	1.67 (0.23)	0.62 (0.36)	80
Central Africa (Cameroon, Central African Republic, and Chad)	Douala–N'Djaména	3.19 (1.10)	1.31 (0.32)	0.57 (0.30)	73
	Douala–Bangui	3.78 (1.30)	1.21 (0.35)	1.08 (0.81)	83
	Ngaoundéré–N'Djaména	5.37 (1.44)	1.83 (0.25)	0.73 (0.44)	118
	Ngaoundéré–Moundou	9.71 (2.58)	2.49 (0.64)	1.55 (0.43)	163
East Africa (Kenya and Uganda)	Mombasa–Kampala	2.22 (1.08)	0.98 (0.47)	0.35 (0.14)	86
	Mombasa–Nairobi	2.26 (1.36)	0.83 (0.17)	0.53 (0.19)	66
Southern Africa (South Africa, Zambia, and Tanzania)	Lusaka–Johannesburg	2.32 (1.59)	1.54 (0.41)	0.34 (0.40)	18
	Lusaka–Dar-es-Salaam	2.55 (0.08)	1.34 (0.52)	0.44 (0.51)	62

Source: World Bank 2008d.
a. Some indicative prices are set by some ministries of transportation in Africa but are not used. Prices set by freight allocation bureaus in Central Africa may be more respected.
b. Data should be interpreted cautiously since some companies may omit some costs or, on the contrary, double count some costs.

Transport infrastructure and service providers are not the only ones extracting bribes and enjoying extranormal profits. The Improved Road Transport Governance Initiative in West Africa monitors road practices harmful to trade on interstate trunk roads between Burkina Faso, Ghana, Mali, and Togo (see map 6.2). In Mali, truckers face 4.6 checkpoints, pay $25, and waste 38 minutes for every 100 kilometers traveled. Internal or distance-related costs are compounded by costs imposed by the divisions of international borders.

National efforts and regional coordination to facilitate trade

Trade facilitation has become the most important policy instrument to achieve gains from international trade—improving the efficiency of ports, harmonizing standards, reducing bureaucratic burdens to cross borders, and coordinating behind the border regulatory norms (see box 6.6). Since August 2004, trade facilitation has moved to the center of the Doha Round

Map 6.2   Crossing borders or climbing walls?
Checkpoints on priority transport corridors

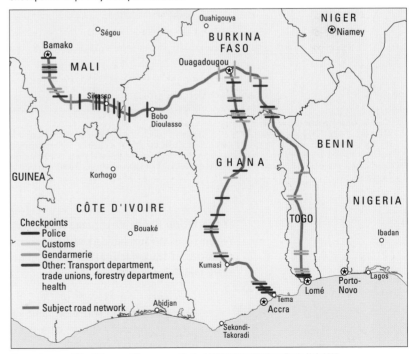

Source: Improved Road Transport Governance Project, USAID West African Trade Hub 2007.

BOX 6.6 *Neighborhoods matter, but so do trade and transport policies*

Proximity to prosperous places can be a blessing, and to poor places, a curse. The box map illustrates the advantage of being in good neighborhoods. It shows the foreign market potential across the world, using an index that combines geographic proximity (distance) and policies to reduce trade barriers (divisions).

But good location is not enough. Even within the geographically fortunate neighborhoods of Central America, North Africa, and Southeast Asia, Mexico, Tunisia, and Malaysia have the highest market access. Their rankings in the World Bank's *Doing Business* indicators—especially those related to trading across borders—are among the highest in their regions. Unsurprisingly, their recent growth performance has been impressive, and their living standards have improved.

Algeria and Indonesia have the same location as Tunisia and Malaysia, but they do not do as well in business and trade policies. Their market access indicators are accordingly lower than those of their neighbors. Sri Lanka and Ghana also do not do well in market access; they have good business and trade policies, but are not fortunate in location.

Sources: Mayer 2008; World Bank 2007d.

Being near prosperous places is important, but not enough
Foreign market potential, 2003

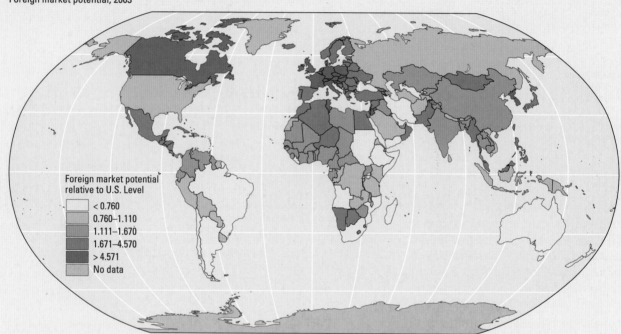

Foreign market potential relative to U.S. Level
- < 0.760
- 0.760–1.110
- 1.111–1.670
- 1.671–4.570
- > 4.571
- No data

Sources: Mayer 2008 for this Report.
Note: To compute foreign market potential, each country is assigned a score for the size of international markets with which it can trade. This is computed by weighting the GDP of other countries by the inverse of a measure that combines physical distance, transport costs, and barriers to trade to show how difficult it is to access these markets. The measure, which is expressed relative to the foreign market potential of the United States, essentially combines the two spatial dimensions of distance and division into a composite of potential market access that does not include the effect of the home market (density). This map is a complement to map 9.2 showing Real Market Access.

of the World Trade Organization. Recent World Bank studies have identified several measures of trade facilitation as the main entry points for policy reform:

- *Port efficiency*—an average of the efficiency of port, inland waterway, and air transport facilities, based on data from the *World Competitiveness Report*
- *Customs regimes*—the hidden import barriers other than published tariffs and quotas, and irregular side payments

or bribes connected with import and export permits

- *Information technology (IT) infrastructure*—a measure of the speed and the cost of Internet access and the contribution of the Internet to the reduction of inventory costs

Improving trade facilitation capacity in 75 countries to half the global average could, as one study suggests, yield a $377 billion increase in world trade.[60] Another study showed that new and old EU member countries would benefit from trade facilitation measures in what were then the accession member countries, Bulgaria, Romania, and Turkey.[61] If these countries reached half the trade facilitation standards of the EU-15 in terms of port efficiency, IT infrastructure, customs regimes, and harmonized regulation, it would lead to $10 billion in overall trade gains. Among the four dimensions of trade facilitiation, improvement of IT infrastructure would result in the highest trade gains (40 percent) followed by port efficiency improvements (30 percent).

Port efficiency improvements require both institutional and infrastructure investments. Maritime transport accounts for 90 percent of world trade by volume.[62] Access to a well-run port may not guarantee export-oriented agglomerations, but these agglomerations certainly will not emerge without it. Private participation will be feasible where trade volumes are sufficiently high, but public support is needed elsewhere. This is also true for other hub infrastructure such as airports, which are increasingly important for trade in low-weight, high-value goods and to support booming export-oriented services that need efficient air travel. In 2007 passenger traffic at Bangalore's airport jumped 35 percent.

With the fall of effective rates in international freight transport, time costs in international transport have become more important relative to the direct money costs.[63] International transport suffers from the extra time cost of border-crossing procedures. These time costs depend not just on the customs and fiscal rules of crossing the border but also on a host of behind-the-border elements concerning regulation and the supply of services.[64]

Among the poorest performers: the time costs of transport range from 46 days in the Democratic Republic of Congo to 104 days in Uzbekistan, set against the Organisation for Economic Co-operation and Development (OECD) average of 9.8 days (see table 6.2).

Table 6.2   Time costs for crossing borders are highest in Central Asia, Central Africa, East Africa, and Southern Africa

Country	Documents for exports	Days	Country	Documents for imports	Days
Iraq	10	102	Uzbekistan	11	104
Kazakhstan	12	89	Chad	9	102
Tajikistan	10	82	Iraq	10	101
Uzbekistan	7	80	Tajikistan	11	83
Chad	6	78	Kazakhstan	14	76
Afghanistan	12	67	Kyrgyz Republic	13	75
Angola	12	64	Afghanistan	11	71
Kyrgyz Republic	13	64	Burundi	10	71
Eritrea	9	59	Eritrea	13	69
Niger	8	59	Rwanda	9	69
Mongolia	10	58	Niger	10	68
Central African Republic	8	57	Zimbabwe	13	67
Azerbaijan	9	56	Central African Republic	18	66
Zambia	8	53	Congo, Dem. Rep. of	9	66
Haiti	8	52	Venezuela, R.B. de	9	65
Zimbabwe	9	52	Mali	11	65
Congo, Rep. of	11	50	Zambia	11	64
Lao PDR	9	50	Congo, Rep. of	12	62
Burundi	9	47	Mongolia	10	59
Rwanda	9	47	Angola	9	58
Congo, Dem. Rep. of	8	46	Azerbaijan	14	56

Sources: World Bank 2007d.

Most of the slowest border crossings occur in Sub-Saharan African or Central Asian countries, many of which are landlocked. Having little control over other aspects of trade costs, such as transport over land to the nearest port, landlocked countries could be more aggressive with the trade facilitation policies that they do have control to improve. They could also benefit from a more explicit regional perspective. A variety of transit rules are recognized by international law and declarations, such as the "Almaty Programme of Action."[65] Corridor facilitation and monitoring initiatives, such as those envisaged under the Sub-Saharan Africa Transport Program, could reduce the risk of coordination failures, but enforcement has been weak.[66]

Even for fairly small coastal countries, regional approaches can be beneficial. Since increases in trade produce scale economies in transport, hub infrastructure is most beneficial if it is shared by as many market participants as possible. Few countries in West or East Africa, if any, can support a medium-size, deep-water container port on their own. But a shared port with a large catchment area would be more likely to support agglomeration, if costs and access are distributed among coastal countries and their landlocked neighbors. Sharing is not easy, however, because of the domestic bias of national infrastructure policies.

Addressing the negative externalities of transport

Efficient transport provides external benefits that go beyond simple time savings or lower maintenance; these benefits are often underappreciated. But transport also has external costs that usually are not internalized by transporters and traders.[67] Congestion and greenhouse gas emissions affect both developed and developing countries, but the direct health-related costs of pollution and poor safety are generally highest in developing countries.

Congestion. The lumpiness of transport infrastructure implies that there is no smooth and immediate supply response when demand increases. With overcapacity, the extra cost could be spread over a larger number of users. With insufficient capacity, congestion causes time and quality losses,

the case in many rapidly growing developing countries. Estimating the costs of congestion is not straightforward, because it occurs mostly during certain times of the day, often caused by specific bottlenecks in the network. One study of Washington, D.C., congestion put these costs at $0.065 per mile.[68]

Emissions. With growing concerns about climate change, the transport sector—a visible consumer of fossil fuels—has been getting more scrutiny. The largest share of these emissions is generated in industrialized countries. But with rising motorization in many developing countries, the world's vehicle fleet will rapidly grow, and so will emissions. Most estimates of greenhouse gas emissions from transport are close to 13.5 percent of the total (see figure 6.6). One integrated assessment study puts the population-weighted expected global costs of a 2.5° C warming in 2100 at 2 percent of world GDP.[69] Half of this is caused by abrupt climate change, including the possible spread of tropical disease, especially in Africa. Other costs are incurred in agriculture (less than 10 percent) and from rising seas (6 percent).

What would internalizing these costs mean for the overall costs of transport? Estimates vary. A meta-analysis of earlier estimates suggests a current upper bound of $50 per ton of carbon.[70] The *Stern Review* (2007) puts the total damage from future warming at 5–20 percent of world GDP in perpetuity and infers a current social cost equivalent of $311 per ton of carbon. With a gallon of gasoline containing 0.0024 tons of carbon, damage of $50 per ton of carbon would translate into $0.12 per gallon of gasoline (or $0.03 per liter) and damage of $300 into $0.72 a gallon ($0.19 a liter). Internalizing the carbon dioxide (CO_2) costs of transport would thus increase transport costs by an amount well within historical gasoline price variations. Efforts to increase fuel efficiency have been under way for the past three decades, aided at least as much by fuel taxes and efficiency regulations as by the rising price of oil.

Pollution. Gasoline vehicles emit carbon monoxide (CO), nitrogen oxides (NOx), and hydrocarbons (HC). CO reduces oxygen in the bloodstream, causing breathing

Figure 6.6   **Transport accounts for about one-seventh of CO₂ emissions**
Sources of greenhouse gas emissions, 2005

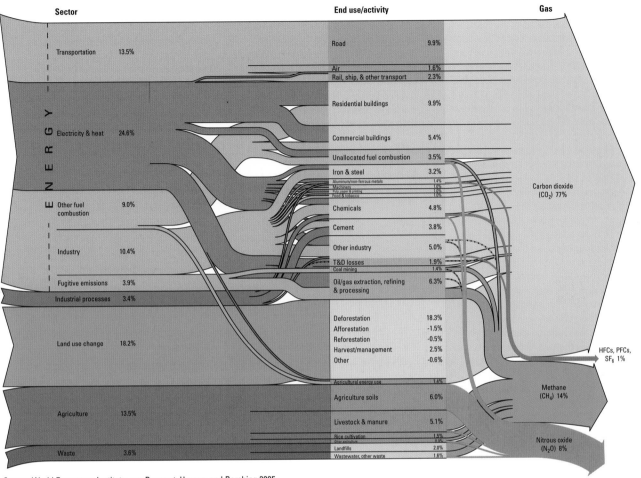

Source: World Resources Institute; see Baumert, Herzog, and Pershing 2005.

difficulty and cardiovascular damage. HC and NOx combine to form ozone, making breathing harder and reducing visibility. NOx and HC also react to form fine particulate matter (PM2.5), small enough to enter lung tissue and increase mortality risks. Vehicle emissions of all local pollutants have fallen in developed countries, but they remain high elsewhere. Diseases related to air pollution contribute to the premature death of more than half a million people each year, imposing a cost of up to 2 percent of GDP in many developing countries. Transport may be responsible for about a quarter of this impact, mainly from private and commercial vehicles.[71]

Accidents. Similar to local air pollution, developed countries with high but stable motorization have reduced road fatalities

and injuries. But in developing and transition countries, these rates are increasing. The rate of road fatalities in the Russian Federation, for example, is five times that of the Netherlands. Some 1.2 million people die in road accidents each year, and 90 percent occur in low- and middle-income countries. World Bank projections suggest an increase by more than 80 percent between 2000 and 2020 in these countries, but a decrease of 30 percent in high-income countries. For every death, there are many cases of injury and disablement. Projected health losses from traffic accidents as a share of the total health losses are highest in the Middle East and North Africa (5 percent)—expected to rise to 8 percent—followed by Latin America and the Caribbean and East Asia and the Pacific (3

BOX 6.7 *Unclogging Latin America's arteries: transport costs now matter more than tariffs*

For the last two decades, the trade policy agenda of Latin America has been dominated by traditional market access and policy barriers issues. It has paid off. Tariffs have come down a lot. Most-favored-nation tariffs fell from more than 40 percent in the mid-1980s to close to 10 percent by 2000. Still, trade agreements continue to dominate policy discussions in the region.

But transport costs are now more important than tariffs. Simple averages of import ad valorem freight range from 6.5 percent in Argentina to 12 percent in Colombia for intraregional freight, and from 7.5 percent in Uruguay to 25 percent in landlocked Paraguay. Freight costs in Latin America and the Caribbean for exports to the United States are—with the exception of Bolivia, Mexico, and República Bolivariana de Venezuela—even higher than intraregional freight.

Low port efficiency and weak competition in the maritime transport sector seem to be the culprits (see figure to the right). On average, transport costs in Latin America would decline by 20 percent if countries in the region had U.S. levels of port efficiency.

A reduction of transport costs would bring about substantial benefits. A 10-percent decrease in trade costs would increase the region's imports by 50 percent and intraregional exports by more than 60 percent. The benefits of better transport policies seem to be much larger than lower tariffs. Compared with a similar reduction in tariffs, the benefits of a fall in transport costs for intraregional exports are almost five times larger and lead to an increase in the number of products exported to the region, which is nine times bigger than a similar reduction in tariffs.

Source: Inter-American Development Bank, forthcoming.

Transport costs now matter more for trade
Percentage change in transport costs by making port efficiency, tariff rates, and number of shippers the same as U.S. levels, base year 2005

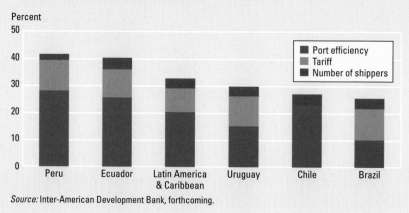

Source: Inter-American Development Bank, forthcoming.

percent), then Africa, Eastern Europe and Central Asia, and South Asia (2 percent).

Fatality risks are highest where motorization rates are rapidly increasing, because of long lags in implementing road safety measures. The transport sector can thus impose a cost on development. To what extent accident costs are "external" depends on how well insurance markets can cover the external costs, but even where those markets do not work well, road safety measures can protect pedestrians, cyclists, and other drivers from the reckless.

Transport: an increasingly important sector

For most modes of transport, costs have declined in many markets. Still, those costs are becoming a larger share of overall trade costs because of steeper declines in tariffs in regions such as Latin America and the Caribbean (see box 6.7). And with fuel costs rising, transport's share will rise even more.

What is needed for transport to continue to contribute to development?

Poor countries become big producers before they become big consumers. Income generation by importing intermediate goods and raw materials and exporting processed goods will be important. The relocation of intermediate production processes to middle- and low-income countries indicates the enormous potential benefits from integration into world markets even for these countries, limited mainly by transport and communications costs. But achieving this raises difficult institutional questions. The provision of access to foreign markets implies that some of the benefits of transport policies will accrue to foreign countries. Coordinating international transport policies thus requires a growing confidence in reciprocal support for international transport.

The increasing returns to scale in transport add two more coordination problems.

The scale of least-cost port and airport investments calls for hub-and-spoke transport systems in which neighboring countries share facilities. Because ownership of large infrastructure facilities provides market power, the sharing of facilities requires credible agreements. Increasing returns in transport operations—with maritime shipping supplied by a small number of firms and logistics services being consolidated in fewer hands—may require regulatory regimes to realize the potential for lower transport costs. The mutual dependence of transport policy and competition policy implies a global effort, such as that started by some multilateral organizations.

Transport and communication costs will remain a principal influence on the speed and efficiency of the spatial transformations needed for growth. Countries at different stages of transformation will have to formulate different policies for reducing transport costs. East, South, and Central Asia illustrate the contrasts:

- Developing countries in East Asia are now closer to world markets, as Japan and the Republic of Korea have prospered, and their transport costs to North America and Western Europe have fallen. They have joined the growing trade in intermediate and final manufactured goods. Countries such as Tunisia can do the same.

- In South Asia, falling trade and communication costs have helped India enter western markets for intermediate services, eliminating some of the disadvantages of being distant. Countries such as South Africa can do the same, exploiting their home market potential.

- In Central Asia—with economies that are small, landlocked, and dependent on exports of primary products such as oil and gas—reducing transport costs will be more difficult. It will also be difficult for smaller countries in divided neighborhoods, such as Burkina Faso, Malawi, Niger, and Rwanda. These countries will need aggressive measures to lessen the trade friction, enforceable agreements with neighbors to share expensive infrastructure, and selected investments to encourage agglomeration and reduce the transport costs for primary goods exports.

Distance and Division in East Asia

When Admiral Zheng He brought a giraffe to Nanjing in 1415, it was believed to be a heavenly beast, associated with great peace and prosperity. It also marked the heyday of Chinese influence in East Asia and the region's wealth relative to the rest of the world. China at the time was probably the world's largest economy, enjoying the highest standard of material, living with flourishing art and education and advances in a range of technologies. Its naval skills had enabled voyages to places as far away as Africa.

China alone may have accounted for one-third of global manufacturing. This was not to last. A hundred years later, a new emperor destroyed Zheng He's navigation logs and slashed the navy to one-tenth its size, believing that the costs of foreign expeditions outweighed the benefits. China entered centuries of self-imposed isolation, broken in infamous and damaging fashion by the British during the Opium Wars of the nineteenth century.

East Asia's age of isolationism

China was not alone in trying to shut out the rest of the world. In Japan, Tokugawa Iemitsu issued the "Closed Country Edict of 1635" and the "Exclusion of the Portuguese, 1639," effectively shutting off Japan to external influences for the next two centuries. The edicts not only prevented foreign entry into Japan but also banned Japanese from going abroad. The dislike of all things Western extended to technology. In an extraordinary attempt to preserve its culture and social hierarchy, Japan gradually abolished the gun in favor of the more elegant and symbolic samurai sword.

These extreme examples show the vast *division* between countries in East Asia, especially after the seventeenth century. Scholars do not agree fully on the economic effects of such division. Some have argued that reductions in living standards were significant during

the Qing and Tokugawa periods. Others believe that it is more apt to characterize these societies as having stagnant rather than declining economies. In any event, wage levels in Japan and China at the start of the nineteenth century were well below those in London or Amsterdam, even in real terms, perhaps by as much as 50 percent.[1] Adam Smith had already recognized this: "The difference between the money price of labour in China and Europe is still greater than that between the money price of subsistence; because the real recompence of labour is higher in Europe than in China."[2]

Smith was correct. Even before the Industrial Revolution, parts of Europe had advanced beyond Asia in their living standards. He was also right in writing about China as a unified economy. The mandarins of China kept exceptional records of wages paid to armorers and other craftsmen providing services to the government. These show little regional difference despite the vast *distances* within imperial China. Only the less dense, sparsely populated northern areas had somewhat higher wages.

By the middle of the nineteenth century, real wages in Canton and Tokyo, the most advanced cities in Asia, were only as high as in small European cities like Milan and Leipzig. Elsewhere in East Asia living standards were lower still. The old Chinese tributary states had been colonized, and Asian countries were further divided (see map G3.1).

Shortly thereafter, most of Europe went through the Industrial Revolution, and the "great divide" between Europe and Asia widened, with widespread advances in European wages and gross domestic product (GDP). According to Angus Maddison (2006), East Asia's share of global GDP, constant at around 40 percent between 1500 and 1800, fell to less than 15 percent by 1950.

Fifty years of Asian integration

Fast forward to today. East Asian economies have become integrated through a dense array of regional production networks. These supply chains started with outsourcing by Japanese multinationals in the 1980s, as wages and land costs in the dense production area of Tokyo grew prohibitive for competitive manufacturing. In fact, economic congestion in Hong Kong, China; Japan; the Republic of Korea; and Taiwan, China, has resulted in spillovers—first to middle-income countries in Southeast Asia, and then to China, as the barriers of economic ideology were reduced. Recently, supply chains have centered on China and the great assembly operations in Guangdong and Shenzhen. As China has matured, it too has become an exporter of intermediates and capital equipment. China is now the main trading partner for Japan and the Republic of Korea and sources more than half its rapidly growing imports from East Asia.

Intraregional trade in East Asia today approximates that within the

Map G3.1   Asia divided: conflict in the middle of the nineteenth century

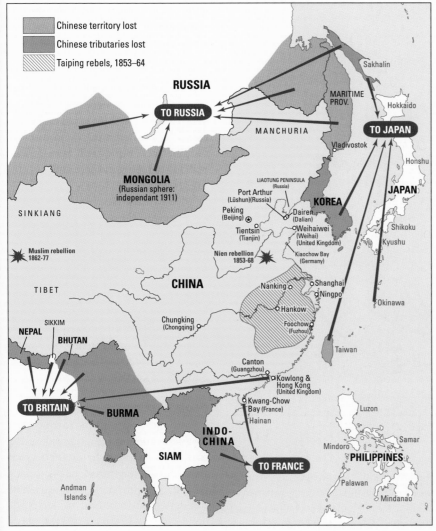

Source: www.fordham.edu/halsall.

European Union (EU), growing consistently faster than that between East Asia and other regions in the world. East Asian countries are the source for almost two-thirds of all foreign investment in the region. Even technology is starting to originate within the region, especially in key export industries such as electronics. East Asian countries are busily driving down divisions between each other in the form of trade barriers and other border costs. They started with world-class logistics in ports and airports—albeit sometimes restricted to special economic zones. And they have continued with improvements in soft infrastructure, such as customs reforms and visa exemptions within the Association of Southeast Asian Nations (ASEAN).

The falling *division* between countries in East Asia has coincided with rapid growth across a diverse spectrum ranging from Lao People's Democratic Republic with a per capita income of $500 in 2006 to Singapore with a per capita income of almost $30,000. Within East Asia, incomes are slowly converging: poor countries are growing faster than rich countries. Most East Asian countries have followed similar paths, starting with agricultural intensification and rural industrialization, followed by urban expansion and manufactured exports. There has been learning from abroad—of new technologies and of new institutions. Exports have become more technologically complex. Middle-income countries have specialized in component production, while rich Asian countries have added more value through innovation, branding, and greater technological sophistication.

As the region has grown, it has developed a dynamic that reinforces growth. ASEAN, China, Japan, and the Republic of Korea are an economic mass comparable to North America in the 1990s. As the center of gravity of the global economy shifts toward the Pacific Rim, global market access for everyone in East Asia has improved.

The degree of intraregional trade in East Asia may be considered surprising given the history of divisive political relationships between many East Asian countries. In the Western Hemisphere, the economic effects of conflict between countries were overcome by formal institutions of codified legal systems and political agreements that governed arm's-length commercial transactions and that could be readily expanded to accommodate rapid growth in commerce and finance. In East Asia these institutions have been slower to develop. Instead, a long history of social networks, communities, and informal institutions—with roots in the migrations over millennia of people from Southeastern China to Southeast Asia—provides the trust to support modern international integration of goods and money (see map G3.2).

The integration ahead— the twin challenges of distance and division

Peering into the future, the region faces challenges on its path of rapid integration.

The shift in *economic density* toward the north poses a special challenge for Southeast Asia. How can it remain

Map G3.2   Asia integrated: trade at the end of the twentieth century

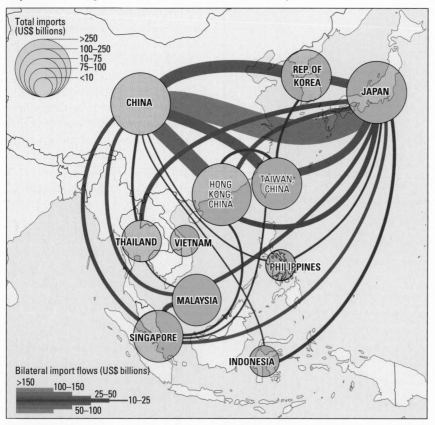

Total imports
(US$ billions)
>250
100–250
10–75
75–100
<10

Bilateral import flows (US$ billions)
>150
100–150
25–50
50–100
10–25

Source: Gill and Kharas 2007.

significant as an economic force in the region? One answer perhaps lies in the development of world-class cities. The major metropolises of Southeast Asia need to develop themselves into "sticky places," attracting and retaining global talent. Meanwhile, the integration of Australia and India into the region might alter the dynamics of place, offsetting to some degree the northward drift of Asia's economic center of gravity.

The problems encountered by countries *distant* from the major markets of the region are echoed in lagging areas within countries. Significant poverty remains in East Asia, with high poverty rates in areas like western China, southern and eastern Philippines, Thailand's northeast, and Vietnam's central highlands. The gap between per capita incomes in the richest and poorest provinces of China—negligible under the imperial dynasties of the past—has swelled to 13.1:1 (compared with 2.1:1 in the United States). Although many have moved closer to prosperous areas, overcoming the geographic *distances* that isolate these populations is still seen as a major challenge.

Within East Asian countries, people are moving to the markets, and markets are developing where people are concentrated. Urbanization is large and rapid in most countries, perhaps adding 25 million city dwellers every year for the next two decades. Most of these people will move to small and medium-size cities of less than 1 million people, not to major metropolitan areas. Managing these small cities efficiently and integrating them into the national economies will be a crucial task for reducing *distance* and sustaining growth.

Meanwhile, East Asia still faces strategic questions about how to bring down *divisions* between countries in the region. ASEAN's two-speed process shows how hard it is for countries with different incomes and economic structures to integrate deeply. No formal process of economic integration brings together all the economies of the region. A first attempt to start a regional dialogue was at the East Asia Summit in Kuala Lumpur, Malaysia, in December 2005. The summit called for financial stability, energy security, poverty eradication, and narrowing gaps between countries. It underscored the challenges that still divide the region: cross-border migration, environmental spillovers, diversity of governance standards, and cultural understanding. Other interesting experiments to foster regional integration are under way, such as within ASEAN+3, but the institutional leadership to forge a common future is fragmented. Even so, leading scholars have noted that "the emergence of an integrated East Asia is inevitable and necessary."[3] The challenge is figuring out how to make this happen quickly.

Contributed by Homi Kharas.

PART THREE
REFRAMING THE POLICY DEBATES

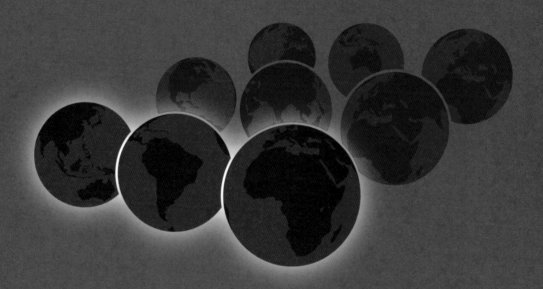

Can crowded cities in developing countries pull people in and power them out of poverty? Does migration help those who move and those left behind? How can trade help the world's wealthy and most destitute? What can policy makers do to address the three big challenges facing the developing world—a billion slum dwellers, a billion people living in remote and underserved areas, and the "bottom billion"? Part three of the Report provides the answer: economic integration. How? By using spatially blind institutions, spatially connective infrastructure, and spatially targeted incentives and calibrating the response to the difficulty of integration. Chapter 7 explains what economic integration means for metropolises, cities, towns, and villages. Chapter 8 proposes how integration between economically leading and lagging areas can benefit everyone. Chapter 9 lays out the difficult steps needed to successfully integrate the world's most isolated countries. In doing so, the chapters in part three revisit and reframe long-standing policy debates on urbanization, territorial development, and international integration.

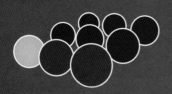

CHAPTER 7

Concentration without Congestion
Policies for an inclusive urbanization

A team of urban experts, as part of a routine exercise in 1974, forecast the size of the world's most populous cities in 2000. Kinshasa, the Democratic Republic of Congo's capital, would grow to 9 million, more than London today. Pakistan's Karachi would expand to 16 million, almost as large as New York City. The forecasts were way off (see figure 7.1). Kinshasa's population is about half of London's today, Karachi's about half of New York City's. Why were the experts, generally good at forecasting national populations, so wrong in predicting city sizes?

The reason: forecasting the spatial distribution of people in a country is not the same thing as predicting the size of its population. As shown in earlier chapters, spatial transformations—the growth of cities and leading areas—are linked closely to changes in the economy, especially the sectoral transformations that accompany growth and the opening of an economy to foreign trade and investment. So predicting the size of a city is *economic forecasting*, a hazardous occupation. Take Guangzhou in China. Its population in 2000 was more than a third larger than the 4.5 million predicted in 1974. Beijing's was half the 19 million predicted. The experts could not have foreseen China's economic liberalization and growth, which quickly would change the country's spatial structure. Simply extrapolating past trends, they should instead have examined the market forces of agglomeration, migration, and specialization—and the government policies that help or hinder them.

Projections now suggest that cities in developing countries will double in three decades, adding another 2 billion people. Indeed, large cities in developing countries will grow bigger to provide the urbanization economies sought by entrepreneurs, workers, and innovators. But this will happen mostly in economies that are doing well. Medium-size cities remain the backbone of urban systems, providing the localization economies that producers with more specialized needs seek. But they will flourish only where economies are industrializing. Smaller cities and towns continue to serve and to depend on surrounding rural settlements. But they will grow rapidly only in areas where farms and village economies are doing well.

The spatial transformations that lead to the rise of cities and towns will not be orderly. Informal settlements—slums and shantytowns—may form and expand as the rising demands of workers and firms outstrip the capacities of governments to institute well-functioning land markets and to invest in infrastructure and accommodation. If today's developed countries are a guide, it takes many decades to address within-city disparities and to absorb informal settlements into more organized city structures. Trying to restrict rural-urban migration can be counterproductive. Why? Because limiting density and diversity stifles innovation and productivity.

Policy makers, if they are not careful, can end up harming these transformations. By not instituting flexible regulation and versatile land use conversion, they can make urban areas inhospitable to firms and investors. By not providing adequate water, sanitation, schools, and health care in rural areas, they can prematurely push villagers to towns and cities. By not investing enough in the infrastructure of rapidly growing cities, they can encourage congestion. More generally, by not responding appropriately to the needs of spatial transformations for different types of places, they cannot reap the full benefits of density and diversity, which congestion and division can undermine.

To help nations benefit from urbanization, this chapter proposes a policy framework—informed by the stylized facts of spatial transformations (chapter 1) and the insights about agglomeration economies that drive these changes (chapter 4). It outlines the policy priorities and their sequencing, using the experiences of countries that have urbanized well and of those that have struggled. The main messages:

- *Rural-urban transformations are best facilitated when policy makers recognize the economic interdependence among settlements.* Within a country's hierarchy of cities, towns, and villages, each specializes in a different function and has strong interrelationships with others. So the policy discussion should be framed not at the extremes of the national level or the individual settlement. Instead, it should be framed at the level of what is termed an "area," usually a state or province. Policy makers should see themselves as managers of the portfolio of places in such an area. An area approach can also inform national urbanization strategies. While area-specific urban shares in the population will determine priorities for all levels of government (central, provincial, and municipal), a nation's urban share can be a good guide to the overall complexity of its challenges.

- *Policy challenges become more complex with urbanization.* Cities and towns provide firms and families the benefits of proximity, but the compactness of activity produces congestion, pollution, and social tension, which can offset those benefits. Whether a policy is desirable depends on if it addresses the market's failures and abets concentration. In countries or areas with low

Figure 7.1   The growth of cities has been grossly overestimated

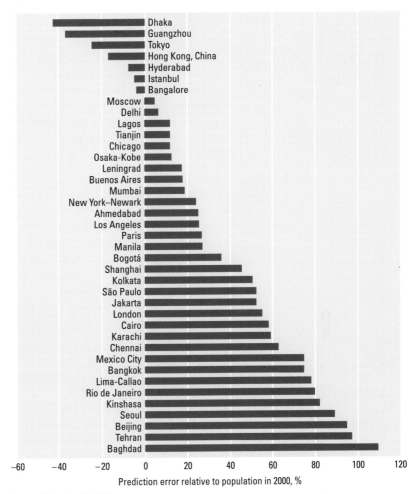

Prediction error relative to population in 2000, %

Source: Satterthwaite 2007.
Note: Comparison of predictions in 1974 with estimates of city populations in 2000. Bar indicates the extent to which the city population was overpredicted in 1974 relative to its size in 2000. A negative number indicates that a city size was greater in 2000 than predicted.

urban shares, for example, traffic congestion and slums may not be the major policy problems. But in rapidly urbanizing areas, congestion can quickly set in. And metropolitan areas may need, in addition, to address within-city divisions posed by shantytowns and slums.

- *Prioritizing and sequencing of policies can help governments facilitate inclusive urbanization even in the early stages of development.* Each dimension of the integration challenge requires a different family of instruments. For areas of incipient urbanization, the policy challenge is one-dimensional: build density with spatially blind institutions. For areas of intermediate urbanization, it is two-dimensional: build density and reduce economic distance with spatially connective infrastructure. And for areas of advanced urbanization, it is three-dimensional: build density, overcome distance, and address the economic and social divisions—caused, say, by slums—with spatially targeted interventions. But at every stage, policy makers should emphasize the spatially blind institutions that encourage density in the right places.

The chapter first summarizes how urbanization policies can help places facilitate agglomeration economies. It next outlines a framework for economic integration to guide the management of a portfolio of places, using the experience of places that have urbanized successfully. It then discusses examples of the framework in action in today's developing countries.

Principles for managing a portfolio of places

Debates about urbanization often evoke images of overcrowded cities, visible concentrations of poverty, and appalling environmental degradation. This can result in a general policy stance to control urban growth and curb rural-urban migration. Geographically targeted interventions to clear or clean up slums that proliferated during low- and middle-income stages of development can end up dominating the discussion.

This chapter reframes the urbanization debate. Historical evidence suggests that urbanization in developing countries will continue to be rapid at early stages of economic growth—much of the rise in urban shares takes place before nations get to upper-middle incomes. But the rising density is to be welcomed if it produces agglomeration economies. The debate should not be mainly about the pace of urbanization, the amount of rural-urban migration, or the ways to eradicate slums with targeted interventions. Instead, it should be about the efficiency and inclusiveness of the processes that transform a rural economy into an urban one. And it should be about how policy can best address the coordination failures that arise at each stage of urbanization. "The poor are gravitating to towns and cities, but more rapid poverty reduction will probably require a faster pace of urbanization, not a slower one—and development policy makers will need to facilitate this process, not hinder it."[1] And because a rural-urban transformation involves both the urban and the rural, urbanization strategies must include measures to improve rural lives and livelihoods (see box 7.1).

The principle: maximize agglomeration economies across the portfolio of places

Concentration, associated with rising density, brings potential benefits from "thick" markets. But it also brings congestion and squalor. The main aim of urban policy is to help settlements deliver agglomeration economies while reducing the grime, crime, and time costs that come with rising concentration. At different stages of urbanization, the binding constraints to promoting concentration

---

BOX 7.1   *Are the policy messages of this Report antirural? No.*

The economic geography of nations does not conform to a simple urban-rural split. A continuum of density gives rise to a portfolio of interrelated places. Symbiosis is the rule. At the head is a country's leading city, and below it, a spectrum of settlements—secondary cities, small urban centers, towns, and villages.

A low-income country's portfolio of places consists of primarily rural areas. At this phase of incipient urbanization, the mainstay of a strategy to facilitate spatial transformations necessary for economic growth is a set of spatially blind policies:

- Versatile and well-implemented regulations governing land markets to enforce property rights, safeguard land tenure, improve land transfers, ease land use conversion to reflect market needs, and bolster land taxation
- Basic and social service provision to improve education and health, increase productivity, and encourage mobility

- Sound macroeconomic policies to reduce market distortions, eliminate biases against agriculture, improve the business climate, stimulate competitiveness, and promote investment and adopt new technologies.

Such "aspatial" policies promote rural development—both in agriculture and the nonfarm economy—so that every place becomes better equipped to participate in industry and services.

These policies will disproportionately benefit rural households because the rural nonfarm economy typically accounts for 30–50 percent of rural employment. Likewise, rural households engage in diverse economic activities, with nonagricultural sources contributing 35–42 percent of household income. Growth in the nonfarm sector will stimulate growth in agriculture as inputs become cheaper, profits are reinvested in agriculture, and technological change allows better farming methods.[a]

Source: WDR 2009 team.
a. Feder and Lanjouw 2001.

while controlling congestion differ, as do the priorities at each stage of urbanization.

- **Incipient.** Areas of incipient urbanization—with urban shares of about 25 percent—are predominantly agricultural or resource based, with low economic density. The priority is simply to facilitate agglomeration forces and to encourage internal economies of scale for plants, mills, and factories in towns. Because it is not yet clear which places will be favored by markets and for what purposes, neutrality between places should be the watchword for policy makers.

- **Intermediate.** As urbanization progresses, economic alliances strengthen within and between urbanized areas. Many firms and plants in the same sector colocate to take advantage of sharing inputs and knowledge spillovers. In such areas—with urban population shares of about 50 percent—the promotion of localization economies is the highest priority. Efficiency in production and transport is the watchword.

- **Advanced.** For highly urbanized areas, productivity and consumption benefits arise from urbanization economies associated with the diversity and intensity of economic activity. While functionality is the goal for industrial towns and cities, the watchword for postindustrial metropolises, with urban shares of about 75 percent, is livability.

The policy rule: sequence and calibrate

The spatial dimensions of density, distance, and division spotlight the policy challenge

in each of these types of place. In predominantly rural neighborhoods, the policy challenge is one dimensional and corresponds to the need to build density. In areas where urbanization has gathered momentum, the challenge is two dimensional. It incorporates the need to promote density and overcome problems of distance caused by congestion. In areas of advanced urbanization, the challenge is three dimensional. For metropolises, again, there is a need to encourage density and overcome distance. To this should be added the need to eliminate divisions within cities, which segregate the poor in informal slums from the rest, in formally settled parts (see figure 7.2).

The unit for deliberating government action: an area

Different parts of a country urbanize at different speeds. Unevenness is the rule, not an exception. And there are synergies and economic interdependencies among settlements of different sizes. Reframing urbanization policies to better meet the economic imperatives at all stages of the rural-urban transformation requires rethinking the spatial scale for deciding policy priorities and design. This Report makes the case for considering policies at an appropriate geographic scale: an "area," or state or province, generally the middle tier of government between the central and municipal. The scale should be big enough to permit both rural-urban and interurban linkages. The experience of Beijing, Shanghai municipality, and Guangdong province supports a deliberately designed area approach to urban strategy. Two other areas

Figure 7.2   The dimensions increase with the level of urbanization

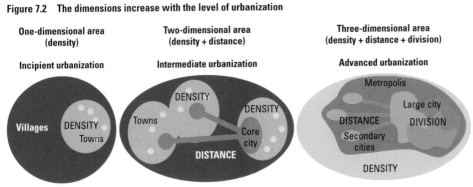

Source: WDR 2009 team.

in western China—Chengdu and Chongqing—are now taking the same approach to urbanization, with some success.

An area approach does not rule out the aggregation of urbanization strategies to a national level. High-density areas tend to have populations concentrated in metropolitan cities, intermediate-density areas in medium-size cities, and low-density areas in small towns and villages. In the same way, more urbanized countries have more of their people in high-density areas, and less urbanized countries have some high-density areas, but most people are in low-density areas. Urbanization policies should incorporate this unevenness of economic development.

A country's aggregate urban share can be a good indicator of the complexity of the urbanization challenges it faces. In the simplest case, one area may characterize an entire country, as for Singapore. For larger countries, a careful aggregation can help determine the priorities at different levels of government.

- In countries where urbanization is incipient, such as Ethiopia, with three-fourths of its population in rural areas, the integration challenge is unidimensional: facilitating density. To be sure, the capital cities and a handful of other cities even in predominantly rural nations face multidimensional challenges in their spatial transformation. But the top priority is the set of aspatial policy instruments that apply universally to all places—establishing market institutions to regulate land use and transactions, and delivering such basic services as security, schools, streets, and sanitation. So in the countries of Sub-Saharan Africa and Central Asia, the role of national governments is pivotal in laying the foundations of inclusive urbanization.
- Where urbanization is intermediate—as in many parts of the countries of East and South Asia such as India and China—central and provincial administrations must also build transport and communication infrastructure.
- Where urbanization is more advanced, as in the countries of Latin America, North Africa, and Eastern Europe, central, state, and municipal governments must synchronize efforts to facilitate the geographic transformations for the push from middle to high incomes.

A framework for integration

As urbanization advances, the policy imperatives change, with the instruments spanning the spectrum from spatially blind to spatially targeted. While the policy debates overemphasize the most spatially explicit of government actions, such as slum-upgrading programs, successful urbanization aimed at integrating every nation's portfolio of places requires the use of the full range of instruments—institutions, infrastructure, and incentives.

Spatially blind "institutions" to facilitate economic density

The responsibility for building institutions that will be the bedrock for urbanization in all parts of the country lies mainly with the central government. Chief among them are those governing the management of land. In this Report, "institutions" encompass three broad sets of measures: law and order (especially the definition and enforcement of property rights), the universal provision of basic services, and macroeconomic stability (see "Navigating This Report" for details). These are core mandates for the central government, and delivering them—or failing to—will alter the geographic distribution of economic activities forever.

The institutions governing land markets include a comprehensive land registry; credible mechanisms for contract enforcement and conflict resolution; flexible zoning laws; and versatile subdivision regulations that help, rather than hinder, the conversion of land for different uses. The transformation of the agricultural sector from one based on communal land rights to individual *property rights* is the sine qua non for urbanization. The evidence clearly shows that once property rights have been established and density is increasing, *land regulation and planning* can ensure the efficient coordination of different land uses. But if regulations are overzealous, they can hinder the benefits of density and agglomeration economies. Similarly, rigid *land use conversion rules,* which may be a consequence of inflexible regulations, can be detrimental to density, as are overly restrictive minimum building standards. The fourth institution is adequate *housing finance*.

Institutions for fluid land markets remain important. The property rights embodied in land titles are essential for converting assets into usable wealth.[2] The practical problems of titling, not least the cost of implementation, should not deter strengthening the legal framework for individual property ownership. Indeed, formal titles are necessary for functioning land and property markets. Although customary systems of tenure still permit informal transactions, the absence of formal titles hinders the conversion of land to areas of higher economic return. Informality is a brake on land development, constraining an efficient spatial transformation.

Consider preindustrial Europe. With more secure individual property rights to land, English cities grew rapidly.[3] Indeed, England may have been the first to industrialize because it introduced such rights before other European countries. The Nobel prize–winning economist Douglass North uses this to spotlight what land institutions can do for long-run growth and development.[4]

The "enclosure" movement made individual private property rights possible. Starting around 1500 open commons were fenced, hedged, or otherwise closed off and deeded or titled to individuals. By 1545 around 40 percent of England's surface area belonged to private individuals. The Enclosure Act of 1604 fostered the conversion of open commons into private plots, which continued until the early twentieth century.[5] Most researchers agree that enclosures in England increased agricultural productivity, which released labor from the land, and provided the food surplus to support the rapidly increasing urban population.[6] This allowed England to become, for a time, the "workshop of the world."[7] More evidence on how aspatial institutions initiate urbanization comes from Denmark (see box 7.2).

Another example of what widespread private property rights can do for growth, and for density, comes from North America and the countries of Latin America and the Caribbean. In the early period of European settlement, Canada and the United States were seen as having economic potential similar to that of other parts of the New World (see "Geography in Motion: Overcoming Distance in North America"). After winning the Anglo-French Seven Years' War of 1756–63, the British vigorously debated whether to claim the small Caribbean islands of Guadeloupe (1,628 square kilometers) or Canada (9.8 million square kilometers) as the spoils of victory.[8]

The development trajectories of North America and Latin America would diverge radically. In Latin America, the Spanish colonialists gave large tracts of land to a handful of individuals, along with the right to tax the local populace. Customary communal property rights determined land use, making people less willing to move. In North America, by contrast, there were few barriers to the acquisition of land, creating

---

BOX 7.2 *Land reform to jump-start urbanization: aiding* villeins *in Denmark*

In central Copenhagen a "pillar of freedom" commemorates land reform. The monument honors the final abolition, in 1788, of "villenage," a form of serfdom common in Western Europe in the Middle Ages. At the beginning of the eighteenth century less than 1 percent of agricultural land was farmed by land-owning peasants, and large amounts of land were common property. Required to work for landlords, "villeins" could not move without their landlord's consent. But starting in 1760, most communal land was transformed into private holdings. Between 1788 and 1807, landlords sold around half of their land to tenants. By 1835 almost 65 percent of the land was owner occupied.[a] A few decades later, Denmark experienced a "take-off" into industrialization and urbanization.

This urbanization did not mean rural squalor. Structural, technological, and institutional changes reduced the value of tenancy to landlords, increasing the economic leverage of tenants. In a 1784 decree the century-old obligation of landlords to collect taxes on behalf of the state was waived on land the landlord sold to their former tenants.

In 1788 the abolition of villeinage further improved the bargaining power of tenants. Policy interventions in the credit market also helped. In 1786 two public credit institutions were established to provide loans for land purchases, complementing an already rather active and efficient private credit market. The result: credit did not constrain many prospective buyers.[b]

Market-based transactions, facilitated by government land policies, formed a large class of owner-occupier farmers, later a driving force behind Denmark's 1849 Constitution and emerging democracy. By promoting education for the poor and for rural residents, they also spread basic services and gave a strong impetus to industrialization and small towns.[c] Denmark's population rose sharply—in preindustrial societies, a growing population is a sign of prospering agriculture. After 1890 agriculture fed a surge of industrial growth in small towns[d] instrumental in Denmark's industrialization.[e]

Contributed by Thomas Markussen.
a. Henriksen 2003. b. Henriksen 2003.
c. Henriksen 2003. d. Pedersen 1990.
e. Christensen 2004, p. 1.

land markets and a predominantly owner-operated agricultural sector on the western frontier.[9] The U.S. Homestead Act of 1862 gave individuals the right to 160 acres of unoccupied public land, the early foundation of a strong property rights system.

Contemporary research confirms the role of well-enforced individual property rights. A study of 80 countries finds that institutional quality does more for long-run growth than either geographic factors or a country's openness to trade.[10] Another study of 75 countries finds that security of property rights, as measured by an index of expropriation risks, aids development. And when such institutional effects are accounted for, physical geography has weak effects on a country's average income.[11]

In incipient urbanization areas or in nations where the rural share is high, the institutions governing property rights may be both the base and the mainstay of the policies for a rapid and sustainable urbanization. By contrast, when there is no secure individual land and property rights, land transactions and urbanization may become divisive. Consider China, where land is collectively owned in rural areas and farmers do not enjoy clearly defined or fully protected land property rights. There, the conversion of land to industrial use generates social conflict because farmers perceive land confiscation as inappropriate without fair compensation. The problems are similar in many Sub-Saharan African countries, where 90 percent of the land is communal.

Land use and building regulations become important as urbanization advances. Governments regulate land markets for two reasons. First, regulation can ensure the appropriate separation of land between different uses, such as preventing the location of heavily polluting industries in residential areas. Second, it can ensure the integration of private and public uses of land, such as providing space for transport infrastructure in densely populated areas. But land use regulation can be overzealous, upsetting the delicate balance between the public interest and private opportunity.

A city's future depends on investor confidence in its prospects and its responsiveness to future changes in the demand for land.

Overly stringent regulations undermine investor confidence and unnecessarily distort housing markets. Consider Mumbai.[12] Overly restrictive land and building regulations have put unnecessary upward pressure on land and property prices, hampering the city's competitiveness. Height regulations hold Mumbai's buildings to only between a fifth and a tenth of the number of floors allowed in major cities in other countries. The city's topography should exhibit a high-density pattern similar to that in Hong Kong, China, but it is instead mostly a low-rise city (see box 7.3). Half of all poor workers commute less than 2 kilometers to work.

Stringent restrictions on land use conversion produce shortages of affordable housing, hurting migrants to a city. For this reason, the average ratio of the median house price to the median annual household income in many African and Asian cities is twice that in many large U.S. cities.[13] Bangladesh has a per capita income of $1,230, less than 3 percent of the U.S. per capita income of $44,070.[14] But in Dhaka prime land prices are similar to those in New York City. As much as 20 percent of the city's inner area is underserviced. Tracts of centrally located, publicly owned land remain idle and underdeveloped, while the rest is allocated for low value-added uses—a cantonment, public housing, and residential areas for government workers.

Stringent land development parameters—including minimum plot sizes and road widths, setbacks, and land for communal facilities—exclude a majority of households from formal land ownership. Indeed, although the underlying plot might be titled, the dwelling may be rendered illegal because of the failure to meet official construction standards. Without a downward revision of standards, the benefits of legal title are lost. Such legal codes also contribute to red tape and excessive housing costs.[15] In Addis Ababa high construction standards have relegated many low-income households, which might otherwise possess a tradable title, to the ownership of "illegal property."[16]

In 1979, the federal government in Brazil, by passing a national land use regulation setting a minimum lot size of 125 square meters and frontage of 5 meters, effectively

BOX 7.3 *Bombay fights the markets, and more than half of Mumbai's residents live in slums*

The city of Mumbai, once known as Bombay, provides sobering lessons. In the 1960s and 1970s, city planners decided that Bombay's population should be controlled at about 7 million. Land regulations and infrastructure policies were designed accordingly. But people flooded into the city anyway, and today the city is more than twice the intended size, with the highest population density of any metropolitan area in the world. Estimates indicate that 54 percent of Mumbai's 16 million people now live in slums, and another quarter in degraded apartments.

The Floor Space Index (FSI)[a] regulations in Mumbai were introduced in 1964, stipulating the maximum building space for every square meter of the plot of land. In Mumbai it was set at 4.5. The standard practice in cities with limited land is to raise the permitted FSI over time to accommodate urban growth, as in Manhattan; Singapore; Hong Kong, China; and Shanghai. Instead, the Municipal Corporation

of Greater Mumbai went the other way, lowering the permitted FSI to 1.33 in 1991. Almost all buildings in Mumbai with an FSI exceeding 4.5 were built before 1964. Under the rules that existed until recently, new buildings, including those in the central business district, were subject to the FSI of 1.33. As a consequence, space consumption in Mumbai averages 4 square meters, much less than the 12 square meters in Shanghai and the more than 20 square meters in Moscow. And about half of its residents are huddled within 2 kilometers of the city center (see the figure below).

Meanwhile, high housing costs account for as much as 15–20 percent of the income of a low-income family. Rent control regulations freeze 30 percent of Mumbai's housing stock, leaving it dilapidated because landlords see little point in investing. Weak property rights imply that only 10 percent of the housing stock has legal title, so land redevelopment

is curtailed. The government relies on property taxes and on inflated real estate prices for revenue, so it has little incentive to fight the groups that resist relaxation of building height restrictions.

The result is a vicious circle of supply shortages and high land prices. Mumbai slipped from 25th place to 40th in the league table of "best cities for business" between 1995 and 1999. It remains India's premier business city—it topped Chennai and Bangalore in investment in 2007 and was the top destination for domestic migrants. But how quickly it reforms its regulations and builds infrastructure will decide how long it will keep this position.

Source: WDR 2009 team; Bertaud 2003.
a. The FSI is the ratio of the total floor space in a building to the area of the plot on which it is built. For example, suppose a building covers half of a plot that is 1,000 square meters in size. If this building has 10 floors, it exhibits an FSI of 5.

Land should be used better in Mumbai, and people should not live so close to work

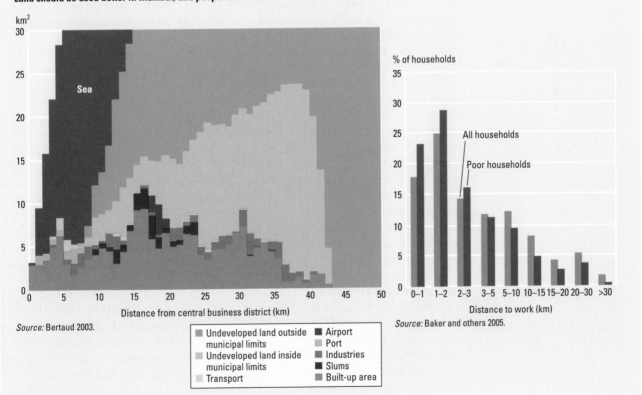

Source: Bertaud 2003.

Source: Baker and others 2005.

excluded many low-income residents from access to land in the formal sector. Many suburban low-income developments could not meet the 125-square-meter requirement, but were built on land owned by developers. Outside the formal sector, such developments could not be legally supplied public services. So more than half the population in regional capitals, such as Recife and Salvador, lives in slums or informal areas.[17,18] After democratization in 1988, cities were encouraged to service the informal sector. Although the national minimum lot size requirement remained in place, areas could be designated as Special Zones of Social Interest and exempted from the requirement as part of a package to secure tenure and improve services.

Land market restrictions can have adverse spillovers on the urban economy and blunt the instruments intended to aid urbanization. Unless basic institutions for land markets and social services are in place, infrastructure development will be hindered, and spatially targeted interventions will likely be ineffective.

Regulations for housing finance affect urbanization. Since the deregulation of financial systems in the second half of the 1980s, market-based housing financing has expanded rapidly. Residential mortgage markets are now equivalent to more that 40 percent of gross domestic product (GDP) in developed countries. But those in developing countries are much smaller, averaging less than 10 percent of GDP.[19] The public role should be to stimulate well-regulated private involvement. For example, private initiatives of the type developed by the Grameen Bank in Bangladesh, Bancosol in Bolivia, and the Housing Development and Finance Corporation in India show that uncollateralized lending can nourish housing finance even in countries with budding financial systems and weak legal and regulatory structures. Establishing the legal foundation for simple, enforceable, and prudent mortgage contracts is a good start. When a country's financial system is more developed and mature, the public sector can encourage a secondary mortgage market, develop financial innovations, and expand the securitization of mortgages.[20]

Occupant-owned housing, usually a household's largest single asset by far, is important in wealth creation, social security, and politics. People who own their house or have secure tenure have a larger stake in their community and thus are more likely to lobby for less crime, stronger governance, and better local environmental conditions.[21]

Spatially connective infrastructure to reduce distance to density

Policies to unify land markets and facilitate labor mobility remain important for the buildup of economic density at all stages of urbanization. But they are not enough for dealing with the more complex challenges of advancing urbanization. In Seoul and Shanghai, downtown traffic averages 8 kilometers an hour; in Bangkok, Manila, and Mexico City, it averages 10 kilometers an hour or slower; in Kuala Lumpur and São Paulo, it averages 15 kilometers an hour or slower. Workers in Jakarta, Kinshasa, Lagos, and Manila spend on average 75 minutes commuting to work.[22] For such areas, congestion can eat away the benefits of rising density. Spatially connective infrastructure must join the spatially blind institutions as priorities for inclusive urbanization.

Connective infrastructure needs institutions. Successful cities react to growing traffic congestion with spatially connective infrastructure. But preceding such infrastructure in all successful cities (or accompanying it in the fastest urbanizers) is a fluid land market and an empowered local government. The sequencing of policies should be spatially blind measures to create conditions suitable for economic concentration, followed by connective policies to deal with congestion.

The United Kingdom in the nineteenth century is illustrative. With systems of governance varying widely across towns, the Reform Act of 1832 and the Municipal Corporations Act of 1835 brought about regularization of municipal government.[23] Municipal authorities could take over privately owned sewerage, water, and gas systems. By the 1880s they had started purchasing land to compete with private utilities, transport, and other services. In doing so, they unified the hodgepodge of preexisting private systems, separating sewage and drainage systems from the water systems, and extending the reach of basic services to poor areas.[24] The Land Enquiry Commission recognized that *"municipal land ownership, town planning and the building up of the system of transit will go hand in hand and each will help the other."*[25] By the end of the nineteenth century, institutions governing land markets were maturing and adapting to the changing urban requirements.[26]

With this as background, the United Kingdom's urbanization was rapid. In 1830 the average GDP per capita was $1,749 (in 1990 international prices), roughly equivalent to Honduras, Mozambique, or Pakistan in 2003.[27] The urban share rose from 28 percent in 1830 to 69 percent in 1910.[28] At the top of the urban hierarchy: London, whose population grew from 2 million in 1830 to 6.6 million in 1900.[29]

Institutions and infrastructure must evolve continually. As areas urbanize and nations develop, the networks for public transit become more complex, and institutions such as legislation governing land use must also adapt. Building a new transport network requires the purchase of contiguous plots of land, and holdouts can extract huge rents or thwart the project entirely. Compulsory purchases ("eminent domain" in the United States) may be necessary, with the safeguard of just compensation for land owners. Another safeguard is that the acquired land be for "public use," although how widely this should be interpreted can be contentious.

The United States, by the mid-nineteenth century, had a reasonably well-defined system of property rights. As New York's transportation network expanded, and the needs of the city changed over the past century, its institutions evolved. The 1916 Zoning Resolution has been amended to respond to shifts in population and land use. Waves of immigration helped swell the city's population from 5 million in 1916 to almost 8 million in 1960. New mass transit routes and growth corridors were created. And with the rise of the mass-produced automobile, car registrations in New York State exploded from 93,000 in 1915 to about

2 million in 1930.[30] To address ever more complex urbanization, the City Planning Commission was created in 1938. After studies and public debate, the 1916 Zoning Resolution was replaced in 1961. The new resolution incorporated parking requirements and emphasized open space.

Although based on the leading planning theories of the day, aspects of those zoning policies have revealed shortcomings over the years. The emphasis on open space has sometimes resulted in buildings that overwhelm their surroundings. Since then, new approaches have been developed to make land use conversion more responsive to changing needs. A more flexible approach at the Department of City Planning encourages a mix of uses that creates lively urban streetscapes that can sustain increased density.[31]

New York City provides an example of the changing spatially blind institutions necessary for spatially connective policies. Indeed, their interaction enabled the density of Manhattan, the Bronx, Brooklyn, and Queens to increase from 230 people per square kilometer in 1820 to more than 5,000 in 1900 and about 12,000 today.

Successful urbanization requires connecting ever wider areas. Inevitably, density brings crowding. New York shows the enormous benefits of an efficient metro system in reducing congestion while encouraging density. The key is an integrated system of mass transport (see box 7.4). Dense city centers and skyscrapers are feasible only when thousands of office workers can be transported efficiently to downtown offices.

Long-term success does not rule out occasional bouts of congestion, but it does require flexible institutions. A British pamphlet published in 1860 observed that

> [F]rom day to day, and from year-to-year, the streets of London become more and more crowded, and must . . . come to a dead-lock between Westminster and the City, unless some more efficient remedy can be provided. The great City lies as it were handcuffed, panting and exhausted under the weight of its own wealth.[32]

London's congestion appeared no closer to resolution in 1939, with traffic averaging

BOX 7.4 *Widening the reach of New York City*

New York's subway system has become one of the busiest and most extensive in the world, serving nearly 5 million passengers every day with 26 train lines operating on 800 miles of track. As New York City spread into a wider metropolitan area, commuter bus networks and rail lines grew. New York City's commuter rail system is the most extensive in the United States, with about 250 stations and 20 rail lines serving more than 150 million commuters annually.[a]

Public transportation in New York City began in the late 1820s with horse-drawn omnibuses. The first steam-driven cable car line opened in 1883. In 1909 electric trolleybuses replaced them, and for 70 years trolleybuses ran in all five boroughs of New York City. The first elevated line ("el") opened in 1868. By 1880 most Manhattan residents were within a 19-minute walk of an "el," which took passengers above the congested streets.

The mid-1880s saw rapid immigration. Overcrowding was rife. As in London, an underground rail network was seen as necessary. But it took a blizzard in March 1888, completely paralyzing the streets, to provide the impetus for an underground rail system. The subway was designed both to move people about within Manhattan, and to connect tracts of undeveloped land.

After years of political wrangling, a plan for a subway was approved in 1894. In 1904, the Interborough Rapid Transit Company opened and carried more than 100,000 passengers on the day of the opening ceremony. Subway trains, at close to 40 miles an hour, were much faster than trolleys (6 miles an hour) and elevated trains (12 miles an hour). More people could now be moved at faster speeds.

It has been a never-ending struggle to expand the transport system fast enough to accommodate population growth. Most of the subway system in use today was built between 1913 and 1931; the number of annual rail passengers jumped from 500 million in 1901 to 2.5 billion in 1929.[b] In 1940 the city unified the three independent subway lines under public ownership, allowing for a more integrated approach to transport development.

The payoff is inclusive and sustainable urbanization. New York's Metropolitan Transportation Authority has served a 5,000-square-mile region since 1968. According to the 2000 U.S. census, New York City is the only locality in the United States where fewer than half of all households own a car—the figure is even lower in Manhattan at fewer than a quarter—compared with 92 percent nationally. One in every three users of mass transit in the United States and two-thirds of the nation's rail riders live in New York City and its suburbs.[c]

Source: WDR 2009 team.
Note: a. The New York City Transit Museum Teacher Resource Center, and the Port Authority of New York and New Jersey Official Web site. b. The New York City Transit Museum Teacher Resource Center. c. The New York City Transit Museum Teacher Resource Center.

8 miles an hour,[33] not so different from the 10–11 miles an hour in central London today.[34] This may suggest an "equilibrium level" of congestion. The city's economic density consistent with this equilibrium depends on the quality of spatially connective infrastructure. In this sense, the value of additional investment in such infrastructure is not as much in the long-run abatement of congestion as in the continually rising economic density for any given level of congestion. Congestion is the result of the substitution of one scarce resource, travel time, for another even more scarce resource, land. It is not efficient to devote so much urban land to roads that congestion is completely eliminated. Some urban congestion is likely to be optimal, if for no other reason than to prompt policy makers to review and update institutions and infrastructure.

As cities specialize, intercity infrastructure becomes a priority in the most dynamic areas. There is a symbiosis between cities and their peripheries, but economic relationships also join other cities in an urban hierarchy. Transport links between cities reinforce agglomeration economies and generate complementary and specialized functions. In the United States the megalopolis stretching from Boston, through New York City, Philadelphia, and Baltimore to Washington along the northeastern coast is linked by highways and rails (the first freight rail link was between Baltimore and Washington in 1827).[35] Japan also invested in spatially connective infrastructure to link its two largest agglomerations Tokyo-Yokohama and Osaka-Kobe (see box 7.5).

In the Republic of Korea, Seoul-Incheon (in the northwest) and Pusan (the second largest city at the southeast tip) were linked as early as 1905 by the Gyeongbu Rail, and in 1970 by the 400-plus-kilometer Gyeongbu Highway. In 2004 the bullet train—the Korea Train Express—connected the two cities in two hours' travel time. In the Pearl River Delta—a region of China studded with factories and interwoven by freeways—the economies of several cities are linked together so effectively that, according to the chief executive officer of a large electronics manufacturer, "In practice, we are a single vast factory scattered across the territory."

Demand management and public transport encourage development of higher density. There are many instruments to increase connectivity, among them—[36]

- Improving transport options—say, through better transit management that increases the use of, or gives preference to, high-occupancy vehicles
- Managing land use—through transit-oriented development or smart growth that gives preference to new develop-

BOX 7.5 *Promoting concentration in Japan between 1860 and 1980: spatially connective policies for Tokyo-Yokohama and Osaka-Kobe*

Japan's manufacturing industries are spatially concentrated—a trend that can be traced to the Meiji era starting in the 1860s. In Tokyo both state-owned factories and private industrial complexes were concentrated along the main river. Gradually small machinery workshops conglomerated, and industries expanded toward the south along the new Tokaido railway connecting Tokyo, Yokohama, and areas farther south.

After World War II, when exports to the United States began to accelerate, industrial production became concentrated in the Keihin industrial zone around Tokyo and Yokohama, and in the Hanshin industrial zone around Osaka and Kobe. This led to heavy traffic congestion, water shortages, and air and water pollution. In 1962 the Japanese government responded by instituting *Zenso*—the Integrated Spatial Development Plan—which aggressively developed the Pacific Ocean Industrial Belt by linking the core agglomerated areas between Tokyo and Osaka and establishing new industrial zones in between. The investments included the bullet train (Shinkansen) and other trunk railways, expressways, and ports (see the map to the right).

Despite heavy infrastructure investments in new industrial clusters in more remote regions, they could not attract industries out of the Pacific Ocean Belt. During the miraculous growth era of the 1950s through 1970s, industries remained spatially concentrated, thanks to the mobility of workers, even though there has been massive relocation of industries from the congested core to surrounding new industrial areas. Enterprises that remained in core urban clusters upgraded from standardized products to high-tech products and new models by taking advantage of urbanization economies accruing from diverse economic activity and a large pool of skill and talent. Other enterprises retained their central management functions in the core agglomerations to benefit from the convenience of face-to-face communications with banks, government offices, and major industrial organizations.

Industries that left the traditional industrial cores were mostly exporters of machinery and electronic appliance plants. They continued to enjoy localization economies from producing similar and related products in new clusters. Their locations alongside the Tomei highway connecting Tokyo and Nagoya gave easy access to markets and high-tech enterprises in the urban centers.

The geographic distribution of industries over several decades of rapid growth reflected the government's efforts to promote concentration while preventing the grime and time costs of rising density. These efforts did not interfere with the profit motives of enterprises, but instead strengthened agglomeration economies. Government policies and market forces reinforced each other spatially to sustain economic growth.

Contributed by Keijiro Otsuka and Megumi Muto.
Sources: Fujita and Tabuchi 1997; Sonobe and Otsuka 2006; Whittaker 1997; Overseas Economic Cooperation Fund 1995.

Connected cities in Japan facilitate agglomeration economies in Tokyo-Yokohama (Keihin) and Osaka-Kobe (Hanshin) by road and rail

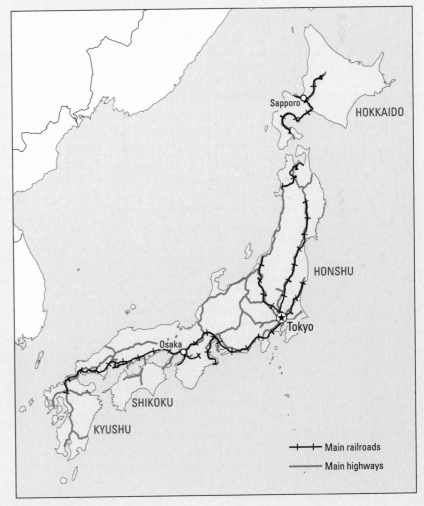

Source: WDR 2009 team.

ments along established public transport routes

- Launching general policies and programs—such as freight transport management and market reforms.

Pricing mechanisms can be most effective in optimizing private car use. Extreme but effective are Singapore's auction permits to purchase cars. Add the car taxes, and the cost of a car in Singapore is four to five times the world price. Amsterdam, London, and Stockholm also have schemes that price road use according to the time of day and level of congestion—substantially reducing peak-time car traffic and car emissions. The revenue streams from congestion charging could be earmarked for reinvestment in public transportation. But such schemes require substantial investment in technology to ensure the efficient collection of fees.

Easier to implement are simple regulations or traffic plans that reduce the number of vehicles in specific parts of a city or overall. In Tehran entry to parts of the city center is restricted to essential traffic. Budapest and Buenos Aires have pedestrian-only zones in the city center, easily reached by public transport. Gothenburg (Sweden) and Bremen (Germany) restrict private car links between different zones ("cells"), encouraging public transit. India's Chandigarh built some 160 kilometers of wide-cycle paths to ease traffic on arterial roads.[37] The most popular restraint limits the use of vehicles on specific days according to their registration plate number, as in Athens, Bogotá, Lagos, Manila, Mexico City, Santiago, São Paulo, Seoul, and Singapore. Such measures have been proven easier to enforce than expected, with widespread public acceptance.[38]

Demand management is the most cost-effective means of increasing mobility. But traffic will increase even with the best policies, especially in rapidly growing cities. Investments in public transport infrastructure can connect different parts of a city and guide land use and urban expansion. Mass rapid transit includes subways, suburban rail, and dedicated busways, all having a capacity and performance far superior to

buses operating on unsegregated and congested roads. But suburban rail and subways require huge investments in fixed capital, so dedicated busways (plus their more sophisticated relation, "bus rapid transit") have been gaining in popularity.

Busways, most common in Latin American cities, cost about $10 million a kilometer to install. Operating in Bogotá, Colombia; Curitiba and São Paulo, Brazil; and Quito, Ecuador, they are being planned or built in many other cities. A more expensive alternative, ranging in cost from $10 million to $30 million a kilometer, is light rail, a modern form of tram covering short distances. It usually feeds a larger system of heavy metro rail. Cities with light rail include Hong Kong, China; Kuala Lumpur; Singapore; Sydney; and Tunis.

The most costly mass rapid transit option is the metropolitan subway system, which has the largest capacity. Building costs average more than $100 million a kilometer, explaining why there are fewer than 200 systems in the world, mostly in industrialized countries.[39] But their number is growing: China, India, and the República Bolivariana de Venezuela have built subways. When cities reach a certain size and density, a subway is the only transport mode capable of moving large numbers of people to concentrated job centers. The benefits that come from enabling such density include efficiency and productivity gains—traditionally in industry, increasingly in services (see chapter 4)—but also lower energy consumption, less pollution, and greater compactness, which increase interaction and encourage nonmotorized transport for short intracity trips. Compact and densely packed cities might also meet the imperatives of climate change (see box 7.6).

Public transport, successful on its own, has encouraged new developments at higher densities, which in turn permit more successful public transport while reducing the economic distance between places. Managing all this takes patience and the discipline to build from the bottom. The establishment and strengthening of land and property market institutions—including secure property rights, flexible land use regulations, and ease of land conversion—is not

BOX 7.6   *Climate change calls for a different urban form, not slower urbanization*

Urbanization is associated with industrialization, which increases emissions of carbon dioxide (CO_2) and other greenhouse gases. And increasing wealth tends to be associated with higher energy consumption, for instance through motorization. But to be concerned about the climate does not mean that urbanization should be slowed. If anything, economic density may need to be encouraged even more.

Historical data going back to the nineteenth century show that today's rich countries experienced rising per capita carbon emissions as they urbanized and industrialized through the twentieth century.[a] Industrialization, motorization, and consequently carbon emissions in developing countries follow the trajectories of developed countries in their earlier stages of development.[b] For instance, per capita carbon emissions in Germany doubled from 0.8 metric tons of carbon in 1880 to 1.6 in 1900. In the United States and the United Kingdom, carbon emissions were about 2.5 in 1900. Today's developing countries have lower average emissions at the equivalent GDPs per capita of Germany, the United Kingdom, and the United States in 1880 and 1900. Botswana's carbon emissions were 0.36 per capita in 1987 and 0.57 in 1996 (see figure at right).

The trend in most developing countries suggests continuing growth in carbon emissions both in total and per capita. The policy response to the projected increases in urbanization and carbon emissions in developing countries should not be to try to prevent the growth of cities. This would not be feasible or desirable in light of the evidence on growth and poverty reduction. Instead, growth in cities—many of which might double in size over the next few decades—should be managed to create urban areas far more carbon efficient than many of today's mature cities.

Monocentric structures and high population densities tend to reduce the length and number of motorized trips.[c] Compact cities use less energy for transport, consume less land for housing, and use less energy for heating. Several studies find that high population density is negatively

correlated with carbon emissions.[d] At the national level, Sweden and Japan have used incentives and regulation to greatly reduce the emissions intensity of their economies. At the urban level, an emphasis on density and smart choices that reduce distance can help do the same. This requires land use policies that favor compactness and transport policies that guide urban form and provide convenient and efficient public transit.[e]

Atlanta and Barcelona illustrate alternative urban growth scenarios. They had similar populations of 2.5 million to 2.8 million, but Atlanta had a density of six people per hectare in 1990, and Barcelona had 176.[f] In Atlanta the longest possible distance between two points within the built-up area is 137 kilometers; in Barcelona, the distance is only 37 kilometers. Per capita CO_2 emission was 400 metric tons in Atlanta, 38 tons in Barcelona.[g] Atlanta's metro network is 74 kilometers long. but only 4 percent of its population is within 800 meters of a metro station. Barcelona's metro

network is 99 kilometers, and 60 percent of its population lives within 600 meters of a metro station. Only 4.5 percent of trips are by mass transit in Atlanta, a fraction of the 30 percent in Barcelona. For Atlanta to achieve Barcelona's metro accessibility would require building an additional 3,400 kilometers of metro tracks and about 2,800 new metro stations. This would allow the Atlanta metro to transport the same number of people that Barcelona does with only 99 kilometers of tracks and 136 stations.

Density makes the difference.

Source: WDR 2009 team.
a. Marland, Boden, and Andres 2007. b. World Bank 2002, figure 2.1; Lanne and Liski 2003, figures 1, 4, and 5; and data in developing countries from http://cdiac.esd.ornl.gov/ftp/ndp030/nation.1751_2004.ems. c. Bento and others 2003. d. Scholz 2006; Vance and Hedel 2006; Golob and Brownstone 2005; Ingram 1997; International Union of Public Transport. e. Bento and others 2003; Scholz 2006; Vance and Hedel 2006; Golob and Brownstone 2005. f. Bertaud 2004. g. Kenworthy 2005.

Countries can change their energy trajectories

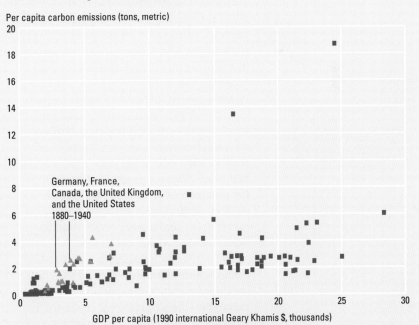

Sources: Carbon emission data worldwide can be found in the Oak Ridge National Laboratory, U.S. Department of Energy at http://cdiac.esd.ornl.gov/ftp/ndp030/nation.1751_2004.ems; Lanne and Liski 2003.

easy. But without the commitment to such institutions, and without investment in connective infrastructure, targeted interventions to deal with slums are unlikely to work.

Spatially targeted interventions to reduce social and economic divisions

For the three-dimensional problem faced by advanced urbanization areas, spatially blind and connective instruments must be supplemented with spatially targeted interventions to address the social and economic division within a city's boundaries—most visibly, slums. The lesson of experience is that spatially targeted efforts succeed when they are applied where land markets work reasonably well, basic social services are widely accessible, and a connective infrastructure links the city's core to its periphery.

Institutions and infrastructure are prerequisites for successful interventions. Successful programs to integrate slums have been built on a foundation of spatially blind and spatially connective policies. This integration included the establishment of institutions to effectively govern the working of the housing market, a spatially blind provision of social and basic services to all settlements, and transport infrastructure investments to connect the newly created housing areas.

Slum clearance requires a legislative basis to empower local authorities to take action and institutions to facilitate an orderly conversion of land from agricultural to residential or other purposes. At the same time, suburban development is made feasible through the provision of basic amenities and social services alongside ongoing improvements in the transport connectivity of cities with their suburbs and surrounding counties.

In London social outcry at the dreadful conditions of Victorian slums provided the impetus for slum clearance and improvement. But the efforts were preceded by steps to improve housing markets and transport systems. The Housing of the Working Classes Act 1890 provided local authorities with the power to build houses for the working classes and to clear areas of unfit housing. An amendment gave local authorities powers to retain the houses built under slum-clearance schemes, paving the way for future public housing schemes. Better transport was part of the solution, evidenced by conferences in 1901 on the subject of "Improved Means of Locomotion as a First Step towards the Cure of the Housing Difficulties of London." The conferences passed a resolution that "a complete system of transportation radiating from urban centers, and which shall be cheap, rapid, and under municipal ownership, is a primary step towards dealing with the housing problem."[40] Londoners obviously understood that connective policies must precede targeted interventions.

Indeed, the link between improvements in spatially connective transport infrastructure and the solution of London's slum problem was made clearly in the policy discourse of the time. In 1890 the Cheap Trains for London Workers Bill proposed extending the provision and further regulating the fares on "workmen's trains." The private railway companies already had been obliged by law to introduce these trains in 1883, to provide an affordable means of commuting to working-class workers who lived in the suburbs but earned their living in central London. By lowering the cost of commuting, the suburbs could be developed, decongesting London's central areas.

Likewise, during the late-nineteenth and early twentieth century, governments across North America and Western Europe implemented large-scale slum clearance and re-housing. Landowners were compensated, and the cleared land was sold for redevelopment. These programs would not have succeeded without a rapid expansion of transport infrastructure. New transport systems helped "open up" the outskirts, or suburbs, of cities, making periurban housing attractive for both real estate developers and urban workers. The resulting flight to the suburbs was also both a cause and a consequence of the relocation of many industries to the peripheries. And it coincided with the spread of basic social services and recreational amenities.

Policies to integrate slums into cities have worked where institutions and infrastructure were adequate. After World

War II, Sweden urbanized rapidly and Stockholm's population grew swiftly, from 741,000 in 1950 to 1.39 million in 1980.[41] Stockholm had an inadequate and dilapidated housing stock, while rents were high relative to most other European cities.[42] In reaction, the Swedish government formed the Royal Housing Commission in 1945. A plan was formulated to demolish slums in Stockholm and other cities, and re-house the displaced slum dwellers in publicly provided rental housing in well-designed high-rise buildings on the city's periphery. The first generation of high-rise residential buildings was integrated with the provision of schools, health clinics, and recreational and shopping facilities, as well as service centers. Spatial connectivity to city centers was ensured through easy access to transport.[43]

Swedish authorities managed to continually upgrade urban living conditions throughout the 1960s and 1970s. With the Million Homes Programme the government set itself the aim of ending innercity squalor and overcrowding by building 100,000 new dwellings a year from 1965 to 1974, adding one-third to Sweden's aggregate housing stock of 3 million units.[44] The new settlements provided basic amenities, including schools and clinics, and were linked to urban employment centers through well-planned traffic systems.[45]

Similar lessons come from the United States. By the end of the nineteenth century, American philanthropists had raised awareness of the hardships facing slum dwellers. They urged building regulations to ensure minimum standards in the construction of new tenements.[46] But it was not until the 1930s that the government became active in the provision of housing.[47] Following the Great Depression, the United States Housing Authority was established by the Wagner-Steagall Housing Act of 1937, which allowed for subsidized loans to be made to local housing authorities for clearing dilapidated areas and building replacement homes. A sound legal framework enabled national and state authorities, civil society organizations, and private developers to deal concertedly with slums. Good intra-urban public transport systems connected the new housing developments to the local city economies. As infrastructure improved even more, particularly after the passage of the Housing and Urban Development Act 1965, the more prosperous residents left the city centers for the suburbs.[48]

Better connective infrastructure is a precondition for applying targeted policies to deal with slum housing. This takes time, but both Hong Kong, China, and Singapore show that it can be done over decades rather than centuries. Regardless of differences in the speed, the sequencing of policies appears to be the same: targeted policies to integrate slums cannot come before the application of geographically blind and connective policies (see box 7.7).

BOX 7.7 *Speeded up, but still in sequence: spatial integration in twentieth-century Hong Kong, China*

Before World War II, Hong Kong, China, developed its administrative structure and legislative framework to govern land markets. In 1935, mounting awareness of poor living conditions in urban slums led to the formation of a Housing Commission. This was followed by the Town Planning Ordinance of 1939, which established a Town Planning Board.

Nevertheless, the proper implementation of the ordinance and town planning in Hong Kong, China, had to wait until after the passage of the Town Planning Regulation in 1954. It was only after the famous Shek Kip Mei slum fire of 1953 that efforts to develop public housing programs went into full swing. In 1965 the Working Party on Slum Clearance was formed. It took Hong Kong, China (a city in a hurry), more than 30 years before it began effectively addressing the problem through spatially targeted interventions. Hong Kong, China, first had to develop and strengthen the spatially blind institutions governing the operation of land and housing markets, and connective infrastructure to improve the use of land.

The first land use strategy and zoning plan—the "Colony Outline Plan and Outline Zoning Plans"— were only drawn up in 1963. The spatially blind institutions had to be adapted over time as the city developed and the urbanization progressed. The 1939 Ordinance was amended in 1958, 1969, and 1974.[a] Having established the necessary planning framework, Hong Kong, China, was better placed to implement spatially connective policies in the 1970s. These policies were a necessary response to the doubling of car registration within a decade and the concomitant increase in congestion that was a product of the city's rapid economic growth of around 10 percent a year.

Institutions and infrastructure went hand in hand. With effective planning laws in place, the government was able to introduce the Temporary Restriction of Building Development Ordinance of 1973 in the Pok Fu Lam and Mid-Levels areas of Hong Kong, China. This in turn paved the way for building the Mass Transit Railway, modifying building height restrictions in the area around the Kai Tak Airport, and accelerating relief for an overloaded transport network.

The result: the city now ranks among the world's top five in infrastructure efficiency, and the slums are gone.[b]

Source: WDR 2009 team.
a. Bristow 1984. b. Cullinane 2002.

***Targeted interventions may have to wait
until institutions and infrastructure have
been improved.*** The experience of developed
countries remains relevant today. Costa Rica,
South Africa, and Singapore show why.

During the 1980s, the combination of
rapid in situ population growth, migration,
and an influx of refugees from war-torn
neighboring countries made Costa Rica's
already acute urban housing shortage even
worse. This led to the creation of a National
Housing Finance System in 1986. The aim
was to provide subsidies to low-income
households for house purchases or construction. Households were able to supplement
the funds that they received with loans from
private institutions, including commercial banks, savings and loans institutions,
and cooperatives. Minimum wage households were entitled to a full subsidy, while
households earning more than four times
the minimum had access to smaller subsidies and loans at near-market conditions.[49]

Costa Rica's housing subsidy succeeded
because the necessary spatially blind institutions and spatially connective infrastructure were in place to facilitate its targeted
interventions. As early as 1869 the government decreed that primary education was
a basic universal right. The 1949 constitution guaranteed free access to secondary
education as well. Costa Rica's government
invests more than 20 percent of its budget
in education each year, and has a literacy
rate of about 95 percent to show for it.
Similar investment in the public medical
system reduced infant mortality rates, with
an average life expectancy at birth of 79
years.[50] Although incomes are much higher
in Costa Rica's central regions, social indicators are similar across the country.[51]

Costa Rica has well-functioning institutions governing the land market. An effective property registry system is in place.
Indeed, more than 80 percent of property
owners possess registered titles, and there is
a high degree of legal security.[52] The capital
city, San José, is linked with the major provincial cities by an efficient and affordable
bus system, and private bus companies connect San José and its outlying suburbs. In
many ways, Costa Rica is a model for other
developing countries.

South Africa's experience is more sobering. When the first post-apartheid South
African government came to power in 1994,
it faced a housing crisis with an estimated
deficit of 1.5 million housing units and
an additional requirement of 170,000 new
units a year. Some 18 percent of households,
or 7.4 million people, lived in slums.[53] The
new housing policy that emerged from
multiparty negotiations was implemented
through the Housing Act of 1997, providing housing-related subsidies to as many
people as possible for renting, purchasing,
constructing, and improving homes.

But the requisite institutions and connective infrastructure were not yet in place.
A range of reforms—including changes to
regional government boundaries, financial
support mechanisms, and housing-related
legislation—were introduced simultaneously. Indeed, the Housing Act repealed,
incorporated, or amended 35 separate
pieces of legislation.[54] The first wave of low-
cost housing developments, on the peripheries of major cities, lacked basic amenities
and transport links to city (and job) centers. These developments failed to amelio-
rate intraurban divisions. Recent shifts in
policy are more encouraging. The Breaking
New Ground national housing program has
focused on integrating low-income communities through improvements in access
to public transportation and basic social
and commercial services.[55]

Improving institutions and infrastructure and intervening at the same time is
a tall order for any government, but Singapore shows it can be done (see box 7.8).
Perhaps the most successful example of how
slums can be eradicated, Singapore is to
some extent an anomaly. It is one of the few
countries that have managed to implement
all three sets of integration policies simultaneously. Singapore was successful because it
had exceptionally rapid economic growth
and a focused government in power since
1965. The fact that it is a city-state helped
greatly, indirectly providing a general lesson: successful urbanization takes coordinated action at all levels of government.

Most countries will not be able to rep-
licate Singapore's efforts—aligning priorities and the effort of central, state, and city

governments is difficult for any country that is not a city-state. More likely, they will have to sequence their policy efforts along the path followed by Costa Rica and earlier developers such as Great Britain, Sweden, and the United States. South Africa shows the difficulties of trying to implement all three sets of policies simultaneously.

"An I for a D"—a policy instrument for each dimension of urbanization's challenge

The sequence of policies corresponds to different levels of urbanization. Incipient urbanization requires mainly the application of spatially blind policies. Intermediate urbanization requires the addition of spatially connective policies. And advanced urbanization requires these and spatially targeted efforts. So the success of the new policy is predicated on the successful implementation of the ones introduced before it.

For a predominantly rural country whose urban share is less than a quarter or so, the portfolio of places is faced with what might be termed a one-dimensional challenge—to facilitate density (see table 7.1). It is not obvious where this density will increase first, and governments are best advised to allow market forces to play themselves out. *Neutrality* between places is the rule, and its urbanization strategy should consist mainly of spatially blind institutions. They include the provision of basic and social services, the establishment of market institutions and law and order, the security of property rights, the efficient operation of the land market, and sound macroeconomic policies. Regulations must be versatile enough to facilitate efficient land use conversion, and standards for building must be enforceable without being overly restrictive. This is a tall order for governments in countries at the low levels of income with which low urbanization rates are associated. They should not make it harder by attempting spatially explicit policies.

For a rapidly urbanizing country with urban shares between one fourth and three fourths, managing its portfolio of places is mainly a two-dimensional challenge—to build density and reduce distance to density. A two-dimensional challenge requires

BOX 7.8 *Singapore: from slums to world city*

At independence in 1965, 70 percent of Singapore's households lived in badly overcrowded conditions, and a third of its people squatted on the city fringes. Unemployment averaged 14 percent, GDP per capita was less than $2,700, and half of the population was illiterate. Falling mortality rates and migration from the Malay Peninsula implied rapid population growth, further increasing the pressure on both housing and employment: 600,000 additional units of housing were needed, and private supply was less than 60,000. An account of this time comes from a contemporary visitor to Singapore:[a]

The undercover walkways are usually taken over by hawker stalls and junk. Laundry hangs from poles thrust out of windows above—just like in old Shanghai. This is Singapore, in the early 1970s. We were all devastated at the time—we who didn't live here. From 1871 to 1931 the city's Chinese population rose from 100,000 to 500,000. By 1960 it is estimated that more than 500,000 Chinese were living in slum-like conditions—indoors. Equipped with only one kitchen and one bathroom, the shophouses were designed for two extended families at most. After extensive partitioning many of them housed up to 50 individuals.

Today, less than 40 years later, Singapore's slums are gone. In their place is one of the cleanest and most welcoming cities in the world. The secret? First, institutional reforms made the government known for its accountability. Then, the government became a major provider of infrastructure and services. The scarcity of land made good planning an imperative. Multiyear plans were produced, implemented, and updated. Finally, the housing authority (HDB) was mandated to undertake a massive program of slum clearance, housing construction, and urban renewal. Public housing has been an integral part of all development plans. At the height of the program, HDB was building a new flat every eight minutes. Of Singapore's population, 86 percent now lives in publicly built units. Most own their flats, encouraged by special housing funds financed from the Employees Provident Fund, a mandatory retirement scheme. Serviced land was made available. Through the Land Amalgamation act, the government acquired almost one-third of city land. Slum dwellers were relocated to public housing.

For a city-state in a poor region, it is not an exaggeration to assert that effective urbanization was responsible for delivering growth rates that averaged 8 percent a year throughout the 1970s and 1980s. It required a combination of market institutions and social service provision, strategic investment in infrastructure, and improved housing for slum dwellers.

Sources: Yuen 2004, Yusuf and Nabeshima 2006.
a. Cockrem 2007.

a two-pronged response: continuing the task of building spatially blind institutions, and investing in spatially connective infrastructure to offset the congestion that might otherwise offset the *efficiency* gains from "localization economies" (see chapter 4).

For a highly urbanized country with urban shares above 75 percent, urbanization should emphasize *livability*, creativity, and urban social integration—the delivery of "urbanization economies." These countries face a three-dimensional challenge—to build density, reduce distance, and diminish divisions. To be sure, these countries have

Table 7.1   An instrument per dimension—a simple framework for urbanization policies

	Area		
	Incipient urbanization	**Intermediate urbanization**	**Advanced urbanization**
Urban shares	Less than 25 percent	About 50 percent	More than 75 percent
Examples	Kampong Speu, Cambodia; Lindi, Tanzania	Chengdu, China; Hyderabad, India	Greater Cairo, the Arab Republic of Egypt; Rio de Janeiro, Brazil
Dimensions of policy challenge	1-D: Build density	2-D: Build density, reduce distance	3-D: Build density, reduce distance, eliminate division
Instruments for integration			
Institutions	Land rights; basic education, health and water and sanitation	Land use regulations; universal provision of basic and social services	Land use regulation and land taxation; universal provision of basic services
Infrastructure		Transport infrastructure	Transport infrastructure; demand management
Interventions			Slum area development; targeted programs to reduce crime and environmental degradation

Source: WDR 2009 team.

a varied economic geography: their portfolio of places consists of a handful of one-dimensional areas, a good proportion face two-dimensional challenges, and some face three-dimensional challenges. Spatially blind and connective policies continue to facilitate agglomeration economies, but now they also are prerequisites for successful interventions to reduce within-city divisions.

The framework in action

Low-density areas should build economic density through rural-urban transformations and stronger links between villages and towns. Rapidly urbanizing areas should ensure that the productivity gains from economic density are not offset by congestion costs. Highly urbanized areas should focus on livability by promoting social integration and the gains from economic concentration. The priorities at the national level correspond with the predominance of one or more of these types of areas.

Incipient urbanizers (one-dimensional areas): institutions for more efficient rural-urban transformations

The recent developers show that success does not require explicitly spatial policies to lay the groundwork for successful urbanization. For areas of incipient urbanization, the policy priorities remain the provision of basic social services and the improvement of land markets.

Emphasize social services. In 1960 the Republic of Korea had a GDP per capita

level roughly the same as Benin, Cambodia, or Tajikistan. Since then it has transformed itself into a leading industrial country.[56] Consistent with the stylized facts of chapter 1, the Republic of Korea's sectoral transformation has been accompanied by an equally radical spatial transformation. In 1960 about 75 percent of all Korean citizens lived in rural areas. By 1990 the country was 75 percent urban, and today the urban share of the population exceeds 80 percent.[57]

Institutions to ensure the universal availability of basic social services helped the nation lay the foundations of rapid and successful urbanization. In 1960 the proportion of the overall population age 15 and over with no schooling was 36 percent, and by 1980, when it had entered the intermediate urbanization stage, this proportion had fallen to less than 15 percent. By 2000, some years after it entered the advanced stage, the proportion was less than 5 percent. The years of schooling of the average member of the labor force had increased from five years in 1960 to nine years in 1980, rising to more than 12 years by 2000.[58] A similar story unfolded for health-related services. In 1980 only 4 percent of children were immunized against measles. By 1989, 95 percent were. In 2006 only one child in every 100 was not immunized.

Matching the universal provision of education and health services has been the nationwide flexibility in land use conversion.[59] In particular, the Republic of Korea's government has been willing to convert agricultural land for industrial purposes. The central government also encouraged local governments to promote the conversion of agricultural land through the formation of smaller, more localized industrial complexes.

While some areas have inevitably been left behind in the Republic of Korea's urbanization process, none has been left disadvantaged. Take Eumseong county, a largely rural area in Chungcheongbukdo province (see map 7.1). As the Republic of Korea industrialized and urbanized, the county experienced a continual outflow of people. In 1968 the population exceeded 120,000, but by 1990 it had fallen to just under 75,000. But even as the people of Eumseong were seeing their neighbors move closer to Korea's major cities, they got better education and health services and improved streets and sanitation. Between 1969 and 1990, middle and high school teachers tripled in Eumseong county from 1,000 to around 3,000. And the number of hospitals per million population in Chungcheongbukdo province doubled from around 400 in 1980 to 800 in 1990, while the water supply coverage increased from less than 30 percent to almost 60 percent. People left Eumseong, but the Korean government did not abandon the county—instead, it continued to emphasize the universal provision of basic and social services.

The Republic of Korea is not the only successful economy to provide evidence of the framework in action. Over the last two decades, China has been gradually putting in place the institutions to improve its urbanization processes. An urban land market has been created, and regulations standardizing the assignment of land use rights have been established.[60] In the 1980s the urban planning law was aimed at controlling the size of large cities, but the 10th Five-Year Plan (2001–05) instead chose to emphasize the synergistic development of China's large, medium, and small cities. The household registration system, which for years had imposed restrictions on rural migrants looking to move to urban areas, has been reformed, and the 11th Five-Year Plan (2006–10) aims to further strengthen land market institutions.

Against this backdrop the urbanization prospects of China's one-dimensional areas have improved. Take Guizhou province. In southwest China, and home to almost 40 million people, Guizhou lags far behind the coastal provinces (see map 7.2). Its GDP per capita in 2005 was only 34 percent of the Chinese average,[61] with almost 75 percent of its population classified as rural. The challenge Guizhou faces is building density to facilitate agglomeration economies. Its 11th Five-Year Plan (2006–10) aims to deliver an urban share of 35 percent by focusing on the area's largest city, Guiyang. With the improvements in spatially blind institutions in China, this

Map 7.1   The Republic of Korea—three areas at different stages of urbanization

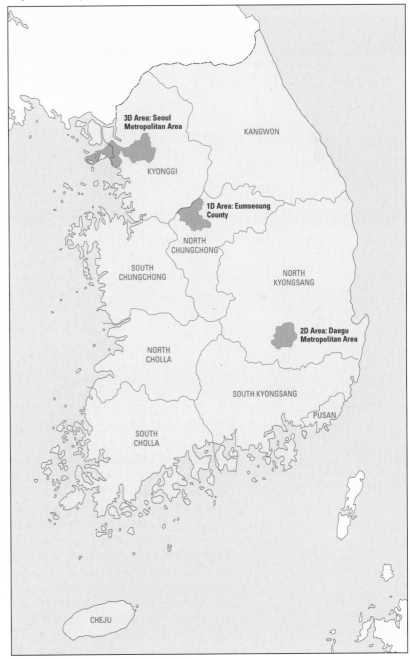

Source: WDR 2009 team.

Map 7.2   China—three areas at different stages of urbanization

Source: WDR 2009 team.

system. The results are more security of tenure—leading to easier transactions, higher land values, and more land investments—and greater mobility to urban areas.

Kampong Speu illustrates the critical issues for areas of incipient urbanizers. Spatially blind policies to encourage rural-urban integration should be the mainstay of a government's strategy: improve land markets and property rights, improve rural and urban social services, and encourage inclusive governance in towns and small cities (box 7.9 discusses the importance of land titling in Cambodia and Vietnam).

Secure tenure promotes greater investment in land and shelter, improves the ability to transfer land, and enhances access to credit. China, Pakistan, and Vietnam confirm its importance for investment in low-density areas. Farmers use more labor and inputs on owned plots than on leased land. They also use land as collateral for new activities and benefit from increases in land prices. In India the prices for titled land are, on average, 15 percent higher than those for untitled land. In the Philippines secure housing commands prices 58 percent higher than housing without title, and in Jakarta prices for secure housing are 73 percent higher.[62]

Despite these obvious advantages, more than 50 percent of the periurban population in Africa and more than 40 percent in Asia lives under informal tenure. In many countries improving land tenure (and registration) is hindered by political and customary tenure arrangements. In Africa, where customary institutions cover between 90 and 98 percent of the land, policies to formalize land tenure must start with customary systems and gradually add features of modern land registration. Once community-recognized rights are obtained in Benin, Ghana, Mozambique, and Namibia, individuals can apply for land certification and full registration, and both can be used for credit.

Improve land administration. Central Asia and Eastern Europe have the most systematic experience in tackling land administration, from Central European countries with old traditions of land markets, to Central Asian countries where no land markets existed. During the transition from plan to market, countries tried to reestablish equity in land and property rights, deepen land

appears to be more realistic now than would have been the case two decades ago.

Define and enforce land rights. Kampong Speu province in Cambodia, about 100 kilometers southwest of Phnom Penh, covers about 7,000 squares kilometers. It has about 700,000 people, and is 10 percent urban. A few market towns serve its farming communes of Mohasaing, Ou, Traeng Trayeung, and others. Many villages are beneficiaries of the land registration and titling begun in 2000. The aims are to strengthen land tenure security and land markets, formulate policies for land administration and management, develop mechanisms for dispute resolution, and establish a national land registration

BOX 7.9 *Titling land for a sustainable rural-urban transformation*

"Application receipts" in Cambodia

Cambodia is formalizing ownership of land through the distribution of land titles, with immediate benefits in higher productivity and land values.[a] Although the courts and other formal institutions to resolve land conflicts are slow, formal land rights documents carry authority in most rural communities. If landholders hold a formal title to a disputed plot of land, their position is considerably strengthened, even if the conflict is resolved through informal means.

In 1989 individual land use in agriculture was codified by law.[b] Rural residents were encouraged to submit applications for land ownership certificates, and applications came in for 4 million plots. Due to the limited administrative capacity and reach of the government, only about half a million titles were actually distributed.[c] But people who applied got an "application receipt," and this document often worked as a formal title.[d]

This view was backed by the 1992 land law, which ruled that an application receipt is a valid claim on the plot. In 2004 the government initiated a comprehensive land management and administration program, and one of its central components includes a systematic titling scheme. By the end of 2005 about 457,000 plots had been registered under this program, and 166,000 titles had been distributed.[e]

"Red books" in Vietnam

In 1981 Vietnam moved to a system similar to the Chinese "household responsibility system," with land users entitled to keep surplus production above a fixed quota. In 1988 some individual property rights to agricultural land were transferred to farmer households. In the 1993 land law, the distribution of land use certificates—known as "red books"—was mandated. Red books come with the rights to sell, rent, mortgage, and bequeath land. So the idea of a land market was formally sanctioned.

Red books increase land market activities, and these activities increase agricultural productivity by transferring land to the most productive users, reducing inefficiencies.[f] The liberalization of the land market has been followed by increased mobility as households sell land to take up new economic opportunities in the wage labor sector.[g] So a more fluid land market has facilitated the ongoing shift in Vietnam from a predominantly agricultural economy to a more diversified and urbanized economy. It is a big part of a strategy that has yielded perhaps the most impressive poverty reduction in any country in recent history.[h]

Contributed by Thomas Markussen.
a. Markussen forthcoming; World Bank 2003b.
b. Boreak 2000.
c. Sophal, Saravi, and Acharya 2001.
d. Sovannarith and others 2001.
e. Deutsch 2006.
f. Deininger and Jin 2003; Ravallion and van de Walle 2006b.
g. Ravallion and van de Walle 2006a.
h. World Bank 2003b.

and capital markets, and improve public functions such as land taxation, planning, and asset management. Now they have to improve mechanisms to enable registrations, valuations, and transactions (see box 7.10).

Instituting mechanisms to govern land use and conversion can be difficult. Some nations fear that land conversion would hurt grain production and food security (China and the Arab Republic of Egypt). Many others are constrained by traditional forms of land tenure, such as the communal systems in Africa and the *ejido* in Mexico. In cases of unclear property title, land conversion tends to benefit the state and the developers at the cost of the farmers or rural households that traditionally held or cultivated this land.

In Mexico the traditional communal land system has evolved to enable land transactions. After the 1917 revolution, Mexico distributed more than 100 million hectares, or 50 percent of its arable area, from large farms to *ejidos*, rural communities organized along the precolonial indigenous social structures. But the redistribution undermined property rights, and the requirement that land be used for self-cultivation precluded rental markets.

BOX 7.10 *Land markets in transition*

In the first phase, Eastern Europe and Central Asia restored property rights, privatized state-owned assets, and promoted equity in housing. Next, they rebuilt the land administration systems for *cadastre* and registration followed. Proper records were needed to stimulate real estate markets and take care of land allocation and consolidation. Information infrastructure, institutional capacity, and databases were the areas of focus. Now some are entering the third phase of collecting property taxes, managing public land, and issuing building permits.

Some lessons:

- Reforming dysfunctional legal and institutional systems such as those in Latin America, may be more difficult than starting anew (the Kyrgyz Republic, Georgia).
- A single agency should be responsible for both registration and *cadastres*. More efficient, a combined system is easier to make self-financing.
- A local champion is needed, preferably not a surveyor or a lawyer. Enthusiastic change managers were instrumental in Moldova and the Czech Republic. Competent officials in the Russian Federation, Serbia, and Turkey were needed to design and implement the new systems. Systematic registration was not necessary because good land records predated socialism, and there were few transactions during the socialist period.
- A solid system with Web-based applications to reduce user transaction costs and the opportunities for corruption can be updated on its own.

Contributed by Cora Shaw and Gavin P. Adlington.

In 1991 the system gave more freedom to *ejidos* to sell and rent land. Of 150,000 hectares used for urban development between 1995 and 2000, more than two-thirds were from *ejidos*. The off-farm income of the farmers increased 45 percent. (Box 7.11 presents promising examples.)

Intermediate urbanization (two-dimensional areas): institutions and infrastructure for increasing density and reducing congestion

Rapidly urbanizing areas expect a continuing influx of migrants and increasing congestion. The priorities include providing social services for rural and urban residents, ensuring fluid land markets, and investing in infrastructure in and around the growing city centers.

Expand administrative jurisdictions to coordinate infrastructure investments. Among the many cities that have absorbed rural Koreans are Seoul and Daegu. Both of these cities were initially able to urbanize against a backdrop of spatially blind policies, but they soon began to face congestion, which required spatially connective policies. Indeed, housing congestion in Seoul became

---

BOX 7.11   *Strengthening land market institutions for rural-urban integration*

Land management on Douala's urban fringe—Cameroon's Mbanga-Japoma Project

Mbanga-Japoma, a land development project in Douala, Cameroon, provides serviced land at a reasonable price and reconciles formal and customary development practices. The first phase, covering 160 hectares 30 kilometers from the city center, started as a partnership among public institutions, formal private investors, and customary owners. The partnership develops the site with primary and secondary infrastructure services (roads, water, sewerage, drainage, electricity), delineating blocks of land of between 1 and 8 hectares. The developer gives back 45 percent of the land to customary landowners, keeping 55 percent. Blocks are then subdivided and sold, either by the developer or by customary owners. The final cost of a serviced plot is much lower than one provided by the formal private sector.

Although there are questions about eligibility for purchasing the serviced plots, the approach provides a new perspective for partnerships in managing rural-urban land use in and near Sub-Saharan cities.

Secondary land rights and farming in central Mali

Secondary land rights—including sharecropping, tenancy, and borrowing land under customary tenure—are often seen as exploitative because they do not give permanent tenure to users. But in some circumstances they can benefit both secondary and permanent rights holders. In the village of Baguinéda, in central Mali,

secondary rights allow small-scale farmers to hire migrant workers in exchange for temporary rights to cultivate plots. The system is highly structured, with specific days of the week designated for laborers and others who are working on the borrowed land. Land tenure in the village is almost exclusively under the customary system, controlled by the village council, allowing for secondary rights allocations. Strong demand from nearby urban markets for horticultural produce makes cultivating of even a small plot profitable and thus attractive to migrants.

Inclusive administration—the Republic of Korea's integrated cities

The Republic of Korea developed the rural-urban integrated city to overcome the shortcomings of earlier rural development initiatives. The integrated city policy incorporates rural counties with cities in a unified spatial framework. It aims to improve local public services and local administration and reduce rural-urban disparities.

Starting in 1994 the government selected 49 cities and 43 counties as candidates. The selection criteria included historical homogeneity, natural topographical conditions, and the potential for balanced development within the integrated city. The selected cities and counties held public hearings and citizen surveys. After this screening, 41 cities and 39 counties were amalgamated into 40 rural-urban integrated cities.

Attitude surveys suggest that residents and local councils see the benefits. Everyone agrees that the integrated city makes

for better land use planning in urban areas. Areas for improvement include the equity of service provision, since rural and urban residents have different needs, and the weak rural voice, since urbanites are believed to be more organized.

Land consolidation in Indonesia

The Land Consolidation Program implemented in Indonesia in the 1990s shows how to facilitate the orderly development of fast-growing areas and to plan the development of vacant areas on the urban fringe.

The mayor has the authority to determine the location of consolidation areas and to manage and supervise the process. But the key actors are the private landowners and the occupiers of (state-owned) land.

The minimum requirement for land consolidation is to have at least 85 percent of landowners representing at least 85 percent of the land area give their agreement. All participants contribute by providing land for infrastructure and services. The amount of land a participant is required to give up is determined by consensus. Small landowners who cannot contribute land can contribute money or labor. The contributions fund infrastructure and utilities—and build a pool of "cost-equivalent land," to be used only by small landowners to enlarge their parcels.

Sources: WDR 2009 team; Groupe Recherche/Actions pour le Développement 2001; and Kim 1998.

a severe problem in 1960 as the area grew through the intermediate stage of urbanization and absorbed a large influx of people from abroad after the country gained independence from Japan and from rural areas in the Republic of Korea. To help tackle this problem, the area of Gangnam, south of the Han River, was absorbed into Seoul's territory in 1963, and the Gangnam Development Program initiated. This program involved a series of spatially connective infrastructure projects spread over 30 years, including several bridges across the Han River and a 54.2-kilometer circular subway line to link Gangnam with central Seoul.

Daegu's story is similar. Between 1950 and 1990, Daegu's population swelled by a factor of six, from 355,000 to nearly 2 million,[63] as its thriving textile industry pulled in rural migrants seeking a better life. The policy response was to integrate Daegu and its hinterland by expanding its administrative zone in 1987 and again in 1995, followed by building a subway system and expanding the city bus system. The city also experienced continual building and upgrading of local roads. In 1980 just over 40 percent of Daegu's local roads were paved, and by 1995, virtually all had been paved.

Combining universal access to the most basic services and reasonable land markets with investments to improve spatial connectivity with other areas of the country, Daegu has thrived. Manufacturing has deconcentrated from Daegu into the surrounding Gyeongsangbukdo province, and the local economy has diversified, reducing its reliance on the textile industry and moving into sectors with higher value added production. Daegu now sits at the center of a vibrant urban system surrounded by five cities, all with easy transport access to the central city, and each having evolved to provide localization economies (see map 7.3). Gumi has been dubbed "Korea's Silicon Valley" for its specialization in electronics, while coastal Pohang and Ulsan, respectively, provide homes for the Pohang Steel Company and Hyundai. Ulsan also houses one of the biggest shipbuilding industries in the world, and both these cities have been on the

Map 7.3   Decentralization and localization economies in Daegu

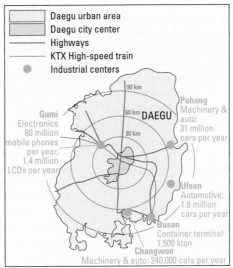

Source: Daegu Metropolitan City.

forefront of the Republic Korea's export-led industrialization.

Other examples are Chongqing and Chengdu, both rapidly urbanizing areas in southwestern China. In line with an unabashedly urbanization-based economic growth strategy, China is piloting the "area approach" in western China. At about 43 percent, they have similar urban shares to the average for China. The objective is to increase those shares to 70 percent in 2020, but in a manner that speeds the concentration of economic activities while reducing rural-urban disparities in living standards. The mainstays of the strategy are institutions and infrastructure (see box 5 in the overview).

If markets favor the two places as much as the central and provincial governments have, the two cities will improve the lives of millions in the Chinese hinterland. The initiatives have already had a local impact. In Chongqing rural incomes in the first half of 2007 increased faster than those of urban residents. Foreign investment is about the same as it was in Shanghai a decade ago. Industries are attracted to the low wages and low cost of land. According to government statistics, average wages, at $2 to $3 a day, are much lower than those in Beijing or Shanghai. In Chengdu farmer concentrations are believed to have increased productivity by 80 percent. Industrialization has been absorbing about 100,000 farmers a year, with some narrowing of rural-urban income differences.

Several areas at the intermediate stage of urbanization in China appear to conform to the principle of an additional instrument for the dimensional challenge of congestion. An example is the tri-city area in the northeast of Hunan province, in central China (see map 7.4). The cluster of three cities—Changsha, Zhuzhou, and Xiangtan—has a combined population of around 13 million and accounts for about one-fifth of the province. With an income exceeding the national average by 17 percent and the Hunan average by 61 percent, this cluster is an intermediate urbanization area with an urban share of half.

An area plan—the first of its kind in inland China—was formulated in 2005.[64] The plan specifies a regulatory land use planning framework within which market prices will be allowed to allocate land for different uses. It also provides planning guidelines including, for example, enforcing land use rights and promoting land

Map 7.4 Changsha, Zhuzhou, and Xiangtan—spatially connective infrastructure in a two dimensional area

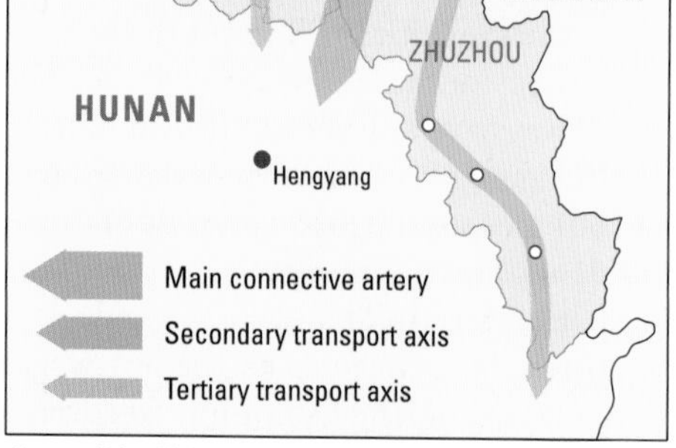

Source: China Urban Planning and Design Institute and Hunan Development and Reform Commission 2005.
Note: The main artery is formed by the Beijing-Guangzhou railway, Beijing-Zhuhai highway, and State Highway 107.

intensification in central city areas. The plan sets out a series of spatially connective policies aiming to promote connectivity between the three cities in the cluster. These include highway and rail-based expressway projects to connect Xiangtan with Zhuzhou and ring roads around each of the three cities. The plan is a good illustration of how the principle of "an *I* for a *D*" can be made operational using an area approach.

Invest in transport connectivity while continuing institutional reform. Developed metropolitan areas rarely leave city growth unplanned. Land and housing markets help allocate residential and office space. Rapidly expanding systems need clear property rights to provide incentives for land transactions and correct land valuation to avoid an urban bias and too much migration to the city. Singapore develops land and housing plans every 10 years and lets the market function once public and private sectors agree on which economic activities to develop and which residential patterns are needed to accommodate firms and workers.

Urban transport, along with urban land management, determines the shape of the city and its ecological footprint. Urban mobility is particularly important for the poor. In Buenos Aires 87 percent of the jobs in the metropolitan area are accessible in 45 minutes. In Mexico City 20 percent of workers spend more than three hours traveling to and from work each day. The urban poor in Beijing and Shanghai spend less than 5 percent of their income on transport because they walk or cycle. If they chose to travel by bus, the costs would be 40 percent of their income.[65] Brazil's *vale de transporte* is an effective way to subsidize poor workers in the absence of good urban transport—financed by the central government and by the employer in equal parts. Several large cities have public transport networks that are used extensively—metro in Delhi, Kolkata, and Mumbai, buses and metro in São Paulo—but the network quickly becomes inadequate and congested because of the rapid population growth. Regular maintenance and new investments in infrastructure are needed to sustain density in urban areas (see box 7.12).

Put infrastructure in the most promising places. Several countries have created new cities to move a capital city (Brasília), to decongest the capital (Seoul), or for economic reasons. Creating new cities with the sole purpose of diverting population from the capital is often risky, evidenced by Brazil, France, República Bolivariana de Venezuela, the United Kingdom, and more recently Egypt and Nigeria.[66] New cities become attractive to private investors only after they reach a threshold, but there is no way to know that threshold.[67] And when cities are created far from main transport networks and business centers, they are unlikely to be economic successes.

When markets identify promising cities, strategic investments in infrastructure and public goods can accelerate their potential for economic growth (see box 7.13). Secondary cities that promote access to markets, improve city management, and build human capital seem a better alternative. And if political concerns dictate the creation of new cities, efficiency concerns will guide locations to be close to growing markets and to have access to infrastructure. Working with existing cities is preferable to creating new cities from scratch. But, if new cities are created, they should be constructed on an appropriate scale, close to markets, and planned to generate demand-side links.

Advanced urbanizers (three-dimensional areas): institutions and infrastructure for higher density and shorter distance, and targeted incentives to address divisions

Successful metropolitan areas in both developed and developing countries have well-functioning land markets, representative management, state-of-the art transport infrastructure, and social policies to integrate low-income residents.

Use an inclusive mix of institutions, infrastructure, and incentives. Colombia's capital, Bogotá, shows the resolve and resources needed for inclusive urbanization in a metropolitan region. Although the area's income places it in upper-middle-income levels, 43 percent of its population of 6.7 million is considered poor. One

BOX 7.12 *Retrofitting transport infrastructure in Bangkok*

In the 1990s it was estimated that the average car in Bangkok spent 44 days each year stationary in traffic. How did this situation come to pass? And how is it being remedied?

A city of around 7 million people, Bangkok is the product of hundreds of years of incremental growth along traditional land configurations. The result is a city woven with narrow lanes, many of them culs-de-sac (called *soi*), but with few arterial roads. Indeed, the arterial roads can be as far as 7 kilometers or more apart. According to a recent estimate, roads account for only about 6.1 percent of Bangkok's land area in the inner city, and only 1.7 percent in its peripheral areas. In high-income countries it is usual for 20 to 30 percent of urban land area to be devoted to roads. Even with this extreme congestion, economic activity has been slow to decentralize to other cities in Thailand, or to suburban districts of Bangkok, because of the enduring attraction of Bangkok's agglomeration economies, sociocultural amenities, and key export infrastructure, including its port.

In recent years several flyovers and elevated expressways have been built, along with an elevated railway system (Skytrain), dedicated bus lanes, and two peripheral ring roads. But car ownership has shot up, too, adding to the traffic and diminishing the impact of remedial investments. Looking to the future, congestion pricing and increased parking fees appear to be promising policy options. Reducing fares on the Skytrain and extending rapid transit to more of Bangkok, perhaps using bus rapid transit, pose greater challenges.

Contributed by Austin Kilroy.
Sources: Angel 2008, Bae and Suthiranart 2003, and Gakenheimer 1999.

of 12 residents lives in a slum, and about one-third of new citizens in recent years are rural migrants. The city has taken steps to make urbanization inclusive. It built better schools, renewed parks, started community centers, and improved main networks for water and sanitation. Since 2000 a public-private bus rapid transit system, the *TransMilenio*, has improved citywide accessibility. Travel times have fallen by an average of 15 minutes, with larger reductions for households in poorer parts of the city (see map 7.5). Aided by these infrastructure improvements, Bogotá's internationally recognized *Programa de Mejoramiento Integral de Barrios* has assisted the poorest neighborhoods to integrate with the city. Begun in 2003 it has already helped 930,000 people. The program is believed to have contributed increases of up to 11 percent in house values.[68]

The Republic of Korea also provides lessons. In the 1950s it had an estimated 136,650 unregistered slum districts, more than 2,200 in the core of Seoul.[69] Spatially targeted policies to redevelop Seoul's slum areas started as early as the mid-1960s.

BOX 7.13   *New cities: escapes from urban jungles, or cathedrals in the desert?*

New cities were attempted in Europe without much success. In the United Kingdom the Barlow Commission Report of 1940 stimulated interest in new towns. Between 1947 and 1968, Britain created 26 new towns to control the growth of London and stimulate development in Scotland and Wales. In 1965 France followed a similar program—nine towns, five in the Paris area and four in lagging areas, were constructed. These programs soon were interrupted and put aside as unsustainable. The new towns never reached their targeted population, nor did they forestall the growth of London or Paris. The experience in developing countries has been mixed.

Failure in the Arab Republic of Egypt

Egypt's program of new cities is the world's largest. In 20 years Egypt has built 20 new cities and is preparing for 45 more. The first set of 24 cities was launched in 1974–75 as a manifestation of the political commitment to conquer the desert and ensure sustainable growth. Large industrial zones were created and generous tax incentives were given to the private sector. Land was virtually free. The "first generation" of new towns included six towns, each with its own industrial base and large target populations.[a] Ten years later—by the mid-1980s—the next program based on satellite settlements was launched, and nine second-generation settlements were launched around Greater Cairo. A third generation included twin towns close to provincial capitals, such as New Thebes.

The performance of the six cities created 30 years ago suggests a mixed record at best. Cities closer to Cairo have attracted businesses and people, though much fewer than anticipated. Cities distant from Cairo (including Sadat City, supposedly the new capital) remain unattractive for skilled labor due to lack of amenities and transport links. The new cities have no more than 1 million inhabitants (1 percent of Egypt's population), compared with the 5 million target set for 2005. The program was also costly: 22 percent of the Ministry of Infrastructure's investment under the Fourth Plan (1997–2001) was spent in these new towns. This will increase if the government continues its policy of developing the urban fringes. The emphasis on attracting investment was not balanced by the need to make cities attractive for skilled labor and accessible from the established urban centers. Eventually, the creation of the new cities had little impact on decongesting greater Cairo.

Success in China

China's approach recognizes the need to create cities with access to major markets and transportation networks. Shenzhen was the first special economic zone (SEZ) to be approved by Deng Xiaoping in 1980. From a small town with 30,000 inhabitants, it grew to 800,000 in 1988 and 7 million in 2000. The new residents include the best-trained professionals in the country, attracted by high salaries, better housing, and education opportunities for their children. GDP per capita increased more than 60 times.

Shenzhen owes its success to its nearness to Hong Kong, China; its connectedness within the area and with other cities in China; and its urban form:

- *Access to foreign markets.* Locating the SEZ close to the city of Hong Kong, China, facilitated foreign investment, technical assistance, and access to foreign markets.
- *Connectedness within the area.* To spread the fruits of development, the boundaries of the municipality were expanded to extend the benefits of the city to all workers. The rural *hukou* was abolished in the municipality, and all urban services became accessible to all residents. Placing the Shenzhen city-area in the Pearl River Delta area ensured the best possible links to its hinterland and other urban nodes in the Delta regions. Complementary decisions to ease the mobility and integration include investments in transport infrastructure and a shift from a road-based to a rail-based system.
- *Functional urban form.* The comprehensive plan for Shenzhen envisions a polycentric metropolis that connects the SEZ to urban nodes through efficient transport.

Sources: WDR 2009 team; Stewart 1996; and World Bank 2007k.
a. For example, Sixth of October had an original target population of 500,000, which was raised in the late 1980s to 1 million, and currently the target is 2.5 million. The actual population is probably less than 200,000.

But without the requisite investments in spatially blind institutions and spatially connective infrastructure in place, these policies succeeded only in relocating the slums to new slum areas such as Mokdang, Nangok, and Shillim near the Guro Industrial Complex, whose textile and other industries provided low-skill employment opportunities for rural migrants.

The Republic of Korea's government would have more luck when it tried again with an expanded set of policies in the 1980s. By this time, the Republic of Korea was closing in on the advanced stage of urbanization, and Seoul's population level had started to stabilize (see map 7.6). Furthermore, enough time had elapsed for the earlier spatially blind and connective policies to take full effect.

Between 1984 and 1990, expanding road capacity struggled to keep up with the growth of vehicle ownership. More extensive plans of city-periphery integration were required, and in 1989 the New City Development plan was launched. Five new cities were encouraged around 25–30 kilometers

Map 7.5   Bogotá's *TransMilenio* has helped to integrate the poor

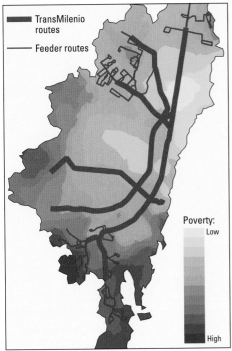

TransMilenio routes

Feeder routes

Poverty:
Low

High

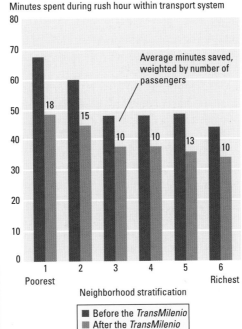

Minutes spent during rush hour within transport system

Average minutes saved, weighted by number of passengers

Neighborhood stratification

1 Poorest   2   3   4   5   6 Richest

■ Before the *TransMilenio*
■ After the *TransMilenio*

Source: Yepes 2008.

from Seoul. Central to the success of this integration were investments in connective infrastructure. The subway system was extended, and a beltway was constructed, easing traffic congestion.

During this period, 93 slum districts covering an area of 427 square kilometers were modernized, including the Wolgoksadong and Mok-dong slum areas.[70] Dwellers in the former benefited from successful in situ upgrading; those in the latter were relocated as the government cleared the area and replaced it with a modern apartment complex. Squatters benefited from moving subsidies of about $2,000 per person and the right to purchase a new apartment at a discount.[71]

Turkey has also transformed itself from a predominantly rural society to a primarily urban one over the past half-century. Since becoming a member of the Organisation for Economic Co-operation and Development (OECD) in 1961, Turkey's urban share increased from around one-third to two-thirds,[72] as GDP per capita more than tripled to about $6,600.[73] Driving this increase in density was the rapid growth of Turkey's cities, foremost among them, Istanbul.

In 1960 Istanbul's population was about 1.5 million, a modern-day Kansas City in the United States. With a population more than 10 million today, Istanbul is now one of Europe's largest cities, about the same

Map 7.6   Economic density in Seoul with good connections to other cities

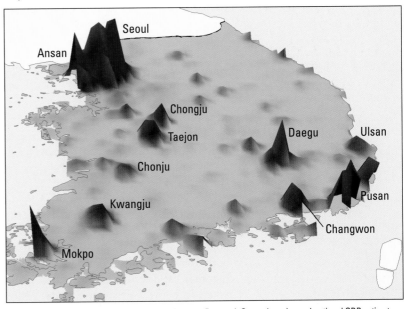

Seoul

Ansan

Chongju

Taejon

Daegu

Ulsan

Chonju

Kwangju

Pusan

Changwon

Mokpo

Source: WDR 2009 team and World Bank Development Research Group, based on subnational GDP estimates for 2005. See also Nordhaus 2006.

size as Chicago.[74] Much of this growth has been accommodated on the Asian side of the city, home to successive waves of rural immigrants. It is now the origin of a daily tidal wave of commuters who make their way across the Bosporus to work on the European side of the city.

Underpinning Turkey's transformation to an urban economy are the spatially blind reforms that accompanied the creation of the modern republic of Turkey. The Turkish constitution of 1924 included the adaptation of European laws to the needs of the new republic, endorsing private property rights. The reforms introduced under Mustafa Kemal Ataturk unified the country's education system, providing the backdrop for better access to education over the last half-century. In 1960 the proportion of the adult population more than 15 years old with no schooling was 67 percent, and in 2000, 18.6 percent.[75] And better health care services helped increase life expectancy from 51 years in 1960 to 71 years in 2005.[76]

The reforms of the 1920s helped to lay the foundation for Istanbul's rapid expansion, but the city has found itself grappling with congestion. In response, the city has improved its connective infrastructure, with 1973 marking the opening of the eight-lane Bosporus Bridge connecting the European and Asian parts of the city. This was followed, in 1988, by the completion of the second Bosporus Bridge. In 1989 the first light metro rail line opened between the areas of Aksaray and Kartaltepe. Meanwhile, a second light metro line opened in 2007, supplementing the 2005 construction of an 11-kilometer metrobus line. More are in the pipeline.

With this prosperity has come division. Much of Istanbul's rapid growth over the last several decades has occurred through the growth of informal settlements, such as Sultanbeyli, Sarigazi, and Paşaköy on the Asian side. These settlements formed as rural migrants took advantage of an ancient legal precept, which survived the Ataturk reforms: no matter who owns the land, if people are able to get their houses built overnight and are moved in by morning, they cannot be evicted without being taken to court. Such settlements, called *gecekondu,* house a large share of Istanbul's

population. Almost half of the city's residents—some 5–6 million people—live in dwellings that are or were *gecekondu.* Although settlements such as Sultanbeyli have integrated themselves into the city, others like Paşaköy have not.[77] Istanbul still needs targeted programs to deal with the divisions associated with the continuing existence of poorly serviced and under-integrated informal communities.[78]

China's Pearl River Delta faces similar challenges. The area consists of nine cities and has a population roughly equal to that of Spain, representing one of China's most advanced urban agglomerations. With an urban share of almost 75 percent in 2006, it is a three-dimensional area with the triple challenge of building density, reducing distance, and overcoming divisions. The divisions are manifest in "urban villages," many of which would be known as slums elsewhere. They lack access to basic sanitation services and are subject to environmental degradation. The cities of the Pearl River Delta area have been introducing spatially targeted policies to deal with urban villages. Guangdong province, where the area is located, began rebuilding urban villages in June 2000. The city of Zhuhai, for example, aims to rebuild 26 administrative villages. An incentive scheme allows the village administration, residents, and developers to share any land appreciation.

Rural-urban integration has been part of post-1978 liberalization in China. Under the township model, the urban core has responsibility for the surrounding rural hinterland. As the city grows and its area of influence expands, the administrative borders of the township also expand. Large cities promote the active inclusion of their surrounding hinterland by financing investment in infrastructure and social services in the small cities and rural areas under their influence (see box 7.14).

Get regulations right. Shanghai, a metropolitan area with special status as a province, has a population of 13 million registered and 4 million permanent residents, spread out over 6,300 square kilometers. The urban share is almost 80 percent, with 18 urban districts and the Chongming rural county. Urban land markets function well in allocating the urban land available under the rural land conversion limits. Floor-area ratios have adapted to changing market needs and increased the space per person from 3 to 12 square meters over the past 20 years. Land leases are a source of revenue.

Shanghai's built-up area has expanded from 300 to 500 square kilometers in the past decade. Passengers on the metro have increased tenfold, from 178,000 to 1.6 million over the past decade, but its share of all trips is just 2.5 percent. Many of the 4 million transient workers in Shanghai live in old urban villages, affordable because they are not subject to regulations for density, height, and public space. Given the difficulties in converting rural land, these urban villages are attractive to developers, but developing them would likely make the housing conditions worse for transient workers.

Less encouraging is Mumbai. Between the 1970s and 1990s, the city resisted the influx of migrants by instituting land use and building regulations that favored incumbents and prevented efficient use of land.[79] The result has been an evenly spread development, but with congested streets and the proliferation of slums.

Integrate slums into cities, using all three instruments—institutions, infrastructure, and incentives. Cities without slums is not a realistic vision for developing countries, as recognized in the midterm appraisal of India's 10th Five-Year plan:

> There has, over the years, been a paradigm shift in government's slum policy prescriptions. Originally, a "slum free cities" policy was prescribed. However, looking at the social dimensions of the whole problem and the various economic activities carried out by the slum dwellers, this concept has given way to rehabilitation of slum dwellers. The rehabilitation involves either relocation or in-situ development of the slum areas. In the initial years of slum development, the focus was on provision of infrastructure in slums through the National Slum Development Program (NSDP) and now there is renewed stress on provision of shelter to urban slum dwellers through the Valmiki Ambedkar Awas Yojana (VAMBAY).[80]

Identifying and implementing policies for managing slum formation is a major concern for policy makers in most

---

BOX 7.14   *Rural-urban integration in Beijing, Guangzhou, and Shanghai*

Beijing, Guangzhou, and Shanghai—all thriving areas—have plans to link rural and urban areas: to provide education and health services, invest in infrastructure and transport networks, and construct townships.

- *Social services.* The governments provide vocational training and other services to support nonagricultural employment and help farmers transition from agriculture to nonagriculture. They also offer incentives for firms that will train people and recruit the trainees after training. And they provide social services such as medical insurance and pensions to rural residents. Beijing subsidized rural cooperative medical insurance. Shanghai increased public spending on rural social services, including education and health to cover farmers (100 percent covered by a rural collective medical insurance plan). Guangzhou will establish a pension scheme to cover all the local residents.

- *Infrastructure investments.* In 2005 Beijing built 304 kilometers of roads and linked all administrative villages. In Shanghai expressways were extended from 200 kilometers in 2003 to 550 kilometers in 2005, and will be extended again to 750 kilometers in 2010. In Guangzhou the provision of roads, electricity, and water to all rural settlements with more than 100 residents was completed in 2007.

- *Integrating surrounding areas.* The three cities have encouraged traditional industries to move from the central business district (where rents are quite high) to the periphery (using fiscal incentives) and allow high value-added industry to move in to the core area. A township construction program was launched to have a city system centered on an inner city of 10 million inhabitants, surrounded by secondary cities, central towns, and villages. In 2003 Guangzhou initiated the building of 10 central towns financed by the city government. Shanghai has begun implementing the "1966 plan," which by 2020 aims to have one main city, nine secondary cities (traditional historical centers), 60 new townships, and 600 central villages with 1,500–3,000 residents each.

Source: WDR 2009 team.

---

developing countries. But there is little consensus on the choice of policies required to improve living conditions and livelihoods of slum dwellers, while not compromising the economic potential of metropolitan areas. Two questions have to be answered. When should slums be improved? And what should be done to develop slums? This Report proposes that the right time to systematically address the problem of slums is when the institutional and infrastructure requirements are in place. And the correct approach is integration of slums into the broader urban economy.

If the problem is crime and squalor, the better strategy would be to upgrade the neighborhood. But if the problem is spatial inefficiency, steps to improve land use efficiency and compensate slum dwellers for disruptions to their livelihoods probably should take precedence. Interventions to improve living conditions in slums include prevention measures, such as sites and services programs and remedial schemes (with slum upgrading being the most common), packages of basic services, paving, shelter, and social integration. The Kampong Improvement Program in Indonesia is probably the oldest, largest, and best-known urban-upgrading initiative in the world. It combines low investment costs of $23 to $118 per person, benefits 15 million people, and uses a participatory approach. The Orangi Project in Pakistan and the Accra District Rehabilitation Project in Ghana are also promising (see table 7.2). But the experiences all show that spatially focused interventions for improving slums are unlikely to be enough for social integration, unless accompanied by infrastructure, institutions, and complementary reform (see box 7.15).

Land use and zoning policies have often excluded the poor from being physically integrated into dynamic labor markets, while deficient transport infrastructure lowers the possibility of connecting distant residents to urban jobs. South African zoning policies under apartheid segregated white and black people in cities. City structure can exacerbate social divisions and hinder efforts to reduce inequality and discrimination. The abolition of apartheid was not enough to reduce the disparities. To offset spatial income inequalities, local governments can subsidize transport costs of poor

Table 7.2   Interventions to integrate the urban poor

Country (city)	Focus and objectives	Key features and lessons
Tunisia (National) Agence de Rehabilitation et de Renovation Urbaine	*Tenure security.* Regularizes tenure, provides infrastructure, house improvement support, plots for displaced households.	Triggered dynamic process of housing improvement; helped explain low proportion of urban population in slums.
Brazil (Goiania) The Goiania Federation for Tenants and Posseiros	*Tenure security.* Public land occupied and tenure secured by appealing to rights of citizens to occupy unused and untitled land.	Covers 100,000 former tenants. Local grassroots organization successfully supported efforts to get tenure security and access to infrastructure and services.
Peru (Ilo) Municipal Government	*Land provision.* Makes serviced plots available for construction by low-income households.	6,000 lots serviced for housing by 2005. Despite a fivefold increase in local population in 1960–2000, no pressure for land invasions.
Argentina (Buenos Aires, San Fernando, and San Jorge) IIED-America Latina	*Land provision.* Serviced land donated to facilitate resettlement and density reduction; plots allocated in community-managed lottery.	Program is the result of a series of actions and initiatives over the past 20 years, supported by an Argentine NGO that lobbies provincial and municipal authorities.
Namibia (Windhoek) Shack Dwellers Federation of Namibia and City Government	*Flexible zoning laws.* Group purchases and leases of land with communal services; plot sizes below official national minimum.	Demonstrates how constraints in the form of urban land use standards and regulations can be overcome to make serviced sites more affordable to low-income households.
Malawi (Lilongwe, Blantyre, Mzuzu) Malawi Homeless People's Federation	*Land provision; flexible regulation.* Lobbied government for land; demonstrated capacity of members to build good quality housing at low cost. Changing official standards important for cost.	Since 2003, approximately 760 plots for housing have been provided and housing construction loans made available to savings groups; slum accommodation containment and land use improvement.
Pakistan (Orangi) Research and Training Institute	*Amenities provision.* Community development of drainage and sewerage systems, financed by local communities and government.	96,994 households in Orangi and 300 locations in Pakistan. All costs can be covered by eliminating contractors and modifying engineering standards.
15 countries (South Asia, East Asia, and Africa) Slum Dwellers International	*Amenities provision.* National federations formed by slum dwellers; initiatives to build and improve homes and basic services.	Savings groups (mostly women) and their collective management of money allow groups to increase capacity for cooperative action; negotiation of partnerships with governments.
Thailand (National) Community Organizations Development Institute	*Amenities provision.* Infrastructure subsidies and housing loans to community organizations formed by low-income slum households.	495 projects in 957 communities covering 52,776 households. Activities identified by each community organization in partnership with local actors; funding sources include community contributions.
Nicaragua (National) Local Development Program (PRODEL)	*Amenities provision.* Cofinance small infrastructure projects (water, sanitation, drainage); house improvement and microenterprise loans and support.	484 projects benefiting some 60,000 households. Funds provided to local governments, NGOs, community organizations, and households.

Source: Sattherthwaite 2008, for this Report.
Note: IIED = International Institute for Environment and Development; NGO = nongovernmental organization.

children, provide private-school vouchers, and increase public-school spending.[81]

A strategy for inclusive urbanization

The Tinbergen principle proposes that one policy instrument is needed to address each policy objective.[82] Applying the principle to the policy issues addressed in this Report implies that as many integration instruments are needed as there are dimensions to a problem. As the integration challenges increase with the stage of urbanization, the number of policy instruments required increases as well. Fortunately for developing nations, the capacity of markets and governments grows as they urbanize. But these policies must be introduced in the right sequence.

The foundations for an inclusive urbanization have to be instituted early in the development process. To do this, governments must be selective. This chapter suggest how they can prioritize and sequence:

- In areas of incipient urbanization, the objective should be to facilitate a natural rural-urban transformation. The core policy instruments are spatially blind institutions that facilitate density in some locations. These instruments include secure land tenure and property rights, basic and social services, and macroeconomic policies that do not favor one productive activity (large industry) over another (small agriculture). Policy makers should aim for neutrality between rural and urban areas.

- In areas of intermediate urbanization, the rapid growth of some cities creates congestion. In addition to spatially blind policies to facilitate density, connective policies to tackle congestion and economic distance become necessary. They include investments in transport infrastructure (to enhance connectivity both within and between cities) and encouragement of socially efficient location decisions by firms.

BOX 7.15 *Slum upgrading and prevention: what works?*

Evidence from policy experience compiled by UN-HABITAT and the Cities Alliance shows that successful initiatives share several attributes. Among them, institutional strengthening and coordination across government levels seem to be the most important.

Stronger institutions. Countries that have been successful in integrating slums into their cities have strengthened their institutions and carried out complementary reforms, which include a broader urban poverty reduction agenda (Indonesia, Islamic Republic of Iran, Mexico, South Africa, and Turkey). Some have implemented policies to integrate the urban poor into the legal and social fabric of cities (Brazil, Chile, and Colombia), others have carried out reforms in land and housing provision (India).

Coordination across government levels and with private agents. Countries that performed well also made an effort to coordinate among central, regional, and local authorities and the private sector (Chile, Egypt, Sri Lanka, Thailand, and Tunisia). But cities and countries that were successful in the delivery of basic services and housing improvements had clear performance monitoring mechanisms that require the involvement of all levels of government. Cambodia, China, and Vietnam, for example, have strict upward accountability regarding municipal implementation on infrastructure. Brazil and Indonesia, on the other hand, have bottom-up performance monitoring, which enhances citizen participation in planning and decision making.[b] Coordination across government levels and with the private sector is also critical for successful scaling up of slum upgrading projects. One example is Indonesia's Kampong Improvement Program, and there are others (for example, Brazil, Colombia, Mexico, South Africa, Thailand, and Tunisia) whose programs began on a modest scale, and were successfully scaled up to the national level because of the involvement of all levels of the government and the private sector.

Based on a contribution by Eduardo López Moreno, chief, Global Urban Observatory, UN-HABITAT.
a. Garau 2008.
b. Bazoglu 2008.

Efficiency should be the watchword of policy makers.

- In areas with advanced urbanization, divisions within cities caused by formal settlements and slums and by grime and crime add to the challenges of density and distance. In addition to spatially blind and spatially connective policies, spatially focused policies for addressing intracity divisions are necessary to target the difficulties of slums, crime, and the environment—and to improve livability.

CHAPTER 8

Unity, Not Uniformity

Effective approaches to territorial development

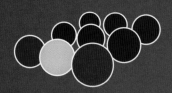

Globalization and liberalization may rearrange production within countries, leaving people concentrated in places no longer favored by markets. In Brazil, China, India, and the Russian Federation, changes in both markets and policies over the last century have altered the fortunes of places. Geographic differences in economic activities encourage migration from lagging areas, concentrating people—including the poor—in leading areas. But geographic unevenness in living standards, by creating or deepening divisions within countries, can also lead to conflict, slowing social and economic development.

Building on the findings and analysis in earlier chapters, this chapter discusses the policy responses to widening or persistent differences in living standards between areas of a country that markets favor with greater economic mass and those that they do not. As in the rest of this report, the term "area" is synonymous with a subnational region or territory, so this chapter deals with the "regional development" (also referred to as the "territorial development") debate. Logic and experience indicate that policy makers should calibrate their responses to the severity of the challenge.

- *In countries where labor and capital are mobile, economic distance between lagging and leading areas should be addressed mainly with spatially blind or universal policies, for which the term "institutions" is used as shorthand.* These policies should make it easier for people to move toward opportunity.

When lagging areas have few people and a small share of the country's poor, measures to enhance migration should be the mainstay of development policy.

- *In countries where lagging areas have large numbers of the poor, but few impediments to their mobility, institutions that promote mobility should be augmented by spatially connective infrastructure.* Some countries have high population densities in lagging areas—and large numbers of the poor—but few cultural, linguistic, or political impediments to labor and capital flows. Investments in infrastructure that increase the flow of goods, people, and information would aid economic concentration and spatial convergence in living standards.

- *In countries fragmented by linguistic, political, religious, or ethnic divisions, spatially targeted interventions may be needed.* When lagging areas face the triple challenge of long distances to economic opportunities in leading areas, large population densities, and large numbers of poor people, as well as domestic divisions that limit the movement of labor and capital, institutions and infrastructure investments could be supplemented by targeted incentives to encourage economic production in lagging areas. But these incentives should not run counter to the integration objectives pursued through institutions that bring people together and infrastructure that connects lagging and leading areas of a nation.

Institutions, infrastructure, and incentives—these are the three parts of a successful policy approach to domestic integration. In deciding among the integration options, governments have to consider the fiscal and opportunity costs of these instruments. This chapter provides an organizing frame for governments to think through these options and find the best combination of policies.

A new approach. Policy discussions about how to improve welfare in lagging areas often begin with a focus on lagging areas—and an emphasis on targeted interventions or policy "incentives" to move production to these places. Instead, territorial development policies should integrate lagging with leading areas, and the discussion of spatially targeted incentives should come last—after considering spatially blind policies such as national revenue-sharing and social expenditure arrangements and spatially connecting initiatives, such as transport and communication systems. The experience of developed and developing countries shows that without these supporting institutions and infrastructure, incentives have been unsuccessful and expensive.

In many countries, the decentralization of administrative and fiscal responsibilities has increased the role of subnational governments in the design and delivery of policies. Resources allocated to subnational governments should come with agreements to ensure that local initiatives improve national welfare along with local welfare (see box 8.1).

In addressing these policy issues, the chapter provides an answer to a question of considerable concern to policy makers: Should countries invest in people or in places? The answer is to invest in activities that produce the highest economic and social returns nationally. In leading areas, emphasize investment in places—durable investments that increase national economic growth. In lagging areas, emphasize investment in people—portable investments that stimulate mobility and accelerate poverty reduction.

People seek opportunities

Throughout history, people have moved from places with harsh geography to those offering a more pleasant climate and better

---

BOX 8.1 *Are the policy messages of this Report "anti-decentralization"? No.*

Spatially blind institutions are the bedrock of economic integration policies seeking spatial efficiency and equity. Regardless of where people live, they should have affordable access to basic services such as primary health care, education, sanitation, and security. How these services are delivered depends on country circumstances.

Decentralization in many countries has made subnational governments more responsible for improving local welfare outcomes. In Vietnam subnational governments were responsible for almost 50 percent of public spending in 2002, up from about 25 percent in 1992. In China the ratio climbed from 67 to 72 percent between 1990 and 2004.[a] In the Philippines the ratio was about 25 percent in 2002, up from 11 percent in 1990.

Problems arise when decentralization gets in the way of delivering spatially blind policies. Rather than allocating resources to social services, subnational

policy makers may be inclined to tilt expenditures toward politically popular activities. In a highly decentralized country such as Brazil, progress on national priorities of eliminating illiteracy and universalizing primary education is monitored using expenditure allocations, with the constitution determining that 25 percent of state and municipal revenues from taxes and transfers be earmarked to finance primary education. But closer inspection shows that around 10 percent of municipalities spend less than the constitutionally recommended amounts.[b]

Large and visible investments are politically expedient signals to voters that their representatives are hard at work. So how can decentralization be consistent with the spatially integrative policies discussed here?

- *Institutions*—resource allocations to subnational governments could be based initially on inputs (expenditures

on public services) but should move as soon as feasible to outcomes (improvements in the national Millennium Development Indicators).

- *Infrastructure*—to maximize synergies from infrastructure investments and to regulate interstate commerce efficiently, design and planning decisions should be jointly made by subnational governments affected by these investments and regulations.

- *Incentives*—while subnational governments may be well suited to assess local economic potential, the decision of *where* to target incentives should lie with a national authority that can prioritize resources to accelerate overall growth. *How* these programs are implemented can be decided locally.

Source: WDR 2009 team.
a. National Bureau of Statistics, China, 2005.
b. Instituto Brasileiro de Geografia e Estatística (IBGE) 2004.

Map 8.1   The poverty rate is high in China's western interior, but most poor people live closer to economic density in the East

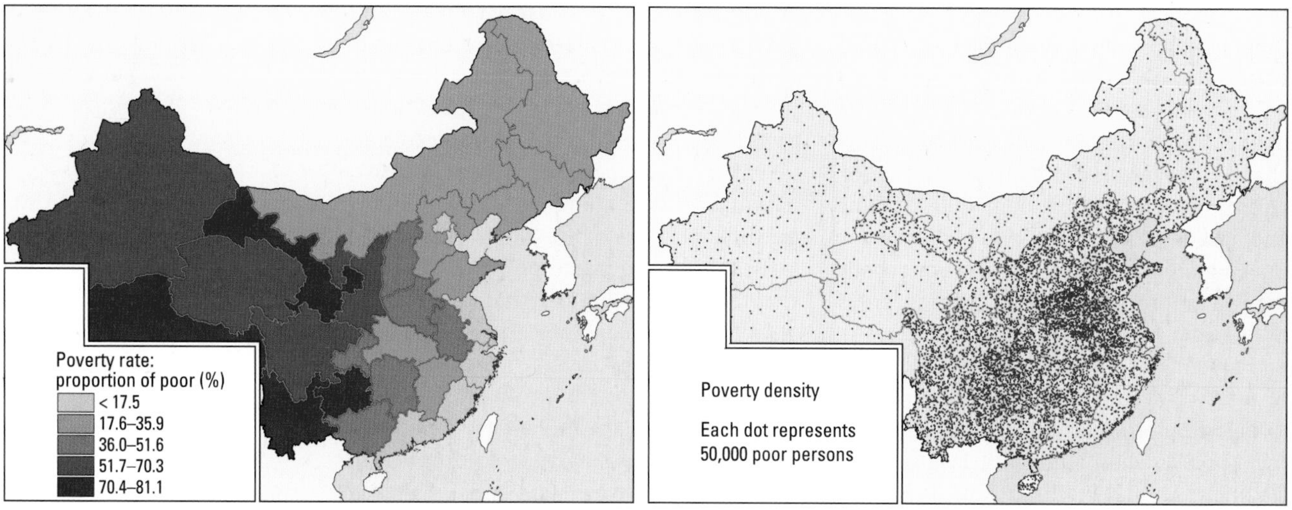

Poverty rate:
proportion of poor (%)
- < 17.5
- 17.6–35.9
- 36.0–51.6
- 51.7–70.3
- 70.4–81.1

Poverty density

Each dot represents
50,000 poor persons

Source: WDR 2009 team.
Note: Poverty rates and counts are estimated for a $2/day poverty line in 2002.

economic opportunities. The concentration of people in areas with hospitable natural environments attracted economic activities to these places, helping many to prosper even when the initial conditions that made these settlements economically attractive became less important. Mobility was not just for the well-off. Poor people also moved to economically dense areas—to seek better lives.

Consider the current distribution of poor people in China (see map 8.1). The percentage of people living below $2 a day is high in the country's lagging western areas. But in absolute terms, many more poor people live in the dynamic coastal southeastern areas—the leaders in China's rapid integration with the global economy. Even before this integration happened, people did not concentrate in places with inhospitable geography, such as the Qinghai-Tibet Plateau with an elevation of 4,000 meters above sea level, or the highlands of the central region with elevations of 2,000 meters. The flat lands and warmer climates along the coast provided better conditions for farming and trade.

Maps of many countries would also show that the poverty mass—the numbers of poor people—and economic mass coincide. Java, the economically leading area in Indonesia, is also the island in the archipelago where most poor people live. The islands of Java and Bali are home to 21 million poor people, about 58 percent of the

country's poor. The numbers on the other islands are much lower: 1.3 million in Kalimantan, 2.6 million in Sulawesi, 2.7 million in Nusa Tenggara, and 1 million in Papua. Chapter 2 showed that Honduras and Vietnam have similar (overlapping) geographic distributions of economic production and poor people.

Using a sharper geographic resolution, a similar distribution of the population can be discerned *within* lagging areas. The northeast of Brazil is the country's poorest area. Per capita incomes in the southeast were 2.9 times that of the northeast in 1939, and 2.8 times in 1992. Eight of the 10 poorest states are in the northeast, two in the north.[1] The poverty rate is clearly high in the rural northeast and Amazon areas (see map 8.2). But even in the northeast, the mass and concentration of poverty—the number of poor people per square kilometer—is much higher in urbanized agglomerations near the coast, from the lagging northeast all the way to the dynamic regions of Rio de Janeiro and São Paulo in the southeast.[2]

In some countries the market forces prompting factor mobility are not quite as strong. Their economic mass and poverty mass do not coincide nearly as much as in countries such as China and Honduras. Consider India, where more than 400 million people live in "lagging states" in the north-central part of the country, which includes—using the country's poverty

Map 8.2 The poverty rate is high in Brazil's Northeast and Amazon areas, but the poor are massed in areas along the coast

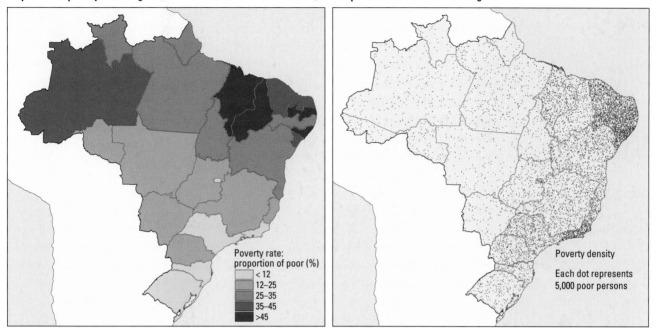

Poverty rate:
proportion of poor (%)

< 12
12–25
25–35
35–45
>45

Poverty density

Each dot represents
5,000 poor persons

Source: State-level poverty rates computed by Phillippe G. Leite, based on the Brazil Household Budget Survey (*Pesquisa de Orcamentos Familiares*) 2002–03 (see World Bank 2007c).

line—60 percent of the nation's poor (see map 8.3).[3] Labor mobility from these areas has been limited due to ethnolinguistic and class-based divisions, perhaps inclining people to stay in their own "enclaves."

People are in these lagging areas for a reason. With rich soils and good internal connections, the fertile Indo-Gangetic plain attracted people. These areas were historically among India's most dynamic locations when the country accounted for a quarter of the world's gross domestic product (GDP), between 1600 and 1700.[4] But historical "accidents," such as making landlords responsible for paying land taxes to the British crown in these areas, eroded agricultural productivity and infrastructure investments.[5] India is now reintegrating into the world economy, resulting in economic dynamism in its coastal and metropolitan areas. These areas offer good access to intermediate inputs and domestic and international markets, provide reliable and high-quality local public services, and have a business environment conducive to entrepreneurship. About half of manufacturing investments in 2005 were concentrated in only 10 of the country's more than 3,000 cities, the ones offering

better access to domestic and international markets.[6]

Should today's policy makers try to correct historical accidents by reviving investments in lagging areas and helping them regain their past glory? Or should they accelerate India's integration with the global economy and help people in lagging areas take advantage of new opportunities in places with greater economic density?

India's national policy discussion in the mid-1970s focused on promoting spatially balanced growth to revive the lagging areas with subsidized finance, investment subsidies, industrial infrastructure, and preferential industrial licensing. India's latest five-year plan recognizes the failures of industrial licensing and its inconsistency with growth. The discussion today is more about integration and the shift toward promoting better health and education in lagging areas, along with strategic interregional infrastructure investments that connect the remote northeast with markets in the rest of the country.[7] Similar regional development policies have been implemented in other countries with internal divisions along religious or ethnic lines, such as Nigeria and Ethiopia.

Map 8.3   Both the poverty rate and poverty mass are high in some of India's lagging states

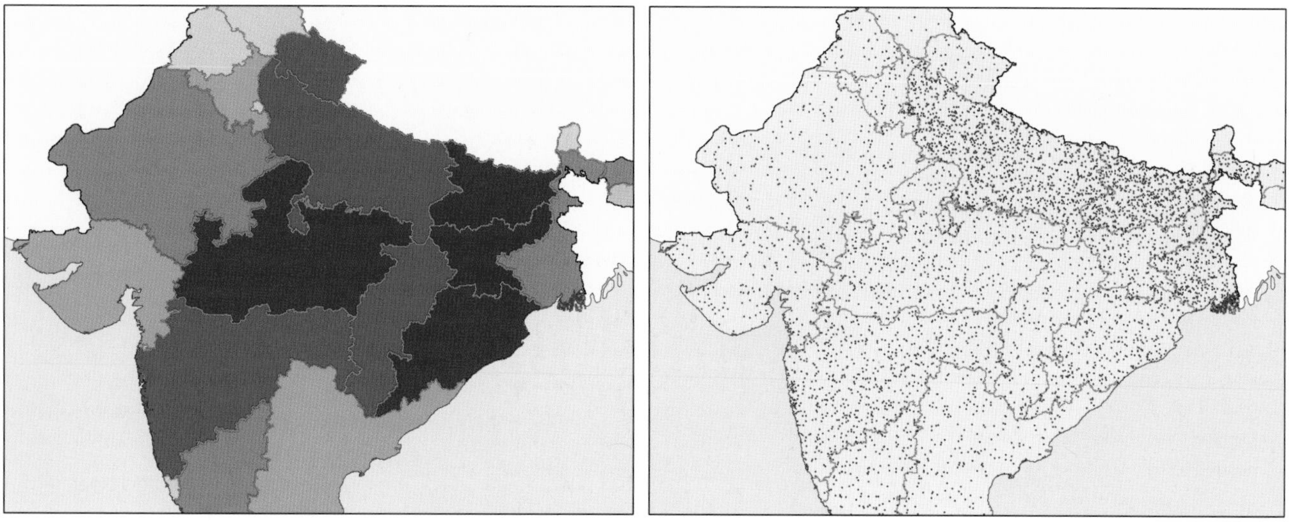

Poverty rate:
proportion of poor (%)
- 6.4–9.7
- 9.8–16.7
- 16.8–24.8
- 24.9–35.4
- 35.5–46.6
- No data

Poverty density

Each dot represents
50,000 poor persons

Source: Based on poverty estimates for 2004–05 from the Planning Commission, Government of India.
Note: State-level poverty rates and counts are based on the sum of the number of urban poor and rural poor in 2004–05, which are calculated using different poverty lines.

Policies aimed at reducing such divisions have reinforced a natural tendency of people to seek places that offer better economic opportunities. Take the well-studied German unification, a merger of two economies with few exchanges of goods and factors that propelled people from the east to the west. The opportunity arose in the summer of 1989, when people could leave East Germany through Hungary. And with the fall of the Berlin wall on November 9, 1989, direct migration from East to West Germany became possible. With the border open, 800,000 people left the east for the west in 1989 and 1990, 5 percent of the eastern population (see box 8.2).[8] Clearly, the German unification started a move to density. It suggests that reducing distance to economic density improves people's welfare, and labor mobility is the strongest natural mechanism for this.

Countries seek unity

Many countries have spatial differences in production and poverty, mostly because of economic distance between lagging and leading areas, and also because of divisions from political, ethnic, religious, and linguistic differences. And all countries seek unity, by lowering the barriers of internal divisions. A review of national constitutions from 20 developing countries shows that promoting unity—reducing divisions—is an important political objective (see box 8.2). In Nigeria an important article of unity is that people will not be discriminated by sex, religion, place of birth, ethnic, or linguistic association. In India Article 16 of the constitution states that "no citizen shall, on grounds only of religion, race, caste, sex, descent, place of birth, residence or any of them, be ineligible for, or discriminated against in respect of, any employment or office under the State." For the most part, constitutions do not make *places* paramount—they focus instead on the welfare and unity of *people* (see box 8.3).

Unity does not mean uniformity. India's national motto, for example, is "unity in diversity." But in many countries, policy makers have viewed uniformity as the main vehicle for unity. The European Union (EU)

BOX 8.2   *The German integration: convergence and concentration with mobile labor*

With the fall of the Berlin wall in 1989, direct migration from East to West Germany became possible. Opening the border led 400,000 people to leave the east to the west in 1989 and again in 1990, about 5 percent of the eastern population (see the left figure). In later years, incomes started to converge and the process slowed. In 2001 a recession in Germany again led about 100,000 people to leave the east for the west. By 2007 more than 1.7 million people had left the east (of about 17 million at the time of the fall of the Berlin wall).

Migration produced one predictable outcome: incomes became more equal between the two areas (see the right figure). While the cross-country distribution of income in 1992 was clearly bimodal, with the counties in the east forming the lower peak, this was smoothed by 2005. Although the counties from the east are still located at the left of the distribution, their economic distance to western counties has shortened.

Convergence in incomes has also produced more surprising outcomes. Almost all counties with more young women than men are in the economically dynamic areas of Germany, which also have better

Migration from East to West Germany was possible after the fall of the Berlin wall
Net migration from East to West Germany, 1991–2005

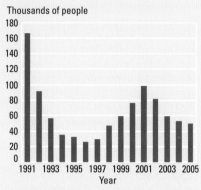

Source: Federal Statistical Office Germany 2007.

Convergence of income across German counties was noticeable between 1992 and 2005

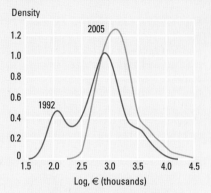

Source: Holzmann, Priebe, and Vollmer 2008.

institutions of higher learning (see the map below). In 2004, in the 18–29 age-group, there were only 90 women for every 100 men in East Germany (including Berlin).

Why did East German women move to the economically dynamic areas, while men stay in the lagging areas? There are two explanations. First, women are on average more successful in school and higher education, which makes it easier

for them to study or to find a job in the economically more dynamic parts of Germany. Second, it is much harder for women to find an attractive job locally in the lagging areas than it is for men, because these areas are typically dominated by traditionally male jobs in agriculture, manufacturing, and construction.

Sources: WDR 2009 team, based on Kroehnert and Vollmer 2008.

Women moved to the west seeking economic opportunity: in 2003, there were fewer women per 100 men in the eastern part of the country (left), and higher taxpayer incomes in the west (right)

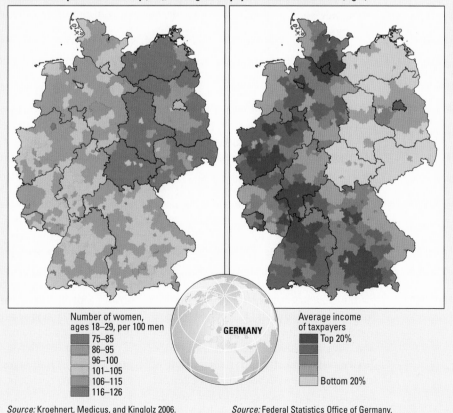

Number of women, ages 18–29, per 100 men
- 75–85
- 86–95
- 96–100
- 101–105
- 106–115
- 116–126

GERMANY

Average income of taxpayers
- Top 20%
- Bottom 20%

Source: Kroehnert, Medicus, and Kinglolz 2006.

Source: Federal Statistics Office of Germany.

BOX 8.3 *Constitutions call for unity, not uniformity*

National constitutions reflect the evolution of political discourse in most countries and define interactions between the state and its citizens. A review of constitutions from 20 developing countries[a] finds that all emphasize national unity as an important national objective. Uniformity in economic outcomes across areas is mentioned only in one—Brazil's constitution. Universal access to primary education and basic health care are constitutional mandates in most countries.

Excerpts from the constitutional articles of three African countries highlight the importance that societies place on national unity and integration:

Nigeria: "The motto of the Federal Republic of Nigeria shall be Unity and Faith, Peace and Progress." Article 15 (2)—"Accordingly, national integration shall be actively encouraged, whilst discrimination on the grounds of place of birth, sex, religion, status, ethnic or linguistic association or ties shall be pro-

hibited." Article 15 (3)—"For the purpose of promoting national integration, it shall be the duty of the State to: (a) provide adequate facilities for and encourage free mobility of people, goods and services throughout the Federation; (b) secure full residence rights for every citizen in all parts of the Federation."

Côte d'Ivoire: Article 30—"The Republic of Côte d'Ivoire shall be one and indivisible, secular, democratic and social. The Republic shall ensure equality before the law to all without distinction as to origin, race, sex or religion. It shall respect all beliefs." Its principle shall be: "Government of the people, by the people and for the people."

Uganda: Article 3—"(i) All organs of the State and people of Uganda shall work towards the promotion of national unity, peace and stability. (ii) Every effort shall be made to integrate all the peoples of Uganda while at the same time recognizing the existence of their ethnic, religious, ideological, political and cultural diversity."

Brazil's constitution calls for regionally balanced economic development, setting out guidelines to promote capital flows to lagging areas. The translation of these guidelines into practice has not produced the expected economic gains. And the programs have been costly. The Constitution Funds—a prominent regional economic development program—provided subsidized credit worth more than $10 billion between 1990 and 2002 to help firms locate in lagging areas. The ineffectiveness of these interventions is evaluated elsewhere in this chapter.

Source: WDR 2009 team; based on a review of constitutions from 20 developing countries. a. The countries are Argentina, Bolivia, Brazil, Colombia, and Mexico (LAC); Côte d'Ivoire, Ghana, Nigeria, and Uganda (AFR); Bangladesh, India, Nepal, and Pakistan (SAR); Kazakhstan, Poland, and the Russian Federation (ECA); China, Indonesia, and the Philippines (EAP); and the Arab Republic of Egypt (MENA).

---

policies to integrate new member states call for "cohesion." But the objective of cohesion—or unity—is pursued through policies for convergence. Convergence targets include eliminating territorial disparities in economic development (economic cohesion) and in access to labor and income (social cohesion). This "cohesion" is matched by the EU regional policy, which allocates about 60 percent of its funding to support areas of low development (less than 75 percent of the EU average GDP per capita).[9]

Accounting for 35 percent of total spending of the EU, the EU cohesion policy is translated into practice through structural funds (90 percent of spending) and the cohesion fund (10 percent). The Agenda 2000 package comes with a price tag of €236 billion, with €195 billion for structural funds; €18 billion for the cohesion funds for Greece, Ireland, Portugal, and Spain; and €22 billion for new member states, in view of their 2004 accession.[10] Agenda 2000's objectives include the development and structural adjustment of lagging areas, the development of border areas and areas in industrial decline, and the adaptation and modernization of education

and training systems.[11] The cohesion policy aims to improve economic performance of specific areas and help them catch up with the rest of the union.

Resource allocations of this scale to support integration may reflect the redistribution preferences of member states (particularly the ones whose residents are footing the bill), but do these policies stimulate overall growth? Are they paying for the "wrong" type of assets? Academic research shows that they are not well suited to maximizing aggregate economic growth because they try to promote spatial evenness and not agglomeration. Nor are they especially well suited to promoting catch-up by lagging areas. Traditional cohesion policies that provide "hard" infrastructure and assistance to firms are unlikely to increase the competitiveness of lagging areas.[12] Moving away from these programs to support education programs and institutional development could do much more.

Trying to use the same instrument to pursue dual challenges of internal and external convergence is likely to make the policy lose focus. The EU's fourth report on economic and social cohesion provides a candid assessment of convergence across its regions and within individual countries.[13] Between 1995 and 2004, there was a tendency of aggregate convergence in the EU, with new member states with lower GDP per capita growing faster than the EU-27 average. But at a more disaggregated Nomenclature of Territorial Units for Statistics (NUTS) 2 regional level—subnational areas larger than administrative units in most countries—the results show little effectiveness of directed interventions in improving economic performance of lagging areas. For the better-off EU-15, the number of people in lagging regions has remained almost unchanged at 32 million, around 8 percent of the total. When the new member states are considered, there has been international convergence in

per capita incomes. But the concentration of economic production within member states—new and old—has been increasing, led by market forces driving faster economic growth in their leading areas. Indeed per capita incomes in several areas in some new member states—Bratislavský kraj in the Slovak Republic, Közép-Magyarország in Hungary, Mazoweickie in Poland, and Zahodna Slovenija in Slovenia—have risen to more than 75 percent of the EU average.

Ireland took a different approach for using EU funds. Rather than try to use the EU funds to achieve both international catch-up and to disperse economic production domestically, Ireland focused on one objective—national economic growth. From being one of Europe's poorest countries, it is now one of the richest (see box 8.4). Between

---

BOX 8.4 *An instrument per objective: Ireland used EU funds for international convergence*

Between 1977 and 2000, Ireland's GDP per capita grew from 72 percent of the EU average to 116 percent. What was behind Ireland's success?

Since joining the European Union in 1973, Ireland received approximately €17 billion in EU Structural and Cohesion Funds through the end of 2003. In the first two rounds of EU funding, the entire country was classified as an Objective One area. Between 1993 and 2003 cohesion funds supported 120 infrastructure projects at the cost of about €2 billion.[a] The choice of projects was based on a national development plan, which focused on investments in economic infrastructure that stimulated long-term national economic growth. These included investments in leading areas and in connecting leading and lagging areas, such as the M50 (Dublin Ring Road), M1 (Dublin-Belfast), and improvements in the N4 (Dublin-Sligo), N7 (Dublin-Limerick), and N11 (Dublin-Rosslare).

The Irish also invested in education, training, and lifelong learning in all of Ireland to provide investors with a good business environment countrywide. With its skilled labor force and good logistics, Ireland has become a popular destination for American firms wishing to reach European markets. In 2004 Irish-based U.S. firms exported $55 billion worth of goods and services, mostly destined for Europe.

Ireland's rapid convergence toward the incomes of Europe's leaders was accompanied by a rising spatial concentration of economic activity. Compared with the other cohesion countries—Greece, Portugal, and Spain—Ireland's economic concentration rose much more (see the figure below). But its per capita income grew much faster too. In 1977 Greece, Ireland, and Spain had per capita incomes of about $9,000; Portugal's was about $6,000. By 2002 Portugal had an income of $11,000, and Greece and Spain close to $15,000. Ireland's per capita income had risen to $27,500.

Today, almost all regions in the new member nations in Eastern Europe qualify for EU financial support. They should consider the Irish example of using the funds for international convergence and not—until later stages—for spatially balanced economic growth within their borders.

Sources: Dall'Erba 2003, WDR 2009 team.
a. Ireland's National Development Plan (NDP) 2000–06.

As Ireland's income rapidly grew, economic concentration increased within the country

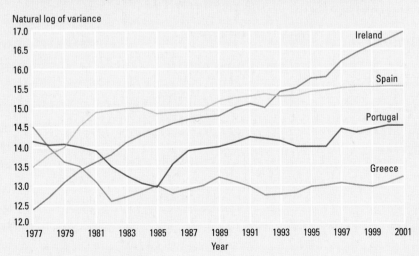

Sources: Dall'Erba 2003; WDR 2009 team.

1991 and 1998 Ireland was just one region for the purposes of Objective One support from the EU.[14] When the country grew past the 75 percent threshold, in July 1999, Ireland created two regional "assemblies"—Border-Midland-Western, and the Southern and Eastern. But spatial concentration of economic production has increased in Ireland relative to Greece, Portugal, and Spain, the other three cohesion countries.[15]

A policy framework for integrating lagging and leading areas

People seek opportunity, and countries seek unity. Policies that integrate lagging and leading areas can help with both. This section outlines a framework to guide policy making. It proposes a calibrated combination of institutions, infrastructure, and incentives to address the domestic challenges posed by density, distance, and division. Used well, a combination of these measures can help countries reap the economic benefits from increasing concentration of economic activity, as well as the social, political, and economic payoffs associated with converging living standards between lagging and leading areas.

Policy makers, often viewing economic concentration as inconsistent with spatial equity in living standards, have sought to reduce concentration through spatially targeted interventions. Many governments fight market forces that promote the concentration of people in economically dense

places. Indonesia's transmigration program tried to relocate people from densely populated Java to less densely populated areas of Kalimantan, Papua, Sulawesi, and Sumatra. At its peak between 1979 and 1984, 535,000 families or almost 2.5 million people were relocated. The objective was to promote "balanced demographic development" and reduce poverty by providing land and new economic opportunities for poor landless settlers. But the program made almost no dent in the population density of Java, nor did the high cost of the program reduce poverty much among the migrants.[16]

Relying solely on spatially targeted interventions is a common mistake. It is far better to rely on institutions that work less noisily. In France the concentration of economic mass and convergence of disposable incomes between leading and lagging areas have been concurrent, producing a "scissors effect" in the geographies of production and disposable income (see figure 8.1).[17] The effect appears to be driven not by spatially focused interventions but by spatially blind or "universal" progressive income taxation, social security, and unemployment benefits. Although space is not explicitly considered in such policies, their effects and outcomes can vary considerably across locations. As the base of economic integration, such "institutions" capture the benefits of spatial concentration of production and deliver convergence in living standards.

Even in the EU as a whole, the rising inequality of market incomes between 1985 and 1995 was partially offset by progressive tax and transfer policies. Increases in the income of skilled people were moderated through higher taxes, and the unskilled were aided with transfers.[18] Similarly, the progressive tax structure in the United States reduced disparities in disposable incomes across states, while production became more concentrated, although the extent has varied greatly over time as government policies changed (see box 8.5).

The experience of the EU and the United States in addressing spatial equity with aspatial tax systems is instructive. Skeptics might counter that the coverage of the tax system is low in developing countries and that weak tax administration and

Figure 8.1 France has benefited from increasing concentration of economic production and declining spatial disparities in disposable income

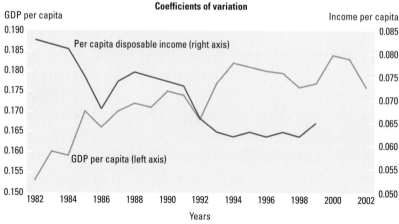

Source: Martin 2005.

BOX 8.5 *Taxation against spatial inequality? The U.S. federal income tax system*

A progressive federal income tax in the United States has reduced income inequalities among people. An unintended effect has been to reduce income inequalities across states, showing that a spatially blind policy can be a sharp instrument for reducing spatial inequalities.

Data from the Internal Revenue Service show how much the income tax reduced spatial inequality. To see this, first, pretax incomes of the top percentile of earners in each state are divided by the U.S. personal income, as published by the Bureau of Economic Analysis. Next, the same income dispersion ratio is calculated with post-tax incomes. Then, the percentage decrease between the pretax and post-

tax income ratios for two groups of 10 states are calculated: one recording the highest pretax incomes (Group 1), and the other the lowest (Group 2).[a] The figure below shows the change in post-tax income differences between the richest and poorest states. Directly imputable to taxation, it shows how the U.S. taxation system has helped to reduce income inequalities across states.

Never had the tax rate been higher than in 1918, at 77 percent to finance the war. After World War I, tax rates declined. Lowered to 24 percent in 1929, the tax rate for top incomes rose again during the Great Depression (–26 percent in 1940 versus –7 percent in 1930 for Group

1). When Congress introduced payroll withholding and quarterly tax payments during World War II, the progressive tax system was reinforced. But these inequality-reducing effects started fading away between 1950 and 1970. A brief rise in these effects during the late 1970s was followed by a fall in the 1980s and 1990s.

Source: WDR 2009 team.
a. Although both groups belong to the richest 1 percent of their respective states, keep in mind the sharp differences from one state to another. In 1940, for instance, an income of about $47,000 made a tax filer part of the wealthiest 1 percent in Mississippi, but part of the wealthiest 10 percent in the District of Columbia.

Without an explicit spatial focus, U.S. federal income taxes reduce spatial disparities

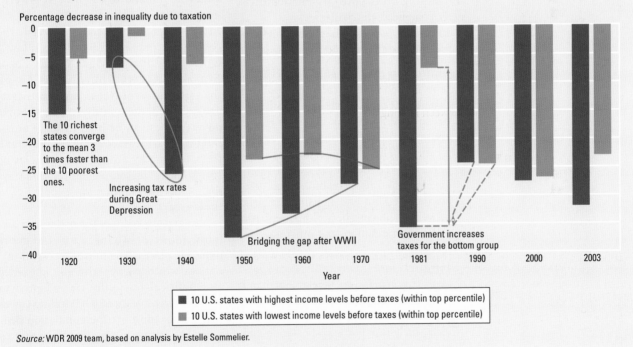

Source: WDR 2009 team, based on analysis by Estelle Sommelier.

widespread informality in the economy will reduce the potential benefits of progressive taxes. But it is worth remembering that a century ago, when its tax system was introduced, the United States exhibited many of the attributes of a developing country today. Its population was mainly rural, with just 28 percent living in metropolitan areas in 1910.[19] Wages were $0.72 an hour in

the automobile industry in 1925.[20] The tax coverage and revenues were low, with only 10 percent of the households filing an individual tax return in 1916; today the ratio is 93 percent.

Some evidence from developing countries points to the fact that income redistribution through a progressive tax system is difficult, and that the targeting of expenditures by individual or household income levels and the level of the average tax rate are more important for the post-transfer income distribution. Thus a high-yield proportional tax system may have a larger equalizing impact than a low-yield progressive tax system.[21]

Spatially blind tax and transfer policies will form the bedrock of public policies to integrate countries spatially and help them benefit from concentration and convergence. But these policies may not be enough. Depending on their conditions, nations need a broader range of instruments for domestic integration. The challenge of economic integration can be seen as reducing the distance between people—especially the poor—and economic opportunity. Misplaced population densities, and barriers to mobility of workers and entrepreneurs between leading and lagging areas posed by internal divisions, complicate the challenge.

In general, a policy framework for economic integration includes the following:

- **Institutions** (spatially blind policies). The term is used here to categorize policies that are not explicitly designed with spatial considerations, but that have effects and outcomes that may vary across locations. These include such national policies as the income tax system, intergovernmental fiscal relations, and governance of land and housing markets, as well as education, health care, basic water and sanitation, and other government initiatives.
- **Infrastructure** (spatially connective policies). The term is used here as shorthand to include all investments that connect places and provide basic business services, such as public transportation and utilities. These include developing interregional highways and railroads to promote trade in goods—and improving information and communication technologies to increase the flow of information and ideas.
- **Incentives** (spatially focused policies). The term is used here to include spatially targeted measures to stimulate economic growth in lagging areas. These include investment subsidies, tax rebates, loca-

tion regulations, local infrastructure development, and targeted investment climate reforms, such as special regulations for export processing zones.

These instruments for integration—institutions, infrastructure, and incentives—span the range between universal and geographically targeted policies. Each of the three categories can include taxes, public spending, and regulations.

Adverse physical geography generally increases economic distance, reducing trade of goods and services and the flow of labor, capital, and information, making delivery of public services harder. In Papua New Guinea, with the transport system fragmented by a rugged mountainous terrain, the average travel time from a rural community to the nearest road is two and a half hours. and to the nearest government station is more than three hours.[22] In the more rugged parts of Peru, the coverage of public infrastructure is low.[23] Other such places include Chile's *Zonas Extremas*, western China, Upper Egypt, the outer areas of Nepal, and northeastern Russia. Because of adverse conditions, poverty rates can be high in these areas. But for the same reasons, unless prevented from leaving by government policies or sociopolitical reasons, or enticed into staying by incentives, not many people live in these areas.

Integration reduces the economic distance between lagging areas and more dynamic places. The most successful initiatives, which balance economic efficiency and political feasibility, are adapted to country circumstances. The circumstances that matter most are the population densities in lagging areas and the extent to which domestic divisions weaken market forces. Where few people live in lagging areas, as in northeastern Russia, integration policies should be different from those in places such as northeastern Brazil, where lagging areas are densely populated. Where lagging and leading areas share a common language and customs, as in Brazil and China, integration policies have to exert less effort than in areas where differences in language, ethnicity, or religion divide one part of a country from another, as in India or Nigeria.

In Brazil the distance between the lagging northeast and the leading southeast is coupled with high population densities in the coastal areas of the northeast. But many *Nordestinos* have found opportunities by moving to the dynamic southeast. As many as 4 million residents of Greater São Paulo are *Nordestinos*.[24] This indicates the high population density in the northeast and the strong market forces of labor mobility, made possible by factors such as a common language and a strong national identity.

Recall the maps of India, where some lagging areas have a high poverty mass and high poverty rate (see map 8.3). Integrating these areas is especially challenging when subnational geographic groupings reflect ethnic, linguistic, or social differences.[25] The movement of people out of these areas has been limited because of local preferences and discrimination against particular groups (see chapter 5). Market forces of factor mobility have been weakened by internal political and social divisions—witness the hostility that Bihari workers have encountered in the more prosperous parts of India. In such nations, the integration challenge involves overcoming economic distance, misplaced density, *and* domestic division.

Using the spatial dimensions of distance, density, and division to characterize conditions in a country, a suggestive taxonomy can be developed to help countries tailor integration policies to their specific economic geography. At least three types of countries can be distinguished:

- *Type 1:* countries with sparsely populated lagging areas
- *Type 2:* unified countries with densely populated lagging areas
- *Type 3:* divided countries with densely populated lagging areas

This taxonomy can characterize lagging areas in most countries, but two qualifications are necessary. First, lagging areas in some countries may be sufficiently heterogeneous that it is difficult to neatly classify them into one of these types. In Thailand the northeast is densely populated and distant from the economically dense capital area, but the sparsely populated south is home to its Muslim minority. In India the lagging northeast is sparsely populated, whereas lagging areas in central India have almost two-thirds of India's poor. Second, countries classified as Type 1 (with sparsely populated lagging areas) can be unified or internally divided. But the strategies for integration in these two types of countries—unified countries with sparsely populated lagging areas such as Russia, or divided countries with sparsely populated lagging areas such as the Philippines—will not be different.

An instrument per dimension

Institutions to overcome distance. In countries with sparsely populated lagging areas, the integration challenge is mainly one of reducing economic distance. Policies that are universal—spatially blind in their design and national in their coverage—can shoulder much of the task of successful economic integration. Developing countries in this category include Chile, China, Ghana, Indonesia, Kenya, Mexico, Mongolia, Kazakhstan, Russia, Sri Lanka, Uganda, and Vietnam. The primary objective of these policies should be to encourage people migrate to places with economic opportunities. For example, as Russia moves further from plan to market, it will have to offset a legacy of policies industrializing its vast territory. Even today, millions of people are subsidized to live in "cold" and isolated places in the northeast (see map 8.4), where they cannot take advantage of new economic opportunities in the dynamic areas of the west.[26]

Correcting land market distortions, removing restrictions on mobility, and providing essential services such as basic education, health care, water, and sanitation should be universal policy priorities. The costs associated with land sales—including fees, survey costs, and transfer fees—can make land transactions prohibitively expensive. In Russia the fees for private surveying are equivalent to two years' minimum wages. These costs could slow migration by

Map 8.4   In the Russian Federation, population densities are highest in the economically vibrant and warmer west, but a communist legacy has left some people in the cold interior

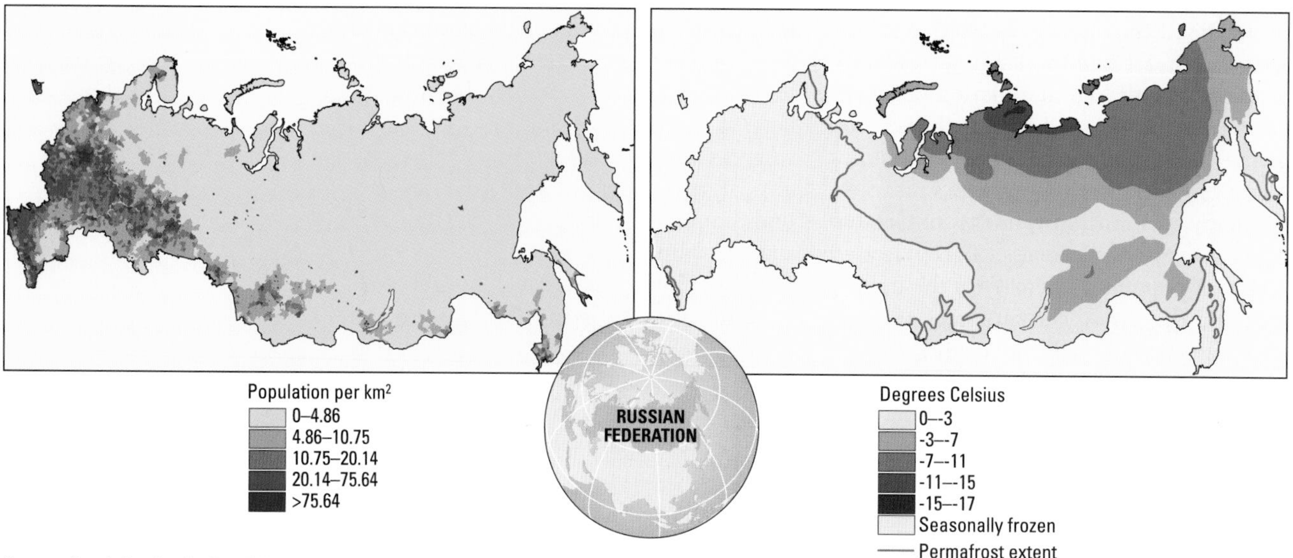

Population per km²
- 0–4.86
- 4.86–10.75
- 10.75–20.14
- 20.14–75.64
- >75.64

RUSSIAN FEDERATION

Degrees Celsius
- 0–-3
- -3–-7
- -7–-11
- -11–-15
- -15–-17
- Seasonally frozen
- Permafrost extent

Sources: Population density: Fay, Felkner, and Lall 2008; Ice Thickness: National Snow and Ice Data Center 2007.

reducing the ability of less wealthy people to transact in land.[27] China's household registration system (the *hukou* system) has been a barrier to rural-urban migration. Not having an urban *hukou* in urban areas means that migrants may not qualify for public education or health benefits. This can produce large interregional wage differences. Recent research indicates that removing such mobility restrictions would reallocate labor across areas, reduce wage differences, and lower income inequality.[28] But the benefits depend on the response of the urban housing market to additional demand from newcomers.

Some countries can have sparsely populated lagging areas and domestic divisions. In Lao People's Democratic Republic, ethnic heterogeneity may make labor less mobile. Vientiane, the leading area, has a relatively low poverty rate, while the provinces in the north and south have higher rates (see map 8.5). But the poor are spread out quite uniformly across the country. In such cases, much of the policy response still should be spatially neutral, with special efforts to ensure equal access to public services to people in these areas. Afghanistan and Tajikistan are other examples of countries with divisions and sparsely populated lagging areas.

Other countries may have just a few lagging areas that are sparsely populated and divided. In Indonesia, an otherwise unified country, places like Aceh are considered lagging areas, with divisions that weaken labor and capital mobility. Policy makers may be tempted to provide economic incentives for firms in these areas to compensate for the lack of factor mobility, but the accompanying risk of creating enclaves of development and deepening existing divisions should be considered. Instead, initiatives that promote economic integration by increasing factor mobility may be better suited for both economic and political reasons. Examples include spatially targeted programs to improve education and equal opportunity legislation to ensure that workers from lagging areas do not face labor market discrimination in other parts of the country.

Institutions and infrastructure to overcome distance and density. When distance is coupled with high population densities in lagging areas, spatially connective infrastructure is also necessary. Countries in this category include Bangladesh, Brazil, Colombia, the Arab Republic of Egypt, Thailand, and Turkey. Isolation from markets in more dynamic parts of the country (or the world) can reduce consumer welfare, as residents face higher prices because of market fragmentation, and workers and producers have less access to markets. In principle, infrastructure investments that connect peripheral areas to markets should improve both consumer welfare and productive efficiency.

With sizable concentrations of the poor in lagging areas, spatially blind institutions that promote the mobility of labor and capital and ensure the provision of basic services must be aided by policies to improve the access of entrepreneurs in lagging areas to markets. Although migration will aid spatial efficiency and equity, with large numbers of the poor in lagging areas, this could take a long time (see chapter 5). Better infrastructural links between lagging and leading areas, by improving market access, may allow some activities to flourish in lagging areas. But they may increase the concentration of economic activity in *leading* areas, because firms that value agglomeration benefits will now be able to serve lagging area markets from farther away (see chapter 6). Activities that respond to better infrastructure in lagging areas are those that do not exhibit agglomeration economies—agriculture, agroprocessing, and labor-intensive manufacturing such as leather and wood products (see chapter 4).

A useful way to conceptualize how infrastructure investments improve connectivity is to think about a measure of market access that captures the size and density of market centers and the quality of transport networks that link different locations to these centers. The measure comes from the gravity model used to analyze trade between areas and countries, with the interaction between two places proportional to their size (population or economic density) and inversely proportional to the distance between them (see box 8.6).

Consider the Arab Republic of Egypt. The location of human settlements has been dictated by a dominant natural geography constraint—access to water. Most people, in leading areas around Cairo and Alexandria as well as lagging areas in Upper Egypt around Aswan and Qena, live along the Nile (see map 8.6). As in the densely populated coastal zone in Brazil, institutions to integrate Egypt need to be complemented with connective infrastructure to ensure both

Map 8.5   In the Lao People's Democratic Republic, the poverty rate is high outside the capital region, but poor people are scattered in remote communities

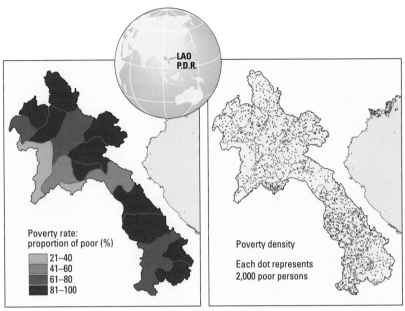

Poverty rate: proportion of poor (%)
- 21–40
- 41–60
- 61–80
- 81–100

Poverty density

Each dot represents 2,000 poor persons

Source: Richter, van der Weide, and Souksavath 2005.
Note: Dots are placed randomly within each province and do not reflect population distribution.

spatial efficiency in production and spatially egalitarian living standards.

There is a long history of using connective infrastructure to integrate peripheral areas with national markets. When accompanied by institutions that integrate nations, such infrastructure investments can pay off. In the United States, the Congress passed the Appalachian Regional Development Act in 1965, relying on spatially blind institutions and connective infrastructure to integrate the 22 million people in this lagging area, which spans 13 states, with the rest of the country.[29] The basic strategy combined regionally coordinated social programs and physical infrastructure. The 1965 Act allocated 85 percent of the funds for highways—seen as critical to meeting other socioeconomic objectives—and, cumulatively, highways have accounted for more than 60 percent of the appropriated funds through the mid-1990s. Other investments included hospitals and treatment centers, land conservation, mineland restoration, flood control and water resource management, vocational education facilities, and sewage treatment works. Between 1965 and 1991, total personal income and earnings

BOX 8.6   *Low market access in Mexico's lagging south*

Quantitative information on regional or local market integration is scarce. Summary statistics—such as the road length in a state or province or the straight-line distance to ports or urban agglomerations—are poor proxies for the complexity of a national or regional transportation network. To improve on them, a geographic representation of Mexico's transport network is used to compute an index of accessibility for each *municipio* in the country as a simple measure of potential market integration.

This index summarizes the size of the potential market that can be reached from a particular point given the density and quality of the transport network in that region. For any point in the country, it is the sum of the population of urban centers surrounding that point, inversely weighted by the travel time to reach

that center. It is computed using an up-to-date digital map of transportation infrastructure from the Mexican statistical agency (*Instituto Nacional de Estadística y Geografía,* INEGI).[a] For each road segment, the database indicates the number of lanes and whether those lanes are paved or unpaved—and for railroad lines, the number of tracks. For each category of road or rail, average travel speeds are estimated to calculate how long it will take to traverse each segment in the transport network.[b] Urban population data from the INEGI database indicate the location and population size of about 700 cities and agglomerations in Mexico. These urban centers accounted for about 68 million of Mexico's 97 million people in 2000.

The map of market access (below) shows high values of the index around

the federal district, thanks to concentrations of people and infrastructure. A quarter of Mexico's GDP is generated within two hours' travel time from the center of the Federal District. The southern states of Chiapas, Guerrero, and Oaxaca, the poorest areas, have low market access.

Source: Deichmann, Fay, Koo, and Lall 2004.
a. The digital road and rail network includes 171,000 kms of roads, of which 84,000 kms are paved roads; 51,000 are unpaved; and 36,000 are paths and breaches. The rail network has an estimated total length of 14,000 kms. These values are calculated by a geographic information system (GIS) from 1:1 million scale digital maps and may not necessarily match official statistics.
b. Using travel time on a transport network provides a more accurate measure of accessibility compared with the computationally much simpler straight-line distance, as employed, for example, by Hanson (1998).

Market access in Mexico is highest around the national capital and low in the lagging southern states

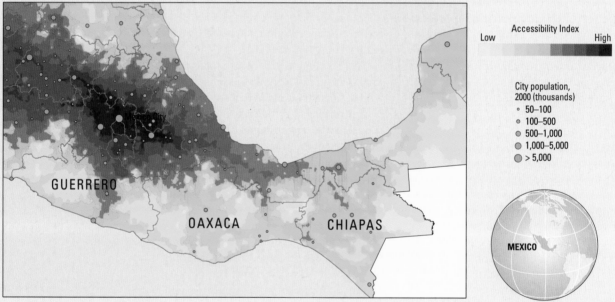

Source: Deichmann, Fay, Koo, and Lall 2004.

grew 48 percentage points faster on average in the Appalachian counties than in their economic "sisters," population grew 5 points faster, and per capita income grew 17 points faster.[30]

Institutions, infrastructure, and incentives to overcome distance, density, and division. When countries face divisions

caused by ethnolinguistic or religious heterogeneity, the forces of factor mobility can be weak even over relatively short distances. Examples include India and Nigeria. In such cases, spatially focused incentives may need to complement institutions and infrastructure to encourage economic production in lagging areas. Commonly used

Map 8.6   In the Arab Republic of Egypt, population densities are high in lagging areas, and connective infrastructure is needed to help spatial integration

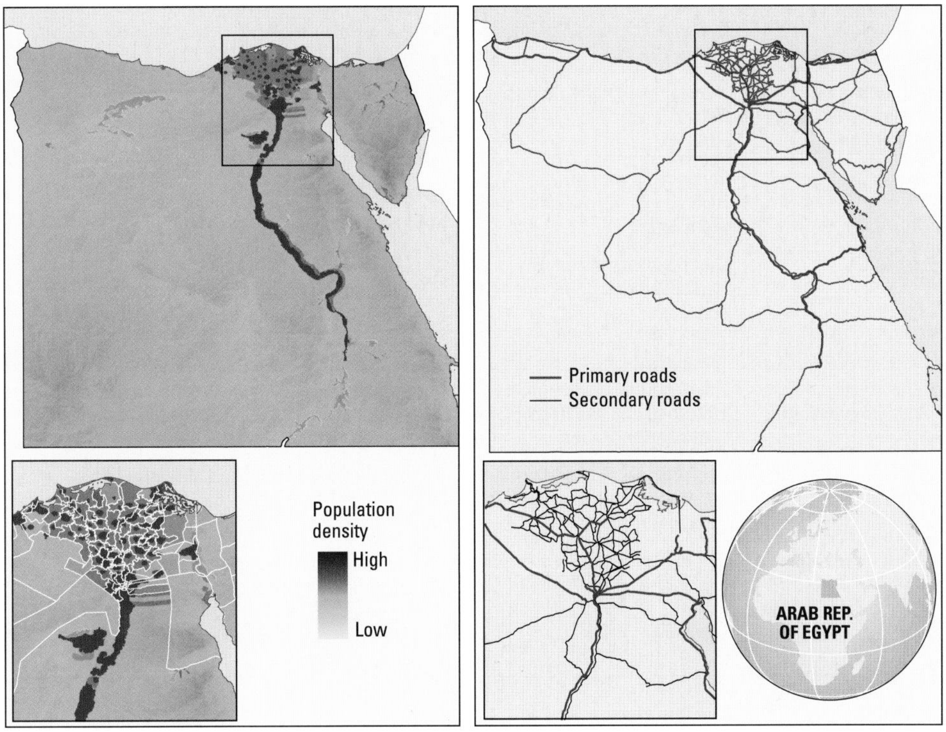

Source: World Bank 2008b.

incentives include fiscal incentives and subsidies, special economic zones, industry location regulations, and investment climate improvements.

Only a few countries face the triple challenges of distance, density, and division. Nevertheless, incentives to promote economic development in lagging areas have been widespread. The experience has been disheartening.[31] In good measure this has been because incentives have been used instead of, rather than in addition to, integrative institutions and infrastructure. More often than not, geographically targeted incentives would not even be necessary if the policy objective was to integrate leading and lagging areas, rather than promote industry in economically unfavorable places.

Table 8.1 summarizes policy options for domestic integration using a calibrated combination of institutions, infrastructure, and incentives. Policy makers should keep three points in mind in designing integration strategies. First, policies should focus primarily on improving the welfare of people, encouraging them to seek economic opportunities *wherever they arise.* Second, they should help unify countries in the long term. Internal divisions may be a short-run constraint for economic integration, but the diminution of division should be a long-term objective. Third, policies that try to offset constraints posed by divisions should not inadvertently strengthen them. For example, making land and labor laws or school systems different in lagging areas may weaken economic and political integration.

The framework in action

This section uses the framework to discuss how countries have used specific policies to integrate lagging and leading areas.

Institutions that promote portable investments

Investing in human capital. Universal primary education and basic health are mandated across a broad range of developing countries, as shown by the review of national constitutions discussed earlier. For

Table 8.1   An instrument per dimension—a framework for area, territorial, or regional development policies

	Country type		
	Sparsely populated lagging areas	**Densely populated lagging areas in united countries**	**Densely populated lagging areas in divided countries**
Examples (countries)	Chile, China, Ghana, Honduras, Pakistan, Peru, Russian Federation, Sri Lanka, Uganda, Vietnam	Bangladesh, Brazil, Colombia, Arab Rep. of Egypt, Mexico, Thailand, Turkey	India, Nigeria
Dimensions of the integration challenge	Economic distance (1-D)	Economic distance High population densities in lagging areas (2-D)	Economic distance High population densities Internal divisions (3-D)
What policies should facilitate	Labor and capital mobility	Labor and capital mobility Market integration for goods and services	Labor and capital mobility Market integration for goods and services Selected economic activities in lagging areas
Policy Priorities			
Spatially blind institutions	Fluid land and labor markets, security, education and health programs, safe water and sanitation	Fluid land and labor markets, security, education and health programs, safe water and sanitation	Fluid land and labor markets, security, education and health programs, safe water and sanitation
Spatially connective infrastructure		Interregional transport infrastructure Information and communication services	Interregional transport infrastructure Information and communication services
Spatially targeted incentives			Incentives to agriculture and agro-based industry Irrigation systems Workforce training Local roads

Source: WDR 2009 team.

example, constitutions state that primary education should be free and universal, regardless of the place of residence, and supplementary national laws specify how many years of instruction are necessary to complete primary education. In conflict-driven or postconflict countries, basic education is viewed as a tool for national reconciliation and ensuring territorial integrity.

Despite such legislation, education, health, and poverty levels vary considerably among areas in many countries, particularly in Asia and Africa. In China, the human development index (a combination of education, health, and income levels) of the leading area in 2003 was 0.97, close to the Republic of Korea's index, and that of the lagging area was 0.59, about the same as Lao PDR's index (see figure 8.2). Chapter 2 pointed out that these gaps were even higher some years ago.

Developing human capital is essential whether policies aim to bring jobs to people or encourage the movement of people to jobs. One of the main gains comes from helping people in lagging areas migrate to areas with better opportunities. In Russia the large economic and physical distances between lagging areas and potential destinations have deterred migration. Reducing economic distance, an additional year of education increases out-migration from remote areas by 40 percent.[32] As Brazil transformed from an agricultural to a manufacturing economy, migration flows from the lagging northeast to the dynamic south and southeast increased between 1960 and 2000. In the northeast people who have at least a primary education migrate more frequently than less educated people.[33]

One of the biggest success stories is in the United States, where a rise in the schooling of African Americans is believed to have been an important causal factor behind their "Great Migration" out of the South. In 1900, 90 percent of African Americans lived in the South, and only 4.3 percent of those born in the region were living elsewhere. By 1950 the proportion in the South had declined to 68 percent, and 19.6 percent of those born in the region had left it. Census data for 1900, 1940, and 1950 show that better-educated people were more likely to migrate because schooling increased their awareness of distant labor market opportunities and their ability to assimilate into a different social and economic environment, thus lowering the costs.[34] In another U.S. study of people tracked between 1968 and 1982, those with high education levels showed less inclination to change professions but were more likely to move geographically. A person with a college education was likely to move three times more often than a person with an eighth-grade education or less.[35]

Opening options for migration stimulates greater human capital investments: people consider not only the local returns to education but also the returns in other locations. If schooling options are available in poor areas, potential migrants will invest in additional human capital, anticipating that jobs in leading areas require higher skills. Employers in those areas are likely to favor educated workers who signal themselves as more "able" than other workers from lagging areas. In the United States, African American school enrollment rates were significantly higher in southern states that previously had experienced high rates of out-migration. An increase in earlier migration rates explains 7.4 percent of the increase in African American enrollment rates between 1910 and 1930. As more African Americans migrated from the South, migration became more common and feasible, and school enrollments rose in response.

Schooling has a strong effect on welfare, as in Brazil. Nine states in the northeast have the worst education attainments, with gains smaller than in the rest of the country. Average illiteracy in the nine states fell 42 percent, less than the 49 percent in other states, and is still twice the national average (18 percent versus 9 percent). Differences in schooling explain more than half the income difference between the northeast and the leading southeast. If the local populace had the same education profile as people in the southeast, average incomes in the northeast would increase by more than half, moving from 62 percent of the Brazilian average to 93 percent.[36]

Government programs, such as that for the universal primary education in Uganda, often reflect national priorities. Uganda's program increased enrollments in the north—the country's poorest area (see box 8.7). But more effort is needed to improve

Figure 8.2   Living standards can vary considerably between leading and lagging areas

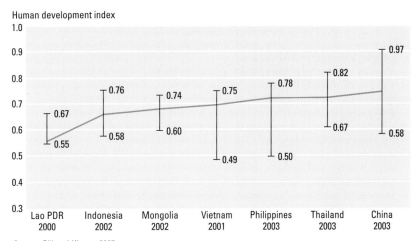

Source: Gill and Kharas 2007.

education quality because of the higher costs of delivering services in the northern region. With poor implementation capacity and underspending in lagging areas, the gap between "regional needs" and allocations from higher levels of government becomes even wider. Although this could be seen as spatial targeting of public spending, an *outcome*-oriented policy framework would regard such efforts as spatially blind.

Transfer mechanisms for public services. Redistributive transfers from higher levels of government can reduce disparities in fiscal capacity and public service provision across subnational jurisdictions. At least three criteria motivate their allocation:

- **Need.** Areas with lower incomes would receive more investment, but richer areas may also demand more resources to meet the needs of population growth and congestion.

- **Efficiency.** Areas with higher returns to investment would receive more allocations.

- **Equality.** Spending is equalized across locations, so that public investments do not give an advantage to any single area.

Need-based transfers can improve public service delivery in lagging areas, because local tax bases may be inadequate to generate enough revenues. Intergovernmental transfers can help provide similar access to public services for residents anywhere in the country. Such transfers are particularly

BOX 8.7 *Universal primary education in Uganda increased access to schools in the northern areas*

President Museveni's decision to implement universal primary education (UPE) in 1996 made Uganda the first African country to institute such a policy. UPE abolished tuition and contributions to parent-teacher associations and school building funds. The impact on primary school enrollment has been large, with those in the poorest quintile gaining most and, within the poorest quintile, the enrollment of girls more than tripled between 1992–93 and 2002–03. In the lagging northern area, girls' enrollment rose from 40 percent to 73 percent.

UPE has had an equalizing effect in access but not in quality and performance. In the northern area, high rates of teacher absenteeism, low financial incentives to teachers, and limited education infrastructure and teaching materials produce low education performance. And the per capita budget allocations to the region do not always reflect the higher costs of delivering services there. A spatially blind program of education that emphasizes outcomes would not be geographically neutral.

Source: Bird and Higgins 2008.

important for subnational governments that depend heavily on federal transfers to cover spending. They finance about 60 percent of subnational spending in developing countries and transition economies, compared with about a third in member countries of the Organisation for Economic Co-operation and Development (OECD). In India central government transfers finance more than 30 percent of state spending. In China central-provincial and provincial-local transfers financed 67 percent of provincial, 57 percent of prefecture, and 66 percent of county and lower-level spending in 2003.[37]

The allocation rules for transfers thus have a direct bearing on the potential for welfare improvement in different areas. But intergovernmental transfers that finance a large share of subnational expenditures are rarely made with spatial equity in mind. Indeed, the large transfers go to areas where people already receive high-quality services (see box 8.8).

Fiscal equalization transfers to lagging areas are financed by a net tax on the residents of leading areas. A common concern in the fiscal competition literature is that higher effective taxes in some areas will stimulate the out-migration of productive factors. The new economic geography provides some hope that tax-induced migration will be limited if residents (both firms

and households) benefit from agglomeration economies in leading areas. External economies induce mobile factors to cluster geographically and turn them into quasi-fixed factors. So if residents see benefits from locating near other similar residents, they become locked into these locations, less sensitive to tax differences. Moderate intergovernmental transfers financed by leading areas thus can finance public services in lagging areas.

Although transfers can bridge short-term fiscal constraints in lagging areas, fiscal dependency is a danger. If intergovernment transfers finance a large share of expenditures, subnational governments are unlikely to improve local revenue collection or be accountable to local residents.[38] OECD countries have recognized these disincentives, and many have reduced the equalization component of revenues and grants (Italy and Spain, for example).

In India, where federal transfers redistribute resources to poor areas, average incomes in low-income states are 40 percent of those in high-income states. With local tax revenues linked to local incomes, the fiscal capacity of low-income states is worse than that of their high-income counterparts.[39] Compensating for this difference is a progressive fiscal redistribution system. Low-income states receive 48 percent of total central government transfers, compared with a 17-percent allocation to high-income states. The progressiveness of transfers is also evident per capita—Bihar, the poorest state receives Rs 501 per person in tax transfers. Maharashtra—a high-income state and home to India's leading urban center, Mumbai—receives only Rs 298 per person. But the translation of resources into services on the ground is not always visible in India's lagging areas.

Many developing countries are collecting and disseminating credible information on service entitlements to increase the accountability of service providers and improve outcomes. Increasing access to reliable quantitative information about service delivery outcomes makes it difficult for providers to ignore this information as anecdotal or irrelevant. Involving community members in identifying concerns and encouraging them to do their own monitoring can create

BOX 8.8 *Improving the spatial progressivity of Nigeria's intergovernmental transfers*

Poverty and service quality in Nigeria are worst in the north, particularly the northeast, and much better in the south, particularly the southwest.[a, b] Nigeria's states rely on fiscal transfers from the center to provide most services. Nigeria's allocation of statutory grants (NGN 700 billion in 2006)[c] is not targeted using a clear principle that supports poverty reduction: 54 percent of the funds are divided equally among all states regardless of population, land area, poverty, or other measures of need.[d] Indicators of health care and education make up only 7 percent of the transfer.

The indicators chosen to direct that small percentage are regressive in that they favor states with the best service delivery and strongest infrastructure. Basing education transfers purely on enrollments favors states that already have education infrastructure and teachers, penalizing those that do not. Basing health transfers purely on hospital beds similarly supports better-off states that have the resources to build more hospitals.

Per capita transfers to states in the north (about NGN 3,300 per person)

are lower than those in the southwest (3,700) despite the north's having the highest overall poverty and worst service delivery.[e] To determine what would happen if transfers were spatially progressive, an illustrative policy experiment was developed by the World Resources Institute to identify the implications. Population and land area, reflecting demand for services, are used to allocate 50 percent of the statutory grant. Equal allocations are reduced to 5 percent (from 54 percent). Education and health care are split between measures to support current service levels and those to support progressive funding for states with the poor services. For education, school enrollment (increased from 4 to 5 percent) is used for the former purpose, and lack of access to schooling (increased from 0 to 5 percent) for the latter. Health care also received a 10 percent weight. The allocation for revenue effort is kept at 2.5 percent. Poverty was added as a category by weighting the number of poor and the poverty rate (headcount ratio) at 2.5 percent apiece.

The proposed changes would shift intergovernmental transfers toward states with the greatest need. The maps below show this shift in per capita terms.

a. National Bureau of Statistics 2006.
b. See numerous measures of service quality and access (National Bureau of Statistics 2006). Core Welfare Indicator Questionnaire (CWIQ). Data can be obtained from the Nigerian Bureau of Statistics electronically from http://www.nigerianstat.gov.ng/cwiq/2006/survey0/index.html.
c. The 13 percent derivation of oil proceeds and disbursements from the oil fund (under which 9 of the 36 southern states where oil is produced receive 13 percent of oil revenues) represents about NGN 330 billion, or about one-third of total transfers to states in 2006. While the derivation strongly shapes Nigeria's overall transfers, this transfer is stipulated by the constitution, not by statute and so is not included here (Nigeria Federal Ministry of Finance, downloaded and compiled from http://www.fmf.gov.ng/portal/detail.php?link=faac).
d. Revenue Mobilization Allocation and Fiscal Commission 2003.
e. National Bureau of Statistics 2004.

Nigeria's statutory grant transfers per capita with actual transfers in 2006 (left) and with equity considerations (right)

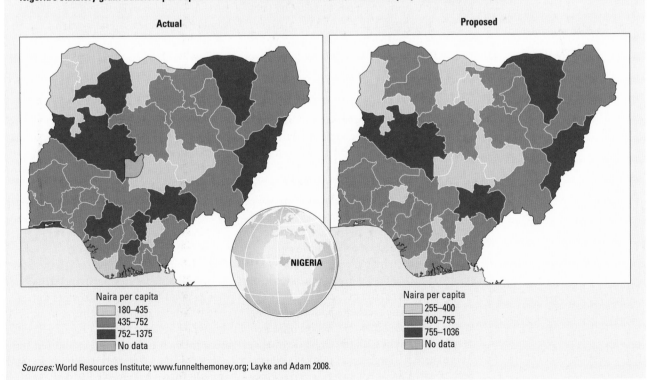

Actual

Proposed

NIGERIA

Naira per capita
- 180–435
- 435–752
- 752–1375
- No data

Naira per capita
- 255–400
- 400–755
- 755–1036
- No data

Sources: World Resources Institute; www.funnelthemoney.org; Layke and Adam 2008.

a constituency of users willing to hold providers accountable.

Effective service delivery thus depends on having enough financial resources and translating them into outcomes on the ground. Investing in public goods in lagging areas reduces migration possibilities in the short term, because it improves the attractiveness of lagging areas. But targeted social investments to develop portable assets can improve the welfare of people and facilitate their longer-term mobility by making them better prepared for work in leading and intermediate areas.

Portable pension benefits. Even with portable assets, people may find it hard to move. In several countries, a lack of pension portability is likely to slow the pace of migration. Facing a potential loss in pension benefits because of differences in schemes or a lack of portability, workers may be less likely to move even when leading areas offer higher wages. The European Commission finds precisely this problem.[40]

Better land market regulations. Well-functioning land markets make it possible for people to acquire land, exchange it with others, and use it effectively.[41] And policies that set up defensible and tradable property rights for land and housing are likely to facilitate people's geographic mobility. The ability to defend rights legally rather than physically allows people to leave their land to take advantage of short-term opportunities. And the ability to use land as collateral or sell it allows them to finance migration costs and benefit from economic and social opportunities elsewhere.

Government involvement in managing land markets and enforcing property rights prevents households from wasting private resources. But too much government involvement can hurt efficiency. Large-scale public ownership can withhold land from the market and artificially increase prices, precluding many poor people from entering the market. And high direct costs and complicated procedures can reduce the incentive for people to formally exchange land.

Policies to safeguard the poor from rising land and housing costs often have hindered market functioning. In the Czech Republic, where there is a large rental market, de facto rent control has kept prices significantly below the market rate and further restricted mobility. Tenants do not want to lose their favorable position in existing contracts.[42] In Chile, meanwhile, the government's success in targeting housing subsidies to the poor in lagging areas has also created a strong incentive for people in these areas not to migrate, impeding convergence across locations even in a country that has a small population and homogenous society.

Institutions and infrastructure to connect lagging and leading areas

Transport infrastructure. Consider Bangladesh, a two-dimensional country, where the most lagging areas are distant from economic density but densely populated. Selected investments in corrective infrastructure can help greatly. The bridge over the Jamuna River opened market access for producers in the northwest around the Rajshahi division. Built at a cost of almost $1 billion, this bridge provides the first road and rail link between the northwest, an intermediate area with the more developed east, which includes the national capital region. Better market access and reduced input prices encouraged farmers to diversify into high-value crops, such as modern varieties of rice and perishable vegetables.[43] The government has complemented connective infrastructure policies with spatially blind institutions to improve coverage of social services. The Expanded Program on Immunization aims to immunize all children less than one year old against the six vaccine-preventable diseases. The Health, Nutrition, and Population Strategic Investment Plan for 2003–10 improves coverage in districts with poor health indicators.[44]

In the Islamic Republic of Iran, another two-dimensional country in the terminology of this Report, connective infrastructure improvements are necessary for spatial integration. In addition, spatially blind education policies of improving schools as well as conditional cash transfers for children to attend schools can improve welfare in lagging areas.[45] Turkey's lagging eastern areas have 44 percent of the land but only 5.7 percent of national motorways, and asphalt road coverage is 40 percent that of the leading regions. The government's Village Infrastructure Support Project (KÖYDES) and Municipal Infrastructure Support Project (BELDES) have improved living standards in rural areas and small towns by paving roads and providing sanitation and drinking water networks.[46] And investments in human capital are likely to benefit potential migrants as well as those who stay behind.

Information and communication technologies. Mobile phones have driven down provision costs, boosting penetration and improving information flows. In 2003 China had more mobile phone users (269 million) than fixed-line users (263 million). For 29 areas in China between 1986 and 2002, telecommunication infrastructure was strongly associated with subnational GDP growth.[47] Because telecommunication investments are subject to diminishing returns, lagging areas can gain the most from them.

New technologies have lowered the costs of delivering financial services, making them more affordable. Many people in lagging areas have limited access to financial services, relying on cash-based transactions outside the banking system. But with rising international and national remittances, better access to financial services can help people in these areas overcome credit constraints. The proliferation of mobile services, even in remote areas, opens new opportunities to provide financial services over a mobile phone network (m-banking). Reports from the Philippines indicate that 3.5 million people have access to mobile phones that can transfer money.[48]

Producers in lagging areas can receive better information on prices they can get for their products. In Kerala, India, mobile phones reduced the dispersion of market prices so much that prices differed only by the transport cost between markets.[49] And in Peru, a ubiquitous but often undervalued communication system is connecting small producers with markets—the postal service (see box 8.9).

Greater benefits in intermediate areas. Intermediate areas closer to centers of economic mass are likely to gain more from connectivity-enhancing infrastructure, and lagging areas are likely to gain less and at a slower pace. Transport connectivity improvements in China's intermediate areas can be economically beneficial for lagging areas. By reducing the transport cost from the west to the coast, infrastructure investments in the central (intermediate) transportation hubs in Henan, Hubei, and Hunan provinces may well have greater effects on the west's development than improvements in the western area itself. But if China's overall growth is the main objective, infrastructure investments in the dynamic economic centers along the coast—Hebei, Jiangsu, and Shandong—could still provide the highest payoffs.[50]

In Brazil improvements to the road network between the 1950s and 1980s did reduce transport and logistics costs. But most of the economic gains accrued to the center-west, with only small gains to the lagging northeast. During this time, its share of the national network increased from 15 percent to 25 percent. Even so, such investments did bring economic density closer to the lagging northeast.

In Colombia, with water and land suitable for agriculture, the mountainous topography makes freight transport difficult. So some intermediate areas are not well integrated

---

BOX 8.9   *Exporting by mail in Peru—connecting small producers to markets*

In many countries small enterprises are often excluded from export chains because they operate in villages or small towns or do not have the needed information to export. In Peru a trade-facilitation program called "Easy Export" connects small producers to markets. The key to this program is the most basic of transport networks—the national postal service.

How does it work? An individual or firm takes a package to the nearest post office, which provides free packaging. The sender fills out an export declaration form, and the post office weighs the package and scans the export declaration form. The sender pays the fee for the type of service desired. Goods with values of $2,000 or less can be exported. The main benefit is that the exporter does not need to use a customs agent, logistics agent, or freight forwarder or to consolidate the merchandise; even the packaging is provided. Firms or individuals need only to go to a post office with a scale and a paper scanner and to use the Internet to complete the export declaration for the tax agency.

Has it made a difference? Within six months of inception, more than 300 firms shipped goods totaling more than $300,000. Most users are new exporters—microentrepreneurs and small firms, producing jewelry, alpaca and cotton garments, food supplements (natural products), cosmetics, wood art and crafts, shoes and leather, and processed food. And many of them are in the poorest areas of the country.

Source: Guasch 2008.

with large domestic and international markets. Casanare, the nation's largest rice producing area, has good potential for biofuels from corn and palm oil. But it takes 18 hours to reach Bogotá and 50 hours to access a main port. Improving road quality would increase market access and help the area's economy. La Mojana, an area with 5,000 square kilometers of flatlands, close to the Atlantic ports and most Colombian cities, is often flooded, because it lies in the buffer zone of two major rivers. Improving ecosystem management along with transport connectivity would improve its access to cities and ports.[51]

Interregional infrastructure improvements can bring higher economic concentration. The potential benefits of improving market access for peripheral areas may instead accrue to firms in larger agglomerations.[52] And improving transport connectivity can further concentrate economic activity. Roads and rails run both ways—better transport connectivity not only provides market access to firms in lagging areas, but also allows firms in leading areas to reach markets. A decline in transport costs helps competitive firms in leading areas easily scale up production to reach these new markets at lower cost relative to local producers in lagging areas. So improving market access may hurt the production of standardized goods in lagging areas. But lower prices and better access to new products are likely to improve consumer welfare.

Experience validates this conjecture. In Italy reducing transport costs between the north and south in the 1950s deprived *Mezzogiorno* firms of their previous protection and accelerated their deindustrialization.[53] And in France, where transport costs within the country fell by 38 percent between 1978 and 1993, the geographic concentration of employment increased.[54]

In addition to growth effects that vary across areas, it is also useful to consider the distributional effects of infrastructure improvements. Are the benefits of infrastructure improvements large enough and distributed progressively enough to reduce overall income inequalities, with more benefits accruing to the poor than the nonpoor? Empirical evidence on this question is limited, but a study from Nepal shows that

the development of extensive rural road networks led to significant economic benefits, with considerable gains to the poor. But the poor's share often is not large enough to significantly reduce income inequality, because the benefits from road extension could be greater for the rich.[55] In Ghana the benefits of improving access to infrastructure by the poor could be increased by complementary spatially blind policies, such as education and health improvements, which would boost the use of that infrastructure.[56]

Institutions, infrastructure, and incentives to overcome the 3-D challenge of distance, density, and division

Incentives to promote economic investments in lagging areas have been widely used by countries to accelerate national economic growth and balance growth outcomes across places. They seem to work better when they reinforce market signals and address coordination failures. They are less successful when governments pick the places to support growth. The following lesson seems to emerge: let markets pick the place, while governments help to push the pace.

Incentives that exploit geographic advantages are more likely to succeed. To stimulate economic growth, many governments have offered tax holidays, reliable infrastructure, and improvements to the business environment. Often the incentives are geographically focused—in special economic zones—to quickly create enclaves of growth, leaving nationwide infrastructure and governance shortfalls to the longer term. There is an ongoing debate over whether focused incentives slow the pace of economic reforms, but the interest here is in identifying where these incentives are more likely to succeed. Is it desirable to provide incentives in areas that already have good geography and human capital? Or should they be remedial measures to offset market forces and help develop lagging areas?

In China and India, spatially targeted incentives are most likely to succeed when they reinforce geographic advantages, particularly in areas advantaged by good access to domestic and international markets (see box 8.10). In Uganda the returns from infrastructure development in highways and power supply are highest in areas that already have a skilled labor force and a diverse mix of industrial activities.[57] These happen to be along the corridor linking the country's two main agglomerations, Kampala and Jinja. Using infrastructure to spread out manufacturing, instead of facilitating its concentration, can slow national economic growth.

Incentives that enhance market links and improve agriculture performance in areas with good natural geography can be a part of development strategies for densely populated lagging areas where factor mobility is constrained. But before offering incentives, agriculture needs to be assessed as an economic driver in the local economy. *World Development Report 2008* provides a useful diagnostic technique to identify subnational areas as agriculture based, transforming, or urbanized—a country's "three worlds" of agriculture—based on the share of aggregate growth originating in agriculture and the share of aggregate poverty in the rural sector. Applying this technique can help identify whether agriculture will remain a prominent feature of lagging areas in the short to medium term.

Consider Malaysia, where agriculture is important in the regional economies of the lagging areas, which account for more than 40 percent of the country's people (Sabah and Sarawak are home to more than 2 million).[58] To encourage agricultural development in the eastern peninsula, the national government has been offering reinvestment allowances for capital expenditures related to farming, providing cold-chain facilities and services for perishable agricultural produce and exempting food processing from tax.[59]

But in Ghana, where the lagging north is mostly in the arid Savannah zone and population densities are low, expanding agriculture is less likely to facilitate territorial integration. Without allowing for large-scale migration or structural transformation, even a sharp acceleration in productivity growth in groundnuts and other northern staples is insufficient to bring the north up to par with the south in the medium term.[60]

Let markets pick the places. The Republic of Korea is one of the few success stories involving spatially targeted incentives. To support economic growth in specific areas, the national government worked with the private sector to identify areas offering production advantages. Consistency between national industrial policy and regional policy objectives was instrumental. Although deconcentrating economic activity from the Seoul metropolitan region was an implicit policy objective in the government's tax sharing, decisions to promote export-oriented "strategic industries" were at the core of industrial and regional policies.[61]

Spatial equity did not guide national industrial policies. In fact, areas picked by the market in different phases of industrialization were encouraged. In the 1960s and 1970s, national industrial policies created new industrial cities—Ansan, Changwon, Kumi, Kwangyang, Pohang, and Ulsan. The private sector (*chaebols*) established large branch plants with imported technology and borrowed foreign capital. Market-driven industrial and regional policy led to different specializations across the country, with chaebol headquarters concentrating in Seoul, and production functions decentralized to areas outside the capital. Since the mid-1980s, industrial policy to support high-technology activities triggered industrial reconcentration in the capital region.

To speed the growth, incentives were complemented by infrastructure investments that connected the southeast to the capital region. The Gyeongbu expressway, which connects Busan, Daegu, Daejeon, and Seoul, enabled industries in the southeast to reach the capital region within five hours. Thus industries producing standardized intermediate goods in the capital and southeast regions benefited from considerable cost reductions. In the Republic of Korea, it may be fair to conclude that markets picked the place and governments pushed the pace.[62]

Many countries have offered incentives to create economic mass in lagging areas. The idea is that to attract firms, lagging areas need to offset higher transport and logistics costs, weaker infrastructure, higher factor prices, and lower levels of public services. European countries have a long history of

BOX 8.10   *Special economic zones bring growth if they exploit advantages in natural and economic geographies*

Many developing countries have locations where infrastructure conditions and economic regulations are more hospitable than those typical in the rest of the country. These locations, often called special economic zones (SEZs), enhance industry competitiveness, attract foreign direct investment, and diversify exports. Recent estimates suggest that there are 2,300 such zones in developing and transition countries.[a]

Look at China

The earliest developing-country SEZs were established in China under Deng Xiaoping's leadership in the early 1980s. In 1978 the government decided to open the country's economy to the outside world. SEZs and "open" coastal cities were integral to this process. In 1980 SEZs were established along the southeastern coast in Shenzhen, Zhuhai, and Shantou in Guangdong Prov-

ince and Xiamen in Fujian Province (see the map below). In 1984 14 coastal cities opened their doors to overseas investment, and in 1988 the entire island of Hainan was assigned SEZ status. Around the same time, the coastal belt around the Yangtze River Delta, the Pearl River Delta, and the Xiamen-Zhangzhou-Quanzhou Triangle in south Fujian opened for business with the world. In the early 1990s the government opened up 11 border cities and six ports along the Yangtze River. The developments reflected a strategy of exploiting the best locations to access external markets.

And at India

A cursory glance at India's SEZs suggests that they were not nearly as well located. In 2007 SEZs were approved in coastal states of Andhra Pradesh, Gujarat, Maharashtra, and Tamil Nadu, as well as inte-

rior states of Haryana, Karnataka, Punjab, and Rajasthan. Even in the coastal states, many SEZs are not along the coast.[b]

Closer inspection reveals considerable diversity across product specialization, which range from standardized manufacturing to information technology and pharmaceuticals. Compared with standardized manufacturing products, human capital–intensive products depend more on reliable telecommunication infrastructure and access to airports, not harbors. Moreover, India's economic zones also target the large domestic market. Take Gurgaon, a satellite town a stone's throw from Delhi's international airport, which 20 years ago was a cluster of villages (*gaon* is the Hindi word for village). Now it is one of the main service-oriented corridors in the country, sitting in the middle of India's largest consumer market. It houses such infor-

China's special economic zones opened the country to external markets

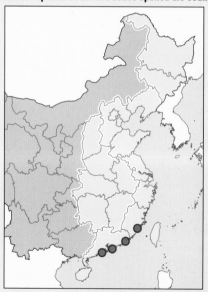 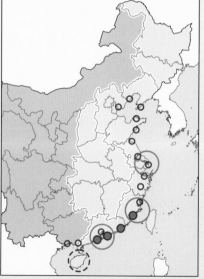 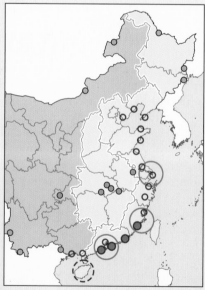

- ◉ 4 first special economic zones (1980)
- ◎ 14 coastal cities (1984)
- ○ 3 deltas (1985)
- ◌ Province of Hainan (1988)
- ◉ 6 ports of Yangtze (1992)
- ◎ 11 border cities (1992)

Source: WDR 2009 team, based on Huang and Luo forthcoming.

BOX 8.10 *Special economic zones bring growth if they exploit advantages in natural and economic geographies—continued*

mation technology service providers as IBM and Microsoft, along with such consumer goods providers as Coca-Cola, Gillette, and Nestlé.

Unlike China's government-led SEZs, India's are being developed by the private sector, by such companies as Infosys and HCL, promoting information technology development,[c] reflecting broader global trends. Of SEZs in developing countries, 62 percent are private, up from 25 percent

in the 1980s. They are generally more profitable and have better social and environmental track records than public zones, except in East Asia's government-run zones.

Location is the key: poor location is the main obstacle to success. It seems to matter more where the zones are located, not who owns and operates them. The lesson from China and India is that spatially directed interventions are more likely to succeed when they exploit

geographic advantages rather than try to offset them.

Source: WDR 2009 team.
a. SEZs take a variety of forms, which include free trade zones, export processing zones, enterprise zones, freeports, and specialized zones (Gauthier 2007).
b. Location of SEZs is based on SEZ INDI-AWEB at http://www.sezindiaweb.com/SEZ_map.html.
c. Information on SEZs in India is drawn from the Indiastat database.

---

using industrial policies to attract firms to lagging areas. But fiscal incentives, while politically efficient, have not transformed the economic fortunes of lagging areas:[63]

- In Italy one of the main objectives of the national economic program begun in 1965 was to eliminate development gaps between the south and the rest of the country. To support this program, financial incentives were provided to firms in the south through partial exemptions of welfare contributions. Through 1992 public infrastructure and financial incentives promoted industrial development in the region.

- In France the Fifth National Plan (1966–70) provided assistance to agriculture and began to direct industrial investment away from Paris toward low-income areas in the west. Light industries—with lower transport costs and higher labor intensity—were targeted for relocation.

- The United Kingdom has supported economic development in northern England, Scotland, Wales, and northern Ireland. During World War II, wartime building controls directed industry out of the south of England and into northern and peripheral areas. During the postwar recession in 1958, employment in coal mining, textiles, and shipbuilding declined, renewing interest in bringing jobs to the north. The 1960s saw regionally differentiated investment

incentives and building grants to lagging areas through the Local Employment Act, along with relocation of 250,000 manufacturing jobs from prosperous to lagging areas.

A common theme in traditional regional policies focusing on taxes, subsidies, and regulations is that they were mainly central government initiatives to create employment and provide infrastructure with the objective of dispersing (or fighting the concentration of) economic activity. They targeted specific firms in the hope that they would become anchors in the local economy and have large multiplier effects.[64] But for the most part, these incentives have not stimulated sustained growth in the lagging areas, imposing large costs on taxpayers.

Most European countries now focus more on "soft" interventions, such as investing in innovation and supporting research institutes and science and technology parks (see table 8.2).[65] Central government programs have been replaced by greater cooperation between the public and private sectors. And rather than target specific firms, coordinated measures are attracting clusters of interrelated firms. Rigorous evaluations of these programs are hard to come by. But innovation policies that bring new information and technologies to lagging areas should in principle help in the long term.

Table 8.2 The OECD's experience with incentives to stimulate lagging areas has been evolving

Strategy	"Traditional" regional policies	"New" regional policies	The economic perspective
Objective	Create jobs and provide large-scale infrastructure	Provide complementary services, subsidize the cost of innovation—research institutes, science and technology parks	Incentives should be provided only to "new" activities—products new to the local economy and new technologies to produce existing products
Main players	Central government	Public-private partnerships	Public sector has limited information on what firms want
Focus area	Incentives to attract individual firms	Encourage development of clusters—both sectors and business development	Public sector support must target activities, not sectors; subsidized activities must have strong spillovers

Source: WDR 2009 team.

The U.S. federal government is also involved in smaller "economic development" programs. A recent review identifies 180 programs of U.S. federal agencies addressing issues as diverse as planning and economic development strategies, industrial parks, infrastructure repair, and building renovation. The agency with the greatest visibility in this group is the Economic Development Administration (EDA) of the U.S. Department of Commerce.[66] The EDA has spent more than $188 billion on economic development, but with little coordination among initiatives, or a common policy objective. The EDA reports that its investments leverage about $37 in private sector investment for every dollar that it spends.[67] No independent evaluation of these programs is available.

Area incentives, popular in developing countries, have produced mixed results at best (see table 8.3). In Brazil, where the goal has been to attract "dynamic" industries to the lagging north and northeast by providing fiscal incentives, expenditures have reached $3 billion to $4 billion a year. A recent impact evaluation shows that the allocation of these "constitutional funds" did induce the entry of footloose manufacturing establishments into lagging regions—but incentives were not attractive enough for vertically integrated industries.[68] Between 1970 and 1980 the Mexican government used fiscal incentives to promote industrial development outside the three largest urban agglomerations. Firms

locating outside these three large cities were eligible for a 50- to 100-percent reduction in import duties and income, sales, and capital gains taxes, as well as accelerated depreciation and lower interest rates. Their impact on economic decentralization was insignificant because import duties on raw materials and capital goods were low to begin with, so the reductions had no effect on location decisions and lost revenues.[69]

In India the Industrial Policy Resolution of 1956 set up a strict licensing system to direct investment into lagging areas. The Indian government decided that no licenses would be issued to new industrial units in the vicinity of large metropolitan areas. And state governments and financial institutions were asked to deny support to new industries in metropolitan areas even when they did not require an industrial license. Large public sector projects (steel plants, for example) were located in the lagging states of Bihar, Madhya Pradesh, and Orissa. Industrial estates (or growth centers) received infrastructure investments and financial incentives for private industrial investment in designated lagging districts. The policies effectively stifled growth in areas that had good market access and human capital and did not allow exit of unproductive activities from lagging areas. Even after more than 30 years of draconian regulation, few districts in backward areas became major industrial centers.

The economic reforms in 1991 scrapped these licensing policies. The decline of production in inland areas continued, and places with good market access and good local business environments flourished. The ten best-performing industrial districts are now located south of the Vindhya mountain range, which divides north from south.[70]

Similarly, in the former Soviet Union, central planners decided where firms would locate and tried to spread economic activity throughout the country's landscape. They spread production facilities across the former Soviet Union's millions of square kilometers. Far from markets and lacking specialization, their productivity suffered. How did the transition to markets change things? New firms located closer to markets and old ones in remote areas closed down. The result was a 2.5 percent gain in firm productivity annually between 1989 and 2004.[71]

Coordinating local and national incentives. Incentives for lagging areas are best coordinated with national sectoral policies: taking stock of various national economic promotion initiatives and aligning spatial interventions with these policies can help. For instance, spatially targeted subsidies represent only 12 percent of Brazil's export promotion and industrialization subsidies, which favor the industrial southeast. Estimates suggest that these industrial subsidies cost $42 billion in 1999, or 4.4 percent of GDP.[72] In Brazil initiatives to recruit firms into the northeast clearly were fighting an uphill battle against broader industrial incentives that were better aligned with market forces.

In India, too, common pricing policies to reduce overall inequalities hurt the economic prospects of lagging areas. The Freight Equalization Policy of 1956 standardized the prices for transporting "essential" items such as coal, steel, and cement nationwide regardless of distance. Lost in the process were the location-based advantages of resource-rich areas. The affected areas included southern Bihar, eastern Madhya Pradesh, and western Orissa, each among the poorest, least industrialized parts of the country. The policy weakened the incentives for private capital to locate production in lagging areas.

Decentralization often has been accompanied by the efforts of subnational governments to create economic mass to meet expenditure responsibilities. They offer fiscal incentives and tax expenditures to attract firms to their jurisdictions. But if not coordinated, these incentives can be wasteful and counterproductive.

Look at the competition between states in Brazil, where Bahia and Rio Grande do Sul competed to attract a Ford Motor Company plant in the 1990s. Rio Grande do Sul offered a package of incentives to Ford that included a R$210 million (around US$200 million) loan from the state at extremely favorable conditions (6 percent interest, 15 years to repay), additional state expenditures of R$234 million on infrastructure

Table 8.3   A range of instruments has been used by governments to create economic mass in lagging areas, with modest results

Instrument	Examples
Investment subsidies	**Brazil:** Constitutional funds (interest rate subsidies)—induced entry of footloose firms, but not for firms in vertically integrated industries (Carvalho, Lall, and Timmins 2005)
Tax holidays	**Thailand:** Income tax exemptions; sales tax reductions for firms locating in secondary cities in the 1970s—unsuccessful as deductions from taxable profits did not induce firms to locate in unprofitable locations (World Bank 1980)
Reductions in import duties	**Mexico:** Import duty and tax exemptions for deconcentrating manufacturing out of the three largest agglomerations—unsuccessful as tax rates were low to begin with (World Bank 1977, Scott 1982)
Industrial estates/ free trade zones	**Chile:** Free trade zones in *zonas extremas* with exemptions for customs, value added tax, corporate profit, and real estate taxes—successful in the high-tax, high-tariff period until the mid-1990s, performance declined with national import duty reduction from 35 percent in the 1980s to 6 percent in 2000 (World Bank 2005b)
Regulation	**India:** Preference to backward areas in industry licensing (1956 industrial policy), with public sector–led industrial growth in lagging areas and regulations to stop industrial expansion in leading areas—few backward areas took off, and when regulations were relaxed, these lagging areas declined further (Chakravorty and Lall 2007)

Source: WDR 2009 team.

and public works, an assured loan from the national development bank of R$500 million, and exemptions from local taxes for 10 years. When the state government tried to renegotiate the deal fearing that it was too generous, Ford moved to Bahia, which offered a package similar to the original one. Evaluations show that these "fiscal wars" cost Brazilian taxpayers around $172,000 per job created—five times the cost of job creation in a General Motors plant in Tennessee.[73]

Thinking through the design of incentives. Before using incentives to promote economic development in lagging areas, national and subnational governments should first find out why some areas are being bypassed by the market. Is it because of the low social returns to economic production in these places, the low ability to capture these returns, or the high cost of finance?[74] Have policies actively or inadvertently blocked local economic growth? The success of incentives depends on how well the problem is diagnosed, perhaps starting with area-specific natural, human, and infrastructure endowments.[75] "Know thy economy," a phrase used in the *World Development Report 2000/01*, should be the motto of subnational governments. Good information can promote constructive debate on development options and build consensus around a development strategy.

If the information and subsequent analysis points to specific opportunities for growth, the next step is to identify whether the planned incentives are to subsidize capital formation or to promote innovation. If they are to attract firms with potential local multipliers, it is important to know whether the product lines value agglomeration economies, which would reduce the power of the incentives. For firms in sectors in which economies of scale and agglomeration are important for production, it is less likely that spatially targeted interventions will attract them to lagging areas. Industrial surveys in Brazil, China, India, Indonesia, and Mexico show that manufacturing firms in many product lines value both internal scale economies from market access and agglomeration economies in deciding their location.[76] Firms producing standardized products serving local markets, and those specializing in natural resources, are less likely to value agglomeration economies than are those depending on skilled labor, business services, and access to information.

And from a national growth perspective, it is important to find out whether relocating "targeted" industries produces net additional employment and output nationally. If not, local efforts of attracting industry may be zero-sum games. If the relocated industries are less productive, policy makers may face a negative sum. If incentives are being used to promote innovation, it is important to ensure that local production processes can accommodate the innovations.

Avoiding Balkanization: the political benefits of economic integration

Economic and political objectives can clash, but more often they coincide. In the Western Balkans, the former republic of Yugoslavia became a federation after World War II but disintegrated when its republics declared themselves independent in the early 1990s. Fueling the disintegration was rising autarky and fragmentation in Yugoslavia since the mid-1970s, with barriers to movements of people and capital across republican borders, limited interrepublic trade, and duplicated economic production. In 1987, for example, 70 percent of all production in Serbia was consumed in the local market.[77]

As discussed in chapter 5, analysis suggests that factor mobility equalizes welfare across areas, weakening incentives to break away from an economic and political union.[78] By contrast, persistent inequalities across areas fuel disintegration movements. Unity, not uniformity, is the valid principle for both political and economic integration.

This chapter has provided a framework for integrating lagging and leading areas as countries address economic distance, misplaced density, and internal divisions. Economic forces are likely to produce spatial divergence in growth outcomes. Economic models of geography and growth show that increasing returns to scale and agglomeration economies can start and sustain a virtuous circle of growth and investment in a few areas.

For valid reasons, though, policy makers are concerned with reducing geographic imbalances soon, sometime between now and the long term. And sometimes, political pressures can be such that widening divergence at any point is unacceptable. The typical territorial development policy response has emphasized targeted incentives and large-scale infrastructure to encourage economic production in lagging areas. However, the evidence reviewed in this chapter shows that many such policies have led to waste. In the meantime, policies that address institutional bottlenecks that can help people seize opportunities elsewhere or improve their living standards locally may be ignored.

Even with such compromises, the biggest part of the policy challenge lies in identifying the outcomes that can be realistically sought, that is, which depend on the stage of development and the fiscal and institutional capacities of a country. Where incomes are low, it may be feasible only to reduce spatial disparities in poverty rates and in access to essential shelter, water, health, nutrition, and education services. China's 11th Five-Year Plan passed by the National People's Congress in 2006 states that "the construction of public finance system should be accelerated . . . to gradually equalize basic public services." In October 2007 the 17th Congress again pointed out that, to narrow regional disparities, equalization of basic public service provision would be the priority. Upper-middle-income countries can be more ambitious in equalizing basic consumption indicators across areas, and developed countries such as those in the EU more ambitious still. Reducing spatial inequality in disposable incomes may be the relevant target for high-income countries.

But at all stages of development, forcing economic production to spread evenly across areas is both elusive and expensive. Growth generally is unbalanced, but it always brings more resources for societies to balance development outcomes. Policy makers should identify and execute strategies that balance development outcomes across areas by means other than resisting the forces of unbalanced growth—because that is tantamount to fighting economic growth itself.

The framework in this chapter is intended to help policy makers identify the policies best suited to addressing domestic integration. The suggested solutions consider country-specific conditions. The main points? First, integration strategies should increase the access of the poor in lagging areas to opportunities, through a set of spatially blind institutions. Second, infrastructure that connects lagging to leading areas is needed when the problem of distance between lagging and leading areas is coupled with misplaced population density in the lagging areas. Third, when the problem of economic distance comes accompanied by both misplaced

Table 8.4 Assessing the performance of area development policies

Performance criteria	Reduce inequalities across regions? (interregional equity)	Pro-poor? (interpersonal equity)	Avoid tradeoff with spatial efficiency?
Institutions	Yes	Yes	Yes
Infrastructure	No	No	Yes
Incentives	No	No	No

Source: World Bank 2008b, based on country-specific case studies.

density and division, targeted incentives are necessary.

This framework was tested using country-specific case studies of spatial integration, which included Brazil, Ghana, India, Mexico, Russia, and Uganda. Each set of integration policies is examined using three criteria: (1) Do they reduce economic distance across subnational areas? (2) Are these policies pro-poor? (3) Are these policies spatially efficient (that is, do these policies avoid tradeoffs with spatial efficiency)? Table 8.4 summarizes the findings. Efforts to strengthen institutions fare well on all three criteria. Although infrastructure investments may not reduce economic distances or help the poor, they can be spatially efficient. Geographically specific incentives do not fare well.

Perhaps most important, the chapter identifies the point at which all discussions of territorial development policies should start—with spatially blind institutions. Infrastructure that connects lagging areas to markets can help nations integrate. Sometimes, not always, these discussions should include spatially targeted incentives. The right mix of integration instruments will bring the benefits that come from both unbalanced growth and inclusive development.

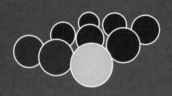

CHAPTER 9

Winners without Borders

Integrating poor countries with world markets

Many leaders in Africa called for a political union of the continent at the time of independence. Félix Houphouët-Boigny, Côte d'Ivoire's first president, was more pragmatic, promoting a gradual increase in economic cooperation with neighboring countries. He proposed one of the first regional economic agreements in Africa, the "Conseil de l'Entente," backed by a solidarity fund provided mainly by Côte d'Ivoire. The key elements of the *Entente* were free trade and free movement of people.[1]

The preferred destination of migrants was, naturally, Côte d'Ivoire. Its share of foreigners increased from 5 percent in 1950 to 26 percent of its 16 million people in 1998—making the country one of the top dozen destinations for international migrants in the world. Côte d'Ivoire benefited as foreign workers contributed to export-led growth in industry and agriculture. Sending countries—especially Benin, Burkina Faso, Niger, and Togo—benefited from remittances and increased trade. The political crisis triggered by a coup in 1999 affected the entire region. But Houphouët-Boigny had vested his country's neighbors in its future, earning the nickname of "The Sage of Africa."

Côte d'Ivoire reflects the main lines of argument in this chapter. In today's developed regions—Europe, North America, and Northeast Asia—most economic activities are highly concentrated, their exports are specialized, and living standards are converging. These regions have overcome national borders and have integrated their economies within their neighborhoods and with the rest of the world. Regional and global integration have been complements, not substitutes, in the development of these regions (see box 9.1).

But in most of the developing world, concentration and convergence have been slow, often because of persisting economic, political, and cultural divisions between countries (see chapter 3). These divisions make it hard for countries to take advantage of scale economies (see chapter 4), mobile labor and capital (see chapter 5), and falling transport costs (see chapter 6). Some developing countries have tried to globalize through unilateral liberalization; others have tried to integrate regionally. There have been successes and failures with both strategies. This chapter deals with ways to combine these strategies by increased cooperation among neighbors and strong connections to world markets, while recognizing and avoiding the tradeoffs that can arise between these two approaches.

The chapter proposes regional integration as a mechanism to increase local supply capacity and global integration to improve access to markets and suppliers. Integration means cooperation between countries in trade, domestic regulations and policies, regional infrastructure, and other cross-border initiatives, including public goods. Regional integration implies cooperation within a neighborhood of countries. Global integration implies cooperation at an even wider international level.

This chapter's framework for policy action uses a taxonomy of neighborhoods to organize thinking about how best to confront the development challenges of each of the developing world's regions.

The main strategies are as follows:

- *Countries close to large world markets should strive to benefit from proximity to high economic density and become an extension of the large markets.* Mexico, the Caribbean, the European Union (EU) accession countries, and the Republic of Korea are linked, respectively, with the U.S., EU, and Japanese markets. But integration must go beyond a simple free trade agreement to gain significant development benefits. The biggest challenge is to make domestic markets attractive enough to investors to be seen as an extension of the large market nearby.

- *Countries with big neighbors but far from world markets should develop their regional market.* This requires two instruments: institutional reforms that facilitate intraregional trade and factor mobility—and infrastructure investments that link lagging to leading countries and the region to major world markets. Regional integration can naturally support regional production networks. These networks maximize production-cost advantages that come with increasing returns to scale, and they allow small countries to specialize in niche products in regional supplier networks. Greater cost efficiency on the supply side makes it easier for such regions to then integrate with global markets.

- *Countries far from world markets in Central Asia, the small Pacific Islands, and Sub-Saharan Africa—the world's "bottom billion"—face the stiffest challenges to economic growth and need a strong commitment for cooperative solutions.* Regional integration can occur in "natural" neighborhoods with three sets of instruments. They need close institutional cooperation and comprehensive regional infrastructure investments, as with the others. But they also may need cross-country compensation mechanisms to sustain the integration effort because deep integration is likely to lead to uneven short-term gains and losses across countries. The international com-

BOX 9.1 *Are the policy messages of this Report anti–global integration? No.*

World Development Report 2009 focuses on regional integration because that is where considerable scope for policy action now lies. But this does not imply that the message is against global integration. Quite the contrary. This chapter argues that regional cooperation boosts the supply capabilities of a neighborhood by providing regional public goods and taking advantage of regional specialization. In this way, it can broaden the gains for each country from global integration. In this sense, regional and global integration are complements, not substitutes. Without global integration, the benefits from regional cooperation would be small or negative, as was true of many past regional agreements. But without regional integration, the benefits from globalization might simply be unattainable for some countries, because they cannot compete on a global scale by themselves.

For many countries, especially in Africa where global export market shares have fallen, the benefits of global integration have been ephemeral. Global integration is sometimes seen as risky, and progress in the Doha Round on several issues central to developing countries, such as agricultural trade, has been slow. In the same vein, past regional cooperation also did not yield significant benefits, and many regional agreements fell apart. Those experiences also highlighted the uneven gains across large and small countries in a neighbor-

hood, which affected the long-term stability of the agreement and the willingness to respond to unexpected events. With many previous efforts at regional integration having failed, the pursuit of further regional agreements has drawn considerable skepticism in development circles.

This chapter argues that, given current conditions, this skepticism is misplaced. Instability stemming from macroeconomic policy and poor governance is far less common today than even a decade ago, so it is less likely that a country will import problems from its neighbor even if their economies are integrated. And with the decline in transport costs and expansion in global trade, the benefits from successful export-led growth are higher than ever. To compete, countries are now more willing to harmonize their policies and institutions with others, so the prospects for regional cooperation have grown substantially. That may be one reason why, in June 2006, 56 regional, 49 regional extension (cooperation between a regional agreement and an individual country), 5 superregional (cooperation between two or more regional agreements), and fully 118 bilateral agreements were signed or initiated under the World Trade Organization (WTO). By acting under the global rules of the game, these agreements strive to recognize and avoid tradeoffs between regional and global integration.

Source: WDR 2009 team.

munity can support these integration efforts through coordinated incentives.

East, Central, and West Africa fall into the third category. Resource-poor coastal countries in these neighborhoods have been the poorest growth performers in the world relative to other world regions.[2] For them, the Report suggests a pact involving regional governments and the international community to improve social services and human capital in lagging countries and to improve infrastructure in leading countries where takeoff is most likely. This should be augmented by preferential access to developed country markets for regional exports. In return, both leading and lagging countries in these "natural neighborhoods" would allow freer intraregional movements of labor, capital, goods, and services.

Today's developing countries, as latecomers, face a stark choice: stay divided and lose ground, or become winners without borders.

Regional integration to scale up supply, global integration to scale up demand

Some countries, such as Chile, Mauritius, and the well-known East Asian tigers, have integrated globally without much cooperation within their world region. They enjoyed significant first-mover advantages. But many other developing countries have found this hard to achieve, and some wonder if the emergence of highly competitive exporters like India and China makes the likelihood of a successful export-led strategy even lower today.

The counterargument is that the range of goods in which a country can develop a comparative advantage has expanded along with the growth in global trade. Intermediate goods and services, more tradable and traded, provide developing countries with a broader range of diversification opportunities than before.[3] Empirical evidence suggests this is true even for Sub-Saharan Africa.[4] Across individual countries within each of nine Sub-Saharan African neighborhoods, imports in the previous year of intermediate goods from neighbors are positively correlated with total exports in the current year. As the level of intermediate imports grows larger and crosses a threshold, this effect becomes noticeably stronger.

These findings show that higher exports occur when countries cooperate regionally (in terms of scale economies, greater factor mobility, and lower transport costs) as well as integrating globally. Regional cooperation means that firms in neighboring countries can produce final goods more cheaply (by building international supply chains) than they can by relying on suppliers in one country alone (see box 9.2). Global integration provides the demand and incentive to develop such efficient regional supply networks. This combination of regional and global integration has produced successful developers in today's rich neighborhoods.

Plant data add further detail to aggregate econometric findings.[5] Firms exporting to regional markets are hurt more by power outages and inefficient border procedures than are firms exporting to global markets, although firms exporting time-sensitive products such as textiles to global markets are hurt by inefficient borders as well. The efficiency of firms dictates where they sell their products: the least efficient sell only in domestic markets, others serve both regional and domestic markets, and the most efficient are involved in domestic, regional, and international markets.[6]

A successful integration policy will concentrate economic activities in places with better access to markets and inputs, whether subnational, national, or regional. Integration could lead to income divergence in a regional neighborhood for a while, before successive waves of lagging countries catch up with the leading countries as growth spills over to the neighborhood. When the integration process is market driven, as in East Asia, production factors will relocate and promote convergence in country per capita incomes within the neighborhood (see chapter 3). But when it is institution driven, as in most developing neighborhoods today, political economy challenges can become major concerns.[7]

Regional and global integration imply tradeoffs

Regional integration agreements, complex to negotiate, implement, and maintain, are intensive in the use of administrative resources. Efforts to align regional institutions through such agreements can come at the expense of domestic administration and unilateral liberalization that can determine a country's integration with the rest of the world. Regional agreements also prevent countries from pursuing more rapid global integration, when some members within a region want to move more slowly.

BOX 9.2 *Diversifying production through regional cooperation*

Diversifying an economy is no easy task. Hidalgo, Barabasi, and Haussman (2007) show that the current export structure of a country determines how easy it will be to diversify its production base over higher-value products. They use the metaphor of a forest representing the product space (the same for all countries in the world). Each tree is a product, and firms are monkeys that can climb higher on a tree to improve their value added (intensive diversification) or jump to another tree with higher value (extensive diversification).

Developing country firms find it easiest to grow through intensive diversification, which builds on capabilities they already possess. The alternative, required at higher incomes or in response to even lower-cost competitors, is to jump to higher value trees. Even if a country is lucky enough to have such higher value trees close to its production base, the jump remains costly and risky. It may require physical infrastructure, specific know-how, knowledge of the tastes and standards in the targeted markets, and easy and cheap access to specific inputs. Haussman and Rodrik (2003) called these initial investment needs "cost discovery," a search by the first firms to explore these new opportunities. Cost discovery can

be facilitated in several ways. Foreign direct investment can provide much of the required information and know-how. So can learning from one's neighbors. Cooperation between neighboring countries can therefore help, providing the scale attractive for foreign investors and the access to critical intermediate goods that makes the leap to a new product less costly and risky. Cooperation can provide an outlet for intermediate goods producers who sell to innovating firms elsewhere in the neighborhood.

When African exports during 1980–2004 are mapped against a global product space of some 800 products (four-digit industries), the Central African Economic and Monetary Community appears to have only a few options for diversification (wood and its manufactures). Members of the East African Community have more options because their exports are more diversified (fruits and vegetables, prepared food, fish, wood and its manufactures, cotton, textiles, low-tech manufactures, metallic products, chemicals, and minerals). Other countries with similar production structures have gone on to diversify into such clusters as cotton, textiles, and garments, which currently enjoy preferences under the African Growth and Opportunity Act in the U.S. market.

Nearly all members of the West African Economic and Monetary Union can benefit from cooperation in at least seven product clusters (fruits and vegetables and their products, wood and its manufactures, cotton, low-tech manufactures, chemicals, and minerals) to reduce their overdependence on traditional agricultural exports, such as coffee and cocoa.

Southern Africa Customs Union members, except for South Africa, can gain significantly more than other unions from cooperation in natural-resource-based and manufacturing clusters, because they have much easier diversification options driven by the logistics, finance, skills, and infrastructure that reflect their middle-income status.

By looking at which areas of economic activity offer the most promise for further development, countries can focus cooperation on sector-specific infrastructure, such as common standards, compliance and metrology systems, and specific curricula to build a skilled labor force and adapt new technologies. That can serve as a complement to the general areas of cooperation in regional infrastructure, better business regulations, and a strong judicial systems.

Based on contributions from Vandana Chandra, Jessica Boccardo, and Israel Osorio.

The regional versus global debate is not new. It revolves around the welfare implications of potential trade diversion and trade creation compared with the first-best welfare- improving effects of unilateral liberalization or multilateralism.[8] Yet a "new regionalism" debate has been launched with the recent proliferation of free trade agreements. One side of this debate sees in regional integration a competitive liberalization process that will ultimately support global integration.[9] The other side sees the emergence of "spaghetti bowls" impeding global integration.[10]

This debate will not be readily concluded. But the lens of the new economic geography gives it a different perspective. Some have argued that when physical geography is properly included in trade models, regional trade agreements can be more welfare improving than multilateral trade agreements if intercontinental transport costs are much higher than intracontinental trade costs.[11] There are also noneconomic gains to regional integration initiatives, such as greater peace and security as well as increased bargaining power in international forums.[12] These noneconomic motives are sometimes more important than the economic in the decision to sign regional integration agreements.

Regional integration can take many forms, from formal treaties regulating many aspects of economic exchange and cooperation to informal, de facto integration that follows from the private sector–led deepening of economic ties. This variety allows for a different dynamic. While global agreements are comprehensive and rare, regional agreements can start small and move at a pace and scope with which each party is comfortable. Each region needs to find the path that allows it to benefit from both regional and global integration.

Developed neighborhoods provide useful insights—think big, start small

Successful neighborhoods in Europe, North America, and Northeast Asia provide three lessons for the design and implementation of regional and global integration initiatives: think global, start small, and compensate the least fortunate.

Think global. For all developing neighborhoods, the most important export markets are outside the region. The Republic of Korea, Mexico, and Romania are fortunate to be close to one of these large world markets, but most nations are not. The main goal of any regional integration process should thus be to promote sound export-led growth. Indeed, the success factor of regional integration agreements is "open regionalism," setting low external tariffs and suppressing all the internal ones.[13] This is a key difference from the first wave of regionalism in the 1970s, which simply extended inward-looking import-substitution policies from countries to regions.

Start small. Regional integration initiatives do not need to address all issues immediately. Nor do they need to involve a whole continent at once. The Latin American and Sub-Saharan experiences in the 1970s show that comprehensive agreements involving a large number of countries often remain "paper agreements."[14] The European Union started with a narrowly focused agreement—the European Coal and Steel Community (see "Geography in Motion, Overcoming Division in Western Europe"). The North American Free Trade Agreement (NAFTA) started with a free trade agreement for automobiles, between the United States and Canada.[15] East Asia's regionalization accelerated in the 1980s, with Japanese multinationals setting up manufacturing export platforms across the region. Often regional integration can start without a formal agreement of any kind but with a statement of intent for strategic cooperation that gives firms comfort that any disputes will be resolved quickly and fairly.

Regional integration implies complementary policy actions by participating countries. The larger the number of participants, the more complex the coordination, with a higher risk of failure. Specific agreements based on country interest can build variable-geometry regional integration in which countries (or areas within countries as with the "growth triangle" in East Asia) deepen their cooperation at their own speed. Such cooperation on trade and nontrade issues can gradually build a stronger neighborhood. This does not preclude specific continentwide initiatives to carry out projects with high fixed costs, such as launching and maintaining a satellite.

Compensate the least fortunate. Regional integration can produce winners and losers across countries—at least in the short term.[16] If two countries with different domestic infrastructure integrate, the country with the better infrastructure will attract more industrial activities, which may deepen differences in income and employment.[17] Building a sustainable neighborhood of countries with different endowments is thus helped by a compensation mechanism to ensure equitable sharing of the gains from integration. In the EU, rich members subsidize infrastructure development in poorer member nations. In the Association of Southeast Asian Nations (ASEAN), richer member countries have programs specifically designed to assist poorer member countries—the Integrated ASEAN Initiative. Some regions also have bilateral aid programs for their poorer neighbors.

One approach to compensation is pooling customs revenues collected in customs unions and redistributing them according to each member's development needs. The West African Economic and Monetary Union (WAEMU) adopted a common external tariff in 2000, and introduced a 1-percent levy on all third-party imports to build a compensation fund. By September 2006, $500 million had been collected and shared. Côte d'Ivoire and Senegal, the richest members of WAEMU, contributed 60 percent of the funds but received only 12 percent. Such transfers are politically feasible if the wealthier countries realize that they will benefit in the long run if their neighborhood prospers. Revenue-sharing initiatives are strengthened by the involvement of a developed country as an external partner willing to subsidize the process. The Economic Partnership Agreements (EPAs) currently being negotiated between the EU and African, Caribbean, and Pacific countries are examples (see box 9.3).

Building integrated neighborhoods: a framework

The "thickness" of country borders is a self-imposed obstacle to development, with isolation increasing the economic distance to markets (see chapter 3). On top of division, some neighborhoods have small countries whose local markets are simply not large enough to trigger or sustain industrialization, or that lack the capabilities to diversify and advance up the value chain. Different countries thus face different problems that require different policy responses to integrate them into the global economy. Integration happens largely through private activity in trade and factor mobility. But most of the institutions or infrastructure needed to connect a region to the global economy are public goods, requiring collective action to overcome coordination problems and externalities.

Three types of policy instruments can be used to pursue regional integration. They also help with global integration.

- *Institutional cooperation* can address coordination problems within neighborhoods and foster greater scale economies.

BOX 9.3　*Economic partnership agreements between the EU and African, Caribbean, and Pacific countries can be made better*

Until 2007 the EU granted nonreciprocal trade preferences to African, Caribbean, and Pacific (ACP) countries. This policy did not comply with the WTO principle of most-favored-nation treatment, but got a temporary waiver that expired in December 2007. The economic partnership agreements (EPAs) between the EU and the ACP countries are a new approach to promoting trade and achieving more general development goals at the same time.

In 2003 the EU started negotiating EPAs with six self-defined ACP regions: the Caribbean (CARIFORUM), Central Africa (CEMAC), Southeast Africa (ESA), West Africa (ECOWAS), Southern Africa (SADC), and the Pacific.

At the core of the EPAs are regional trade agreements between the EU and each of the six regions. The export structure from these regions to the EU is heterogeneous, often reflecting dependency on just a few products. But the EPAs are broader in scope. They will extend 100 percent duty-free and quota-free market access into the EU from each region (with simplified EU rules of origin) while permitting ACP countries to open their markets to a lesser extent (on average 80 percent within 15 years).

The goal is ambitious. The EPAs give incentives to ACP countries to increase regional trade and cooperation, unlike the previous arrangements that favored a hub-and-spoke structure, discouraging interaction with neighbors. And while the previous trade preferences were determined unilaterally by the EU, the EPAs are jointly negotiated. Understandably, some countries are unwilling to cooperate on issues in which they might lose. But the EU can provide incentives—like aid—to help overcome such differences.

Experience shows, however, that (North-South) trade liberalization alone does not promote economic development. So the EPAs try to improve the coherence between trade and development. Besides trade in goods, the EPAs include trade in services as well as investment, public procurement, and competition law. Although the agreements on trade of goods and services are about mutual—though asymmetric—trade liberalization, the trade-related issues follow another route. They aim to support regional integration by common regional regulation, harmonization, and implementation,

thus improving political and economic stability and creating a better business and investment climate.

One of the most difficult issues is the expected loss in tariff revenues, which are, on average, about 2 percent of gross domestic product (GDP) for Sub-Saharan countries. But for some, the loss can be 4 to 6 percent of GDP, a sizable fraction of the public purse. A phased reduction in tariffs is designed to mitigate big declines in government revenues. Over the long term, the lost tariff revenues need to be replaced through reforms of domestic tax and tax administration. A more radical approach would be for the EU to provide budget support to the most affected countries over a predetermined transition period.

Another issue involves complicated rules of origin that need to be simplified and liberalized. Technical assistance is also needed to enable developing countries to fulfill EU standards and stimulate a supply response to enhanced market access. "Aid-for-trade" programs provide resources for such efforts.

Contributed by Sebastian Vollmer.

- *Regional infrastructure,* strategically linking the neighborhood to the leading world markets, can reduce transport costs.
- *Coordinated incentives* involving all the neighborhood's stakeholders and donors from the leading world markets can promote factor mobility and converging living standards between leading and lagging countries in the neighborhood.

Institutional cooperation

Behind-the-border reforms. Institutional cooperation—such as mutual recognition agreements on technical and business procedures, adoption of international standards, and macroeconomic convergence frameworks—expands the size of regional markets, supporting scale economies. Indeed, domestic and foreign firms assess investment opportunities and related government policies and the business environment—such as property rights, regulation, taxes, finance, infrastructure, corruption, and macroeconomic stability—as part of a package that determines a country's attractiveness for investment.[18] Another part is the quality of the legal system, which increases equity investments and firm sizes.[19] These effects spill over even to countries with better institutional endowments in leading world markets. The less

attractive the neighborhood of a country, the less attractive the individual country, particularly when its local market is tiny.

Now that tariff preferences have fallen, behind-the-border barriers are more important determinants of the pattern of trade. And by aligning domestic and international standards and institutions, a neighborhood can improve its attractiveness for foreign direct investment (FDI) and increase its opportunities for trade, particularly important given the need to connect to regional and global production networks and markets. For instance, the crisis facing the fish-processing sector in Kenya in the 1990s would have been less severe if raw and semi-processed fish providers in Kenya, Tanzania, and Uganda had all cooperated to adjust to EU hygiene standards.[20] Many countries in Sub-Saharan Africa are now aiming for such cooperation.[21]

At-the-border policies. Facilitating the flow of capital, labor, and intermediate inputs is a precondition for cross-border production networks. The WTO provides a framework for such liberalization that permits the scope of agreements to vary. Almost all new regional trade agreements include provisions on service liberalization, but some of these services are embodied in people and require corresponding agreement on labor mobility, on which there is little uniformity (see table 9.1).[22] Movement of labor raises economic and political concerns that appear to be far higher than for traded goods or investments, so few agreements provide the kind of mobility required for countries and people to benefit fully.

Financial and monetary cooperation improves capital mobility and increases a region's attractiveness to FDI, especially for small countries.[23] Indeed, small financial markets tend to be less competitive and less efficient because they cannot exploit the substantial economies of scale in financial markets. Some market segments may be missing, and small markets are less able to diversify investments and operational risks. The regulatory structure tends to be more costly and of lower quality in small markets, and ancillary services such as credit information are more difficult to maintain. Regional and global trade in financial services is the best

Table 9.1   Few regional agreements provide for full mobility of labor

Degree of mobility stipulated	Agreement
Full labor mobility	European Union, Agreement on the European Economic Area, European Free Trade Association, Australia–New Zealand Closer Economic Relations, Economic Community of West African States
Market access for certain groups	Caribbean Community, North American Free Trade Agreement, Europe agreements, Group of Three, and Canada-Chile, U.S.-Singapore, U.S.-Chile, Japan-Singapore Free Trade Agreements
Based on GATS mode 4, with additional provisions or limitations	ASEAN Free Trade Area, Euro-Med Association Agreements, New Zealand–Singapore Closer Economic Partnership, Southern Common Market agreement, and EU-Mexico, EU-Chile, MERCOSUR, U.S.-Jordan Free Trade agreements
No effective provisions for labor mobility	Asia Pacific Economic Cooperation Forum, South Asian Association for Regional Cooperation, Central European Free Trade Agreement, and Common Market for Eastern and Southern Africa

Source: World Bank 2004a, updated by the WDR 2009 team.
Note: ASEAN = Association of Southeast Asian Nations; GATS = General Agreement on Trade in Services; MERCOSUR = Southern Common Market.

way to cope with being small—by opening national markets to foreign financial intermediaries, by fully or partially integrating with a regional financial system, and by gradually opening national markets to international capital flows. The benefits of regional financial integration increase as a group of countries moves toward a single currency, a single central bank, and a single licensing and regulatory system for financial services firms.[24] But such integration also reduces the policy flexibility in responding to shocks.

Efforts beyond borders. Developing countries, particularly the landlocked, are hurt by high transport costs due to expensive and unreliable freight services. They have overregulated transport sectors, inefficient logistics services, oligopolistic freight forwarders, as well as roadblocks and demands for bribes along international corridors.[25] Each day a product is delayed before being shipped is estimated to translate into an increase in the distance to its trading partners by 70 kilometers, reducing its trade volume by 1 percent.[26] Landlocked countries, in particular, would enjoy greater exports if their neighbors improved the quality of their transport logistics and customs procedures: it is estimated that a one standard deviation improvement in a landlocked country's logistics together with one standard deviation improvement in its neighbors' logistics would raise the landlocked country's exports by 74 percent.[27]

Beyond-the-border institutional reforms facilitating trade and transport in a neighborhood can greatly increase the efficiency and reliability of logistics chains. Central Asia and Sub-Saharan Africa, whose international competitiveness is seriously affected by high transport costs, are now exploring corridor approaches that have worked well elsewhere, as in Southeastern Europe.[28]

In 1998 six countries asked for World Bank support in designing a regional program of trade and transport facilitation in Southeast Europe. By 2004 eight countries were involved: Albania, Bosnia and Herzegovina, Bulgaria, Croatia, FYR Macedonia, Moldova, Romania, and Serbia and Montenegro. The initiative reduces transport costs, fights corruption, and helps customs

administrations gradually align their procedures with EU standards. The goals are to reduce the processing time for traders and transporters, reduce facilitation payments, reduce corruption related to international transport and trade, and improve the effectiveness of controls and antismuggling efforts. The results provide an encouraging precedent for replicating and scaling up regional trade elsewhere.

Regional infrastructure

Regional transport infrastructure reduces the economic distance between trading partners, both within the neighborhood and between the neighborhood and leading world markets. Electricity, water, telephone lines, and Internet access all raise productivity but are severely inadequate in many developing regions (see table 9.2). Many countries could benefit by coordinating and cooperating in infrastructure provision. Hydropower development launched in 1997 by Mali, Mauritania, and Senegal lowered costs and improved access, reliability, and quality of electricity supply.[29] The East Caribbean telecommunications project, implemented in 1998, increased access to telecom services, reduced prices, and increased employment opportunities.

Table 9.2 Sub-Saharan Africa, South Asia, and the Middle East and North Africa are most affected by unreliable infrastructure, East Asia the least

	World regions						
	EAP	ECA	LAC	MNA	SAR	SSA	OECD
Delay in obtaining an electrical connection (days)	19.4	9.3	32.9	53.7	**56.3**	43.8	9.7
Number of electrical outages (days)	9.3	14.0	17.8	46.1	**121.5**	56.4	1.5
Value lost due to electrical outages (% of sales)	2.5	3.1	3.6	4.2	5.6	**5.7**	2.3
Number of water supply failures (days)	3.5	7.5	14.5	41.7	12.0	**37.2**	0.3
Delay in obtaining a mainline telephone connection (days)	15.8	13.4	45.1	49.9	**66.3**	58.4	9.0
Firms using the Web in interaction with clients/suppliers (%)	23.7	56.7	40.9	34.2	29.2	**20.4**	80.2

Source: World Bank ICA database.
Note: EAP = East Asia and the Pacific; ECA = Europe and Central Asia; LAC = Latin America and the Caribbean; MNA = Middle East and North Africa; SAR = South Asia Region; SSA = Sub-Saharan Africa; OECD = Organisation for Economic Co-operation and Development.

Regional infrastructure is an important part of regional integration, but it often requires considerable outside financial support because the upfront costs can be high. Cross-border project preparation is complex, and individual countries may not have local capacity to conceptualize the technical design and to build a consensus.[30] And the legal and regulatory framework to facilitate the provision of cross-border infrastructure is often lacking. All these constraints can prevent promising regional infrastructure projects from getting to the bankable stage.

Three types of regional infrastructure and related services enhance scale economies, factor mobility, and trade between countries.

Productivity-enhancing regional infrastructure. Power, mobile phones, Internet connectivity, and major trunk roads can all generate revenue through fees. The productivity increases from these infrastructure services translate into a high willingness to pay. Private firms will provide regional infrastructure when it is profitable—as with the South Atlantic 3 (SAT3) marine cable connecting West Africa to the global fiber optic network, or the Regional African Satellite Communications Organization (RASCOM) public-private partnership to provide satellite telecommunications coverage in Africa. Regional cooperation can provide a sound regulatory framework that, for example, permits free access of

neighboring countries to the backbone infrastructure and free entry by firms into national markets. But the rapid spread of mobile phone coverage in Africa still leaves out many areas (see map 9.1).

Mobility-enhancing regional infrastructure. Cooperation in higher education and training can not only increase the endowment of skilled workers but also enhance labor mobility as students from different countries establish cross-country networks.[31] French cooperation and the EU Commission sponsor a network of three statistical schools in Abidjan (*Ecole Nationale Supérieure de Statistique et d'Economie Appliquée*, ENSEA), Dakar (*Ecole Nationale d'Economie Appliqué*, ENEA), and Yaoundé (*Institut Sous-regional de Statistique et d'Economie Appliqué*, ISSEA), training highly qualified statisticians for French-speaking African private and public enterprises.[32] Recognizing the importance of mobility-enhancing regional infrastructures, a high-level panel of the African Development Bank has proposed centers of excellence in research, tertiary education, and vocational training in collaboration with the private sector.[33]

Trade-enhancing regional infrastructure. Good transport infrastructure reduces transport costs, which in turn increases trade flows.[34] Some observers have argued that there is little potential for intraregional trade within developing neighborhoods

Map 9.1 Mobile phone coverage has spread rapidly in Africa
Global System for Mobile communications network coverage

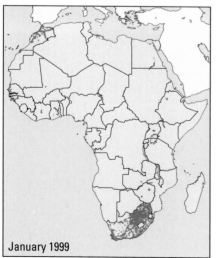
January 1999

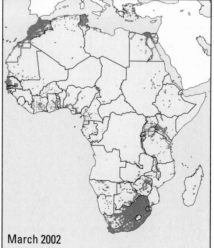
March 2002

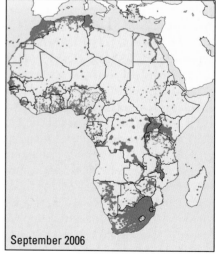
September 2006

Source: Buys and others 2008.

because the small size of economies will not create significant trade flows.[35] If so, improving the quality of regional roads would have no impact on intraregional trade. But recent studies suggest otherwise.

Trade models show that regional investments to pave all the unpaved interstate roads would increase the intraregional trade of West African countries threefold—and boost the region's trade with the rest of the world.[36] Upgrading the main highway network in Sub-Saharan Africa could expand overland trade by about $250 billion over 15 years, with major benefits for the rural poor, while requiring about $20 billion for initial upgrades and $1 billion annually for maintenance.[37] In Central Asia road upgrades could increase trade by half, exceeding the expected gains from tariff reductions or trade facilitation programs of comparable scope. Total intraregional trade in Eastern Europe and Central Asia could be increased 30 percent by upgrading roads in just Albania, Hungary, and Romania.[38]

Coordinated incentives

Coordinated incentives can address market failures and disputes between countries in a regional association. The Central American Common Market, created in 1960 by El Salvador, Guatemala, Honduras, and Nicaragua, faced periodic complaints about redistributing benefits to Honduras and Nicaragua. The agreement collapsed in 1969 following conflict between El Salvador and Honduras. Some studies suggest that the underlying

reason for the collapse was that El Salvador gained much more from regional cooperation because of its better infrastructure.[39] In 1977 the East African Community of Kenya, Tanzania, and Uganda also collapsed after disagreements over the benefits that would be received from common regional services such as airline, harbors, and telecommunications—as well as over ideological differences.[40] Sound compensation mechanisms and better communication about longer-term gains for all participants can reduce the risk of failure of such initiatives.[41]

Consider a taxonomy that incorporates the three essential properties of public goods: nonrivalry, nonexcludability, and aggregated contributions (see table 9.3).[42]

- *Nonrivalry* implies that several groups or individuals can consume the good without diminishing its value. Clean air and water are common examples.
- *Nonexcludability* means that no one can be prevented from consuming the good. There is an incentive to leave the cost of provision to a third party.
- *Aggregated contributions* relate to resource pooling to finance public goods. Commonly, the willingness to contribute decays over time.

Each of these properties requires a coordinated response or some mechanism for equitably matching benefits and costs, or else the good will be underprovided. The quantity and quality of the public good both depend on member contributions. In some instances,

Table 9.3 Regional "club goods" can easily be provided because costless exclusion is possible
Regional public goods, types, and examples

Impact of aggregated contributions	Pure public goods (nonrival, nonexcludable)	Impure public goods	
		Goods for which exclusion is easy	Shared public services
Each contribution has the same impact on the quality and quantity	A clean lake	Transnational park	Preserving the rain forest
Countries more interested in the good can contribute more	Curbing the spread of HIV/AIDS	Power grid	Eliminating transnational terrorist threats
Contribution of weakest member determines the quantity and quality	Implementing international financial standards	Airport hub-spoke network	Preventing and mitigating natural disasters
Contributions of weaker members determines the quantity and quality	Forestalling the spread of pests	Transport infrastructure	Providing Internet connectivity
Contribution of leading countries determines the quantity and quality	Eradication of a disease	Satellite launch facility	Regional peacekeeping
Contribution of strongest member determines the quantity and quality	Discovering an effective treatment	Biohazard facility	Agricultural research and bioprospecting

Sources: Sandler 2002, adapted by the WDR 2009 team.

each member is equally important. In others, the public good depends on the weakest or strongest member, or some combination. This taxonomy suggests that the nature of regional cooperation varies depending on the goal.

When the regional public good is sensitive to the performance of the weaker members, as in a hub-and-spoke airport network, the challenge for the other members is to raise the performance of the weaker links to an acceptable standard. This can be done through cross-country subsidies, as in the EU structural funds. In poor neighborhoods, foreign aid may be the only feasible way to ensure the provision of such public goods. If the good depends on the best-performing member of the neighborhood, such as targeted agricultural research, the weaker members may be asked to contribute to stronger members, or foreign assistance can facilitate its provision.[43]

Trust is especially important in regional cooperation. For the waters of the Nile, the Arab Republic of Egypt and Sudan, two countries that were culturally and politically closer, built the Aswan High Dam near their common border instead of cooperating with Ethiopia, where a dam might have been more efficient for the electricity and water needs of all three countries.[44] International organizations can help build trust, as in the Aral Sea Basin rehabilitation. Another example is the "development diplomacy" used to resolve the Indus River Basin dispute between India and Pakistan, with the World Bank facilitating cooperation. This diplomacy was recognized by the then–World Bank President Eugene Black as "the most important thing the Bank has ever done, by far."[45]

Specific regional agreements can get things started, but they can also lead to multiple and at times overlapping agreements, weakening coordination. Many developing regions need to rationalize their regional economic communities and clarify relations with river basin or power pool organizations.[46] Broader regional agreements can foster trust, provide an institutional framework for compensation that facilitates bargaining, and allow for more effective sanctions.[47] The Southern African

Development Community (SADC), for instance, promoted the Southern Africa Power Pool to take advantage of the distribution of power sources in the region. The Central American Electricity Connection System was initiated in 2005 under the umbrella of the Central American Common Market (CACM). So an umbrella agreement can spawn smaller agreements, or small agreements can be consolidated into umbrella agreements. The path is a tactical choice.

In the same vein, there is a choice between starting with aggregate political agreements, as in the EU enlargement, or starting with economic ties, as in East Asia, with ASEAN+3. Both approaches have seen success and failure. The United Arab Republic joining Egypt and Syria in 1958 foundered in part because of its limited economic advantages. The First East African Community started in 1967 as an economic grouping, but collapsed 10 years later because of political divisions between the major countries. It has since been revived, but the forces for economic and political union remain divided.

The geography of regional integration

Looking at the world's neighborhoods through the lens of market access highlights the role of the three major world markets: Europe, North America, and Northeast Asia, rich neighborhoods where most of the world GDP is clustered (see chapter 3). Proximity to these markets, the thickness of borders, and the fragmentation of world regions reveal the potential market access of all countries (see map 9.2).[48]

Adding up the country scores for potential market access produces three broad types of developing regions:

- *Type 1 countries are in regions close to large world markets*, where the market access score is dominated by proximity to the densest areas in the world. They include those on the periphery of the two largest markets: North America and Western Europe. The neighborhoods are Central America and the Caribbean, Eastern Europe, and the Middle East and North Africa.

Map 9.2　Density, distance, and division combine to determine access to markets
Real market access, relative to the United States in 2003

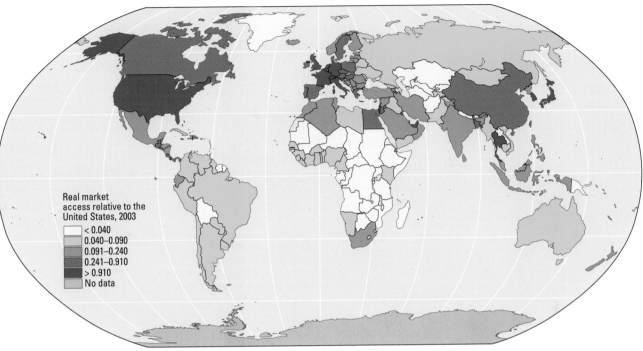

Source: Mayer 2008 for this Report.
Note: To compute potential market access: Each country is assigned a score for the size of its own market (real GDP) and the size of international markets with which it can trade. This is computed by weighting the GDP of other countries by the inverse of a measure that combines physical distance, transport costs, and barriers to trade to show how difficult it is to access these markets. The measure, which is expressed relative to the market access of the United States, essentially combines all three spatial dimensions of density, distance, and division into a composite of potential market access. This map is a complement to the map showing foreign market access in box 6.6.

For these countries, the major problem is division between themselves and major markets. The main instruments for integration will be *institutional:* formal regional trade agreements, more limited sector-specific agreements (on labor mobility or natural resource-sharing), and harmonization of standards and regulations—all implemented with or without formal regional bodies.

- *Type 2 countries are in regions with big neighbors far from world markets.* They include the neighborhoods of the developing world's giants—Brazil, China, India, and South Africa. Although these are potentially large markets, growth has not yet been sustained long enough and many domestic distortions remain.[49] Integration with them runs a risk—to different degrees in different parts of the world—of exposing a neighbor to volatility and of importing inefficiency from the large neighbors' domestic structures. But because their market potential is attractive to enterprises in Europe and

North America, they can serve as a conduit to accessing markets everywhere. In some regions, like those in South Asia, political considerations also preclude economic integration of all the countries in the neighborhood.

These countries have moderate market access potential (see map 9.3). Their distance from major markets holds down their overall score, but the presence of large developing country neighbors can offset this score to some degree. Brazil, China, Nigeria, the Russian Federation, and South Africa are examples of large emerging economies that add considerably to the market access scores of their immediate neighbors. For countries in these neighborhoods, division is compounded by distance. Appropriate instruments include *institutional* and *infrastructure* development, including regionally shared utilities, transport corridors and hubs, and a range of other regional public goods.

Map 9.3   Potential access to major world markets distinguishes the developing world's regions

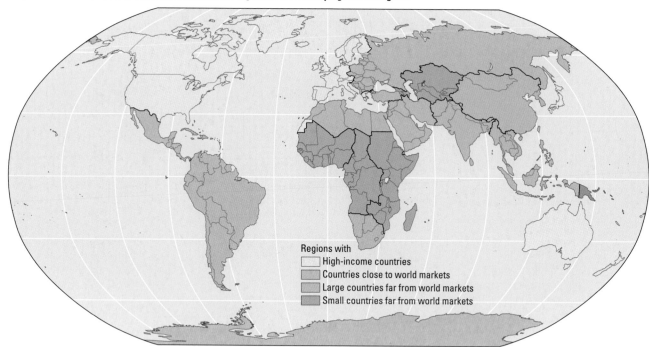

Regions with
- High-income countries
- Countries close to world markets
- Large countries far from world markets
- Small countries far from world markets

Source: WDR 2009 team.

- *Type 3 countries are in regions far from world markets, without a big neighbor.* They make up the "bottom billion" described in Collier (2007) and consist of Central Africa, Central Asia and Caucasus, East Africa, the small Pacific Islands, and West Africa. Many of these countries are falling behind because they are trapped in conflict, suffer from a natural resource curse, are landlocked with bad neighbors, or are small with bad governance.

A range of countries, mostly small, have low market access potential. Having to contend with being far from major markets, these countries face division, distance, and low economic density. In addition to *institutional* and *infrastructure* instruments, they need coordinated *incentives* for regional integration. The incentives include transfers from customs unions and other revenue sources, direct aid, and preferential market access, such as relaxed rules of origin.

All three types of countries have much lower market access potential than rich countries, implying considerable potential for more effective economic integration. But their persistent divisions from major world markets pose barriers to the beneficial flows of people, goods, capital, and ideas.

For each of these country types, the economic integration strategies and priorities will differ (see table 9.4). As the potential for market access becomes lower, the complexity of the integration problem becomes greater, and a broader range of instruments is required to manage integration effectively. For each dimension of the integration challenge, this chapter proposes an instrument for integration—"an I for a D."

Some countries do not fit neatly into any of these three types, such as Chile and Russia. Chile is a relatively small country far from major markets. But it has grown by exporting to world markets without significant regional integration. Russia is another special case because of its peculiar economic geography that spans eleven time zones, connected to Europe at its most populated and most developed western part, and connected with Northeast Asia through the inhospitable and sparsely populated Siberia.[50] One part of Russia, and some of the former Soviet republics with political and economic ties, could be considered a neighborhood with a big country far from world markets. But given that its economic center is in the western part, Russia is more

Table 9.4 An instrument per dimension—a simple framework for regional integration

	Region or neighborhood		
	Close to world markets	**With big countries far from world markets**	**Small countries far from world markets**
World neighborhoods	Central America and Caribbean, North Africa, Middle East	South America, Southern Africa, East Asia, South Asia	Central Africa, East Africa, West Africa, Central Asia and Caucasus, small Pacific Islands
Dimensions of the regional integration challenge	International division (1-D)	Regional division, economic distance (2-D)	International division, economic distance, low density (3-D)
What policy instruments should facilitate	Integration with large nearby markets	Regional integration Regional and global connectivity	Regional integration Regional and global connectivity Regional compensation mechanisms
Priority instruments			
Institutions	Agreements on trade and factor mobility within region and with large markets nearby	Agreements on trade and factor mobility within region and with large markets nearby Regional provision of public goods	Agreements on trade and factor mobility within region Shared facilities (research, central banks, regulatory bodies)
Infrastructure		Transport corridors connecting to large regional economy Regional power grids, telecoms, water management	Hub-and-spoke infrastructure Regional power grids, telecoms, water management
Incentives			Subsidized human development investments in lagging countries and areas Productive investments in leading countries and areas Preferential market access

Source: WDR 2009 team.

appropriately considered close to world markets.

Russia also highlights the point that the concept of market potential is not country-wide but more spatially specific. It is convenient to measure it as a single number for all localities within a country, but many developing economies have areas where markets in other countries are potentially more accessible than their own domestic markets because of poor local infrastructure. Northern areas of Pakistan are closer to Afghanistan and western China than to the major markets in Karachi and Lahore. Medan in Indonesia is closer to Penang in Malaysia than it is to its own capital city. The principles of economic integration in the real world and the use of the instruments can be applied as readily at the subnational level as at the country level (see table 9.4).

The framework in action

What concrete steps can countries take toward regional integration to build better neighborhoods and increase global competitiveness?

Integration options for countries close to world markets

Market access is essential for growth, and proximity is an asset for just-in-time production. Many examples in car manufacturing and in segments of the garment industry demand short-term repeat orders. Perishable goods (fresh fruits and vegetables) are easier to export to nearby markets. Tradable services—such as marketing, research, and complex information technology tasks—benefit from frequent face-to-face interaction, easier if the client is nearby. Countries close to world markets thus have an intrinsic advantage in connecting to markets, suppliers, and ideas. Conversely, for the wealthy world regions—Europe, North America, and Northeast Asia—neighboring developing regions expand their growth potential as domestic markets mature, while also delivering lower-cost platforms for their firms. There are mutual gains to regional cooperation and ongoing processes to further deepen integration.

The Euro-Mediterranean Forum is a long-standing coordination mechanism between Europe, the Middle East, and North Africa. The Caribbean Basin has benefited from privileged access to the U.S. market through various preferential trade schemes, including NAFTA, the Caribbean Basin Initiative, and the Dominican Republic–Central America Free Trade Agreement (DR-CAFTA). China, Japan, and the Republic of Korea are intensifying their relations with Southeast Asian countries through the ASEAN+3 initiative. The long-term benefits are clear to all sides, but the short-term risks and adjustment costs have to be managed.

Institutional reform. The key for countries close to world markets is to undertake institutional reforms and improve domestic governance to fully integrate with the large markets nearby. Free trade alone does not bring the full benefits of integration. Although Turkey has had a free trade agreement with the EU for many years, it did not receive significant FDI until it embarked on major institutional reforms associated with membership talks. The policies and governance standards in countries close to large world markets have to converge with those in the nearby high-income region. Indeed, multinational firms are more likely to locate in a country if it has both institutional and physical connections to a larger market. The large market nearby also has a strong incentive to foster sound policy and governance frameworks in nearby small markets to ensure the stability of its neighborhood. These two factors make the coordination of national policies in neighborhoods close to large world markets both desirable and feasible. The prospect of joining the EU has accelerated the pace of reform in Central Europe. And the prospect of better access to the U.S. market triggered policy reforms in Mexico long before NAFTA took effect.[51]

Institutional reforms include moving to a sound macroeconomic environment that contains inflation and an efficient fiscal system that does not rely on distorted trade policies for budget revenues. They also include establishing a sound institutional framework that limits corruption and improves governance. The Stabilization

and Association Agreements between the EU and the Balkans specify the legal and regulatory reforms to be undertaken before joining the EU. The Balkans also have signed an intraregional free trade agreement, the Central European Free Trade Agreement (CEFTA), to replace the patchwork of 32 bilateral agreements formerly governing their intraregional trade. The new agreement simplifies and harmonizes rules of origin and extends the trade and transport facilitation initiative launched in 2000. The region has also established a common power market and signed an open sky agreement with the EU that could boost tourism.

The Balkan region is close enough to the EU to permit tight integration of its companies into pan-European production networks. Governments can facilitate regional production chains linking their supply capacity to that of the EU by signing mutual recognition agreements, conformity assessments, and other trade-related coordination initiatives. Besides trade promotion, government policies can attract direct investment by multinationals to help countries move from agriculture and basic manufacturing to higher technology production. In the 1990s El Salvador and Costa Rica diversified their exports from traditional products (coffee for El Salvador and bananas for Costa Rica) by developing export processing zones, tax incentives, and FDI promotion in high-tech activities. They more than doubled their exports in a decade. In Costa Rica and Mexico, human capital and FDI have jointly stimulated knowledge-intensive manufacturing activities.[52]

Small countries usually lack the economic and political weight to bargain with wealthier regions. But the Caribbean Regional Negotiating Machinery, created in 1997, has the goal of formulating and implementing a joint Caribbean negotiating strategy in international trade forums.[53] The countries now have technical specialists to deal with each area of negotiations in the WTO. The machinery also facilitates the transition of Caribbean Community (CARICOM) countries toward a single market, with a common external tariff as the basis for a common trade policy. And it has been involved in the negotiations of the EPA between the EU and CARICOM.

To enter the world market for tradable accounting and back-office functions, countries need an efficient telecommunication system and a highly educated workforce. The small countries of the Caribbean region have pooled resources to establish the Eastern Caribbean Telecommunications Authority (ECTEL) and the Caribbean Knowledge and Learning Network (CKLN).

Contrast that with the lack of coordination in the Middle East and North Africa. The regional economy is based mainly on oil revenue and cannot create enough jobs for the 4.2 million people added to the labor force every year.[54] Governments in the region have started the transition to manufacturing and services, but the region's investment climate is still weak. The Pan-Arab Free Trade Area (PAFTA) and the Arab Maghreb Union (AMU) have had little impact on export performance. The declining imports from the rest of the world accompanying the increase in intra-PAFTA and intra-AMU exports suggest that the agreements have been more trade diverting than trade creating.[55] The region could take greater advantage of its proximity to European markets by increasing exports of high-value agricultural products, especially in the winter. But agricultural expansion will put pressure on scarce water resources, so regional agreements for water management and use are essential.[56]

Integration options for countries with big neighbors but distant from world markets

A large home market gives countries an advantage in attracting industrial activities. If this market is also well connected to world markets, this advantage is reinforced. But the second group of countries is far from world markets. South America is farther than Central America and the Caribbean from the U.S. market and even farther from the EU and Northeast Asian markets. South Asia is far from Northeast Asia. Southern Africa is far from all three large world markets. Countries in these

distant regions should try to bridge the gap with world markets by reducing border barriers, but they suffer from late-mover disadvantages in major markets. They can complement their global integration with efforts to build a stronger regional market centered on a large neighbor.

The competitive advantage of neighborhoods with big countries is size: large local markets, abundant human capital, and substantial remittances. Economic activities generating scale economies—such as petroleum and coal products, refineries, pharmaceuticals, electric and electronic machinery, iron and steel, instruments, and nonelectrical machinery—benefit from being concentrated in leading countries that have strong agglomeration economies and better market access.[57] Because most investment in these sectors will go to those countries, usually the largest in the region, this creates tensions. The challenges are to balance political and economic concerns between leading and lagging countries, to ensure spillovers of direct and indirect benefits to lagging countries, and to compete with neighborhoods close to world markets and such emerging economic powers as China and Russia.

Meeting these challenges of division and distance requires institutions to ensure policies and governance that promote trade, factor mobility, and regional growth—and *infrastructure* to connect lagging and leading countries, link regional economic centers, and favor regional production networks integrated with the global economy.

Institutional reform to improve regional integration. The provision of public goods within a region depends on each member to a differing degree according to the good (see table 9.3). Although regional cooperation is sometimes seen as a process to be led by the strongest member economy, this is valid only for certain types of regional public goods, perhaps peacekeeping, research, and specialized shared infrastructure, such as biohazard facilities or satellite launch sites. For other types of goods, mainly network related, institutional reforms depend on the contributions of the weaker members of the region. In these cases, some assistance to build the capabilities of weaker member states can promote overall regional integration.

Countries grow faster when other countries in their neighborhood are also growing, as several studies confirm.[58] For small countries far from world markets but close to a large developing country, their best prospects often lie in growth in the dominant economy.[59] Regional growth centers are one reason for regional economic groupings and for regional peer surveillance. What happens in one's neighborhood, good or bad, is too important to one's own development prospects to ignore.

Economic advantage may not be the sole determinant of regional integration prospects. Conflict in South Asia after the end of the British colonial rule in 1947 prevented the neighborhood from taking advantage of its market size, more than a fifth of the world's people. It took four decades before trade volumes between India and Pakistan passed those of the early 1950s.[60] A recent study estimates that trade between India and Pakistan would increase by 405 percent if the territorial and political disputes were resolved.[61] In 2004 the two countries engaged in the "Composite Dialogue" on peace and security issues, including terrorism and drug trafficking, confidence-building, economic and commercial cooperation, and friendly exchanges in various fields. On a broader regional basis, the South Asian Association for Regional Cooperation is a forum to discuss development challenges, such as cooperation in energy production and water basin management. The burden is on India, the largest country by far in the neighborhood, to take the lead in promoting the common agenda.[62]

Zimbabwe's political instability since 1998 has dimmed growth prospects in the Southern African neighborhood. Attempts to mediate by the African Union and the SADC have brought limited results. South Africa, the largest country in the Southern Africa Customs Union, has a large interest in a stable neighborhood. But the large rents from natural resources along regional transport corridors are realized even during conflict, though most of the benefits are not shared widely. So economic reasons may be unlikely to provide enough

incentives, and the growing political crisis poses risks to the effectiveness of deeper regional integration.

Investments in cross-country infrastructure to connect regional markets. In neighborhoods with big countries distant from world markets, the costs and benefits of cross-country infrastructure can differ between large and small countries in the neighborhood. Where the distribution of benefits differs from the proposed sharing of the costs, there may be underinvestment in such infrastructure. One example is a landlocked country such as Bolivia or Paraguay that needs access to the coast to export its products. International transit agreements guarantee this right to landlocked countries, but since they are not always enforced, support from the international community, or from regional institutions, may be necessary. Another example is the potential for better infrastructure to link India's northeastern lagging regions and Bangladesh, Bhutan, and Nepal. The South Asia Subregional Economic Cooperation (SASEC) initiative of the Asian Development Bank suggests that such cross-border cooperation can be beneficial for all these countries.

Several major cross-border infrastructure projects are being developed. The Maputo Development Corridor between South Africa and Mozambique was initiated in 1995 to rehabilitate the primary infrastructure network along the corridor (road, rail, port, and border posts), attract investment in the corridor's catchment area, and provide employment opportunities for disadvantaged populations (see map 9.4). Its structure, led by South Africa, promotes fast-track design and implementation of bankable private investment projects and public-private partnerships. But it risks failing to address the social service needs of local communities.[63] Some ongoing evaluations of the corridor show that border-crossing costs and delays are common impediments, possibly diverting freight to domestic corridors. This suggests that more formal institutional cooperation between the countries could generate additional benefits.

South America has been much more ambitious in its plans with the Initiative

Map 9.4   Building regional infrastructure in Southern Africa
The Maputo Development Corridor

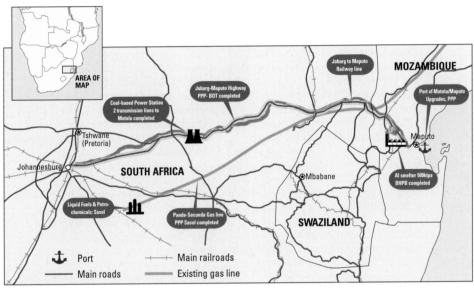

Source: MINTEK 2007.

for Integration of Regional Infrastructure, launched in 2000 to promote the integration and modernization of the 12 countries' physical infrastructure in the energy, telecommunications, and transport sectors, with the goal of improving global competitiveness. The initiative focuses on 10 hubs of economic integration across the continent and on harmonizing regulatory frameworks. It has identified 40 megaprojects and hundreds of smaller infrastructure improvement projects for potential financing, with an aggregate cost in the tens of billions of dollars. Implementation has been slow, however.

Integration options for countries distant from world markets and with small neighbors

Central Asia has the highest proportion of landlocked countries (see box 9.4) with many common problems that could be more effectively tackled through better regional cooperation. The small Pacific Islands are the most geographically fragmented, making them "sealocked," with limited accessibility to world markets (see box 9.5). And Africa between the tropics has the largest number of landlocked countries, many small in population and

GDP, most among the world's poorest, and far too many prone to conflict. These neighborhoods face divisions and barriers to trade and factor mobility, are distant from major markets, and lack the density of economic production to benefit from agglomeration economies. Collier (2007) identifies their populations as the "bottom billion."

The challenge for countries in isolated neighborhoods is to find ways to integrate regionally and globally. Their geographic situation implies that the degree of integration rarely will be as high as in other countries, so the prospects for manufactured trade are more limited. Conversely, their isolation provides them with natural protection of their home markets.

Many of these economies have minerals and other natural resources, such as water, that can best be exploited on a regional basis. While there is evidence of growth spillover from resource-rich countries to their neighbors in Sub-Saharan Africa,[64] regional integration is the key to getting resource-led growth going and to spreading benefits more broadly. These countries face the triple challenges of division, distance, and density. Addressing them will require institutional reform, scaling

BOX 9.4 *Integration in Central Asia*

Central Asia has five landlocked countries: Kazakhstan, the Kyrgyz Republic, Tajikistan, Turkmenistan, and Uzbekistan. The countries vary in population, type of government, and willingness to cooperate with each other and the rest of the world. But the region has established national identities and institutions, avoided violent conflicts, established the foundations for market-based economies, and sustained an economic recovery since the end of the 1990s.

Consider many regional institutions and initiatives. The Central Asia Cooperation Organization (CACO) comprises Kazakhstan, the Kyrgyz Republic, Russia, Tajikistan, Turkmenistan, and Uzbekistan, which merged with EURASEC (Eurasian Economic Community) in 2005. The Central Asia Regional Economic Cooperation Initiative (CAREC) comprises Azerbaijan, China, Kazakhstan, the Kyrgyz Republic, Mongolia, Tajikistan, and Uzbekistan. The Shanghai Cooperation Organisation (SCO) comprises China, Kazakhstan, the Kyrgyz

Republic, Russia, Tajikistan, and Uzbekistan. Then there are the Commonwealth of Independent States (CIS), the Collective Security Treaty Organization (CSTO), the Economic Cooperation Organization (ECO), and the Special Programme for the Economies of Central Asia (SPECA).

The sheer number of regional agreements illustrate the problems that can arise from a disjointed regional approach. Regional initiatives in Central Asia can foster integration but add duplication and complexity to reform. The ongoing WTO accession for many of these countries could help, because the WTO has clear rules on regional trade agreements. Also needed are trade and transport facilitation initiatives and behind-the-border reforms to improve the countries' attractiveness to FDI and bolster their global integration. (Countries with the highest cost of business entry have lower imports, exports, and FDI inflows.) Regional forums for business communities could offer suggestions

and feedback on the design and implementation of trade and related policies.

The region loses an estimated 3 percent of GDP annually because of poor water management. Agreements are also needed for oil and gas resources to reach international markets. Many environmental problems remain as a legacy from the Soviet era, such as radioactivity from abandoned uranium mines and dangerous remnants of biological and nuclear tests. Regional organizations could be rationalized around these key themes of trade and transport facilitation, water, energy, and environment management. They could develop long-term plans for these issues, bringing civil society and academic institutions into the fray. The international community could facilitate the strengthening of institutions with clear mandates and targets.

Sources: Linn and Tiomkin 2006; Broadman 2005; United Nations 2005a.

BOX 9.5 *Integrating the small and distant Pacific Islands with world markets*

Small island developing states face a great risk of marginalization in the global economy because of their small size, remoteness from large markets, and vulnerability to economic and natural shocks. And with their fragile ecosystems, they are highly vulnerable to domestic pollution and rising seas. Their share in global merchandise trade fell from 0.4 percent of world exports of goods in 1980 to 0.2 percent in 2003, while their share of global services trade remained at 0.7 percent.

One effort to deal with the special problems of small islands is the South

Pacific Regional Trade and Economic Cooperation Agreement (SPARTECA), a nonreciprocal trade agreement for which Australia and New Zealand offer duty-free, unrestricted, or concessional access for almost all products originating from the countries of the Pacific Islands Forum. To qualify for preferential access, goods exported to Australia and New Zealand must meet the rules of origin set out in SPARTECA.

The textiles, clothing, and footwear industry has been a major beneficiary. But Australia and New Zealand are planning to adopt free trade by 2010, ending

this preferential access to their markets. Without significant trade preferences, the Pacific Islands need other ways to integrate with their large neighbors. More radical approaches, including consideration of greater labor mobility, could be required. Children in island families receiving remittances from overseas family members show strong improvements in education and health outcomes, suggesting labor mobility could be a powerful driver for longer-term development in these countries.

Sources: UNCTAD 2002; SPARTECA 1996.

up infrastructure investments, and targeted incentives to encourage regional integration.

Identifying natural neighborhoods for institutional reform. Neighborhoods with small countries distant from world markets need to focus on specific institutional needs that drive their cooperation. There is no shortage of international agreements.

But these agreements are often poorly implemented, their effectiveness tends to be low, and they overlap in responsibilities. The administrative costs of participating in such agreements are high in relation to the small benefits, given the small size of the participating economies. The African Union has spotlighted the inefficiencies of 13 or 14 overlapping regional economic communities and has called for their rationalization.[65]

Regional integration can be rooted in the traditional economic and sociocultural interactions within natural neighborhoods, as building blocks for broader integration. Trust can be built on a shared language. East African countries share Swahili, which has facilitated trade in the neighborhood for centuries. Free trade was established between Kenya and Uganda during colonial times.[66] West African countries share the Dioula, Haoussa, and Peuhl cultures, which, nurtured by Islam, developed an impressive trade network.[67]

Interactions between neighboring areas or cities across countries can also provide the base for broader integration—a form of transfrontier regionalism that could follow European models.[68] Sub-Saharan Africa has many pairs of large cities that are near each other but separated by a national border (see map 9.5). This carries hidden economic costs that can be overcome through

cross-border agreements. Cameroon shares twin cities with West African neighbors, but none in its Central African neighborhood. Similarly, local integration initiatives, such as growth triangles starting in the early 1980s in East Asia, can take advantage of the economic complementarities in bordering regions.

A succession of large coastal cities along the Gulf of Guinea spans from Abidjan in Côte d'Ivoire to Douala in Cameroon, and includes Accra, Cotonou, Lagos, and Lomé. When discussing "growth champions," it may be worth keeping in mind the potential of such multicountry agglomerations, rather than thinking of some nations as regional growth leaders. When seen through the lens of economic geography, the regional integration priorities change to prioritizing regional infrastructure investments in leading areas that span several countries.

Regional trade in agricultural products can be another entry point for broader regional integration. This requires a revival

Map 9.5 Twin cities for local integration
City pairs in bordering regions within 150 kilometers and with more than 100,000 inhabitants

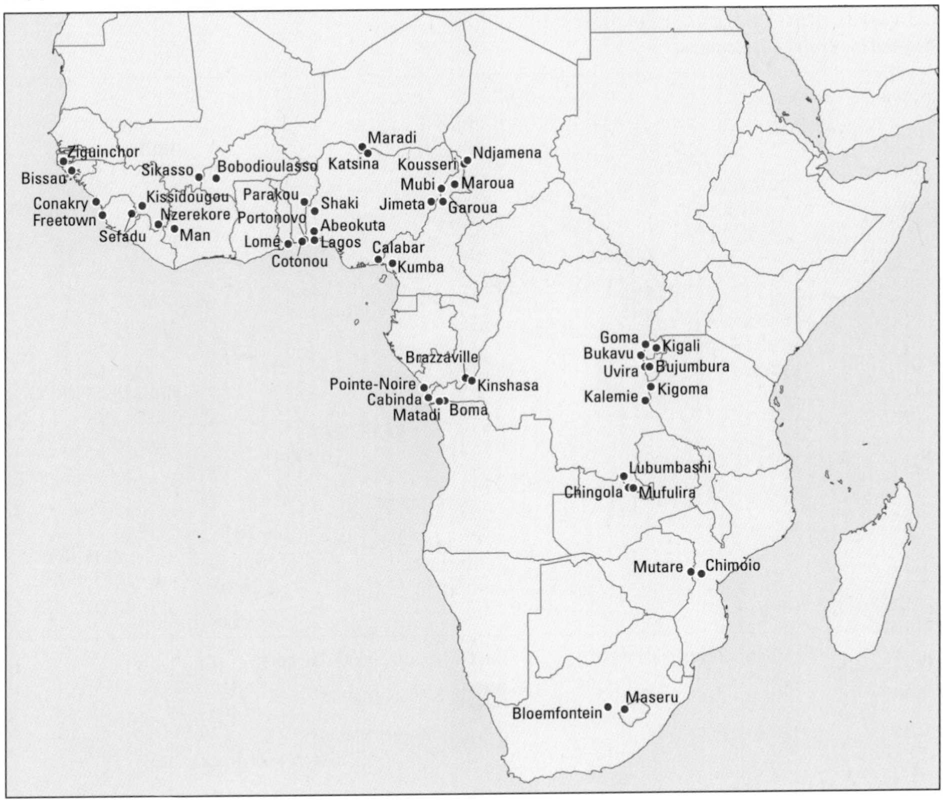

Source: WDR 2009 team.

of regional trade agreements, adequate cross-country infrastructure, institutional reforms, and nonmarket institutions such as farmer cooperatives.[69] The Horn of Africa could build on its livestock trade, though security poses a problem.[70] West Africa could build on cotton, if leading agricultural areas across several countries can be integrated into a single, efficient production and processing zone: the Sahelian cotton basin in the border region of Burkina Faso, Côte d'Ivoire, and Mali (see map 9.6). This region, dominated by Dioula ethnic groups, is anchored by three cities—Bobodioulasso in Burkina Faso, Korhogo in Côte d'Ivoire, and Sikasso in Mali.[71] In 2000 the population of this area was 4 million (11 percent of the total in the three countries), with an estimated gross regional product of 1,000 billion CFA francs (10 percent of aggregate national GDPs).

The areas in this region have complementary economic endowments. Bobodioulasso has an international airport with storage facilities. Korhogo has a regional airport, a specialized university, and training centers in agricultural science. Sikasso

is the center of the cotton basin, with the most production. Rails connect Ouagadougou and the port of Abidjan, and roads link all three cities. And many ginneries and textile industries are located in the region. By upgrading and pooling infrastructure within a regional industrial development program, input costs could fall and cotton-based industries such as textile and garments could become competitive in the global market. Such an initiative would require a strong commitment from the participating countries and support from regional associations and the international community.

Institutional development to increase scale, support labor and capital mobility, and improve market access. Some regions have taken concrete steps toward integration. ECOWAS has signed protocols for the free movement of people, abolishing visa and entry permit requirements. In fact, labor mobility has always been a hallmark of Sub-Saharan Africa, where tradition or colonial laws have favored circular labor mobility. Nomads moved across countries in response to seasonal climatic change,

Map 9.6   West Africa has potential for cotton-led industrial development

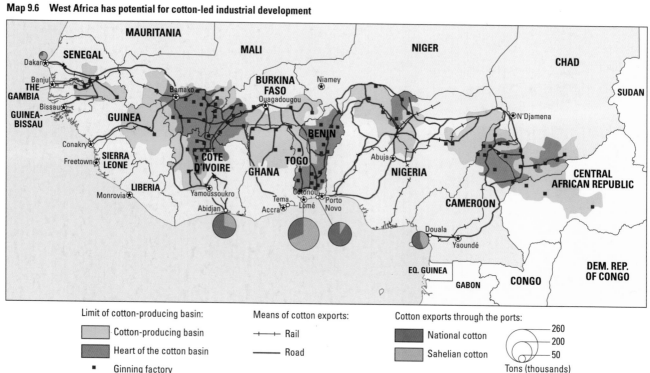

Limit of cotton-producing basin:
- Cotton-producing basin
- Heart of the cotton basin
- ■ Ginning factory

Means of cotton exports:
- +—+—+ Rail
- —— Road

Cotton exports through the ports:
- National cotton
- Sahelian cotton

260
200
50

Tons (thousands)

Sources: Atlas on Regional Integration in West Africa. ECOWAS; Sahel and West Africa Club/OECD 2006.

while sedentary farmers also moved seasonally in search of supplementary income during the dry season.[72] But the skills of the workforce need to improve. For higher education, technical training, and research, cooperation within the neighborhood can support institutions beyond the means of individual countries. And a better local business climate and new opportunities in regional growth centers may induce African migrants with technical and business know-how to return from abroad.

Invest in regional infrastructure. The New Partnership for Africa's Development (NEPAD) spatial development initiative identified the Bas-Congo development corridor involving Angola, the Democratic Republic of Congo, and the Republic of Congo as a region where deep integration would have large benefits, based on enormous hydroelectric power potential.[73] Two other development corridors also have promise in West and East Africa:

- The Gulf of Guinea development corridor—linking Benin, Côte d'Ivoire, Ghana, Liberia, Nigeria, and Togo—could integrate West African economies through transport and energy. It could also connect five large coastal cities with a critical mass of economic activities and administrative service provision: Abidjan, Accra, Cotonou, Lagos, and Lomé.

- The Mombasa development corridor—linking the Democratic Republic of Congo, Kenya, Sudan, and Uganda—could use established infrastructure links such as the Northern Corridor to unlock natural resources in the Democratic Republic of Congo and southern Sudan.

Even with more regional infrastructure, better human capital, and greater factor mobility, these neighborhoods still face being latecomers in the global market, where other developing countries with low-cost advantage dominate the market for basic manufactures. African countries need to diversify their export base to reduce dependence on natural resources. Many of these neighborhoods need to design explicit export diversification strategies to capture a larger share of the world market (see box 9.2). Success requires

institutional cooperation as well as specific infrastructure among countries in the neighborhood.

Providing a regional public good is less complex politically if it is based on a mutually beneficial and profitable project, as in much of energy, communications, and irrigation infrastructure. But for small isolated countries, regional infrastructure projects require considerable outside support. Traffic volumes are too small in most parts of Africa for toll roads to be feasible. And regional infrastructure may be more beneficial for one country, even though most of the investment costs are incurred in another. In addition to reinvigorating public-private partnerships in infrastructure, there is a need for scaling up International Development Association (IDA) contributions to regional integration, systematizing Aid-for-Trade initiatives[74] and rationalizing the interaction between regional development banks and global financial institutions. Less than 3 percent of all international development support now goes for regional programs.[75]

Use coordinated incentives to facilitate regional integration. African countries need to make a strong commitment to regional integration, sharing the costs and benefits from opening borders in natural neighborhoods. Multilateral agencies and donors need to commit to long-term support of these initiatives by providing financial and technical assistance and better access to markets. Concrete steps can be sequenced, gradually ensuring the irreversibility of policy reforms in leading and lagging countries. Preferential trade agreements and aid flows could be tied to cooperation among recipient countries, with the proposed EPAs with the EU as one model (see box 9.3). In cases in which incentives for regional cooperation are insufficient for some partners—such as facilitating access for a landlocked economy to a port in its neighboring country—conditional aid flows with clear performance targets may be required.

A key incentive for policy reform in Africa is temporary preferential access to OECD markets.[76] Africa cannot wait for a big wage difference with Asia before starting to attract greater productive investment

BOX 9.6 *A contract with Africa? The give and take of the world's biggest development challenge*

Better understanding of the geography of development can lead to more effective development aid. This Report advocates different strategies for Africa's landlocked countries and its resource-poor coastal economies. The former have natural disadvantages associated with geography and a large distance to market that reduces their potential growth by as much as half a percentage point per year. But what is unusual in Africa is that resource-poor coastal countries have underperformed. These are the types of countries that act as engines of growth in other world regions. Africa's growth poles are still weak.

This Report argues, to exaggerate somewhat, that development strategies for leading areas should invest in places, and strategies for lagging areas should invest in people. Seen through the lens of economic geography, the thrust of development assistance to Africa that focused on education, health, and other social infrastructure in the late 1990s seems correct for the lagging, landlocked countries. But this assistance appears to focus on the wrong priorities for coastal countries, which need physical infrastructure and better integration with global markets.

A better contract between donors and countries would be to differentiate approaches across countries depending on their potential market access. This Report proposes a tailored approach, which would lay out the rights and responsibilities of countries according to their potential

regional role. For each of Sub-Saharan Africa's regions, the contract would include specific obligations and actions that encourage regional development. The governments of East, West, and Central Africa would commit to the following:

- Establishing "Regional Economic Areas" that would tie the economic interests of leading and lagging countries in Africa's regional neighborhoods tightly together and provide a framework for the provision of regional public goods.
- Pursuing freer movements of labor, capital, goods, and services within these areas.
- Maintaining and protecting access routes between landlocked countries and outlets for trade.

The strategy would combine institutional cooperation, investment in regional infrastructure, and coordinated interventions that may require giving up some hard-won and jealously guarded attributes of national sovereignty.

In exchange for these actions, bilateral and multilateral development partners would commit to the following:

- A large increase in international financial assistance for improved social services and other life-sustaining infrastructure aimed at raising living standards and creating portable human capital in lagging countries.
- Increased financial support for growth-sustaining infrastructure—including

ports, transport links, and information and communication technology—in the coastal countries, as well as corridor infrastructure to link coastal and interior markets.

- Preferential access for Sub-Saharan Africa's exports, with liberalized rules of origin that encourage regional supply chains.

Things are already headed in this direction. In 2007 the Government of the United Kingdom, through its Department for International Development, allocated $1.4 billion over the coming decade to efforts by the governments of Burundi, Kenya, Rwanda, Tanzania, and Uganda and to revitalize the East African Economic Community. The European Commission is also adopting a regional approach with its economic partnership agreements. But all donors could be bolder in their approaches.

The experience of Europe after World War II illustrates how national determination to prioritize reconstruction coupled with international assistance can pay off. Regional integration in Europe did not go smoothly initially. But encouraged by the tough terms of cooperation in the Marshall Plan, a process of integration that would have been impossible a generation earlier, created the largest common market for capital, labor, and ideas today.

Source: WDR 2009 team.

and larger export shares, especially with multilateral trade negotiations at the WTO driving down tariffs at a fast pace. Initiatives such as the U.S. Africa Growth and Opportunity Act and the EU Everything But Arms could be extended to all Sub-Saharan countries, with more liberal rules of origin and a longer time span. This may allow at least some of these countries to break into world markets and could jump-start export diversification in African neighborhoods. A "contract with Africa" could be a framework for supporting such coordinated incentives (see box 9.6).

Over the past centuries, East, Central, and West Africa have suffered a series of "formative disasters" (see "Geography in Motion, Density, Distance, and Division in Sub-Saharan Africa"). Today, they pose an especially difficult development challenge spanning the three development dimensions—density, distance, and division. To reshape their economic geography, the policy response has to be commensurately calibrated. A three-dimensional challenge demands employing all three instruments of integration—institutions, infrastructure, and incentives.

Density, Distance, and Division in Sub-Saharan Africa

In November 1884, Chancellor Otto von Bismarck of Germany convened a meeting of 14 European colonial powers in Berlin. After four centuries of competition and hostility, the time had come to negotiate and settle territorial claims. Britain, France, Germany, and Portugal were the main players; no Africans were invited. Four months later, the borders of African countries had been charted in a pattern still recognizable today (see map G4.1). Bismarck's disciplined solution remained until the end of World War I, when the League of Nations confiscated Germany's four colonies and gave other colonizers the mandate of governing them. At independence in the 1950s and 1960s, Sub-Saharan Africa had almost 50 countries, many of them called "artificial states," with borders cutting across physical geographic features and partitioning ethnic groups into more than one country.[1]

For Sub-Saharan Africa, the Berlin conference was just the last in a long line of what geographers have termed "formative disasters," unfavorably altering the human, physical, and political geography of the continent, creating continentwide problems of low density, long distances, and divided countries.

- *Low density.* Sub-Saharan Africa has long been a continent where people are scarce. Its population in the eighteenth century was about 90 million. Eurasia, with an area about twice that of Africa, had more than five times as many people. But these initial conditions were tragically worsened by the slave trade. Between 1700 and 1810, an estimated 15 million Africans—one of every six—were taken to the Americas. Some areas were depopulated, and many more mired in devastating conflict as the price put on humans turned Africans against each another. Europe finally put an end to the slave trade, and replaced it with colonialism in the eighteenth century. A rapacious trade in men was then replaced by a plundering of the continent for minerals. But even with new settlers, the continent still suffered from low density in most places.

- *Long distances.* Since the Holocene Age that began about 18,000 years ago, the Sahara has been an inhospitable desert, separating northern Africa from what we now call "Sub-Saharan" Africa. The global warming of that period had other major consequences. It cut contact between most of Africa and the emerging civilizations in the Arab Republic of Egypt and the Middle East. It turned Equatorial Africa from a temperate savannah into a hot and humid place where malaria and yellow fever thrived. Proximity to wild animals and the absence of frost—a natural disinfectant—increased human vulnerability to diseases. And when Africans settled in healthy, fertile places, they were again displaced by colonial settlers. Since the 1950s armed conflicts in pre- and postindependence movements have aggravated the problem of refugees. The result: movements of people that have left many in remote areas far from the centers of economic activity. The long distance to density still affects the growth potential of a large part of the African population.

- *Deep divisions.* The partitioning of Africa in 1884 left the continent with the most countries per square kilometer of any region in the world. Each African country has an average of four neighbors; in Latin America the average is 2.3. There are also religious divisions, between and within countries. Chad, Côte d'Ivoire, Ethiopia, Nigeria, Somalia, and Sudan, for example, are fragmented into Islamic and non-Islamic parts. Islam came from the Middle East into North and West Africa by land and into East Africa by sea. Later, European colonialists brought Christianity. The superimposition of these great world religions on top of traditional beliefs reinforced the continent's divide and may have added to conflict.[2]

Sub-Saharan Africa today suffers from the triple disadvantages of low density, long distance, and deep division that put the continent at a developmental disadvantage. These spatial dimensions reduce proximity between economic agents within Sub-Saharan Africa, and between Africa and the rest of the world. "Cumulative causation" between these forces catches many countries in Sub-Saharan Africa in a "proximity trap."[3]

Low density is linked to weak agglomeration forces

The average population density on the continent (77 people per square kilometer) is among the lowest in the world.[4] A sparsely inhabited continent can overcome this by using its land and people well and by concentrating resources in urban agglomerations. But Sub-Saharan

Map G4.1   Africa's borders were charted before World War I

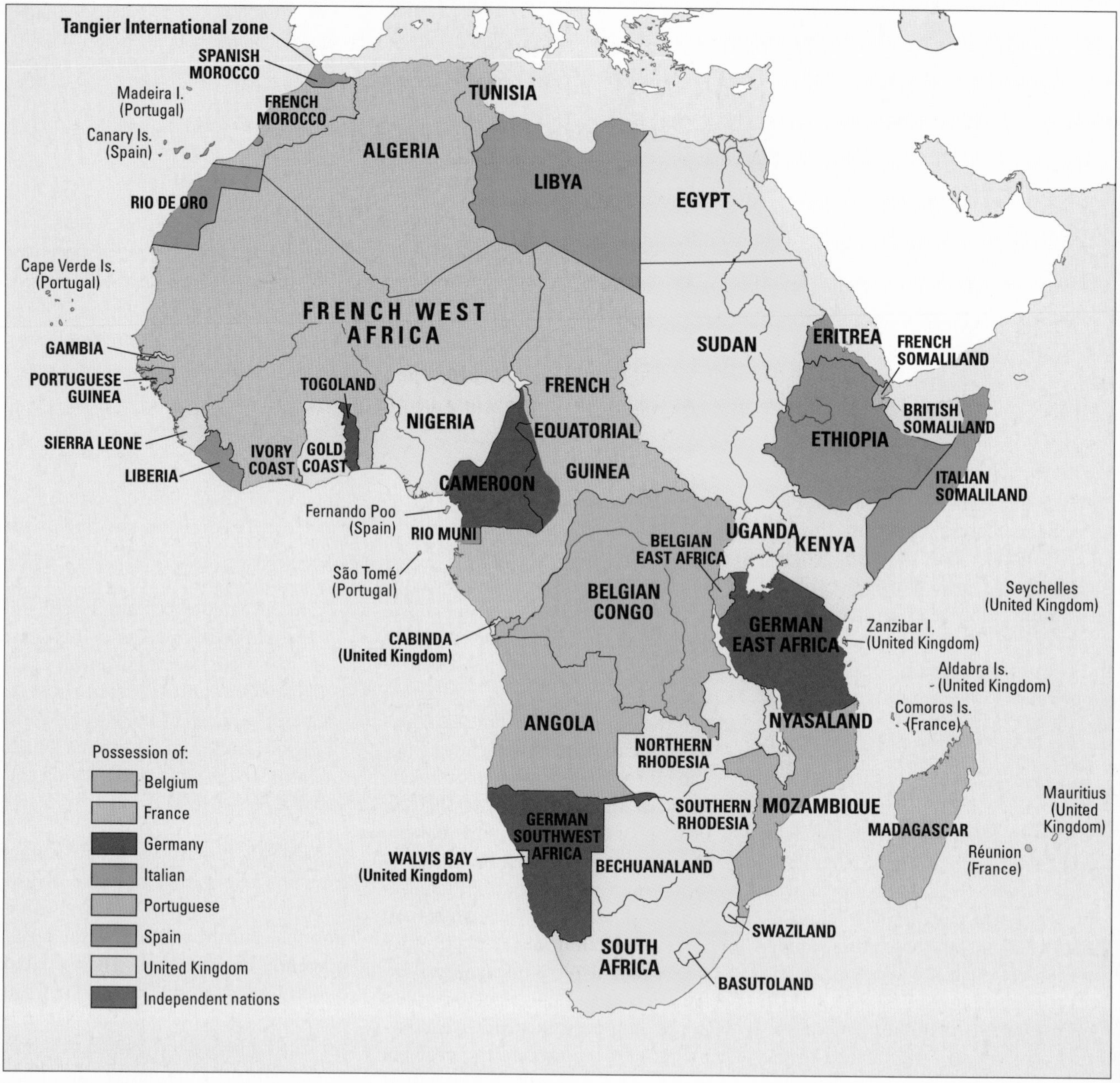

Source: WDR 2009 team, based on Pakenham 1992.

Africa is the world's least urbanized continent, with only one-third of the population living in urban areas in 2000, according to the UN's *World Urbanization Prospects.* Due to the lack of regular and recent censuses, even this may overstate the urbanization in Africa.[5] The agglomeration index in chapter 1 gives Africa a score of 30 percent, compared with about 50 percent for the rest of the world.

Divisions between countries in Africa can distort the pattern of urbanization. One simulation suggests that if Africa's 50 countries were 50 states in one country, like the United States, the largest cities would be even bigger than they are today, capable of sustaining diversified economies and incubating entrepreneurship, skills, and innovation. Without such prospects Africa's skilled labor has migrated to other continents.

Long distances raise transport costs and reduce factor mobility

Distance reinforces the effects of low population density on productivity in Africa. While much is made of Africa's distance from world markets, the primary problem is domestic—long distances within countries.[6] Table G4.1 indicates that Africa has one of the lowest road densities in the world, second only

Table G4.1 The most distant and divided regions—trading and transport are expensive

Region	Trading time across borders for exports (days)[a]	Average transport costs ($ per container to Baltimore)[b]	Population in landlocked countries (%)[b]	Ratio of number countries to surface area[b]	Road density (km² of road per surface area) (1999)[c]	Estimated number of civil conflicts, (1940–2000)[d]
East Asia & Pacific	24	3,900	0.42	1.44	0.72	8
Europe & Central Asia	29	–	23.00	1.17	–	13
Latin America & Caribbean	22	4,600	2.77	1.52	0.12	15
Middle East & North Africa	27	2,100	0	1.60	0.33	17
South Asia	34	3,900	3.78	1.67	0.85	24
Sub-Saharan Africa	40	7,600	40.20	2.00	0.13	34

Sources: a. World Bank 2006b, p. 44; b. Ndulu and others 2007, p. 101; c. Ndulu and others 2007, p. 29; d. Fearon and Laitin 2003, pp. 7–10.
Note: – = not available

to Latin America. But unlike Latin America—where the population lives largely along the coast, making it unnecessary to build roads into the interior—Africa has a third of its population in landlocked countries and even more far from access to global markets. Economic distance in Africa—in the sense of market access (see chapter 2)—is further lengthened by armed conflicts and linguistic diversity (see map G4.1). Economic distance has isolated a large proportion of Africans from access to domestic and global markets. Physical factors, such as the relative absence of navigable rivers and natural harbors, have been serious barriers to trade. Low levels of domestic and international trade, in turn, limit the potential for growth.

Deep divisions raise transport costs

Sub-Saharan Africa is a highly fragmented continent with many borders, many neighbors, and high transport costs. Africa is as physically close to global markets as is East Asia—about 7,500 kilometers—and closer than Latin America (9,000 kilometers).[7] But it still costs almost twice as much to ship a container to the east coast of the United States from Africa as from other regions (see table G4.1). Compounding expensive access to global markets is costly access to regional markets. It takes an African exporter about 40 days to cross the border into a neighboring country, compared with 22 days for a Latin American counterpart. For the

third of Africans who live in landlocked countries, the costs of division are even greater. They must move goods long distances over land—expensive, because each 1 percent increase in distance increases transport costs by approximately 0.25 percent.[8] And landlocked countries must rely on the goodwill (and efficient investment) of neighbors for access to ports and markets.

Meeting the challenge—better urbanization, more domestic specialization, and more regional integration

Africa can reduce the limitations of its poor economic geography. Better urban agglomerations can deliver scale efficiencies. Transport links can help domestic markets grow. And regional and global integration can promote trade. Regional integration, labor mobility, investments in trade, communication and transport infrastructure, and peace and stability should remain high on the agenda. They create good neighborhoods, and better neighborhoods will facilitate investment, trade, and factor mobility in a cycle of prosperity.

- **Urbanization.** Contrary to some thinking, urbanization, done right, can help development *more* in Africa than elsewhere. Despite five decades of low-quality urbanization, living standards in Africa's cities are much higher than in the countryside. If urbanization can be managed better, along the lines proposed in chapter 7,

significant gains can be expected in productivity and poverty reduction.
- **Territorial development.** The guidance from economic geography is unambiguous: firms and workers seek agglomeration, and migration is a natural way to increase density and reduce distance to markets. Chapter 8 proposes some principles and priorities for countries where lagging areas are sparsely populated and divided along ethnic, linguistic, or religious lines. Agriculture is one priority, but policies to help *leading* areas exploit scale economies may be especially important in Africa as a latecomer to economic development.
- **Regional integration.** Given its history, political regionalism may have to take the lead in African regional integration. The experience of Western Europe summarized earlier in this Report spotlights the importance of starting small and keeping expectations realistic. Regional integration takes time and will not happen in all parts of Africa at once. Infrastructure projects are a good place to start. But through regional integration, Africa can undo some of what Bismarck and his guests did in 1884. Chapter 9 showed that many African countries have taken the first steps, outlining what the rest of the world can do to help.

Based on a contribution by Wim Naudé.

Bibliographical Note

This Report draws on a wide range of World Bank documents and on numerous outside sources. Background papers and notes were prepared by Maria Abreu, Stephen Adam, Yusuf Ahmad, M Alva, Alberto Behar, Sarah Boeckmann, Marius Brulhart, Massimiliano Cali, Yang Chen, Michael Clemens, Kirsten Cornelson, Souleymane Coulibaly, Nicholas Crafts, Edward Feser, John Felkner, Kali Glen-Haley, Geoffrey J.D. Hewings, Austin Kilroy, Melissa Klink, Christian Layke, Philip Manners, Robert Margo, Thomas Markussen, Thierry Mayer, John McCombie, Topher McDougal, Claudio E. Montenegro, Megumi Muto, Andrew Nelson, B. Nelson, Wim Naudé, Park Sam Ock, Jinhwan Oh, Keijiro Otsuka, Ken Poole, Lant Pritchett, Diego Puga, David Satterthwaite, Andrey Treyvish, Hirotsugu Uchida, Dirk Willem Te Velde, Cam Vidler, and Nong Zhu.

Background papers for the Report are available either on the World Wide Web www.worldbank.org/wdr2009 or through the World Development Report office. The views expressed in these papers are not necessarily those of the World Bank or of this Report.

Many people inside and outside the World Bank gave comments to the team. Valuable comments, guidance, support, and contributions were provided by James Adams, Uma Adusumilli, Theodore Ahlers, Alexis Albion, Junaid Ahmed, Halil Ibrahim Akca, Mohamad Al-Arief, Riad Al Khoury, Asad Alam, Ritu Anand, Candra Fajri Ananda, Inger Andersen, Martin Andersson, Patricia Clarke Annez, Jorge Saba Arbache, Omar Arias, Jean Eric Aubert, Fouad Awada, Jit Bajpai, George Banjo, Luca Barbone, Elena Bardasi, Alberto Behar, Connie Bernard, Anthony Bigio, S. A. Dan Biller, Kate Bird, Alessandro Magnoli Bocchi, Zeljko Bogetic, Laurent Bossard, Carlos Braga, Milan Brahmbhatt, Marie-H. P. Bricknell, Robert Buckley, Thomas Buckley, Derek Byerlee, Fernando Cabezas, Francisco Carneiro, Mauricio Carrizosa, Shyam Chainani, Nadereh Chamlou, Jaime Saavedra Chanduvi, Robert Chase, Ken Chomitz, Abderrahmane Chorfi, Luc Christiaensen, Marie-Helene Collion, Hector Valdes Conroy, Jean-Marie Cour, Xavier Crépin, Aude de Amorim, Augusto de la Torre, Christopher Delgado, Christian Delvoie, Gabriel Demombynes, Sebastien Dessus, Jaime de Melo, Mamadou Dem, Banu Demir, Michele de Nevers, Jean-Jacques Dethier, Shantayanan Devarajan, Makhtar Diop, Ndiame Diop, Frederique Docquier, Paul Dorosh, Cuney Duzyol, William Easterly, Ibrahim Elbadawi, Lewis Eldridge, Antonio Estache, Warren Evans, Shahrokh Fardoust, Marianne Fay, Wolfgang Fengler, Alexander Ferguson, Francisco Ferreira, Melissa Fossberg, Vivien Foster, Bernard G. Funck, Saurabh Garg, Kristalina Georgieva, Ejaz Ghani, Marcelo Giugale, Sudarshan Gooptu Jose Luis Guasch, Sumila Gulyani, Jonathan Halpern, Simon Hay, Rui Hao, Jesko S. Hentschel, Santiago Herrera, Andre Herzog, Kate Higging, Larry Hinkle, Mun S. Ho, Bernard Hoekman, Vivian Hon, Yukon Huang, David Hummels, Djibrilla Issa, Narasimham Vijay Jagannathan, Zelena Jagdeo, Rachid Jamali, Emmanuel Jimenez, Steen Jorgensen, Abha Joshi-Ghani, Ellis J. Juan, Stephen George Karam, Shigeo Katsu, Phil Keefer, Christine Kessides, Peyvand Khaleghian, Homi Kharas, Nadim Khouri, Jacob Kolster, Aart Kraay, Alexander Kremer, K. L. Krishna, Kathy Krumm, Alice Kuegler, Praveen Kumar, Caterina Laderchi, Amina Lahreche, Peter Lanjouw, Hedi Larbi, Frannie Leautier, Phillippe Leite, Jeffrey Lewis, Maureen Lewis, Johannes Linn, Laszlo Lovei, Xubei Luo, William Maloney, Jean-Michel Marchat, Katharine Martingale, Ernesto May, David McKenzie, Elisabeth Mealey, Shomik Raj Mehndiratta, Barjor Mehta, Mukesh Mehta, Abel Mejia, Taye Mengistae, Dino Merotto, Stephen Mink, Pradeep Mitra, Keiko Miwa, Celestin Monga, Nasser Munjee, Zafer Mustafaoglu, Abdu Muwonge, Ijaz Nabi, Mustapha Kamel Nabli, Gobind Nankani, Ashish Narain, Benno N'dulu, Vikram Nehru, Eric Neumayer, Cecile Niang, John Overholt, Caglar Ozden, Nicolas Perrin, Abhay Pethe, Axel Peuker, Vidyadhar Phatak, Brian Pinto, Mark Povey, Habib Nasser Rab, Madhu Raghunath, Robin Rajack, Anupam Rastogi, Dilip Ratha, S. K. Rao, Martin Ravallion, Jean-Louis Reiffers, Jose Guilherme Reis, Frederic Robert-Nicoud, Klaus Rohland, Jamal Saghir, Maurice Schiff, Emily M. Schmidt, Annemarie Schneider. Harris Selod, Marcelo Selowsky, Ethel Sennhauser, Claudia Sepulveda, Shekhar Shah, Zmarak Shalizi, Sudhir Shetty, Vera Songwe, Manju Sood, Andrew Steer, Jack Stein, Andy Tatem, Ahmet Tiktik, Christopher Timmins, Tim Thomas, Vinod Thomas, Peter Thomson, Mark Tomlinson, Yvonne Tsikata, Laura Tuck, Carolyn Turk, Sanjay Ubale, Sameh Wahba, Linda Van Gelder, Juergen Voegele, Hyoung Gun Wang, David Wheeler, Dirk Willem te Velde, Jan von der Goltz, Jorge Wilheim, John Wilson, Zelai Xu, Ahmet Yaman, Evgeny Yasin, Tito Yepes, Yutaka Yoshino, Shahid Yusuf, Ulrich Zachau, Albert Zeufack, Yan Zhang, and Ekaterina Zhuravskaya.

We have also benefited from suggestions and feedback of participants at consultation and discussion workshops held during the drafting stage of the report. In particular, we would like to thank Olav Seim and Marianne Berg of Ministry of Foreign Affairs (Norway); Per Ronnas, Klas Groth, and Christina Hartler of SIDA (Sweden); Pekka Hukka and Elina Levaniemi of Ministry of Foreign

Affaires (Finland); participants in the Berlin workshop: Tanja Boerzel, Mantang Cai, Angel de la Fuente Moreno, Nicola De Michelis, Manfred Fischer, Grzegorz Gorzelak, Eduardo Haddad, Steven Haggblade, Michael Hofmann, Robert Kappel, Aehyung Kim, Adama Konseiga, Frauke Kraas, Astrid Kuehl, Rolf J. Langhammer, Ingo Liefner, Roman Mogilevsky, Hassen Mohamed, Peter Nijkamp, Nils-Henning Meyer, Ulrich Nitschke, Boris Pleskovic, and Gerhard Ressel; participants in the Marseille workshop: Mona Yafi, Jean-Eric Aubert, Gilles Pipien, Rachid Afirat, Erfan Ali, Michel Arnaud, Jean-Dominique Assie, Fouad Awada, Mohamed Basyouny, AbdelKébir Berkia, Morched Chabbi, Abderrahmane Chorfi, Simon Compaore, Jean-Pierre Elong Mbassi, Kamal Hamdan, Gamal Hamid, Rachid El-Jamali, Rabea Kharfi, Hugues Kouadio, Frannie Léautier, Abdellah Lehzam, Pierre Mayet, Jean-Louis Reiffers, Wafaa Sobhy, Kian Tajbakhsh, Pierre Veltz, Xavier Crépin, Luc Dassonville, Thierry Desclos, Olivier Mourareau, Joan Parpal, Elizabeth Peri, Michele Reynaud, Paul-Henri Schipper, Serge Snrech, Louis-Jacques Vaillant, Nathalie Tchoumba Bitnga, Loraine Falconetti, Fabien Marry, and Olivier Lavinal; participants in the Dar-es-Salaam workshop: Tom Okurut, Samuel Wangwe, Elly Manjale, Mr. Raphael Mwai, Audance Ndayizeye, Professor Semboja, Dennis Rweyemamu, Amos Majule, Mr Kweyamba, Professor Kishimba, Furaha Lugoe, Haji Semboja, Dr Shechambo, Cosmos Sokoni, Prof Yanda, Marc Kabandama, H. B. Lunogelo, Vivian Kazi, Irene Alenga, Stina Peteson, and Monica Hangi; participants in the Abidjan workshop: Mohamadou Abdoul, Kasségné Adjonou, Stéphane Aka Anghui, Alban Alphonse Emmanuel Ahourse, Jean-Marie Akpoue, Koffi Attahi, Djerkbary Bambah, Toyidi Bello, Joseph Coulibaly, Konan Kouakou Noel Dahoua, Alhassane Coster Diaw, Anne Marcelle Douka, Jacques Esso, Siaka Fofana, Agnès Gnamon-Adiko, Joachim Hunlede, John Igue, Prosper Kedagni, Constant Koidou, Hugues Kouadio, Alexane Kouame, Kouassi Jean-Baptiste Kouma, Mibanan Hippolithe Kone, Jean Claude Koutou, Gabin Kponhassia, Owusu-Bonsu Kwame, Moussa Ladan, Youayou Marital Laguidahi, Konon Jules Lella, Edmond Manouan, Isaac F. Mensa-Bonsou, Yao Kouadio Antoine N'Gbala, Jérôme Aloko N'Guessan, N'Da N'Guessan Kouadio, Sidi Ould Cheikh Abdallahi, Guillaume Poirel, Adama Sall, Kanon Seri, Adama Sissouma, Soumaïla Sogodogo, Fidel Yapi Amoncou, and François Yatta; organizers of the Mumbai and Hyderabad workshops: Infrastructure Development Finance Corporation and Bombay Chamber of Commerce and Industry; and Administrative Staff College of India; participants at the Mumbai workshop: Jairaj Phatak, Sanjay G. Ubale, Manu Kumar Srivastava, Sanjay Sethi,

P. R. K. Murthy, Uma Adusumilli, Vidyadhar K. Phatak, G. S. Gill, Satyendra Sinha, C. S. Deshpande, Mukesh Mehta, Mridula Krishna, Arun Mokashi, Siddharth Roy, Veena Mishra, Rajan Divekar, Dilip Karmarkar, Dinkar Samant, Shishirkumar Rai, John Alexander, Ramakant Jha, Rahul Srivastava, Shyam H. Chainani, Gerson D'Cunha, Jockin Arputham, Abhay Pethe, Niranjan Rajadhyaksha, Sarosh Bana, Darryl D'Monte, Ashley D'Mello, Dilip D'Souza, Neha Batura, Sadashiv Rao, M. K. Sinha, A. K. T. Chari, Sonia Sethi, Ashish Chandak, Anupam Rastogi, Lavi D'Costa, Ritu Anand, Nasser Munjee, Manju Sood, C. B. Juvekar, and R. Ganesh; participants at the Hyderabad workshop: Kamal Kumar, M. Govinda Rao, K. L. Krishna, B. G. Verghese, Mahendra Dev, Subhashish Gangopadhyay, Narhari Rao, Sanjaya Baru, C. Rammanohar Reddy, Amitabh Kundu, Ravi Bhoothalingam, Amb. S. Narayanan, Ranjana Kumar, Alakh N. Sharma, Rameshwar Singh, A. K. Singh, Sri. B. C. Mohapatra, R. Radhakrishna, K. Krishnamurthy, Mahesh Mishra, Santosh Mahrotra, D. C. Sah, Surjit Singh, Prabhat P. Ghosh, G. C. Paul, Jang Pangi, Yaduvendra Mathur, Shubas Chandra Garg, Umesh Sinha, Gautam Pingle, S. K. Rao, Mohammed A. Abid, Surendar Reddy, Nirmalaya Bagchi, and Anand Akundy; participants at the Moscow workshop: Evgeny Yasin, Vladimir Mau, Vladimir Nazarov, Ilya Mazayev, Mikhail Dmitriev, Ksenia Yudaeva, Ekaterina Zhuravskaya, Evsei Gurvich, Evgennii Gavrlienkov, Galina Kurlyandskaya, Nadezhda Kosareva, Lidiya Ovhcharova, Natalia Zubarevich, Vladimir Drebentsov, Eugenii Gontmacher, Aleksey Prazdnichnykh, Aleksander Morozov, Andrey Treyvish, Vitaly Shipov, Dmitry Aratsky, Tatyana Popova, Irina Makeeva, Oksana Sergienko, Oleg Zasov, Marina Vasilieva, and Vladislava Nemova; the organizers of the Ankara workshop, State Planning Organization, and participants: Necla Akça, Didem Akman, Enver Aksoy, Ayhan Atli, Yavuz Cabbar, Abdullah Çelik, Ayda Eraydin, Oguz Isik, Serap Kayasu, Vural Kural, Cenk Oguzsoy, Elvan Ongun, Mevlüt Özen, Ibrahim Hakki Polat, Gül Polat, Faruk Sahin, Zekeriya Sarbak, Zafer Yavan, and Hami Yildirim

Jeff Lecksell, Siobhan Murray, and Brian Blankespoor prepared the maps for this Report. Other valuable assistance was provided by Gytis Kanchas, Polly Means, Nacer Mohamed Megherbi, Grace P. Sorensen, Catalina Tejada, and Roula I. Yazigi. Merrell J. Tuck-Primdahl, Kavita Watsa, and Prianka Nandy assisted the team with consultations and dissemination.

Despite efforts to compile a comprehensive list, some who contributed may have been inadvertently omitted. The team apologizes for any oversights and reiterates its gratitude to all who contributed to this Report.

Background papers for the World Development Report 2009

Behar, Alberto. 2008. "Neighborhood Growth Effects: An Annual Panel Data Approach."

Brulhart, Marius. 2008. "An Account of Global Intra-Industry Trade, 1962-2006."

Cali, Massimiliano. 2007. "Urbanisation, Inequality and Economic Growth: Evidence from Indian States."

Clemens, Michael A., Claudio E. Montenegro, and Lant Pritchett. 2008. "The Great Discrimination: Borders as a Labor Market Barrier."

Coulibaly, Souleymane. 2008. "On the Complementarity of Regional and Global Trade."

Hewings, Geoffrey, E. Feser, and K. Poole. 2007. "Spatial/Territorial Development Policies in the United States."

Kilroy, Austin. 2007. "Intra-Urban Spatial Inequalities: Cities as 'Urban Regions.'"

Kroehnert, Steffen, and Sebastian Vollmer. 2008. "Where Have All Young Women Gone?"

Mayer, Thierry. 2008. "Market Potential and Development."

Montenegro, Claudio E., and Maximilian L. Hirn. 2008. "A New Disaggregated Set of Labor Market Indicators using Standardized Household Surveys from Around the World."

Nelson, Andrew. 2007. "Accessibility Model and Population Estimates."

Nelson, B., and A. Behar. 2008. "Natural Resources, Growth and Spatially-Based Development: A View of the Literature."

Roberts, Mark. 2008. "Congestion and spatially connective infrastructure: the case of London in the 19th and early 20th century."

Roberts, Mark, and Uwe Deichmann. 2008. "Regional Spillover Estimation."

Uchida, Hirotsugu, and Andrew Nelson. 2008. "Agglomeration Index: Towards a New Measure of Urban Concentration."

Background notes for the World Development Report 2009

Abreu, Maria. 2008. "Effectively Dealing with Slums."

Alva, M., and A. Behar. 2008. "Factors That Contribute to (or Detract from) Successful Outcomes in African Regional Agreements."

Andersson, Martin. 2007. "Spatial Disparities in Taiwan."

Cali, Massimiliano. 2008. "Urban Agglomeration Policy in China."

Chen, Yang. 2008. "China: A Case Study of 1D-2D-3D areas."

Cornelson, Kirsten. 2008. "Egypt and South Africa: A Case Study of 1D-2D-3D areas."

Crafts, Nicholas. 2007. "European Growth in the Age of Regional Economic Integration: Convergence Big Time?"

Crafts, Nicholas. 2007. "Spatial Disparities in 19th Century British Industrialization."

Hay, Simon I., Dave L. Smith, and Robert W. Snow. 2008. "Is a Future for Human Malaria Inevitable?"

Kilroy, Austin. 2008. "The Role of Cities in Postwar Economic Recovery."

Klink, Melissa. 2008. "Nigeria and South Africa: A Case Study of 1D-2D-3D areas."

Layke, Christian, and Stephen Adam. 2008. "Spatial Allocation of Public Expenditures in Nigeria."

Manners, P., and A. Behar. 2007. "Trade in Sub-Saharan Africa and Opportunities for Low Income Countries."

Markussen, Thomas. 2008. "Policies for improved land use in developing countries."

Naudé, Wim. 2007. "Density, Distance and Division Spotlight on Sub-Saharan Africa."

Oh, Jinhwan. 2008. "Korea: A Case Study of 1D-2D-3D areas."

Roberts, Mark. 2008. "Social and Spatial Equity."

Satterthwaite, David. 2007. "Expanding the Supply and Reducing the Cost of Land for Housing in Urban Areas in Low- and Middle-Income Nations."

Te Velde, Dirk Willem. 2007. "Regional Integration, Growth and Concentration."

Treyvish, Andrey. 2008. "The Downfall of the Soviet Union: A Spatial Explanation."

Vidler, Cam, 2008. "Turkey and Russia: A Case Study of 1D-2D-3D areas."

Endnotes

Overview

1. Clemens, Montenegro, and Pritchett (2008), background paper for this Report.

2. Collier (2007).

3. In Zambia a person in a settlement with more than 5,000 people is considered urban; in India the threshold is 20,000. To compare urbanization across countries, this Report pioneers a new measure of population density, the "agglomeration index" (see chapter 1).

4. See World Bank 2007k.

5. Fujita 2007.

6. Mukherjee 2007.

7. Koh and Chang 2005.

8. de Blij 2005.

9. Khanna 2008.

10. World Bank 2008e.

11. Throughout this Report, what is often called "regional development" or "territorial development" is referred to as "area development." These policies must contend with even greater spatial unevenness as their scope widens to encompass a country.

Navigating This Report

1. http://nobelprize.org/nobel_prizes/economics/laureates/1971.

2. http://nobelprize.org/nobel_prizes/economics/laureates/1971/kuznets-lecture.html.

3. Brown and others 2008.

GIM 1

1. See Engerman and Sokoloff (2000a) and Acemoglu, Johnson, and Robinson (2002).

2. For a more detailed discussion of U.S. economic geography, see Kim and Margo (2004).

3. Fogel (1979) suggests that no single technology was responsible for this reduction in cost. For example, he estimates that U.S. output in 1890 would have been only 4 percent lower if goods were transported by water rather than rail.

4. McCallum (1995).

Chapter 1

1. Farvacque-Vitkovic, Casalis, and Eghoff (2007), p. 37.

2. United Nations/Wilbur Smith Associates (1980), p. 2.

3. Siegel (1997), p. 61.

4. NUTS provides a single uniform classification of territorial units for producing regional statistics for the European Union. The first two administrative levels in most member states correspond to NUTS 2 and NUTS 3. NUTS 1, a larger unit representing the major socioeconomic regions, often does not correspond to existing administrative units within member states.

5. The figures in this paragraph are derived from data on total land area, proportion of land area dedicated to agricultural uses, total employment, proportion of employment in agriculture, GDP, and proportion of gross value added (GVA) generated in agriculture (*Eurostat* 2005; Belgium's Office of National Statistics 2006).

Employment figures are for 2003, population figures for 2002, and GDP figures for 2005. All GDP figures are quoted using purchasing power standard (PPS) exchange rates.

6. Population figures are for year 2007 (www.citypopulation.de/world.htm).

7. The tendency for the populations of the primate or largest few cities in a country to considerably outweigh the populations of cities down the hierarchy of places is reflected in the tendency of the rank-size rule to break down at the top end of the size distribution of cities.

8. These definitions of the rank-size rule and Zipf's law are approximate. For more precise definitions see Gabaix and Ioannides (2004).

9. Eeckhout 2004.

10. Martin 2005. Even in the United Kingdom, which has a highly spatially and institutionally concentrated financial sector, large cities such as Birmingham, Manchester, Leeds, and Edinburgh have fairly large concentrations of venture capital firms, although regional stock exchanges had been abolished by the beginning of the 1970s.

11. Kim and Margo 2004.

12. Office of the Deputy Prime Minister 2003.

13. Thanh, Anh, and Tacoli 2005.

14. Tiffen 2003.

15. Glaeser and Kahn 2001, p. 21.

16. Baker and others 2005, p. 15.

17. Peng, Zhu, and Song 2008, p. 7.

18. Glaeser and Kahn 2001.

19. Estimated from the gross product of the world's major cities published in www.citymayors.com; Price Waterhouse Cooper 2007.

20. This is equal to the excess of GVA measured on a workplace basis over GVA measured on a residence basis for London. Calculation is based on data from Office of National Statistics (2006).

21. Figures on flows of earnings associated with commuting come from the U.S. Bureau of Economic Analysis.

22. Quote taken from the glossary of the World Urbanization Prospects: The 2007 Revision Population Database (http://esa.un.org/unup/.).

23. Even with time-series analysis, some care needs to be exhibited with the World Urbanization Prospects database. For some countries the official definition of an urban area has changed over time. In China, for example, the urban share in 1999 could have been 24 percent, 31 percent, or 73 percent depending on the official definition of urban population used (Satterthwaite 2007).

24. Glaeser, Kolko, and Saiz 2001.

25. Statistics taken from Price Waterhouse Cooper 2007.

26. The estimates of urban consumption shares are based on available household surveys of different years, and the per capita GDP estimates are in 2000 U.S. dollars for the respective years (the data set is described in detail in Montenegro and Hirn 2008).

27. Maddison 2008b.

28. Kim and Margo 2004.

29. This is the so-called home market effect of the new economic geography, also discussed in chapter 4. The concentration of economic activity in urban areas also entails additional productivity-enhancing effects, as discussed in chapter 4.

30. This tendency for urbanization to produce a divergence in basic welfare indicators in favor of urban areas distinguishes the modern-day developing countries from the industrializers of the nineteenth and early twentieth centuries, discussed below.

31. Based on 2003 data from Maddison (2008b).

32. European Commission 2001.

33. Miles 2007.

34. As measured in constant 1990 international dollars using data from Maddison (2008b).

35. An area is defined as predominantly urban (rural) if more than 50 percent of its population lives in urban (rural) areas. An area is also classed as predominantly urban if its urban population share is between 15 and 50 percent and it has an urban center of more than 500,000 inhabitants (1 million for Japan) representing in excess of 25 percent of the area's population.

36. Some care is required in this case. The increase in the U.S. urban wage premium during this period might have had less to do with better lives in cities than with the effects of large declines in the relative prices of agricultural commodities (Barro and Sala-I-Martin 2004, p. 470).

37. These estimates of urban consumption and urban shares of population are based on country household surveys of different years, depending on availability.

38. As illustrated later for China, however, this is not the case for all developing countries. Although there is a negative relationship across Chinese provinces between the urban share and the ratio of urban to rural income, this relationship has shifted upward since the late 1990s.

39. "Access to water" is defined here as any access to improved water sources. These sources vary according to the local context, but include wells, communal taps, piped water, and trucks selling water. Similarly, "sanitation" refers to a range of qualified items such as latrines and outhouses.

40. The countries included in the sample are Bangladesh, Benin, Bolivia, Burkina Faso, Cameroon, Chad, Colombia, the Dominican Republic, the Arab Republic of Egypt, Ghana, Guatemala, Haiti, India, Indonesia, Kazakhstan, Kenya, Malawi, Mali, Morocco, Mozambique, Namibia, Nepal, Nicaragua, Nigeria, Peru, the Philippines, Tanzania, Turkey, Uganda, Vietnam, Zambia, and Zimbabwe.

41. Gwatkin and others 2007.

42. Satterthwaite and others 2007.

43. *The Economist* 2007a.

44. Satterthwaite and others 2007.

45. Satterthwaite and others 2007.

46. Data on Delhi's population comes from United Nations (2006).

47. Smith 1989.

48. Crafts 2008.

49. Williamson 1982.

50. *The Economist* 2007a.

51. Satterthwaite and others 2007.

52. This figure, together with all other historical urban share figures quoted in this section, is based on the definition of an urban area as a city with more than 5,000 inhabitants and taken from Bairoch and Goertz (1986). All figures on urban shares and populations for contemporary developing countries in this section have been taken, or calculated using data, from the United Nations (2006c). As previously noted, using this database to compare *changes* in urban share across countries is not as problematic as using it to compare *levels* of urban shares across countries.

53. This sample consists of Belgium, Denmark, Finland, France, Germany, Greece, Italy, the Netherlands, Norway, Portugal, Spain, Sweden, Switzerland, and the United Kingdom. Its composition was determined by the availability of historical data from Bairoch and Goertz (1986).

54. Figure 1.13 illustrates a number of countries that, according to the United Nations (2006), experienced positive change in urban share between 1985 and 2005. A handful of countries with populations greater than 1 million experienced "negative urbanization" over this period (for example, Armenia, Estonia, Georgia, Kyrgystan, Latvia, Moldova, Tajikistan and Uzbekistan). Although the definitions of an urban area have not changed for these countries, the pattern of declining urban shares may, in these cases, be related to the dissolution of the Soviet Union. A further two of the countries (the Czech Republic and the Slovak Republic) were parts of the former Czechoslovakia, and the dissolution of this country, along with the transition away from a planned economy, may likewise have affected their urban shares. For the remaining six countries (Iraq, Mauritius, Papua New Guinea, Sri Lanka, the United Arab Emirates, and Zambia), a number have unconventional or changing definitions of an urban area. For example, Papua New Guinea's definition of an urban area is a center with 500 inhabitants or more, an unusually small threshold, while the United Arab Emirates' urban population is measured as the population of nine cities.

55. Satterthwaite 2007.

56. United Nations 2006c.

57. This conclusion is based on historical estimate of U.S. urban population growth derived by combining historical data on urban shares from Bairoch and Goertz (1986) with historical data on country population sizes from Maddison (2008b).

58. Gwatkin and others 2007.

59. Gwatkin and others 2007.

60. Woods 2000.

61. Williams and Galley 1995.

62. Orwell 1937.

63. Crafts 2008.

64. Williamson 1990.

65. Stockel 2002.

66. Kim and Margo 2004.

Chapter 2

1. Armstrong and Taylor 2000. See, in particular, chapter 8.

2. Beaumier 1998.

3. Krugman (1991a), pp. 11–13.

4. See, for example, Barro and Sala-I-Martin (2004).

5. OECD (2007), p. 14.

6. Blanchard and Katz 1992.

7. OECD (2006), p. 13.

8. France's National Statistics Office's Web site (www.insee.fr/fr/default.asp).

9. Länder National Accounts Working Group (http://www.statistik-portal.de).

10. This pattern is familiar to development specialists as the "Kuznets curve," named for the Nobel economist Simon Kuznets. Although the Kuznets curve depicts a relationship between a country's economic development and its interpersonal income inequality, the hypothesis Kuznets forwarded to explain this relationship corresponds to that underlying the relationship between spatial inequality and development documented in this chapter.

11. Poncet 2006.

12. Buys, Deichmann, and Wheeler 2006.

13. Poncet 2005.

14. Poncet 2006.

15. Tobler 1970.

16. Angeriz, McCombie, and Roberts 2008.

17. Lipsey and Nakamura 2006.

18. Henderson, Kuncoro, and Nasution 1996.

19. Deichmann and others forthcoming.

20. Henderson, Shalizi, and Venables 2001.

21. U.S. Bureau Census, various years.

22. Aghion and Williamson (1998), pp. 144–51.

23. Taylor and Williamson 2006.

24. Angeriz, McCombie, and Roberts 2008.

25. Fingleton 2003.

26. Deichmann and others 2005.

27. Hering and Poncet 2006.

28. Da Mata and others 2007.

29. Paillacar 2007.

30. Head and Mayer 2006.

31. Collier 2007.

32. Estimates generated from Nordhaus's Geographically Based Economic Database (http://gecon.yale.edu/), compiled from information gathered in 1990.

33. Time-series data on spatial concentration were assembled for 10 countries—some, however, with only two observations. Countries in the sample are Canada (1890–2006), Spain (1850–2000), France (1801–1999), the Netherlands (1850–2006), Japan (1900–2000), United States (1960–2000), Brazil (1960–2004), Chile (1975–2004), Thailand (1975–2004), Indonesia (1989–2005), and the Philippines (1980–2005. Except France, Spain, and the Netherlands, where population is used, economic mass is measured based on GDP. Data come from a variety of sources. But, as explained below, this combination of information sources does not constitute a significant problem because the concentration measure—a ratio—is robust to various indicators.

34. In what follows, the concentration measure is defined according to the following method. First, we estimate an area's hypothetical share of national GDP under the assumption that this GDP exhibits a uniform spatial distribution. Second, we identify the area with the highest actual share of national GDP. Third, we divide the actual GDP share of this leading area by its hypothetical (uniformly spatially distributed) share to get our measure of spatial concentration. For example, if the leading area has an actual share of 10 percent and a hypothetical share of 2 percent, then the measure of concentration is equal to 5.

35. The concentration measure in this section focuses only on the level of concentration (density) in the leading area of each country. It does not provide information for the spatial distribution of density across the remaining areas.

36. GDP per capita figures are taken from Maddison (2008b).

37. Krugman (1991a), pp. 11–13.

38. Ingram and Whitehead 2008.

39. The source of information is a set of more than 120 household surveys in 75 countries, with some countries having two years of observations. For each country and year, we estimate household consumption for individual households. In some countries, only household incomes are available. Then, we aggregate the household consumption into total household consumption for each census region of the country. The concentration measure for a country is proxied by the highest regional share of total household consumption.

40. The source of information is Yale University's William Nordhaus's Geographically Based Economic Database (http://gecon.yale.edu/). This database of population, gross product, and land area of subnational areas covers more than 90 countries.

41. In cross-country comparisons, use of a standardized grid cell helps avoid the cross-level fallacy, in which the number of partitions can affect the variance of the measure. Like the procedure for estimating the spatial Gini coefficient, we rank the terrestrial grid cells in descending order according to their GDP density and plot the cumulative land area on the horizontal axis against cumulative gross product on the vertical axis. Then a polynomial function is fitted to the data to predict the share of GDP within the densest 5 percent of the country's land area.

42. Spatial Gini coefficients consider the distribution of density across a country's *entire* land area. The coefficient equals zero if economic density is evenly distributed across space, while it equals one if all production takes place within a single terrestrial grid cell. Spatial Gini coefficients of GDP density are computed in three steps. First, grid cells are ranked in descending order according to density of economic mass (GDP per square kilometer). Second, cumulative shares of land area are derived, plus a corresponding series of cumulative shares of GDP, by grid cell. Third, these two measures are plotted against each other to produce a Lorenz curve, and the spatial Gini coefficient is calculated as the ratio of the area between the uniform distribution line and the Lorenz curve to the area below the uniform distribution line.

43. Krugman 1993.

44. Based on constant 1990 international Geary-Khamis dollars in Maddison (2008b).

45. The coefficient of variation increased from 0.107 to 0.148 (Crafts 2005).

46. Comparison based on GDP per capita figures from Maddison (2008b).

47. Roberts 2004.

48. Barro and Sala-I-Martin 1992.

49. Green 1969.

50. We define the welfare measure as per capita gross cell product, and spatial disparity as the ratio of the highest-to-lowest per capita gross cell product. Other measures of spatial inequality—such as the difference between the 90th percentile and the 10th percentile and that between the mean for the top 10 grid cells and the

mean for the bottom 10 grid cells—and coefficients of variation show similar stylized patterns.

51. For each country and year, we estimate a Mincerian-type regression with per capita household consumption as the dependent variable, a set of location dummies as the independent variables, and standard observable household characteristics (such as household size and household head's education, gender, age, and marital status) as control variables. The location variables are broad census regions. The difference between the maximal and minimal coefficients on the location dummy variables is our disparity measure in consumption between leading and lagging areas, purely because of location.

52. We estimate the relationship between spatial disparity and GDP per capita by pooling the disparity estimates from each household survey in a regression analysis that also controls for the number of census regions within each country and each country's land area. The inverse relationship between spatial disparities in consumption and the level of development was found to be robust to various model specifications (to the use of different sets of control variables).

53. These estimates are in 2000 U.S. dollars for the years of the household surveys during the 2000s.

54. Yemtsov 2005.

55. Kanbur and Zhang 2005; Milanovic 2005.

56. Demurger and others 2002.

57. World Bank 2007.

58. Georgia was the only country in the region not to enjoy a reduction in absolute poverty over the period. Douthat, Poe, and Cutler (2006), p. 52, and World Bank (2005e).

59. Ferreira 2000.

60. GDP per capita figures taken from Maddison 2008b.

61. Naudé and Krugell 2006.

62. Cárdenas and Pontón 1995.

63. Hill, Resosudarmo, and Vidyattama 2007.

64. Wisaweisuan forthcoming.

65. Son forthcoming.

66. Based on United Nations (1997) and United Nations (2005).

67. Garcia-Verdu 2005; Fuentes and Montes 2004.

68. Public Administration Research and Consultation Centre (PARC) 2004.

69. Government of India Planning Commission 2002b.

70. Sri Lanka National Council for Economic Development and UNDP (2005).

71. Government of Sri Lanka 2008.

72. Kenya Ministry of Planning and National Development and UNDP (2005).

73. Smith (1976), p. 122.

74. Venables 2006.

75. Chang 2005.

76. Hanson 1998b.

77. Demurger and others 2002.

78. He forthcoming.

79. Venables 2006.

80. Crafts (2005), table 4, p. 59.

81. Calculations are for 2005, based on data from the *China Statistical Yearbook* (2006), (http://www.stats.gov.cn/tjsj/ndsj/2006/indexeh.htm).

82. GDP per capita figures for Shanghai and Guizho have been calculated for 2005 by multiplying the estimates for relative provincial performance by Maddison's estimate of national GDP per capita. The figures are in 1990 international dollars. Comparisons with Britain are likewise based on Maddison's data from Maddison (2008b).

Chapter 3

1. Figures are based on Maddison (2006). Between 1820 and 1998, GDP increased from $694.4 billion to $33,725.9 billion in 1990 international dollars. Population during that time grew from 1.04 billion to 5.3 billion, a fivefold increase at about 1 percent per year.

2. These estimates are based on the G-Econ project database assembled at Yale University (see Nordhaus 2006). The database provides estimates for 1990 of GDP, population, and land area of regular grid cells that are about 100 by 100 kilometers at the equator. These figures likely underestimate actual concentration.

3. Ohmae 1990.

4. The numbers include land borders between nation-states only. So, borders between colonies in the nineteenth or early twentieth century are not considered.

5. Blake 2005.

6. The measure summarizes four indicators representing restrictions to the flow of goods, capital, people, and ideas: (1) average tariffs (World Bank data), (2) capital openness (Chinn and Ito 2006), (3) proportion of countries that need a visa to visit that country (Neumayer 2006), and (4) a press freedom index that includes information such as Internet filtering (Reporters without Borders for Press Freedom 2007). These measures are discussed in more detail later in the chapter. All indicators were normalized and rescaled from more open to more closed borders and summed. An index based on rank sizes provides similar results. The data typically refer to 2005 or 2006, but in a few instances they refer to 2004. For a few countries with only three of the four indicators were available, the missing values were replaced by the overall mean. Among the larger countries, this affected Afghanistan, Cuba, the Democratic Republic of Congo, Serbia and Montenegro, Tajikistan, and the Republic of Yemen. The index captures many but not all barriers and divisions. For instance, incompatible laws and regulations can have an impact on country well-being.

7. There are several globalization indexes that capture similar aspects of international barriers. One example is the KOF Index of Globalization (globalization.kof.ethz.ch). However, these indexes typically mix country regulations such as tariff levels with outcome variables such as the share of exports in GDP. For the illustrative analysis in this chapter, we are strictly interested in how countries themselves manage economic interaction.

8. See McCallum (1995) and Helliwell (2002).

9. Anderson and van Wincoop 2003; 2004.

10. Bhagwati and Srinivasan 2002; Alcalá and Ciccone 2004.

11. Rodriguez and Rodrik 2000; Slaughter 2001.

12. World Bank 2007j.

13. Kee, Nicita, and Olarreaga (2006) develop measures of trade restrictions that include some of these aspects. Available for a smaller set of countries than the average tariff index, this subset shows a high correlation with the average tariff index.

14. See Chinn and Ito (2006). The Chinn-Ito index of capital openness is derived from the IMF's *Annual Report on Exchange Arrangements and Exchange Restrictions* (AREAER). It is the first principle component of four binary variables reported: existence of multiple exchange rates, restrictions on current account, capital account transactions, and requirement of the surrender of export proceeds. See Chinn and Ito (2006). The original index values were rescaled between 0 (lowest restrictions among all countries) and 100 (highest restrictions). The regional averages are unweighted.

15. McKenzie 2001; Kose, Prasad, Rogoff, and Wei 2006; Chinn and Ito 2006; Henry 2007.

16. Quinn and Toyoda 2006.

17. Bekaerta, Harvey, and Lundblad 2005.

18. Kose, Prasad, Rogoff, and Wei 2006.

19. Pritchett 2006.

20. Quantifying these benefits is difficult. But a recent study estimates that a 3 percent increase in the labor force of industrial countries could provide a $356 billion gain (World Bank 2005).

21. Pritchett 2006.

22. Neumayer 2006.

23. McKenzie 2007.

24. Linden, Kraemer, and Dedrick 2007. Another example of the importance of knowledge-intensive activities is given by Oppenheimer (2008): Of each cup of Latin American–grown coffee that U.S. consumers buy, only 3 percent of the price goes to the region's farmers. The rest funds genetic engineering, processing, branding, marketing, and other knowledge-based activities, which are mostly based outside the region.

25. Criscuolo, Haskel, and Slaughter 2004.

26. Brunettia and Weder 2003; Keefer and Khemani 2005.

27. Data available online at www.rsf.org.

28. Gallup, Sachs, and Mellinger 1999.

29. See Collier 2007.

30. Alesina and Spolaore (2003), p. 81.

31. Winters and Martins 2004.

32. Bertram 2004; World Bank 2006a.

33. Alesina, Devleeschauwer, Easterly, Kurlat, and Wacziarg 2003.

34. Collier 2007.

35. Spolaore and Wacziarg 2005.

36. Simmons 2006.

37. Blake 2005.

38. Collier 2003; 2007. Miguel, Satyanath, and Sergenti (2004) show that the impact can also be in the opposite direction. Based on data for African countries from 1981–99 and using rainfall data to correct for potential endogeneity, they estimate that a negative growth shock of 5 percent increases the likelihood of conflict by one-half in the following year.

39. See endnote 2 for data source. These data by grid cells may still underestimate concentration, because the estimates are based on data for 1990 and high-concentration areas have likely grown faster than low-concentration areas.

40. Maddison 2006.

41. Bairoch 1982.

42. Tilly 1990.

43. Maddison 2006.

44. See box 0.2 for definitions of WDR regions.

45. Disdier and Head 2008.

46. Leamer (2007) highlights this point.

47. Bourguignon and Morrisson 1998; World Bank 2007a.

48. Morrisson and Murtin 2005.

49. Maddison 2006.

50. Bourguignon and Morrisson 2002.

51. Collier 2007.

52. Cutler, Deaton, and Lleras-Muney (2006) discuss the drivers of falling mortality rates that led to these increases in longevity.

53. Morrisson and Murtin 2005.

54. The inequality numbers may underestimate the true disparities in human capital outcomes. "Years of schooling" relates only to primary and secondary education and therefore has an inherent maximum value. Many developed countries have essentially achieved a natural maximum some time ago, but they have made further progress in improving the quality of education and in expanding tertiary education. Developing countries have been catching up on primary and secondary education, but less so in other dimensions of human capital.

55. Cohen and Soto 2007.

56. These numbers may overstate improvements somewhat, because no data are available for several countries that are likely among the worst performers.

57. Baumol 1986; De Long 1988; Barro and Sala-I-Martin 1992; Quah 1996.

58. Maddison 2006. Pre-1990 data for Eastern Europe are likely somewhat less reliable.

59. Lederman, Maloney, and Servén 2005.

60. Pallage and Robe 2003.

61. Nordhaus 2006.

62. Snow, Craig, Deichmann, and Marsh 1999.

63. Caselli 2005.

64. Easterly and Levine 2001.

65. Baldwin, Martin, and Ottaviano 2001.

66. Puga and Venables 1999; Shatz and Venables 2005.

67. Levinson 2006.

68. Economic Intelligence Unit 2007.

69. Wolf 2004. Others, however, such as Bordo, Eichengreen, and Irwin (1999), think trade and capital markets are more integrated today.

70. Leamer 2007.

71. According to UN Comtrade data for 2004 and using figures reported by China—for example, Japan has a trade surplus in manufacturing of US$21 billion with China, the Republic of Korea US$34 billion, Thailand US$6 billion, the Philippines US$5 billion, and Indonesia US$1 billion.

72. *New York Times*, February 22, 1999.

GIM 2

1. Baldwin and Wyplosz 2006; Crafts and Toniolo 1996.

2. Baldwin 2008.

3. Baldwin 1995.

Chapter 4

1. Smith (1976), p. 21.

2. See Glaeser, Kolko, and Saiz 2001; Sinai and Waldfogel 2004.

3. Discussion of agglomeration economies dates as far back as Smith's consideration of specialization and the division of labor (Smith (1976)); Marshall's information spillovers, searching and

matching processes, and input-sharing (Marshall (1890)); and more recently, interindustry supply linkages (Chinitz (1961)); learning-by-doing (Arrow (1962)); and cross-fertilization of ideas and innovation (Jacobs (1970)).

4. McCann (2001), p. 56.

5. See, for example, Henderson (1986); Henderson, Kuncoro, and Turner (1995); Nakamura (1985); Hammond and von Hagen (1994); Sveikauskas, Gowdy, and Funk (1988); Greytak and Blackley (1985); Glaeser and others (1992); and Bernstein and Nadiri (1988).

6. Prateen 1988.

7. Junius 1997.

8. Of 27 estimated scale coefficients, 23 show increasing returns to scale, most above 4 percent, robust to various specifications of the production function (Griliches and Ringstad 1971, and Ringstad 1978).

9. Baldwin and Gorecki 1986.

10. Owen (1983) for Europe, and Scherer (1980) and Hall (1988; 1990) for the United States.

11. Industry-level scale returns in the range of 1.30 are found for many U.S. manufacturing industries (see Paul and Siegel 1999), and Chilean plant-level data for eight industries exhibit a comparable scale elasticity of between 1.20 and 1.44 (Levinsohn and Petrin 1999).

12. Antweiler and Trefler (2002) for 71 countries over the period 1972–92.

13. The average scale elasticity estimate of 1.051 is within the bounds of estimates in the United States (Basu and Fernald 1997) and in Canada (Fuss and Gupta 1981).

14. See Roeger (1995) for the United States, and Martins, Scarpetta, and Pilat (1996) for the Organisation for Economic Co-operation and Development.

15. Junius 1997.

16. Roeger 1995.

17. Hughes and Mester (1998) detect that, as scale increases, banks economize on resources to manage risks, preserve capital, and signal institutional strength. Calem (1994) and Hughes and others (1999) suggest that geographic expansion of bank branches produces scale efficiency gains from lower deposit volatility, higher expected returns, and more diversified risk. There is also evidence of increasing returns to scale in data processing activities (for example, Hancock, Humphrey, and Wilcox (1999) for payment system).

18. Bossone and Lee (2004), using a sample of 875 commercial banks drawn from the FitchLBCA's Bank Scope database.

19. Named after three economists: Alfred Marshall, Kenneth Arrow, and Paul Romer (Glaeser and others 1992).

20. Hanson 1996.

21. See www.referenceforbusiness.com/industries/Textile-Mill/Women-s-Full-Length-Knee.html.

22. Donsky 1990.

23. U.S. Bureau of Census website.

24. Henderson (1986), based on cross-sectional data for the United States and Brazil.

25. Jacobs 1970.

26. Henderson, Kuncoro, and Turner 1995. Henderson (1997a) finds the largest effects on productivity from own-industry employment are lagged two to five years, because it takes time to learn from neighbors. Jaffe, Trajtenberg, and Henderson (1993) corroborate

the slow diffusion over space of location- and industry-specific information.

27. Carlton 1983; Wheeler and Mody 1992; Carlino 1979; and Hay (1979) find that concentration of industrial activity is favorable for influencing U.S. firms investment and location decisions.

28. World Bank 2006c.

29. Burchfield and others 2006.

30. Instituto de Pesquisa Economica Aplicada (ipeadata.gov.br).

31. Data from World Bank (2007j).

32. Devereux, Griffith, and Simpson (2004) for the United Kingdom; Ellison and Glaeser (1997) for the United States; and Maurel and Sédillot (1999) for France.

33. Rosenthal and Strange 2004.

34. Kim 1995.

35. Duranton and Overman 2002.

36. Henderson, Shalizi, and Venables 2001.

37. Henderson, Shalizi, and Venables 2001.

38. Henderson, Lee, and Lee 2001.

39. Krugman (1991b) notes that "the most spectacular examples of localization in today's world are, in fact, based on services rather than manufacturing . . . and technology . . . will promote more localization of services" (p. 66).

40. In 2004, the rest of the nonfarm employment went to transport and trade (22 percent) and forestry, utilities, and construction (7 percent) (Kolko 2007).

41. Audretsch and Feldman 1996.

42. Feldman (1994) documents that, in the United States, services, such as innovative or knowledge-intensive activity, are far more densely packed than manufacturing. Audretsch and Feldman (1996), using a count of new product introductions by the Small Business Administration in 1982, find that knowledge-oriented industries have more spatially concentrated innovative activity. Dekle and Eaton (1999) provide evidence that external economies from clustering are even stronger for business services than for manufacturing activities. Feldman and Audretsch (1999) find that sectors in which R&D, university research, and skilled labor are important inputs tend to be more spatially concentrated.

43. Kolko 2007.

44. Fafchamps and Desmet 2000.

45. Desmet and Fafchamps 2006.

46. At the upper tail of the distribution, however, the opposite is true, with large cities losing jobs in favor of intermediate size urban areas (Carlino and Chatterjee 2001; Desmet and Fafchamps 2003).

47. Kolko 1998.

48. Martin, R. 2005.

49. See, for example, Holmes and Stevens (2002).

50. Head, Reis, and Swenson (1995) and Smith Jr. and Florida (1994) find strong preferences of Japanese automotive assemblers to locate near each other to take advantage of backward and forward linkages. Hammond and von Hagen (1994) examining employment in four U.S. cities and three two-digit industries, find that labor-sharing tends to be stronger in expanding markets while asset-sharing is more important in mature markets. Holmes (1999) offers the most direct and compelling evidence of input-sharing as a source of agglomeration economies: the pantyhose industry is concentrated in North Carolina with 62 percent of national employment, and purchased input intensity of 53 percent, compared with 40 percent nationally. This pattern is found for other concentrated

industries as well. Holmes (1999) examines the textile industry, finding evidence in support of input-sharing. In particular, he finds a positive relationship between the size of the textile industry at a location and the presence of local specialized input suppliers to the industry.

51. Costa and Kahn 2000.

52. See Bikhchandani, Hirshleifer, and Welch (1998), and Sobel (2000) for surveys of the literature on social learning.

53. Marshall (1890) emphasizes how cities favor the diffusion of innovations and ideas while Jacobs (1970) stresses how the environment offered by cities improves the prospects for generating new ideas. Lucas Jr. (1988) also suggests that learning encompasses, not just of cutting-edge technology, but incremental mundane knowledge (knowing how, knowing who, etc.) through intended and unintended communications, and cities are the best place for knowledge transmission.

54. Marshall 1890.

55. Jaffe, Trajtenberg, and Henderson 1993. Jaffe (1986) finds evidence for local research and development (R&D) spillovers among 432 U.S. firms where the number of patents per dollar of R&D spending is higher for firms located in areas with above-average R&D spending.

56. Rauch (1993) shows that wages are higher where average education levels are high, because workers will be more productive and employers will be willing to pay high wages in competing for them. Moretti (2004a) finds a positive effect of college graduates on a city's wages. Charlot and Duranton (2004) use survey data to show that workplace communication is more extensive in urban areas and that this communication increases wages.

57. This is known as the home market effects in the literature.

58. Holmes and Stevens (2002) look at the relationship between firm size and city size across county-industries in the United States, and interpret their findings as evidence of increased productivity associated with concentration that allows the plants to become larger.

59. Holmes 1999; Henderson 2005a.

60. Davis and Weinstein (1999), examining production across Japanese prefectures, find that an industry's production is concentrated where the demand for that industry's good is relatively high. Wheat (1986) and Glaeser and others (1992) find evidence that manufacturing employment grows faster in subnational areas with more rapid population growth. Justman (1994) finds strong positive comovements of local supply and local demand for manufacturing industries in U.S. cities.

61. See, for example, Shefer (1973); Mera (1973); Segal (1976); Kawashima (1975); Sveikauskas (1975); Moomaw (1981) and Moomaw (1983); and Bartelsman, Caballero, and Lyons (1994).

62. Henderson, Shalizi, and Venables 2001).

63. As Glaeser and others (1992) observe "intellectual breakthroughs must cross hallways and streets more easily than oceans and continents" (p. 1127).

64. Feldman and Audretsch 1999.

65. Angeriz, McCombie, and Roberts 2008.

66. On this point see Feldman and Audretsch (1999), pp. 409–29.

67. On this point see Venables (2006), pp. 61–85.

68. There were, of course, some exceptions, most notably in the work of Young (1928) and Kaldor (see, for example, Kaldor 1972).

These economists failed, however, to provide the technical solutions associated with the modeling of increasing returns to scale.

69. Krugman 1991b.

70. Warsh (2006) provides an entertaining and accurate account of intellectual progress in dealing with increasing returns to scale. The advances are based on the special features of ideas, highlighted elegantly in Romer (1994). An idea, once developed, may be used costlessly by others as a starting point for new ideas, making it "nonrival," unlike labor, capital, land, and other inputs for production. Though ideas are nonrival, however, they are generally neither free nor nonexcludable. Coming up with useful ideas usually requires effort, and through secrecy or the enforcement of intellectual property rights, it is possible to exclude people from using ideas to improve products or production processes, even if temporarily. This excludability results in knowledge that confers a monopoly power on the creators of the knowledge. By adding knowledge explicitly to formulations of economic growth, economists are able to recognize the centrality of ideas and the importance of increasing returns, but this also requires recognizing the proliferation of imperfect competition.

71. Dixit and Stiglitz 1977.

72. Henderson 1974.

73. Black and Henderson 1999; Calem and Carlino 1991; Combes 2000; Desmet and Fafchamps 2006; Duranton and Puga 2005; Duranton and Puga 2004; Feldman and Audretsch 1999; Fujita and Ishii 1999; and Glaeser and others 1992.

74. Glaeser and Maré 2001; Henderson 1986; Henderson, Kuncoro, and Turner 1995; Henderson 1997b; Henderson 1997a; Henderson 2003b; Moomaw 1981; Moomaw 1983; Kolko 1999; Nakamura 1985; Rosenthal and Strange 2001; Rosenthal and Strange 2003; Sveikauskas, Gowdy, and Funk 1988.

75. Black and Henderson 1999; Dumais, Ellison, and Glaeser 2002; Eaton and Eckstein 1997; Henderson 1997a; Henderson 2003a; and Kim 1995.

76. This has been recognized in geography as long ago as since Christaller (1933) and Lösch (1940).

77. Duranton and Puga 2000.

78. Henderson (1997b) for the United States, Fujita and Ishii (1999) for Japan, and Kolko (1999) and Henderson, Lee, and Lee (2001) for the Republic of Korea.

79. Henderson 1997b.

80. Glaeser, Scheinkman, and Schleifer 1995; Fafchamps and Desmet 2000.

81. Henderson 2005b and Henderson, Kuncoro, and Nasution 1996.

82. Glaeser and Kahn 2001.

83. Diversity is measured by the inverse of the Herfindal Index of local employment shares of different sectors.

84. Feldman and Audretsch 1999.

85. Fujita and Ishii 1999 and Duranton and Puga 2001.

86. Duranton and Puga 2005.

87. Chandler Jr. 1977 and Kim 1999.

88. Toffler 1980; Naisbitt 1995; Negroponte 1995; and Knoke 1996.

89. Feldman and Audretsch 1999 and Venables 2006.

90. Kolko 2000.

91. Glaeser and others 1992; Henderson, Kuncoro, and Turner 1995.

92. Black and Henderson (2003) show that cities that dramatically grew (the Phoenix population multiplied 10-fold during 1950–90) or shrank (the Detroit population halved during the same period) are the exceptions, as relative sizes of U.S. cities have been stable over the last century. Eaton and Eckstein (1997) and Dobkins and Ioannides (2001) also find a pattern of overall stability in France, Japan, and the United States. They observe that the relative populations of the top 40 urban areas in France (1876–1990) and Japan (1925–85) remained essentially unchanged.

93. Henderson (1997b). Kim (1995) shows a high (0.64) correlation coefficient of regional localization for two-digit industries in the United States between 1860 and 1987 at the state level. Dumais, Ellison, and Glaeser (2002) also find that, for most industries, agglomeration patterns were strikingly stable over 1972–92. Henderson (2003a) finds stable specialization patterns over 30 years in a study of nine three-digit industries.

94. See, Dunne, Roberts, and Samuelson (1989b); Dunne, Roberts, and Samuelson (1989a); Davis and Haltiwanger (1992); and Herzog Jr. and Schlottmann (1991).

95. Brezis and Krugman 1997.

96. Henderson, Kuncoro, and Turner 1995.

97. Van der Linde 2003.

98. Kolko 1998.

99. United Nations (2006c), Fact Sheet 9.

100. Gribbin (2000), pp. 30–31.

101. Quote from a top UN official, Lars Reutersward, Nairobi-based director of the UN Human Settlements Program.

102. Quoting Lars Reutersward in Ward 2006.

103. United Nations 2004b.

104. Gill and Kharas 2007.

105. Au and Henderson 2006a.

106. Rosenthal and Strange 2004 cited from Hoover and Vernon 1959.

107. Santos and Shaffer 2004.

108. McCrae 2006.

109. World Bank 2002a.

Chapter 5

1. Bureau of Transport Statistics 2003.

2. While returns to capital vary by place (between urban and rural areas, leading and lagging regions, and rich and poor countries), lower marginal returns in a given location can be explained by inadequate complementary factors (Caselli and Feyrer 2007).

3. In 2000 China sent only 458,000 migrants abroad, while 120 million people migrated internally. In the second half of 1990s, fewer than 300,000 people emigrated from Vietnam, while 4.3 million people migrated internally. See Anh, Tacoli, and Thanh (2003) in Deshingkar and Grimm (2004).

4. Migration from rural areas to cities accounts for only about a third for the growth of urban areas worldwide. Nam, Serow, and Sly (1990) and Deshingkar and Grimm (2004) show that the largest flows of internal migrants in developing countries are from rural areas to other rural areas. In India, where permanent migration seems to have stabilized, temporary "circular" migration—particularly by workers in poor households—is increasing.

5. More than half the migrants to the United States come from Central and South America. About the same portion of migrants to the EU-15 come from Europe and Central Asia. And up to 70 per-

cent of migrants to Japan come from other countries in East Asia and the Pacific.

6. The largest share of emigrants in Sub-Saharan Africa (more than 63 percent) and South Asia (34 percent) settle in countries within the same region, typically in an adjacent country. See Ratha and Shaw (2007). This phenomenon is in part a colonial legacy, because borders were drawn arbitrarily across traditional lands dividing long-standing trading partners and even people of the same ethnic groups.

7. Obstfeld, Shambaugh, and Taylor 2004.

8. Taylor 1996; Obstfeld and Taylor 2002.

9. See Caselli and Feyrer 2007.

10. See de Blij (2005) for a review of the geographic and climatic drivers of early migrations.

11. See Massey (2003) for a review of the modern history of international migration.

12. Comparable statistics of emigration from European countries and Japan are available in Massey (1988).

13. Massey (1988) calculates a correlation coefficient of 0.59 between the onset of industrialization (proxied by the year when rail track exceeded 1,000 kilometers), and the initiation of large-scale international movement of labor (defined as the period when emigration first exceeded 10,000 people).

14. See the International Organization of Immigration (IOM) Web page for updated statistics, at http://www.iom.org. An international migrant is defined as a person living in a country other than where he or she was born (Ozden and Schiff 2007).

15. Massey 2003.

16. Ratha and Shaw 2007.

17. The notable exceptions are Australia, because of isolation, and Israel, because of the religious and political nature of the decision to immigrate.

18. Experts point out that although appealing to governments in high-income countries, selective immigration policies are probably not transferable to other popular destinations. A crucial element to the viability of these policies in Canada and Australia is the relative geographic isolation of these countries, which makes movement across their borders easier to monitor and control.

19. Timmer and Williamson (1998), cited in Massey (2003).

20. The best data currently available are still likely to underestimate the internal mobility of labor. Census and survey data used to track internal migration are notoriously inadequate. Census and survey instruments typically fail to capture seasonal movement to part-time and temporary jobs; movement of migrants who find jobs in the informal economy or who reside in informal settlements; and movement between rural areas. For a detailed discussion of the limitations of data on internal migration see Nam, Serow, and Sly (1990), Lucas (1997), Bell (2003), and Deshingkar and Grimm (2004).

21. Lucas (1997) cites quantitative studies by Connell and others (1976) and Skeldon (1986) to support this assertion.

22. Rodriguez 2004.

23. Deshingkar and Grimm (2004) give a detailed description of biases in data collection instruments that lead to a systematic underestimation of rural-to-rural migration, and particularly of temporary "circular" migration, which leads to the "invisibility" of a large portion of internally labor movements to policy makers that is captured only in qualitative village-level studies. Lucas

(1997) points out that the failure of the early literature on internal migration to capture the dominant rural-to-rural movement can be explained by the greater visibility of urban growth, and by the portrayal of rural sectors in the early theoretical models as homogenous, within which migration did not confer any real benefits.

24. Borjas 1990; Borjas, Bronars, and Trejo 1992; Dunlevy and Bellante 1983.

25. Deshingkar and Grimm 2004; United Nations 2006b.

26. Lucas 1997; 2003; McKenzie and Rapoport 2007.

27. Schiff and Özden 2006.

28. Docquier 2006.

29. Lucas 1997.

30. Solow 1956; Swan 1956.

31. Romer 1986; Lucas Jr. 1988.

32. A recent comprehensive review of economic theories and empirical evidence on internal labor migration is available in Lall, Selod, and Shalizi (2006), on which this subsection is based.

33. Todaro 1969.

34. Harris and Todaro 1970.

35. Lucas 1997.

36. Cole and Sanders 1985; Packard 1997.

37. Romer (1986) and Lucas Jr. (1988), originally delivered as an address in 1985.

38. Lucas Jr. 1988.

39. Lucas Jr. (1988) with an acknowledgment of Jacobs (1970).

40. Moretti 2004b; Rosenthal and Strange 2004; Ciccone and Peri 2006.

41. As discussed in other chapters of this Report, urban economics provide a range of arguments in favor of clustering that are independent of spillovers to human capital. For example, cities provide the large markets for producers to exploit productivity gains from scale, as shown by Faini (1996), as well as "thick" labor markets that lower hiring costs for employers. Clustering workers adds to growth by increasing backward and forward linkages, as shown by Adelman and Robinson (1978) in a study of the Republic of Korea.

42. Clemens, Montenegro, and Pritchett 2008.

43. Ratha and Xu 2008.

44. Pritchett 2006.

45. Andrews, Clark, and Whittaker 2007.

46. Cited in Andrews, Clark, and Whittaker (2007).

47. In the United States, rates of internal migration among the native born declined from 1850 to 1940 but accelerated significantly thereafter coinciding with the rapid rate of economic growth after World War II. See Rosenbloom and Sundstrom (2003).

48. Schmertmann 1992.

49. Fujita and Tabuchi 1997.

50. Xenos 2004.

51. Anh 2003.

52. Timmins 2005.

53. Au and Henderson 2006a; 2006b.

54. Shukla and Stark 1986.

55. For evidence on nineteenth-century labor market integration in the United States, see Lebergott (1964) and Margo (2000).

56. Coe and Emery 2004.

57. Hunt 1986.

58. Gallaway and Vedder 1971.

59. Rosenbloom and Sundstrom 2003.

60. McInnis 1966.

61. European Commission 2007.

62. Decressin and Fatás (1994) examine regional labor markets dynamics in Europe and the United States. They analyze the adjustment mechanisms that a typical region's specific shock triggers in regional labor markets. In Europe they find that for the first three years, most of the shock is absorbed by changes in the participation rate, while in the United States, it is immediately reflected in migration.

63. Tabuchi 1988.

64. Barro and Sala-I-Martin 1992; Brown 1997.

65. Fujita and Tabuchi 1997. However, the authors observe that inequality then rose in a third stage, after 1975, as the impact of agglomeration economies accelerated income growth in large metropolitan areas, such as Tokyo.

66. De Brauw and Giles (2008) on China, and McKenzie and Rapoport (2007) on Mexico.

67. Overseas Development Institute 2006.

68. Soto and Torche 2004.

69. Timmins 2005.

70. Koola and Özden 2008.

71. Beegle, De Weerdt, and Dercon 2008.

72. Adams Jr. (2006) as cited in Özden and Schiff (2007).

73. Acosta, Fajnzylber, and Lopez (2007) in Özden and Schiff (2007).

74. Yang 2008.

75. World Bank 2007k.

76. Garrett 2005.

77. De Brauw and Giles 2008.

78. Zhu and Luo 2008.

79. Iliffe (1995) on the historical impact of drought on population distribution in Africa; Bryceson (1999) on the Sahel and Sudan; Hardoy and Satterthwaite (1989) on Mauritania.

80. Wandschneider and Mishra (2003), cited in Deshingkar and Grimm (2004), on the drought-induced migration of 60,000 people out of Bolangir, in the Indian state of Orissa, in 2001.

81. Venables and Kanbur 2005.

82. Deshingkar and Grimm 2004; Rodriguez 2004.

83. Docquier, Beine, and Rapoport 2006.

84. Docquier 2006.

85. Easterly and Nyarko 2008.

86. Sahn and Stifel 2003.

87. Anderson and Pomfret 2005.

Chapter 6

1. Some of these trends were due to the rise in trade with Europe as a share of GDP. But non-European trade declined even as a share of GDP.

2. Krugman 1991b; see also Krugman 2007.

3. See, for example, Antweiler and Trefler (2002), who find that international trade is fueled as much by scale economies as by differences in factor endowments.

4. Limão and Venables 2001.

5. Gallup, Sachs, and Mellinger 1999.

6. World Bank 2007d.

7. Anderson and van Wincoop 2004.

8. It has also meant a change in long-distance trade, mainly in a rise in manufacturing exports (based on differences in labor abun-

dance) and a fall in the share of agricultural goods (based on climatic differences) from developing countries.

9. Rostow 1960.
10. Williamson 1974.
11. Mitchell 1964.
12. Crafts, Mills, and Mulatu 2007.
13. Metzer 1974.
14. Hurd 1975.
15. Roy 2002.
16. Mohammed and Williamson 2004.
17. Harley 1980.
18. O'Rourke and Williamson 1994.
19. Yasuba 1978.
20. Krueger 2006.
21. Baldwin and Martin 1999.
22. Krugman 2007.
23. Combes and Lafourcade 2005. Costs are approximated by ad valorem shares of trade values between geographic regions and distance and take into account that the real price for transportation depends on the physical transportation network, technology, traffic conditions, and structure of the market for transport services.
24. Ivaldi and McCullough 2007.
25. Gordon 1990.
26. Hummels 2007.
27. United Nations Conference on Trade and Development (various years).
28. Tolofari 1986.
29. Button 1999.
30. United Nations 1970.
31. Gilman 1984.
32. Tramp prices are set in competitive markets and quoted in U.S. dollars. Two deflators are used to compute the development of real prices: the U.S. GDP deflator and the price index for bulk commodities that typically are shipped by tramp.
33. Levinson 2006.
34. Hummels 2007.
35. Harrigan 2005.
36. Hummels 2001.
37. Evans and Harrigan 2005. For a similar analysis on trade between East and West Europe compare Nordas, Pinali, and Grosso (2006).
38. Harrigan and Venables 2006.
39. Krugman 1995; Venables 2001.
40. Freund and Weinhold 2004.
41. Fink, Mattoo, and Neagu 2005.
42. Rauch 1999.
43. Antras, Garicano, and Rossi-Hansberg 2006.
44. Rajan and Wei 2004.
45. Amiti and Wei 2005.
46. Bairoch 1988.
47. Christaller 1966.
48. Feenstra and Hanson 1997.
49. Evans and Harrigan 2005.
50. Duranton and Puga 2004.
51. Leamer and Storper 2001.
52. Storper and Venables 2007.
53. Winston 1993.
54. Nikomborirak 2007.

55. Hulten, Bennathan, and Srinivasan (2003), summarized in Hummels, Lugovsky, and Skiba (2007). Scale economies in the manufacturing sector derive from the benefits of many independent producers with relatively small market shares moving close together and interacting (monopolistic competition). Indivisibility and network effects, by contrast, favor monopolies or oligopolies in which one or a few providers generate scale economies that are internal to a private or public transport provider that dominates a port, airport, or railway.
56. Estache, Gonzalez, and Trujillo 2002.
57. Hulten 2007.
58. Canning and Bennathan (2007), for example, find a large variation across countries but a general tendency of middle-income countries to have a deficit in infrastructure investment, in particular road infrastructure. The macroeconomic rates of return calculated in these studies derive from the agglomeration and specialization benefits provided by the lowering of transport costs. These benefits increase with an increasing level of development. See Estache and Fay (2007) for a review of these studies.
59. Brushett 2005.
60. Wilson, Mann, and Otsuki 2004.
61. Wilson, Luo, and Broadman 2006.
62. World Bank 2008.
63. Evans and Harrigan 2005; Harrigan and Venables 2006.
64. Martinez-Zarzoso and Marquez-Ramos 2007.
65. Arvis, Raballand, and Marteau 2007.
66. Arnold 2006.
67. World Bank 2008.
68. Fischer, Harrington, and Parry forthcoming.
69. Nordhaus and Boyer 2000.
70. Tol 2005.
71. World Bank 2008.

GIM 3

1. Allen and others 2007.
2. Smith (1979), p. 189.
3. Kuroda 2007.

Chapter 7

1. Ravallion 2007.
2. Soto 2000.
3. De Long and Shleifer 1993.
4. A passage explicitly mentioning the land law is found in North (1971), p. 123.
5. Wordie 1983.
6. Craft 1989; Turner 1986; Wordie 1983; Wrigley 1985.
7. Craft 1989.
8. Sokoloff and Engerman 2000b.
9. Sokoloff and Engerman 2000b.
10. Rodrik, Subramanian, and Trebbi 2004.
11. Acemoglu, Johnson, and Robinson 2001.
12. This discussion of Mumbai is drawn from Buckley, Bertaud, and Phatak 2005; Buckley and Kalarickal 2006.
13. United Nations 2001; www.mymoneyblog.comarchives/2006.
14. World Bank 2007j; purchasing power parity adjusted per capita gross national income (GNI).
15. Brueckener 2007; Henderson 2007.
16. Buckley and Kalarickal (2006), box 3.4.

17. In 2002, a Ministry of Cities was established to overhaul the regulatory framework allowing cities to more effectively manage land use and subdivision and be more responsive to changes in market needs.

18. World Bank 2007b.

19. Chiquier, Hassler, and Lea 2004.

20. World Bank 2006d.

21. Lall and others 2004.

22. World Bank 2002a.

23. The discussion is based on the historical collection of transport pamphlets the London School of Economics library has converted into digital format and made available for public download (www.lse.ac.uk/library/pamphlets/Transport/transportpamphletpages/urban_transport.htm). These pamphlets cover London transport history (eight pamphlets), transport policy in London (nine pamphlets), the tramways (three pamphlets), and urban transport policy more generally (three pamphlets). These pamphlets were issued by a variety of organizations, including private-sector providers of transport, local political parties, and what might now be called think-tanks. See Roberts (2008), a background paper for this Report.

24. Hargan 2007.

25. Land Enquiry Commission 1914.

26. Offer (1981), p. 291.

27. GDP per capita figures have been taken from Maddison's (2007) historical database (http://www.ggdc.net/maddison/). They are quoted in 1990 international Geary-Khamis dollars.

28. Bairoch and Goertz (1986), table 3, p. 288.

29. Staff City Population Database, Human Settlements Group, International Institute for Environment and Development (IIED).

30. Mumford 1963.

31. Dunlap 1992.

32. Lane 1860.

33. O'Gorman 1939a; 1939b.

34. Santos and Shaffer 2004.

35. Meyer 1917.

36. Victoria Transport Policy Institute 2007.

37. Pucher and others 2005.

38. World Bank 2002a.

39. Metro Bits (http://mic-ro.com/metro).

40. Booth 1901.

41. Abreu 2008, a note prepared for this Report.

42. Nesslein 2003.

43. Borgegård and Kemeny 2004.

44. Hall and Vidén 2005.

45. Swedish Council for Building Research 1990; Borgegård and Kemeny 2004.

46. Hoffman 1996.

47. Hall 2002; Chandler 1992.

48. Chandler 1992.

48. Imparato and Ruster 2003; Abreu 2008.

50. World Bank 2007j.

51. Hall 1984.

52. Trackman, Fisher, and Salas 1999.

53. Mackay 1999; Jones and Datta 2000, based on Abreu 2008.

54. Mackay 1999, based on Abreu 2008.

55. Goodlad 1996; Mackay 1999; Jones and Datta 2000.

56. These comparisons are based on data from Maddison 2006.

57. *World Urbanisation Prospects: The 2007 Revision Population Database* (http://esa.un.org/unup/).

58. Cohen and Soto 2001.

59. The discussion that follows is largely based on Oh (2008), a note prepared for this Report.

60. The discussion that follows is based in part on Chen (2008), a note prepared for this Report.

61. Figure derived from *China Statistical Yearbook 2007*.

62. World Bank 2003b; 2007k; Bertaud 2004.

63. *World Urbanisation Prospects: The 2007 Revision Population Database* (http://esa.un.org/unup/).

64. Human Development and Reform Commission 2005; Changsha-Zhuzhou-Xiangtan Cluster Regional Plan.

65. Kilroy 2007.

66. Lall 2005.

67. Lall 2005.

68. Yepes and Lall 2008.

69. Sohn 2003, based on Oh 2008.

70. Evans 2002, Sohn 2003, respectively.

71. *World Urbanisation Prospects: The 2007 Revision Population Database* (http://esa.un.org/unup/).

72. Maddison 2006. GDP per capita is quoted in constant 1990 international dollars.

73. Comparisons based on urban agglomeration population data from *World Urbanisation Prospects*.

74. Cohen and Soto 2007.

75. World Bank 2007j.

76. Neuwirth 2007, based on Vidler 2008.

77. BBC World Service, Thursday, April 27, 2000 (http://news.bbc.co.uk/1/hi/sci/tech/727966.stm).

78. The discussion of Turkey above is based on Vidler (2008), a note prepared for this Report.

79. Bertaud 2003.

80. Government of India Planning Commission 2002a.

81. Selod 2007.

82. Tinbergen 1952.

Chapter 8

1. Azzoni, Menezes-Filho, Menezes, and Silveira-Neto (2000), World Bank 1998.

2. World Bank (2007b), figure 8.2 comes from this Report.

3. World Bank 2007a.

4. Estimate based on figures reported in Maddison (2008). In 1700 India's GDP was $90,750 million compared with a world GDP of $371,369 million in 1990 international dollars (Maddison 2008).

5. In landlord systems, the landlord was responsible for collecting revenues from villages after retaining part of the revenue he collected; in individual systems, British government officers collected revenue directly from cultivators; in village systems, a village community body bore the responsibility for revenue collection (Banerjee and Iyer 2005).

6. Lall, Wang, and Deichmann 2008b.

7. Government of India 2006.

8. Hunt 2000.

9. Gorzelak 2007.

10. European Commission 2002.

11. Between 1994 and 1999 structural funds allocated resources to areas on the basis of five "objectives": supporting development

and structural adjustment of areas whose development is lagging, helping frontier areas or parts of areas seriously affected by industrial decline, combating long-term unemployment and facilitating labor market integration of persons excluded from the labor market, speeding adjustment of agricultural structures as part of common agriculture policy reform and structural adjustment of rural areas, and promoting development and structural adjustment in areas with low population density.

12. Rodríguez-Pose and Fratesi 2004.
13. European Commission 2007.
14. Objective One is to help regions (called "areas" in this Report) whose development is lagging to catch up. Some 50 regions, representing 22 percent of the EU's population, are included.
15. Dall'Erba 2003.
16. Estimates suggest that resettlement costs were US$7,000 per family in the mid-1980s (Adhiati and Bobsien 2001).
17. Davezies (2001), Martin (2005). This figure shows that the coefficient of variation of per capita GDP (orange line, left axis) across NUTS 2 areas in France rises between 1982 and 2002; whereas the coefficient of variation of per capita disposable incomes falls (blue line, right axis).
18. Morrisson and Murtin 2005.
19. United States Census Bureau 2002.
20. About $8 an hour in 2007 U.S. dollars.
21. Engel, Galetovic, and Raddatz 1998.
22. Gibson and Rozelle 2003.
23. Escobal and Torero 2000.
24. Baer 1995.
25. Stewart 2008.
26. Hill and Gaddy 2003.
27. Rolfes 2002.
28. Whalley and Zhang 2007.
29. Hewings, Feser, and Poole 2008; population figure for 1996.
30. Rephann and Isserman (1994). One of the first ex post evaluations of regional development programs ever conducted in the United States using an experimental design.
31. Specific examples are discussed later in this chapter.
32. Andrienko and Guriev 2003.
33. Based on recent research using census micro data for Brazil between 1960 and 2000.
34 . Margo 1988.
35. Borsch-Supan 1987.
36. Duarte, Ferreira, and Salvato Jr. 2004. The labor force in the northeast has 4.6 years of schooling compared with the average of 6.4 years nationwide, and 7.3 years in the southeast.
37. Shah and Shen 2006.
38. They will be accountable to the higher levels of government providing these transfers.
39. Numbers are for 2000 (Chakraborty 2003).
40. Euractiv (2008).
41. World Bank (2003b) provides a comprehensive treatment of land management practices and policies in different parts of the world, and how specific policies promote development and reduce poverty.
42. Palacin and Shelburne 2005.
43. Bayes 2007.
44. World Bank 2008b.
45. World Bank 2008a.

46. World Bank 2008e.
47. Econometric analysis based on panel data (Lei and Haynes 2004).
48. Kloeppinger-Todd 2007. Overall, there are more than 20 million mobile phone subscribers in the Philippines.
49. Jensen 2007.
50. Luo 2004.
51. Yepes and Lall 2008.
52. Baldwin, Forslid, Martin, Ottaviano, and Robert-Nicoud 2003. The predictions of new economic geography models are as follows: Infrastructure policies that facilitate interregional trade between leading and lagging areas will increase spatial concentrations of economic activity in leading areas. These policies will also increase growth in the whole economy while reducing nominal income inequalities between areas and between workers and capital owners. By contrast, infrastructure policies that improve connectivity within lagging areas may enhance local economic growth but can slow the growth of the whole economy.
53. Faini 1983.
54. Combes and Lafourcade 2001.
55. Jacoby 2000.
56. World Bank 2008b.
57. Lall, Schroeder, and Schmidt 2008.
58. Government of Malaysia 2001.
59. Malaysia Industrial Development Authority (http://www.mida.gov.my/).
60. Al-Hassan and Diao 2007.
61. Park forthcoming.
62. Lee (2008).
63. The following examples are based on background research for this report.
64. Donoso-Clark and Leninhan (2008) call these centrally administered policies to disperse economic activity "first-generation" approaches to territorial development.
65. Donoso-Clark and Leninhan 2008.
66. Drabenstott 2005.
67. Hewings, Feser, and Poole 2008.
68. Carvalho, Lall, and Timmins 2006. Constitutional funds were created in 1989 to finance economic activities in the north and northeast regions.
69. World Bank 1977; Scott 1982.
70. Chakravorty and Lall 2005.
71. Fay, Felkner, and Lall 2008.
72. Based on research done by the Secretary of Economic Policy, reported in Calmon (2003) and World Bank (2005a).
73. Details are provided in Calmon (2003).
74. Haussman, Rodrik, and Velasco 2005.
75. Donoso-Clark and Leninhan 2008 point out that a feature of the failed "first-generation" territorial development programs of the 1960s and 1970s was that they depended on external inputs and expertise, rather than exploiting local assets and comparative advantage.
76. A recent paper on firm location in developing countries summarizes the findings from empirical work on the main factors influencing location choices (see Deichmann, Lall, Redding, and Venables forthcoming).
77. Uvalic 1993.
78. Bolton and Roland 1997.

Chapter 9

1. Woronoff (1972), p. 141. The *Entente* was created in 1959 and designed to promote the economic development of members by raising funds, guaranteeing loans, and encouraging trade and investment. It operates through the Mutual Aid and Loan Guarantee Fund headquartered in Abidjan, Côte d'Ivoire. The original member states were Dahomey (now Benin), Côte d'Ivoire, Niger, and Upper Volta (now Burkina Faso); Togo joined in 1966.

2. Collier 2007.

3. See Brülhart (2008) for a detailed analysis on intermediate goods.

4. Coulibaly 2008.

5. See Yoshino (2008), using both the World Bank enterprise survey database and the *Doing Business* database.

6. Melitz 2003.

7. See Schiff and Winters (2003) for a detailed development on these points.

8. Viner 1950; Meade 1956; Balassa 1967; Aitken 1973; among others.

9. Baier and Bergstrand 2004; Bond 2005; Evenett 2005; Bergstrand 2006.

10. Bhagwati 1995; Bhagwati, Greenaway, and Panagariya 1998; Krishna 1998.

11. Krugman 1991; Frankel, Stein, and Wei 1996; Carrere 2005.

12. Martin, Mayer, and Thoenig (2008) estimate that countries trading a lot with their neighbors are less likely to have an armed conflict with them than countries trading mainly with distant partners.

13. World Bank 2004a; United Nations 2007.

14. Also in the 1970s, Sub-Saharan Africa was made up of vast countries, mostly rural with a few isolated, densely populated areas (mostly on the coast) and no interconnecting infrastructure—hardly conducive to regional integration (CSAO/ECOWAS 2005).

15. The current WTO rules specify that regional trade agreements should cover substantially all sectors, which excludes sector-specific trade deals for today's developing countries. But the principle of starting with focused areas of cooperation is still valid.

16. Venables (2003) shows that regional integration between low-income countries tends to lead to income divergence between the least developed and the relatively more advanced member countries. Goyal and Staal (2004) show that small countries are more in favor of integration, whereas large countries prefer integrating with countries of equal size.

17. Coulibaly 2006.

18. World Bank 2004b.

19. Laeven and Woodruff 2007.

20. Box 3.3 of the report on food safety and agricultural health standards (World Bank 2005c).

21. Gibbon and Ponte 2005; Chandra 2006; Broadman 2006; Czubala, Shepherd, and Wilson 2007.

22. Fink and Mattoo 2004; Hoekman 2006.

23. Chow and others 2005; World Bank 2007g.

24. World Bank 2007f.

25. Arvis, Raballand, and Marteau 2007.

26. Djankov, Freund, and Pham 2006.

27. Behar and Manners 2008.

28. World Bank 2004b.

29. Both examples are from a World Bank Independent Evaluation Group report on regional programs.

30. Leigland and Roberts 2007.

31. World Bank 2006n.

32. N'Guessan and Chitou 2006.

33. African Development Bank 2007.

34. Bougheas, Demetriades, and Morgenroth 1999; Limão and Venables 2001.

35. For instance, Foroutan and Pritchett (1993) make this argument for Sub-Saharan Africa.

36. Coulibaly and Fontagné 2006.

37. Buys, Deichmann, and Wheeler 2006.

38. Shepherd and Wilson 2006.

39. Vargas-Hidalgo 1979; Wionczek 1970.

40. Hazelwood 1979; Kasekende and Ng'eno 1999.

41. Brandts and Cooper (2007) show that effective communication is a more powerful coordination mechanism than purely financial incentives.

42. Sandler 2002.

43. Arce 2001; 2004; Arce and Sandler 2002.

44. Schiff and Winters 2002.

45. In Kraske and others (1996), p. 95.

46. See the International Development Association and World Bank (2008) for a thorough discussion of these issues.

47. Schiff and Winters 2002.

48. Mayer 2008.

49. Note that Northeast Asia is an exceptional case, because of its proximity to Japan. Its main markets are still North America and the European Union. For purposes of market access, given its trade links with China, Southeast Asia should be considered as part of the same neighborhood as China.

50. Hill and Gaddy 2003.

51. International Monetary Fund (1998) for the EU enlargement; Schiff and Wang (2003) for NAFTA.

52. World Bank 2002b.

53. Jessen 2002.

54. World Bank (2003a) report on trade and investment.

55. Assessment made using the methodology proposed by Coulibaly (2007). The trade impact of the Gulf Cooperation Council (GCC) is not faring better from this assessment, even if its members took the important step to launch a common market on January 1, 2008.

56. World Bank 2007g.

57. Antweiler and Trefler 2002.

58. See for instance Moreno and Trehan (1997).

59. Arora and Vamvakidis (2005) show the impact of South Africa on its neighbors, while Behar and Collier emphasize on the impact of resource-rich countries on their neighbors in Sub-Saharan Africa.

60. Nabi and Nasim 2001.

61. Naqvi and Schuler 2007.

62. World Bank 2007h.

63. Söderbaum 2001.

64. Behar and Collier 2008.

65. United Nations (2004a) and United Nations and African Union (2006) report on regional integration.

66. N'Dulu 2001.

67. Gregoire and Labazee 1993.

68. Ladman 1979; Asiwaju 2005.

69. Dorosh, Haggblade, and Dradri 2007; Jayne and others 2005; Tschirley and others 2004; Negri and Porto 2007.

70. Little 2007.

71. Gregoire and Labazee 1993; Yade and others 1999.

72. Adebusoye 2006.

73. Jourdan and NEPAD 2006.

74. Hoekman and Njinkeu 2007.

75. Independent Evaluation Group (IEG) 2007.

76. Collier and Venables 2007.

GIM 4

1. Alesina, Easterly, and Matuszeski 2006.

2. de Blij 2005.

3. Naudé 2007.

4. Ndulu and others (2007), p. 101.

5. Satterthwaite 2007.

6. Naudé and Matthee 2007.

7. Ramos 2007.

8. Martínez-Zarzoso, García-Menéndez, and Suárez-Burguet 2003.

References

The word "processed" describes informally reproduced works that may not be commonly available through libraries.

Abreu, María. 2008. "Effectively Dealing with Slums." Background note for the WDR 2009.

Acemoglu, Daron, Simon Johnson, and James A. Robinson. 2001. "The Colonial Origins of Comparative Development: An Empirical Investigation." *American Economic Review* 91 (5): 1369–401.

———. 2002. "Reversal of Fortune: Geography and Institutions in the Making of the Modern World Income Distribution." *Quarterly Journal of Economics* 117 (4): 1231–94.

Acosta, Pablo, Pablo Fajnzylber, and J. Humberto Lopez. 2007. "The Impact of Remittances on Poverty and Human Capital: Evidence from Latin America Household Surveys." In *International Migration, Economic Development, and Policy*, ed. Caglar Özden and Maurice Schiff. Washington, DC, and New York: World Bank and Palgrave Macmillan.

Adams, David, and E. M. Hastings. 2001. "Urban Renewal in Hong Kong: Transition From Development Corporation to Renewal Authority." *Land Use Policy* 18(3):245–58.

Adams, Richard H. Jr. 2006. "Remittances, Poverty, and Investment in Guatemala." In *International Migration, Remittances, and the Brain Drain*, ed. Caglar Özden and Maurice Schiff. Washington, DC, and New York: World Bank and Palgrave Macmillan.

Adebusoye, Paulina Makinwa. 2006. "Geographic Labour Mobility in Sub-Saharan Africa." Globalization, Growth, and Poverty Working Paper Series 1, IDRC, Ottawa.

Adelman, Irma, and Sherman Robinson. 1978. "Migration, Demographic Change, and Income Distribution in a Model of a Developing Country." In *Research in Population Economics*, vol. I, ed. Julian Simon. Greenwich, CT: JAI Press.

Adhiati, M. Adriana Sri, and Armin Bobsien. 2001. *Indonesia's Transmigration Programme—An Update: A Report Prepared for Down to Earth*. London: International Campaign for Ecological Justice in Indonesia.

Africa Development Bank (ADB). 2007. *Report of the High Level Panel: Investing in Africa's Future*. Abidjan, Côte d'Ivoire: ADB.

Aghion, Philippe, Robin Burgess, Stephen J. Redding, and Fabrizio Zilibotti. 2006. "The Unequal Effects of Liberalization: Evidence from Dismantling the License Raj in India." NBER Working Paper 12031, National Bureau of Economic Research, Cambridge, MA.

Aghion, Philippe, and Peter Howitt. 1992. "A Model of Growth Through Creative Destruction." *Econometrica* 60(2):323–51.

———. 2005. "Growth With Quality-Improving Innovations: An Integrated Framework." In *Handbook of Economic Growth, Volume 1A*, ed. Philippe Aghion and Steven Durlauf. Amsterdam, Netherlands: North-Holland.

Aghion, Philippe, and Jeffrey G. Williamson. 1998. *Growth, Inequality and Globalization: Theory, History, and Policy*. New York: Cambridge University Press.

Aitken, Norman D. 1973. "The Effects of the EEC and the EFTA on European Trade: A Temporal Cross-Section Analysis." *American Economic Review* 63 (5): 881–92.

Al-Hassan, Ramatu M., and Xinshen Diao. 2007. "Regional Disparities in Ghana: Policy Options and Public Investment Implications." IFPRI Working Paper 693, Internationhal Food Policy Research Institute, Washington, DC.

Alcalá, Francisco, and Antonio Ciccone. 2004. "Trade and Productivity." *Quarterly Journal of Economics* 119 (2): 613–46.

Alderman, Harold, Miriam Babita, Gabriel Demombynes, Nthabiseng Makhatha, and Berk Özler. 2002. "How Low Can You Go? Combining Census and Survey Data for Mapping Poverty in South Africa." *Journal of African Economies* 11 (2): 169–200.

Alesina, Alberto, Arnaud Devleeschauwer, William Easterly, Sergio Kurlat, and Romain Wacziarg. 2003. "Fractionalization." *Journal of Economic Growth* 8 (2): 155–94.

Alesina, Alberto, William Easterly, and Janina Matuszeski. 2006. "Artificial States." Working Paper 2115, Harvard Institute of Economic Research, Cambridge, MA.

Alesina, Alberto, and Enrico Spolaore. 2003. *The Size of Nations.* Cambridge, MA, and London: MIT Press.

Allen, Robert, Jean-Pascal Bassino, Debin Ma, Christine Moll-Murata, and Jan Luiten Van Zanden. 2007. "Wages, Prices, and Living Standards in China, 1738–1925: In Comparison with Europe, Japan, and India." Economics Working Paper 316, University of Oxford, Oxford, U.K.

Alston, Lee, and T. J. Hatton. 1991. "The Earnings Gap between Agricultural and Manufacturing Laborers, 1925–1941." *Journal of Economic History* 51 (1): 83–99.

Amiti, Mary, and Shang-Jin Wei. 2005. "Fear of Service Outsourcing: Is It Justified?" *Economic Policy* 20 (42): 308–47.

Anderson, James E., and Eric van Wincoop. 2003. "Gravity with Gravitas: A Solution to the Border Puzzle." *American Economic Review* 93 (1): 170–92.

———. 2004. "Trade Costs." *Journal of Economic Literature* 42 (3): 691–751.

Anderson, Kathryn H., and Richard Pomfret. 2005. "Spatial Inequality and Development in Central Asia." In *Spatial Disparities in Human Development: Perspectives from Asia*, ed. Ravi Kanbur, Anthony J. Venables, and Guanghua Wan. Tokyo and New York: United Nations University Press.

Andrews, Martyn, Kenneth Clark, and William Whittaker. 2007. "The Employment and Earnings of Migrants in Great Britain."

Working Paper 3068, Institute for the Study of Labor, Bonn, Germany.

Andrienko, Yuri, and Sergei M. Guriev. 2003. "Determinants of Interregional Mobility in Russia: Evidence from Panel Data." Working Paper 3835, Centre for Economic Policy Research, London.

Angel, Shlomo. 2008. "Preparing for Urban Expansion: A Proposed Strategy for Intermediate Cities in Ecuador." In *The New Global Frontier: Cities, Poverty and Environment in the 21st Century*, ed. G. Martine, G. McGranahan, M. Montgomery, and R. Castilla-Fernandez. London: IIED/UNFPA and Earthscan.

Angeriz, Alvaro, John McCombie, and Mark Roberts. 2008. "New Estimates of Returns to Scale and Spatial Spillovers for EU Regional Manufacturing, 1986–2002." *International Regional Science Review* 31 (1): 62–87.

Anh, Dang Nguyen. 2003. "Migration and Poverty in Asia, with Reference to Bangladesh, China, the Philippines, and Viet Nam." Paper presented at the Ad Hoc Expert Group Meeting on Migration and Development, Bangkok, Thailand, August 27.

Anh, Dang Nguyen, Cecilia Tacoli, and Hoang Xuan Thanh. 2003. "Migration in Vietnam: A Review of Information on Current Trends and Patterns, and Their Policy Implications." Paper presented at the Regional Conference on Migration, Development and Pro-poor Policy Choices in Asia, Dhaka, Bangladesh.

Antràs, Pol, Luis Garicano, and Esteban Rossi-Hansberg. 2006. "Offshoring in a Knowledge Economy." *Quarterly Journal of Economics* 121 (1): 31–77.

Antweiler, Werner, and Daniel Trefler. 2002. "Increasing Returns and All That: A View from Trade." *American Economic Review* 92 (1): 93–119.

Arce, Daniel M. 2001. "Leadership and the Aggregation of International Collective Action." *Oxford Economic Papers* 53 (1): 114–37.

———. 2004. "Asymmetric Leadership and International Public Goods." *Public Finance Review* 32 (5): 528–58.

Armstrong, Harvey, and Jim Taylor. 2000. *Regional Economics and Policy*. Oxford, U.K.: Blackwell.

Arnold, John. 2006. "Best Practices in Management of International Trade Corridors." Transport Working Paper TM-13, World Bank, Washington, DC.

Arora, Vivek, and Athanasios Vamvakidis. 2005. "The Implications of South African Economic Growth for the Rest of Africa." *South African Journal of Economics* 73 (2): 229–42.

Arrow, Kenneth J. 1962. "Economic Welfare and the Allocation of Resources for Invention." In *The Rate and Direction of Inventive Activity: Economic and Social Factors*, ed. Conference of the Universities and the National Bureau Committee for Economic Research. Princeton, NJ: Princeton University Press.

Arvis, Jean-François, Gael Raballand, and Jean-François Marteau. 2007. "The Cost of Being Landlocked: Logistics Cost and Supply Chain Reliability." Policy Research Working Paper 4258, World Bank, Washington, DC.

Asiwaju, Anthony I. 2005. "Transfrontier Regionalism: The European Union Perspective on Postcolonial Africa, with Special Reference to Borgu." In *Holding the Line. Borders in a Global World*, ed. Heather N. Nicol and Ian Townsend-Gault. Vancouver, Canada: University of British Columbia Press.

Atkinson, Michael M., and Richard A. Powers. 1987. "Inside the Industrial Policy Garbage Can: Selective Subsidies to Business in Canada." *Canadian Public Policy* 13 (2): 208–17.

Au, Chun-Chung, and J. Vernon Henderson. 2006a. "Are Chinese Cities Too Small?" *Review of Economic Studies* 73 (3): 549–76.

———. 2006b. "How Migration Restrictions Limit Agglomeration and Productivity in China." *Journal of Development Economics* 80 (2): 350–88.

Audretsch, David B., and Maryann P. Feldman. 1996. "R&D Spillovers and the Geography of Innovation and Production." *American Economic Review* 86 (3): 630–40.

Azzoni, Carlos, Naercio Menezes-Filho, Tatiane A. De Menezes, and Raul Silveira-Neto. 2000. "Geography and Income Convergence among Brazilian States." Research Network Working Paper R-395, Inter-American Development Bank, Washington, DC.

Bae, Chang-Hee Christine, and Yaourai Suthiranart. 2003. "Policy Options towards a Sustainable Urban Transportation Strategy for Bangkok." *International Development Planning Review* 25 (1): 31–51.

Baer, Werner. 1995. *The Brazilian Economy: Growth and Development*, 4th ed. Westport, CT: Praeger Publishers.

Baier, Scott L., and Jeffrey H. Bergstrand. 2004. "Economic Determinants of Free Trade Agreements." *Journal of International Economics* 64 (1): 29–63.

Bairoch, Paul. 1982. "International Industrialization Levels from 1750 to 1980." *Journal of European Economic History* 11 (2): 269–333.

———. 1988. *Cities and Economic Development: From the Dawn of History to the Present*. Chicago: University of Chicago Press.

Bairoch, Paul, and Gary Goertz. 1986. "Factors of Urbanization in the Nineteenth-Century Developed Countries: A Descriptive and Econometric Analysis." *Urban Studies* 23 (4): 285–305.

Baker, Jim. 1999. *Crossroads: A Popular History of Malaysia and Singapore*. Singapore: Times Books International.

Baker, Judy, Rakhi Basu, Maureen Cropper, Somik V. Lall, and Akie Takeuchi. 2005. "Urban Poverty and Transport: The Case of Mumbai." Policy Research Working Paper 3693, World Bank, Washington, DC.

Baker, Kevin. 2001. "The First Slum in America." *New York Times*, September 30.

Balassa, Bela. 1967. "Trade Creation and Trade Diversion in European Common Market." *Economic Journal* 77 (305): 1–21.

Baldwin, John R., and Paul K. Gorecki. 1986. *Role of Scale in Canada–U.S. Productivity Differences in the Manufacturing Sector 1970–1979*. Buffalo, NY, and Toronto, Canada: University of Toronto Press.

Baldwin, Richard E. 1995. "A Domino Theory of Regionalism." In *Expanding Membership of the European Union*, ed. Richard E. Baldwin, Pertti Haaparanta, and Jaakko Kiander. Cambridge, MA, and New York: Cambridge University Press.

———. 2008. "Sequencing and Depth of Regional Economic Integration: Lessons for the Americas from Europe." *World Economy* 31 (1): 5–30.

Baldwin, Richard E., Rikard Forslid, Philippe Martin, Gianmarco I. P. Ottaviano, and Frederic Robert-Nicoud. 2003. *Economic*

Geography and Public Policy. Princeton, NJ: Princeton University Press.

Baldwin, Richard E., and Philippe Martin. 1999. "Two Waves of Globalization: Superficial Similarities, Fundamental Differences." In *Globalization and Labor*, ed. Horst Siebert. Tuebingen, Germany: Mohr Siebeck.

Baldwin, Richard E., Philippe Martin, and Gianmarco I. P. Ottaviano. 2001. "Global Income Divergence, Trade, and Industrialization: The Geography of Growth Take-Offs." *Journal of Economic Growth* 6 (1): 5–37.

Baldwin, Richard E., and Charles Wyplosz. 2006. *The Economics of European Integration*, 2nd ed. London: McGraw-Hill Education.

Balisacan, Arsenio, Hal Hill, and Sharon Faye Piza. Forthcoming. "Spatial Disparities and Development Policy in the Philippines." In *Reshaping Economic Geography in East Asia*, ed. Yukon Huang and Alessandro Magnoli Bocchi. Washington, DC: World Bank, EAP Companion Volume to the WDR 2009.

Balk, Deborah L., Uwe Deichmann, Gregory Yetman, Francesca Pozzi, Simon I. Hay, and Andrew Nelson. 2006. "Determining Global Population Distribution: Methods, Applications, and Data." *Advances in Parasitology* 62: 119–56.

Banerjee, Abhijit, and Lakshmi Iyer. 2005. "History, Institutions, and Economic Performance: The Legacy of Colonial Land Tenure Systems in India." *American Economic Review* 95 (4): 1190–213.

Barro, Robert J., and Xavier Sala-I-Martin. 1992. "Convergence." *Journal of Political Economy* 100 (2): 223–51.

———. 2004. *Economic Growth*, 2nd ed. Cambridge, MA: MIT Press.

Barro, Robert J., Xavier Sala-I-Martin, Olivier J. Blanchard, and Robert E. Hall. 1991. "Convergence across States and Cities." *Brookings Papers on Economic Activity* 1991 (1): 107–82.

Bartelsman, Eric J., Ricardo J. Caballero, and Richard K. Lyons. 1994. "Customer and Supplier-Driven Externalities." *American Economic Review* 84 (4): 1075–84.

Basu, Susanto, and John G. Fernald. 1997. "Returns to Scale in U.S. Production: Estimates and Implications." *Journal of Political Economy* 105 (2): 249–83.

Baumert, Kevin A., Timothy Herzog, and Jonathan Pershing. 2005. *Navigating the Numbers: Greenhouse Gas Data and International Climate Policy*. Washington, DC: World Resources Institute.

Baumol, William J. 1986. "Productivity Growth, Convergence, and Welfare: What the Long-Run Data Show." *American Economic Review* 76 (5): 1072–85.

Bayes, Abdul. 2007. *Impact Assessment of Jamuna Multipurpose Bridge Project (JMBP) on Poverty*. Dhaka: Japan Bank for International Cooperation.

Bazoglu, Nefise. 2008. *Cities in Transition: Demographics and the Development of Cities*. Philadelphia: Pennsylvania State University.

Beaumier, Guy. 1998. *Regional Development in Canada*. Ottawa: Government of Canada.

Beegle, Kathleen, Joachim De Weerdt, and Stefan Dercon. 2008. "Migration and Economic Mobility in Tanzania: Evidence from a Tracking Survey." World Bank, Washington, DC. Processed.

Behar, Alberto, and Paul Collier. 2008. "Does Proximity Matters More Than Wealth?" CSAE, Oxford, U.K.

Behar, Alberto, and Phil Manners. 2008. "Logistics and Exports." Department of Economics and CSAE Working Paper 2008-13, University of Oxford, Oxford, U.K.

Bekaert, Geert, Campbell R. Harvey, and Christian Lundblad. 2005. "Does Financial Liberalization Spur Growth?" *Journal of Financial Economics* 77 (1): 3–55.

Bell, Martin. 2003. "Comparing Internal Migration between Countries: Measures, Data Sources, and Results." Working Paper 2003/02, University of Queensland Centre for Population Research, Brisbane, Australia.

Bento, Antonio M., Maureen L. Cropper, Ahmed Mushfiq Mobarak, and Katja Vinha. 2003. "The Impact of Urban Spatial Structure on Travel Demand in the United States." Policy Research Working Paper 3007, World Bank, Washington, DC.

Bergstrand, Jeffrey H. 2006. "Regional Integration as a Development Strategy." Paper presented at The New Regionalism: Progress, Setbacks, and Challenges, Washington, DC.

Bernstein, Jeffrey I., and M. Ishaq Nadiri. 1988. "Inter-industry R&D Spillovers, Rates of Return, and Production in High-Tech Industries." *American Economic Review* 78 (2): 429–34.

Bertaud, Alain. 2003. "Order without Design." World Bank, Washington, DC. Processed.

———. 2004. "The Spatial Organization of Cities: Deliberate Outcome or Unforeseen Consequence?" Working Paper WP-2004-01, Institute of Urban and Regional Development, Berkeley, CA.

Bertram, Geoffrey. 2004. "On the Convergence of Small Island Economies with their Metropolitan Patrons." *World Development* 32 (2): 343–64.

Bhagwati, Jagdish. 1995. "U.S. Trade Policy: The Infatuation with Free Trade Areas." In *The Dangerous Drift to Preferential Trade Agreements*, ed. Jagdish Bhagwati and Anne O. Krueger. Washington, DC: American Enterprise Institute.

Bhagwati, Jagdish, David Greenaway, and Arvind Panagariya. 1998. "Trading Preferentially: Theory and Policy." *Economic Journal* 108 (449): 1128–48.

Bhagwati, Jagdish, and T. N. Srinivasan. 2002. "Trade and Poverty in the Poor Countries." *American Economic Review* 92 (2): 180–3.

Biedermann, Rob. 2007. "Sinvin Realty Handles Meatpacking District Deal in NYC." *crefeed.com*, October 29.

Bikhchandani, Sushil, David Hirshleifer, and Ivo Welch. 1998. "Learning from the Behavior of Others: Conformity, Fads, and Informational Cascades." *Journal of Economic Perspectives* 12 (3): 151–70.

Bird, Kate, and Kate Higgins. 2008. "Regional Inequality and Primary Education in Northern Uganda, Policy Brief 2." Background paper for the WDR 2009.

Black, Duncan, and J. Vernon Henderson. 1999. "A Theory of Urban Growth." *Journal of Political Economy* 107 (2): 252–84.

———. 2003. "Urban Evolution in the USA." *Journal of Economic Geography* 3 (4): 343–72.

Blake, Gerald. 2005. "Boundary Permeability in Perspective." In *Holding the Line: Borders in a Global World*, ed. Heather N. Nicol and Ian Townsend-Gault. Vancouver, Canada: University of British Columbia Press.

Blanchard, Olivier J., Lawrence F. Katz, Robert E. Hall, and Barry Eichengreen. 1992. "Regional Evolutions." *Brookings Papers on Economic Activity* 1992 (1): 1–75.

Boltho, Andrea, Wendy Carlin, and Pasquale Scaramozzino. 1997. "Will East Germany Become a New Mezzogiorno?" *Journal of Comparative Economics* 24 (3): 241–64.

Bolton, Patrick, and Gerard Roland. 1997. "The Breakup of Nations: A Political Economy Analysis." *Quarterly Journal of Economics* 112 (4): 1057–90.

Bond, Eric W. 2005. "The Sequencing of Trade Liberalization in the Presence of Adjustment Costs." Paper presented at the Sequencing of Regional Economic Integration: Issues in the Breadth and Depth of Economic Integration in the Americas, Notre Dame, IN.

Booth, Charles. 1901. *Improved Means of Locomotion as a First Step Towards the Cure of the Housing Difficulties of London*. London: Macmillan.

Bordo, Michael D., Barry Eichengreen, and Douglas A. Irwin. 1999. "Is Globalization Today Really Different Than Globalization a Hundred Years Ago?" NBER Working Paper 7195, National Bureau of Economic Research, Cambridge, MA.

Boreak, Sik. 2000. "Land Ownership, Sales, and Concentration in Cambodia. A Preliminary Review of Secondary Data and Primary Data from Four Recent Surveys." Working Paper 16, Development Resource Institute, Phnom Penh.

Borgegård, Lars-Erik, and Jim Kemeny. 2004. "Sweden: High-Rise Housing for a Low-Density Country." In *High-Rise Housing in Europe: Current Trends and Future Prospects*, ed. R. Turkington, R. van Kempen, and E. Wassenberg. Delft, Netherlands: Delft University Press.

Borjas, George J. 1990. *Friends or Strangers: The Impact of Immigration on the U.S. Economy*. New York: Basic Books.

Borjas, George J., Stephen G. Bronars, and Stephen J. Trejo. 1992. "Self Selection and Internal Migration in the United States." *Journal of Urban Economics* 32 (2): 159–85.

Borsch-Supan, Axel. 1987. "The Role of Education: Mobility Increasing or Mobility Impeding?" NBER Working Paper 2329, National Bureau of Economic Research, Cambridge, MA.

Bossone, Biagio, and Jong-Kun Lee. 2004. "In Finance, Size Matters: The 'Systemic Scale Economies' Hypothesis." *IMF Staff Papers* 51 (1): 19–46.

Bougheas, Spiros, Panicos O. Demetriades, and Edgar L. W. Morgenroth. 1999. "Infrastructure, Transport Costs, and Trade." *Journal of International Economics* 47 (1): 169–89.

Bourguignon, François, and Christian Morrisson. 1998. "Inequality and Development: The Role of Dualism." *Journal of Development Economics* 57 (2): 233–57.

———. 2002. "Inequality among World Citizens: 1820–1992." *American Economic Review* 92 (4): 727–44.

Brahmbhatt, Milan. 2004. *Strong Fundamentals to the Fore: Regional Overview*. Washington, DC: World Bank, East and Pacific Region.

Brakman, Steven, Harry Garretsen, and Charles van Marrewijk. 2001. *An Introduction to Geographical Economics: Trade, Location, and Growth*. New York: Cambridge University Press.

Brandts, Jordi, and David J. Cooper. 2007. "It's What You Say, Not What You Pay: An Experimental Study of Manager-Employee Relationships in Overcoming Coordination Failure." *Journal of the European Economic Association* 5 (6): 1223–68.

Brezis, Elise S., and Paul R. Krugman. 1997. "Technology and the Life Cycle of Cities." *Journal of Economic Growth* 2 (4): 369–83.

Bristow, R. 1984. *Land-Use Planning in Hong Kong: History, Policies, and Procedures*. Hong Kong: Oxford University Press.

Broadman, Harry G. 2005. *From Disintegration to Reintegration: Eastern Europe and the Former Soviet Union in International Trade*. Washington, DC: World Bank.

———. 2006. *Africa's Silk Road: China and India's New Economic Frontier*. Washington, DC: World Bank.

Brockerhoff, M., and P. Hewett. 2000. "Inequality of Child Mortality among Ethnic Groups in Sub-Saharan Africa." *Bulletin of the World Health Organization* 78 (1): 30–41.

Brown, Annette N. 1997. "The Economic Determinants of the Internal Migration Flows in Russia During Transition." Working Paper 89, William Davidson Institute, Ann Arbor, MI.

Brown, David, Marianne Fay, John Felkner, Somik V. Lall, and Hyoung Gun Wang. 2008. "The Death of Distance? Economic Implications of Infrastructure Improvement in Russia." World Bank, Office of the Chief Economist, Europe and Central Asia Region, Washington, DC.

Brueckner, Jan K. 2007. "Government Land-Use Interventions: An Economic Analysis." Paper presented at the World Bank 4th Urban Research Symposium, Washington, DC.

Brülhart, Marius. 2008. "An Account of Global Intra-Industry Trade, 1962–2006." Working Paper 2008-08, University of Nottingham, Nottingham, U.K.

Brunetti, Aymo, and Beatrice Weder. 2003. "A Free Press Is Bad News for Corruption." *Journal of Public Economics* 87 (7–8): 1801–24.

Brushett, Stephen. 2005. "Management and Financing of Road Transport Infrastructure in Africa." Sub-Saharan Africa Transport Policy Working Paper 4, World Bank, Washington, DC.

Bryceson, Deborah Fahy. 1999. "Sub-Saharan Africa Betwixt and Between: Rural Livelihood Practices and Policies." Working Paper 43, African Studies Centre, Leiden, Netherlands.

Buckley, Robert, Alain Bertaud, and V. K. Phatak. 2005. "Property Rights and Interlocking Policy Constraints Urban Land Markets: Reforming Mumbai's Real Estate Raj." Paper presented at the Land Policies and Administration for Accelerated Growth and Poverty Reduction, New Delhi.

Buckley, Robert, and Jerry Kalarickal, eds. 2006. *Thirty Years of World Bank Shelter Lending: What Have We Learned?* Washington, DC: World Bank.

Burchfield, Marcy, Henry G. Overman, Diego Puga, and Matthew Turner. 2006. "Causes of Sprawl: A Portrait from Space." *Quarterly Journal of Economics* 121 (2): 587–633.

Burkey, Mark L. 2006. "Gini Coefficients for the 2000 Census." North Carolina A&T State University, Department of Economics and Transportation-Logistics, Greensboro, NC.

Button, Kenneth. 1999. "Shipping Alliances: Are They at the Core of Solving Instability Problems in Shipping?" Paper presented at the 1999 Meeting of the International Association of Maritime Economists, Halifax, Canada.

Buys, Piet, Susmita Dasgupta, Timothy S. Thomas, and David Wheeler. 2008. "Determinants of a Digital Divide in Sub-Saharan Africa: A Spatial Econometric Analysis of Cell Phone Coverage." Policy Research Working Paper 4516, World Bank, Washington, DC.

Buys, Piet, Uwe Deichmann, and David Wheeler. 2006. "Road Network Upgrading and Overland Trade Expansion in Sub-Saharan Africa." Policy Research Working Paper 4097, World Bank, Washington, DC.

Cabinet Council. 1972. *New Integrated Spatial Development Plan (Japanese)*. Tokyo: Cabinet Council.

Calem, Paul S. 1994. "The Impact of Geographic Deregulation on Small Banks." *Business Review* (November/December): 17–31.

Calem, Paul S., and Gerald A. Carlino. 1991. "Urban Agglomeration Economies in the Presence of Technical Change." *Journal of Urban Economics* 29 (1): 82–95.

Cali, Massimiliano. 2008. "Urbanization, Inequality, and Economic Growth: Evidence from Indian States." Background paper for the WDR 2009.

Calmon, Paulo Carlos Du Pin. 2003. "Evaluation of Subsidies in Brazil: An Overview." World Bank, Washington, DC.

Canning, David, and Esra Bennathan. 2007. "The Rate of Return to Transportation Infrastructure." In *Transport, Infrastructure Investment and Economic Productivity*, ed. OECD/ECMT. Paris: Organisation for Economic Co-operation and Development.

Cárdenas, Mauricio, and Adriana Pontón. 1995. "Growth and Convergence in Colombia: 1950–1990." *Journal of Development Economics* 47 (1): 5–37.

Carlino, Gerald A. 1979. "Increasing Returns to Scale in Metropolitan Manufacturing." *Journal of Regional Science* 19 (3): 369–72.

Carlino, Gerald A., and Satyajit Chatterjee. 2001. "Employment Deconcentration: A New Perspective on America's Postwar Urban Evolution." Working Paper 01-4, Federal Reserve Bank of Philadelphia, Philadelphia.

Carlton, Dennis W. 1983. "The Location and Employment Choices of New Firms: An Econometric Model with Discrete and Continuous Endogenous Variables." *Review of Economics and Statistics* 65 (3): 440–49.

Carrère, Céline. 2007. "Regional Agreement and the Welfare in the South: When Scale Economies in Transport Matters." Working Paper 2007-26, CERDI, Clermont-Ferrand, France.

Carvalho, Alexandre S., Somik V. Lall, and Christopher Timmins. 2006. "Regional Subsidies and Industrial Prospects of Lagging Regions." Policy Research Working Paper 3843, World Bank, Washington, DC.

Caselli, Francesco. 2005. "Accounting for Cross-Country Income Differences." In *Handbook of Economic Growth*, vol. I, ed. Philippe Aghion and Steven N. Durlauf. Amsterdam: North-Holland.

Caselli, Francesco, and James Feyrer. 2007. "The Marginal Product of Capital." *Quarterly Journal of Economics* 122 (2): 535–68.

Cashin, Paul A. 1995. "Economic Growth and Convergence across the Seven Colonies of Australasia: 1861–1991." *Economic Record* 71 (2): 132–44.

Catin, Maurice, and Christophe Van Huffel. 2003. "Inégalités Régionales et Développement Economique: le Cas Français (1850–2000)." *La Revue d'Economie Régionale e Urbaine* Part 5: 1–18.

Chakraborty, Pinaki. 2003. "Unequal Fiscal Capacities across Indian States: How Corrective Is the Fiscal Transfer Mechanism?" Paper presented at the WIDER project conference on Spatial Inequality in Asia at United Nations University Headquarters, Tokyo.

Chakravorty, Sanjoy, and Somik V. Lall. 2005. "Industrial Location and Spatial Inequality: Theory and Evidence from India." *Review of Development Economics* 9 (1): 47–68.

———. 2007. *Made in India: The Economic Geography and Political Economy of Industrialization*. New Delhi and New York: Oxford University Press.

Chandler, Alfred Dupont Jr. 1977. *The Visible Hand: The Managerial Revolution in American Business*. Cambridge, MA: Belknap Press.

Chandler, Mittie Olion. 1992. "Public Housing Desegregation: What Are the Options?" *Housing Policy Debate* 3 (2): 509–34.

Chandler, Tertius. 1987. *Four Thousand Years of Urban Growth: An Historical Census*. Lampeter, U.K.: Edwin Mellen Press.

Chandler, Tertius, and Gerald Fox. 1974. *Three Thousand Years of Urban Growth*. New York and London: Academic Press.

Chandra, Vandana, ed. 2006. *Technology Adaptation and Exports: How Some Developing Countries Got It Right*. Washington, DC: World Bank.

Chang, Ha-Joon. 2005. "Policy Space in Historical Perspective—with Special Reference to Trade and Industrial Policies." Paper presented at the Queen Elizabeth House 50th Anniversary Conference: The Development of Threats and Promises, Oxford, U.K.

Charlot, Sylvie, and Gilles Duranton. 2004. "Communication Externalities in Cities." *Journal of Urban Economics* 56 (3): 581–613.

Chase-Dunn, Christopher, Yukio Kawano, and Benjamin D. Brewer. 2000. "Trade Globalization since 1795: Waves of Integration in the World System." *American Sociological Review* 65 (1): 77–95.

Chen, Yang. 2008. "China: A Case Study of 1D-2D-3D Areas." Background note for the WDR 2009.

———. 2008. "Urban Agglomeration Policy in China." Background note for the WDR 2009.

Chinitz, Benjamin J. 1961. "Contrasts in Agglomeration: New York and Pittsburgh." *American Economic Review* 51 (2): 279–89.

Chinn, Menzie D., and Hiro Ito. 2006. "What Matters for Financial Development? Capital Controls, Institutions, and Interactions." *Journal of Development Economics* 81 (1): 163–92.

Chiquier, Loic, Olivier Hassler, and Michael Lea. 2004. "Mortgage Securities in Emerging Markets." Policy Research Working Paper 3370, World Bank, Washington, DC.

Chomitz, Kenneth M., Piet Buys, and Timothy S. Thomas. 2005. "Quantifying the Rural-Urban Gradient in Latin America and the Caribbean." Policy Research Working Paper 3634, World Bank, Washington, DC.

Chow, Hwee K., Peter N. Kriz, Roberto S. Mariano, and Augustine H. H. Tan. 2005. *Trade, Investment, and Financial Integration in East Asia*. Tanglin, Singapore: Association of Southeasrtern Asian Nations + 3 Secretariat.

Christaller, Walter. 1933. *Central Places in Southern Germany*. Englewood Cliffs, NJ: Prentice Hall.

Christensen, Dan Charly. 2004. "Physiocracy: The Missing Link." In *Modernisation and Tradition European Local and Manorial Societies 1500–1900*, ed. K. Sundberg, T. Germundsson, and K. Hansen. Lancaster, U.K.: Nordic Academic Press.

Ciccone, Antonio. 2002. "Agglomeration Effects in Europe." *European Economic Review* 46(2):213–27.

Ciccone, Antonio, and Robert E. Hall. 1996. "Productivity and the Density of Economic Activity." *American Economic Review* 86(1):54–70.

Ciccone, Antonio, and Giovanni Peri. 2006. "Identifying Human-Capital Externalities: Theory with Applications." *Review of Economic Studies* 73 (2): 381–412.

Clark, Colin. 1957. *The Conditions of Economic Progress*, 3rd ed. London: Macmillan.

Clemens, Michael A., Claudio E. Montenegro, and Lant Pritchett. 2008. "The Place Premium: Wage Differences for Identical Workers across the U.S. Border." Policy Research Working Paper 4671, World Bank, Washington, DC. Background paper for the WDR 2009.

Cockrem, Tom. 2007. "Singapore's Slum Deal." *The Sun-Herald*, April 8.

Coe, Patrick J., and J. C. Herbert Emery. 2004. "The Disintegrating Canadian Labour Market? The Extent of the Market Then and Now." *Canadian Journal of Economics* 37 (4): 879–97.

Cohen, Daniel, and Marcelo Soto. 2007. "Growth and Human Capital: Good Data, Good Results." *Journal of Economic Growth* 12 (1): 51–76.

Cole, William E., and Richard D. Sanders. 1985. "Internal Migration and Urban Employment in the Third World." *American Economic Review* 75 (3): 481–94.

Collier, Paul. 2003. *Breaking the Conflict Trap: Civil War and Development Policy*. Washington, DC, and New York: World Bank and Oxford University Press.

———. 2007. *The Bottom Billion: Why the Poorest Countries Are Failing and What Can Be Done about It*. New York and Oxford, U.K.: Oxford University Press.

Collier, Paul, and Stephen A. O'Connel. 2008. "Opportunities and Choices." In *The Political Economy of Economic Growth in Africa, 1960–2000*, vol. 1, ed. Benno J. Ndulu, Stephen A. O'Connel, Robert H. Bates, Paul Collier, and Charles C. Soludo. Cambridge, U.K.: Cambridge University Press.

Collier, Paul, and Anthony J. Venables. 2007. "Rethinking Trade Preferences: How Africa Can Diversify Its Exports." *World Economy* 30 (8): 1326–45.

Combes, Pierre-Philippe. 2000. "Marshall-Arrow-Romer Externalities and City Growth." Working Paper 99-06, Centre d'Étude et de Recherche en Action Sociale, Paris.

Combes, Pierre-Philippe, and Miren Lafourcade. 2001. "Transport Cost Decline and Regional Inequalities: Evidence from France."

Working Paper 2894, Centre for Economic Policy Research, London.

———. 2005. "Transport Costs: Measures, Determinants, and Regional Policy Implications for France." *Journal of Economic Geography* 5 (3): 319–49.

Commission for Africa (CFA). 2005. *Our Common Interest: Report of the Commission for Africa*. London: CFA.

Connell, J., B. Dasgupta, R. Laishley, and M. Lipton. 1976. *Migration from Rural Areas: The Evidence from Village Studies*. Delhi: Oxford University Press.

Costa, Dora L., and Matthew E. Kahn. 2000. "Power Couples: Changes in the Locational Choice of the College Educated, 1940–1990." *Quarterly Journal of Economics* 115 (4): 1287–315.

Coulibaly, Souleymane. 2006. "Regional Integration and the Persistent Uneven Spread of Economic Activities in Developing Areas." *Economie Internationale* 106 (2): 5–23.

———. 2007. "Evaluating the Trade Impact of Developing RTAs: A Semi-Parametric Approach." Policy Research Working Paper 4220, World Bank, Washington, DC.

———. 2008. "On the Complementarity of Regional and Global Trade." Background paper for the WDR 2009.

Coulibaly, Souleymane, and Lionel Fontagné. 2006. "South-South Trade: Geography Matters." *Journal of African Economies* 15 (2): 313–41.

Crafts, Nicholas. 2005. "Regional GDP in Britain, 1871–1911: Some Estimates." *Scottish Journal of Political Economy* 52 (1): 54–64.

———. 2008. "Spatial Disparities in 19th-Century British Industrialization." Background note for the WDR 2009.

Crafts, Nicholas, Terence C. Mills, and Abay Mulatu. 2007. "Total Factor Productivity Growth on Britain's Railways, 1852–1912: A Reappraisal of the Evidence." *Exploration in Economic History* 44 (4): 608–34.

Crafts, Nicholas, and Gianni Toniolo. 1996. *Economic Growth in Europe since 1945*. Cambridge, U.K., and New York: Cambridge University Press.

Crafts, Nicholas F. R. 1989. "British Industrialization in an International Context." *Journal of Interdisciplinary History* 19 (3): 415–28.

Criscuolo, Chiara, Jonathan E. Haskel, and Mattew J. Slaughter. 2004. "Why Are Some Firms More Innovative? Knowledge Inputs, Knowledge Stocks, and the Role of Global Engagement." Tuck School of Business, Hanover, NH.

CSAO-ECOWAS. 2005. *Atlas des Transports et des Telecommunications dans la West African States*. Paris and Abuja: Club Du Sahel et de L'Afrique de L'Ouest and Economic Community of West African States.

Cullinane, Sharon. 2002. "The Relationship between Car Ownership and Public Transport Provision: A Case Study of Hong Kong." *Transport Policy* 9 (1): 29–39.

Cutler, David, Angus Deaton, and Adriana Lleras-Muney. 2006. "The Determinants of Mortality." *Journal of Economic Perspectives* 20 (3): 97–120.

Czubala, Witold, Ben Shepherd, and John S. Wilson. 2007. "Help or Hindrance? The Impact of Harmonized Standards on African Exports." Policy Research Working Paper 4400, World Bank, Washington, DC.

Da Mata, Daniel, Uwe Deichmann, J. Vernon Henderson, Somik V. Lall, and Howard G Wang. 2007. "Determinants of City Growth in Brazil." *Journal of Urban Economics* 62 (2): 252–72.

Dall'Erba, Sandy. 2003. "The Trade-off Efficiency-Equity as an Explanation of the Mitigated Success of the European Regional Development Policies." Working Paper 2 (3), EUC, Urbana, IL.

Davezies, Laurent. 2001. *Policies for Sound Development*. Paris: Organisation for Economic Co-operation and Development.

Davis, Donald R., and David E. Weinstein. 1999. "Economic Geography and Regional Production Structure: An Empirical Investigation." *European Economic Review* 43 (2): 379–407.

Davis, Steven J., and John C. Haltiwanger. 1992. "Gross Job Creation, Gross Job Destruction, and Employment Reallocation." *Quarterly Journal of Economics* 107 (3): 819–63.

de Blij, Harm. 2005. *Why Geography Matters: Three Challenges Facing America: Climate Change, the Rise of China, and Global Terrorism*. New York: Oxford University Press.

De Brauw, Alan, and John Giles. 2008. "Migrant Labor Markets and the Welfare of Rural Households in the Developing World: Evidence from China." Policy Research Working Paper 4585, World Bank, Washington, DC.

de la Fuente, Angel. 2000. "Convergence across Countries and Regions: Theory and Empirics." Working Paper 2465, Centre for Economic Policy Research, London.

———. 2004. "Second-Best Redistribution through Public Investment: A Characterization, an Empirical Test and an Application to the Case of Spain." *Regional Science and Urban Economics* 34 (5): 489–503.

de la Fuente, Angel, Xavier Vives, Juan J. Dolado, and Riccardo Faini. 1995. "Infrastructure and Education as Instruments of Regional Policy: Evidence from Spain." *Economic Policy* 10 (20): 11–51.

De Long, J. Bradford. 1988. "Productivity Growth, Convergence, and Welfare: Comment." *American Economic Review* 78 (5): 1138–54.

De Long, J. Bradford, and Andrei Shleifer. 1993. "Princes and Merchants: European City Growth before the Industrial Revolution." *Journal of Law and Economics* 36 (2): 671–702.

de Soto, Hernando. 2000. *The Mystery of Capital: Why Capitalism Triumphs in the West and Fails Everywhere Else*. London: Bantan Press.

Decressin, Jörg, and Antonio Fatás. 1994. "Regional Labour Market Dynamics in Europe." Working Paper DP1085, Centre for Economic Policy Research, London.

Deichmann, Uwe, Marianne Fay, Jun Koo, and Somik V. Lall. 2004. "Economic Structure, Productivity, and Infrastructure Quality in Southern Mexico." *Annals of Regional Science* 38 (3): 361–85.

Deichmann, Uwe, Kai Kaiser, Somik V. Lall, and Zmarak Shalizi. 2005. "Agglomeration, Transport, and Regional Development in Indonesia." Policy Research Working Paper 3477, World Bank, Washington, DC.

Deichmann, Uwe, Somik V. Lall, Stephen J. Redding, and Anthony J. Venables. 2008. "Industrial Location in Developing Countries." *World Bank Research Observer* 23(2): 219–46.

Deininger, Klaus W., and S. Jin. 2003. "Land Sales and Rental Markets in Transition. Evidence from Rural Vietnam." Policy Research Working Paper 3013, World Bank, Washington, DC.

Dekle, Robert, and Jonathan Eaton. 1999. "Agglomeration and Land Rents: Evidence from the Prefectures." *Journal of Urban Economics* 46 (2): 200–14.

Demurger, Sylvie, Jeffrey D. Sachs, Wing Thye Woo, Shuming Bao, Gene Chang, and Andrew Mellinger. 2002. "Geography, Economic Policy and Regional Development in China." *Asian Economic Papers* 1 (1): 146–97.

Deshingkar, Priya, and Sven Grimm. 2004. *Voluntary Internal Migration: An Update*. London: Overseas Development Institute.

Desmet, Klaus, and Marcel Fafchamps. 2003. "What Are Falling Transport Costs Doing to Spatial Concentration across U.S. Counties?" Working Paper 3853, Centre for Economic Policy Research, London.

———. 2006. "Employment Concentration across U.S. Counties." *Regional Science and Urban Economics* 36 (4): 482–509.

Deutsch, Robert. 2006. "Beneficiary Assessment of Land Titles Recipients under Land Management and Administrative Project (LMAP)."

Devereux, Michael P., Rachel Griffith, and Helen Simpson. 2004. "The Geographic Distribution of Production Activity in the U.K." *Regional Science and Urban Economics* 34 (5): 533–64.

Dillinger, William. 2007. "Poverty and Regional Development in Eastern Europe and Central Asia." Working Paper 118, World Bank, Washington, DC.

Disdier, Anne-Celia, and Keith Head. 2008. "The Puzzling Persistence of the Distance Effect on Bilateral Trade." *Review of Economics and Statistics* 90 (1): 37–48.

Dixie, G. 2002. *Review of Current and Future Airfreight Situation from Bangladesh*. Dhaka: Accord Associates for the Hortex Foundation.

Dixit, Avinash K., and Joseph E. Stiglitz. 1977. "Monopolistic Competition and Optimum Product Diversity." *American Economic Review* 67 (3): 297–308.

Djankov, Simeon, Caroline L. Freund, and Cong S. Pham. 2006. "Trading on Time." Policy Research Working Paper 3909, World Bank, Washington, DC.

Dobkins, Linda Harris, and Yannis M. Ioannides. 2001. "Spatial Interactions among U.S. Cities, 1900–1990." *Regional Science and Urban Economics* 31 (6): 701–31.

Docquier, Frédéric. 2006. "Brain Drain and Inequality across Nations." Paper presented at the EUDN-AFD Conference on Migration and Development, Paris.

Docquier, Frédéric, Michel Beine, and Hillel Rapoport. 2006. "Brain Drain and Human Capital Formation in Developing Countries: Winner and Losers." Working Paper 2006-23, Université Catholique de Louvain, Département des Sciences Economiques, Louvain-la-Neuve, Belgium.

Dongguan Government. 2005. *Guangdong Statistical Yearbook 2005*. Beijing, China: China Statistics Press.

Donoso Clark, M., and M. Leninhan. 2008. "A Space-Based Development Framework: A Bottom-Up Approach to Economic Integration." World Bank, Environmentally and Socially Sustainable

Development Unit, Europe and Central Asia Regional Office, Washington, DC.

Donsky, Martin. 1990. "Putting a Spin on the Yarn Business: Macfield Tries to Get a Leg Up on Its Competition." *Business North Carolina*, September 1.

Dorosh, Paul A., Steven Haggblade, and Simon Dradri. 2007. "Cotton in Zambia: Alternative Instruments for Ensuring Food Security and Price Stability in Zambia." Collaborative Working Paper ZM-FSRP-WP-29, International Development, East Lansing, MI.

Douthat, Ross, Marshall Poe, and Abigail Cutler. 2006. "The Poor get Richer." *Atlantic Monthly*.

Drabenstott, Mark. 2005. *A Review of the Federal Role in Regional Economic Development*. Kansas City, MO: Federal Reserve Bank of Kansas City.

Duarte, Angelo José Mont Alverne, Pedro Cavalcanti Gomes Ferreira, and Marcio Antonio Salvato Jr. 2004. "Regional or Educational Disparities? A Counterfactual Exercise." Working Paper 532, Fundação Getulio Vargas Department of Economics, Sâo Paulo.

Dumais, Guy, Glenn Ellison, and Edward L. Glaeser. 2002. "Geographic Concentration as a Dynamic Process." *Review of Economics and Statistics* 84 (2): 193–204.

Dumke, Rolf H. 1994. "Urban Inequality in Wilhemine Germany." Institut für Volkswirtscaftslehre, Universitat der Bundeswehr Munchen, Munich, Germany.

Dunlap, David W. 1992. "Some Land-Use History Highlights." *New York Times*, April 12.

Dunlevy, James A., and Don Bellante. 1983. "Net Migration, Endogenous Incomes and the Speed of Adjustment to the North-South Differential." *Review of Economics and Statistics* 65 (1): 66–75.

Dunne, Timothy, Mark J. Roberts, and Larry Samuelson. 1989a. "Plant Turnover and Gross Employment Flows in the U.S. Manufacturing Sector." *Journal of Labor Economics* 7 (1): 48–71.

———. 1989b. "The Growth and Failure of U.S. Manufacturing Plants." *Quarterly Journal of Economics* 104 (4): 671–98.

Duranton, Gilles, and Henry G. Overman. 2002. "Testing for Localization Using Micro-Geographic Data." Working Paper 540, Centre for Economic Performance, London.

———. 2007. "Testing for Localization Using Micro-Geographic Data." *Review of Economic Studies* 72(4):1077–106.

Duranton, Gilles, and Diego Puga. 2000. "Diversity and Specialization in Cities: Why, Where, and When Does It Matter?" *Urban Studies* 37 (3): 533–55.

———. 2001. "Nursery Cities: Urban Diversity, Process Innovation, and the Life Cycle of Products." *American Economic Review* 91 (5): 1454–77.

———. 2004. "Micro-Foundations of Urban Agglomeration Economies." In *Handbook of Urban and Regional Economies*, vol. 4, ed. J. Vernon Henderson and Jacque Thisse. Amsterdam: North-Holland.

———. 2005. "From Sectoral to Functional Urban Specialization." *Journal of Urban Economics* 57 (2): 343–70.

Easterly, William, and Ross Levine. 2001. "What Have We Learned from a Decade of Empirical Research on Growth? It's Not Factor Accumulation: Stylized Facts and Growth Models." *World Bank Economic Review* 15 (2): 177–219.

Easterly, William, and Yaw Nyarko. 2008. "Is the Brain Drain Good for Africa?" Working Paper 19, Brookings Global Economy and Development, Washington, DC.

Eaton, Jonathan, and Zvi Eckstein. 1997. "Cities and Growth: Theory and Evidence from France and Japan." *Regional Science and Urban Economics* 27 (4–5): 443–74.

The Economist. 2007a. "A Flourishing Slum." *The Economist*, December 9.

———. 2007b. "Chile and Peru. Neighbours, But Not Yet Friends." *The Economist*, June 28.

The Economist Economic Intelligence Unit. 2007. *China/India Technology: Leapfrogging or Piggybacking?* London: *The Economist*.

Eeckhout, Jan. 2004. "Gibrat's Law for (All) Cities." *American Economic Review* 94 (5): 1429–51.

Ellison, Glenn, and Edward L. Glaeser. 1997. "Geographic Concentration in U.S. Manufacturing Industries: A Dartboard Approach." *Journal of Political Economy* 105 (5): 889–927.

Engel, Eduardo, Alexander Galetovic, and Claudio Raddatz. 1998. "Taxes and Income Distribution in Chile: Some Unpleasant Redistributive Arithmetic." Documentos de Trabajo 41, Centro de Economía Aplicada, Universidad de Chile, Santiago, Chile.

Engels, Friedrich. 1987. *The Condition of the Working Class in England*. New York: Penguin Books (original published in German in 1945).

Escobal, Javier, and Maximo Torero. 2000. "Does Geography Explain Differences in Economic Growth in Peru?" Research Network Working Paper R-404, Inter-American Development Bank, Washington, DC.

Estache, Antonio, and Marianne Fay. 2007. "Current Debates on Infrastructure Policy." Policy Research Working Paper 4410, World Bank, Washington, DC.

Estache, Antonio, Marianela González, and Lourdes Trujillo. 2002. "Efficiency Gains from Port Reform and the Potential for Yardstick Competition: Lessons from Mexico." *World Development* 30 (4): 545–60.

Ethier, Wilfred J. 1982. "National and International Returns to Scale in the Modern Theory of International Trade." *American Economic Review* 72(3):389–405.

Euractiv. 2008. *Commission Defends Proposal on Pension 'Portability.'* Brussels: Euractiv.

European Commission. 2001. *Unity, Solidarity, Diversity for Europe, its People and its Territory: Second Report on Economic and Social Cohesion*. Brussels: European Commission.

———. 2002. *European Union Public Finance*. Luxembourg: European Commission, Office for Official Publications of the European Communities.

———. 2007. *Growing Regions, Growing Europe*. Brussels: European Communities.

Evans, Carolyn L., and James E. Harrigan. 2005. "Distance, Time, and Specialization: Lean Retailing in General Equilibrium." *American Economic Review* 95 (1): 292–313.

Evans, Peter. 2002. *Livable Cities? Urban Struggles for Livelihood and Sustainability.* Berkeley, CA: University of California Press.

Evenett, Simon J. 2005. "Competitive Liberalization: A Tournament Theory-Based Interpretation." Paper presented at the Sequencing of Regional Economic Integration: Issues in the Breadth and Depth of Economic Integration in the Americas, Notre Dame, IN.

Ezcurra, Roberto, and Pedro Pascual. 2007. "Spatial Disparities in Productivity in Central and Eastern Europe." *Eastern European Economics* 45 (3): 5–32.

Fafchamps, Marcel, and Klaus Desmet. 2000. "The Changing Spatial Distribution of Economic Activity across U.S. Counties." Economic Working Paper 43, Oxford, U.K.

Faini, Riccardo. 1983. "Cumulative Process of Deindustrialization in an Open Region: the Case of Southern Italy." *Journal of Development Economics* 12 (3): 277–301.

———. 1996. "Increasing Returns, Migration, and Convergence." *Journal of Development Economics* 49 (1): 121–36.

Faini, Riccardo, Curzio Giannini, and Giampaolo Galli. 1993. "Finance and Development: The Case of Southern Italy." In *Finance and Development: Issues and Experience*, ed. Alberto Giovannini. Cambridge, U.K.: Cambridge University Press.

Fan, Shenggen, Xiaobo Zhang, and Neetha Rao. 2004. "Public Expenditure, Growth, and Poverty Reduction in Rural Uganda." IFPRI Working Paper 4, International Food Policy Research Institute, Washington, DC.

Farvacque-Vitkovic, Catherine, Alicia Casalis, Christian Eghoff, and Mahine Diop. 2007. "Development of the Cities of Mali: Challenges and Priorities." Africa Region Working Paper 104, World Bank, Washington, DC.

Fay, Marianne, John Felkner, and Somik V. Lall. 2008. "Market Access and Firm Productivity in the Russian Federation." World Bank, Washington, DC. Processed.

Fay, Marianne, and Charlotte Opal. 2000. "Urbanization without Growth: A Not-So-Uncommon Phenomenon." Policy Research Working Paper 2412, World Bank, Washington, DC.

Fearon, James D., and David D. Laitin. 2003. "Additional Tables for Ethnicity, Insurgency, and Civil War." Stanford University, Palo Alto, CA.

Feder, Gershon, and Peter Lanjouw. 2001. "Rural Non-farm Activities and Rural Development: From Experience towards Strategy." Rural Development Strategy Background Paper 4, World Bank, Washington, DC.

Feenstra, Robert C., and Gordon H. Hanson. 1997. "Foreign Direct Investment and Relative Wages: Evidence from Mexico's Maquiladoras." *Journal of International Economics* 42 (3–4): 371–93.

Feldman, Maryann P. 1994. *The Geography of Innovation.* Boston, MA: Kluwer.

Feldman, Maryann P., and David B. Audretsch. 1999. "Innovation in Cities: Science-Based Diversity, Specialization, and Localized Competition." *European Economic Review* 43 (2): 409–29.

Ferreira, Afonso. 2000. "Convergence in Brazil: Recent Trends and Long-Run Prospects." *Journal of Applied Economics* 3 (4): 479–89.

Fingleton, Bernard. 2003. "Increasing Returns: Evidence from Local Wages in Great Britain." *Oxford Economic Papers* 55 (4): 716–39.

Fink, Carsten, and Aaditya Mattoo. 2004. "Regional Agreements and Trade in Services: Policy Issues." *Journal of Economic Integration* 19 (4): 742–79.

Fink, Carsten, Aaditya Mattoo, and Ileana Cristina Neagu. 2005. "Assessing the Impact of Communication Costs on International Trade." *Journal of International Economics* 67 (2): 428–45.

Fischer, Carolyn, Winston Harrington, and Ian W. H. Parry. 2007. "Should Automobile Fuel Economy Standards Be Tightened?" *Energy Journal* 28 (4): 1–30.

Fogel, Robert W. 1979. "Notes on the Social Savings Controversy." *Journal of Economic History* 39 (1): 1–54.

Fontagné, Lionel, Thierry Mayer, and Soledad Zignago. 2005. "Trade in the Triad: How Easy Is the Access to Large Markets?" *Canadian Journal of Economics* 38 (4): 1401–30.

Foroutan, Faezeh, and Lant Pritchett. 1993. "Intra-Sub-Saharan African Trade: Is It Too Little?" *Journal of African Economies* 2 (1): 74–105.

Frankel, Jeffrey A., Ernesto Stein, and Shang-Jin Wei. 1996. "Regional Trade Arrangements: Natural or Supernatural." *American Economic Review* 86 (2): 52–6.

Freund, Caroline L., and Diana Weinhold. 2004. "The Effect of the Internet on International Trade." *Journal of International Economics* 62 (1): 171–89.

Fuentes, Ricardo, and Andrés Montes. 2004. "Mexico and the Millennium Development Goals in a Subnational Level." *Journal of Human Development* 5 (1): 97–120.

Fujita, Masahisa, ed. 2007. *Regional Integration in East Asia: From the Viewpoint of Spatial Economics.* New York: Palgrave Macmillan.

Fujita, Masahisa, and Ryoichi Ishii. 1999. "Global Location Behavior and Organizational Dynamics of Japanese Electronics Firms and Their Impact on Regional Economies." In *The Dynamic Firm: The Role of Technology, Strategy, Organization, and Regions*, ed. Alfred D. Chandler Jr., Peter Hagstrom, and Orjan Solvell. Oxford, U.K.: Oxford University Press.

Fujita, Masahisa, and Takatoshi Tabuchi. 1997. "Regional Growth in Post War Japan." *Regional Science and Urban Economics* 27 (6): 643–70.

Fujita, Masahisa, Paul Krugman, and Anthony J. Venables. 2001. *The Spatial Economy. Cities, Regions, and International Trade.* Cambridge, MA: MIT Press.

Fuss, Melvyn A., and Vinod K. Gupta. 1981. "A Cost Function Approach to the Estimation of Minimum Efficient Scale, Returns to Scale, and Suboptimal Capacity: With an Application to Canadian Manufacturing." *European Economic Review* 15 (2): 123–35.

Gabaix, Xavier, and Yannis M. Ioannides. 2004. "Evolution of City Size Distributions." In *Handbook of Urban and Regional Economics*, vol. 4, ed. J. Vernon Henderson and Jacque-Francois Thisse. Amsterdam: Elsevier.

Gakenheimer, Ralph. 1999. "Urban Mobility in the Developing World." *Transportation Research Part A: Policy and Practice* 33 (7): 671–89.

Gallaway, Lowell E., and Richard K. Vedder. 1971. "Mobility of Native Americans." *Journal of Economic History* 31 (3): 613–49.

Gallup, John L., Jeffrey D. Sachs, and Andrew D. Mellinger. 1999. "Geography and Economic Development." *International Regional Science Review* 22 (2): 179–232.

Garau, Pietro. 2008. *Notes for the State of the World's Cities Report 2008: Policy Analysis and Recommendations.* Nairobi: UN-HABITAT.

García-Verdú, Rodrigo. 2005. "Income, Mortality, and Literacy Distribution Dynamics across States in Mexico: 1940–2000." *Cuadernos de Economía* 42 (125): 165–92.

Garrett, James. 2005. *Mobility, Migration, and Rural-Urban Changes, Brief 2.* Washington, DC: International Food Policy Research Institute.

Garrett, Power. 2002. "Slums of Baltimore." In *From Mobtown to Charm City: New Perspectives on Baltimore's Past,* ed. Jessica L. Elfenbein, John R. Breihan, and Thomas L. Hollowak. Baltimore, MD: Maryland Historical Society.

Gaspar, Jess, and Edward L. Glaeser. 1998. "Information Technology and the Future of Cities." *Journal of Urban Economics* 43(1):136–56.

Gastner, Michael T. and Mark E. J. Newman. 2004. "Diffusion-based method for producing density-equalizing maps." *Proceedings of the National Academy of Sciences,* 101, 20:7499–7504.

Gauthier, Jean-Paul. 2007. *Special Economic Zones: Performance, Lessons Learned, and Implications for Zone Development.* Washington, DC: World Bank, Foreign Investment Advisory Service.

Gibbon, Peter, and Stefano Ponte. 2005. *Trading Down: Africa, Value Chains, and the Global Economy.* Philadelphia: Temple University Press.

Gibson, John, and Scott Rozelle. 2003. "Poverty and Access to Roads in Papua New Guinea." *Economic Development and Cultural Change* 52 (1): 159–85.

Gill, Indermit, and Homi Kharas. 2007. *An East Asia Renaissance: Ideas for Economic Growth.* Washington, DC: World Bank.

Gilman, Sidney. 1984. *The Competitive Dynamics of Container Shipping.* Liverpool, U.K.: Gower Publishing.

Glaeser, Edward L., and Matthew E. Kahn. 2001. "Decentralized Employment and the Transformation of the American City." Working Paper 1912, Harvard Institute of Economic Research, Cambridge, MA.

Glaeser, Edward L., Hedi D. Kallal, José A. Scheinkman, and Andrei Shleifer. 1992. "Growth in Cities." *Journal of Political Economy* 100 (6): 1126–52.

Glaeser, Edward L., Jed Kolko, and Albert Saiz. 2001. "Consumer City." *Journal of Economic Geography* 1 (1): 27–50.

Glaeser, Edward L., and David C. Maré. 2001. "Cities and Skills." *Journal of Labor Economics* 19 (2): 316–42.

Glaeser, Edward L., José A. Scheinkman, and Andrei Schleifer. 1995. "Economic Growth in a Cross-Section of Cities." *Journal of Monetary Economics* 36 (1): 117–43.

Golob, Thomas F., and David Brownstone. 2005. "The Impact of Residential Density on Vehicle Usage and Energy Consumption." Energy Institute Policy and Economics Working Paper EPE-011, University of California, Berkeley, CA.

Good, David F. 1986. "Uneven Development in the Nineteenth Century: A Comparison of the Habsburg Empire and the United States." *Journal of Economic History* 46 (1): 137–51.

Goodlad, R. 1996. "The Housing Challenge in South Africa." *Urban Studies* 33 (9): 1629–45.

Gordon, Robert J. 1990. *The Measurement of Durable Goods Prices.* Chicago: University of Chicago Press.

Gorzelak, Grzegorz. 2007. "Cohesion and Convergence: Synonyms or Two Different Notions?" Paper presented at the Policy Workshop "Spatial Disparities and Development Policy," Berlin.

Gottman, Jean. 1977. "Megalopolis and Antipolis: The Telephone and the Structure of the City." In Ithiel de Sola Pool, (eds.), *The Social Impact of the Telephone.* Cambridge, MA: Massachusetts Institute of Technology.

Government of India Planning Commission. 2002a. *10th Five Year Plan (2002–2007).* New Delhi: Government of India, Planning Commission.

———. 2002b. *National Human Development Report 2001.* New Delhi: Government of India, Planning Commission.

———. 2006. *Towards Faster and More Inclusive Growth: An approach to the Eleventh Five Year Plan 2007–2012.* New Delhi: Government of India.

Government of Malaysia. 2001. *Eight Malaysia Plan: 2001–2005.* Kuala Lumpur: Malaysia Economic Planning Unit.

Government of Nigeria, Federal Ministry of Science and Technology. 2003. *Multi-Disciplinary Committee Report of the Techno-Economic Survey on Wood and Wood Products Sector, 2003, 4th Update.* Lagos: Government of Nigeria, Federal Ministry of Science and Technology.

Government of Sri Lanka. 2008. *Poverty Indicators Household Income and Expenditure Survey, 2006–07.* Colombo: Sri Lanka Department of Census and Statistics, Ministry of Planning and Finance.

Goyal, Sanjeev, and Klaas Staal. 2004. "The Political Economy of Regionalism." *European Economic Review* 48 (3): 563–93.

Green, Alan G. 1969. "Regional Inequality, Structural Change, and Economic Growth in Canada, 1890–1956." *Economic Development and Cultural Change* 17 (4): 567–83.

Gregoire, Emmanuel, and Pascal Labazee. 1993. *Grands Commerçants d'Afrique de l'Ouest.* Paris: Karthala-Orstom.

Greytak, David, and Paul Blackley. 1985. "Labor Productivity and Local Industry Size: Further Issues in Assessing Agglomeration Economies." *Southern Economic Journal* 51 (4): 1121–29.

Gribbin, August. 2000. "Overpopulated Megacities Face Frightening Future: Overpopulation in Developing Countries Impact on the West." *Insight on the News,* August 21.

Griliches, Zvi, and Vidar Ringstad. 1971. *Economies of Scale and the Form of the Production Function: An Econometric Study of Norwegian Manufacturing Establishment Data.* Amsterdam: North-Holland.

Grossman, Gene M., and Elhanan Helpman. 1991. "Quality Ladders in the Theory of Growth." *Review of Economic Studies* 58(1):43–61.

———. 1995. "Technology and Trade." In Gene M. Grossman and Kenneth Rogoff, (eds.), *Handbook of International Economics, Volume III.* Amsterdam, Netherlands: North-Holland.

Groupe Recherche—Actions pour le Développement. 2001. "Potentialités et Conflits dans les Zones Péri-urbaines: Le Cas de Bamako au Mali." Rural-Urban Interactions and Livelihood Strategies Working Paper 5, IIED, London.

Guasch, Juan Luis. 2008. *Exporting by Mail: An Innovative Trade Facilitation Tool.* Washington, DC: World Bank, IFC Smart Lessons.

Guerra, Carlos A., Priscilla W. Gikandi, Andrew J. Tatem, Abdisalan M. Noor, Dave L. Smith, Simon I. Hay, and Robert W. Snow. 2008. "The Limits and Intensity of Plasmodium Falciparum Transmission: Implications for Malaria Control and Elimination Worldwide." *Plos Medicine* 5 (2): e38–e38.

Gupta, Vinod K. 1983. "Labor Productivity, Establishment Size, and Scale Economies." *Southern Economic Journal* 49(3):853–9.

Gwatkin, Davidson R., Shea Rutstein, Kiersten Johnson, Eldaw Suliman, Adam Wagstaff, and Agbessi Amouzou. 2007. *Socio-Economic Differences in Health, Nutrition, and Population within Developing Countries: An Overview.* Washington, DC: World Bank.

Hall, Carolyn. 1984. "Regional Inequalities in Well-Being in Costa Rica." *Geographical Review* 74 (1): 48–62.

Hall, Peter. 2002. *Cities of Tomorrow.* Oxford, U.K.: Blackwell Publishing.

Hall, Robert E. 1988. "The Relation between Price and Marginal Cost in U.S. Industry." *Journal of Political Economy* 96 (5): 921–47.

———. 1990. "Invariance Properties of Solow's Productivity Residual." In *Growth, Productivity, Unemployment: Essays to Celebrate Bob Solow's Birthday*, ed. Peter Diamond. Cambridge, MA: MIT Press.

Hall, Thomas, and Sonja Vidén. 2005. "The Million Homes Programme: A Review of the Great Swedish Planning Model." *Planning Perspectives* 20 (3): 301–28.

Hamaguchi, Nobuaki. Forthcoming. "Regional Integration, Agglomeration, and Income Distribution in East Asia." In *Reshaping Economic Geography in East Asia*, ed. Yukon Huang and Alessandro Magnoli Bocchi. Washington, DC: World Bank, EAP Companion Volume to the WDR 2009.

Hammond, George William, and Jürgen von Hagen. 1994. "Industrial Localization: An Empirical Test for Marshallian Localization Economies." Working Paper 917, Centre for Economic Policy Research, London.

Hancock, Diana, David B. Humphrey, and James A. Wilcox. 1999. "Cost Reductions in Electronic Payments: The Roles of Consolidation, Economies of Scale, and Technical Change." *Journal of Banking and Finance* 23 (2–4): 391–421.

Hansen, Eric R. 1990. "Agglomeration Economics and Industrial Decentralization: The Wage-Productivity Trade-Offs." *Journal of Urban Economics* 28(2):140–59.

Hanson, Gordon H. 1996. "Agglomeration, Dispersion, and the Pioneer Firm." *Journal of Urban Economics* 39 (3): 255–81.

———. 1998a. "North American Economic Integration and Industry Location." *Oxford Review of Economic Policy* 14 (2): 30–44.

———. 1998b. "Regional Adjustment to Trade Liberalization." *Regional Science and Urban Economics* 28 (4): 419–44.

Hardoy, Jorge E., and David Satterthwaite. 1989. *Squatter Citizen: Life in the Urban Third World.* London: Earthscan.

Hargan, Jim. 2007. "Prince Charles Poundbury." *Brittish Heritage.* May, 2007.

Harley, C. Knick. 1980. "Transportation, the World Wheat Trade, and the Kuznets Cycle, 1850–1913." *Explorations in Economic History* 17 (3): 218–50.

Harrigan, James E. 2005. "Airplanes and Comparative Advantage." NBER Working Paper 11688, National Bureau of Economic Research, Cambridge, MA.

Harrigan, James E., and Anthony J. Venables. 2006. "Timeliness and Agglomeration." *Journal of Urban Economics* 59 (2): 300–16.

Harris, John R., and Michael P. Todaro. 1970. "Migration, Unemployment, and Development: A Two-Sector Analysis." *American Economic Review* 60 (1): 126–42.

Hau, Timothy. 1990. "Electronic Road Pricing: Developments in Hong Kong, 1983–1989." *Journal of Transport Economics and Policy* 24 (2): 203–14.

Haussmann, Ricardo, and Dani Rodrik. 2003. "Economic Development as Self-Discovery." *Journal of Development Economics* 72 (2): 603–33.

Haussmann, Ricardo, Dani Rodrik, and Andrés Velasco. 2005. "Growth Diagnostics." Center for International Development, Cambridge, MA.

Hay, Donald Andrew. 1979. "The Location of Industry in a Developing Country: The Case of Brazil." *Oxford Economic Papers* 31 (1): 93–120.

Hay, Simon I., Carlos A. Guerra, Andrew J. Tatem, Abdisalan M. Noor, and Robert W. Snow. 2004. "The Global Distribution and Population at Risk of Malaria: Past, Present, and Future." *Lancet Infectious Diseases* 4 (6): 327–36.

Hay, Simon I., David L. Smith, and Robert W. Snow. 2008. "Measuring Malaria Endemicity from Intense to Interrupted Transmission." *Lancet Infectious Diseases* 8 (6): 369–78.

Hayashi, Takehisa. 2003. *Readings on Local Public Finance.* Tokyo: Toyo Keizai Shinposya.

Hazlewood, Arthur. 1979. "The End of the East African Community: What Are the Lessons for Regional Integration Schemes?" *Journal of Common Market Studies* 18 (1): 40–58.

He, Canfei. Forthcoming. "Industrial Agglomeration and Economic Performance in the Transitional China." In *Reshaping Economic Geography in East Asia*, ed. Yukon Huang and Alessandro Magnoli Bocchi. Washington, DC: World Bank, EAP Companion Volume to the WDR 2009.

Head, Charles Keith, and Thierry Mayer. 2006. "Regional Wage and Employment Responses to Market Potential in the EU." *Regional Science and Urban Economics* 36 (5): 573–94.

Head, Charles Keith, John Reis, and Deborah Swenson. 1995. "Agglomeration Benefits and Location Choice: Evidence from Japanese Manufacturing Investment in the United States." *Journal of International Economics* 38 (3–4): 223–47.

Heideloff, Christel, and Manfred Zachcial. 2006. *Shipping Statistical Yearbook 2006.* Bremen, Germany: Institute of Shipping Economics and Logistics.

Helliwell, John F. 2002. "Measuring the Width of National Borders." *Review of International Economics* 10 (3): 517–24.

Helpman, Elhanan, and Paul Krugman. 1987. *Market Structure and Foreign Trade.* Cambridge, MA: MIT Press.

Henderson, J. Vernon. 1974. "The Sizes and Types of Cities." *American Economic Review* 64 (4): 640–56.

——. 1986. "Efficiency of Resources Usage and City Size." *Journal of Urban Economics* 19 (1): 47–70.

——. 1994. "Where Does an Industry Locate?" *Journal of Urban Economics* 35(1):83–104.

——. 1997a. "Externalities and Industrial Development." *Journal of Urban Economics* 42 (3): 449–70.

——. 1997b. "Medium Size Cities." *Regional Science and Urban Economics* 27 (6): 583–612.

——. 2003a. "Marshall's Scale Economies." *Journal of Urban Economics* 53 (1): 1–28.

——. 2003b. "The Urbanization Process and Economic Growth: The So-What Question." *Journal of Economic Growth* 8 (1): 47–71.

——. 2005a. "Development and Growth." In *Handbook of Economic Growth*, vol. 1, part B, ed. Philippe Aghion and Steven N. Durlauf. Amsterdam: North-Holland.

——. 2005b. "Urbanization and Growth." In *Handbook of Economic Growth*, ed. Philippe Aghion and Steven N. Durlauf. Amsterdam: North-Holland.

——. 2007. *Urbanization in China: Policy Issues and Options.* New York: China Economic Research and Advisory Programme.

Henderson, J. Vernon, Ari Kuncoro, and Damhuri Nasution. 1996. "The Dynamics of Jabotabek Development." *Bulletin of Indonesian Economic Studies* 32 (1): 71–95.

Henderson, J. Vernon, Ari Kuncoro, and Matthew Turner. 1995. "Industrial Development in Cities." *Journal of Political Economy* 103 (5): 1067–90.

Henderson, J. Vernon, Todd Lee, and Yung Joon Lee. 2001. "Scale Externalities in Korea." *Journal of Urban Economics* 49 (3): 479–504.

Henderson, J. Vernon, Zmarak Shalizi, and Anthony J. Venables. 2001. "Geography and Development." *Journal of Economic Geography* 1 (1): 81–105.

Henriksen, Ingrid. 2003. "Freehold Tenure in Late Eighteenth Century Denmark." In *Advances in Agricultural Economic History*, ed. Kyle D. Kaufman. New York: JAI Press.

Henry, Peter Blair. 2007. "Capital Account Liberalization: Theory, Evidence, and Speculation." *Journal of Economic Literature* 45 (4): 887–935.

Hering, Laura, and Sandra Poncet. 2006. "Market Access and Individual Wages: Evidence from China." Working Paper 2006-23, Centre d'Études Prospectives et d'Informations Internationales, Paris.

Herzog, Henry W. Jr., and Alan M. Schlottmann, eds. 1991. *Industry Location and Public Policy.* Knoxville, TN: University of Tennessee.

Hewings, G., E. Feser, and K. Poole. 2008. "Spatial/Territorial Development Policies in the United States." Background paper for the WDR 2009.

Hidalgo, C. A., B. Klinger, A. L. Barabási, and R. Hausmann. 2007. "The Product Space Conditions for the Development of Nations." *Science* 317 (5837): 482–87.

Hill, Fiona, and Clifford Gaddy. 2003. *The Siberia Curse: How Communist Planners Left Russia out in the Cold.* Washington, DC: Brookings Institution Press.

Hill, Hal, Budy Resosudarmo, and Yogi Vidyattama. 2007. "Indonesia's Changing Economic Geography." Working Papers in Economics and Development Studies 2007-13, Bandung, Indonesia.

Hoekman, Bernard. 2006. "Liberalizing Trade in Services: A Survey." Policy Research Working Paper 4030, World Bank, Washington, DC.

Hoekman, Bernard, and Dominique Njinkeu. 2007. "Aid for Trade and Export Competitiveness: New Opportunities for Africa." World Bank, Washington, DC.

Holmes, Thomas J. 1999. "Localization of Industry and Vertical Disintegration." *Review of Economics and Statistics* 81 (2): 314–25.

Holmes, Thomas J., and John J. Stevens. 2002. "Geographic Concentration and Establishment Scale." *Review of Economics and Statistics* 84 (4): 682–91.

Holzmann, Hajo, and Sebastian Vollmer. 2008. "The Distribution of Income across German Counties, 1992–2005." University of Goettingen, Goettingen, Germany.

Hoover, Edgar M., and Raymond Vernon. 1959. *Anatomy of a Metropolis: The Changing Distribution of People and Jobs within the New York Metropolitan Area.* Cambridge, MA: Harvard University Press.

Huang, Yukon, and Xubei Luo. Forthcoming. "Reshaping Economic Geography in China." In *Reshaping Economic Geography in East Asia*, ed. Yukon Huang and Alessandro Magnoli Bocchi. Washington, DC: World Bank.

Huber, Peter W. 1995. "New York, Capital of the Information Age." *New York City Journal* 5(1):12–22.

Hughes, Joseph P., William W. Lang, Loretta J. Mester, and Choon-Geol Moon. 1999. "The Dollars and Sense of Bank Consolidation." *Journal of Banking and Finance* 23 (2–4): 291–324.

Hughes, Joseph P., and Loretta J. Mester. 1998. "Bank Capitalization and Cost: Evidence of Scale Economies in Risk Management and Signaling." *Review of Economics and Statistics* 80 (2): 314–25.

Hulten, Charles R. 2007. "Transportation Infrastructure, Productivity and Externalities." In *ECMT Round Tables No. 132: Transport, Infrastructure Investment and Economic Productivity*, ed. OECD/ECMT. Paris: Organisation for Economic Co-operation and Development.

Hummels, David. 2001. *Time as a Trade Barrier.* West Lafayette, IN: Purdue University Press.

——. 2007. "Transportation Costs and International Trade in the Second Era of Globalization." *Journal of Economic Perspectives* 21 (3): 131–54.

Hummels, David, Volodymyr Lugovskyy, and Alexandre Skiba. 2007. "The Trade Reducing Effect of Market Power in International Shipping." NBER Working Paper 12914, National Bureau of Economic Research, Cambridge, MA.

Hunt, Edward H. 1986. "Industrialization and Regional Inequality: Wages in Britain, 1760–1914." *Journal of Economic History* 46 (4): 935–66.

Hunt, Jennifer. 2000. "Why Do People Still Live in East Germany?" NBER Working Paper 7564, National Bureau of Economic Research, Cambridge, MA.

Hurd, John II. 1975. "Railways and the Expansion of Markets in India, 1861–1921." *Explorations in Economic History* 12 (3): 263–88.

Iliffe, John. 1995. *Africans: The History of a Continent*. Cambridge, U.K.: Cambridge University Press.

Independent Evaluation Group (IEG). 2007. "The Development Potential of Regional Programs: An Evaluation of World Bank Support of Multicountry Operations." Paper presented at the IEG Conference on Unlocking the Potential of Regional Development Programs, Washington, DC.

Ingram, Gregory. 1997. "Patterns of Metropolitan Development: What Have We Learned?" Policy Research Working Paper 1841, World Bank, Washington, DC.

Ingram, Gregory, and John Whitehead. 2008. "The Distribution and Concentration of Population in the U.S., 1900–2000." Working Paper WP08GI1, Lincoln Institute of Land Policy, Cambridge, MA.

Instituto Brasileiro de Geografia e Estatística (IBGE). 2004. *Perfil Dos Municipios Brasileiros*. Rio de Janeiro: IBGE.

Inter-American Development Bank. Forthcoming. *Unclogging the Arteries: A Report on the Impact of Transport Costs on Latin American and Caribbean Trade*. Cambridge, MA: Harvard University Press.

International Air Transport Association. 2007a. *Aviation Economic Benefits: Issues Briefing No. 8*. Montreal, Canada: International Air Transport Association.

———. 2007b. *Economics Briefing: Air Freight Market Outlook*. Montreal, Canada: International Air Transport Association.

International Development Association, and World Bank. 2008. *Regional Integration Assistance Strategy*. Washington, DC: World Bank.

International Monetary Fund. 1998. *World Economic Outlook. Financial Crises: Causes and Indicators*. Washington, DC: International Monetary Fund.

———. 2007. *Directions of Trade*. Washington, DC: International Monetary Fund.

Ivaldi, Marc, and Gerard McCullough. 2007. "Railroad Pricing and Revenue-to-Cost Margins in the Post-Staggers Era." In *Research in Transportation Economics*, ed. Scott Dennis and Wayne Talley. Amsterdam: Elsevier.

Jacobs, Jane. 1970. *The Economy of Cities*. New York: Vintage.

Jacoby, Hanan G. 2000. "Access to Markets and the Benefits of Rural Roads." *Economic Journal* 110 (465): 713–37.

Jaffe, Adam B. 1986. "Technological Opportunity and Spillover of R&D: Evidence from Firms' Patents, Profits, and Market Value." *American Economic Review* 76 (5): 984–1001.

Jaffe, Adam B., Manuel Trajtenberg, and Rebecca Henderson. 1993. "Geographic Localization of Knowledge Spillovers as Evidence by Patent Citations." *Quarterly Journal of Economics* 108 (3): 577–98.

Jayne, Thomas S., B. Zulu, D. Mather, E. Mghenyi, E. Chirwa, and David L. Tschirley. 2005. "Maize Marketing and Trade Policy in a Pro-Poor Agricultural Growth Strategy: Insights from Household Surveys in Eastern and Southern Africa." Paper presented at Toward Improved Maize Marketing and Trade Policies in the Southern Africa Region, Centurion, South Africa.

Jensen, Robert. 2007. "The Digital Provide: Information (Technology), Market Performance, and Welfare in the South Indian Fisheries Sector." *Quarterly Journal of Economics* 122 (3): 879–924.

Jessen, Anneje. 2002. "Regional Public Goods and Small Economies: The Caribbean Regional Negotiating Machinery." In *Regional Public Goods: From Theory to Practice*, ed. Antoni Estevadeordal, Brian Frantz, and Tam R. Nguyen. Washington, DC: Inter-American Development Bank and Asian Development Bank.

Jones, Gareth A., and Kavita Datta. 2000. "Enabling Markets to Work? Housing Policy in the 'New' South Africa." *International Planning Studies* 5 (3): 393–416.

Jourdan, Paul, and NEPAD. 2006. "Regional Strategies. The Case for a Resource-Based Spatial Development Programme." Paper presented at the U.S.–Africa Infrastructure Conference, Washington, DC.

Junius, Karsten. 1997. "Economies of Scale: A Survey of Empirical Literature." Working Paper 813, Kiel Institute of World Economics, Kiel, Germany.

Justman, Moshe. 1994. "The Effect of Local Demand on Industry Location." *Review of Economics and Statistics* 76 (4): 742–53.

Kaldor, Nicholas. 1972. "The Irrelevance of Equilibrium Economics." *Economic Journal* 82 (328): 1237–55.

Kamada, Kimiyoshi, Nobuhiro Okuno, and Ritsuko Futagami. 1998. "Decisions on Regional Allocation of Public Investment: the Case of Japan." *Applied Economic Letters* 5 (8): 503–6.

Kanbur, Ravi, and Anthony J. Venables. 2005. *Rising Spatial Disparities and Development: Why Do they Matter?* Oxford, U.K.: Oxford University Press, UNU-WIDER Studies in Development Economics.

Kanbur, Ravi, and Xiaobo Zhang. 2005. "Fifty Years of Regional Inequality in China: A Journey through Central Planning, Reform, and Openness." *Review of Development Economics* 9 (1): 87–106.

Kasekende, Louis A., and Nehemiah Ng'eno. 1999. "Regional Integration and Economic Liberalization in Eastern and Southern Africa." In *Regional Integration and Trade Liberalization in Sub-Saharan Africa, Volume 3: Regional Case-Studies*, ed. Ademola Oyejide, Ibrahim Elbadawi, and Stephen Yeo. London: Palgrave Macmillan Press.

Kawashima, Tatsuhiko. 1975. "Urban Agglomeration Economies in Manufacturing Industries." *Papers in Regional Science* 34 (1): 157–72.

Kearns, Kevin C. 2006. *Dublin's Lost Heroines: Mammies and Grannies in a Vanished Dublin*. Park West, Dublin: Gill and Macmillan.

Kee, Hiau Looi, Alessandro Nicita, and Marcelo Olarreaga. 2006. "Estimating Trade Restiveness Indices." Policy Research Working Paper 3840, World Bank, Washington, DC.

Keefer, Philip, and Stuti Khemani. 2005. "Democracy, Public Expenditures, and the Poor: Understanding Political Incentives for Providing Public Services." *World Bank Research Observer Advance Access* 20 (1): 1–27.

Kenworthy, Jeff. 2005. "Transport Energy Use and Greenhouse Gases in Urban Passenger Transport Systems: A Study of 84

Global Cities." Institute for Sustainability and Technology Policy, Murdoch University, Murdoch, Australia.

Kenya Ministry of Planning and National Development and UNDP. 2005. *Millennium Development Goals Country Report 2005: Kenya*. Nairobi: United Nations and Kenya Ministry of Planning and National Development.

Khanna, Tarun. 2008. *Billions of Entrepreneurs: How China and India Are Reshaping Their Futures—and Yours*. Cambridge, MA: Harvard Business School Press.

Kilkenny, Maureen. 1998. "Economies of Scale. Lecture for Economics 376: Rural, Urban and Regional Economics." Iowa State University. Ames, IA.

Kilroy, Austin. 2008. "Intra-Urban Spatial Inequalities: Cities as 'Urban Regions.'" Background paper for the WDR 2009.

Kim, Sukkoo. 1995. "Expansion of Markets and the Geographic Distribution of Economic Activities: The Trends in U.S. Regional Manufacturing Structure, 1860–1987." *Quarterly Journal of Economics* 110 (4): 881–908.

———. 1999. "Regions, Resources, and Economics Geography: Sources of U.S. Regional Comparative Advantage, 1880–1987." *Regional Science and Urban Economics* 29 (1): 1–32.

Kim, Sukkoo, and Robert A. Margo. 2004. "Historical Perspectives on U.S. Economic Geography." In *Handbook of Regional and Urban Economics, Volume 4: Cities and Geography*, ed. J. Vernon Henderson and Jacque-Francois Thisse. Amsterdam: North-Holland.

Kim, Won Bae. 1998. "Korea's Policy of Rural-Urban Integrated Cities." Paper presented at the International Workshop on Rural and Urban Linkages, Curitiba, Brazil.

Kloeppinger-Todd, Renate. 2007. "ICT and Rural Access to Finance." Paper presented at the *info*Dev/ARD Workshop on Using ICT to Support Rural Livelihoods, Washington, DC.

Knoke, William. 1996. *Bold New World: The Essential Road Map to the Twenty-First Century*. New York: Kodansha International.

Koh, Tommy, and Li Lin Chang, eds. 2005. *The Little Red Dot: Reflections by Singapore's Diplomats*. Singapore: World Scientific Publishing.

Kolko, Jed. 1998. "New England at Your Service: The New Geography of Service Industries." *Regional Review* 1998 (Q4): 6–11.

———. 1999. "Can I Get Some Service Here? Information Technology, Service Industries, and the Future of Cities." Ph.D. thesis, Harvard University, Cambridge, MA.

———. 2000. "The Death of Cities? The Death of Distance? Evidence from the Geography of Commercial Internet Usage." In *The Internet Upheaval*, ed. Ingo Vogelsang and Benjamin Compaine. Cambridge, MA: MIT.

———. 2007. "Agglomeration and Co-Agglomeration of Services Industries." Munich Personal RePEc Archive (MPRA) Working Paper 3362, Munich, Germany.

Koola, J., and Caglar Özden. 2008. "Making the Move: The Effect of Migration on Welfare in Uganda." World Bank, Washington, DC.

Kose, M. Ayhan, Eswar Prasad, Kenneth Rogoff, and Shang-Jin Wei. 2006. "Financial Globalization: A Reappraisal." Working Paper 06/189, International Monetary Fund, Washington, DC.

Kraske, Jochen, William H. Becker, William Diamond, and Louis Galambos. 1996. *Bankers with a Mission: The Presidents of the World Bank, 1946–91*. Oxford, U.K.: Oxford University Press.

Krishna, Pravin. 1998. "Regionalism and Multilateralism: A Political Economy Approach." *Quarterly Journal of Economics* 113 (1): 227–50.

Kroehnert, Steffen, Franziska Medicus, and Reiner Kinglolz. 2006. *Die Demografische Lage der Nation. Wie Zukunftsfaehig sind Deutschlands Regionen? Daten, Fakten, Analysen*. Berlin: Berlin Institute for Population and Development.

Kroehnert, Steffen, and Sebastian Vollmer. 2008. "Where Have All Young Women Gone?" Background paper for the WDR 2009.

Krueger, Anne O. 2006. "Globalization and International Locational Competition." Paper presented at the Symposium in Honor of Herbert Giersch, Kiel, Germany.

Krugman, Paul R. 1980. "Scale Economies, Product Differentiation, and the Pattern of Trade." *American Economic Review* 70(5):950–9.

———. 1981. "Intraindustry Specialization and the Gains from Trade." *Journal of Political Economy* 89(5):959–73.

———. 1991a. *Geography and Trade*. Cambridge, MA: MIT Press.

———. 1991b. "Increasing Returns and Economic Geography." *Journal of Political Economy* 99 (3): 483–99.

———. 1991c. "Is Bilateralism Bad?" In *International Trade and Trade Policy*, ed. Elhanan Helpman and Assaf Razin. Cambridge, MA: MIT Press.

———. 1993. "First Nature, Second Nature, and Metropolitan Location." *Journal of Regional Science* 33 (2): 129–44.

———. 1995. "Innovation and Agglomeration: Two Parables Suggested by City-Size Distributions." *Japan and the World Economy* 7 (4): 371–90.

———. 2007. "The 'New' Economic Geography: Where Are We?" In *Regional Integration in East Asia*, ed. Masahisa Fujita. New York: Palgrave Macmillan.

Kuncoro, Ari. Forthcoming. "Spatial Agglomeration, Site Productivity and Local Governance: Indonesian Experience from 1980 to 2003." In Yukon Huang and Alessandro Magnoli Bocchi (eds.) *Reshaping Economic Geography in East Asia*. Washington, DC: World Bank, EAP Companion Volume to the WDR 2009.

Kuroda, Haruhiko. 2007. "Toward an Integrated, Poverty-Free and Peaceful East Asia." In *East Asia Visions: Perspectives on Economic Development*, ed. Indermit Gill, Yukon Huang, and Homi Kharas. Washington, DC, and Singapore: World Bank.

Ladman, Jerry R. 1979. "The Economic Interdependence of Contiguous Border Cities: The Twin City Multiplier." *Annals of Regional Science* 13 (1): 23–28.

Laeven, Luc, and Christopher Woodruff. 2007. "The Quality of the Legal System, Firm Ownership, and Firm Size." *Review of Economics and Statistics* 89 (4): 601–14.

Lall, Somik V. 2005. "City Performance and Policy Actions." In *Inputs for a Strategy of Cities in Brazil*, ed. World Bank. Washington, DC: World Bank.

Lall, Somik V., Uwe Deichmann, Mattias K. A. Lundberg, and Nazmul Chaudhury. 2004. "Tenure, Diversity, and Commitment: Community Participation for Urban Service Provision." *Journal of Development Studies* 40 (3): 1–26.

Lall, Somik V., Elizabeth Schroeder, and Emily Schmidt. 2008. "Geographically Prioritizing Infrastructure Improvements to Accelerate Growth in Uganda." World Bank, Washington, DC.

Lall, Somik V., Harris Selod, and Zmarak Shalizi. 2006. "Rural-Urban Migration in Developing Countries: A Survey of Theoretical Predictions and Empirical Findings." Policy Research Working Paper 3915, World Bank, Washington, DC.

Lall, Somik V., Hyoung Gun Wang, and Uwe Deichmann. 2008. "Infrastructure and City Competitiveness in India." Policy Research Working Paper, World Bank, Washington, DC.

Land Enquiry Commission. 1914. *The Land*, vol. II. London: Hodder and Stoughton.

Landes, David S. 1998. *The Wealth and Poverty of Nations: Why Some Are So Rich and Some So Poor*. New York: W. W. Norton.

Lane, C. B. 1860. *Railway Communication in London and the Thames Embankment*. London: James Ridgway.

Lanne, Markku, and Matti Liski. 2003. "Trends and Breaks in Per-Capita Carbon Dioxide Emissions, 1870–2028." Working Paper 0302, Center for Energy and Environmental Policy Research, Cambridge, MA.

Layke, Christian, and Stephen Adam. 2008. "Spatial Allocation of Public Expenditures in Nigeria." Background paper for the WDR 2009.

Leamer, Edward E. 2007. "A Flat World, a Level Playing Field, a Small World After All, or None of the Above? A Review of Thomas L. Friedman's *The World Is Flat*." *Journal of Economic Literature* 45 (1): 83–126.

Leamer, Edward E., and Michael Storper. 2001. "The Economic Geography of the Internet Age." *Journal of International Business Studies* 32 (4): 641–65.

Lebergott, Stanley. 1964. *Manpower in Economic Growth: The American Record since 1800*. New York: McGraw Hill.

Lederman, Daniel, William F. Maloney, and Luis Servén. 2005. *Lessons from NAFTA for Latin America and the Caribbean*. Washington, DC, and Palo Alto, CA: World Bank and Stanford University Press.

Lee, Annabel. 2008. "A History of Korea's Spatial Transformation and Economic Growth." Washington, DC.

Lei, Ding, and Kingsley E. Haynes. 2004. "The Role of Telecommunications Infrastructure in Regional Economic Growth of China." Paper presented at the Telecommunications Policy Research Conference, Washington, DC.

Leigland, James, and Andrew Roberts. 2007. "The African Project Preparation Gap." Note 18.

Levinsohn, James, and Amil Petrin. 1999. "When Industries Become More Productive, Do Firms?" NBER Working Paper 6893, National Bureau of Economic Research, Cambridge, MA.

Levinson, Marc. 2006. *The Box: How the Shipping Container Made the World Smaller and the World Economy Bigger*. Princeton, NJ: Princeton University Press.

Limão, Nuno, and Anthony J. Venables. 2001. "Infrastructure, Geographical Disadvantage, Transport Costs, and Trade." *World Bank Economic Review* 15 (3): 451–79.

Linden, Greg, Kenneth L. Kraemer, and Jason Dedrick. 2007. "Who Captures Value in a Global Innovation System? The Case of the Apple's iPod." Personal Computing Industry Center, Irvine, CA.

Linn, F. Johannes, and David Tiomkin. 2006. "The New Impetus toward Economic Integration between Europe and Asia." *Asia Europe Journal* 4 (1): 31–41.

Lipsey, Richard G., and Alice Nakamura, eds. 2006. *Services Industries and the Knowledge-Based Economy*. Calgary, Canada: University of Calgary Press.

Little, Peter D. 2007. "Unofficial Cross-Border Trade in Eastern Africa." Paper presented at the Staple Food Trade and Market Policy Options for Promoting Development in Eastern and Southern Africa, Rome.

Lösch, Auguste. 1940. *The Economics of Location*. New Haven, CT: Yale University Press.

Lucas, Robert E. Jr. 1988. "On the Mechanics of Economic Development." *Journal of Monetary Economics* 22 (1): 3–42.

———. 2004. "Life Earnings and Rural-Urban Migration." *Journal of Political Economy* 112 (S1): S29–S59.

———. 2007. "Trade and the Diffusion of the Industrial Revolution." NBER Working Paper 13286, National Bureau of Economic Research, Cambridge, MA.

Lucas, Robert E. B. 1997. "Internal Migration in Developing Countries." In *Handbook of Population and Family Economics*, ed. Mark Rosenzweig and Oded Stark. Amsterdam: North-Holland.

———. 2003. "Migration and Lagging Regions." Boston University, Boston. Processed.

———. 2006. "Migration and Economic Development in Africa: A Review of Evidence." *Journal of African Economies* 15 (2): 337–95.

Luo, Xubei. 2004. "The Role of Infrastructure Investment Location in China's Western Development." Policy Research Working Paper 3345, World Bank, Washington, DC.

Lutz, Vera. 1962. *Italy: A Study in Economic Development*. London: Oxford University Press.

Lynch, Sarah N., and Eugene Mulero. 2007. "Williamsburg's Most Recent Reinvention: The Makeover in Brooklyn." *The Cooperator*. Nov., 2007.

Lysenko, A. J., and I. N. Semashko. 1968. "Geography of Malaria: A Medico-Geographic Profile of an Ancient Disease [in Russian]." In *Medicinskaja Geografija*, ed. A. W. Lebedew. Moscow: Russian Academy of Sciences.

Mackay, C. J. 1999. "Housing Policy in South Africa: The Challenge of Delivery." *Housing Studies* 14 (3): 387–99.

MacMillan, Margaret. 2002. *Paris 1919: Six Months That Changed the World*. New York: Random House.

Maddison, Angus. 2006. *The World Economy*. Paris: Organisation for Economic Co-operation and Development.

———. 2008a. *The World Economy: Volume 1: A Millennial Perspective*. Paris: OECD.

———. 2008b. "World Population, GDP, and Per Capita GDP, 1–2003 AD." University of Gröningen Growth and Development Centre, Gröningen, Netherlands.

Malaysia Economic Planning Unit. 2008. *Malaysia Achieving the MDGs*. Kuala Lumpur: Malaysia Economic Planning Unit, Primer Minister's Office.

Malinowski, Matthew. 2007. "Cold Snap Prompts Chile to Seek Gas Deal with Old Foe Bolivia." *Christian Science Monitor,* August 8.

Margo, Robert A. 1988. "Schooling and the Great Migration." NBER Working Paper 2697, National Bureau of Economic Research, Cambridge, MA.

———. 2000. *Wages and Labor Markets in the United States, 1820–1860.* Chicago: University of Chicago Press.

———. 2004. "The North-South Wage Gap, Before and After the Civil War." In *Slavery in the Development of the Americas,* ed. David Eltis, Frank D. Lewis, and Kenneth L. Sokoloff. New York: Cambridge University Press.

Markussen, T. Forthcoming. "Property Rights, Productivity, and Common Property Resources: Insights from Rural Cambodia." *World Development.*

Marland, Gregg, Tom Boden, and Robert Andres. 2007. "National CO_2 Emissions from Fossil-Fuel Burning, Cement Manufacture, and Gas Flaring: 1751–2004." Carbon Dioxide Information Analysis Center, Oakridge National Laboratory, Oak Ridge, TN.

Marshall, Alfred. 1890. *Principles of Economics.* London: Macmillan.

Martin, Philippe. 2005. "The Geography of Inequalities in Europe." *Swedish Economic Policy Review* 12: 83–108.

Martin, Philippe, Thierry Mayer, and Mathias Thoenig. 2008. "Civil Wars and International Trade." *Journal of the European Economic Association* 6 (2–3): 541–50.

Martin, Ronald L. 2005. "Centralized Versus Decentralized Financial Systems: Is There a Case for Local Capital Markets?" Paper presented at the Cambridge-MIT Institute Conference on Venture Capital, Finance and Regional Development, Cambridge, U.K., June 17.

Martinez-Galarraga, Julio. 2007. "New Estimates on Regional GDP in Spain, 1860–1930." Working Paper 177, Universitat de Barcelona Espai de Recerca en Economia, Barcelona.

Martínez-Zarzoso, Inmaculada, L. García-Menéndez, and C. Suárez-Burguet. 2003. "Impact of Transport Costs on International Trade: The Case of Spanish Ceramic Exports." *Maritime Economics and Logistics* 5 (2): 179–98.

Martínez-Zarzoso, Inmaculada, and Laura Marquez-Ramos. 2007. "The Effect of Trade Facilitation on Sectoral Trade." Working Paper 167, Ibero-America Institute for Economic Research, Göttingen, Germany.

Martins, Joaquim Oliveira, Stefano Scarpetta, and Dirk Pilat. 1996. "Mark-up Ratios in Manufacturing Industries: Estimates for 14 OECD Countries." Working Paper 162, Organisation for Economic Co-operation and Development, Paris.

Massey, Douglas S. 1988. "International Migration and Economic Development in Comparative Perspective." *Population and Development Review* 14 (3): 383–413.

———. 2003. "Patterns and Processes of International Migration in the 21st Century." Paper presented at the Conference on African Migration in Comparative Perspective, Johannesburg.

Maurel, Françoise, and Béatrice Sédillot. 1999. "A Measure of the Geographic Concentration in French Manufacturing Industries." *Regional Science and Urban Economics* 29 (5): 575–604.

Mayer, Thierry. 2008. "Market Potential and Development." Background paper for the WDR 2009.

McCallum, John. 1995. "National Borders Matter: Canada-U.S. Regional Trade Patterns." *American Economic Review* 85 (3): 615–23.

McCann, Philip. 2001. *Urban and Regional Economics.* Oxford, U.K.: Oxford University Press.

McCrae, Ian. 2006. "Uncertainties in Road Transport Emissions in Developing Countries." HM Treasury, London.

McInnis, R. Marvin. 1966. "Regional Income Differentials in Canada, 1911–1961." *Journal of Economic History* 26 (4): 586–88.

McKenzie, David J. 2001. "The Impact of Capital Controls on Growth Convergence." *Journal of Economic Development* 26 (1): 1–25.

———. 2007. "Paper Walls Are Easier to Tear Down: Passport Costs and Legal Barriers to Emigrations." *World Development* 35 (11): 2026–39.

McKenzie, David J., and Hillel Rapoport. 2007. "Self-Selection Patterns in Mexico-U.S. Migration: The Role of Migration Networks." Policy Research Working Paper 4118, World Bank, Washington, DC.

Meade, James E. 1956. "The Theory of Customs Union." *American Economic Review* 46 (4): 724–26.

Melitz, J. Marc. 2003. "The Impact of Trade on Intra-industry Reallocations and Aggregate Industry Productivity." *Econometrica* 71 (6): 1695–725.

Mera, Koichi. 1973. "Regional Production Function and Social Overhead Capital: An Analysis of the Japanese Case." *Regional and Urban Economics* 3 (2): 157–86.

Metzer, Jacob. 1974. "Railroad Development and Market Integration: The Case of Tsarist Russia." *Journal of Economic History* 34 (3): 529–50.

Meybeck, Michel, Pamela Green, and Charles Vorosmarty. 2001. "A New Typology for Mountains and Other Relief Classes." *Mountain Research and Development* 21 (1): 34–45.

Meyer, Balthasar H. 1917. *History of Transportation in the United States before 1860.* Washington, DC: Carnegie Institution of Washington.

Miguel, Edward, Shanker Satyanath, and Ernest Sergenti. 2004. "Economic Shocks and Civil Conflict: An Instrumental Variables Approach." *Journal of Political Economy* 112 (4): 725–53.

Milanovic, Branko. 2005. *Worlds Apart. Measuring International and Global Inequality.* Princeton, NJ: Princeton University Press.

Miles, Alice. 2007. "What's That Whimpering from the Fields?" *London Times,* July 17.

Mills, Edwin S., and James MacKinnon. 1973. "Notes on the New Urban Economics." *Bell Journal of Economics and Management Science* 4(2):593–601.

Minot, Nicholas, Bob Baulch, and Michael Epprecht. 2003. *Poverty and Inequality in Vietnam: Spatial Patterns and Geographic Determinants.* Washington, DC: International Food Policy Research Institute and Inter-ministerial Poverty Mapping Task Force.

Mints, A. A. 1974. *Prognoznaya Hypoteza Razvitiya Narodnogo Khozyastva Evropeyskoy Chasti SSSR [A Forecast Hypothesis of* the Development of the European USSR Economy]. Moscow: Resursy, Sreda, Rasselenie, Nauka.

Mitchell, Brian R. 1964. "The Coming of the Railway and the United Kingdom Economic Growth." *Journal of Economic History* 24 (3): 315–36.

Mohammed, Saif I., and Jeffrey G. Williamson. 2004. "Freight Rates and Productivity Gains in British Tramp Shipping, 1869–1950." *Explorations in Economic History* 41 (2): 172–203.

Montenegro, Claudio E., and Maximilian L. Hirn. 2008. "A New Disaggregated Set of Labor Market Indicators Using Standardized Household Surveys from Around the World." Background paper for the WDR 2009.

Moomaw, Ronald L. 1981. "Productivity and City Size: A Critique of the Evidence." *Quarterly Journal of Economics* 96 (4): 675–88.

———. 1983. "Is Population Scale a Worthless Surrogate for Business Agglomeration Economies?" *Regional Science and Urban Economics* 13 (4): 525–45.

Moreno, Ramón, and Bharat Trehan. 1997. "Location and the Growth of Nations." *Journal of Economic Growth* 2 (4): 399–418.

Moretti, Enrico. 2004a. "Estimating the Social Return to Higher Education: Evidence from Longitudinal and Repeated Cross-Sectional Data." *Journal of Econometrics* 121 (1–2): 175–212.

———. 2004b. "Workers' Education, Spillovers, and Productivity: Evidence from Plant-Level Production Functions." *American Economic Review* 94 (3): 656–90.

Morrisson, Christian, and Fabrice Murtin. 2005. "The World Distribution of Human Capital, Life Expectancy and Income: A Multi-dimensional Approach." London School of Economics, London.

Mukherjee, Andy. 2007. "India's Answer to Shenzhen Needs Political Will." *Bloomberg.com*, March 15.

Mumford, Lewis. 1963. *The Highway and the City*. New York: Harcourt Brace and World Bank.

Mutlu, Servet. 1991. "Regional Disparities, Industry and Government Policy in Japan." *Development and Change* 22 (3): 547–86.

N'Dulu, Benno J. 2001. "From Vision to Reality of African Economic Integration: Priority Actions and the Institutional Framework for the Way Forward." World Bank, Washington, DC.

N'Guessan, Koffi, and Bassirou Chitou. 2006. "ENSEA of Abidjan: in the Heart of Statistical Training in Francophone Africa." *African Statistical Journal* 2: 151–56.

Nabi, Ijaz, and Anjum Nasim. 2001. "Trading with the Enemy: A Case for Liberalizing Pakistan-India Trade." In *Regionalism and Globalization: Theory and Practice*, ed. Sajal Lahiri. New York: Routledge.

Naisbitt, John. 1995. *The Global Paradox*. New York: Avon Books.

Nakajima, Tomio. 1982. *Public Investment: Theory and Practice*. Tokyo: Gyosei.

Nakamura, Ryohei. 1985. "Agglomeration Economies in Urban Manufacturing Industries: A Case of Japanese Cities." *Journal of Urban Economics* 17 (1): 108–24.

Nam, Charles B., William J. Serow, and David F. Sly. 1990. *International Handbook on Internal Migration*. New York: Greenwood Press.

Naqvi, Zareen F., and Philip Schuler. 2007. *The Challenges and Potential of Pakistan-India Trade*. Washington, DC: World Bank.

Naudé, Wim A. 2007. "Geography and Development in Africa: Overview and Implications for Regional Cooperation." WIDER Working Paper Series 2007/03, United Nations, Helsinki.

Naudé, Wim A., and W. F. Krugell. 2006. "Sub-national Growth Rate Differentials in South Africa: An Econometric Analysis." *Papers in Regional Science* 85 (3): 443–57.

Naudé, Wim A., and Marianne Matthee. 2007. "The Significance of Transport Costs in Africa." United Nations University, Tokyo. Processed.

Ndulu, Benno J., Lopamudra Chakraborty, Lebohang Lijane, Vijaya Ramachandran, and Jerome Wolgin. 2007. *Challenges of African Growth: Opportunities, Constraints and Strategic Directions*. Washington, DC: World Bank.

Negri, Mariano, and Guido Porto. 2007. "Burley Tobacco Clubs in Malawi: Non-market Institutions for Export." World Bank, Washington, DC.

Negroponte, Nicholas. 1995. *Being Digital*. New York: Vintage Books.

Nelson, Andrew. 2008. "Accessibility Model and Population Estimates." Background paper for the WDR 2009.

Nesslein, Thomas S. 2003. "Markets versus Planning: An Assessment of the Swedish Housing Model in the Post-War Period." *Urban Studies* 40 (7): 1259–82.

Neumayer, Eric. 2006. "Unequal Access to Foreign Spaces: How States Use Visa Restrictions to Regulate Mobility in a Globalised World." Paper presented at the Annual Meeting of the International Studies Association, San Diego, CA.

Neuwirth, Robert. 2007. "Security of Tenure in Istanbul: The Triumph of the 'Self-Service' City." United Nations Habitat. Case study prepared for Enhancing Urban Safety and Security, Global Report on Human Settlements 2007.

Nigeria National Bureau of Statistics. 2004. *National Nigeria Living Standard Survey (NLSS)*. Abuja: Nigeria National Bureau of Statistics.

———. 2006. *Poverty Profile for Nigeria*. Abuja: National Bureau of Statistics, Federal Republic of Nigeria.

Nikomborirak, Deunden. 2007. "Liberalization of Air Transport and Competition Concerns in ASEAN." In *Market Access, Trade in Transport Services and Trade Facilitation*, ed. OECD/ECMT. Paris: Organisation for Economic Co-operation and Development.

Nordas, Hildegunn Kyvik, Enrico Pinali, and Massimo Geloso Grosso. 2006. "Logistics and Time as a Trade Barrier." Trade Policy Working Paper 35, Organisation for Economic Co-operation and Development, Paris.

Nordhaus, William D. 2006. "Geography and Macroeconomics: New Data and New Findings." *Proceedings of the National Academy of Science* 103 (10): 3510–17.

Nordhaus, William D., and Joseph Boyer. 2000. *Warming the World: Economic Models of Global Warming*. Cambridge, MA: MIT Press.

North, Douglass C. 1971. "Institutional Change and Economic Growth." *Journal of Economic History* 31 (1): 118–25.

O'Gorman, Marvin. 1939a. "Square Deals for London Traffic: A Study of London's Traffic Problem with Suggested Solutions. Part 1." *Highways and Bridges*, March 29.

———. 1939b. "Square Deals for London Traffic: A Study of London's Traffic Problem with Suggested Solutions. Part 2." *Highways and Bridges*, April 5.

O'Rourke, Kevin H., and Jeffrey Williamson. 1994. "Late Nineteenth-Century Anglo-American Factor-Price Convergence: Were Heckscher and Ohlin Right?" *Journal of Economic History* 54 (4): 892–916.

Obstfeld, Maurice, Jay C. Shambaugh, and Alan M. Taylor. 2004. "Monetary Sovereignty, Exchange Rates, and Capital Controls: The Trilemma in the Interwar Period." NBER Working Paper 10393, National Bureau of Economic Research, Cambridge, MA.

Obstfeld, Maurice, and Alan M. Taylor. 2002. "Globalization and Capital Markets." NBER Working Paper 8846, National Bureau of Economic Research, Cambridge, MA.

Offer, A. 1981. *Property and Politics, 1870–1914*. Cambridge, U.K.: Cambridge University Press.

Office of the Deputy Prime Minister. 2003. *Cities, Regions, and Competitiveness*. London: Office of the Deputy Prime Minister.

Oh, Jinhwan. 2008. "Korea: A Case Study of 1D-2D-3D Areas." Background note for the WDR 2009.

———. 2008. "Spatially Blind and Connective Policies in a 1D Region: The Case of Eumseong County in South Korea." Background note for the WDR 2009.

Ohmae, Kenichi. 1990. *The Borderless World: Power and Strategies in the Interlinked Economy*. New York: Harper Business.

Okuma, Ichiro, ed. 1980. *Readings in Public Finance*. Tokyo: Toyo Kenzai Shinposya.

Openshaw, Stan, and Paul Taylor. 1979. "A Million or So Correlation Coefficients: Three Experiments on the Modifiable Areal Unit Problem." In *Statistical Applications in the Spatial Sciences*, ed. Neil Wrigley. London: Pion.

Oppenheimer, Andrés. 2008. "Latin America Is Lagging. Someone Tells Its Leaders." *Washington Post*, January 13.

Organisation for Economic Co-operation and Development (OECD). 2003. *Place-Based Policies for Rural Development: The Micro-Regions Strategy, Mexico (Case Study)*. Background paper for the OECD's Horizontal Review of Place-Based Policies for Development, Paris.

———. 2006. *Territorial Reviews: Competitive Cities in the Global Economy*. Paris: Organisation for Economic Co-operation and Development.

———. 2007. *OECD: Regions at a Glance*. Paris: Organisation for Economic Co-operation and Development.

Orwell, George. 1937. *The Road to Wigan Pier*. London: Victor Gollancz.

Overseas Development Institute. 2006. *What's Next in International Development?* London: Overseas Development Institute.

Owen, Nicholas. 1983. *Economies of Scale, Competitiveness, and Trade Patterns within the European Community*. Oxford, U.K.: Clarendon Press.

Özden, Caglar, and Maurice Schiff. 2007. *International Migration, Economic Development and Policy*. Washington, DC: World Bank.

Paci, Pierella, Erwin R. Tiongson, Mateusz Walewski, Jacek Liwinski, and Maria M. Stoilkova. 2007. "Internal Labor Mobility in Central Europe and the Baltic Region." Policy Research Working Paper 105, World Bank, Washington, DC.

Packard, Truman. 1997. "Adjustment, Migration and Economic Informality in Latin America." M.S. Economic for Development thesis, Queen Elizabeth House, University of Oxford.

Paillacar, Rodrigo. 2007. "Market Potential and Worker Heterogeneity as Determinants of Brazilian Wages." Université de Paris I Panthéon-Sorbonne. Paris.

Pakenham, Thomas. 1992. *The Scramble for Africa*. New York: Harper Collins.

Palacin, Jose, and Robert C. Shelburne. 2005. "The Private Housing Market in Eastern Europe and the CIS." Working Paper 2005-5, United Nations Commission for Europe, Geneva.

Pallage, Stéphane, and Michel A. Robe. 2003. "On the Welfare Cost of Economic Fluctuation in Developing Countries." *International Economic Review* 44 (2): 677–98.

Park, Sam Ock. Forthcoming. "A History of Korea's Spatial Transformation and Economic Growth." In *Reshaping Economic Geography in East Asia*, ed. Yukon Huang and Alessandro Magnoli Bocchi. Washington, DC: World Bank, EAP Companion Volume to the WDR 2009.

Parsons, Christopher R., Ronald Skeldon, Terrie L. Walmsley, and L. Alan Winters. 2007. "Quantifying International Migration: A Database of Bilateral Migrant Stocks." In *International Migration, Economic Development and Policy*, ed. Caglar Özden and Maurice Schiff. Washington, DC: World Bank.

Paul, Catherine J. Morrison, and Donald S. Siegel. 1999. "Scale Economies and Industry Agglomeration Externalities: A Dynamic Cost Function Approach." *American Economic Review* 89 (1): 272–90.

Pedersen, P. O. 1990. "The Role of Small Rural Towns in Development." In *Small Town Africa, Seminar Proceedings No. 23*, ed. Jonathan Baker. Uppsalla: Scandinavian Institute of African Studies.

Peng, Zhong-Ren, Yi Zhu, and Shunfeng Song. 2008. "Mobility of the Chinese Urban Poor: A Case Study of Hefei City." *Chinese Economy* 41 (1): 36–57.

Phillips, Truman P., Daphne S. Taylor, Lateef Sanni, and Malachy O. Akoroda. 2004. *The Global Cassava Development Strategy*. Rome: Food and Agriculture Organization of the United Nations.

Policy Research Institute for Land, Infrastructure Transport, and Tourism Research. 2001. *Discussion on Equity and Social Capital Improvement*. Tokyo: Policy Research Institute for Land, Infrastructure, Transport, and Tourism.

Poncet, Sandra. 2005. "A Fragmented China: Measures and Determinants of Chinese Domestic Market Integration." *Review of International Economics* 13 (3): 409–30.

———. 2006. "Provincial Migration Dynamics in China: Borders, Costs, and Economic Motivations." *Regional Science and Urban Economics* 36 (3): 385–98.

Prateen, Cliff. 1988. "Survey of the Economies of Scale." Economic Papers 67, Commission of the European Communities, Brussels.

PricewaterhouseCoopers. 2007. *Which Are the Largest City Economies in the World and How Might This Change by 2020?* London: PricewaterhouseCoopers: UK Economic Outlook.

Pritchett, Lant. 2006. *Let Their People Come: Breaking the Gridlock on Global Labor Mobility.* Washington, DC: Center for Global Development.

Public Administration Research and Consultation Centre. 2004. *Egypt Millennium Development Goals: Second Country Report.* Cairo: United Nations and Egypt Ministry of Planning.

Pucher, John, Nisha Korattyswaropam, Neha Mittal, and Neenu Ittyerah. 2005. "Urban Transport Crisis in India." *Transport Policy* 12 (3): 185–98.

Puga, Diego. 2002. "European Regional Policies in Light of Recent Location Theories." *Journal of Economic Geography* 2 (4): 373–406.

Puga, Diego, and Anthony J. Venables. 1999. "Agglomeration and Economic Development: Import Substitution vs. Trade Liberalization." *Economic Journal* 109 (455): 292–311.

Quah, Danny T. 1996. "Twin Peaks: Growth and Convergence in Models of Distribution Dynamics." *Economic Journal* 106 (437): 1045–55.

Quinn, Dennis P., and A. María Toyoda. 2006. "Does Capital Account Liberalization Lead to Growth?" Georgetown University, Washington, DC.

Rajan, Raghuram, and Shang-Jin Wei. 2004. "The Non-Threat That Is Outsourcing." *Business Times (Singapore).*

Ratha, Dilip, and William Shaw. 2007. "South-South Migration and Remittances." Working Paper 102, World Bank, Washington, DC.

Ratha, Dilip, and Zhimei Xu. 2008. *Migration and Remittances Factbook 2008.* Washington, DC: World Bank.

Rauch, James E. 1993. "Productivity Gains from Geographic Concentration of Human Capital: Evidence from the Cities." *Journal of Urban Economics* 34 (3): 380–400.

———. 1999. "Networks versus Markets in International Trade." *Journal of International Economics* 48 (1): 7–35.

Ravallion, Martin. 2007. "Inequality Is Bad for the Poor." In *Inequality and Poverty Re-Examined,* ed. Steven Jenkins and John Micklewright. New York: Oxford University Press.

Ravallion, Martin, and Dominique van de Walle. 2006a. "Does Rising Landlessness Signal Success or Failure for Vietnam's Agricultural Transition?" Policy Research Working Paper 3871, World Bank, Washington, DC.

———. 2006b. "Land Reallocation in an Agrarian Transition." *Economic Journal* 116 (514): 924–42.

Redding, Stephen J., and Anthony J. Venables. 2004. "Economic Geography and International Inequality." *Journal of International Economics* 62 (1): 53–82.

Rephann, Terance, and Andrew Isserman. 1994. "New Highways as Economic Development Tools: An Evaluation Using Quasi-Experimental Matching Methods." *Regional Science and Urban Economics* 24 (6): 723–51.

Reporters without Borders for Press Freedom. 2007. *Freedom of the Press Worldwide in 2007.* Paris: Reporters without Borders for Press Freedom.

Revenue Mobilization Allocation and Fiscal Commission. 2003. *States and Local Governments 2003 Revenue Allocation Indices.* Abuja, Nigeria: Revenue Mobilization Allocation and Fiscal Commission.

Richter, K., R. van der Weide, and Phonesaly Souksavath. 2005. *Lao PDR Poverty Trends 1992/93–2002/03.* Washington, DC: National Statistics Centre and World Bank.

Roberts, Leslie, and Martin Enserink. 2007. "María: Did They Really Say ... Eradication?" *Science* 318 (5856): 1544–45.

Roberts, Mark. 2004. "The Growth Performances of the GB Counties: Some New Empirical Evidence for 1977–1993." *Regional Studies* 38 (2): 149–65.

Roberts, Mark, and Uwe Deichmann. 2008. "Regional Spillover Estimation." Background paper for the WDR 2009.

Robles, Marcos. 2003. *Estimación de Indicadores de pobreza y Desigualdad a Nivel Municipal en Honduras.* Tegucigalpa: BID-MECOVI and Instituto Nacional de Estadísticas de Honduras.

Rodríguez, Francisco, and Dani Rodrik. 2000. "Trade Policy and Economic Growth: A Skeptic's Guide to the Cross-National Evidence." In *NBER Macroeconomics Annual 2000,* ed. Ben S. Bernanke and Kenneth Rogoff. Cambridge, MA: National Bureau of Economic Research.

Rodríguez, Jorge. 2004. "Migración Interna en América Latina y el Caribe: Estudio Regional del Período 1980–2000." Serie Población y Desarrollo 50, ECLAC, Santiago.

Rodríguez-Pose, Andrés, and Ugo Fratesi. 2004. "Between Development and Social Policies: The Impact of European Structural Funds in Objective 1 Regions." *Regional Studies* 38 (1): 97–113.

Rodrik, Dani, Arvind Subramanian, and Francesco Trebbi. 2004. "Institutions Rule: The Primacy of Institutions over Geography and Integration in Economic Development." *Journal of Economic Growth* 9 (2): 131–65.

Roeger, Werner. 1995. "Can Imperfect Competition Explain the Difference between Primal and Dual Productivity Measures? Estimates for U.S. Manufacturing." *Journal of Political Economy* 103 (2): 316–30.

Rohwedder, Cecilie, and Keith Johnson. 2008. "Pace-Setting Zara Seeks More Speed to Fight Its Rising Cheap-Chic Rivals." *Wall Street Journal,* February 20.

Rolfes, L. Jr. 2002. "Making the Legal Basis for Private Land Rights Operational and Effective." Paper presented at the World Bank Regional Land Policy Workshop, Budapest, April 6.

Romer, Paul M. 1986. "Increasing Returns in Long-Run Growth." *Journal of Political Economy* 94 (5): 1002–37.

———. 1990. "Endogenous Technological Change." *Journal of Political Economy* 98(5):71–102.

———. 1994. "The Origins of Endogenous Growth." *Journal of Economic Perspectives* 8 (1): 3–22.

Rose, Andrew K. 2005. "Cities and Countries." Discussion Paper 5235, Centre for Economic Policy Research, London.

Rosenbloom, Joshua L., and William A. Sundstrom. 2003. "The Decline and Rise of Interstate Migration in the United States: Evidence from the IPUMS, 1850–1990." NBER Working Paper 9857, National Bureau of Economic Research, Cambridge, MA.

Rosenthal, Stuart S., and William C. Strange. 2001. "The Determinants of Agglomeration." *Journal of Urban Economics* 50 (2): 191–229.

———. 2003. "Geography, Industrial Organization, and Agglomeration." *Review of Economics and Statistics* 85 (2): 377–93.

———. 2004. "Evidence on the Nature and Sources of Agglomeration Economies." In *Handbook of Regional and Urban Economics*, vol. IV, ed. J. Vernon Henderson and Jacque Thisse. Amsterdam: North-Holland.

Rossi-Hansberg, Esteban, and Mark L. J. Wright. 2007. "Urban Structure and Growth." *Review of Economic Studies* 74(2):597–624.

Rostow, Walt Whitman. 1960. *The Stages of Economic Growth.* Cambridge, U.K.: Cambridge University Press.

Roy, Tirthankar. 2002. "Economic History and Modern India: Redefining the Link." *Journal of Economic Perspectives* 16 (3): 109–30.

Ruster, Jeff, and Ivo Imperato. 2003. *Slum Upgrading and Participation: Lessons from Latin America.* Washington, DC: World Bank.

Sachs, Jeffrey D., and Pia Malaney. 2002. "The Economic and Social Burden of Malaria." *Nature* 415 (6872): 680–5.

Sahn, David E., and David C. Stifel. 2003. "Urban-Rural Inequality in Living Standards in Africa." *Journal of African Economies* 12 (4): 564–97.

Sakamaki, Tetsuro. 2006. "Regional Disparities and National Land Development Policy in East Asian Countries." *Journal of Japan Bank for International Cooperation Institute* 29: 84–122.

Sánchez, Ricardo J., Jan Hoffmann, Alejandro Micco, Georgina V. Pizzolitto, Martín Sgut, and Gordon Wilmsmeier. 2003. "Port Efficiency and International Trade: Port Efficiency as a Determinant of Maritime Transport Costs." *Maritime Economics and Logistics* 5 (2): 199–218.

Sandler, Todd. 2002. "Demand and Institutions for Regional Public Goods." In *Regional Public Goods: From Theory to Practice*, ed. Antoni Estevadeordal, Brian Frantz, and Tam R. Nguyen. Washington, DC: Inter-American Development Bank and Asian Development Bank.

Sandler, Todd, and Daniel M. Arce. 2002. "A Conceptual Framework for Understanding Global and Transnational Public Goods for Health." *Fiscal Studies* 23 (2): 195–222.

Santos, Georgina, and Blake Shaffer. 2004. "Preliminary Results of the London Congestion Charging Scheme." *Public Work Management and Policy* 9 (2): 164–81.

Sassen, Saskia. 1991. *The Global City: New York, London, Tokyo.* Princeton, NJ: Princeton University Press.

Satterthwaite, David. 2007. "The Transition to a Predominantly Urban World and Its Underpinnings." Paper presented at the UNU-WIDER International Workshop on Beyond the Tipping Point: Development in an Urban World, London, October 19.

———. 2008. "Expanding the Supply and Reducing the Cost of Land for Housing in Urban Areas in Low and Middle Income Nations." Background note for the WDR 2009.

Satterthwaite, David, Saleemul Hug, Mark Pelling, Hannah Reid, and Patricia Romero-Lankao. 2007. *Adapting to Climate Change in Urban Areas: The Possibilities and Constraints in Low and Middle Income Nations.* London: International Institute for Environment and Development.

Schacter, Jason P. 2004. "Geographical Mobility: 2002 to 2003." Current Population Report, U.S. Census Bureau, Washington, DC. March.

Scherer, Frederic M. 1980. *Industrial Market Structure and Economic Performance.* Boston: Houghton Mifflin.

Schiff, Maurice, and Caglar Özden. 2006. *International Migration, Remittances and the Brain Drain.* Washington, DC: World Bank and Palgrave Macmillan.

Schiff, Maurice, and Yanling Wang. 2003. "Regional Integration and Technology Diffusion: The Case of North American Free Trade Agreement." Policy Research Working Paper 3132, World Bank, Washington, DC.

Schiff, Maurice, and L. Alain Winters. 2002. "Regional Cooperation and the Role of International Organizations and Regional Integration." Policy Research Working Paper 2872, World Bank, Washington, DC.

———. 2003. *Regional Integration and Development.* New York: Oxford University Press.

Schmertmann, Carl P. 1992. "Estimation of Historical Migration Rates from a Single Census: Interregional Migration in Brazil, 1900–1980." *Population Studies* 46 (1): 103–20.

Schneider, A., M. A. Friedl, and D. Potere. Forthcoming. "A New Map of Global Urban Extent from MODIS Data." *Geophysical Research Letters.*

Scholz, Stephan. 2006. "The POETICS of Industrial Carbon Dioxide Emissions in Japan: An Urban and Institutional Extension of the IPAT Identity." *Carbon Balance and Management* 1 (11): 1–10.

Schwenning, Gustav. 1927. "An Attack on Shanghai Slums." *Social Forces* 6 (1): 125–31.

Scott, Ian. 1982. *Urban and Spatial Development in Mexico.* Baltimore, MD: Johns Hopkins University.

Seeman, Helene Zuckerman, and Alanna Siegfried. 1978. "The Evolution of SoHo." In Helene Zuckerman Seeman and Alanna Siegfried, (eds.), *SoHo: A Guide.* New York, NY: Neal-Schuman Publishers, Inc.

Segal, David. 1976. "Are There Returns to Scale in City Size?" *Review of Economics and Statistics* 58 (3): 339–50.

Selod, Harris. 2007. "Land Policies and Urban Segregation." World Bank, Washington, DC.

Shah, Anwar, and Chunli Shen. 2006. "The Reform of the Intergovernmental Transfer System to Achieve a Harmonious Society and a Level Playing Field for Regional Development in China." Policy Research Working Paper 4100, World Bank, Washington, DC.

Shatz, Howard J., and Anthony J. Venables. 2005. "The Geography of International Investment." In *Oxford Handbook of Economic Geography*, ed. Gordon L. Clark, Meric S. Gertler, and Maryann P. Feldman. Oxford, U.K.: Oxford University Press.

Shaw, Dan. 2007. "Meatpacking District: What a Difference 38 Years Make." *The New York Times*, October 14.

Shefer, Daniel. 1973. "Localization Economies in SMSA's: A Production Function Analysis." *Journal of Regional Science* 13 (1): 55–64.

Shepherd, Ben, and John S. Wilson. 2006. "Road Infrastructure in Europe and Central Asia: Does Network Quality Affects Trade?" Policy Research Working Paper 4104, World Bank, Washington, DC.

Showers, Victor. 1979. *World Facts and Figures.* Chichester, U.K.: John Wiley and Sons.

Shukla, Vibhooti, and Oded Stark. 1986. "Urban External Economies and Optimal Migration." In *Migration, Human Capital, and Development,* ed. Oded Stark. Greenwich, CT: JAI Press.

Sicsic, Pierre. 1992. "City-Farm Wage Gaps in Late Nineteenth-Century France." *Journal of Economic History* 52 (3): 675–95.

Siegel, Fred. 1997. *The Future Once Happened Here: New York, D.C., L.A., and the Fate of America's Big Cities.* Florence, MA: Free Press.

Simmons, Beth A. 2005. "Rules over Real Estate: Trade, Territorial Conflict, and International Borders as Institutions." *Journal of Conflict Resolution* 49 (6): 823–48.

Sinai, Todd, and Joel Waldfogel. 2004. "Geography and the Internet: Is the Internet a Substitute or Complement for Cities?" *Journal of Urban Economics* 56 (1): 1–24.

Sinn, Hans-Werner, and Frank Westermann. 2001. "Two Mezzogiornos." NBER Working Paper 8125, National Bureau of Economic Research, Cambridge, MA.

Skeldon, Ronald. 1986. "On Migration Patterns in India during the 1970s." *Population and Development Review* 12 (4): 759–79.

Slaughter, Mattew J. 2001. "Trade Liberalization and Per Capita Income Convergence: A Difference-in-Differences Analysis." *Journal of International Economics* 55 (1): 203–28.

Smith, Adam. 1976 [1776]. *An Inquiry into the Nature and Causes of the Wealth of Nations.* Chicago: University of Chicago Press (Cannan's edition of the *Wealth of Nations* was originally published in 1904 by Methuen & Co. Ltd. First Edition in 1776).

Smith, Donald F. Jr., and Richard Florida. 1994. "Agglomeration and Industrial Location: An Econometric Analysis of Japanese-Affiliated Manufacturing Establishments in Automotive-Related Industries." *Journal of Urban Economics* 36 (1): 23–41.

Smith, P. J. 1989. "The Rehousing/Relocation Issue in an Early Slum Clearance Scheme: Edinburgh 1865–1885." *Urban Studies* 26 (1): 100–14.

Snow, Robert W., Marlies Craig, Uwe Deichmann, and Karen Marsh. 1999. "Estimating Mortality, Morbidity, and Disability Due to Malaria among Africa's Non-Pregnant Population." *Bulletin of the World Health Organization* 77 (8): 624–40.

Sobel, Robert. 2000. *How a Generation of Americans Created the World's Most Prosperous Society.* New York: St. Martin's Press.

Söderbaum, Fredrik. 2001. "Institutional Aspects of the Maputo Development Corridor." Development Policy Research Unit Working Paper 9675, University of Cape Town, Cape Town, South Africa.

Sohn, Jeongmok. 2003. *Seoul Dosi Hoek Iyagi [Seoul: The Story of Urban Planning].* Seoul: Hanul.

Sokoloff, Kenneth L., and Stanley L. Engerman. 2000a. "History Lessons: Institutions, Factor Endowments, and Paths of Development in the New World." *Journal of Economic Perspectives* 14 (3): 217–32.

———. 2000b. "Institutions, Factor Endowments, and Paths of Development in the New World." *Journal of Economic Perspectives* 14 (3): 217–32.

Solow, Robert M. 1956. "A Contribution to the Theory of Economic Growth." *Quarterly Journal of Economics* 70 (1): 65–94.

Soltow, Lee. 1989. "The Rich and the Destitute in Sweden, 1805–1855: A Test of Tocqueville's Inequality Hypotheses." *Economic History Review* 42 (1): 43–63.

Son, Dang Kim. Forthcoming. "Rural Development and Issues in Vietnam: Spatial Disparities and Some Recommendations." In *Reshaping Economic Geography in East Asia,* ed. Yukon Huang and Alessandro Magnoli Bocchi. Washington, DC: World Bank, EAP Companion Volume to the WDR 2009.

Sonobe, Tetsushi, and Keijiro Otsuka. 2006. *Cluster-Based Industrial Development: An East Asian Model.* Hampshire, U.K.: Palgrave Macmillan.

Sophal, Chan, Tep Saravi, and Sarthi Acharya. 2001. "Land Tenure in Cambodia: A Data Update." Working Paper 19, Development Resource Institute, Phnom Penh.

Soto, Raimundo, and Arístides Torche. 2004. "Spatial Inequality, Migration, and Economic Growth in Chile." *Cuadernos de Economía* 41 (124): 401–24.

Sovannarith, So, Real Sopheap, Uch Utey, Sy Rathmony, Brett Ballard, and Sarthi Acharya. 2001. "Social Assessment of Land in Cambodia: A Field Study." Prepared for the Ministry of Land Management, Urban Planning, and Construction, Royal Government of Cambodia, Cambodia Development Resource Institute, Phnom Penh.

SPARTECA. 1996. *Rules of Origin Requirements of the South Pacific Trade and Economic Co-operation Agreement.* Suva: South Pacific Regional Trade and Economic Co-operation Agreement, Forum Secretariat.

Spence, A. Michael. 1976. "Product Selection, Fixed Costs, and Monopolistic Competition." *Review of Economic Studies* 43(2):217–35.

Spolaore, Enrico, and Romain Wacziarg. 2005. "Borders and Growth." *Journal of Economic Growth* 10 (4): 331–86.

Squire, Lyn. 1981. *Employment Policy in Developing Countries.* Oxford, U.K.: Oxford University Press.

Sri Lanka National Council for Economic Development, and UNDP. 2005. *Millennium Development Goals Country Report 2005: Sri Lanka.* Colombo: Sri Lanka National Council for Economic Development.

Stewart, Dona J. 1996. "Cities in the Desert: The Egyptian New Town-Program." *Annals of the Association of American Geographers* 86 (3): 459–80.

Stewart, Frances. 2008. "Horizontal Inequalities: A Neglected Dimension of Development." Queen Elizabeth House Working Paper 81, Oxford University, Oxford, U.K.

Stinnett, Douglas M., Jaroslav Tir, Philip Schafer, Paul F. Diehl, and Charles Gochman. 2002. "The Correlates of War Project Direct Contiguity Data, Version 3." *Conflict Management and Peace Science* 19 (2): 58–66.

Stockel, Sigrid. 2002. "Infant Mortality and Concepts of Hygiene: Strategies and Consequences in the Kaiserreich and the Weimar

Republic—The Example of Berlin." *History of the Family* 7 (4): 601–16.

Storper, Michael, and Anthony J. Venables. 2007. "Buzz: Face-to-Face Contact and the Urban Economy." In *Clusters, Networks and Innovation*, ed. Stefano Breschi and Franco Malerba. Oxford, U.K.: Oxford University Press.

Sveikauskas, Leo A. 1975. "The Productivity of Cities." *Quarterly Journal of Economics* 89 (3): 393–413.

Sveikauskas, Leo A., John Gowdy, and Michael Funk. 1988. "Urban Productivity: City Size or Industry Size." *Journal of Regional Science* 28 (2): 185–202.

Sveikauskas, Leo A., Peter M. Townroe, and Eric R. Hansen. 1985. "Intraregional Productivity Difference in Sao Paulo State Manufacturing Plants." *Weltwirtschaftliches Archiv* 121(4):722–40.

Swan, Trevor W. 1956. "Economic Growth and Capital Accumulation." *Economic Record* 32 (2): 334–61.

Swedish Council for Building Research. 1990. *Housing Research and Design in Sweden*. Stockholm: Swedish Council for Building Research.

Tabuchi, Takatoshi. 1988. "Interregional Income Differentials and Migration: Their Interrelationships." *Regional Studies* 22 (1): 1–10.

Taira, Koji. 1969. "Urban Poverty, Ragpickers, and the 'Ants' Villa' in Tokyo." *Economic Development and Cultural Change* 17 (2): 155–77.

Taylor, Alan M. 1996. "International Capital Mobility in History: Purchasing-Power Parity in the Long Run." NBER Working Paper 5742, National Bureau of Economic Research, Cambridge, MA.

Taylor, Alan M., and Jeffrey Williamson. 2006. "Convergence in the Age of Mass Migration." *European Review of Economic History* 1 (1): 27–63.

Thanh, Hoang Xuan, Dang Nguyen Anh, and Cecilia Tacoli. 2005. "Livelihood Diversification and Rural-Urban Linkages in Vietnam's Red River Delta." IFPRI Working Paper 193, International Food Policy Research Institute, Washington, DC.

Tiffen, Mary. 2003. "Transitions in Sub-Saharan Africa: Agriculture, Urbanization, and Income Growth." *World Development* 31 (8): 1343–66.

Tilly, Richard H. 1990. *Vom Zollverein zum Industriestaat: Die wirtschaftlich-soziale Entwicklung Deutschlands 1834 bis 1914*. Munich, Germany: Deutscher Taschenbuch Verlag.

Timmer, Ashley S., and Jeffrey G. Williamson. 1998. "Immigration Policy prior to the 1930s: Labor Markets, Policy Interactions, and Globalization Backlash." *Population and Development Review* 24 (4): 739–71.

Timmins, Christopher. 2005. "Estimable Equilibrium Models of Locational Sorting and Their Role in Development Economics." *Journal of Economic Geography* 5 (1): 83–100.

Tinbergen, J. 1952. *On the Theory of Economic Policy*. Amsterdam: North-Holland.

Tobler, W. R. 1970. "A Computer Movie Simulating Urban Growth in the Detroit Region." *Economic Geography* 46 (Supplement): 234–40.

Todaro, Michael P. 1969. "A Model of Labor Migration and Urban Unemployment in Less Developed Countries." *American Economic Review* 59 (1): 138–48.

Toffler, Alvin. 1980. *The Third Wave*. New York: Bantam Books.

Tol, Richard S. J. 2005. "The Marginal Damage Costs of Carbon Dioxide Emissions: An Assessment of the Uncertainties." *Energy Policy* 33 (16): 2064–74.

Tolofari, Sonny R. 1986. *Open Registry Shipping: A Comparative Study of Costs Freight Rates*. New York: Routledge.

Trackman, B., W. Fisher, and L. Salas. 1999. *The Reform of Property Registration Systems in Costa Rica: A Status Report*. Cambridge, MA: Law School Harvard University.

Tschirley, David L., Jan J. Nijhoff, Pedro Arlindo, Billy Mwinga, Michael T. Weber, and Thomas S. Jayne. 2006. "Anticipating and Responding to Drought Emergencies in Southern Africa: Lessons from the 2002–2003 Experience." International Development Working Paper 89, East Lansing, MI.

Turner, Michael. 1986. "English Open Fields and Enclosures: Retardation or Productivity Improvements." *Journal of Economic History* 46 (3): 669–92.

Uchida, Hirotsugu, and Andrew Nelson. 2008. ""Agglomeration Index: Towards a New Measure of Urban Concentration." Background paper for the WDR 2009.

United Nations. 1949. *Demographic Yearbook 1948*. New York: United Nations.

———. 1952. *Demographic Yearbook 1952*. New York: United Nations.

———. 1969. *Growth of the World's Urban and Rural Population, 1920–2000*. New York: United Nations, Population Division.

———. 1970. "Unitization of Cargo." Paper presented at the United Nations Conference on Trade and Development, Geneva.

———. 1997. *China Human Development Report 1997: Human Development and Poverty Reduction*. New York: United Nations Development Program.

———. 2001. "Istanbul+5: Reviewing and Appraising Progress Five Years after Habitat II in June 2001." United Nations, New York.

———. 2004a. *Assessing Regional Integration in Africa*. Addis Ababa: United Nations Economic Commission for Africa.

———. 2004b. *State of the World's Cities Report 2004/2005*. Nairobi: United Nations.

———. 2005a. *Bringing Down Barriers: Regional Cooperation for Human Development and Human Security*. Bratislava: United Nations Development Programme.

———. 2005b. *China Human Development Report 2005: Development with Equity*. New York: United Nations Development Program.

———. 2006a. *State of the Worlds Cities 2006/7: The Millennium Development Goals and Urban Sustainability: 30 Years of Shaping the Habitat Agenda (UN Habitat)*. Nairobi: UN-Habitat.

———. 2006b. *The 2004 Vietnam Migration Survey: The Quality of Life of Migrants in Vietnam*. Hanoi: United Nations Population Fund.

———. 2006c. "World Urbanization Prospects: The 2005 Revision." United Nations, Department of Economic and Social Affairs, Population Division, New York.

———. 2007. "Trade and Development Report 2007: Regional Cooperation for Development." Paper presented at the United Nations Conference on Trade and Development, New York.

United Nations and African Union. 2006. *Assessing Regional Integration in Africa II: Rationalizing Regional Economic Communities.* Addis Ababa: United Nations Commission for Africa and African Union.

U.S. Bureau of Transport Statistics. 2003. *America on the Go: U.S. Holiday Travel.* Washington, DC: U.S. Department of Transportation, Research, and Innovative Technology Administration.

U.S. Census Bureau. 2002. *Demographic Trends in the 20th Century. Census 2000 Special Reports.* Washington, DC: U.S. Census Bureau.

Uvalic, Milica. 1993. "The Disintegration of Yugoslavia: Its Costs and Benefits." *Post-Communist Economies* 5 (3): 273–93.

Van der Linde, Claas. 2003. "The Demography of Clusters: Findings from the Cluster Meta-Study." In *Innovation Clusters and Interregional Competition*, ed. Johannes Brocker, Dirk Dohse, and Rudiger Soltwedel. Berlin: Springer.

Vance, Colin, and Ralf Hedel. 2006. "On the Link between Urban Form and Automobile Use: Evidence from German Survey Data." Working Paper 0048, Rheinisch-Westfälisches Institut für Wirtschaftsforschung, Essen, Germany.

Vargas-Hidalgo, Rafael. 1979. "The Crisis for the Andean Pact: Lessons for Integration among Developing Countries." *Journal of Common Market Studies* 17 (3): 213–26.

Venables, Anthony J. 2001. "Geography and International Inequalities: the Impact of New Technologies." *Journal of Industry, Competition and Trade* 1 (2): 135–59.

———. 2003. "Winners and Losers from Regional Integration Agreements." *Economic Journal* 113 (490): 747–61.

———. 2006. "Shifts in Economic Geography and Their Causes." *Economic Review* 2006 (Q IV): 61–85.

Venables, Anthony J., and Ravi Kanbur. 2005. *Spatial Inequality and Development, Overview of the UNU-WIDER Project.* New York: Oxford University Press.

Victoria Transport Policy Institute. 2007. *Online TDM Encyclopedia.* Victoria, Canada: Victoria Transport Policy Institute.

Vidler, Cam. 2008. "Turkey: A Case Study of 1D-2D-3D Areas." Background note for the WDR 2009.

Vigdor, Jacob L. 2006. "The New Promised Land: Black-White Convergence in the American South, 1960–2000." NBER Working Paper 12143, National Bureau of Economic Research, Cambridge, MA.

Villarreal, Roberto. 2005. "Regional Development Policies in Mexico." Paper presented at the Sustainable Regional Policy and Planning Roundtable, Beijing, December 14.

Viner, Jacob. 1950. *The Customs Union Issue.* New York: Carnegie Endowment of International Peace.

von Hoffman, A. 1996. "High Ambitions: The Past and Future of American Low-Income Housing Policy." *Housing Policy Debate* 7 (3): 423–46.

Wandschneider, Tiago, and Pravas Mishra. 2003. *Rural Non-Farm Economy and Livelihood Enhancement.* Washington, DC: National Resources Institute.

Ward, Doug. 2006. "Urbanization Is a World Concern." *Vancouver Sun*, June 14.

Warsh, David. 2006. *Knowledge and the Wealth of Nations: A Story of Economic Discovery.* New York: W.W. Norton and Company.

Weber, Adna. 1899. *The Growth of Cities in the Nineteenth Century: A Study in Statistics.* New York: Macmillan.

Whalley, John, and Shunming Zhang. 2007. "A Numerical Simulation Analysis of (Hukou) Labour Mobility Restrictions in China." *Journal of Development Economics* 83 (2): 392–410.

Wheat, Leonard F. 1986. "The Determinants of 1963–77 Regional Manufacturing Growth: Why the South and West Grow." *Journal of Regional Science* 26 (4): 635–59.

Wheeler, David, and Ashoka Mody. 1992. "International Investment Location Decisions: The Case for U.S. Firms." *Journal of International Economics* 33 (1–2): 57–76.

Whittaker, D. Hugh. 1997. *Small Firms in the Japanese Economy.* Cambridge, U.K.: Cambridge University Press.

Wilbur Smith Associates and United Nations. 1980. *Master Plan for Metropolitan Lagos.* New York: United Nations.

Williams, Naomi, and Chris Galley. 1995. "Urban-Rural Differentials in Infant Mortality in Victorian England." *Population Studies* 49 (3): 401–20.

Williamson, Jeffrey. 1965. "Regional Inequality and the Process of National Development: A Description of the Patterns." *Economic Development and Cultural Change* 13 (4): 1–84.

———. 1974. *Late Nineteenth Century American Development: A General Equilibrium History.* New York: Cambridge University Press.

———. 1982. "Was the Industrial Revolution Worth It? Disamenities and Death in 19th-Century British Towns." *Exploration in Economic History* 19 (3): 221–45.

———. 1987. "Did English Factor Markets Fail during the Industrial Revolution?" *Oxford Economic Papers* 39 (4): 641–78.

———. 1990. *Coping with City Growth during the British Industrial Revolution.* Cambridge, U.K.: Cambridge University Press.

Wilson, John S., Xubei Luo, and Harry J. Broadman. 2006. "Trade and Transport Facilitation: European Accession and Capacity Building Priorities." Paper presented at the Transport and International Trade, Report of the 130th Round Table on Transport Economics, Paris.

Wilson, John S., Catherine L. Mann, and Tsunehiro Otsuki. 2004. "Assessing the Potential Benefit of Trade Facilitation: A Global Perspective." Policy Research Working Paper 3224, World Bank, Washington, DC.

Winston, Clifford. 1993. "Economic Deregulation: Days of Reckoning for the Microeconomists." *Journal of Economic Literature* 31 (3): 1263–89.

Winters, L. Alain, and Pedro Martins. 2004. "When Comparative Advantage Is Not Enough: Business Costs in Small Remote Economies." *World Trade Review* 3 (3): 347–83.

Wionczek, Miguel S. 1970. "The Rise and Decline of Latin American Economic Integration." *Journal of Common Market Studies* 9 (1): 49–66.

Wisaweisuan, Nitinant. Forthcoming. "Spatial Disparities in Thailand: Does Government Policy Aggravate or Alleviate the Problem?" In *Reshaping Economic Geography in East Asia*, ed. Yukon Huang and Alessandro Magnoli Bocchi. Washington, DC: World Bank, EAP Companion Volume to the WDR 2009.

Wolf, Martin. 2004. *Why Globalization Works.* New Haven, CT: Yale University Press.

Woods, Robert. 2000. *The Demography of Victorian England and Wales.* Cambridge, U.K.: Cambridge University Press.

Wordie, J. R. 1983. "The Chronology of English Enclosure, 1500–1914." *Economic History Review* 36 (4): 483–505.

World Bank. 1977. *Spatial Development in Mexico.* Report No. 1081-ME. Washington, DC: World Bank.

———. 1980. *The Development of Regional Cities in Thailand.* Report No. 2900-TH. Washington, DC: World Bank.

———. 1998. *Public Expenditure for Poverty Alleviation in North-east Brazil: Promoting Growth and Improving Services.* Washington, DC: World Bank.

———. 2002a. *Cities on the Move: A World Bank Urban Transport Strategy Review.* Washington, DC: World Bank.

———. 2002b. *From Natural Resources to the Knowledge Economy: Trade and Job Quality.* Washington, DC: World Bank, Latin American and Caribbean Region.

———. 2003a. *Trade, Investment, and Development in the Middle East and North Africa: Engaging with the World.* Washington, DC: World Bank.

———. 2003b. *World Bank Policy Research Report 2003: Land Policies for Growth and Poverty Reduction.* New York: Oxford University Press.

———. 2004a. *Global Economic Prospects 2005: Trade, Regionalism, and Development.* Washington, DC: World Bank.

———. 2004b. *World Development Report 2005: A Better Investment Climate for Everyone.* New York: Oxford University Press.

———. 2005a. *Brazil: Regional Economic Development—(Some) Lessons from Experience.* Washington, DC: World Bank.

———. 2005b. *Chile: Zonas Extremas Policies and Beyond—An Assessment of Costs and Impact with Recommendations of Avenues for Policy Reform.* Report No. 27357-CH. Washington, DC: World Bank.

———. 2005c. *Food Safety and Agricultural Health Standards: Challenges and Opportunities for Developing Country Exports.* Washington, DC: World Bank, PREM, and ARD.

———. 2005d. *Global Economic Prospects 2006. Economic Implications of Remittances and Migration.* Washington, DC: World Bank.

———. 2005e. *Growth, Poverty and Inequality: Eastern Europe and the Former Soviet Union.* Washington, DC: World Bank.

———. 2006a. *At Home and Away: Expanding Job Opportunities for Pacific Islanders through Labour Mobility.* Washington, DC: World Bank, East Asia and Pacific Region.

———. 2006b. *Doing Business in 2007: How to Reform.* Washington, DC: World Bank.

———. 2006c. *Governance, Investment Climate, and Harmonious Society: Competitiveness Enhancements for 120 Cities in China.* Washington, DC: World Bank.

———. 2006d. *Housing Finance in Emerging Economies.* Washington, DC: World Bank.

———. 2006e. *Labor Migration in the Greater Mekong Sub-Region, Synthesis Report Phase I.* Washington, DC: World Bank, Regional Office for East Asia and the Pacific.

———. 2006f. *Trends in Average Applied Tariff Rates in Developing and Industrial Countries, 1981–2005.* Washington, DC: World Bank, Development Research Group (digital file).

———. 2006g. *World Development Indicators 2006.* Washington, DC: World Bank.

———. 2006h. *World Development Report 2007: Development and the Next Generation.* Washington, DC: World Bank.

———. 2007a. *Accelerating Growth and Development in the Lagging Regions of India.* Washington, DC: World Bank, ESW Report.

———. 2007b. *Brazil: Inputs for a Strategy for Cities in Brazil.* Report No. 35749-BR. Washington, DC: World Bank.

———. 2007c. *Brazil: Measuring Poverty using Household Consumption.* Report No. 36358-BR. Washington, DC: World Bank, Poverty Reduction and Economic Management Sector Unit, Latin America, and the Caribbean Region.

———. 2007d. *Doing Business in 2008: Making a Difference.* Washington, DC: World Bank.

———. 2007e. *East Asia and Pacific Update: Will Resilience Overcome Risk?* Washington, DC: World Bank.

———. 2007f. *Making Finance Work for Africa.* Washington, DC: World Bank, Africa Region.

———. 2007g. *Making the Most of Scarcity: Accountability for Better Water Management in the Middle East and North Africa.* Washington, DC: World Bank, Middle East and North Africa Region.

———. 2007h. *South Asia: Growth and Regional Integration.* New Delhi: World Bank.

———. 2007i. *World Bank Policy Research Report 2007: At Loggerheads? Agricultural Expansion, Poverty Reduction, and Environment in the Tropical Forests.* Washington, DC: World Bank.

———. 2007j. *World Development Indicators 2007.* Washington, DC: World Bank.

———. 2007k. *World Development Report 2008: Agriculture for Development.* Washington, DC: World Bank.

———. 2008a. "Iran: Spatial Patterns of Poverty and Economic Activity." World Bank, Washington, DC.

———. 2008b. "Shrinking Distance: Identifying Priorities and Assessing Trade-offs for Territorial Development Policies—SDN Flagship Report, Spatial and Local." World Bank, Washington, DC.

———. 2008c. *Transport for Development: The World Bank's Transport Business Strategy for 2008–2012.* Washington, DC: World Bank.

———. 2008d. *Transport Prices and Costs in Africa: A Review of the Main International Corridors.* Washington, DC: World Bank.

———. 2008e. *Turkey: Country Economic Memorandum, Sustaining High Growth—Selected Issues.* Report No. 39194. Washington, DC: World Bank.

Woronoff, Jon. 1972. *West African Wager.* Metuchen, NJ: Scarecrow Press.

Wrigley, E. Anthony. 1985. "Urban Growth and Agricultural Change: England and the Continent in the Early Modern Period." *Journal of Interdisciplinary History* 15 (4): 683–728.

Xenos, Peter. 2004. "Demographic Forces Shaping Youth Populations in Asian Cities." In *Youth Poverty, and Conflict in Southeast Asian Cities*, ed. Lisa Hanley, Blair Ruble, and Joseph Tulchin. Washington, DC: Woodrow Wilson International Center for Scholars.

Yade, Mbaye, Anne Chohin-Kuper, Valerie Kelly, John Staatz, and James Tefft. 1999. "The Role of Regional Trade in Agricultural Transformation." Paper presented at the Workshops on Structural Transformation in Africa, Nairobi.

Yamauchi, Futoshi, Megumi Muto, Reno Dewina, and Sony Sumaryanto. Forthcoming. "Spatial Networks, Incentives, and the Dynamics of Village Economy: Evidence from Indonesia." In *Reshaping Economic Geography in East Asia*, ed. Yukon Huang and Alessandro Magnoli Bocchi. Washington, DC: World Bank, EAP Companion Volume to the WDR 2009.

Yang, Dean. 2008. "International Migration, Remittances and Household Investment: Evidence from Philippine Migrants' Exchange Rate Shocks." *Economic Journal* 118 (528): 591–630.

Yao, Yang. Forthcoming. "The Political Economy of Government Policies Toward Regional Inequality in China." In *Reshaping Economic Geography in East Asia*, ed. Yukon Huang and Alessandro Magnoli Bocchi. Washington, DC: World Bank, EAP Companion Volume to the WDR 2009.

Yasuba, Yasukichi. 1978. "Freight Rates and Productivity in Ocean Transportation for Japan, 1875–1943." *Explorations in Economic History* 15 (1): 11–39.

Yemtsov, Ruslan. 2005. "Quo Vadis? Inequality and Poverty Dynamics across Russian Regions." In *Spatial Inequality and Development*, ed. Ravi Kanbur and Anthony J. Venables. Oxford, U.K.: Oxford University Press.

Yepes, Tito. 2008. "Inclusive Growth for Latin America." World Bank, Washington, DC.

Yepes, Tito, and Somik V. Lall. 2008. "Evaluating the Impact of Upgrading Informal Settlements on Land Markets: Evidence from Bogota." World Bank, Washington, DC.

Yoshino, Yutaka. 2008. "Domestic Constraints, Firm Characteristics, and Geographical Diversification of Firm-Level Manufacturing Exports in Africa." Policy Research Working Paper 4575, World Bank, Washington, DC.

Young, Allyn. 1928. "Increasing Returns and Economic Progress." *Economic Journal* 38 (152): 527–42.

Yuen, Belinda. 2004. "Planning Singapore Growth for Better Living." In *Enhancing Urban Management in East Asia*, ed. Belinda Yuen and Mila Freire. Hampshire, U.K.: Ashgate Publishing.

Yusuf, Shahid, and Kaoru Nabeshima. 2006. *Post-industrial East Asian Cities, Innovation for Growth*. Palo Alto, CA, and Washington, DC: World Bank and Stanford University Press.

Zhu, Nong, and Xubei Luo. 2008. "Impact of Remittances on Rural Poverty and Inequality in China." World Bank, East Asia and Pacific Regional Office, Washington, DC.

Selected Indicators

Table A1 Geography and access

Economy	Location	Surface area (km²)	Arable land (% of land area)	Forest land (% of land area)	Coastline (kms)	Land boundaries (kms)	Airports with paved runway (number)	Ports and terminals (number)	Rail density (rail km per 100 km²)	Road density (road km per 100 km²)	National average distance to capital city (kms)
	2007	2007	2007	2007	2007	2007	2007	2007	2000–06 [a]	2000–06 [a]	2000
Afghanistan	33 00 N, 65 00 E	652,090	12.1	1.3	0	5,529	11	0	..	5.3	418
Albania	41 00 N, 20 00 E	28,750	21.1	29.0	362	720	3	4	1.6	65.7	84
Algeria	28 00 N, 3 00 E	2,381,740	3.2	1.0	998	6,343	52	9	0.2	4.5	1,108
American Samoa	14 20 S, 170 00 W	200	10.0	90.0	116	0	2	1	..	..	7
Andorra	42 30 N, 1 30 E	470	2.1	34.2	0	120	0	0	..	..	10
Angola	12 30 S, 18 30 E	1,246,700	2.6	47.4	1,600	5,198	31	3	0.2	4.1	711
Antigua and Barbuda	17 03 N, 61 48 W	440	18.2	20.5	153	0	2	1	..	264.8	30
Argentina	34 00 S, 64 00 W	2,780,400	10.2	12.1	4,989	9,861	154	8	1.2	14.6	971
Armenia	40 00 N, 45 00 E	29,800	17.6	10.0	0	1,254	11	0	3.0	27.1	87
Aruba	12 30 N, 69 58 W	180	10.5	..	69	0	1	3	..	..	8
Australia	27 00 S, 133 00 E	7,741,220	6.4	21.3	25,760	0	311	11	0.5	10.5	1,946
Austria	47 20 N, 13 20 E	83,870	16.8	46.8	0	2,562	25	0	7.7	162.4	204
Azerbaijan	40 30 N, 47 30 E	86,600	22.3	11.3	0	2,013	27	0	2.6	71.5	219
Bahamas, The	24 15 N, 76 00 W	13,880	0.8	51.4	3,542	0	29	3	..	..	230
Bahrain	26 00 N, 50 33 E	710	2.8	0.0	161	0	3	2	..	492.7	25
Bangladesh	24 00 N, 90 00 E	144,000	61.1	6.7	580	4,246	15	2	2.1	183.8	165
Barbados	13 10 N, 59 32 W	430	37.2	4.7	97	0	1	1	..	372.1	14
Belarus	53 00 N, 28 00 E	207,600	26.3	38.0	0	2,900	41	0	2.7	45.0	185
Belgium	50 50 N, 4 00 E	30,530	27.9	22.1	67	1,385	25	6	11.7	498.1	78
Belize	17 15 N, 88 45 W	22,970	3.1	72.5	386	516	5	2	..	..	74
Benin	9 30 N, 2 15 E	112,620	24.0	21.3	121	1,989	1	1	0.7	17.2	398
Bermuda	32 20 N, 64 45 W	50	20.0	20.0	103	0	1	2	..	..	7
Bhutan	27 30 N, 90 30 E	47,000	3.4	68.0	0	1,075	16	0	..	17.1	99
Bolivia	17 00 S, 65 00 W	1,098,580	2.8	54.2	0	6,940	16	0	0.3	5.8	521
Bosnia and Herzegovina	44 00 N, 18 00 E	51,210	19.5	42.7	20	1,459	8	1	1.2	..	103
Botswana	22 00 S, 24 00 E	581,730	0.7	21.1	0	4,013	10	0	0.2	4.3	441
Brazil	10 00 S, 55 00 W	8,514,880	7.0	56.5	7,491	16,885	714	9	0.3	20.7	1,378
Brunei Darussalam	4 30 N, 114 40 E	5,770	2.7	52.8	161	381	1	3	..	..	61
Bulgaria	43 00 N, 25 00 E	111,000	29.2	33.4	354	1,808	132	2	4.0	40.5	190
Burkina Faso	13 00 N, 2 00 W	274,000	17.7	24.8	0	3,193	2	0	0.2	5.6	220
Burundi	3 30 S, 30 00 E	27,830	38.6	5.9	0	974	1	0	..	48.0	84
Cambodia	13 00 N, 105 00 E	181,040	21.0	59.2	443	2,752	6	2	0.3	21.7	206
Cameroon	6 00 N, 12 00 E	475,440	12.8	45.6	402	4,591	11	2	0.2	10.7	363
Canada	60 00 N, 95 00 W	9,984,670	5.0	34.1	202,080	8,893	509	8	0.5	15.5	2,449
Cape Verde	16 00 N, 24 00 W	4,030	11.4	20.8	965	0	7	3	..	33.5	156
Cayman Islands	19 30 N, 80 30 W	260	3.8	46.2	160	0	2	2	..	..	15
Central African Republic	7 00 N, 21 00 E	623,000	3.1	36.5	0	5,203	3	0	..	..	450
Chad	15 00 N, 19 00 E	1,284,000	2.9	9.5	0	5,968	7	0	..	..	671
Channel Islands		190	0.0	..	..	..	..	..	..	..	..
Chile	30 00 S, 71 00 W	756,630	2.6	21.5	6,435	6,339	73	8	0.9	10.6	1,149
China	35 00 N, 105 00 E	9,598,088	11.1	21.2	14,500	22,117	403	7	0.8	20.7	1,668
Colombia	4 00 N, 72 00 W	1,141,750	1.8	54.7	3,208	6,309	101	7	0.3	..	456
Comoros	12 10 S, 44 15 E	1,861	35.9	2.2	340	0	4	2	..	..	59
Congo, Dem. Rep.	0 00 N, 25 00 E	2,344,860	3.0	58.9	37	10,730	25	11	0.2	6.8	1,006
Congo, Rep.	1 00 S, 15 00 E	342,000	1.4	65.8	169	5,504	4	6	0.3	5.1	479
Costa Rica	10 00 N, 84 00 W	51,100	4.4	46.8	1,290	639	32	2	0.5	69.2	105
Côte d'Ivoire	8 00 N, 5 00 W	322,460	10.4	32.7	515	3,110	7	4	0.2	25.2	236
Croatia	45 10 N, 15 30 E	56,540	19.8	38.2	1,777	2,197	23	5	4.9	50.9	144
Cuba	21 30 N, 80 00 W	110,860	27.9	24.7	3,735	29	78	3	3.8	..	398
Cyprus	35 00 N, 33 00 E	9,250	10.8	18.8	648	0	13	3	..	130.5	48
Czech Republic	49 45 N, 15 30 E	78,870	39.4	34.3	0	2,290	46	0	12.4	165.2	134
Denmark	56 00 N, 10 00 E	43,090	52.7	11.8	7,314	68	28	12	6.2	169.3	195
Djibouti	11 30 N, 43 00 E	23,200	0.0	0.3	314	516	3	1	0.4	..	85
Dominica	15 25 N, 61 20 W	750	6.7	61.3	148	0	2	2	..	..	20
Dominican Republic	19 00 N, 70 40 W	48,730	22.7	28.4	1,288	360	14	4	1.1	..	119
Ecuador	2 00 S, 77 30 W	283,560	4.9	39.2	2,237	2,010	98	5	0.3	15.6	266
Egypt, Arab Rep.	27 00 N, 30 00 E	1,001,450	3.0	0.1	2,450	2,665	72	3	0.5	9.3	558
El Salvador	13 50 N, 88 55 W	21,040	31.9	14.4	307	545	4	2	2.7	..	68
Equatorial Guinea	2 00 N, 10 00 E	28,050	4.6	58.2	296	539	3	1	..	..	301
Eritrea	15 00 N, 39 00 E	117,600	5.6	15.4	1,151	1,626	4	2	0.3	..	184
Estonia	59 00 N, 26 00 E	45,230	13.9	53.9	3,794	633	12	5	2.3	134.1	128
Ethiopia	8 00 N, 38 00 E	1,104,300	11.1	13.0	0	5,328	14	0	0.1	3.6	425
Faeroe Islands	62 00 N, 7 00 W	1,400	2.1	..	1,117	0	1	1	..	..	25
Fiji	18 00 S, 175 00 E	18,270	10.9	54.7	1,129	0	3	3	3.3	..	113
Finland	64 00 N, 26 00 E	338,150	7.3	73.9	1,250	2,681	76	10	1.9	25.7	417
France	46 00 N, 2 00 E	551,500	33.6	28.3	3,427	2,889	292	10	5.3	172.9	365
French Polynesia	15 00 S, 140 00 W	4,000	0.8	28.7	2,525	0	39	1	..	..	472
Gabon	1 00 S, 11 45 E	267,670	1.3	84.5	885	2,551	11	5	0.3	3.6	317
Gambia, The	13 28 N, 16 34 W	11,300	31.5	47.1	80	740	1	1	..	37.4	123
Georgia	42 00 N, 43 30 E	69,700	11.5	39.7	310	1,461	19	2	2.3	29.1	156
Germany	51 00 N, 9 00 E	357,050	34.1	31.8	2,389	3,621	332	10	13.8	..	334
Ghana	8 00 N, 2 00 W	238,540	18.4	24.2	539	2,094	7	2	0.4	21.0	344
Greece	39 00 N, 22 00 E	131,960	20.4	29.1	13,676	1,228	66	6	2.0	89.2	249
Greenland	72 00 N, 40 00 W	410,450	0.0	..	44,087	0	9	1	..	..	1,031
Grenada	12 07 N, 61 40 W	340	5.9	11.8	121	0	3	1	..	..	11
Guam	13 28 N, 144 47 E	540	3.6	47.3	126	0	4	1	..	..	14
Guatemala	15 30 N, 90 15 W	108,890	13.3	36.3	400	1,687	11	2	0.8	..	175
Guinea	11 00 N, 10 00 W	245,860	4.5	27.4	320	3,399	5	1	0.3	18.0	348
Guinea-Bissau	12 00 N, 15 00 W	36,120	10.7	73.7	350	724	3	4	..	12.3	97
Guyana	5 00 N, 59 00 W	214,970	2.4	76.7	459	2,949	9	1	..	..	314

Economy	Location	Surface area (km²)	Arable land (% of land area)	Forest land (% of land area)	Coastline (kms)	Land boundaries (kms)	Airports with paved runway (number)	Ports and terminals (number)	Rail density (rail km per 100 km²)	Road density (road km per 100 km²)	National average distance to capital city (kms)
		2007	2007	2007	2007	2007	2007	2007	2000–06 [a]	2000–06 [a]	2000
Haiti	19 00 N, 72 25 W	27,750	28.3	3.8	1,771	360	4	1	..	..	99
Honduras	15 00 N, 86 30 W	112,090	9.5	41.5	820	1,520	11	4	0.6	..	167
Hong Kong, China	22 15 N, 114 10 E	1,092	0.0		733	30	3	1	..	186.5	..
Hungary	47 00 N, 20 00 E	93,030	51.3	22.1	0	2,271	20	0	9.0	178.0	137
Iceland	65 00 N, 18 00 W	103,000	0.1	0.5	4,970	0	5	5	..	12.9	235
India	20 00 N, 77 00 E	3,287,260	53.7	22.8	7,000	14,103	243	8	2.1	113.8	992
Indonesia	5 00 S, 120 00 E	1,904,570	12.7	48.8	54,716	2,830	159	9	0.4	20.3	1,519
Iran, Islamic Rep.	32 00 N, 53 00 E	1,745,150	9.8	6.8	2,440	5,440	129	2	0.5	11.0	654
Iraq	33 00 N, 44 00 E	438,320	13.1	1.9	58	3,650	77	3	0.5	..	281
Ireland	53 00 N, 8 00 W	70,270	17.6	9.7	1,448	360	15	5	4.7	140.2	165
Isle of Man	54 15 N, 4 30 W	570	0.0	5.2	160	0	1	3	11.4	..	13
Israel	31 30 N, 34 45 E	22,070	14.6	7.9	273	1,017	30	4	3.9	80.6	110
Italy	42 50 N, 12 50 E	301,340	26.3	33.9	7,600	1,932	98	8	6.6	164.8	353
Jamaica	18 15 N, 77 30 W	10,990	16.1	31.3	1,022	0	11	5	..	193.9	67
Japan	36 00 N, 138 00 E	377,910	12.0	68.2	29,751	0	145	10	6.4	323.0	531
Jordan	31 00 N, 36 00 E	88,780	2.1	0.9	26	1,635	15	1	0.6	8.5	171
Kazakhstan	48 00 N, 68 00 E	2,724,900	8.3	1.2	0	12,012	67	0	0.5	3.3	823
Kenya	1 00 N, 38 00 E	580,370	8.2	6.2	536	3,477	15	1	0.5	11.1	372
Kiribati	1 25 N, 173 00 E	810	2.7	2.7	1,143	0	3	1	..	..	25
Korea, Dem. Rep.	40 00 N, 127 00 E	120,540	23.3	51.4	2,495	238	36	12	4.3	..	211
Korea, Rep.	37 00 N, 127 30 E	99,260	16.6	63.5	2,416	462	69	5	3.5	101.6	187
Kuwait	29 30 N, 45 45 E	17,820	0.8	0.3	499	462	4	6	..	32.3	67
Kyrgyz Republic	41 00 N, 75 00 E	199,900	6.7	4.5	0	3,878	18	0	0.2	9.8	255
Lao PDR	18 00 N, 105 00 E	236,800	4.3	69.9	0	5,083	9	0	..	13.5	311
Latvia	57 00 N, 25 00 E	64,590	17.5	47.2	531	1,368	24	2	3.7	111.6	140
Lebanon	33 50 N, 35 50 E	10,400	16.6	13.3	225	454	5	4	3.9	..	60
Lesotho	29 30 S, 28 30 E	30,350	10.9	0.3	0	909	3	0	..	..	98
Liberia	6 30 N, 9 30 W	111,370	4.0	32.7	579	1,585	2	2	0.5	..	196
Libya	25 00 N, 17 00 E	1,759,540	1.0	0.1	1,770	4,348	60	6	..	..	910
Liechtenstein	47 16 N, 9 32 E	160	25.0	43.8	0	76	0	0	5.6	..	6
Lithuania	56 00 N, 24 00 E	65,300	30.4	33.5	90	1,613	34	1	2.8	126.6	143
Luxembourg	49 45 N, 6 10 E	2,590	23.2	33.6	0	359	1	0	10.6	201.8	25
Macao, China	22 10 N, 113 33 E	28	0.0	..	41	0	1	1	..	1284.0	..
Macedonia, FYR	41 50 N, 22 00 E	25,710	22.3	35.6	0	766	10	0	2.7	..	76
Madagascar	20 00 S, 47 00 E	587,040	5.1	22.1	4,828	0	29	4	0.1	..	385
Malawi	13 30 S, 34 00 E	118,480	26.0	36.2	0	2,881	6	0	0.8	16.4	230
Malaysia	2 30 N, 112 30 E	329,740	5.5	63.6	4,675	2,669	37	9	0.6	30.0	873
Maldives	3 15 N, 73 00 E	300	13.3	3.3	644	0	2	1	..	..	276
Mali	17 00 N, 4 00 W	1,240,190	3.9	10.3	0	7,243	9	0	0.1	1.5	804
Malta	35 50 N, 14 35 E	320	28.1	..	197	0	1	1	..	704.4	9
Marshall Islands	9 00 N, 168 00 E	180	11.1	..	370	0	4	1	..	..	..
Mauritania	20 00 N, 12 00 W	1,030,700	0.5	0.3	754	5,074	8	2	0.1	..	686
Mauritius	20 17 S, 57 33 E	2,040	49.3	18.2	177	0	2	1	..	99.3	51
Mayotte	12 50 S, 45 10 E	374	0.0	13.4	185	0	1	1	..	..	13
Mexico	23 00 N, 102 00 W	1,964,380	13.0	33.7	9,330	4,353	228	7	0.9	17.7	886
Micronesia, Fed. Sts.	6 55 N, 158 15 E	700	5.7	90.0	6,112	0	6	1	..	..	134
Moldova	47 00 N, 29 00 E	33,840	56.2	10.0	0	1,389	6	0	3.5	38.7	87
Monaco	43 44 N, 7 24 E	2	0.0	0.0	4	4	0	1	..	..	..
Mongolia	46 00 N, 105 00 E	1,566,500	0.8	6.5	0	8,220	12	0	0.1	3.1	617
Montenegro	42 30 N, 19 18 E	14,026	0.0	..	294	625	3	1	1.8	..	..
Morocco	32 00 N, 5 00 W	446,550	19.0	9.8	1,835	2,018	26	6	0.4	12.9	369
Mozambique	18 15 S, 35 00 E	799,380	5.5	24.6	2,470	4,571	22	3	0.4	..	1,112
Myanmar	22 00 N, 98 00 E	676,580	15.3	49.0	1,930	5,876	21	3	0.6	5.1	619
Namibia	22 00 S, 17 00 E	824,290	1.0	9.3	1,572	3,936	21	2	0.3	5.1	407
Nepal	28 00 N, 84 00 E	147,180	16.5	25.4	0	2,926	10	0	0.0	12.2	236
Netherlands	52 30 N, 5 45 E	41,530	26.8	10.8	451	1,027	20	7	8.3	372.2	95
Netherlands Antilles	12 15 N, 68 45 W	800	10.0	1.3	364	0	5	4	..	..	36
New Caledonia	21 30 S, 165 30 E	18,580	0.3	39.2	2,254	0	11	1	..	..	157
New Zealand	41 00 S, 174 00 E	267,710	5.6	31.0	15,134	0	45	5	1.5	34.7	418
Nicaragua	13 00 N, 85 00 W	130,000	15.9	42.7	910	1,231	11	3	0.0	15.4	192
Niger	16 00 N, 8 00 E	1,267,000	11.4	1.0	0	5,697	9	0	..	1.1	896
Nigeria	10 00 N, 8 00 E	923,770	33.5	12.2	853	4,047	36	3	0.4	21.2	380
Northern Mariana Islands		460	0.0	69.2	..	..	..	..	..	..	16
Norway	62 00 N, 10 00 E	323,800	2.8	30.8	2,650	2,542	67	8	1.4	30.2	507
Oman	21 00 N, 57 00 E	309,500	0.1	0.0	2,092	1,374	6	2	..	11.3	462
Pakistan	30 00 N, 70 00 E	796,100	27.6	2.5	1,046	6,774	91	2	1.1	33.5	661
Palau	7 30 N, 134 30 E	460	8.7	87.0	1,519	0	1	1	..	..	11
Panama	9 00 N, 80 00 W	75,520	7.4	57.7	2,490	555	53	3	0.5	15.6	179
Papua New Guinea	6 00 S, 147 00 E	462,840	0.5	65.0	5,152	820	21	3	..	..	536
Paraguay	23 00 S, 58 00 W	406,750	7.7	46.5	0	3,995	12	0	0.0	..	363
Peru	10 00 S, 76 00 W	1,285,220	2.9	53.7	2,414	7,461	54	2	0.2	6.2	690
Philippines	13 00 N, 122 00 E	300,000	19.1	24.0	36,289	0	83	6	0.3	67.1	555
Poland	52 00 N, 20 00 E	312,690	39.6	30.0	491	3,056	83	4	7.5	138.5	237
Portugal	39 30 N, 8 00 W	92,120	16.8	41.3	1,793	1,214	43	4	3.0	85.8	237
Puerto Rico	18 15 N, 66 30 W	8,950	8.0	46.0	501	0	17	3	1.1	289.1	60
Qatar	25 30 N, 51 15 E	11,000	1.6	0.0	563	60	3	1	..	..	55
Romania	46 00 N, 25 00 E	238,390	40.4	27.7	225	2,508	25	4	5.0	86.4	246
Russian Federation	60 00 N, 100 00 E	17,098,240	7.4	49.4	37,653	20,097	616	10	0.5	3.3	4,322
Rwanda	2 00 S, 30 00 E	26,340	48.6	19.5	0	893	4	0	..	56.8	65
Samoa	13 35 S, 172 20 W	2,840	21.2	60.4	403	0	3	1	..	82.6	51

Table A1   Geography and access—continued

Economy	Location	Surface area (km²)	Arable land (% of land area)	Forest land (% of land area)	Coastline (kms)	Land boundaries (kms)	Airports with paved runway (number)	Ports and terminals (number)	Rail density (rail km per 100 km²)	Road density (road km per 100 km²)	National average distance to capital city (kms)
	2007	2007	2007	2007	2007	2007	2007	2007	2000–06 ª	2000–06 ª	2000
San Marino	43 46 N, 12 25 E	60	16.7	..	0	39	0	0	..	..	3
Sao Tome and Princip	1 00 N, 7 00 E	960	8.3	28.1	209	0	2	1	..	..	45
Saudi Arabia	25 00 N, 45 00 E	2,000,000	1.8	1.4	2,640	4,431	73	4	0.1	7.6	593
Senegal	14 00 N, 14 00 W	196,720	12.8	45.0	531	2,640	9	1	0.5	7.1	328
Serbia		88,361	0.0	..	..	..	..	..	4.3	..	..
Seychelles	4 35 S, 55 40 E	460	2.2	87.0	491	0	8	1	..	99.6	413
Sierra Leone	8 30 N, 11 30 W	71,740	8.0	38.5	402	958	1	3	..	15.8	170
Singapore	1 22 N, 103 48 E	699	0.9	2.9	193	0	9	1	..	462.7	11
Slovak Republic	48 40 N, 19 30 E	49,030	28.9	40.1	0	1,524	18	0	7.6	89.4	199
Slovenia	46 07 N, 14 49 E	20,270	8.7	62.8	47	1,382	6	1	6.1	190.9	65
Solomon Islands	8 00 S, 159 00 E	28,900	0.6	77.6	5,313	0	2	5	..	0.0	214
Somalia	10 00 N, 49 00 E	637,660	1.7	11.4	3,025	2,340	7	5	..	..	623
South Africa	29 00 S, 24 00 E	1,219,090	12.1	7.6	2,798	4,862	146	6	1.7	30.0	608
Spain	40 00 N, 4 00 W	505,370	27.4	35.9	4,964	1,918	96	8	3.0	133.5	306
Sri Lanka	7 00 N, 81 00 E	65,610	14.2	29.9	1,340	0	14	2	2.2	150.5	157
St. Kitts and Nevis	17 20 N, 62 45 W	260	19.4	13.9	135	0	2	2	13.9	..	8
St. Lucia	13 53 N, 60 58 W	620	6.6	27.9	158	0	2	3	..	..	15
St. Vincent and the Grenadines	13 15 N, 61 12 W	390	17.9	28.2	84	0	5	1	..	212.6	11
Sudan	15 00 N, 30 00 E	2,505,810	7.2	28.4	853	7,687	15	1	0.3	0.0	699
Suriname	4 00 N, 56 00 W	163,270	0.4	94.7	386	1,703	5	1	..	2.8	248
Swaziland	26 30 S, 31 30 E	17,360	10.3	31.5	0	535	1	0	1.8	20.9	64
Sweden	62 00 N, 15 00 E	450,290	6.6	67.1	3,218	2,233	155	9	2.8	103.6	439
Switzerland	47 00 N, 8 00 E	41,280	10.3	30.5	0	1,852	42	0	12.1	178.0	99
Syrian Arab Republic	35 00 N, 38 00 E	185,180	26.5	2.5	193	2,253	26	2	1.5	51.6	289
Taiwan, China	23 30 N, 121 00 E	35,980	0.0	..	1,566	0	38	5	7.8	115.6	168
Tajikistan	39 00 N, 71 00 E	142,550	6.6	2.9	0	3,651	17	0	0.3	19.8	240
Tanzania	6 00 S, 35 00 E	947,300	4.5	39.9	1,424	3,861	11	3	0.4	8.9	395
Thailand	15 00 N, 100 00 E	513,120	27.7	28.4	3,219	4,863	66	4	0.8	11.2	428
Timor-Leste	8 50 S, 125 55 E	14,870	8.2	53.7	706	228	3	1	..	..	..
Togo	8 00 N, 1 10 E	56,790	46.1	7.1	56	1,647	2	2	1.0	..	300
Tonga	20 00 S, 175 00 W	750	20.8	5.6	419	0	1	1	..	..	108
Trinidad and Tobago	11 00 N, 61 00 W	5,130	14.6	44.1	362	0	3	3	..	..	48
Tunisia	34 00 N, 9 00 E	163,610	18.0	6.8	1,148	1,424	14	4	1.4	12.4	335
Turkey	39 00 N, 35 00 E	783,560	31.0	13.2	7,200	2,648	89	8	1.1	55.5	442
Turkmenistan	40 00 N, 60 00 E	488,100	4.7	8.8	0	3,736	22	0	0.5	..	344
Uganda	1 00 N, 32 00 E	241,040	26.4	18.4	0	2,698	5	0	0.6	35.9	223
Ukraine	49 00 N, 32 00 E	603,550	56.0	16.5	2,782	4,663	193	8	3.9	29.2	373
United Arab Emirates	24 00 N, 54 00 E	83,600	0.8	3.7	1,318	867	23	7	..	..	141
United Kingdom	54 00 N, 2 00 W	243,610	23.7	11.8	12,429	360	334	8	6.8	160.2	361
United States	38 00 N, 97 00 W	9,632,030	19.0	33.1	19,924	12,034	5119	12	2.5	70.2	2,595
Uruguay	33 00 S, 56 00 W	176,220	7.8	8.6	660	1,648	8	5	1.2	34.3	275
Uzbekistan	41 00 N, 64 00 E	447,400	11.0	7.7	0	6,221	34	0	0.9	..	564
Vanuatu	16 00 S, 167 00 E	12,190	1.6	36.1	2,528	0	3	3	..	..	250
Venezuela, RB	8 00 N, 66 00 W	912,050	2.9	54.1	2,800	4,993	129	5	0.1	..	549
Vietnam	16 00 N, 106 00 E	329,310	21.3	41.7	3,444	4,639	26	2	0.8	71.7	646
Virgin Islands (U.S.)	18 20 N, 64 50 W	350	5.7	28.6	188	0	2	2	..	..	10
West Bank and Gaza	32 00 N, 35 15 E	6,020	17.8	1.5	0	404	3	0	..	83.0	..
Yemen, Rep.	15 00 N, 48 00 E	527,970	2.9	1.0	1,906	1,746	16	2	..	..	406
Zambia	15 00 S, 30 00 E	752,610	7.1	57.1	0	5,664	10	0	0.3	12.3	436
Zimbabwe	20 00 S, 30 00 E	390,760	8.3	45.3	0	3,066	17	0	0.8	25.1	285

a. Data are for the latest year available in the period shown.

Table A2 Urbanization

Economy	Urbanization				Population density			Rural-urban disparities			
	Agglomeration index, 0 (low) to 100 (high)	Urban population (% of total pop.)	Urban population (% of total pop.)	Urban population (% of total pop.)	Population density (number of people per km²)	Pop. in cities > 1 million (% of total pop.)	Pop. in largest city (% of urban pop.)	% of urban population with water access	% of rural population with water access	% of urban population with sanitation services	% of rural population with sanitation services
	2000	2000	2005	2015	2006	2005	2005	2004	2004	2004	2004
Afghanistan	25.0	21.3	22.9	27.1	..	..	..	63	31	49	29
Albania	52.7	41.8	45.4	52.8	115	..	..	99	94	99	84
Algeria	58.7	59.8	63.3	69.3	14	9.7	15.4	88	80	99	82
American Samoa	..	88.8	91.3	94.1	292	..	..	..	..	..	..
Andorra	..	92.4	90.6	87.8	141	..	..	100	100	100	100
Angola	26.8	50.0	53.3	59.7	13	17.2	32.2	75	40	56	16
Antigua and Barbuda	..	37.3	39.1	44.7	189	..	..	95	89	98	94
Argentina	72.1	89.2	90.1	91.6	14	39.1	35.9	98	80	92	83
Armenia	69.6	65.1	64.1	64.1	107	36.5	57.0	99	80	96	61
Aruba	..	46.7	46.6	47.6	557	..	..	100	100	..	..
Australia	75.9	87.2	88.2	89.9	3	60.4	24.1	100	100	100	100
Austria	67.9	65.8	66.0	67.7	100	27.4	41.6	100	100	100	100
Azerbaijan	48.7	50.9	51.5	52.8	102	22.1	42.9	95	59	73	36
Bahamas, The	57.8	88.8	90.4	92.2	32	..	..	98	86	100	100
Bahrain	94.9	94.6	96.5	98.2	1021	..	..	100	..	100	..
Bangladesh	48.0	23.2	25.1	29.9	1178	11.8	32.3	82	72	51	35
Barbados	91.3	49.9	52.7	58.8	679	..	..	100	100	99	100
Belarus	60.6	70.0	72.3	76.7	47	18.2	25.2	100	100	93	61
Belgium	89.8	97.1	97.2	97.5	347	9.7	9.9	100	..	..	..
Belize	1.8	47.7	48.3	51.2	13	..	..	100	82	71	25
Benin	37.5	38.4	40.1	44.6	77	..	..	78	57	59	11
Bermuda	..	100.0	100.0	100.0	1271	..	..	..	..	..	..
Bhutan	3.8	9.6	11.1	14.8	14	..	..	86	60	65	70
Bolivia	55.7	61.8	64.2	68.8	8	31.0	25.9	95	68	60	22
Bosnia and Herzegovina	37.7	43.2	45.8	51.8	76	..	..	99	96	99	92
Botswana	27.9	53.3	57.4	64.6	3	..	..	100	90	57	25
Brazil	63.6	81.2	84.2	88.2	22	36.9	11.7	96	57	83	37
Brunei Darussalam	63.8	71.2	73.5	77.6	71	..	..	..	..	..	..
Bulgaria	64.9	68.9	70.0	72.8	71	14.1	20.2	100	97	100	96
Burkina Faso	12.8	16.6	18.3	22.8	51	..	36.3	94	54	42	6
Burundi	31.7	8.6	10.0	13.5	306	..	..	92	77	47	35
Cambodia	23.8	16.9	19.7	26.1	79	9.8	49.6	64	35	53	8
Cameroon	40.2	50.0	54.6	62.7	38	18.2	18.1	86	44	58	43
Canada	70.5	79.4	80.1	81.4	4	44.5	20.5	100	99	100	99
Cape Verde	44.4	53.4	57.3	64.3	126	..	..	86	73	61	19
Cayman Islands	..	100.0	100.0	100.0	173	..	..	..	..	..	..
Central African Republic	19.7	37.6	38.1	40.4	7	..	..	93	61	47	12
Chad	12.1	23.4	25.3	30.5	8	..	34.6	41	43	24	4
Channel Islands	..	30.5	30.5	31.5	782	..	..	..	..	..	..
Chile	74.8	86.0	87.6	90.1	22	34.9	39.8	100	58	95	62
China	37.2	35.8	40.4	49.2	140	17.7	2.8	93	67	69	28
Colombia	62.1	71.2	72.7	75.7	41	36.0	23.7	99	71	96	54
Comoros	..	33.8	37.0	44.0	323	..	..	92	82	41	29
Congo, Dem. Rep.	25.6	29.8	32.1	38.6	26	16.2	32.1	82	29	42	25
Congo, Rep.	54.2	58.3	60.2	64.2	11	32.5	54.0	84	27	28	25
Costa Rica	54.0	59.0	61.7	66.9	85	28.1	45.6	100	92	89	97
Côte d'Ivoire	35.1	43.1	45.0	49.8	58	19.2	42.8	97	74	46	29
Croatia	37.3	55.6	56.5	59.5	79	..	..	100	100	100	100
Cuba	64.2	75.6	75.5	74.7	103	19.4	25.7	95	78	99	95
Cyprus	62.1	68.7	69.3	71.5	82	..	..	100	100	100	100
Czech Republic	73.8	74.0	73.5	74.1	132	11.4	15.6	100	100	99	97
Denmark	48.8	85.1	85.6	86.9	128	20.1	23.5	100	100	..	..
Djibouti	40.6	83.4	86.1	89.6	35	..	..	76	59	88	50
Dominica	..	71.1	72.9	76.4	96	..	..	100	90	86	75
Dominican Republic	71.7	62.4	66.8	73.6	196	21.4	32.0	97	91	81	73
Ecuador	49.2	60.3	62.8	67.6	47	29.9	29.1	97	89	94	82
Egypt, Arab Rep.	90.4	42.5	42.8	45.4	73	20.5	35.7	99	97	86	58
El Salvador	73.7	58.4	59.8	63.2	322	22.7	38.0	94	70	77	39
Equatorial Guinea	21.4	38.8	38.9	41.1	17	..	..	45	42	60	46
Eritrea	21.4	17.8	19.4	24.4	45	..	..	74	57	32	3
Estonia	45.3	69.4	69.1	70.1	32	..	..	100	99	97	96
Ethiopia	11.9	14.9	16.0	19.1	75	3.8	24.1	81	11	44	7
Faeroe Islands	..	36.3	38.8	41.5	35	..	..	..	..	..	..
Fiji	17.7	48.3	50.8	56.1	45	..	..	43	51	87	55
Finland	52.4	61.1	61.1	62.7	17	20.8	34.0	100	100	100	100
France	72.5	75.8	76.7	79.0	111	22.4	21.0	100	100	..	..
French Polynesia	45.8	52.4	51.7	52.3	70	..	..	100	100	99	97
Gabon	35.9	80.2	83.6	87.7	5	..	..	95	47	37	30
Gambia, The	44.0	49.1	53.9	61.8	162	..	..	95	77	72	46
Georgia	50.2	52.7	52.2	53.8	64	23.4	44.8	96	67	96	91
Germany	79.6	75.1	75.2	76.3	236	7.7	5.5	100	100	100	100
Ghana	34.1	44.0	47.8	55.1	99	15.5	18.4	88	64	27	11
Greece	57.5	58.8	59.0	61.0	86	29.1	49.3	..	..	..	..
Greenland	..	81.6	82.9	85.5	0	..	..	..	..	..	..
Grenada	..	31.0	30.6	32.2	313	..	..	97	93	96	97

Table A2   Urbanization—continued

	Urbanization			Population density			Rural-urban disparities			
	Agglomeration index, 0 (low) to 100 (high)	Urban population (% of total pop.)	Urban population (% of total pop.)	Urban population (% of total pop.)	Population density (number of people per km²)	Pop. in cities > 1 million (% of total pop.)	Pop. in largest city (% of urban pop.)	% of urban population with water access	% of rural population with water access	% of urban population with sanitation services	% of rural population with sanitation services
Economy	2000	2000	2005	2015	2006	2005	2005	2004	2004	2004	2004
Guam	2.4	93.2	94.1	95.3	312	..	..	100	100	99	98
Guatemala	36.6	45.1	47.2	52.0	117	..	16.4	99	92	90	82
Guinea	15.0	31.0	33.0	38.1	37	15.8	48.0	78	35	31	11
Guinea-Bissau	20.9	29.7	29.6	31.1	57	..	..	79	49	57	23
Guyana	36.1	28.6	28.2	29.4	4	..	..	83	83	86	60
Haiti	33.9	35.6	38.8	45.5	337	22.9	59.0	52	56	57	14
Honduras	41.6	44.4	46.5	51.4	61	..	29.2	95	81	87	54
Hong Kong, China	99.8	100.0	100.0	100.0	6539	103.3	103.3	..	..	..	..
Hungary	71.9	64.6	66.3	70.3	113	16.8	25.3	100	98	100	85
Iceland	57.1	92.3	92.8	93.6	3	..	..	100	100	100	100
India	52.4	27.7	28.7	32.0	368	11.6	5.8	95	83	59	22
Indonesia	55.2	42.0	48.1	58.5	122	11.6	12.5	87	69	73	40
Iran, Islamic Rep.	60.9	64.2	66.9	71.9	42	22.9	15.8	99	84	..	..
Iraq	69.9	67.8	66.9	66.9	..	..	..	97	50	95	48
Ireland	45.8	59.2	60.5	63.8	60	24.9	41.2	100	..	..	..
Isle of Man	..	51.8	51.8	52.8	133	..	..	..	..	..	..
Israel	81.3	91.4	91.6	91.9	320	43.5	47.5	100	100	100	..
Italy	78.0	67.2	67.6	69.5	199	17.4	8.5	100	..	..	..
Jamaica	69.4	51.8	53.1	56.7	245	..	..	98	88	91	69
Japan	90.9	65.2	65.8	68.2	351	47.8	41.9	100	100	100	100
Jordan	77.9	80.4	82.3	85.3	61	23.9	29.0	99	91	94	87
Kazakhstan	50.6	56.3	57.3	60.3	6	7.6	13.3	97	73	87	52
Kenya	25.4	19.7	20.7	24.1	63	7.8	37.6	83	46	46	41
Kiribati	..	43.0	47.4	55.4	122	..	..	77	53	59	22
Korea, Dem. Rep.	46.2	60.2	61.6	65.5	196	18.9	23.0	100	100	58	60
Korea, Rep.	86.4	79.6	80.8	83.1	489	50.6	24.7	97	71	..	..
Kuwait	85.2	98.2	98.3	98.5	142	71.4	72.6	..	..	..	..
Kyrgyz Republic	34.0	35.4	35.8	38.1	27	..	43.3	98	66	75	51
Lao PDR	13.5	18.9	20.6	24.9	25	..	..	79	43	67	20
Latvia	52.6	68.1	67.8	68.9	37	..	..	100	96	82	71
Lebanon	79.0	86.0	86.6	87.9	392	44.3	51.2	100	100	100	87
Lesotho	23.1	17.9	18.7	22.0	65	..	..	92	76	61	32
Liberia	17.8	54.3	58.1	64.8	36	..	46.8	72	52	49	7
Libya	80.4	83.1	84.8	87.4	3	54.3	41.8	..	..	97	96
Liechtenstein	..	15.1	14.6	14.7	217	..	..	..	..	..	..
Lithuania	56.1	67.0	66.6	66.8	54	..	..	..	..	..	..
Luxembourg	75.1	83.8	82.8	82.1	176	..	..	100	100	..	..
Macao, China	58.8	100.0	100.0	100.0	16776	..	..	..	..	..	..
Macedonia, FYR	63.5	64.9	68.9	75.2	80	..	..	..	..	..	..
Madagascar	19.5	26.0	26.8	30.1	32	8.5	31.7	77	35	48	26
Malawi	23.8	15.1	17.2	22.1	141	..	..	98	68	62	61
Malaysia	68.0	61.8	67.3	75.4	78	5.5	8.1	100	96	95	93
Maldives	..	27.5	29.6	34.8	984	..	..	98	76	100	42
Mali	18.4	27.9	30.5	36.5	10	11.8	38.6	78	36	59	39
Malta	91.5	93.4	95.3	97.2	1261	..	..	100	100	100	..
Marshall Islands	..	65.8	66.7	69.3	351	..	..	82	96	93	58
Mauritania	26.3	40.0	40.4	43.1	3	..	..	59	44	49	8
Mauritius	92.1	42.7	42.4	44.1	612	..	..	100	100	95	94
Mayotte	0.0	..	..	..	481	..	..	..	..	..	..
Mexico	68.4	74.7	76.0	78.7	53	35.0	24.8	100	87	91	41
Micronesia, Fed. Sts.	..	22.3	22.3	23.6	157	..	..	95	94	61	14
Moldova	49.4	46.1	46.7	50.0	118	..	..	97	88	86	52
Monaco	..	100.0	100.0	100.0	16667	..	..	100	..	100	..
Mongolia	34.4	56.6	56.7	58.8	2	..	59.6	87	30	75	37
Montenegro	37.4	..	..	..	44	..	..	..	..	..	..
Morocco	53.0	55.1	58.7	65.0	68	15.9	17.7	99	56	88	52
Mozambique	24.1	30.7	34.5	42.4	26	6.4	18.6	72	26	53	19
Myanmar	33.1	28.0	30.7	37.4	73	8.6	28.0	80	77	88	72
Namibia	13.3	32.4	35.1	41.1	2	..	..	98	81	50	13
Nepal	26.0	13.4	15.8	20.9	189	..	19.0	96	89	62	30
Netherlands	88.2	76.8	80.2	84.9	482	13.8	8.8	100	100	100	100
Netherlands Antilles	81.5	69.3	70.4	73.4	233	..	..	..	..	..	..
New Caledonia	50.6	61.9	63.7	67.4	13	..	..	..	..	..	..
New Zealand	64.7	85.7	86.2	87.4	15	27.8	32.2	100	..	..	..
Nicaragua	48.0	57.2	59.0	63.0	45	21.3	36.2	90	63	56	34
Niger	14.3	16.2	16.8	19.3	10	..	38.1	80	36	43	4
Nigeria	40.8	43.9	48.2	55.9	155	13.3	16.0	67	31	53	36
Northern Mariana Islands	..	93.3	94.5	95.9	175	..	..	98	97	94	96
Norway	46.8	76.1	77.4	78.6	15	..	22.4	100	100	..	..
Oman	68.5	71.6	71.5	72.3	8	..	..	..	..	97	..
Pakistan	53.6	33.2	34.9	39.6	202	17.8	21.4	96	89	92	41
Palau	..	69.6	69.7	70.9	44	..	..	79	94	96	52
Panama	52.6	65.8	70.8	77.9	43	37.6	53.1	99	79	89	51
Papua New Guinea	3.5	13.2	13.4	15.0	13	..	..	88	32	67	41
Paraguay	45.7	55.3	58.5	64.4	15	31.5	53.8	99	68	94	61

Economy	Urbanization				Population density			Rural-urban disparities			
	Agglomeration index, 0 (low) to 100 (high)	Urban population (% of total pop.)	Urban population (% of total pop.)	Urban population (% of total pop.)	Population density (number of people per km²)	Pop. in cities > 1 million (% of total pop.)	Pop. in largest city (% of urban pop.)	% of urban population with water access	% of rural population with water access	% of urban population with sanitation services	% of rural population with sanitation services
	2000	2000	2005	2015	2006	2005	2005	2004	2004	2004	2004
Peru	52.1	71.6	72.6	74.9	21	26.3	36.3	89	65	74	32
Philippines	56.1	58.6	62.7	69.6	284	14.2	20.2	87	82	80	59
Poland	67.2	61.7	62.1	64.0	125	4.4	7.1	100	..	..	..
Portugal	62.6	54.4	57.6	63.6	115	38.6	45.4	..	..	..	..
Puerto Rico	90.3	94.7	97.6	99.3	441	66.6	68.2	..	..	..	..
Qatar	87.1	95.0	95.4	96.2	72	..	..	100	100	100	100
Romania	65.2	54.6	53.7	56.1	94	8.9	16.6	91	16	89	..
Russian Federation	64.8	73.4	73.0	72.6	9	19.2	10.2	100	88	93	70
Rwanda	14.3	13.8	19.3	28.7	374	..	43.7	92	69	56	38
Samoa	..	21.9	22.4	24.9	65	..	..	90	87	100	100
San Marino	60.0	93.5	97.2	99.3	470	..	..	..	..	..	..
Sao Tome and Princip	46.2	53.4	58.0	65.8	159	..	..	89	73	32	20
Saudi Arabia	75.7	79.9	81.0	83.2	12	36.2	22.4	97	..	100	..
Senegal	43.0	40.6	41.6	44.7	61	18.3	44.1	92	60	79	34
Serbia	60.5	..	..	..	84	..	..	..	..	..	..
Seychelles	..	51.1	52.9	58.2	180	..	..	100	75	..	100
Sierra Leone	29.3	37.0	40.7	48.2	78	..	35.2	75	46	53	30
Singapore	96.2	100.0	100.0	100.0	6302	99.6	99.6	100	..	100	..
Slovak Republic	59.3	56.3	56.2	58.0	112	..	..	100	99	100	98
Slovenia	48.1	50.8	51.0	53.3	99	..	..	..	..	..	..
Solomon Islands	6.9	15.7	17.0	20.5	17	..	..	94	65	98	18
Somalia	21.4	33.3	35.2	40.1	13	16.1	45.7	32	27	48	14
South Africa	50.2	56.9	59.3	64.1	39	30.0	11.7	99	73	79	46
Spain	76.7	76.3	76.7	78.3	87	24.0	16.8	100	100	100	100
Sri Lanka	38.2	15.7	15.1	15.7	304	..	..	98	74	98	89
St. Kitts and Nevis	..	32.8	32.2	33.5	185	..	..	99	99	96	96
St. Lucia	75.4	28.0	27.6	29.0	270	..	..	98	98	89	89
St. Vincent and the Grenadines	..	44.4	45.9	50.0	305	..	..	..	93	..	96
Sudan	31.9	36.1	40.8	49.4	16	12.2	30.0	78	64	50	24
Suriname	70.4	72.1	73.9	77.4	3	..	..	98	73	99	76
Swaziland	20.2	23.3	24.1	27.5	66	..	..	87	54	59	44
Sweden	54.4	84.0	84.2	85.1	22	18.9	22.5	100	100	100	100
Switzerland	75.8	73.1	75.2	78.8	186	15.4	20.5	100	100	100	100
Syrian Arab Republic	57.2	50.1	50.6	53.4	103	25.4	26.4	98	87	99	81
Taiwan, China	84.1	..	..	..	705	..	..	..	..	..	..
Tajikistan	36.2	25.9	24.7	24.6	47	..	..	92	48	70	45
Tanzania	28.2	22.3	24.2	28.9	43	7.0	28.7	85	49	53	43
Thailand	35.6	31.1	32.3	36.2	123	10.5	32.4	98	100	98	99
Timor-Leste	0.0	24.5	26.5	31.2	66	..	..	77	56	66	33
Togo	35.7	36.6	40.1	47.4	115	21.4	53.4	80	36	71	15
Tonga	..	23.2	24.0	27.4	138	..	..	100	100	98	96
Trinidad and Tobago	81.6	10.8	12.2	15.8	258	..	..	92	88	100	100
Tunisia	48.7	63.4	65.3	69.1	65	..	..	99	82	96	65
Turkey	60.1	64.7	67.3	71.9	94	25.6	20.0	98	93	96	72
Turkmenistan	42.6	45.1	46.3	50.8	10	..	..	93	54	77	50
Uganda	28.0	12.1	12.6	14.5	147	4.6	36.2	87	56	54	41
Ukraine	63.9	67.2	67.8	70.2	81	13.1	8.4	99	91	98	93
United Arab Emirates	61.0	77.4	76.7	77.4	49	32.4	42.2	100	100	98	95
United Kingdom	84.4	89.4	89.7	90.6	249	26.1	15.7	100	100	..	..
United States	71.9	79.1	80.8	83.7	32	43.3	7.8	100	100	100	100
Uruguay	64.1	91.4	92.0	93.1	19	38.2	41.6	100	100	100	99
Uzbekistan	54.2	37.3	36.7	38.0	62	8.3	22.7	95	75	78	61
Vanuatu	..	21.7	23.5	28.1	18	..	..	86	52	78	42
Venezuela, RB	80.5	91.1	93.4	95.9	30	36.9	11.7	85	70	71	48
Vietnam	47.1	24.3	26.4	31.6	268	13.4	23.1	99	80	92	50
Virgin Islands (U.S.)	..	92.6	94.2	96.0	311	..	..	..	..	..	..
West Bank and Gaza	57.9	71.5	71.6	72.9	602	..	..	94	88	78	61
Yemen, Rep.	23.0	25.4	27.3	31.9	40	8.5	31.3	71	65	86	28
Zambia	30.8	34.8	35.0	37.0	15	11.0	31.4	90	40	59	52
Zimbabwe	33.4	33.8	35.9	40.9	34	11.5	32.2	98	72	63	47

Table A3 Territorial development

		Leading area: defined as the area with the highest measure of welfare (income or consumption or gdp) per capita						Lagging area: defined as the area with the lowest measure of welfare (income or consumption or gdp) per capita				
Economy	Area name	Poverty Incidence 1995–2006[a]	Area's number of poor as percentage of total country poor 1995–2006[a]	Area's welfare measure as a % of country's average welfare measure 1995–2006[a]	Area (km²) 2007	Population density (number of people per km²) latest census	Area name	Poverty Incidence 1995–2006[a]	Area's number of poor as percentage of total country poor 1995–2006[a]	Area's welfare measure as a % of country's average welfare measure 1995–2006[a]	Area (km²) 2007	Population density (number of people per km²) latest census
Albania	Tirane	21.8	13.0	111	1,193	439	Bulqize	56.2	2.8	66	718	60
Argentina	Ciudad Autonoma de Buenos Aires	18.7	5.4	256	203	13,676	Santiago del Estero	31.4	2.6	38	136,351	6
Armenia	Yerevan	44.7	34.2	124	210	5,196	Armavir	52.0	9.3	68	1,241	20
Australia	Australian Capital Territory	14.8	0.9	139	2,432	129	Tasmania	31.1	2.8	89	68,127	7
Azerbaijan	Baku	49.0	25.1	109	2,130	944	Nakhchivan AR	45.0	4.1	90	5,500	65
Bangladesh	Dhaka	46.7	30.0	157	30,772	1,257	Rajshahi	56.7	28.2	22	13,218	2,269
Belarus	Minsk	13.3	14.4	107	40,800	38	Gomel	17.3	18.5	93	40,400	38
Belize	Belize	24.5	21.8	123	4,204	16	Toledo	57.6	17.5	74	4,649	5
Benin	Littoral	8.9	2.5	185	79	6,795	Mono	58.6	8.5	64	1,396	201
Bolivia	Santa Cruz	40.6	17.8	131	370,621	5	Potosi	76.6	11.8	56	118,218	6
Brazil	Sao Paulo	17.8	12.6	154	248,177	149	Piaui	57.1	3.1	31	251,312	11
Bulgaria	Sofia-city	3.2	4.4	111	1,349	858	Kardzhali	19.3	3.7	81	3,209	50
Burkina Faso	Centre	22.3	4.9	197	2,805	413	Centre Sud	66.1	6.1	61	11,313	43
Burundi	Muramvya	37.6	3.5	141	696	363	Ruyigi	55.4	6.2	62	2,339	130
Cambodia	Phnom Penh	11.9	3.6	249	375	2,547	Siemreap	53.7	11.8	63	10,299	67
Cameroon	Douala (capital of Littoral)	10.9	2.6	183	..	..	Extreme-Nord	56.3	24.9	67	34,246	80
Canada	Alberta	13.3	8.6	111	661,848	5	Newfoundland	18.7	1.9	77	405,212	1
Chad	Ennedi	21.0	0.01	295	..	..	Mayo-Dala	79.0	4.9	68	..	..
Chile	Region Metropolitana	13.5	28.9	130	15,782	384	Maule	23.1	7.4	70	30,518	30
Costa Rica	Central	17.1	34.8	117	10,669	47	Huetar Atlantic	23.6	10.8	38	9,189	12
Côte d'Ivoire	Lagunes	17.9	6.1	160	14,200	230	Marahoue	56.4	5.4	62	8,500	59
Croatia	Grad Zagreb	2.7	4.1	133	641	1,216	Viroviticko-Podravska zupanija	19.8	3.6	68	2,024	46
Djibouti	Ali Sabieh	92.4	7.0	192	2,600	6	Djibouti	36.2	58.3	92	600	528
Dominican Republic	Distrito Nacional	21.5	6.2	159	91	9,897	Elias Pina	74.0	1.5	39	1,397	46
Ecuador	Pichincha	5.1	7.9	144	9,110	259	Pastaza	34.7	1.6	49	29,774	2
El Salvador	San Salvador	6.8	12.6	151	886	1,668	Cabanas	32.6	5.5	45	1,104	123
Estonia	Harjumaa	7.9	33.7	228	4,333	120	Hiiumaa	11.4	1.0	2	1,023	10
Ethiopia	Addis Ababa City	57.0	4.0	197	530	4,574	Benishangul Gumuz	71.0	1.1	72	49,289	11
Gabon	Estuaire	23.0	35.8	121	20,740	29	Ogooue-Ivindo	59.9	7.4	55	46,075	1
Gambia, The	Banjul	50.0	19.2	183	88	4,060	Upper River	80.0	15.7	52	2,070	88
Ghana	Greater Accra	2.4	1.4	182	2,593	1,121	Upper East	79.6	14.9	35	8,842	104
Guatemala	Guatemala	11.7	4.6	212	2,126	810	San Marcos	86.7	12.5	39	3,791	166
Guinea	Conakry	24.4	7.6	140	308	3,523	Labe	66.3	15.1	75	24,144	33
Haiti	Ouest	57.0	25.7	162	4,595	543	Nord-Est	94.0	4.2	41	1,698	147
Honduras	Islas de la Bahia	57.6	0.4	154	261	120	Lempira	94.7	5.2	43	4,290	57
India	Kerala	15.0	1.7	140	38,863	819	Bihar	41.4	12.2	76	99,200	837
Indonesia	Jakarta	4.3	0.8	289	664	12,516	Jawa Central	28.4	18.3	16	32,549	930
Jamaica	Saint Andrew and Kingston	16.4	16.8	138	431	1,282	Saint Ann	33.8	10.3	61	1,213	136
Jordan	Amman	7.8	28.6	124	8,231	236	Al-Mafraq	29.2	13.5	72	26,435	9
Kenya	Nairobi Province	44.0	6.5	244	684	3,133	Eastern Province	57.6	18.5	65	159,891	29
Kyrgyz Republic	Chuy Oblast	33.1	9.4	136	20,200	38	Naryn	98.1	9.0	65	45,200	6
Madagascar	Antananarivo	61.7	25.3	158	58,283	79	Fianarantsoa	81.1	24.4	65	102,373	33
Malawi	Southern Region	68.1	48.7	119	31,754	146	Northern Region	62.5	11.9	81	26,931	46
Mali	Bamako	28.2	5.2	174	267	3,952	Sikasso	76.4	21.7	78	71,741	24
Mauritania	Nouakchott	29.0	15.3	130	1,000	498	Guidimakha	71.6	10.8	60	10,300	14
Mexico	Distrito Federal	31.8	5.6	182	1,479	5,896	Oaxaca	68.0	4.8	49	93,952	37
Mongolia	Ulaanbaatar	26.0	22.5	116	..	..	West	49.0	23.8	79	..	..
Morocco	Grand Casablanca	4.0	3.0	159	1,615	1,870	Gharb-Chrarda-Beni Hssen	23.3	9.2	47	8,805	182
Mozambique	Maputo (city)	47.8	4.2	192	602	1,631	Inhambane	82.6	8.6	70	68,615	17
Namibia	Khomas	23.5	5.1	274	36,805	7	Ohangwena	85.8	16.9	38	10,582	22
Nepal	Western	27.1	17.1	119	29,398	155	Far Western	41.0	12.4	76	19,539	112
Nicaragua	Managua	3.6	4.3	161	3,465	314	Esteli	23.4	4.5	21	2,230	78
Niger	Niamey	26.2	2.7	180	670	1,065	Maradi	80.4	26.2	64	38,581	58
Nigeria	Bayelsa	26.2	0.6	162	9,363	182	Jigawa	89.5	5.4	36	23,415	186
Pakistan	Punjab	32.4	54.1	104	205,344	359	Azad Kashmir	15.6	1.0	85	11,639	241
Panama	Panamá	22.7	29.0	127	9,633	140	Ngöbe Buglé	98.7	10.3	15	6,673	16
Paraguay	Asuncion	24.8	6.2	135	117	4,244	San Pedro	51.1	8.1	72	20,002	16
Peru	Lima	24.5	16.8	137	32,137	254	Huancavelica	88.7	3.5	39	22,131	21
Philippines	National Capital region (NCR)	5.7	2.6	216	630	15,766	Region V (Bicol region)	49.0	10.5	63	14,544	321
Poland	Mazowieckie	10.8	9.1	163	35,728	142	Lubelskie	21.2	7.9	67	25,115	89

Economy	Leading area: defined as the area with the highest measure of welfare (income or consumption or gdp) per capita						Lagging area: defined as the area with the lowest measure of welfare (income or consumption or gdp) per capita					
	Area name	Poverty Incidence	Area's number of poor as percentage of total country poor	Area's welfare measure as a % of country's average welfare measure	Area (km²)	Population density (number of people per km²)	Area name	Poverty Incidence	Area's number of poor as percentage of total country poor	Area's welfare measure as a % of country's average welfare measure	Area (km²)	Population density (number of people per km²)
		1995–2006[a]	1995–2006[a]	1995–2006[a]	2007	latest census		1995–2006[a]	1995–2006[a]	1995–2006[a]	2007	latest census
Romania	Bucharest	3.0	2.2	216	1,821	1,186	North-East	25.0	31.4	69	36,850	100
Russian Federation	Saint Petersburg	7.8	1.1	117	23,900	197	Republic Tyva	66.5	0.6	56	37,300	8
Rwanda	Prefecture de la Ville de Kigali	12.3	0.6	379	313	753	Gikongoro	77.2	8.0	70	1,974	237
Sierra Leone	Western Area	80.8	19.0	200	557	1,707	Eastern	80.0	23.5	65	15,553	76
Slovak Republic	Bratislava	9.4	10.3	172	2,052	292	Presov	9.7	14.0	73	8,981	88
South Africa	Gauteng	19.0	6.6	186	17,010	520	Northern Province (Limpopo)	77.0	18.0	46	123,910	40
Sri Lanka	Colombo	6.0	3.7	179	642	3,480	Monaragala	37.0	4.0	51	7,133	56
Tajikistan	Dushanbe (City)	43.5	6.9	144	300	1,873	Khatlon (Qurghonteppa)	73.3	44.8	79	24,600	87
Tanzania	Dar Es Salaam	19.1	4.3	188	1,393	1,793	Rukwa	36.4	3.8	68	68,635	17
Thailand	Krung Thep Maha Nakhon (Bangkok)	0.5	1.2	174	1,569	13,016	Nong Bua Lam Phu	35.2	2.1	39	3,859	125
Turkmenistan	Lebap	28.5	17.4	116	93,800	11	Ahal	34.8	12.4	79	95,400	6
Uganda	Central	22.3	17.1	146	..	..	Northern	63.3	29.9	54	..	..
United States	New Jersey	8.7	1.9	129	20,168	429	Mississippi	21.0	1.5	73	123,515	23
Venezuela, RB	Capital	15.0	13.6	126	9,880	518	Zuliana	25.2	15.7	83	63,100	56
Vietnam	Ho Chi Minh city	5.3	1.0	241	2,090	2,409	Lai Chau	79.8	1.7	46	9,065	65
Yemen, Rep.	Sana'a	16.6	4.2	184	380	4,827	Al Jawf	40.8	2.7	71	39,500	12
Zambia	Lusaka	52.0	10.0	170	21,898	64	Western	89.0	9.4	59	126,386	6

340   WORLD DEVELOPMENT REPORT 2009

Table A4   International integration

	People				Ideas			Trade			
Economy	Countries that need a visa to visit this country (number)	Countries for which this country's residents need a visa (number)	Cost of obtaining a passport relative to GDP per capita (%)	International migration stock (% of foreigners) (%)	International voice traffic (incoming and outgoing, minutes per person) (minutes)	International Internet bandwith (bits per person) (bits)	Telephone average cost of call to the US (US$ per three minutes) (US$)	Total trade as share of GDP (%)	Index of shipping difficulties (Index)	Average tariffs and custom duties (% of import value) (%)	Share of trade with neighboring countries (% of total trade) (%)
	2004	2004	2005	2005	2000–06a	2000–06a	2000–06a	2005–06a	2008	2005	Average 2000–2005
Afghanistan	192	168	..	0.1	0.6	0.2	0.39	68.1	174	11.2	..
Albania	142	159	2.2	2.6	160.0	3.8	1.34	74.2	70	7.6	71.9
Algeria	183	157	..	0.7	16.9	4.8	2.08	71.4	114	3.0	10.5
American Samoa	192	156	..	35.0	..	..	..	..	..	..	0.0
Andorra	132	89	..	79.1	..	6344.4	..	..	..	..	0.0
Angola	191	162	4.9	0.4	6.7	11.5	3.23	111.7	164	..	..
Antigua and Barbuda	105	121	0.2	22.0	596.4	16588.0	..	130.8	55	..	17.4
Argentina	124	88	0.7	3.9	32.5	689.9	..	43.9	107	15.8	35.9
Armenia	162	144	0.0	7.8	127.8	22.5	2.42	58.5	118	3.3	10.4
Aruba	..	..	..	24.4	..	1794.6	..	..	..	..	5.4
Australia	161	59	0.4	20.2	213.8	11593.4	0.68	42.1	34	1.8	0.0
Austria	132	57	0.3	15.0	264.7	6633.5	0.71	109.7	12	0.0	81.3
Azerbaijan	181	143	2.5	2.2	32.6	35.7	4.18	111.3	173	,,	26.7
Bahamas, The	119	119	0.2	9.8	585.0	278.4	..	..	..	55.0	0.0
Bahrain	140	139	0.3	40.7	587.1	564.3	1.74	127.0	..	3.7	23.7
Bangladesh	19	155	5.2	0.7	6.4	8.0	2.02	44.2	112	32.6	8.9
Barbados	72	113	0.7	9.7	565.2	2055.3	1.95	117.8	..	8.0	22.6
Belarus	179	141	..	12.2	64.0	191.7	1.90	124.1	137	7.2	68.9
Belgium	132	54	0.3	6.9	316.3	11278.5	0.75	172.8	48	..	73.8
Belize	120	127	0.4	13.9	178.2	604.8	2.59	125.4	116	..	14.1
Benin	167	144	8.6	2.1	6.4	5.4	4.80	39.6	124	24.5	20.4
Bermuda	..	..	..	29.6	..	8699.1	..	..	..	..	0.0
Bhutan	191	153	..	1.5	40.9	33.9	0.66	76.8	149	1.5	..
Bolivia	140	110	6.7	1.3	48.7	43.3	1.89	75.1	115	2.1	50.8
Bosnia and Herzegovina	154	154	7.0	1.0	207.6	39.6	3.62	72.3	53	0.0	57.9
Botswana	139	138	0.1	4.5	74.1	16.1	2.88	83.8	145	..	50.2
Brazil	140	85	1.3	0.3	11.7	149.9	0.71	26.4	93	..	13.2
Brunei Darussalam	157	89	..	33.2	142.7	1453.1	..	96.2	36	..	7.3
Bulgaria	147	103	0.7	1.3	71.7	1756.1	0.57	147.0	89	2.4	25.5
Burkina Faso	175	147	12.7	5.8	10.8	15.0	1.14	35.8	170	12.7	40.7
Burundi	191	163	50.9	1.3	1.6	0.5	2.45	58.7	167	..	14.8
Cambodia	191	159	..	2.2	9.5	1.3	2.94	144.6	139	21.6	10.2
Cameroon	184	157	11.4	0.8	8.8	8.7	..	52.7	132	..	12.4
Canada	149	57	0.3	18.9	438.7	6731.9	..	72.0	39	1.3	73.0
Cape Verde	174	145	..	2.2	139.5	46.3	6.08	74.6	51	..	1.1
Cayman Islands	121	156	..	35.8	1630.2	..	..	..	..	..	0.0
Central African Republic	173	153	17.7	1.9	2.3	0.4	1.99	35.5	172	19.4	16.1
Chad	181	154	60.2	4.5	2.0	0.5	9.11	97.3	157	..	..
Channel Islands	..	..	..	45.8	..	..	2.90	..	..	..	0.0
Chile	114	84	1.5	1.4	48.3	779.6	2.18	76.3	43	1.6	12.4
China	191	161	2.9	0.0	7.3	195.7	2.90	72.4	42	−16.2	15.4
Colombia	64	150	1.5	0.3	68.2	560.2	..	47.3	105	8.8	19.2
Comoros	192	158	..	11.2	33.1	3.3	..	47.3	119	..	0.0
Congo, Dem. Rep.	190	162	125.0	0.9	5.3	0.1	..	70.4	154	27.4	..
Congo, Rep.	169	151	8.5	7.2	..	0.3	5.39	137.0	171	6.6	..
Costa Rica	125	100	0.4	10.2	126.8	176.2	1.93	105.5	54	5.0	7.6
Cote d'Ivoire	169	145	..	13.1	16.9	3.0	2.25	92.3	147	43.6	20.2
Croatia	131	105	2.0	14.9	231.2	1073.7	..	104.6	96	1.6	50.0
Cuba	169	153	..	0.7	30.6	13.8	7.49	..	..	..	0.4
Cyprus	137	80	0.3	15.3	693.2	593.8	0.33	..	..	0.7	8.5
Czech Republic	136	95	0.1	4.4	94.8	2169.8	1.06	148.3	30	0.0	61.8
Denmark	132	53	0.4	7.2	318.0	34796.1	0.89	100.8	2	..	74.9
Djibouti	192	159	..	2.6	26.7	56.0	4.73	97.2	66	..	..
Dominica	0	130	1.0	6.3	..	419.8	..	107.2	80	..	30.5
Dominican Republic	130	152	..	1.7	218.5	6.1	0.22	73.5	35	13.9	..
Ecuador	27	139	3.6	0.9	215.6	227.2	1.75	67.5	131	..	15.4
Egypt, Arab Rep.	60	156	1.9	0.2	30.1	126.4	1.45	61.5	26	6.4	5.4
El Salvador	120	108	0.4	0.3	409.9	22.9	2.40	74.0	68	6.0	29.1
Equatorial Guinea	191	159	..	1.2	..	34.7	..	144.7	133	..	..
Eritrea	190	163	..	0.3	8.7	1.7	3.59	58.1	159	..	4.5
Estonia	132	98	0.2	15.0	109.0	11174.9	0.90	169.3	7	0.0	54.6
Ethiopia	190	163	31.1	0.8	3.5	0.1	4.01	57.5	150	26.6	6.6
Faeroe Islands	..	..	..	11.1	..	3312.6	..	..	..	..	3.1
Fiji	94	131	1.6	2.0	112.1	87.0	2.84	127.6	111	15.9	1.3
Finland	132	55	0.2	3.0	178.3	4311.2	1.80	82.3	5	0.0	65.4
France	132	54	0.2	10.6	182.8	3285.5	0.84	55.1	25	0.0	62.4
French Polynesia	..	..	..	13.1	..	887.2	3.67	29.1	..	..	0.0
Gabon	174	156	..	17.7	74.0	152.6	2.77	89.1	106	..	2.4
Gambia, The	41	135	6.0	15.3	..	5.6	1.81	110.2	73	..	4.1
Georgia	131	143	..	4.3	57.5	7.2	0.68	89.9	64	4.0	39.4

Economy	People				Ideas			Trade			
	Countries that need a visa to visit this country (number)	Countries for which this country's residents need a visa (number)	Cost of obtaining a passport relative to GDP per capita (%)	International migration stock (% of foreigners) (%)	International voice traffic (incoming and outgoing, minutes per person) (minutes)	International Internet bandwith (bits per person) (bits)	Telephone average cost of call to the US (US$ per three minutes) (US$)	Total trade as share of GDP (%)	Index of shipping difficulties (Index)	Average tariffs and custom duties (% of import value) (%)	Share of trade with neighboring countries (% of total trade) (%)
	2004	2004	2005	2005	2000–06[a]	2000–06[a]	2000–06[a]	2005–06[a]	2008	2005	Average 2000–2005
Germany	132	54	0.3	12.3	190.8	6863.8	0.43	84.7	10		63.6
Ghana	171	142	1.4	7.5	20.1	9.3	0.39	103.0	61	28.5	10.7
Greece	132	56	0.4	8.8	181.8	586.5	1.09	45.6	65	0.0	56.4
Greenland	..	..	1.0	21.4		106.8	2.41	..	..	..	0.0
Grenada	11	127	..	10.2	624.5	3976.0	..	109.0	52	..	25.9
Guam	..	..	..	66.9				..	..	..	0.0
Guatemala	118	110	1.8	0.4	194.7	55.5	1.21	46.2	116	8.9	21.4
Guinea	171	146		4.5	6.8	0.2	4.61	67.4	102		10.1
Guinea-Bissau	176	150	..	1.2	8.9	1.2	..	95.4	109	..	..
Guyana	158	127	0.6	0.1	118.3	48.7	..	211.8	101	..	25.2
Haiti	4	157	..	0.4		16.7	2.15	57.3	153	..	..
Honduras	128	110	3.4	0.4	96.4	6.0	2.52	107.3	103	6.3	20.6
Hong Kong, China	42	89	0.2	43.2	1178.7	13438.6	0.77	399.4	3	..	49.1
Hungary	132	85	0.3	3.1	105.1	993.3	1.01	155.1	45	0.0	26.5
Iceland	132	59	0.2	7.8	240.0	7289.6	0.84	83.1	11	1.1	0.7
India	189	160	3.6	0.5	3.0	24.3	1.19	48.8	79	14.6	9.9
Indonesia	162	148	1.9	0.1	5.3	6.8	2.79	56.9	41	3.0	4.1
Iran, Islamic Rep.	188	166	..	2.9	8.8	53.2	0.55	75.2	135	5.5	4.8
Iraq	..	..		0.1					175	..	..
Ireland	107	57	0.3	14.1	709.5	5911.6	0.71	149.9	20	0.1	60.6
Isle of Man	..	..	..	48.6							0.0
Israel	123	88	0.3	38.4	364.2	2455.4	0.59	88.4	8	0.7	0.9
Italy	132	55	0.2	4.3	236.0	2044.0	0.79	56.5	62	..	59.4
Jamaica	80	126	1.4	0.7	233.2	15822.2	0.87	108.8	92	7.7	0.8
Japan	137	56	0.2	1.6	43.4	1037.8	1.63	27.3	18	..	0.0
Jordan	61	159	..	41.1	138.8	57.3	1.44	146.6	59	10.4	31.8
Kazakhstan	175	141	..	16.5	26.4	62.5	..	91.6	178	6.0	34.4
Kenya	21	140	1.2	1.0	5.6	20.8	3.00	62.2	148	10.2	13.8
Kiribati	168	133	..	2.6	24.2	5.4	8.82	133.3	97	..	0.0
Korea, Dem. Rep.	192	163		0.2							0.0
Korea, Rep.	89	78	0.3	1.1	91.6	1027.8	0.76	85.3	13	3.4	0.0
Kuwait	154	135	..	65.8		347.9	1.51	98.0	99	1.3	..
Kyrgyz Republic	144	143	..	5.6	29.5	38.9	5.40	115.7	177	13.2	35.8
Lao PDR	192	158	11.8	0.4	6.6	3.5	1.11	78.2	158	..	..
Latvia	132	98	..	19.5	66.7	3229.7	1.63	108.6	19	0.6	55.0
Lebanon	100	169	4.0	16.4	279.1	111.0	2.19	63.6	83	7.6	9.9
Lesotho	127	135	1.5	0.3	18.1	2.2	3.28	149.0	129	49.5	66.4
Liberia	176	151		1.5		0.1	..	99.6	98	..	..
Libya	177	163	..	10.5	65.6	20.6	..	84.1	..	..	8.6
Liechtenstein	117	74	..	33.7		4298.0					..
Lithuania	132	100	0.4	4.8	49.0	2714.4	1.55	129.8	23	0.5	48.0
Luxembourg	132	55	0.0	38.0	1399.1	20459.0	15.96	326.6	32	..	89.1
Macao, China	0	122	..	55.9	497.2	6491.7	1.12	150.5	..	..	39.9
Macedonia, FYR	148	141	..	6.0	63.3	16.7	0.59	118.3	72	..	45.8
Madagascar	0	156	..	0.3	1.3	1.8	..	70.7	126	24.8	0.0
Malawi	123	139	..	2.2	4.8	1.5	3.56	46.4	161	..	16.4
Malaysia	23	63	1.7	6.5	87.9	124.5	0.71	217.0	21	5.6	22.0
Maldives	3	134	..	1.0	91.2	179.5	5.86	178.1	110	23.6	10.7
Mali	172	148	..	0.3	7.4	25.9	12.28	72.3	162	3.8	25.1
Malta	132	73	0.3	2.6	222.4	4729.1	0.77	179.6	..	0.1	19.5
Marshall Islands	162	144	..	2.6	76.5	26.2	..	113.7	46	..	0.0
Mauritania	169	141	8.7	2.1	20.3	29.6	..	113.7	152	..	2.1
Mauritius	88	131	0.5	1.7	149.8	153.2	1.59	127.1	17	16.8	0.0
Mayotte	..	..	..	..						..	0.0
Mexico	139	92	1.2	0.6	174.0	109.0	0.83	65.1	76	4.1	72.3
Micronesia, Fed. Sts.	0	146	2.5	3.2	80.8	54.5	6.00		85	..	0.0
Moldova	149	141	..	11.4	109.9	147.4	1.46	139.2	122	4.1	39.7
Monaco	132	88	..	75.8				125.0	168	..	..
Mongolia	174	155	..	0.4	4.8	13.3	4.92	128.9	113	5.7	64.7
Montenegro	..	..	..	6.4						..	..
Morocco	134	147	2.1	0.4	65.1	377.1	1.69	71.4	67	9.4	16.6
Mozambique	0	158	..	2.1	12.7	0.9	1.17	88.9	140	..	43.7
Myanmar	192	161	2.3	0.2	2.8	1.9	0.17			2.3	..
Namibia	141	145	1.0	7.1	58.0	17.8	4.28	110.0	144	31.8	63.1
Nepal	0	158	26.3	3.0	5.6	4.6	2.04	45.3	151	18.2	60.5
Netherlands	132	56	0.2	10.0	310.8	20501.3	0.32	140.6	14	0.8	56.4
Netherlands Antilles	..	..	..	26.5						..	0.0
New Caledonia	..	..	..	18.4	215.0	562.9	3.13			..	0.4
New Zealand	146	59	0.2	15.7	361.1	1106.7	1.30	58.2	16	1.7	0.0
Nicaragua	38	116	3.0	0.5	61.7	1.1	3.15	92.1	87	4.6	28.4

Table A4   International integration—continued

	People				Ideas			Trade			
Economy	Countries that need a visa to visit this country (number)	Countries for which this country's residents need a visa (number)	Cost of obtaining a passport relative to GDP per capita (%)	International migration stock (% of foreigners) (%)	International voice traffic (incoming and outgoing, minutes per person) (minutes)	International Internet bandwith (bits per person) (bits)	Telephone average cost of call to the US (US$ per three minutes) (US$)	Total trade as share of GDP (%)	Index of shipping difficulties (Index)	Average tariffs and custom duties (% of import value) (%)	Share of trade with neighboring countries (% of total trade) (%)
	2004	2004	2005	2005	2000–06[a]	2000–06[a]	2000–06[a]	2005–06[a]	2008	2005	Average 2000–2005
Niger	167	144	19.8	0.9	2.0	2.3	8.77	38.9	163	..	20.7
Nigeria	174	149	10.0	0.7	2.3	1.1	1.49	91.1	138	..	4.4
Northern Mariana Islands	157	153	..	6.5	..	..	..	..	..	..	0.0
Norway	132	56	0.3	7.4	192.9	9304.8	0.31	75.0	4	0.2	18.8
Oman	128	141	0.2	24.4	189.1	173.6	1.87	99.2	104	2.8	32.1
Pakistan	184	165	4.2	2.1	10.5	4.6	1.03	38.6	94	13.0	11.1
Palau	0	148	0.7	15.1	..	..	..	153.5	121	..	0.0
Panama	130	107		3.2	54.9	286.6	3.64	144.5	9	8.6	9.7
Papua New Guinea	114	138	5.3	0.4	8.0	1.0	4.32	134.8	82	26.4	1.7
Paraguay	163	103		2.9	31.3	83.1	0.90	115.2	123	8.2	41.4
Peru	97	135	2.6	0.1	99.1	366.6	1.80	48.5	71	5.7	21.5
Philippines	44	144	0.8	0.5	28.3	38.0	1.20	94.0	57	20.4	0.0
Poland	132	86	0.5	1.8	60.6	560.2	1.35	82.0	40	0.4	52.7
Portugal	132	57	0.4	7.2	178.1	829.0	1.04	70.0	31	0.0	28.2
Puerto Rico	..	..		10.7	..	511.2	..	181.2	95	..	0.0
Qatar	156	136	..	78.3	842.9	943.6	1.95	101.7	..	3.2	9.2
Romania	145	107	1.1	0.6	49.1	1503.2	0.82	78.5	38	3.0	18.7
Russian Federation	183	134	0.4	8.4	15.3	100.3	2.03	55.1	155	29.2	33.1
Rwanda	180	156	41.5	1.3	..	7.4	2.43	43.2	166	..	43.2
Samoa	0	129	2.1	5.0	149.7	49.0	1.36	78.1	108	..	6.5
San Marino	132	82	..	33.4	6448.4	5419.6	..	..	..	1.7	..
Sao Tome and Princip	0	155	..	4.8	51.3	25.8	5.11	..	91	..	3.1
Saudi Arabia	187	142	0.8	27.5	215.8	126.1	2.40	92.9	33	..	3.2
Senegal	151	146	4.1	2.8	39.4	102.7	1.02	69.8	136	33.1	9.1
Serbia	..	..		6.4	..	94.6	..	73.4	58	..	..
Seychelles	0	131	1.1	5.8	..	307.3	3.78	244.5	84	10.7	0.0
Sierra Leone	124	139	..	2.2	..	0.1	..	59.4	130	27.0	2.3
Singapore	32	66	0.2	42.4	1045.4	7052.4	0.69	473.5	1	0.1	14.7
Slovak Republic	131	95	0.5	2.3	90.0	2912.6	1.06	176.0	90	0.0	66.8
Slovenia	132	92	0.3	8.4	..	1254.7	0.65	139.1	69	0.1	67.1
Solomon Islands	123	130	..	0.7	23.2	17.1	..	102.2	74	..	0.0
Somalia	192	165	..	3.4	..	0.4	..	..	..	..	..
South Africa	120	118	0.7	2.4	27.6	18.8	0.79	63.1	134	4.2	2.9
Spain	132	55	0.1	11.0	173.3	2775.7	0.60	58.4	47	0.0	64.7
Sri Lanka	114	156	2.4	1.9	27.9	25.1	2.11	74.8	60	14.6	0.6
St. Kitts and Nevis	92	120	0.2	9.3	571.6	42.5	..	113.5	22	31.3	15.5
St. Lucia	130	121	0.5	5.3	217.9	94.9	..	117.6	88	..	22.8
St. Vincent and the Grenadines	122	124	0.6	8.7	288.5	25.0	3.97	125.0	75	..	33.8
Sudan	190	166	..	1.8	12.2	5.4	39.18	42.8	143	..	5.2
Suriname	171	137	..	1.2	276.7	439.3	1.33	76.3	86	..	4.4
Swaziland	137	138	0.3	4.0	47.5	0.9	2.97	167.5	146	47.7	80.0
Sweden	132	54	0.2	12.4	..	17468.5	0.41	94.5	6	..	25.9
Switzerland	119	57	0.2	22.3	664.8	9609.1	0.32	89.0	37	1.1	61.4
Syrian Arab Republic	160	163	..	5.2	44.0	8.0	4.81	75.0	127	..	16.0
Taiwan, China	..	..		..	292.3	6569.5	0.51	134.0	29	..	10.8
Tajikistan	..	..	13.4	4.7	10.4	0.3	7.84	80.7	176	11.1	..
Tanzania	35	142	13.4	2.1	1.4	0.4	3.17	55.1	100	..	8.5
Thailand	136	146	1.0	1.6	14.1	156.2	0.67	143.5	50	6.2	7.5
Timor-Leste	..	..	..	0.6	..	..	..	..	78	..	..
Togo	0	148	..	3.0	21.5	15.6	3.98	83.9	81	..	28.1
Tonga	142	135	2.4	1.1	..	20.1	1.09	54.3	44	..	0.0
Trinidad and Tobago	47	119	0.3	2.9	375.7	370.2	2.19	108.0	49	4.8	10.3
Tunisia	126	142	1.1	0.4	72.6	126.4	2.28	108.7	28	6.2	26.3
Turkey	118	126	8.9	1.8	27.1	630.7	2.40	64.1	56	1.1	9.3
Turkmenistan	174	148	..	4.6	6.0	15.7	..	126.2		..	..
Uganda	0	145	..	1.8	3.1	4.4	3.21	44.4	141	20.5	26.1
Ukraine	181	139	2.7	14.5	56.6	17.3	1.65	97.3	120	4.3	40.6
United Arab Emirates	155	136	..	70.9	..	2371.4	1.73	170.6	24	..	..
United Kingdom	104	55	0.2	9.0	262.2	13062.0	0.77	61.6	27	..	55.2
United States	158	52	0.2	12.9	279.5	3306.6	..	26.8	15	1.1	30.7
Uruguay	134	98	..	2.5	120.7	484.0	0.52	60.2	125	5.1	36.2
Uzbekistan	184	148	..	4.8	12.4	8.7	13.95	63.4	165	..	..
Vanuatu	106	137	3.4	0.5	..	23.2	7.45	100.3	142	..	0.0
Venezuela, RB	131	95	0.5	3.8	23.1	50.3	0.84	57.6	156	4.9	14.6
Vietnam	185	160	2.3	0.0	8.4	84.1	1.95	150.3	63	..	11.7
Virgin Islands (U.S.)	..	..	..	33.7	..	414.0	..	..		..	0.0
West Bank and Gaza	..	..	..	46.3	65.7	198.7	1.17	85.4	77	..	..
Yemen, Rep.	145	161	..	1.3	12.0	0.3	2.39	79.4	128	..	7.6
Zambia	18	142	3.7	2.4	6.9	10.9	1.41	67.8	160	9.0	14.1
Zimbabwe	117	141	..	3.9	24.9	4.2	4.36	129.8	169	..	53.9

a. Data are for the latest year available in the period shown.

Table A5   Other indicators

	Terrain characteristics					Geography and people			
Economy	plains (% of total land area)	lowlands (% of total land area)	plateaus (% of total land area)	hills (% of total land area)	mountains (% of total land area)	Population living at less than 25 kms from an international border (%)	Population living at less than 75 kms from an international border (%)	Population living at less than 25 kms from a coastline (%)	Population living at less than 75 kms from a coastline (%)
	2007	2007	2007	2007	2007	2000	2000	2000	2000
Afghanistan	0.9	0.0	8.7	0.3	90.1	11.2	37.1	0.0	0.0
Albania	0.0	0.4	0.0	33.6	66.0	29.2	83.2	41.9	87.2
Algeria	12.4	4.2	51.7	5.1	26.6	3.3	13.0	35.8	63.4
American Samoa	0.0	100.0	0.0	0.0	0.0	0.0	0.0	100.0	100.0
Andorra	0.0	0.0	0.0	0.0	100.0	100.0	100.0	0.0	0.0
Angola	16.9	3.0	47.0	6.0	27.1	5.2	11.5	23.0	26.9
Antigua and Barbuda	0.0	100.0	0.0	0.0	0.0	0.0	0.0	100.0	100.0
Argentina	33.0	9.4	8.7	11.0	37.9	5.0	10.4	33.3	42.8
Armenia	0.0	0.0	0.0	0.0	100.0	70.5	100.0	0.0	0.0
Aruba	35.4	64.6	0.0	0.0	0.0	0.0	0.0	100.0	100.0
Australia	29.7	23.3	33.5	8.8	4.8	0.0	0.0	69.1	87.5
Austria	0.0	0.2	0.0	26.7	73.1	38.7	97.4	0.0	0.0
Azerbaijan	0.7	31.2	0.0	5.6	62.5	26.9	61.9	0.0	0.0
Bahamas, The	100.0	0.0	0.0	0.0	0.0	0.0	0.0	100.0	100.0
Bahrain	57.3	42.7	0.0	0.0	0.0	0.0	0.0	100.0	100.0
Bangladesh	67.1	20.3	0.0	10.8	1.8	28.2	78.8	25.3	48.1
Barbados	0.0	100.0	0.0	0.0	0.0	0.0	0.0	100.0	100.0
Belarus	37.8	58.7	3.5	0.0	0.0	18.3	53.5	0.0	0.0
Belgium	19.2	45.5	0.0	35.3	0.0	53.4	100.0	18.1	69.9
Belize	1.4	51.5	7.7	39.5	0.0	37.9	94.2	57.9	94.4
Benin	13.3	15.5	65.2	6.0	0.0	42.7	96.0	27.7	46.0
Bermuda	100.0	0.0	0.0	0.0	0.0	0.0	0.0	100.0	100.0
Bhutan	0.0	0.4	0.0	16.2	83.4	54.8	99.9	0.0	0.0
Bolivia	26.3	8.4	14.8	13.1	37.3	5.0	22.5	0.0	0.0
Bosnia and Herzegovina	0.0	6.0	0.0	23.0	71.0	40.5	90.1	0.8	12.4
Botswana	49.4	0.0	48.5	0.0	2.1	34.2	66.2	0.0	0.0
Brazil	21.1	20.8	37.6	8.0	12.5	1.0	2.4	25.4	46.5
Brunei Darussalam	0.3	75.7	0.0	0.0	23.9	98.9	100.0	80.8	99.3
Bulgaria	0.0	21.9	0.0	45.4	32.7	19.1	80.5	9.4	15.8
Burkina Faso	34.4	0.1	65.6	0.0	0.0	14.4	42.2	0.0	0.0
Burundi	0.0	0.0	15.9	0.0	84.1	60.9	100.0	0.0	0.0
Cambodia	6.5	74.3	0.0	17.9	1.4	18.1	57.0	4.9	12.1
Cameroon	2.2	2.0	44.7	20.7	30.4	17.5	40.2	15.8	20.8
Canada	6.7	20.8	27.9	21.3	23.2	17.6	61.8	20.6	23.1
Cape Verde	0.7	40.9	0.0	31.7	26.8	0.0	0.0	100.0	100.0
Cayman Islands	100.0	0.0	0.0	0.0	0.0	0.0	0.0	100.0	100.0
Central African Republic	17.6	0.0	78.5	0.0	3.9	31.4	58.5	0.0	0.0
Chad	35.9	0.0	42.4	3.7	18.0	23.6	51.5	0.0	0.0
Channel Islands	0.0	100.0	0.0	0.0	0.0	0.0	0.0	100.0	100.0
Chile	0.0	9.0	0.0	26.9	64.1	3.3	48.9	26.2	53.1
China	3.9	10.2	8.9	12.7	64.2	1.1	3.7	11.6	21.8
Colombia	24.0	23.1	9.7	12.5	30.7	4.7	11.1	11.5	24.9
Comoros	0.0	0.0	12.4	26.2	61.4	0.0	0.0	100.0	100.0
Congo, Dem. Rep.	17.1	0.3	61.1	1.0	20.5	24.9	46.5	0.6	1.8
Congo, Rep.	29.1	1.2	58.6	8.2	2.8	50.5	91.8	19.8	21.5
Costa Rica	0.0	1.9	0.0	62.0	36.1	11.3	29.4	22.1	97.7
Cote d'Ivoire	0.0	0.1	0.1	72.9	27.0	11.3	30.0	26.0	33.7
Croatia	6.8	25.3	60.8	6.4	0.6	68.1	98.1	31.2	36.3
Cuba	0.0	41.3	0.0	25.7	32.9	1.3	11.4	63.5	100.0
Cyprus	5.8	80.1	0.0	14.2	0.0	0.0	0.0	90.1	100.0
Czech Republic	0.0	44.1	0.0	55.9	0.0	38.3	88.0	0.0	0.0
Denmark	30.1	69.9	0.0	0.0	0.0	2.0	9.1	94.8	100.0
Djibouti	0.0	18.6	0.0	30.0	51.4	86.3	100.0	79.8	99.1
Dominica	0.0	0.0	0.0	100.0	0.0	0.0	0.0	100.0	100.0
Dominican Republic	0.1	31.2	0.0	33.2	35.5	3.7	17.3	61.2	96.7
Ecuador	7.4	6.1	9.7	28.1	48.7	5.2	15.8	33.7	49.0
Egypt, Arab Rep.	5.7	27.8	41.4	16.4	8.7	0.2	0.5	16.4	36.9
El Salvador	0.0	1.1	0.0	52.5	46.4	25.4	96.7	26.7	94.7
Equatorial Guinea	0.0	20.6	18.6	7.7	53.1	35.6	77.9	41.3	59.5
Eritrea	0.1	11.6	0.0	14.6	73.8	16.7	56.2	11.1	51.8
Estonia	39.8	60.2	0.0	0.0	0.0	13.7	48.1	64.4	78.5
Ethiopia	0.7	0.3	14.1	4.8	80.1	3.0	9.1	0.0	0.0
Faeroe Islands	0.0	100.0	0.0	0.0	0.0	0.0	0.0	100.0	100.0
Fiji	0.0	43.2	0.0	56.8	0.0	0.0	0.0	88.3	100.0
Finland	2.0	71.7	6.3	19.2	0.8	4.7	14.2	48.1	67.4
France	3.9	41.0	3.0	30.1	21.9	12.0	23.2	20.8	36.2
French Polynesia	0.0	9.2	6.2	84.5	0.0	0.0	0.0	100.0	100.0
Gabon	5.2	21.3	52.0	15.7	5.7	13.2	32.7	44.9	53.0
Gambia, The	100.0	0.0	0.0	0.0	0.0	92.2	100.0	74.2	85.7
Georgia	0.0	0.0	0.0	6.9	93.0	21.8	91.7	15.2	28.1

Table A5   Other indicators—continued

Economy	Terrain characteristics					Geography and people			
	plains (% of total land area)	lowlands (% of total land area)	plateaus (% of total land area)	hills (% of total land area)	mountains (% of total land area)	Population living at less than 25 kms from an international border (%)	Population living at less than 75 kms from an international border (%)	Population living at less than 25 kms from a coastline (%)	Population living at less than 75 kms from a coastline (%)
	2007	2007	2007	2007	2007	2000	2000	2000	2000
Germany	3.1	45.2	4.6	34.3	12.8	15.2	52.0	7.3	12.6
Ghana	15.2	41.8	24.0	19.0	0.0	14.7	33.3	25.9	39.9
Greece	0.0	7.4	0.0	50.6	41.9	7.1	27.2	81.4	96.4
Greenland	0.3	3.0	33.6	8.1	54.9	0.0	0.0	100.0	100.0
Grenada	0.2	99.8	0.0	0.0	0.0	0.0	0.0	100.0	100.0
Guam	0.0	100.0	0.0	0.0	0.0	0.0	0.0	100.0	100.0
Guatemala	0.3	19.1	7.6	22.8	50.2	18.0	57.2	5.6	28.5
Guinea	5.9	11.9	23.7	20.9	37.6	25.0	63.3	19.0	26.4
Guinea-Bissau	71.9	24.6	0.0	3.5	0.0	26.0	96.5	60.9	86.5
Guyana	9.7	49.6	16.8	18.7	5.1	10.2	23.3	56.9	81.5
Haiti	0.0	0.8	0.0	67.1	32.2	16.3	63.3	80.9	99.8
Honduras	2.1	12.4	0.0	40.0	45.4	19.8	77.6	22.0	46.1
Hong Kong, China	0.0	100.0	0.0	0.0	0.0	49.4	100.0	100.0	100.0
Hungary	15.8	66.6	0.0	16.4	1.2	30.5	91.4	0.0	0.0
Iceland	0.0	9.6	0.0	43.2	47.2	0.0	0.0	99.2	100.0
India	13.2	17.8	27.4	22.8	18.7	5.6	16.1	10.3	19.7
Indonesia	13.3	30.5	0.1	32.3	23.8	0.1	0.7	52.2	90.4
Iran, Islamic Rep.	1.1	4.3	0.3	4.9	89.4	6.0	21.3	2.2	5.5
Iraq	19.2	27.2	35.1	12.0	6.4	9.2	28.7	0.7	5.1
Ireland	0.0	100.0	0.0	0.0	0.0	7.5	31.4	73.4	98.0
Isle of Man	0.0	100.0	0.0	0.0	0.0	0.0	0.0	100.0	100.0
Israel	0.0	31.1	0.0	49.1	19.8	90.6	100.0	66.4	95.2
Italy	0.0	14.5	0.0	49.8	35.7	6.8	28.4	45.2	68.3
Jamaica	0.0	23.3	0.0	76.7	0.0	0.0	0.0	91.3	100.0
Japan	0.1	17.3	0.0	64.6	18.0	0.0	0.0	69.3	95.3
Jordan	0.0	0.0	53.3	9.8	36.9	33.6	100.0	1.5	1.8
Kazakhstan	22.7	22.4	27.4	7.9	19.6	14.2	45.8	0.0	0.0
Kenya	9.4	10.3	10.7	3.3	66.4	8.5	32.0	6.1	7.5
Kiribati	100.0	0.0	0.0	0.0	0.0	0.0	0.0	100.0	100.0
Korea, Dem. Rep.	0.0	19.4	0.0	34.5	46.1	12.8	28.9	43.9	89.2
Korea, Rep.	0.0	35.2	0.0	52.5	12.3	1.3	37.3	62.3	70.7
Kuwait	7.9	70.9	21.2	0.0	0.0	13.7	100.0	88.5	97.7
Kyrgyz Republic	0.0	0.0	0.2	0.0	99.8	55.3	94.9	0.0	0.0
Lao PDR	0.0	11.0	0.0	25.3	63.7	49.0	91.3	0.0	0.0
Latvia	8.5	91.5	0.0	0.0	0.0	19.4	94.3	50.0	73.5
Lebanon	0.0	0.0	0.0	0.0	100.0	35.0	100.0	84.3	100.0
Lesotho	0.0	0.0	0.0	0.0	100.0	60.5	100.0	0.0	0.0
Liberia	2.1	45.9	31.8	17.1	3.2	28.2	55.2	39.7	54.7
Libya	23.5	11.4	52.8	2.6	9.7	1.2	4.8	73.6	86.5
Liechtenstein	0.0	0.0	0.0	0.0	100.0	100.0	100.0	0.0	0.0
Lithuania	3.5	96.5	0.0	0.0	0.0	28.7	87.1	9.1	14.8
Luxembourg	0.0	0.0	0.0	100.0	0.0	100.0	100.0	0.0	0.0
Macao, China	0.0	100.0	0.0	0.0	0.0	100.0	100.0	100.0	100.0
Macedonia, FYR	0.0	0.0	0.0	0.0	100.0	67.5	100.0	0.0	0.0
Madagascar	0.3	20.2	3.8	31.0	44.7	0.0	0.0	23.2	45.0
Malawi	0.0	0.3	0.0	6.0	93.7	34.3	98.8	0.0	0.0
Malaysia	2.9	48.2	0.0	29.5	19.5	8.2	25.1	59.0	95.6
Maldives	99.0	0.0	0.0	0.0	0.0	0.0	0.0	100.0	100.0
Mali	59.3	2.4	36.6	1.8	0.0	12.6	38.1	0.0	0.0
Malta	0.0	100.0	0.0	0.0	0.0	0.0	0.0	100.0	100.0
Marshall Islands	96.2	0.0	0.0	0.0	0.0	0.0	0.0	100.0	100.0
Mauritania	56.0	13.4	29.6	1.1	0.0	22.4	46.8	27.0	32.6
Mauritius	0.0	5.3	0.0	94.2	0.0	0.0	0.0	100.0	100.0
Mayotte	0.0	100.0	0.0	0.0	0.0	0.0	0.0	100.0	100.0
Mexico	5.1	12.9	5.4	14.7	62.0	5.8	8.0	11.2	23.5
Micronesia, Fed. Sts.	0.0	100.0	0.0	0.0	0.0	0.0	0.0	100.0	100.0
Moldova	0.0	85.4	14.6	0.0	0.0	52.7	100.0	0.0	0.0
Monaco	0.0	0.0	0.0	0.0	100.0	100.0	100.0	100.0	100.0
Mongolia	0.0	0.0	14.3	0.0	85.7	5.8	18.1	0.0	0.0
Montenegro	0.0	0.0	0.0	1.3	98.7				
Morocco	1.3	4.8	6.7	17.8	69.5	4.6	13.2	39.5	59.7
Mozambique	6.5	30.2	6.6	28.4	28.3	8.9	34.6	32.7	52.1
Myanmar	2.8	18.8	0.0	31.7	46.6	3.5	15.2	26.0	42.7
Namibia	22.4	0.9	26.4	3.0	47.4	26.8	54.1	6.0	6.7
Nepal	0.0	5.5	0.0	19.5	75.0	44.1	95.2	0.0	0.0
Netherlands	40.0	58.3	0.0	1.8	0.0	33.2	85.6	53.8	88.6
Netherlands Antilles	74.1	25.9	0.0	0.0	0.0	0.0	0.0	100.0	100.0
New Caledonia	10.9	4.7	0.0	84.5	0.0	0.0	0.0	100.0	100.0
New Zealand	0.0	19.1	0.0	28.3	52.6	0.0	0.0	87.0	98.3
Nicaragua	7.9	53.2	0.0	23.5	15.4	10.6	39.1	17.3	63.2

	Terrain characteristics					Geography and people			
	plains (% of total land area)	lowlands (% of total land area)	plateaus (% of total land area)	hills (% of total land area)	mountains (% of total land area)	Population living at less than 25 kms from an international border (%)	Population living at less than 75 kms from an international border (%)	Population living at less than 25 kms from a coastline (%)	Population living at less than 75 kms from a coastline (%)
Economy	2007	2007	2007	2007	2007	2000	2000	2000	2000
Niger	50.2	0.0	41.8	0.0	7.9	21.5	55.5	0.0	0.0
Nigeria	16.1	21.8	35.4	17.5	9.2	5.3	24.4	12.3	20.9
Northern Mariana Islands	0.0	100.0	0.0	0.0	0.0	0.0	0.0	100.0	100.0
Norway	0.0	9.8	0.0	42.7	47.5	5.2	48.7	82.3	92.4
Oman	31.3	17.9	14.4	20.0	16.3	4.7	15.1	66.5	81.5
Pakistan	21.9	10.2	0.9	15.6	51.4	13.8	42.2	7.1	8.3
Palau	0.0	100.0	0.0	0.0	0.0	0.0	0.0	100.0	100.0
Panama	0.2	30.8	0.0	53.6	15.4	8.6	17.2	78.8	100.0
Papua New Guinea	13.1	17.1	0.0	25.9	43.9	1.0	3.4	35.8	53.3
Paraguay	51.3	22.3	23.6	2.8	0.0	53.0	73.1	0.0	0.0
Peru	24.5	4.2	8.5	11.0	51.9	2.5	11.8	39.0	50.4
Philippines	0.1	26.4	0.0	56.4	17.0	0.0	0.0	78.3	98.9
Poland	10.8	63.5	12.2	10.4	3.2	12.8	44.0	5.9	11.2
Portugal	0.0	37.4	0.0	36.4	26.2	6.4	32.4	65.1	89.8
Puerto Rico	0.0	38.9	0.0	61.1	0.0	0.0	0.0	94.1	100.0
Qatar	79.2	20.8	0.0	0.0	0.0	0.4	18.6	94.0	100.0
Romania	0.9	37.9	0.6	21.5	39.1	20.1	61.5	3.4	5.1
Russian Federation	10.0	36.0	6.4	22.1	25.5	3.5	13.0	8.0	10.7
Rwanda	0.0	0.0	15.5	0.0	84.5	57.8	100.0	0.0	0.0
Samoa	0.0	8.0	0.0	92.0	0.0	0.0	0.0		
San Marino	0.0	0.0	0.0	100.0	0.0	100.0	100.0	0.0	0.0
Sao Tome and Princip	0.0	0.6	31.2	35.9	32.3	0.0	0.0	100.0	100.0
Saudi Arabia	0.0	16.4	0.0	83.6	0.0	2.8	9.0	27.0	38.3
Senegal	19.7	5.2	48.0	3.4	23.6	20.2	39.9	48.6	74.4
Serbia	84.2	10.0	2.2	3.6	0.0	..	..	..	..
Seychelles	1.4	18.8	0.0	39.3	40.5	0.0	0.0	100.0	100.0
Sierra Leone	35.4	64.6	0.0	0.0	0.0	15.0	68.1	35.0	55.3
Singapore	0.2	53.3	2.8	43.7	0.0	..	..	100.0	100.0
Slovak Republic	0.0	100.0	0.0	0.0	0.0	57.0	100.0	0.0	0.0
Slovenia	0.0	5.2	0.0	67.5	27.2	68.4	100.0	4.3	14.0
Solomon Islands	0.0	0.0	0.0	49.4	50.6	0.0	0.0	100.0	100.0
Somalia	0.1	51.4	0.0	48.4	0.0	8.0	25.2	30.5	52.7
South Africa	13.1	19.2	36.1	11.6	20.1	5.0	14.8	23.4	35.9
Spain	1.8	3.7	29.1	7.4	58.0	4.7	15.3	48.1	63.5
Sri Lanka	0.0	2.8	3.7	31.6	61.8	0.0	0.0	47.3	88.0
St. Kitts and Nevis	20.3	43.6	0.0	36.0	0.0	0.0	0.0	100.0	100.0
St. Lucia	0.0	100.0	0.0	0.0	0.0	0.0	0.0	100.0	100.0
St. Vincent and the Grenadines	0.0	71.5	0.0	28.5	0.0	0.0	0.0	100.0	100.0
Sudan	0.0	0.0	0.0	100.0	0.0	5.9	14.2	1.8	2.6
Suriname	29.7	0.3	51.1	3.1	15.9	3.4	14.1	86.8	97.3
Swaziland	9.5	65.2	16.8	8.5	0.0	60.5	100.0	0.0	0.0
Sweden	0.0	5.3	0.0	8.0	86.7	1.0	7.1	63.9	82.9
Switzerland	2.3	37.8	4.4	34.4	21.1	63.8	100.0	0.0	0.0
Syrian Arab Republic	0.0	0.0	0.0	0.5	99.5	25.3	85.8	11.3	28.5
Taiwan, China	0.0	5.1	0.0	12.6	82.3	0.0	0.0	71.4	100.0
Tajikistan	0.0	0.0	0.3	0.7	99.0	49.9	96.2	0.0	0.0
Tanzania	1.5	5.1	29.2	7.2	57.1	10.9	32.3	13.6	17.3
Thailand	5.0	41.1	2.3	38.4	13.2	10.5	34.4	18.2	37.6
Timor-Leste	..	..	..	..	..	..	..	..	..
Togo	0.0	58.2	14.8	27.0	0.0	72.5	100.0	26.8	38.6
Tonga	89.3	10.7	0.0	0.0	0.0	0.0	0.0	100.0	100.0
Trinidad and Tobago	0.0	100.0	0.0	0.0	0.0	0.0	0.0	100.0	100.0
Tunisia	1.2	40.5	17.4	36.4	4.4	6.6	22.4	55.8	79.4
Turkey	0.0	4.3	0.6	9.1	86.0	4.2	12.7	37.8	52.7
Turkmenistan	36.5	34.6	11.1	8.1	9.7	27.4	54.9	0.0	0.0
Uganda	10.2	0.0	40.8	0.0	49.1	21.3	53.1	0.0	0.0
Ukraine	23.0	51.1	18.1	4.3	3.5	10.1	41.1	11.2	16.4
United Arab Emirates	29.8	50.7	0.0	19.5	0.0	23.3	83.7	54.8	84.4
United Kingdom	2.3	67.4	0.0	30.3	0.0	0.7	2.1	45.5	87.6
United States	12.6	13.1	24.6	12.8	36.9	3.1	6.9	28.9	41.4
Uruguay	17.4	82.5	0.0	0.0	0.0	10.7	17.5	65.7	77.4
Uzbekistan	23.5	27.2	12.4	17.6	19.4	55.8	86.6	0.0	0.0
Vanuatu	0.3	7.9	1.4	90.4	0.0	0.0	0.0	100.0	100.0
Venezuela, RB	11.0	31.9	4.0	27.2	25.9	3.7	9.8	35.4	64.8
Vietnam	8.4	25.3	0.0	30.5	35.9	9.9	44.7	42.0	73.2
Virgin Islands (U.S.)	0.0	100.0	0.0	0.0	0.0	0.0	0.0	100.0	100.0
West Bank and Gaza	0.0	10.1	0.0	89.9	0.0	100.0	100.0	34.8	66.3
Yemen, Rep.	2.5	1.8	21.5	3.7	70.4	2.0	7.9	13.3	43.7
Zambia	20.3	0.0	46.4	0.0	33.3	22.7	52.6	0.0	0.0
Zimbabwe	2.2	0.0	35.9	0.0	61.9	11.7	28.8	0.0	0.0

Sources and Definitions

Table A1   Geography and access

Column		Source	Notes
1	Location	CIA Factbook	This entry includes rounded latitude and longitude figures for the purpose of finding the approximate geographic center of an entity and is based on the Gazetteer of Conventional Names, Third Edition, August 1988, US Board on Geographic Names and on other sources.
2	Surface area (sq. km)	World Bank	Surface area is a country's total area, including areas under inland bodies of water and some coastal waterways. Food and Agriculture Organization, Production Yearbook and data files.
3	Arable land (% of land area)	World Bank	Arable land includes land defined by the FAO as land under temporary crops (double-cropped areas are counted once), temporary meadows for mowing or for pasture, land under market or kitchen gardens, and land temporarily fallow.
4	Forest land (% of land area)	World Bank	Forest area is land under natural or planted stands of trees, whether productive or not.
5	Coastline (kms)	CIA Factbook	Total length of the boundary between the land area (including islands) and the sea.
6	Land boundaries (kms)	CIA Factbook	*Total* length of all land boundaries and the individual lengths for each of the contiguous *border countries.* When available, official lengths published by national statistical agencies are used. Because surveying methods may differ, country border lengths reported by contiguous countries may differ.
7	Airports with paved runway (number)	CIA Factbook	Total number of airports with paved runways (concrete or asphalt surfaces) by length. For airports with more than one runway, only the longest runway is included according to the following five groups - (1) *over 3,047 m,* (2) *2,438 to 3,047 m,* (3) *1,524 to 2,437 m,* (4) *914 to 1,523 m,* and (5) *under 914 m.* Only airports with usable runways are included in this listing. Not all airports have facilities for refueling, maintenance, or air traffic control.
8	Ports and terminals (number)	CIA Factbook	Number of ports
9	Rail density (rail km per 100 km^2)	CIA Factbook	Total route length of the railway network and of its component parts by gauge (*broad, standard, narrow,* and *dual) divided by the country size (in % terms).*
10	Road density (road km per 100 km^2)	WB and CIA Factbook	Total length of the road network and includes the length of the *paved* and *unpaved* portions divided by the country size (in % terms).
11	National average distance to capital city (kms)	WDR 2009 Team	Population weighted average distance to the capital city

Table A2   Urbanization

Column		Source	Notes
12	Agglomeration index	WDR 2009 Team	See chapter 1
13	% of urban population to total population (2000)	UN	Urban population as a % of total population in 2000
14	% of urban population to total population (2005)	UN	Urban population as a % of total population in 2005
15	% of urban population to total population (2015)	UN	Urban population as a % of total population in 2015
16	Population density (number of people per km^2)	World Bank	Number of people per km^2
17	Pop. in cities > 1 million (% of total pop.)	World Bank	Proportion of the population living in cities bigger than 1 million people
18	% of Population in largest city (% of urban pop.)	World Bank	Proportion of the population living in the largest city (as % of the urban population)
19	% of urban population with water access	World Bank	Percentage of the urban population with reasonable access to an adequate amount of water from an improved source, such as a household connection, public standpipe, borehole, protected well or spring, and rainwater collection. Reasonable access is defined as the availability of at least 20 liters a person a day from a source within one kilometer of the dwelling.
20	% of rural population with water access	World Bank	Percentage of the urban population with reasonable access to an adequate amount of water from an improved source, such as a household connection, public standpipe, borehole, protected well or spring, and rainwater collection. Reasonable access is defined as the availability of at least 20 liters a person a day from a source within one kilometer of the dwelling.
21	% of urban population with sanitation services	World Bank	Percentage of the urban population with at least adequate access to excreta disposal facilities that can effectively prevent human, animal, and insect contact with excreta. Improved facilities range from simple but protected pit latrines to flush toilets with a sewerage connection. To be effective, facilities must be correctly constructed and properly maintained.
22	% of rural population with sanitation services	World Bank	Percentage of the rural population with at least adequate access to excreta disposal facilities that can effectively prevent human, animal, and insect contact with excreta. Improved facilities range from simple but protected pit latrines to flush toilets with a sewerage connection. To be effective, facilities must be correctly constructed and properly maintained.

Table A3   Territorial development

Column		Source	Notes
23	Leading area: Area name	WDR 2009 Team	Name of the leading area. Leading area is defined as the area with the highest measure of welfare (income or consumption or gdp) per capita
24	Leading area: Poverty Incidence	WDR 2009 Team	The poverty incidence is the proportion of the population living below the poverty line
25	Leading area: Poor in area as % of total country poor	WDR 2009 Team	Proportion of the country's poor residing in the leading area
26	Leading area: Welfare measure in area (as a % of country's average welfare measure)	WDR 2009 Team	Leading measure of welfare (income, consumption or gdp) per capita, relative to the national measure of welfare (income, consumption or gdp) per capita
27	Leading area: Area (km2)	Statoids	Surface area of the leading area
28	Leading area: Population density (number of people per km2)	Statoids	People per km2 in the leading area
29	Lagging area: Area name	WDR 2009 Team	Name of the lagging area. Lagging area is defined as the area with the lowest measure of welfare (income or consumption or gdp) per capita
30	Lagging area: Poverty Incidence	WDR 2009 Team	The poverty incidence is the proportion of the population living below the poverty line
31	Lagging area: Poor in area as % of total country poor	WDR 2009 Team	Proportion of the country's poor residing in the lagging area
32	Lagging area: Welfare measure in area (as a % of country's average welfare measure)	WDR 2009 Team	Lagging measure of welfare (income, consumption or gdp) per capita, relative to the national measure of welfare (income, consumption or gdp) per capita
33	Lagging area: Area (km2)	Statoids	Surface area of the lagging area
34	Lagging area: Population density (number of people per km2)	Statoids	People per km2 in the leading area

Table A4   International integration

Column		Source	Notes
35	Countries that need a visa to visit this country	Neumayer (2005)	Number of countries for which their nationals need a visa to visit this country.
36	Countries for which this country's residents need a visa	Neumayer (2005)	Number of countries for which the nationals of this country need a visa.
37	Cost of obtaining a passport relative to GDP per capita	McKenzie (2005)	The price of a standard passport standardized using the GNI per capita
38	International migration stock (% of foreigners)	World Bank	Migration stock is the number of people born in a country other than that in which they live. It also includes refugees
39	International voice traffic (incoming and outgoing, minutes per person)	World Bank	International voice traffic is the sum of international incoming and outgoing telephone traffic (in minutes).
40	International internet bandwith (bits per person)	World Bank	International Internet bandwidth is the contracted capacity of international connections between countries for transmitting Internet traffic.
41	Telephone average cost of call to the US (US$ per three minutes)	World Bank	Cost of international call to U.S. is the cost of a three-minute, peak rate, fixed line call from the country to the United States.
42	Total trade as share of GDP	World Bank	Trade is the sum of exports and imports of goods and services measured as a share of gross domestic product.
43	Index of shipping difficulties	WB Doing Business	Indicator of shipping difficulties (border delays, read carpet, fees, red tape, etc)
44	Average tariffs and custom duties (% of import value)	World Bank	Average tariffs
45	Share of trade with neighboring countries (% of total trade)	WDR 2009 Team	The proportion of trade with neighboring countries as a proportion of the total trade of the country. Calculation using COMTRADE data.

Table A5 Other indicators

Column		Source	Notes
46	% of terrain: plains	Nelson (2007)	% of terrain: plains
47	% of terrain: lowlands	Nelson (2007)	% of terrain: lowlands
48	% of terrain: plateaus	Nelson (2007)	% of terrain: plateaus
49	% of terrain: hills	Nelson (2007)	% of terrain: hills
50	% of terrain: mountains	Nelson (2007)	% of terrain: mountains
51	Population living less than 25 kms from an international border	WDR 2009 Team	Proportion of the total population living in less than 25 kms from an international border
52	Population living less than 75 kms from an international border	WDR 2009 Team	Proportion of the total population living in less than 75 kms from an international border
53	Population living less than 25 kms from a coastline	WDR 2009 Team	Proportion of the total population living in less than 25 kms from a coastline
54	Population living less than 75 kms from a coastline	WDR 2009 Team	Proportion of the total population living in less than 75 kms from a coastline

Selected World Development Indicators

In this year's edition, development data are presented in five tables showing the comparative socioeconomic data for more than 130 economies for the most recent year for which data are available and, for some indicators, for an earlier year. An additional table presents basic indicators for 77 economies with sparse data or with populations of less than 3 million.

The indicators presented here are a selection from more than 800 included in *World Development Indicators 2008*. Published annually, *World Development Indicators* (WDI) reflects a comprehensive view of the development process. The WDI's six sections recognize the contribution of a wide range of factors: progress on the Millennium Development Goals and human capital development, environmental sustainability, macroeconomic performance, private sector development and the investment climate, and the global links that influence the external environment for development.

World Development Indicators is complemented by a separately published database that gives access to more than 1,000 data tables and 800 time-series indicators for 222 economies and regions. This database is available through an electronic subscription (*WDI Online*) or as a CD-ROM.

Data sources and methodology

Socioeconomic and environmental data presented here are drawn from several sources: primary data collected by the World Bank, member country statistical publications, research institutes, and international organizations such as the United Nations and its specialized agencies, the International Monetary Fund (IMF), and the Organisation for Economic Co-operation and Development (OECD) (see the *Data Sources* following the *Technical notes* for a complete listing). Although international standards of coverage, definition, and classification apply to most statistics reported by countries and international agencies, there are inevitably differences in timeliness and reliability arising from differences in the capabilities and resources devoted to basic data collection and compilation. For some topics, competing sources of data require review by World Bank staff to ensure that the most reliable data available are presented. In some instances, where available data are deemed too weak to provide reliable measures of levels and trends or do not adequately adhere to international standards, the data are not shown.

The data presented are generally consistent with those in *World Development Indicators 2008*. However, data have been revised and updated wherever new information has become available. Differences may also reflect revisions to historical series and changes in methodology. Thus data of different vintages may be published in different editions of World Bank publications. Readers are advised not to compile data series from different publications or different editions of the same publication. Consistent time-series data are available on *World Development Indicators 2008* CD-ROM and through *WDI Online*.

All dollar figures are in current U.S. dollars unless otherwise stated. The various methods used to convert from national currency figures are described in the *Technical notes*.

Because the World Bank's primary business is providing lending and policy advice to its low- and middle-income members, the issues covered in these tables focus mainly on these economies. Where available, information on the high-income economies is also provided for comparison. Readers may wish to refer to national statistical publications and publications of the OECD and the European Union for more information on the high-income economies

Classification of economies and summary measures

The summary measures at the bottom of most tables include economies classified by income per capita and by region. Gross national income (GNI) per capita is used to determine the following income classifications: low-income, $935 or less in 2007; middle-income, $936 to $11,455; and high-income, $11,456 and above. A further division at GNI per capita $3,705 is made between lower-middle-income and upper-middle-income economies. The classification of economies based on per capita income occurs annually, so the country composition of the income groups may change annually. When these changes in classification are made based on the most recent estimates, aggregates based on the new income classifications are recalculated for all past periods to ensure that a consistent time series is maintained. See the table on classification of economies at the end of this volume for a list of economies in each group (including those with populations of less than 3 million).

Summary measures are either totals (indicated by **t** if the aggregates include estimates for missing data and nonreporting countries, or by an **s** for simple sums of the data available), weighted averages (**w**), or median values (**m**) calculated for groups of economies. Data for the countries excluded from the main tables (those presented in table 5) have been included in the summary measures, where data are available, or by assuming that they follow the trend of reporting countries. This gives a more consistent aggregated measure by standardizing country coverage for each period shown. Where missing information accounts for a

third or more of the overall estimate, however, the group measure is reported as not available. The section on *Statistical methods* in the *Technical notes* provides further information on aggregation methods. Weights used to construct the aggregates are listed in the technical notes for each table.

Terminology and country coverage

The term *country* does not imply political independence but may refer to any territory for which authorities report separate social or economic statistics. Data are shown for economies as they were constituted in 2007, and historical data are revised to reflect current political arrangements. Throughout the tables, exceptions are noted. Unless otherwise noted, data for China do not include data for Hong Kong, China; Macao, China; or Taiwan, China. Data for Indonesia include Timor-Leste through 1999 unless otherwise noted. Montenegro declared independence from Serbia and Montenegro on June 3, 2006. When available, data for each country are shown separately. *However, some indicators for Serbia continue to include data for Montenegro through 2005; these data are footnoted in the tables.* Moreover, data for most indicators from 1999 onward for Serbia exclude data for Kosovo, a territory within Serbia that is currently under international administration pursuant to UN Security Council Resolution 1244 (1999); any exceptions are noted.

Technical notes

Because data quality and intercountry comparisons are often problematic, readers are encouraged to consult the *Technical notes,* the table on Classification of Economies by Region and Income, and the footnotes to the tables. For more extensive documentation, see *World Development Indicators 2008.*

Readers may find more information on the WDI 2008, and orders can be made online, by phone, or fax as follows:

For more information and to order online: http://www.worldbank.org/data/wdi2006/index.htm.

To order by phone or fax: 1-800-645-7247 or 703-661-1580; Fax 703-661-1501.

To order by mail: The World Bank, P.O. Box 960, Herndon, VA 20172-0960, U.S.A.

Classification of economies by region and income, FY2009

East Asia and the Pacific		Latin America and the Caribbean		South Asia		High income OECD
American Samoa	UMC	Argentina	UMC	Afghanistan	LIC	Australia
Cambodia	LIC	Belize	UMC	Bangladesh	LIC	Austria
China	LMC	Bolivia	LMC	Bhutan	LMC	Belgium
Fiji	UMC	Brazil	UMC	India	LMC	Canada
Indonesia	LMC	Chile	UMC	Maldives	LMC	Czech Republic
Kiribati	LMC	Colombia	LMC	Nepal	LIC	Denmark
Korea, Dem. People's Rep. of	LIC	Costa Rica	UMC	Pakistan	LIC	Finland
Lao PDR	LIC	Cuba	UMC	Sri Lanka	LMC	France
Malaysia	UMC	Dominica	UMC			Germany
Marshall Islands	LMC	Dominican Republic	LMC			Greece
Micronesia, Fed. States of	LMC	Ecuador	LMC	**Sub-Saharan Africa**		Hungary
Mongolia	LMC	El Salvador	LMC	Angola	LMC	Iceland
Myanmar	LIC	Grenada	UMC	Benin	LIC	Ireland
Palau	UMC	Guatemala	LMC	Botswana	UMC	Italy
Papua New Guinea	LIC	Guyana	LMC	Burkina Faso	LIC	Japan
Philippines	LMC	Haiti	LIC	Burundi	LIC	Korea, Rep. of
Samoa	LMC	Honduras	LMC	Cameroon	LMC	Luxembourg
Solomon Islands	LIC	Jamaica	UMC	Cape Verde	LMC	Netherlands
Thailand	LMC	Mexico	UMC	Central African Republic	LIC	New Zealand
Timor-Leste	LMC	Nicaragua	LMC	Chad	LIC	Norway
Tonga	LMC	Panama	UMC	Comoros	LIC	Portugal
Vanuatu	LMC	Paraguay	LMC	Congo, Dem. Rep. of	LIC	Slovak Republic
Vietnam	LIC	Peru	LMC	Congo, Rep. of	LMC	Spain
		St. Kitts and Nevis	UMC	Côte d'Ivoire	LIC	Sweden
		St. Lucia	UMC	Eritrea	LIC	Switzerland
Europe and Central Asia		St. Vincent and the Grenadines	UMC	Ethiopia	LIC	United Kingdom
Albania	LMC	Suriname	UMC	Gabon	UMC	United States
Armenia	LMC	Uruguay	UMC	Gambia, The	LIC	
Azerbaijan	LMC	Venezuela, R.B.	UMC	Ghana	LIC	
Belarus	UMC			Guinea	LIC	**Other high income**
Bosnia and Herzegovina	LMC			Guinea-Bissau	LIC	Andorra
Bulgaria	UMC	**Middle East and North Africa**		Kenya	LIC	Antigua and Barbuda
Croatia	UMC	Algeria	LMC	Lesotho	LMC	Aruba
Georgia	LMC	Djibouti	LMC	Liberia	LIC	Bahamas, The
Kazakhstan	UMC	Egypt, Arab Rep. of	LMC	Madagascar	LIC	Bahrain
Kyrgyz Republic	LIC	Iran, Islamic Rep. of	LMC	Malawi	LIC	Barbados
Latvia	UMC	Iraq	LMC	Mali	LIC	Bermuda
Lithuania	UMC	Jordan	LMC	Mauritania	LIC	Brunei Darussalam
Macedonia, FYR	LMC	Lebanon	UMC	Mauritius	UMC	Cayman Islands
Moldova	LMC	Libya	UMC	Mayotte	UMC	Channel Islands
Montenegro	UMC	Morocco	LMC	Mozambique	LIC	Cyprus
Poland	UMC	Syrian Arab Republic	LMC	Namibia	LMC	Equatorial Guinea
Romania	UMC	Tunisia	LMC	Niger	LIC	Estonia
Russian Federation	UMC	West Bank and Gaza	LMC	Nigeria	LIC	Faeroe Islands
Serbia	UMC	Yemen, Rep. of	LIC	Rwanda	LIC	French Polynesia
Tajikistan	LIC			São Tomé and Príncipe	LIC	Greenland
Turkey	UMC			Senegal	LIC	Guam
Turkmenistan	LMC			Seychelles	UMC	Hong Kong, China
Ukraine	LMC			Sierra Leone	LIC	Isle of Man
Uzbekistan	LIC			Somalia	LIC	Israel
				South Africa	UMC	Kuwait
				Sudan	LMC	Liechtenstein
				Swaziland	LMC	Macao, China
				Tanzania	LIC	Malta
				Togo	LIC	Monaco
				Uganda	LIC	Netherlands Antilles
				Zambia	LIC	New Caledonia
				Zimbabwe	LIC	Northern Mariana Islands
						Oman
						Puerto Rico
						Qatar
						San Marino
						Saudi Arabia
						Singapore
						Slovenia
						Taiwan, China
						Trinidad and Tobago
						United Arab Emirates
						Virgin Islands (U.S.)

This table classifies all World Bank member economies and all other economies with populations of more than 30,000. Economies are divided among income groups according to 2007 GNI per capita, calculated using the World Bank Atlas method. The groups are low income (LIC), $935 or less; lower middle income (LMC), $936–3,705; upper middle income (UMC), $3,706–11,455; and high income, $11,456 or more.
Source: World Bank data.

Table 1 Key indicators of development

	Population			Population age composition % ages 0–14 2007	GNI[a]		PPP GNI[b]		Gross domestic product per capita % growth 2006–07	Life expectancy at birth		Adult literacy rate % ages 15 and older 2005	Carbon dioxide emissions per capita metric tons 2004
	Millions 2007	Average annual % growth 2000–07	Density people per sq. km 2007		$ billions 2007	$ per capita 2007	$ billions 2007	$ per capita 2007		Male years 2006	Female years 2006		
Afghanistan	..	..	..	..	10.1	..[c]	27.2[d]	..[d]	..	..	..	..	0.0
Albania	3	0.5	116	25	10.5	3,290	20.9	6,580	5.7	73	80	99	1.2
Algeria	34	1.5	14	28	122.5	3,620	258.8[d]	7,640[d]	1.6	71	73	70	6.0
Angola	17	2.9	14	46	43.6	2,560	74.9	4,400	20.1	41	44	67	0.5
Argentina	40	1.0	14	26	238.9	6,050	513.0	12,990	7.6	71	79	97	3.7
Armenia	3	−0.4	106	19	7.9	2,640	17.7	5,900	14.0	68	75	99	1.2
Australia	21	1.3	3	19	755.8	35,960	700.6	33,340	2.9	79	83	..	16.2
Austria	8	0.5	101	15	355.1	42,700	316.8	38,090	3.0	77	83	..	8.5
Azerbaijan	9	0.9	104	23	21.9	2,550	54.6	6,370	18.0	70	75	..	3.8
Bangladesh	159	1.8	1,218	34	75.1	470	212.7	1,340	4.8	63	65	47	0.3
Belarus	10	−0.4	47	15	40.9	4,220	104.2	10,740	8.5	63	74	..	6.6
Belgium	11	0.5	352	17	432.5	40,710	373.1	35,110	2.1	77	82	..	9.7
Benin	9	3.2	82	44	5.1	570	11.9	1,310	1.5	55	57	35	0.3
Bolivia	10	1.9	9	37	12.0	1,260	39.4	4,140	2.8	63	67	87	0.8
Bosnia and Herzegovina	4	0.3	74	17	14.3	3,790	28.6	7,280	6.8	72	77	97	4.0
Brazil	192	1.4	23	27	1,133.0	5,910	1,795.7	9,370	4.2	69	76	89	1.8
Bulgaria	8	−0.8	70	13	35.1	4,590	85.4	11,180	6.9	69	76	98	5.5
Burkina Faso	15	3.1	54	46	6.4	430	16.5	1,120	1.0	50	53	24	0.1
Burundi	8	3.5	331	44	0.9	110	2.8	330	−0.3	48	50	59	0.0
Cambodia	14	1.8	82	36	7.9	540	24.5	1,690	8.4	57	61	74	0.0
Cameroon	19	2.2	40	41	19.5	1,050	39.2	2,120	1.3	50	51	68	0.2
Canada	33	1.0	4	17	1,300.0	39,420	1,164.2	35,310	1.7	78	83	..	20.0
Central African Republic	4	1.7	7	42	1.7	380	3.2	740	2.3	43	46	49	0.1
Chad	11	3.4	9	46	5.8	540	13.8	1,280	−2.1	49	52	26	0.0
Chile	17	1.1	22	24	138.6	8,350	209.0	12,590	4.1	75	81	96	3.9
China	1,320	0.6	142	21	3,120.9	2,360	7,083.5	5,370	11.2	70	74	91	3.9
Hong Kong, China	7	0.5	6,647	14	218.9	31,610	305.1	44,050	5.3	79	85	..	5.5
Colombia	46	1.4	42	29	149.9	3,250	306.2	6,640	6.2	69	76	93	1.2
Congo, Dem. Rep. of	62	3.0	28	47	8.6	140	17.9	290	3.5	45	47	67	0.0
Congo, Rep. of	4	2.3	11	42	5.8	1,540	10.4	2,750	−3.6	54	56	85	1.0
Costa Rica	4	1.8	87	27	24.8	5,560	47.7[d]	10,700[d]	4.8	76	81	95	1.5
Côte d'Ivoire	19	1.7	61	41	17.5	910	30.7	1,590	−0.1	47	49	49	0.3
Croatia	4	−0.2	79	15	46.4	10,460	66.8	15,050	5.6	73	79	98	5.3
Czech Republic	10	0.1	134	14	149.4	14,450	225.5	21,820	5.0	73	80	..	11.5
Denmark	5	0.3	129	19	299.8	54,910	200.6	36,740	1.4	76	80	..	9.8
Dominican Republic	10	1.6	202	33	34.6	3,550	61.8[d]	6,340[d]	7.0	69	75	87	2.1
Ecuador	13	1.2	48	32	41.2	3,080	93.9	7,040	0.9	72	78	91	2.3
Egypt, Arab Rep. of	75	1.8	76	33	119.4	1,580	407.6	5,400	5.2	69	73	71	2.2
El Salvador	7	1.4	331	33	19.5	2,850	38.6[d]	5,640[d]	2.8	69	75	81	0.9
Eritrea	5	3.9	48	43	1.1	230	2.5[d]	520[d]	−2.3	55	60	..	0.2
Ethiopia	79	2.6	79	44	17.6	220	61.7	780	8.4	51	54	36	0.1
Finland	5	0.3	17	17	234.8	44,400	186.5	35,270	4.0	76	83	..	12.6
France	62	0.7	112	18	2,447.1	38,500[e]	2,065.4	33,470	1.6	77	84	..	6.2
Georgia	4	−1.0	63	18	9.3	2,120	21.0	4,770	13.4	67	75	..	0.9
Germany	82	0.0[f]	236	14	3,197.0	38,860	2,782.7	33,820	2.6	76	82	..	9.8
Ghana	23	2.2	103	38	13.9	590	31.2	1,330	4.3	59	60	58	0.3
Greece	11	0.4	87	14	331.7	29,630	364.1	32,520	3.6	77	82	96	8.7
Guatemala	13	2.5	123	43	32.6	2,440	60.4[d]	4,520[d]	3.2	66	74	69	1.0
Guinea	9	1.9	38	43	3.7	400	10.5	1,120	−0.6	54	57	29	0.2
Haiti	10	1.6	349	37	5.4	560	11.1[d]	1,150[d]	1.4	59	62	..	0.2
Honduras	7	1.9	63	39	11.3	1,600	25.7[d]	3,620[d]	4.5	66	73	80	1.1
Hungary	10	−0.2	112	15	116.3	11,570	175.2	17,430	1.5	69	77	..	5.7
India	1,123	1.4	378	32	1,069.4	950	3,078.7	2,740	7.7	63	66	61	1.2
Indonesia	226	1.3	125	28	373.1	1,650	807.9	3,580	5.1	66	70	90	1.7
Iran, Islamic Rep. of	71	1.5	44	27	246.5	3,470	766.9	10,800	6.2	69	72	82	6.4
Iraq	..	..	..	..	..[g]		..	..	..	..	..	..	3.0
Ireland	4	2.0	63	21	210.2	48,140	161.7	37,040	2.8	77	82	..	10.4
Israel	7	1.9	331	28	157.1	21,900	186.0	25,930	3.4	78	82	..	10.5
Italy	59	0.6	202	14	1,991.3	33,540	1,775.3	29,900	0.8	78	84	98	7.7
Japan	128	0.1	351	14	4,813.3	37,670	4,420.6	34,600	2.1	79	86	..	9.8
Jordan	6	2.5	65	36	16.3	2,850	29.5	5,160	2.6	71	74	91	3.1
Kazakhstan	15	0.6	6	24	78.3	5,060	150.1	9,700	7.3	61	72	..	13.3
Kenya	38	2.6	66	43	25.6	680	57.8	1,540	4.1	52	55	74	0.3
Korea, Rep. of	49	0.5	492	18	955.8	19,690	1,201.1	24,750	4.7	75	82	..	9.7
Kyrgyz Republic	5	0.9	27	30	3.1	590	10.2	1,950	6.4	64	72	..	1.1
Lao PDR	6	1.6	25	38	3.4	580	11.4	1,940	5.3	63	65	69	0.2
Lebanon	4	1.2	401	28	23.7	5,770	41.2	10,050	1.0	70	74	..	4.1
Liberia	4	2.9	39	47	0.6	150	1.1	290	4.3	44	46	52	0.1
Libya	6	2.0	4	30	55.5	9,010	90.6[d]	14,710[d]	4.8	71	77	84	10.3
Lithuania	3	−0.5	54	16	33.5	9,920	58.0	17,180	9.4	65	77	100	3.9
Madagascar	20	2.8	34	43	6.3	320	18.2	920	3.7	57	61	71	0.2
Malawi	14	2.6	148	47	3.5	250	10.5	750	4.7	47	48	..	0.1
Malaysia	27	1.9	81	30	173.7	6,540	360.2	13,570	4.0	72	76	89	7.0
Mali	12	3.0	10	48	6.1	500	12.8	1,040	−0.3	52	56	24	0.1
Mauritania	3	2.8	3	40	2.6	840	6.3	2,010	−0.6	62	66	51	0.9
Mexico	105	1.0	54	30	878.0	8,340	1,324.2	12,580	2.3	72	77	92	4.3
Moldova	4	−1.3	115	19	4.3	1,260[h]	11.1	2,930	4.1	65	72	99	2.0
Morocco	31	1.2	69	29	69.4	2,250	123.3	3,990	1.1	69	73	52	1.4
Mozambique	21	2.3	27	44	6.8	320	14.8	690	5.0	42	43	..	0.1
Myanmar	49	0.9	74	26	..	..[c]	..	..	4.1	59	65	90	0.2

| | Population | | | Population age composition % ages 0–14 2007 | GNI[a] | | PPP GNI[b] | | Gross domestic product per capita % growth 2006–07 | Life expectancy at birth | | Adult literacy rate % ages 15 and older 2005 | Carbon dioxide emissions per capita metric tons 2004 |
	Millions 2007	Average annual % growth 2000–07	Density people per sq. km 2007		$ billions 2007	$ per capita 2007	$ billions 2007	$ per capita 2007		Male years 2006	Female years 2006		
Nepal	28	2.0	197	38	9.7	340	29.2	1,040	0.8	63	64	49	0.1
Netherlands	16	0.4	484	18	750.5	45,820	647.1	39,500	3.3	78	82	..	8.7
New Zealand	4	1.3	16	21	121.7	28,780	111.4	26,340	2.3	78	82	..	7.7
Nicaragua	6	1.3	46	37	5.5	980	14.1[d]	2,520[d]	2.9	70	76	77	0.7
Niger	14	3.5	11	48	4.0	280	9.0	630	–0.1	57	56	29	0.1
Nigeria	148	2.4	162	44	137.1	930	262.5	1,770	4.0	46	47	69	0.8
Norway	5	0.7	15	19	360.0	76,450	252.8	53,690	2.4	78	83	..	19.1
Pakistan	162	2.3	211	36	141.0	870	417.5	2,570	4.2	65	66	50	0.8
Panama	3	1.8	45	30	18.4	5,510	35.4[d]	10,610[d]	9.4	73	78	92	1.8
Papua New Guinea	6	2.3	14	40	5.4	850	11.8[d]	1,870[d]	4.2	55	60	57	0.4
Paraguay	6	1.9	15	35	10.2	1,670	26.8	4,380	4.6	69	74	93	0.7
Peru	28	1.2	22	31	96.2	3,450	201.9	7,240	7.8	69	74	88	1.2
Philippines	88	2.0	295	35	142.6	1,620	327.8	3,730	5.3	69	74	93	1.0
Poland	38	–0.1	124	15	374.6	9,840	593.3	15,590	6.7	71	80	..	8.0
Portugal	11	0.5	116	16	201.1	18,950	219.0	20,640	1.7	75	82	94	5.6
Romania	22	–0.6	94	15	132.5	6,150	236.6	10,980	6.4	69	76	97	4.2
Russian Federation	142	–0.5	9	15	1,071.0	7,560	2,039.1	14,400	8.8	59	73	99	10.6
Rwanda	10	2.5	395	43	3.1	320	8.4	860	3.0	44	47	65	0.1
Saudi Arabia	24	2.3	12	34	373.5	15,440	554.3	22,910	1.2	71	75	83	13.7
Senegal	12	2.6	64	42	10.2	820	20.3	1,640	1.9	61	65	39	0.4
Serbia	7[i]	–0.3[i]	95[i]	18	35.0	4,730[i]	75.5	10,220	6.9	70[i]	76[i]	..	..
Sierra Leone	6	3.7	82	43	1.5	260	3.9	660	4.6	41	44	35	0.2
Singapore	5	1.9	6,660	18	149.0	32,470	222.7	48,520	3.3	78	82	93	12.5
Slovak Republic	5	0.0[f]	112	16	63.3	11,730	104.3	19,330	10.3	70	78	..	6.7
Somalia	9	3.0	14	44	..	..[c]	..	..	..	47	49	..	..
South Africa	48	1.1	39	32	274.0	5,760	454.8	9,560	4.4	49	53	..	9.4
Spain	45	1.6	90	15	1,321.8	29,450	1,351.1	30,110	2.0	78	84	..	7.7
Sri Lanka	20	0.4	309	23	30.8	1,540	84.0	4,210	6.5	72	78	91	0.6
Sudan	39	2.1	16	40	37.0	960	72.6	1,880	7.8	57	60	61	0.3
Sweden	9	0.4	22	17	421.3	46,060	327.9	35,840	1.8	79	83	..	5.9
Switzerland	8	0.7	189	16	452.1	59,880	325.3	43,080	2.2	79	84	..	5.5
Syrian Arab Republic	20	2.7	108	36	35.0	1,760	87.0	4,370	4.0	72	76	81	3.7
Tajikistan	7	1.3	48	38	3.1	460	11.5	1,710	6.2	64	69	99	0.8
Tanzania	40	2.5	46	44	16.3	400[j]	48.7	1,200	4.5	51	53	69	0.1
Thailand	64	0.7	125	21	217.4	3,400	503.1	7,880	4.1	66	75	93	4.3
Togo	7	2.8	121	43	2.4	360	5.2	800	–0.5	56	60	53	0.4
Tunisia	10	1.0	66	25	32.8	3,200	73.0	7,130	5.1	72	76	74	2.3
Turkey	74	1.3	96	27	592.9	8,020	893.1	12,090	3.2	69	74	87	3.2
Turkmenistan	5	1.4	11	30	..[g]	..	21.0[d]	4,350[d]	..	59	67	..	8.8
Uganda	31	3.2	157	49	10.5	340	28.5	920	2.9	50	51	67	0.1
Ukraine	46	–0.8	80	14	118.4	2,550	315.9	6,810	8.2	62	74	99	7.0
United Arab Emirates	4	4.2	52	20	..[k]	..	..	..	4.4	77	82	89	37.8
United Kingdom	61	0.5	252	18	2,608.5	42,740	2,097.9	34,370	2.3	77	81	..	9.8
United States	302	0.9	33	20	13,886.5	46,040	13,829.0	45,850	1.5	75	81	..	20.6
Uruguay	3	0.1	19	23	21.2	6,380	36.6	11,040	7.3	72	80	..	1.7
Uzbekistan	27	1.2	63	32	19.7	730	65.3[d]	2,430[d]	7.9	64	71	..	5.3
Venezuela, R.B. de	27	1.7	31	31	201.2	7,320	327.5	11,920	6.6	72	77	93	6.6
Vietnam	85	1.3	275	28	67.2	790	216.9	2,550	7.2	68	73	..	1.2
West Bank and Gaza	4	3.8	643	45	4.5	1,230	..	..	–4.9	71	74	92	..
Yemen, Rep.	22	3.0	42	45	19.4	870	49.3	2,200	0.6	61	64	54	1.0
Zambia	12	1.9	16	46	9.5	800	14.6	1,220	4.0	41	42	..	0.2
Zimbabwe	13	0.8	35	38	4.5	340	..	..	–6.0	43	42	89	0.8
World	6,612s	1.2w	51w	28w	52,621.4t	7,958w	65,144.4t	9,852w	2.6w	66w	70w	82w	4.3w
Low income	1,296	2.2	61	39	748.8	578	1,935.2	1,494	4.3	56	58	61	0.6
Middle income	4,260	1.0	57	27	12,234.7	2,872	25,353.6	5,952	6.9	67	71	90	3.2
Lower middle income	3,437	1.1	100	27	6,485.0	1,887	15,613.9	4,543	8.6	67	70	89	2.6
Upper middle income	823	0.7	20	24	5,749.6	6,987	9,765.9	11,868	5.1	67	74	93	5.5
Low and middle income	5,556	1.3	58	29	12,985.9	2,337	27,283.9	4,911	6.5	64	68	79	2.6
East Asia & Pacific	1,914	0.8	121	23	4,173.5	2,180	9,449.8	4,937	9.6	69	73	91	3.3
Europe & Central Asia	445	0.0[f]	19	19	2,693.7	6,051	4,947.7	11,115	6.7	64	74	97	7.1
Latin America & the Caribbean	563	1.3	28	29	3,118.0	5,540	5,245.9	9,321	4.5	70	76	90	2.6
Middle East & North Africa	313	1.8	36	32	875.6	2,794	2,314.7	7,385	4.0	68	72	73	3.8
South Asia	1,520	1.6	318	33	1,338.6	880	3,856.7	2,537	7.0	63	66	58	1.1
Sub-Saharan Africa	800	2.5	34	43	761.6	952	1,496.1	1,870	3.7	49	52	59	0.9
High income	1,056	0.7	32	18	39,682.1	37,566	38,133.5	36,100	2.0	76	82	99	13.1

a. Calculated using the World Bank Atlas method. b. PPP is purchasing power parity; see *Technical notes*. c. Estimated to be low income ($935 or less). d. The estimate is based on regression; others are extrapolated from the latest International Comparison Program benchmark estimates. e. The GNI and GNI per capita estimates include the French overseas departments of French Guiana, Guadeloupe, Martinique, and Réunion. f. Less than 0.05. g. Estimated to be lower middle income ($936 to $3,705). h. Excludes data for Transnistria. i. Excludes data for Kosovo and Metohija. j. Data refer to mainland Tanzania only. k. Estimated to be high income ($11.456 or more).

Table 2   Millennium Development Goals: eradicating poverty and improving lives

	Eradicate extreme poverty and hunger				Achieve universal primary education		Promote gender equality		Reduce child mortality		Improve maternal health				Combat HIV/AIDS and other diseases
	Share of poorest quintile in national consumption or income %[b]	Prevalence of child malnutrition % of children under 5		Primary completion rate[a] %		Ratio of girls to boys enrollments in primary and secondary school[a] %		Under-five mortality rate per 1,000		Births attended by skilled health staff % of total		Contraceptive Prevalence rate % of married women ages 15–49		HIV prevalence % of population ages 15–49
	1992–2005	1990	2000–07[b]	1991	2006	1991	2006	1990	2006	1990	2000–07[b]	1990	2000–07[b]	2005
Afghanistan	..	..	..	..	..	..	..	..	..	..	..	..	..	..
Albania	8.2[c]	..	17.0	..	96	96	97	45	17	..	100	..	60	0.2
Algeria	7.0[c]	..	10.2	80	85	83	99	69	38	77	95	47	61	0.1
Angola	..	..	27.5	35	..	..	..	260	260	..	45	..	6	3.7
Argentina	3.1[d,e]	..	2.3	..	97	..	104	29	16	96	99	..	..	0.6
Armenia	8.5[c]	..	4.2	..	91	..	104	56	24	..	98	..	53	0.1
Australia	5.9[e]	..	..	..	..	101	97	10	6	100	100	..	..	0.3
Austria	8.6[e]	..	..	..	103	95	97	10	5	..	..	..	..	0.3
Azerbaijan	7.4[c]	..	14.0	..	92	100	96	105	88	..	100	..	55	0.1
Bangladesh	8.8[c]	..	39.2	49	72	..	103	149	69	..	20	31	58	<0.1
Belarus	8.8[c]	..	1.3	94	95	..	101	24	13	..	100	..	73	0.3
Belgium	8.5[e]	..	..	79	87	101	98	10	4	..	..	78	..	0.3
Benin	7.4[c]	..	21.5	21	64	49	73	185	148	..	79	..	17	1.8
Bolivia	1.5[e]	8.9	5.9	..	101	..	98	125	61	43	67	30	58	0.1
Bosnia and Herzegovina	7.0[c]	..	1.6	..	..	..	..	22	15	97	100	..	36	<0.1
Brazil	2.9[e]	..	3.7	93	106	..	103	57	20	72	97	59	..	0.5
Bulgaria	8.7[c]	..	1.6	84	98	99	97	19	14	..	99	..	..	<0.1
Burkina Faso	6.9[c]	..	35.2	20	31	62	80	206	204	..	54	..	17	2.0
Burundi	5.1[c]	..	38.9	46	36	82	89	190	181	..	34	..	9	3.3
Cambodia	6.8[c]	..	28.4	..	87	73	89	116	82	..	44	..	40	1.6
Cameroon	5.6[c]	..	15.1	53	52	83	83	139	149	58	63	16	29	5.5[g]
Canada	7.2[c]	..	..	..	..	99	98	8	6	..	100	..	..	0.3
Central African Republic	2.0[c]	..	21.8	27	24	60	..	173	175	..	53	..	19	10.7
Chad	..	..	33.9	18	31	42	61	201	209	..	14	..	3	3.5
Chile	3.8[c]	..	..	..	95	100	99	21	9	..	100	56	..	0.3
China	4.3[e]	..	6.8	105	..	87	100	45	24	50	98	71	87	0.1[h]
Hong Kong, China	5.3[e]	..	..	102	100	103	98	..	..	..	100	86	..	..
Colombia	2.9[e]	..	5.1	70	105	108	104	35	21	82	96	66	78	0.6
Congo, Dem. Rep. of	..	..	33.6	46	..	..	..	205	205	..	74[k]	8	21[k]	3.2
Congo, Rep.	..	..	11.8	54	73	85	90	103	126	..	86	..	44	5.3
Costa Rica	4.1[e]	..	..	79	89	101	102	18	12	98	99	..	96	0.3
Côte d'Ivoire	5.2[c]	..	20.2	43	43	65	..	153	127	..	57	..	13	7.1
Croatia	8.8[c]	..	..	..	92	102	102	12	6	100	100	..	69	<0.1
Czech Republic	10.3[e]	..	2.1	..	94	98	101	13	4	..	100	78	..	0.1
Denmark	8.3[e]	..	..	98	101	101	101	9	5	..	..	78	..	0.2
Dominican Republic	4.1[e]	8.4	4.2	..	83	..	104	65	29	93	96	56	61	1.1
Ecuador	3.3[c]	..	6.2	..	106	..	100	57	24	..	75	53	73	0.3
Egypt, Arab Rep. of	8.9[c]	..	5.4	..	98[k]	81	95	91	35	37	74	38	59	<0.1
El Salvador	2.7[e]	11.1	6.1	41	88	102	99	60	25	52	92	47	67	0.9
Eritrea	..	..	34.5	..	49	..	72	147	74	..	28	..	8	2.4
Ethiopia	9.1[c]	..	34.6	26	46[k]	68	83[k]	204	123	..	6	4	15	1.4[i]
Finland	9.6[e]	..	..	97	97	109	102	7	4	..	100	77	..	0.1
France	7.2[e]	..	..	104	..	102	100	9	4	..	..	81	..	0.4
Georgia	5.4[c]	..	..	..	85	98	103	46	32	..	92	..	47	0.2
Germany	8.5[e]	..	..	100	97	99	98	9	4	..	100	75	..	0.1
Ghana	5.6[c]	24.1	18.8	61	71	79	95[k]	120	120	40	50	13	17	2.3
Greece	6.7[e]	..	..	99	103	99	98	11	4	..	..	..	..	0.2
Guatemala	3.9[e]	..	17.7	..	77	..	92	82	41	..	41	..	43	0.9
Guinea	7.0[c]	..	22.5	17	64	45	74	235	161	31	38	..	9	1.5
Haiti	2.4[c]	..	18.9	27	..	..	94	152	80	23	26	10	32	2.2[j]
Honduras	3.4[c]	..	8.6	64	89	106	109	58	27	45	67	47	65	1.5
Hungary	8.6[c]	2.3	..	93	96	100	99	17	7	..	100	..	..	0.1
India	8.1[c]	..	43.5	64	86	70	91	115	76	..	47	43	56	0.9
Indonesia	7.1[c]	31.0	24.4	91	99	93	98	91	34	32	72	50	57	0.1
Iran, Islamic Rep. of	6.5[c]	..	..	91	101	85	105	72	34	..	90	49	74	0.2
Iraq	..	..	..	58	..	78	..	53	..	54	..	14	..	..
Ireland	7.4[e]	..	..	..	96	104	103	9	5	..	100	60	..	0.2
Israel	5.7[e]	..	..	..	101	105	101	12	5	..	..	68	..	0.2
Italy	6.5[e]	..	..	104	100	100	99	9	4	..	99	..	..	0.5
Japan	10.6[e]	..	..	101	..	101	100	6	4	100	100	58	56	<0.1
Jordan	6.7[c]	4.8	3.6	72	99	101	102	40	25	87	100	40	56	0.2
Kazakhstan	7.4[c]	..	..	..	101[k]	102	99[k]	60	29	..	100	..	51	0.1
Kenya	6.0[c]	..	16.5	..	93	94	96	97	121	50	42	27	39	6.1
Korea, Rep. of	7.9[e]	..	..	98	101[k]	99	96[k]	9	5	98	100	77	..	<0.1
Kyrgyz Republic	8.9[c]	..	..	..	99	..	100	75	41	..	98	..	48	0.1
Lao PDR	8.1[c]	..	36.4	46	75	76	85	163	75	..	19	..	32	0.1
Lebanon	..	..	3.4	..	80	..	103	37	30	..	98	..	58	0.1
Liberia	..	..	22.8	..	63	..	..	235	235	..	51	..	10	..
Libya	..	..	..	..	..	..	105	41	18	..	..	..	..	0.2
Lithuania	6.8[c]	..	..	..	93	..	100	13	8	..	100	..	..	0.2
Madagascar	4.9[c]	35.5	36.8	33	57	98	96	168	115	57	51	17	27	0.5
Malawi	7.0[c]	24.4	18.4	29	55	81	100	221	120	55	54	13	42	14.1
Malaysia	4.4[e]	..	..	91	98	101	104	22	12	..	98	50	..	0.5
Mali	6.1[c]	..	30.1	13	49	57	74	250	217	..	41	..	8	1.7
Mauritania	6.2[c]	..	30.4	34	47	71	102	133	125	40	57	3	8	0.7
Mexico	4.3[c]	13.9	3.4	88	104	97	99	53	35	..	83	..	71	0.3
Moldova	7.8[c]	..	3.2	..	98	106	103	37	19	..	100	..	68	1.1
Morocco	6.5[c]	8.1	9.9	48	84	70	87	89	37	31	63	42	63	0.1
Mozambique	5.4[c]	..	21.2	26	42	71	85	235	138	..	48	..	17	16.1
Myanmar	..	..	29.6	..	95	97	101	130	104	..	68	17	34	1.3

	Eradicate extreme poverty and hunger			Achieve universal primary education		Promote gender equality		Reduce child mortality		Improve maternal health				Combat HIV/AIDS and other diseases
	Share of poorest quintile in national consumption or income % [b]	Prevalence of child malnutrition % of children under 5		Primary completion rate[a] %		Ratio of girls to boys enrollments in primary and secondary school[a] %		Under-five mortality rate per 1,000		Births attended by skilled health staff % of total		Contraceptive Prevalence rate % of married women ages 15–49		HIV prevalence % of population ages 15–49
	1992–2005	1990	2000–07[b]	1991	2006	1991	2006	1990	2006	1990	2000–07[b]	1990	2000–07[b]	2005
Nepal	6.0[c]	..	38.8	51	76	59	93	142	59	7	19	23	48	0.5
Netherlands	7.6[e]	..	..	..	..	97	98	9	5	..	100	76	..	0.2
New Zealand	6.4[e]	..	..	100	..	100	103	11	6	..	97	..	..	0.1
Nicaragua	5.6[c]	..	7.8	42	73	109	102	68	36	..	67	..	69	0.2
Niger	2.6[c]	41.0	39.9	18	33	53	70	320	253	15	18	4	11	1.1
Nigeria	5.0[c]	35.1	27.2	..	76	77	83	230	191	33	36	6	13	3.9
Norway	9.6[e]	..	..	100	96	102	100	9	4	100	..	74	..	0.1
Pakistan	9.1[c]	39.0	31.3	..	62	..	78	130	97	19	31	15	28	0.1
Panama	2.5[e]	..	..	86	94	..	101	34	23	..	91	..	..	0.9
Papua New Guinea	4.5[c]	..	..	46	..	80	..	94	73	..	42	..	..	1.8
Paraguay	2.4[e]	2.8	..	68	95	98	99	41	22	66	77	48	73	0.4
Peru	3.7[e]	8.8	5.2	..	101	96	101	78	25	80	87	59	46	0.6
Philippines	5.4[c]	..	20.7	86	94	100	102	62	32	..	60	36	49	<0.1
Poland	7.4[c]	..	..	98	97	101	99	18	7	..	100	49	..	0.1
Portugal	5.8[e]	..	..	95	104	103	101	14	5	98	100	..	..	0.4
Romania	8.2[c]	..	3.5	96	101	99	100	31	18	..	98	..	70	<0.1
Russian Federation	6.1[c]	..	..	..	94	104	99	27	16	..	99	34	..	1.1
Rwanda	5.3[c]	24.3	18.0	35	35	92	102	176	160	26	39	21	17	3.0[j]
Saudi Arabia	..	..	..	55	..	84	..	44	25	..	96	..	..	0.2
Senegal	6.6[c]	..	14.5	42	49	69	92	149	116	..	52	..	12	0.7[j]
Serbia	8.3[c,f]	..	1.8	..	81[k]	67	86[k]	..	8	..	99	..	41	0.2[f]
Sierra Leone	6.5[c]	..	24.7	..	..	95	..	290	270	..	43	..	5	1.6
Singapore	5.0[e]	..	3.3	..	..	95	..	8	3	..	100	65	..	0.3
Slovak Republic	8.8[e]	..	..	96	93	..	100	14	8	..	100	74	..	<0.1
Somalia	..	..	32.8	..	..	..	..	203	145	..	33	1	15	0.9
South Africa	3.5[c]	..	..	76	100	104	100	60	69	..	92	57	60	18.8
Spain	7.0[e]	..	..	..	103	104	103	9	4	..	..	..	..	0.6
Sri Lanka	7.0[c]	..	22.8	102	108	102	..	32	13	..	96	..	70	<0.1
Sudan	..	..	38.4	42	47	77	89	120	89	69	49	9	8	1.6
Sweden	9.1[e]	..	..	96	..	102	100	7	3	..	..	..	..	0.2
Switzerland	7.6[e]	..	..	53	88	97	97	9	5	..	100	..	..	0.4
Syrian Arab Republic	..	..	8.5	89	115	85	95	38	14	..	93	..	58	0.2
Tajikistan	7.8[c]	..	..	..	106	..	88	115	68	..	83	..	38	0.1
Tanzania	7.3[c]	25.1	16.7	62	85[k]	97	..	161	118	53	43	10	26	6.5
Thailand	6.3[c]	..	7.0	..	..	97	104	31	8	..	97	..	77	1.4
Togo	..	21.2	..	35	67	59	73	149	108	31	62	34	17	3.2
Tunisia	6.0[c]	8.5	..	74	120	86	104	52	23	69	90	50	63	0.1
Turkey	5.3[c]	..	3.5	90	96	81	90	82	26	..	83	63	71	0.2
Turkmenistan	6.1[c]	..	..	..	..	..	..	99	51	..	100	..	48	<0.1
Uganda	5.7[c]	19.7	19.0	..	54	82	98	160	134	38	42	5	24	6.4[l]
Ukraine	9.0[c]	..	4.1	94	105	..	99	25	24	..	100	..	66	1.4
United Arab Emirates	..	..	..	103	100	104	101	15	8	..	100	..	..	0.2
United Kingdom	6.1[e]	..	..	..	..	102	102	10	6	..	..	..	84	0.2
United States	5.4[e]	..	1.1	..	95	100	100	11	8	99	99	71	..	0.6
Uruguay	4.5[d,e]	..	6.0	94	99	..	106	23	12	..	99	..	..	0.5
Uzbekistan	7.2[c]	..	4.4	..	100	94	98[k]	74	43	..	100	..	65	0.2
Venezuela, R.B. de	3.3[e]	..	..	43	96	105	103	33	21	..	95	..	..	0.7
Vietnam	7.1[c]	..	20.2	..	..	..	104	53	17	..	88	53	76	0.5[j]
West Bank and Gaza	..	..	..	..	95	..	104	40	22	..	99	..	50	..
Yemen, Rep.	7.2[c]	..	41.3	..	60	..	66	139	100	16	27	10	23	0.2
Zambia	3.6[c]	21.2	23.3	..	84	..	93	180	182	51	43	15	34	17.0
Zimbabwe	4.6[c]	8.0	14.0	97	..	92	97	76	105	70	80	43	60	18.1[j]
World	..w	..w	23.9w	79w	86w	..w	95w	92w	72w	49w	65w	57w	60w	1.0w
Low income	..	..	28.9	49	65	76	88	164	135	33	41	22	33	2.5
Middle income	..	..	22.9	82	93	86	97	75	49	48	73	61	69	0.7
Lower middle income	..	..	25.2	83	91	83	96	81	54	44	69	63	69	0.5
Upper middle income	..	..	..	88	101	99	100	46	26	79	94	50	67	1.6
Low and middle income	..	..	24.9	77	85	84	94	101	79	45	62	54	60	1.1
East Asia & Pacific	..	..	13.3	101	98	90	100	56	29	47	87	75	79	0.2
Europe & Central Asia	..	..	..	90	98	98	97	49	26	81	95	44	63	0.6
Latin America & the Caribbean	..	..	5.1	82	100	99	101	55	26	75	88	57	67	0.6
Middle East & North Africa	..	..	..	77	90	79	93	78	42	48	77	42	60	0.1
South Asia	..	..	41.3	62	80	70	90	123	83	30	41	40	53	0.7
Sub-Saharan Africa	..	..	26.8	51	60	82	87	184	157	44	45	15	22	5.8
High income	..	..	..	..	97	100	99	12	7	..	99	71	..	0.4

a. Because of the change from International Standard Classification of Education 1976 (ISCED76) to ISCED97, data before 1998 are not fully comparable with data from 1999 onward. b. Data are for the most recent year available. c. Refers to expenditure shares by percentiles of population, ranked by per capita expenditure. d. Urban data. e. Refers to income shares by percentiles of population, ranked by per capita income. f. Includes Montenegro. g. Survey data, 2004. h. Includes Hong Kong, China. i. Survey data 2005. j. Survey data 2005–2006. k. Data are for 2007. l. Survey data, 2004–2005.

Table 3   Economic activity

	Gross domestic product		Agricultural tchr productivity		Value added as % of GDP			Household final cons. expenditure	General gov't. final cons. expenditure	Gross capital formation	External balance of goods and services	GDP implicit deflator
	Millions of dollars	Avg. annual % growth	Agricultural value added per worker 2000 $		Agriculture	Industry	Services	% of GDP	% of GDP	% of GDP	% of GDP	Avg. annual % growth
	2007	2000–07	1990–92	2003–05	2007	2007	2007	2007	2007	2007	2007	2000–07
Afghanistan	11,627	11.5	..	..	36	24	39	111	10	28	–49	5.9
Albania	10,569	5.3	778	1,449	23	22	56	90	9	27	–26	3.5
Algeria	135,285	4.5	1,911	2,225	8	61	30	34	12	30	24	8.8
Angola	58,547	13.1	165	174	10	68	22	59	..[a]	14	26	55.3
Argentina	262,331	4.7	6,767	10,072	8	36	56	59	12	24	6	12.3
Armenia	9,177	12.7	1,476[b]	3,692	18	44	38	74	9	32	–15	4.2
Australia	821,716	3.3	20,838	29,924	3	28	69	57	18	27	–1	3.7
Austria	377,028	1.9	12,048	22,203	2	31	67	56	18	21	6	1.8
Azerbaijan	31,248	17.2	1,084[b]	1,143	6	62	32	32	13	27	27	9.3
Bangladesh	67,694	5.8	254	338	19	29	53	77	6	24	–7	4.3
Belarus	44,771	8.3	1,977[b]	3,153	9	40	51	62	20	28	–9	27.6
Belgium	448,560	1.9	21,479	41,631	1	24	75	53	23	22	3	2.0
Benin	5,428	3.8	326	519	32	13	54	78	15	20	–13	2.9
Bolivia	13,120	3.6	670	773	14	32	54	68	13	13	5	6.8
Bosnia and Herzegovina	14,661	5.3	..	8,270	10	26	64	76	24	18	–18	3.8
Brazil	1,314,170	3.3	1,506	3,126	5	31	64	48	28	22	2	8.5
Bulgaria	39,549	5.7	2,500	7,159	8	33	59	75	12	35	–22	5.0
Burkina Faso	6,767	5.8	110	173	33	22	44	75	22	18	–15	2.2
Burundi	974	2.7	108	70	35	20	45	91	29	17	–37	8.4
Cambodia	8,628	9.8	..	306	30	26	44	82	3	21	–7	3.8
Cameroon	20,644	3.5	389	646	19	29	52	73	9	17	1	2.2
Canada	1,326,376	2.7	28,243	43,055	..	..	..	55	19	22	4	2.0
Central African Republic	1,712	0.1	287	381	56	16	28	88	10	9	–7	1.9
Chad	7,085	12.2	173	215	23	44	32	60	6	19	15	8.2
Chile	163,915	4.5	3,600	5,308	4	48	48	55	10	21	14	7.0
China	3,280,053	10.2	254	401	12	48	40	34	14	44	8	3.7
Hong Kong, China	206,706	5.2	..	..	0	9	91	60	8	21	11	–2.3
Colombia	171,979	4.5	3,405	2,847	11	29	60	63	13	24	–1	6.3
Congo, Dem. Rep. of	8,955	5.0	184	149	42	28	29	82	9	18	–9	31.0
Congo, Rep. of	7,646	4.1	..	..	5	60	35	29	14	27	30	5.7
Costa Rica	25,225	5.2	3,143	4,499	9	31	60	75	5	27	–7	9.8
Côte d'Ivoire	19,570	0.2	598	795	23	26	51	73	8	10	8	3.1
Croatia	51,277	4.8	4,921[b]	9,987	7	32	61	56	20	33	–8	3.7
Czech Republic	168,142	4.5	..	5,423	3	39	58	48	21	27	3	2.1
Denmark	308,093	1.8	15,190	40,780	2	26	72	49	26	23	3	2.2
Dominican Republic	36,686	4.8	2,268	4,586	12	28	60	80	7	20	–6	17.4
Ecuador	44,184	5.0	1,686	1,676	7	35	58	67	13	21	–1	9.6
Egypt, Arab Rep. of	128,095	4.5	1,528	2,072	13	36	51	75	11	22	–8	6.9
El Salvador	20,215	2.7	1,633	1,638	11	29	60	93	11	16	–21	3.4
Eritrea	1,201	2.3	..	61	18	24	58	81	42	19	–42	14.8
Ethiopia	19,395	7.5	146	158	46	13	40	84	11	25	–19	6.6
Finland	246,020	3.1	18,822	31,214	3	32	65	51	21	21	7	0.9
France	2,562,288	1.7	22,234	44,017	2	21	77	57	24	21	–1	2.0
Georgia	10,176	8.3	2,443[b]	1,790	11	24	65	75	22	29	–26	6.9
Germany	3,297,233	1.1	13,724	26,549	1	30	69	58	18	18	5	1.0
Ghana	15,246	5.5	293	320	36	25	38	78	13	33	–23	19.5
Greece	360,031	4.3	7,668	9,011	3	21	76	68	14	26	–8	3.4
Guatemala	33,432	3.6	2,119	2,350	12	27	60	87	9	20	–16	4.7
Guinea	4,564	2.8	142	190	17	45	38	84	6	13	–2	18.1
Haiti	6,137	0.2	..	..	..	..	..	91	9	29	–29	16.5
Honduras	12,279	5.3	1,193	1,483	13	28	58	79	15	28	–23	6.2
Hungary	138,182	4.0	4,105	6,987	4	29	66	66	10	22	2	5.1
India	1,170,968	7.8	324	392	18	29	53	55	10	38	–3	4.4
Indonesia	432,817	5.1	484	583	14	47	39	63	8	25	4	10.1
Iran, Islamic Rep. of	270,937	5.9	1,954	2,542	9	42	49	47	14	37	3	16.9
Iraq	..	–11.4	..	1,756	..	..	..	..	..	..	..	
Ireland	254,970	5.2	..	17,879	2	36	62	44	16	27	13	3.1
Israel	161,822	3.3	..	..	..	..	..	56	26	20	–1	1.2
Italy	2,107,481	0.8	11,542	23,967	2	27	71	59	20	21	–1	2.7
Japan	4,376,705	1.7	20,445	35,517	2	30	69	57	18	23	1	–1.2
Jordan	15,832	6.3	1,892	1,360	3	32	65	89	20	26	–35	3.0
Kazakhstan	103,840	10.0	1,795[b]	1,557	7	44	49	48	11	31	9	14.3
Kenya	29,509	4.4	333	332	23	19	58	75	16	20	–10	6.0
Korea, Rep. of	969,795	4.7	5,679	11,286	3	39	58	55	15	29	1	1.7
Kyrgyz Republic	3,505	4.0	675[b]	979	33	20	47	101	19	17	–37	5.8
Lao PDR	4,008	6.6	360	458	42	32	26	65	9	33	–6	9.4
Lebanon	24,001	3.3	..	30,099	6	23	71	89	15	12	–16	2.0
Liberia	725	–2.7	..	..	66	16	18	86	11	16	–14	10.0
Libya	58,333	3.7	..	..	..	..	..	..	..	..	..	21.0
Lithuania	38,328	8.0	..	4,703	5	33	61	66	17	30	–12	2.9
Madagascar	7,326	3.3	186	174	27	15	58	81	10	29	–19	11.6
Malawi	3,552	3.2	72	116	34	20	45	71	12	28	–11	21.3
Malaysia	180,714	5.1	3,803	5,126	9	51	41	50	13	23	14	4.8
Mali	6,863	5.4	208	241	37	24	39	76	11	23	–10	3.6
Mauritania	2,644	5.4	574	356	13	47	41	61	20	26	–7	11.3
Mexico	893,364	2.6	2,256	2,792	4	25	71	71	9	23	–2	6.3
Moldova	4,396	6.5	1,286[b]	816	17	15	67	97	18	30	–44	11.5
Morocco	73,275	4.9	1,430	1,775	12	29	59	58	16	32	–6	1.1
Mozambique	7,752	8.0	109	153	28	27	45	72	12	24	–8	7.8
Myanmar	..	9.2	..	..	..	..	..	..	..	..	..	21.2

	Gross domestic product		Agricultural tchr productivity		Value added as % of GDP			Household final cons. expenditure	General gov't. final cons. expenditure	Gross capital formation	External balance of goods and services	GDP implicit deflator
	Millions of dollars	Avg. annual % growth	Agricultural value added per worker 2000 $		Agriculture	Industry	Services	% of GDP	% of GDP	% of GDP	% of GDP	Avg. annual % growth
	2007	2000–07	1990–92	2003–05	2007	2007	2007	2007	2007	2007	2007	2000–07
Nepal	10,207	3.2	191	207	35	16	49	82	9	25	−16	5.6
Netherlands	754,203	1.6	24,914	42,198	2	25	73	47	25	20	8	2.1
New Zealand	129,372	3.2	19,204	25,109	..	..	..	60	18	25	−3	2.4
Nicaragua	5,676	3.5	..	2,071	20	30	51	92	9	29	−30	7.6
Niger	4,170	3.9	152	157[b]	..	..	..	75	12	23	−9	2.1
Nigeria	165,690	6.7	..	..	33	39	28	..	..	..	9	17.8
Norway	381,951	2.5	19,500	37,776	2	45	54	41	19	22	18	4.0
Pakistan	143,597	5.8	593	695	20	27	54	75	10	23	−8	6.5
Panama	19,740	6.0	2,363	3,914	7	16	77	71	7	23	−1	1.8
Papua New Guinea	6,261	2.4	500	595	36	45	19	47	12	20	21	7.2
Paraguay	12,004	3.3	1,596	2,052	26	20	54	74	9	21	−4	10.6
Peru	109,088	5.4	930	1,498	6	35	59	63	9	20	8	3.8
Philippines	144,129	5.1	905	1,075	14	31	55	80	10	15	−5	5.1
Poland	420,321	4.1	1,502[b]	2,182	4	30	66	63	17	22	−1	2.4
Portugal	220,241	0.8	4,612	5,980	3	25	72	65	21	22	−8	3.0
Romania	165,980	6.1	2,196	4,646	8	26	65	77	14	22	−13	18.0
Russian Federation	1,291,011	6.6	1,825[b]	2,519	5	39	57	50	17	25	8	16.7
Rwanda	3,320	5.8	168	182	36	14	50	85	11	22	−18	9.7
Saudi Arabia	381,683	4.1	7,875	15,780	3	65	32	28	23	22	27	8.1
Senegal	11,151	4.5	225	215	15	22	63	76	10	32	−18	2.2
Serbia	41,581	5.5	..	..	13	26	62	73	22	25	−20	19.5
Sierra Leone	1,672	11.2	..	..	44	24	32	84	13	17	−14	8.9
Singapore	161,347	5.8	22,695	40,419	0	31	69	38	10	23	29	1.0
Slovak Republic	74,932	6.0	..	5,026	3	37	60	55	18	27	0	3.9
Somalia	..	..	..	..	..	..	..	..	..	..	..	..
South Africa	277,581	4.3	1,786	2,484	3	31	66	64	20	20	−4	6.6
Spain	1,429,226	3.4	9,511	19,030	3	30	67	58	18	31	−6	4.0
Sri Lanka	32,354	5.3	679	702	12	30	58	68	15	27	−10	10.0
Sudan	47,632	7.1	418	666	32	28	41	68	14	24	−6	9.6
Sweden	444,443	2.8	21,463	33,023	1	29	70	47	27	18	8	1.5
Switzerland	415,516	1.6	22,344	23,418	1	28	70	60	11	22	7	0.9
Syrian Arab Republic	38,081	4.5	2,344	3,261	20	32	48	71	12	16	2	6.2
Tajikistan	3,712	8.8	397[b]	465	21	28	51	113	9	23	−45	20.5
Tanzania[c]	16,181	6.7	238	295	45	17	37	73	16	17	−6	9.0
Thailand	245,818	5.4	497	621	11	44	45	57	10	30	4	2.9
Togo	2,493	2.6	312	347	43	23	34	85	10	18	−13	0.8
Tunisia	35,020	4.8	2,422	2,719	11	27	62	64	13	23	0	2.7
Turkey	657,091	5.9	..	1,846	9	28	63	71	12	22	−5	18.8
Turkmenistan	12,933	..	1,222[b]	..	..	..	..	46	13	23	17	..
Uganda	11,214	5.7	184	229	29	18	53	80	14	24	−19	6.2
Ukraine	140,484	7.6	1,195[b]	1,702	7	32	61	66	15	22	−4	14.0
United Arab Emirates	129,702	8.2	10,454	25,841	2	56	42	46	11	24	18	4.9
United Kingdom	2,727,806	2.6	22,659	26,933	1	24	75	64	22	18	−4	2.6
United States	13,811,200	2.7	20,793	41,797	1	23	76	71	16	19	−6	2.6
Uruguay	23,087	3.3	5,714	7,973	9	32	59	73	11	18	−2	9.4
Uzbekistan	22,308	6.2	1,272[b]	1,800	24	27	49	54	16	20	10	26.5
Venezuela, R.B. de	228,071	4.7	4,483	6,292	..	..	..	48	11	24	17	26.8
Vietnam	71,216	7.8	214	305	20	42	38	67	6	35	−8	6.7
West Bank and Gaza	4,007	0.4	..	..	..	..	..	96	33	23	−52	3.0
Yemen, Rep. of	22,523	4.0	271	328[b]	..	..	..	..	..	..	..	13.5
Zambia	11,363	−5.7	159	204	22	38	40	59	10	24	6	18.3
Zimbabwe	3,418	−4.4	240	222	19	24	57	72	27	17	−16	232.0
World	54,347,038t	3.2w	730w	911w	3w	28w	69w	61w	17w	22w	0w	
Low income	810,300	5.6	259	321	25	28	48	74	9	24	−6	
Middle income	13,342,194	6.2	454	654	8	32	59	60	15	25	0	
Lower middle income	6,888,343	8.0	370	509	13	41	46	49	13	35	3	
Upper middle income	6,450,429	4.3	2,134	2,954	5	31	64	59	17	23	1	
Low and middle income	14,155,882	6.2	417	583	10	32	59	61	15	25	−1	
East Asia & Pacific	4,438,135	8.9	303	446	12	47	41	41	13	38	7	
Europe & Central Asia	3,155,221	6.1	1,588	2,109	7	33	60	61	16	24	−1	
Latin America & the Caribbean	3,444,374	3.6	2,155	3,053	5	29	66	60	17	22	1	
Middle East & North Africa	828,691	4.5	1,583	2,205	11	35	53	62	14	26	−1	
South Asia	1,438,594	7.3	335	406	18	29	53	59	10	35	−4	
Sub-Saharan Africa	842,914	5.0	246	281	15	32	54	67	16	21	−3	
High income	40,197,253	2.4	14,586	25,456	2	26	72	62	18	21	−1	

a. Data on general government final consumption expenditure are not available separately; they are included in household final consumption expenditure. b. Data for all three years are not available. c. Data refer to mainland Tanzania only.

Table 4 Trade, aid, and finance

	Merchandise trade		Manufactured exports	High technology exports	Current account balance	Foreign direct investment net inflows	Official development assistance[a]	External debt		Domestic credit provided by banking sector	Net migration
	Exports	Imports	% of total merchandise exports	% of manufactured exports				Total $ millions	Present value % of GNI	% of GDP	thousands
	$ millions	$ millions			$ millions	$ millions	$ per capita				
	2007	2007	2006	2006	2007	2006	2006	2006	2006	2007	2000–05[b]
Afghanistan	480	2,950	..	..	..	..	..	1,771	18[d]	0	1,112
Albania	1,072	4,196	27	13	−671	325	101	2,340	21	64	−110
Algeria	59,518	27,439	1	2	..	1,795	6	5,583	5	−3	−140
Angola	38,100	11,400	..	..	10,690	−38	10	9,563	33	2	175
Argentina	55,933	44,780	32	7	7,210	4,840	3	122,190	68	29	−100
Armenia	1,219	3,282	56	1	−571	343	71	2,073	29	12	−100
Australia	141,079	165,331	23	12	−56,783	26,599	..	..	..	142	593
Austria	162,204	161,800	80	13	12,031	157	..	..	..	124	180
Azerbaijan	9,300	6,050	8	2	9,019	−584	24	1,900	12	18	−100
Bangladesh	12,360	18,470	92	0	1,196	697	8	20,521	22	59	−500
Belarus	24,339	28,674	50	3	−2,944	354	7	6,124	17	27	..
Belgium	432,327	415,752	77	8[c]	8,254	61,990	..	..	..	114	180
Benin	590	1,110	9	0	−226	63	43	824	12[d]	9	99
Bolivia	4,485	3,446	7	4	1,319	240	62	5,292	20[d]	54	−100
Bosnia and Herzegovina	4,155	9,726	62	3	−1,939	423	126	5,669	43	56	115
Brazil	160,649	126,581	51	12	1,460	18,782	0	194,150	26	96	−229
Bulgaria	18,450	30,034	53	6	−8,592	5,172	..	20,925	74	59	−43
Burkina Faso	660	1,700	8	10	..	26	61	1,142	11[d]	12	100
Burundi	55	350	6	4	−135	0	51	1,411	105	38	192
Cambodia	4,400	5,300	97	0	−506	483	37	3,527	48	13	10
Cameroon	3,750	3,760	3	3	..	309	93	3,171	4[d]	6	6
Canada	418,493	389,670	56	15	12,815	69,068	..	..	..	166	1,041
Central African Republic	195	230	36	0	..	24	31	1,020	53[d]	18	−45
Chad	3,450	1,500	..	..	..	700	27	1,772	23[d]	0	219
Chile	68,296	46,108	11	7	7,200	7,952	5	47,977	42	90	30
China	1,217,939[e]	955,845	92[e]	30	249,866	78,095	1	322,845	14	136	−1,900
Hong Kong, China	349,663	370,733	91	11	27,405	42,891	..	..	..	126	300
Colombia	29,360	32,897	37	4	−5,851	6,463	22	39,698	32	50	−120
Congo, Dem. Rep. of	2,600	2,950	..	..	..	180	34	11,201	119[d]	5	−237
Congo, Rep. of	6,100	2,900	..	..	903	344	69	6,130	108[d]	−10	−10
Costa Rica	9,367	12,955	65	45	−1,499	1,469	5	6,832	35	48	84
Côte d'Ivoire	8,400	6,100	15	42	−146	315	13	13,840	72[d]	21	−339
Croatia	12,360	25,830	66	10	−4,412	3,376	45	37,480	93	83	100
Czech Republic	122,414	117,980	89	14	−4,586	6,021	..	..	..	55	67
Denmark	103,307	99,375	65	20	4,279	3,343	..	..	..	207	46
Dominican Republic	6,700	13,100	..	..	−2,231	1,183	6	8,905	35	54	−148
Ecuador	13,751	13,565	10	8	1,503	271	14	16,536	52	19	−400
Egypt, Arab Rep. of	16,201	27,064	21	1	2,635	10,043	12	29,339	28	91	−525
El Salvador	3,980	8,677	55	3	−855	204	23	9,136	55	46	−143
Eritrea	15	515	..	..	..	4	28	800	49[d]	139	229
Ethiopia	1,290	5,320	..	..	−1,786	364	25	2,326	8[d]	47	−140
Finland	89,656	81,145	81	22	11,402	5,311	..	..	..	85	33
France	552,193	613,224	79	21	−30,567	81,045	..	..	..	123	722
Georgia	1,240	5,217	48	16	−1,931	1,060	81	1,964	22	32	−248
Germany	1,326,521	1,059,439	83	17	150,746	43,410	..	..	..	126	1,000
Ghana	4,320	7,980	31	0	−1,040	435	51	3,192	21[d]	33	12
Greece	23,574	75,553	52	11	−29,565	5,401	..	..	..	95	154
Guatemala	6,926	13,578	35	3	−1,592	354	37	5,496	18	42	−300
Guinea	1,100	1,190	..	..	..	108	18	3,281	58[d]	16	−425
Haiti	550	1,550	..	..	1	160	62	1,189	22[d]	25	−140
Honduras	2,160	6,760	21	1	−195	385	84	4,076	25[d]	51	−150
Hungary	94,160	94,792	84	24	−7,421	6,098	..	107,677	100	75	65
India	145,228	216,682	70	5	−9,415	17,453	1	153,075	15	63	−1,350
Indonesia	118,163	91,715	45	13	11,009	5,580	6	130,956	45	41	−1,000
Iran, Islamic Rep. of	83,000	45,000	10	6	..	901	2	20,113	10	48	−1,250
Iraq	36,400	29,020	..	..	..	..	..	..	..	..	−375
Ireland	121,068	81,678	85	34	−12,695	−882	..	..	..	199	188
Israel	54,065	58,950	82	14	4,994	14,302	..	..	..	76	115
Italy	491,532	504,591	85	7	−51,032	38,884	..	..	..	129	1,125
Japan	712,839	620,967	91	22	210,490	−6,784	..	..	..	294	270
Jordan	5,760	13,310	71	1	−1,909	3,219	105	8,000	58	124	130
Kazakhstan	46,540	32,940	13	21	−7,184	6,143	11	74,148	132	41	−200
Kenya	4,140	9,210	26	3	−526	51	26	6,534	26	34	25
Korea, Rep. of	371,554	356,648	89	32	5,954	3,645	..	..	..	110	−80
Kyrgyz Republic	1,105	2,475	46	3	−234	182	60	2,382	52[d]	15	−75
Lao PDR	980	1,400	..	..	..	187	63	2,985	87	8	−115
Lebanon	3,574	12,251	70	2	−2,046	2,794	174	23,963	116	190	..
Liberia	157	490	..	..	−138	−82	75	2,674	1,128[d]	92	−119
Libya	45,000	8,600	..	..	22,170	..	6	..	..	−70	10
Lithuania	17,173	24,116	58	8	−3,218	1,812	..	18,955	79	61	−30
Madagascar	1,190	2,590	41	1	−554	230	39	1,453	13[d]	9	−5
Malawi	670	1,380	13	11	..	30	49	850	6[d]	16	−30
Malaysia	176,211	146,982	74	54	28,931	6,064	9	52,526	39	117	150
Mali	1,620	2,000	10	4	−231	185	69	1,436	15[d]	15	−134
Mauritania	1,360	1,510	0	..	..	−3	62	1,630	93[d]	..	30
Mexico	272,044	296,578	76	19	−1,993	19,222	2	160,700	21	43	−3,983
Moldova	1,370	3,720	31	5	−695	242	60	2,416	65	40	−250
Morocco	14,646	31,468	68	10	1,851	2,699	34	18,493	30	92	−550
Mozambique	2,650	3,210	5	2	−634	154	77	3,265	12[d]	10	−20
Myanmar	5,350	3,250	..	..	802	279	3	6,828	47	28	−99

	Merchandise trade Exports $ millions 2007	Merchandise trade Imports $ millions 2007	Manufactured exports % of total merchandise exports 2006	High technology exports % of manufactured exports 2006	Current account balance $ millions 2007	Foreign direct investment net inflows $ millions 2006	Official development assistance[a] $ per capita 2006	External debt Total $ millions 2006	External debt Present value % of GNI 2006	Domestic credit provided by banking sector % of GDP 2007	Net migration thousands 2000–05[b]
Nepal	888	2,904	..	..	6	−7	19	3,409	27[d]	49	−100
Netherlands	550,636	490,582	66	28	50,706	7,197	..	..	..	208	110
New Zealand	26,950	30,890	27	11	−10,233	7,941	..	..	..	152	102
Nicaragua	1,210	3,510	9	7	−855	282	132	4,391	30[d]	74	−210
Niger	650	970	15	11	−312	20	29	805	8[d]	7	−29
Nigeria	66,500	27,500	..	..	24,202	5,445	79	7,693	9	4	−170
Norway	139,424	80,347	16	19	64,070	4,653	..	..	..	..	84
Pakistan	17,457	32,598	81	1	−8,253	4,273	14	35,909	26	46	−1,239
Panama	1,200	7,010	10	0	−1,577	2,574	9	9,989	77	88	8
Papua New Guinea	4,610	2,950	..	..	640	32	45	1,675	35	23	..
Paraguay	3,374	7,280	16	8	−217	189	9	3,426	43	20	−45
Peru	27,956	20,185	14	2	2,589	3,467	17	28,174	42	16	−510
Philippines	50,276	57,160	87	68	5,897	2,345	7	60,324	57	41	−900
Poland	137,609	160,804	79	4	−15,794	19,198	..	125,831	41	47	−200
Portugal	50,994	77,050	74	9	−18,281	7,366	..	..	..	174	276
Romania	40,257	69,712	79	4	−23,136	11,394	..	55,114	58	36	−270
Russian Federation	355,177	223,059	17	9	78,310	30,827	..	251,067	34	25	917
Rwanda	165	600	..	..	−147	11	62	419	8[d]	9	43
Saudi Arabia	228,550	94,235	8	1	99,066	660	1	..	..	18	285
Senegal	1,650	4,250	44	6	..	58	68	1,984	14[d]	25	−100
Serbia	8,780	18,295	..	4	..	5,128	214	13,831	52	30	−339
Sierra Leone	260	420	..	..	−101	59	63	1,428	10[d]	10	472
Singapore	299,271[e]	263,150	80[e]	58	36,326	24,191	..	..	..	81	200
Slovak Republic	58,082	60,103	85	6	..	4,165	..	27,085	58	52	3
Somalia	..	..	..	..	..	96	46	2,836	..	..	100
South Africa	69,788	90,990	53[f]	6	−20,631	−120	15	35,549	15	89	75
Spain	241,962	373,585	76	6	−145,275	20,167	..	..	..	194	2,846
Sri Lanka	7,750	10,840	70	2	−1,334	480	40	11,446	40	47	−442
Sudan	8,160	8,450	0	1	−4,722	3,534	55	19,158	77[d]	0	−532
Sweden	168,223	150,039	78	16	28,413	27,299	..	..	..	135	152
Switzerland	171,621	160,798	91	22	72,354	27,185	..	..	..	194	100
Syrian Arab Republic	11,330	14,820	32	1	920	600	1	6,502	23	33	200
Tajikistan	1,468	2,455	..	..	−21	339	36	1,154	36	15	−345
Tanzania	2,005	5,337	18	0	−1,442	474	46	4,240	16[d,g]	13	−345
Thailand	152,469	141,347	76	27	14,921	9,010	−3	55,233	30	96	231
Togo	690	1,450	58	0	−461	57	12	1,806	68[d]	22	−4
Tunisia	15,029	18,980	75	4	−634	3,270	43	18,480	66	72	−29
Turkey	107,154	169,987	42	..	−32,774	20,070	8	207,854	61	49	−30
Turkmenistan	8,920	4,460	..	..	..	731	5	881	11	..	−10
Uganda	1,530	3,350	21	34	−745	392	52	1,264	6[d]	9	−5
Ukraine	49,100	60,440	73	3	−5,927	5,604	10	49,887	58	62	−173
United Arab Emirates	154,000	121,100	..	..	..	..	..	..	..	59	577
United Kingdom	435,615	617,178	77	34	−115,243	139,745	..	..	..	194	948
United States	1,163,183	2,016,978	79	30	−738,641	180,580	..	..	..	240	6,493
Uruguay	4,480	5,480	32	3	−186	1,346	6	9,804	66	25	−104
Uzbekistan	8,040	4,470	..	..	..	164	6	3,892	26	..	−300
Venezuela, R.B. de	69,165	48,591	5	2	20,001	−543	2	44,635	34	23	40
Vietnam	48,387	60,830	50	5	−6,992	2,315	22	20,202	33	96	−200
West Bank and Gaza	..	..	..	..	..	..	384	..	..	9	11
Yemen, Rep. of	7,160	5,890	1	5	206	1,121	13	5,563	25	10	−100
Zambia	4,876	4,014	6	2	−505	575	122	2,325	9[d]	17	−82
Zimbabwe	2,050	2,420	38	2	..	40	21	4,677	110	93	−75
World	13,899,267t	14,107,100t	74w	20w	..	1,352,442s	16w	..s	167w	..w[h]	
Low income	230,215	251,819	..	..	..	20,380	35	201,382	30		−2,858
Middle income	3,919,104	3,641,914	60	20	..	334,242	9	2,642,418	77		−15,770
Lower middle income	2,179,289	1,947,080	69	25	..	162,047	9	1,080,416	102		−11,295
Upper middle income	1,738,728	1,690,142	52	16	..	172,195	7	1,562,002	55		−4,475
Low and middle income	4,149,329	3,893,700	60	20	..	354,621	19	2,843,800	75		−18,629
East Asia & Pacific	1,783,695	1,475,731	80	33	..	104,972	4	659,985	119		−3,847
Europe & Central Asia	874,122	935,854	39	8	..	114,318	14	912,265	38		−1,798
Latin America & the Caribbean	750,092	732,907	53	12	..	70,457	12	734,499	63		−6,811
Middle East & North Africa	297,678	234,252	19	5	..	26,551	54	136,499	49		−2,618
South Asia	184,991	286,021	72	4	..	22,916	6	227,303	60		−2,484
Sub-Saharan Africa	261,373	237,971	..	..	..	15,408	52	173,248	48		−1,070
High income	9,752,088	10,219,990	77	21	..	997,821	0.1	..	..	196	18,522

a. The distinction between official aid, for countries on the Part II list of the OECD Development Assistance Committee (DAC), and official development assistance was dropped in 2005. Regional aggregates include data for economies not listed in the table. World and income group totals include aid not allocated by country or region. b. Total for the 5-year period. c. Includes Luxembourg. d. Data are from debt sustainability analysis undertaken as part of the Heavily Indebted Poor Countries (HIPC) initiative. e. Includes re-exports. f. Data on total exports and imports refer to South Africa only. Data on export commodity shares refer to the South African Customs Union (Botswana, Lesotho, Namibia, and South Africa). g. GNI refers to mainland Tanzania only. h. World total computed by the UN sums to zero, but because the aggregates shown here refer to World Bank definitions, regional and income group totals do not equal zero.

Table 5 Key indicators for other economies

	Population				Gross national income (GNI)[a]		PPP gross national income (GNI)[b]		Gross domestic product per capita % growth	Life expectancy at birth		Adult literacy rate % ages 15 and older	Carbon dioxide emissions per capita metric tons
	Thousands	Avg. annual % growth	Density people per sq. km	Population age composition % ages 0–14	Millions of dollars	per capita dollars	Millions of dollars	per capita dollars		Male years	Female years		
	2007	2000–2007	2007	2007	2007	2007	2007	2007	2006–2007	2006	2006	2005	2004
American Samoa	60	1.4[c]	301	..	..	d	..	..	..	..	..	..	5.1
Andorra	67	0.5[c]	143	..	..	e	..	..	..	..	..	..	..
Antigua and Barbuda	85	1.4	193	..	977	11,520	1,494	17,620[f]	2.9	..	..	..	5.1
Aruba	101	0.5[c]	561	22	..	e	..	..	..	..	..	97	21.8
Bahamas, The	331	1.3	33	27	..	e	..	..	..	70	76	..	6.3
Bahrain	753	2.1	1,060	25	14,022	19,350	24,869	34,310	5.6	74	77	87	23.8
Barbados	294	0.4	684	18	..	e	4,711[f]	16,140[f]	..	74	80	..	4.4
Belize	304	2.8	13	37	1,157	3,800	1,886[f]	6,200[f]	0.1	70	74	..	2.8
Bermuda	64	0.4	1,280	..	..	e	..	..	..	76	81	..	8.7
Bhutan	657	2.3	14	31	1,166	1,770	3,276	4,980	17.5	64	67	60	0.7
Botswana	1,881	1.2	3	35	10,991	5,840	23,369	12,420	2.5	50	50	81	2.4
Brunei Darussalam	389	2.2	74	29	10,287	26,930	19,059	49,900	2.9	75	80	93	24.1
Cape Verde	530	2.3	132	38	1,287	2,430	1,558	2,940	4.6	68	74	81	0.6
Cayman Islands	47	2.1[c]	180	..	..	e	..	..	..	..	..	..	7.1
Channel Islands	149	0.2	785	16	..	e	..	..	..	76	81	..	..
Comoros	626	2.1	336	42[g]	425	680	721	1,150	-2.9	62[g]	64[g]	..	0.2
Cuba	11,257	0.1	103	18	..	d	..	..	..	76	80	100	2.3
Cyprus	787	1.8	85	19	19,617	24,940	20,741	26,370	2.5	77	82	97	9.1
Djibouti	833	1.9	36	37	908	1,090	1,886	2,260	2.2	53	56	..	0.5
Dominica	73	0.3	97	..	310	4,250	540[f]	7,410[f]	0.4	..	..	..	1.5
Equatorial Guinea	508	2.3	18	42	6,527	12,860	10,773	21,230	9.9	50	52	87	11.5
Estonia	1,342	-0.3	32	15	17,706	13,200	26,399	19,680	7.3	67	78	100	14.0
Faeroe Islands	48	0.2[c]	35	..	..	e	..	..	..	77	81	..	13.7
Fiji	838	0.6	46	32	3,189	3,800	3,666	4,370	-5.0	66	71	..	1.3
French Polynesia	263	1.5	72	27	..	e	..	..	..	71	77	..	2.7
Gabon	1,330	1.7	5	35	8,876	6,670	17,395	13,080	4.0	56	57	84	1.1
Gambia, The	1,707	3.0	171	41	544	320	1,951	1,140	4.3	58	60	..	0.2
Greenland	57	0.1	0[h]	..	..	e	..	..	..	..	..	..	10.0
Grenada	108	0.9	318	33	505	4,670	747[f]	6,910[f]	3.0	..	..	..	2.0
Guam	173	1.6	321	29	..	e	..	..	..	73	78	..	25.0
Guinea-Bissau	1,695	3.0	60	48	331	200	790	470	-0.3	45	48	..	0.2
Guyana	739	0.1	4	31	959	1,300	2,129[f]	2,880[f]	5.5	63	69	..	2.0
Iceland	311	1.4	3	22	16,826	54,100	10,592	34,060	1.4	79	83	..	7.6
Isle of Man	77	0.9	136	..	3,088	40,600	2,568[f]	33,750[f]	4.9	..	..	..	..
Jamaica	2,677	0.5	247	31	9,923	3,710	16,612	6,210	1.7	70	73	..	4.0
Kiribati	102	1.7	126	..	120	1,170	228[f]	2,240[f]	0.8	..	..	..	0.3
Korea, Dem. People's Rep. of	23,783	0.5	198	23	..	i	..	..	..	65	69	..	3.4
Kuwait	2,663	2.8	149	23	80,221	31,640	126,703	49,970	6.7	76	80	93	40.4
Latvia	2,276	-0.6	37	14	22,595	9,930	38,452	16,890	10.9	65	77	100	3.1
Lesotho	2,006	0.9	66	40	2,007	1,000	3,783	1,890	4.3	43	43	82	..
Liechtenstein	35	0.8[c]	220	..	..	e	..	..	..	..	..	..	..
Luxembourg	480	1.3	185	18	36,420	75,880	30,909	64,400	1.9	76	82	..	24.9
Macao, China	480	1.2	17,026	14	..	..	..	..	26.6	78	83	91	4.7
Macedonia, FYR	2,037	0.2	80	19	7,052	3,460	17,344	8,510	5.1	72	76	96	5.1
Maldives	305	1.6	1,018	32	977	3,200	1,540	5,040	3.8	67	69	96	2.5
Malta	409	0.7	1,279	17	6,216	15,310	8,523	20,990	2.7	77	81	..	6.1
Marshall Islands	67	3.3	369	..	204	3,070	..	..	1.8	..	..	..	..
Mauritius	1,263	0.9	622	24	6,878	5,450	14,381	11,390	3.9	70	77	84	2.6
Mayotte	194	3.8[c]	518	..	..	d	..	..	..	..	..	..	..
Micronesia, Fed. States	111	0.5	159	38	274	2,470	363[f]	3,270[f]	1.5	68	69	..	..
Monaco	33	0.3[c]	16,769	..	..	e	..	..	..	..	..	..	..
Mongolia	2,612	1.2	2	27	3,362	1,290	8,246	3,160	8.7	66	69	98	3.4
Montenegro	600	-1.6	43	19	3,109	5,180	6,175	10,290	7.6	72	77	..	..
Namibia	2,074	1.4	3	37	6,970	3,360	10,608	5,120	4.6	52	53	85	1.2
Netherlands Antilles	191	0.8	239	21	..	e	..	..	..	71	79	..	22.2
New Caledonia	242	1.8	13	26	..	e	..	..	..	73	78	..	11.2
Northern Mariana Islands	84	2.4[c]	182	..	..	e	..	..	..	..	..	..	..
Oman	2,600	1.1	8	32	27,887	11,120	49,487	19,740	4.6	74	77	81	12.5
Palau	20	0.8[c]	44	..	167	8,210	..	..	2.0	..	..	..	11.9
Puerto Rico	3,943	0.5	445	21	..	e	..	..	..	74	83	90	0.5
Qatar	836	4.3	76	21	..	e	..	..	1.8	75	76	89	69.2
Samoa	187	0.7	66	40	454	2,430	735[f]	3,930[f]	2.2	68	75	99	0.8
San Marino	29	1.1[i]	482	..	1,291	45,130	1,046[f]	37,080[f]	3.5	79	85	..	..
São Tomé and Príncipe	158	1.7	165	41	138	870	258	1,630	4.1	63	67	85	0.6
Seychelles	85	0.7	185	..	762	8,960	1,313[f]	15,450[f]	5.8	69	76	92	6.6
Slovenia	2,018	0.2	100	14	42,306	20,960	53,756	26,640	5.5	74	81	100	8.1
Solomon Islands	495	2.5	18	40	363	730	831[f]	1,680[f]	3.2	63	64	..	0.4
St. Kitts and Nevis	49	1.4	188	..	470	9,630	650[f]	13,320[f]	2.5	..	..	..	2.7
St. Lucia	168	1.1	275	27	929	5,530	1,584[f]	9,430[f]	2.0	73	76	..	2.3
St. Vincent and the Grenadines	120	0.5	309	28	507	4,210	863[f]	7,170[f]	6.2	69	74	..	1.7
Suriname	458	0.7	3	29	2,166	4,730	3,499[f]	7,640[f]	4.7	67	73	90	5.1
Swaziland	1,145	1.3	67	39	2,951	2,580	5,649	4,930	1.7	42	40	80	0.9
Timor-Leste	1,066	4.4	72	45	1,604	1,510	3,281[f]	3,080[f]	4.1	56	58	..	0.2
Tonga	101	0.4	140	37	233	2,320	367[f]	3,650[f]	-4.3	72	74	..	1.2
Trinidad and Tobago	1,333	0.4	260	21	18,795	14,100	29,981	22,490	5.6	68	72	98	24.7
Vanuatu	226	2.5	19	39	417	1,840	771[f]	3,410[f]	2.6	68	72	..	0.4
Virgin Islands (U.S.)	108	0.0[k]	310	23	..	e	..	..	..	77	80	..	124.3

a. Calculated using the World Bank Atlas method. b. PPP is purchasing power parity; see *Definitions*. c. Data are for 2003–2007. d. Estimated to be upper middle ($3,706 to $11,455). e. Estimated to be high income ($11,456 or more). f. The estimate is based on regression; others are extrapolated from the latest International Comparison Program benchmark estimates. g. Includes the island of Mayotte. h. Less than 0.5. i. Estimated to be low income ($935 or less). j. Data are for 2004–2007. k. More than –0.05.

Technical notes

These technical notes discuss the sources and methods used to compile the indicators included in this edition of Selected World Development Indicators. The notes follow the order in which the indicators appear in the tables.

Sources

The data published in the Selected World Development Indicators are taken from *World Development Indicators 2008*. Where possible, however, revisions reported since the closing date of that edition have been incorporated. In addition, newly released estimates of population and gross national income (GNI) per capita for 2007 are included in table 1 and table 5.

The World Bank draws on a variety of sources for the statistics published in the *World Development Indicators*. Data on external debt for developing countries are reported directly to the World Bank by developing member countries through the Debtor Reporting System. Other data are drawn mainly from the United Nations and its specialized agencies, from the International Monetary Fund (IMF), and from country reports to the World Bank. Bank staff estimates are also used to improve currentness or consistency. For most countries, national accounts estimates are obtained from member governments through World Bank economic missions. In some instances these are adjusted by staff to ensure conformity with international definitions and concepts. Most social data from national sources are drawn from regular administrative files, special surveys, or periodic censuses.

For more detailed notes about the data, please refer to the World Bank's *World Development Indicators 2008*.

Data consistency and reliability

Considerable effort has been made to standardize the data, but full comparability cannot be assured, and care must be taken in interpreting the indicators. Many factors affect data availability, comparability, and reliability: statistical systems in many developing economies are still weak; statistical methods, coverage, practices, and definitions differ widely; and cross-country and intertemporal comparisons involve complex technical and conceptual problems that cannot be unequivocally resolved. Data coverage may not be complete because of special circumstances or for economies experiencing problems (such as those stemming from conflicts) affecting the collection and reporting of data. For these reasons, although the data are drawn from the sources thought to be most authoritative, they should be construed only as indicating trends and characterizing major differences among economies rather than offering precise quantitative measures of those differences. Discrepancies in data presented in different editions reflect updates by countries as well as revisions to historical series and changes in methodology. Thus readers are advised not to compare data series between editions or between different editions of World Bank publications. Consistent time series are available from the *World Development Indicators 2008* CD-ROM and in *WDI Online*.

Ratios and growth rates

For ease of reference, the tables usually show ratios and rates of growth rather than the simple underlying values. Values in their original form are available from the *World Development Indicators 2008* CD-ROM. Unless otherwise noted, growth rates are computed using the least-squares regression method (see *Statistical methods* below). Because this method takes into account all available observations during a period, the resulting growth rates reflect general trends that are not unduly influenced by exceptional values. To exclude the effects of inflation, constant price economic indicators are used in calculating growth rates. Data in italics are for a year or period other than that specified in the column heading—up to two years before or after for economic indicators and up to three years for social indicators, because the latter tend to be collected less regularly and change less dramatically over short periods.

Constant price series

An economy's growth is measured by the increase in value added produced by the individuals and enterprises operating in that economy. Thus, measuring real growth requires estimates of GDP and its components valued in constant prices. The World Bank collects constant price national accounts series in national currencies and recorded in the country's original base year. To obtain comparable series of constant price data, it rescales GDP and value added by industrial origin to a common reference year, 2000 in the current version of the *World Development Indicators*. This process gives rise to a discrepancy between the rescaled GDP and the sum of the rescaled components. Because allocating the discrepancy would give rise to distortions in the growth rate, it is left unallocated.

Summary measures

The summary measures for regions and income groups, presented at the end of most tables, are calculated by simple addition when they are expressed in levels. Aggregate growth rates and ratios are usually computed as weighted averages. The summary measures for social indicators are weighted by population or subgroups of population, except for infant mortality, which is weighted by the number of births. See the notes on specific indicators for more information.

For summary measures that cover many years, calculations are based on a uniform group of economies so that the composition of the aggregate does not change over time. Group measures are compiled only if the data available for a given year account for at least two-thirds of the full group, as defined for the 2000 benchmark year. As long as this criterion is met, economies for which data are missing are assumed to behave like those that provide estimates. Readers should keep in mind that the summary measures are estimates of representative aggregates for each topic and that nothing meaningful can be deduced about behavior at the country level by working back from group indicators. In addition, the estimation process may result in discrepancies between subgroup and overall totals.

Table 1. Key indicators of development

Population is based on the de facto definition, which counts all residents, regardless

of legal status or citizenship, except for refugees not permanently settled in the country of asylum, who are generally considered part of the population of the country of origin.

Average annual population growth rate is the exponential rate of change for the period (see the section on *Statistical methods* below).

Population density is midyear population divided by land area. Land area is a country's total area excluding areas under inland bodies of water and coastal waterways. Density is calculated using the most recently available data on land area.

Population age composition, ages 0–14 refers to the percentage of the total population that is ages 0–14.

Gross national income (GNI) is the broadest measure of national income; it measures total value added from domestic and foreign sources claimed by residents. GNI comprises gross domestic product (GDP) plus net receipts of primary income from foreign sources. Data are converted from national currency to current U.S. dollars using the World Bank Atlas method. This involves using a three-year average of exchange rates to smooth the effects of transitory exchange rate fluctuations. (See the section on *Statistical methods* below for further discussion of the Atlas method.)

GNI per capita is GNI divided by midyear population. It is converted into current U.S. dollars by the Atlas method. The World Bank uses GNI per capita in U.S. dollars to classify economies for analytical purposes and to determine borrowing eligibility.

PPP gross national income, which is GNI converted into international dollars using purchasing power parity (PPP) conversion factors, is included because nominal exchange rates do not always reflect international differences in relative prices. At the PPP rate, one international dollar has the same purchasing power over domestic GNI that the U.S. dollar has over U.S. GNI. PPP rates allow a standard comparison of real price levels between countries, just as conventional price indexes allow comparison of real values over time. The PPP conversion factors used here are derived from price surveys covering 146 countries conducted in 2005 by the International Comparison Program. For OECD countries, data come from the most recent round of surveys, completed in 1999; the rest are either from the 1996 survey, or data from the 1993 or earlier round and extrapolated to the 1996 benchmark. Estimates for countries not included in the surveys are derived from statistical models using available data.

PPP GNI per capita is PPP GNI divided by midyear population.

Gross domestic product (GDP) per capita growth is based on GDP measured in constant prices. Growth in GDP is considered a broad measure of the growth of an economy. GDP in constant prices can be estimated by measuring the total quantity of goods and services produced in a period, valuing them at an agreed set of base year prices, and subtracting the cost of intermediate inputs, also in constant prices. See the section on *Statistical methods* for details of the least-squares growth rate.

Life expectancy at birth is the number of years a newborn infant would live if patterns of mortality prevailing at its birth were to stay the same throughout its life. Data are presented for males and females separately.

Adult literacy rate is the percentage of persons aged 15 and above who can, with understanding, read and write a short, simple statement about their everyday life. In practice, literacy is difficult to measure. To estimate literacy using such a definition requires census or survey measurements under controlled conditions. Many countries estimate the number of literate people from self-reported data. Some use educational attainment data as a proxy but apply different lengths of school attendance or level of completion. Because definition and methodologies of data collection differ across countries, data need to be used with caution.

Carbon dioxide emissions (CO_2) measures those emissions stemming from the burning of fossil fuels and the manufacture of cement. These include carbon dioxide produced during consumption of solid, liquid, and gas fuels and from gas flaring. Carbon dioxide per capita is CO_2 divided by the mid-year population.

The Carbon Dioxide Information Analysis Center (CDIAC), sponsored by the U.S. Department of Energy, calculates annual anthropogenic emissions of CO_2. These calculations are derived from data on fossil fuel consumption, based on the World Energy Data Set maintained by the UNSD, and from data on world cement manufacturing, based on the Cement Manufacturing Data Set maintained by the U.S. Bureau of Mines. Each year the CDIAC recalculates the entire time series from 1950 to the present, incorporating its most recent findings and the latest corrections to its database. Estimates exclude fuels supplied to ships and aircraft engaged in international transportation because of the difficulty of apportioning these fuels among the countries benefiting from that transport.

Table 2. Millennium Development Goals: eradicating poverty and improving lives
Share of poorest quintile in national consumption or income is the share of the poorest 20 percent of the population in consumption or, in some cases, income. It is a distributional measure. Countries with more unequal distributions of consumption (or income) have a higher rate of poverty for a given average income. Data are from nationally representative household surveys. Because the underlying household surveys differ in method and type of data collected, the distribution data are not strictly comparable across countries. The World Bank staff have made an effort to ensure that the data are as comparable as possible. Wherever possible, consumption has been used rather than income.

Prevalence of child malnutrition is the percentage of children under five whose weight for age is less than minus two standard deviations from the median for the international reference population ages 0–59 months. The table presents data for the new child growth standards released by the World Health Organization (WHO) in 2006. Estimates of child malnutrition are from national survey data. The proportion of children who are underweight is the most common indicator of malnutrition. Being underweight, even mildly, increases the risk of death and inhibits cognitive development in children. Moreover, it perpetuates the problem from one generation to the next, as malnourished women are more likely to have low-birth-weight babies.

Primary completion rate is the percentage of students completing the last year of primary school. It is calculated by taking the total number of students in the last grade of primary school, minus the number of repeaters in that grade, divided by the total number of children of official graduation age. The primary completion rate reflects the primary cycle as defined by the International Standard Classification of Education (ISCED), ranging from three or four years of primary education (in a very small number of countries) to five or six years (in most countries) and seven (in a small number of countries). Because curricula and standards for school completion vary across countries, a high rate of primary completion does not necessarily mean high levels of student learning.

Ratio of girls to boys enrollments in primary and secondary school is the ratio of the female gross enrollment rate in primary and secondary school to the male gross enrollment rate.

Eliminating gender disparities in education would help to increase the status and capabilities of women. This indicator is an imperfect measure of the relative accessibility of schooling for girls. With a target date of 2005, this is the first of the targets to fall due. School enrollment data are reported to the UN Educational, Scientific, and Cultural Organization (UNESCO) Institute for Statistics by national education authorities. Primary education provides children with basic reading, writing, and mathematics skills along with an elementary understanding of such subjects as history, geography, natural science, social science, art, and music. Secondary education completes the provision of basic education that began at the primary level and aims at laying foundations for lifelong learning and human development by offering more subject-or skill-oriented instruction using more specialized teachers.

Under-five mortality rate is the probability that a newborn baby will die before reaching age five, if subject to current age-specific mortality rates. The probability is expressed as a rate per 1,000. The main sources of mortality date are vital registration systems and direct or indirect estimates based on sample surveys or censuses. To produce harmonized estimates of under-five mortality rates that make use of all available information in a transparent way, a methodology that fits a regression line to the relationship between mortality rates and their reference dates using weighted least squares was developed and adopted by both UNICEF and the World Bank.

Births attended by skilled health staff are the percentage of deliveries attended by personnel trained to give the necessary supervision, care, and advice to women during pregnancy, labor, and the postpartum period; to conduct deliveries on their own; and to care for newborns. The share of births attended by skilled health staff is an indicator of a health system's ability to provide adequate care for pregnant women. Data are from UNICEF and household surveys. Good prenatal and postnatal care improves maternal health and reduces maternal and infant mortality. But data may not reflect such improvements because health information systems are often weak, maternal deaths are underreported, and rates of maternal mortality are difficult to measure.

Contraceptive prevalence rate is the percentage of women married or in-union ages 15–49 who are practicing, or whose sexual partners are practicing, any form of contraception. Safe and effective contraception is one of the indispensable means to achieve reproductive health, helping women avoid unintended pregnancies while preventing sexually transmitted diseases. Contraceptive prevalence reflects all methods—ineffective traditional methods as well as highly effective modern methods. Contraceptive prevalence rates are obtained mainly from household surveys.

Prevalence of HIV is the percentage of people ages 15–49 who are infected with HIV. Adult HIV prevalence rates reflect the rate of HIV infection in each country's population. Low national prevalence rates can be very misleading, however. They often disguise serious epidemics that are initially concentrated in certain localities or among specific population groups and threaten to spill over into the wider population. In many parts of the developing world, most new infections occur in young adults, with young women especially vulnerable. The estimates of HIV prevalence are based on extrapolations from data collected through surveys and from surveillance of small, nonrepresentative groups.

Table 3. Economic activity

Gross domestic product (GDP) is gross value added, at purchasers' prices, by all resident producers in the economy plus any taxes and minus any subsidies not included in the value of the products. It is calculated without deducting for depreciation of fabricated assets or for depletion or degradation of natural resources. Value added is the net output of an industry after adding up all outputs and subtracting intermediate inputs. The industrial origin of value added is determined by the International Standard Industrial Classification (ISIC) revision 3. The World Bank conventionally uses the U.S. dollar and applies the average official exchange rate reported by the IMF for the year shown. An alternative conversion factor is applied if the official exchange rate is judged to diverge by an exceptionally large margin from the rate effectively applied to transactions in foreign currencies and traded products.

Gross domestic product average annual growth rate is calculated from constant price GDP data in local currency.

Agricultural productivity refers to the ratio of agricultural value added, measured in constant 1995 U.S. dollars, to the number of workers in agriculture.

Value added is the net output of an industry after adding up all outputs and subtracting intermediate inputs. The industrial origin of value added is determined by the International Standard Industrial Classification (ISIC) revision 3.

Agriculture value added corresponds to ISIC divisions 1–5 and includes forestry and fishing.

Industry value added comprises mining, manufacturing, construction, electricity, water, and gas (ISIC divisions 10–45).

Services value added correspond to ISIC divisions 50–99.

Household final consumption expenditure is the market value of all goods and services, including durable products (such as cars, washing machines, and home computers), purchased by households. It excludes purchases of dwellings but includes imputed rent for owner-occupied dwellings. It also includes payments and fees to governments to obtain permits and licenses. Here, household consumption expenditure includes the expenditures of nonprofit institutions serving households, even when reported separately by the country. In practice, household consumption expenditure may include any statistical discrepancy in the use of resources relative to the supply of resources.

General government final consumption expenditure includes all government current expenditures for purchases of goods and services (including compensation of employees). It also includes most expenditures on national defense and security, but excludes government military expenditures that are part of government capital formation.

Gross capital formation consists of outlays on additions to the fixed assets of the economy plus net changes in the level of inventories and valuables. Fixed assets include land improvements (fences, ditches, drains, and so on); plant, machinery, and equipment purchases; and the construction of buildings, roads, railways, and the like, including commercial and industrial buildings, offices, schools, hospitals, and private dwellings. Inventories are stocks of goods held by firms to meet temporary or unexpected fluctuations in production or sales, and "work in progress." According to the 1993 System of National Accounts (SNA), net acquisitions of valuables are also considered capital formation.

External balance of goods and services is exports of goods and services less imports of goods and services. Trade in goods and services comprise all transactions between residents of a country and the rest of the world involving a change in ownership of general merchandise, goods sent for processing and repairs, nonmonetary gold, and services.

The **GDP implicit deflator** reflects changes in prices for all final demand categories, such as government consumption, capital formation, and international trade, as well as the main component, private final consumption. It is derived as the ratio of current to constant price GDP. The GDP deflator may also be calculated explicitly as a Paasche price index in which the weights are the current period quantities of output.

National accounts indicators for most developing countries are collected from national statistical organizations and central banks by visiting and resident World Bank missions. Data for high-income economies come from the OECD.

Table 4. Trade, aid, and finance

Merchandise exports show the free on board (f.o.b.) value of goods provided to the rest of the world valued in U.S. dollars.

Merchandise imports show the c.i.f. value of goods (the cost of the goods including insurance and freight) purchased from the rest of the world valued in U.S. dollars. Data on merchandise trade come from the World Trade Organization (WTO) in its annual report.

Manufactured exports comprise the commodities in Standard Industrial Trade Classification (SITC) sections 5 (chemicals), 6 (basic manufactures), 7 (machinery and transport equipment), and 8 (miscellaneous manufactured goods), excluding division 68.

High-technology exports are products with high research and development (R&D) intensity. They include high-technology products such as in aerospace, computers, pharmaceuticals, scientific instruments, and electrical machinery.

Current account balance is the sum of net exports of goods and services, net income, and net current transfers. Data are drawn from the IMF's *Balance of Payments Statistics Yearbook*.

Foreign direct investment is net inflows of investment to acquire a lasting management interest (10 percent or more of voting stock) in an enterprise operating in an economy other than that of the investor. It is the sum of equity capital, re-investment of earnings, other long-term capital, and short-term capital, as shown in the balance of payments. Data on FDI are based on balance-of-payments data reported by the IMF, supplemented by World Bank staff estimates using data reported by the United Nations Conference on Trade and Development, and official national sources.

Official development assistance or official aid from the high-income members of the OECD are the main source of official external finance for developing countries, but official development assistance (ODA) is also disbursed by some important donor countries that are not members of OECD's Development Assistance Committee (DAC). DAC has three criteria for ODA: it is undertaken by the official sector; it promotes economic development or welfare as a main objective; and it is provided on concessional terms, with a grant element of at least 25 percent on loans (calculated at a 10-percent discount rate). Official development assistance comprises grants and loans, net of repayments, that meet the DAC definition of ODA and are made to countries and territories on of the DAC list of aid recipients. The new DAC list of recipients is organized on more objective needs-based criteria than its predecessors, and includes all low- and middle-income countries, except those that are members of the G8 or the EU (including countries with a firm date for EU admission).

Total external debt is debt owed to nonresidents repayable in foreign currency, goods, or services. It is the sum of public, publicly guaranteed, and private non-guaranteed long-term debt, use of IMF credit, and short-term debt. Short-term debt includes all debt having an original maturity of one year or less and interest in arrears on long-term debt.

Present value of debt is the sum of short-term external debt plus the discounted sum of total debt service payments due on public, publicly guaranteed, and private nonguaranteed long-term external debt over the life of existing loans. Data on external debt come mainly from reports to the World Bank through its Debtor Reporting System via member countries that have received IBRD loans or IDA credits, with additional information from the files of the World Bank, the IMF, the African Development Bank and African Development Fund, the Asian Development Bank and Asian Development Fund, and the Inter American Development Bank. Summary tables of the external debt of developing countries are published annually in the World Bank's *Global Development Finance.*

Net migration is the total net number of migrants during the period, that is, the number of immigrants less the number of emigrants, including both citizens and non-citizens. Data shown in the table are five-year estimates. Data are from the United Nations Population Division's *World Population Prospects: The 2006 Revision.*

Domestic credit provided by banking sector includes all credit to various sectors on a gross basis, with the exception of credit to the central government, which is net. The banking sector includes monetary authorities, deposit money banks, and other banking institutions for which data are available (including institutions that do not accept transferable deposits but do incur such liabilities as time and savings deposits). Examples of other banking institutions include savings and mortgage loan institutions and building and loan associations. Data are from the IMF's *International Finance Statistics.*

Table 5. Key indicators for other economies

See *Technical notes* for table 1, key indicators.

Statistical methods

This section describes the calculation of the least-squares growth rate, the exponential (endpoint) growth rate, and the World Bank's Atlas methodology for calculating the conversion factor used to estimate GNI and GNI per capita in U.S. dollars.

Least-squares growth rate

Least-squares growth rates are used wherever there is a sufficiently long time series to permit a reliable calculation. No growth rate is calculated if more than half the observations in a period are missing.

The least-squares growth rate, r, is estimated by fitting a linear regression trendline to the logarithmic annual values of the variable in the relevant period. The regression equation takes the form

$$\ln X_t = a + bt$$

which is equivalent to the logarithmic transformation of the compound growth equation,

$$X_t = X_o (1 + r)^t$$

In this equation, X is the variable, t is time, and $a = \log X_o$ and $b = \ln (1 + r)$ are the parameters to be estimated. If b^* is the least-squares estimate of b, the average annual growth rate, r, is obtained as $[\exp(b^*) - 1]$ and is multiplied by 100 to express it as a percentage.

The calculated growth rate is an average rate that is representative of the available observations over the entire period. It does not necessarily match the actual growth rate between any two periods.

Exponential growth rate

The growth rate between two points in time for certain demographic data, notably labor force and population, is calculated from the equation

$$r = \ln (p_n / p_1)/n$$

where p_n and p_1 are the last and first observations in the period, n is the number of years in the period, and ln is the natural logarithm operator. This growth rate is based on a model of continuous, exponential growth between two points in time. It does not take into account the intermediate values of the series. Note also that the exponential growth rate does not correspond to the annual rate of change measured at a one-year interval which is given by

$$(p_n - p_{n-1})/p_{n-1}$$

World Bank Atlas method

In calculating GNI and GNI per capita in U.S. dollars for certain operational purposes, the World Bank uses the Atlas conversion factor. The purpose of the Atlas conversion factor is to reduce the impact of exchange rate fluctuations in the cross-country comparison of national incomes. The Atlas conversion factor for any year is the average of a country's exchange rate (or alternative conversion factor) for that year and its exchange rates for the two preceding years, adjusted for the difference between the rate of inflation in the country and that in Japan, the United Kingdom, the United States, and the Euro Zone. A country's inflation rate is measured by the change in its GDP deflator. The inflation rate for Japan, the United Kingdom, the United States, and the Euro Zone, representing international inflation, is measured by the change in the SDR deflator. (Special drawing rights, or SDRs, are the IMF's unit of account.) The SDR deflator is calculated as a weighted average of these countries' GDP deflators in SDR terms, the weights being the amount of each country's currency in one SDR unit. Weights vary over time because both the composition of the SDR and the relative exchange rates for each currency change. The SDR deflator is calculated in SDR terms first and then converted to U.S. dollars using the SDR to dollar Atlas conversion factor. The Atlas conversion factor is then applied to a country's GNI. The resulting GNI in U.S. dollars is divided by the midyear population to derive GNI per capita.

When official exchange rates are deemed to be unreliable or unrepresentative of the effective exchange rate during a period, an alternative estimate of the exchange rate is used in the Atlas formula (see below).

The following formulas describe the calculation of the Atlas conversion factor for year t:

$$e_t^* = \frac{1}{3}\left[e_{t-2}\left(\frac{p_t}{p_{t-2}} / \frac{p_t^{s\$}}{p_{t-2}^{s\$}} \right) + e_{t-1}\left(\frac{p_t}{p_{t-1}} / \frac{p_t^{s\$}}{p_{t-1}^{s\$}} \right) + e_t \right]$$

and the calculation of GNI per capita in U.S. dollars for year t:

$$Y_t^\$ = (Y_t/N_t)/e_t^*$$

where e_t^* is the Atlas conversion factor (national currency to the U.S. dollar) for year t, e_t is the average annual exchange rate (national currency to the U.S. dollar) for year t, p_t is the GDP deflator for year t, $p_t^{s\$}$ is the SDR deflator in U.S. dollar terms for year t, $Y_t^\$$ is the Atlas GNI per capita in U.S. dollars in year t, Y_t is current GNI (local currency) for year t, and N_t is the midyear population for year t.

Alternative conversion factors

The World Bank systematically assesses the appropriateness of official exchange rates as conversion factors. An alternative conversion factor is used when the official exchange rate is judged to diverge by an exceptionally large margin from the rate effectively applied to domestic transactions of foreign currencies and traded products. This applies to only a small number of countries, as shown in the primary data documentation table in *World Development Indicators 2007*. Alternative conversion factors are used in the Atlas methodology and elsewhere in the Selected World Development Indicators as single-year conversion factors.

Index